P9-CCI-782

JUSTICE IN JERUSALEM

JUSTICE IN JERUSALEM

By GIDEON HAUSNER

HARPER & ROW, PUBLISHERS
NEW YORK

LIBRARY OF CONGRESS CATALOG CARD NUMBER: 63-20290

I-Q

To my wife, Yehudith, without whose love and inspiration this book could not have been written

To my wife, Yehudith, without whose love and inspiration
this book could not have been written

ACKNOWLEDGMENTS

I was the beneficiary of generous help in the preparation of this book. Joel Carmichael of New York offered most valuable editorial criticism and made numerous constructive suggestions. Misha Louvish of Jerusalem was very helpful in different phases of the preparation of the manuscript. He also translated into English the lullaby appearing in Chapter 17. Yehuda Reshef of Haifa led me to much useful material and has passed a fine-tooth comb through the work to fend off errors. Julian Meltzer of Rehovoth contributed to the evolution of Chapter 1.

I wish to acknowledge a debt of gratitude to Yad Vashem, Martyrs' and Heroes' Memorial Authority, Jerusalem, for making the facilities of the institution available to me. Special thanks are due to some members of Yad Vashem's staff: to Rachel Auerbach for her assistance in filling several gaps, to Nachman Blumenthal for advice on material regarding the reaction of non-Jews to Nazi methods, and to the librarians Mrs. Ora Alkalay and Mrs. Perla Bauman for the heavy use I made of the institution's library.

Last, and not least, I have to acknowledge my debt to Yehudith Hausner, who, during the span of almost three years, when this work was in preparation, provided incisive critical insights and keen observations as well as the incentive to proceed with the work. In more than one sense this is a joint book by both of us.

Jerusalem
January, 1966

GIDEON HAUSNER

CONTENTS

ACKNOWLEDGMENTS vii

PART I: THE MASK AND THE MAN

CHAPTER 1 The Mask 3
CHAPTER 2 The Pathology of Hatred and Its Organization 14
CHAPTER 3 The Beginnings of a Man and Bureaucrat 27
CHAPTER 4 Overture to Destruction: Eichmann Wins His Spurs 33

PART II: THE CRIME

CHAPTER 5 Deportation into Ghettos 53
CHAPTER 6 A Slaughterhouse on Wheels: The *Einsatzgruppen* 69
CHAPTER 7 The Final Solution 84
CHAPTER 8 The Great Deporter I: Germany and Occupied Europe 98
CHAPTER 9 The Great Deporter II: Hungary 132
CHAPTER 10 The Death Camps 156
CHAPTER 11 Under the Heel 176
CHAPTER 12 The Great Powers and the Little Man 226

PART III: THE MILLS OF JUSTICE

CHAPTER 13 Escape and Capture 265
CHAPTER 14 The Preparation of a Case 277
CHAPTER 15 Some Prosecution Problems 288
CHAPTER 16 The Opening Battle 305
CHAPTER 17 The Case for the Prosecution 322
CHAPTER 18 The Case for the Defense 352
CHAPTER 19 The Defense Witnesses 374

CHAPTER 20 The Summations 388
CHAPTER 21 The Judgment 409
CHAPTER 22 Appeal and Aftermath 433
CHAPTER 23 Reflections—Three Years Later 447

APPENDIX I Reactions to the Trial 455
APPENDIX II Notes 473
APPENDIX III Bibliography 511
INDEX 513

ILLUSTRATIONS

The following are grouped in a separate section after page 242.

Adolf Eichmann's false identity card
The accused
Eichmann, Robert Servatius and Dieter Wechtenbruch
Gideon Hausner
Hausner, Jacob Baror, Gabriel Bach and Jacob Robinson
Abraham Selinger
Michael Goldmann
Moshe Landau
Benjamin Halevy
Yitzhak Raveh
Heinrich Karl Grueber
Jacob Wernik
Zivia Lubetkin Zuckerman
Michael A. Musmanno
Unidentified spectators at the trial
Courtroom scene

AUTHOR'S NOTE

This book contains, in addition to the evidence brought out at the Eichmann trial, a mass of additional material.

To avoid burdening the reader with constant annotations, I have listed the references for quotations and specific statements at the back of the book by chapter and page number, identifying them by an excerpt from the text or an indication of the subject matter.

G. H.

PART I

The Mask and the Man

CHAPTER 1

The Mask

The Valley of Decision, which runs between the steep banks of the Mount of Olives and the four sacred hills on which old Jerusalem stands, presented its customary peaceful appearance that fine spring morning. It was here, according to the ancient prophecy, in the deep gorge below the gray-lichened walls adorning the proud heights of the Holy City, that multitudes would be gathered and the mighty ones brought down to be judged for shedding the innocent blood of Judah's sons and daughters. Here, proclaimed the prophet Joel, the nations will assemble, their men of war will draw near and the sun and moon and stars be darkened on judgment day.

There was nothing untoward about the serene dawn to distinguish it from any other in the spring of the year, nor any visible indication down in the inert, slumbering valley itself that Joel's eschatological prophecy was about to be fulfilled. No multitudes were assembling to answer for their misdeeds toward Judah's scattered children, nor did the sun turn into darkness but rose in superb and shining majesty to herald the new morn with streamers of golden fire that lit up the jagged peaks of Moab to the east.

Yet in Jerusalem itself, the new city outside the walls, this was no ordinary April day. Within a handsome modern edifice of marble and smooth white stone, a trumpet call from the brooding Valley of Decision, a court of justice was about to convene for the arraignment of a man who had been charged with crimes never surpassed in legal annals for their magnitude and ferocity. They were crimes that, in their totality as genocide, had plunged the oft-persecuted Jewish people into the greatest calamity recorded in the long, blood-drenched history of their race—the deliberate, systematic murder of over six million, more than a third of their entire number throughout the world. Behind the marble and stone façade, in a hall furnished with the trappings and panoply of a court of law, the whole somber panorama of German Nazi oppression was to be revealed over the coming few months in all its fiendishness.

Figuratively, if not physically, other multitudes were about to gather here.

They were the wraiths of the millions of victims, men, women and children; the accusers, not the accused; the innocents who had been butchered methodically, insensately, inhumanly in a vast blood bath which to this day numbs the imagination.

Those who came into the hall of justice for the first time that morning, judges and counselors at law, court attendants and witnesses, spectators and world newsmedia representatives, were conscious of the epochal drama that was to be unfolded there. But none could foresee the impact upon world opinion, and upon history, of the revelations which were to crowd the hall with the ghosts from a great celestial Valley of Decision and indite their relentless horror upon the tablets of scarcely believing minds.

Nor could anyone assess the prisoner at the bar of the court. Could this rather nondescript individual in his middle fifties, lean and of medium height, who might have passed for any minor employee, really be a mass murderer? Who was Adolf Eichmann, the man behind the mask?

For more than two decades, until the moment he was called to account for his share in the man-made holocaust that virtually expunged European Jewry from the map of the world's communities, Eichmann had been one of the foremost mystery figures in the Nazi constellation. It was only toward the end of World War II that the full extent of his sinister role in the execution of "the Final Solution of the Jewish question" in Europe began to emerge. Clearly he was the key official in the hierarchy upon whom his superiors had imposed the principal responsibility for carrying out this diabolical policy. But while the pattern of his activities in directing the liquidation of the Jews of Europe began to be pieced together, he himself disappeared among the debris of the Third Reich and remained in hiding until captured in Argentina fifteen years later.

What was the true character of this man who was about to fight for his life before a court in Jerusalem?

Could he be a hypnotized follower of an evil genius, the blind and unwilling tool of a wicked spirit to which he had sworn unswerving allegiance, the victim of a tremendous whirlwind of inexorable historical forces sweeping away all that stood in its ravaging path?

Or was he a cold-blooded, scheming plotter, one of the gang of hardened Nazis set upon clambering over pyramids of corpses to the pinnacle of world conquest? Had he embarked upon a criminal career eagerly and with malice prepense, motivated by vicious personal impulses and vile ambitions, and pursued it to the point where he became the key figure in the annihilation of European Jewry?

These were not just rhetorical or academic questions, but vital issues between the prosecution and the defense. They were part of the core and substance of the case against him.

Both during his pretrial interrogation and the testimony which he gave in court, Eichmann depicted himself as a decent, easygoing sort of person, somewhat fond of the bottle, it was true, but otherwise quite humane and well-meaning: a model family man. The trouble was, he contended, that he had been caught up in a chain of unfortunate circumstances—a succession of bad luck—and compelled to participate against his will in events over which he could exercise no control.

Truth to tell, he claimed, he had never wished to harm a single Jew; he had sought only to promote a humane solution to the problem of a homeless nation. All he had ever wanted was to find some place for them to dwell permanently, to provide some firm ground beneath their feet. The utmost he had ever planned, he said, was to put them into a favorable position. This, according to him, occurred in the early days of his activity when, as head of the Central Bureau for Jewish Emigration, he forced Jews to leave the Reich in order to seek a secure domicile elsewhere in the world. Toward this goal, he said, he had worked with joy and satisfaction.

When "other ways and means"—actual physical extirpation—were ordered by higher authority later on, he felt himself bound by his oath of allegiance and his duty to his country to carry out such commands as he received; in his opinion these had nothing whatever to do with the actual extermination itself. The measures imposed were against his own good judgment, but he was seized at the time in the iron grasp of necessity, coerced into compliance by a cruel fate he could not evade and by rules of war he could not alter.

He stressed again and again that he was only happy that the duties he performed had nothing to do with the actual murder of human beings. He only deported people to concentration camps. In any event, he never did anything of his own accord; whatever he did, however he acted, was on the orders of the Chief of the Gestapo, Heinrich Mueller. His was only an insignificant and marginal participation in what he readily admitted was one of the major crimes in human history; in expiation of the sins that had been committed he was prepared to hang himself in public to warn the anti-Semites of the world of the consequences of such dastardly actions.

Whenever this ingenuous self-portrayal was probed by questioning, he went to great lengths to maintain the image he gave of himself. He admitted that, as a high-ranking officer and head of the Jewish Department in the Reich's Main Security Office, he had the right to command and to reach decisions, "but never made use of it." He always brought matters before his superiors and asked for instructions, he said. He not only refrained from taking decisions on his own but even refused to offer any suggestions to his superiors.

Indeed, he had repeatedly applied to his superior officers at headquarters to release him from his onerous work, even asking to be assigned to combat duty on the front. But here again he was visited by hard luck. They would not hear of it.

In short, he asserted, his guiding moral principle in life had been formed by the Kantian categorical imperative: to behave in such a way that one's conduct might become a model for legislation.

Eichmann's sanctimonious argumentations, delivered in a righteous tone of voice, took in a great deal of moral and ethical territory.

*

At the time of Adolf Eichmann's interrogation in Israel I was the Attorney General; it fell to me to prepare the indictment and to prosecute him before the Jerusalem District Court.

For many months I lived with him vicariously, studying the details of his background and his past. A mass of facts, data, figures and minute particulars was accumulated by the prosecution; from them we re-created the story of his whole life. We probed into secrets he had sedulously guarded, discovered and brought to light hidden records and unknown instruments. We collected hundreds of documents bearing his signature and gathered all available statements about him by his associates. We traced the memoranda of conferences in which he had played a leading part, unearthed records of his secret conversations and open pronouncements. We even studied the marginal observations he used to scribble in books while reading. Finally we submitted him to extensive psychological tests.

From the information in our possession I knew Eichmann to be a cunning, flinthearted plotter, with a demonic personality which certainly was completely indifferent to the suffering he inflicted, either collectively or individually, and which reveled in the exercise of personal power.

From a purely legal point of view, Eichmann's inner attitude to his crime was not decisive, at least not so far as obtaining his conviction was concerned. It was his actual deeds that counted, not the alacrity with which he perpetrated them. But for a moral analysis and appreciation of the man it was vital to ascertain whether all his excuses were just empty talk and an assumed outer mask or whether they reflected his real feelings. This might also be of prime significance for the next stage when, after his conviction, which I hoped to achieve, the sentence and the punishment were to be considered.

As soon as we started our legal preparations, we realized that Eichmann might plead insanity. To counter such a maneuver I directed that he be examined by psychiatrists. One of the tests applied had been devised by the well-known Hungarian psychologist Professor L. Szondi. It consists of showing the person under examination a number of photographs arranged in groups. Each group contains pictures of a convicted murderer, a proven sadist, a certified lunatic. The person being examined is asked to select from each group photographs of two people who attract and two others who repel him.

Eichmann was given the test ten times over a period of forty days. In all, he selected faces he liked and disliked 240 times.

To be certain of the proper interpretation of the results, the examining psychiatrists decided to send them to the author of the tests, Professor Szondi himself, then resident in Switzerland, without revealing the identity of the selector.

The psychologist's reply was, to put it mildly, astonishing. He began by saying that he never analyzed tests of people who had not been identified for him, but added that on glancing at the present results he found them so extraordinary that he had undertaken a complete analysis.

The person who took the test, he said, revealed in all phases a man obsessed with an urge for power and an insatiable tendency to kill. "You have on your hands a most dangerous person," Dr. Szondi wrote. In every single group the subject had unerringly picked out the most negative types as those appealing to him. Dr. Szondi said this had never happened in his twenty-four years of practice, in the course of which he had tested more than six thousand criminals. He requested a full case report.

Other psychological tests produced similar results. They all confirmed that Eichmann, though legally sane and fully responsible for his actions, was possessed of a dangerous, perverted personality, with an unusual and unlimited capacity for using his fellow men as inanimate objects for the attainment of his goals.

It became increasingly evident to me that the principal values that really mattered to Eichmann were those concerned with the façade and formalities of conduct. The inner significance of his incredible acts never troubled him; certainly he had little remorse, or never showed any, over the untold suffering and anguish he had inflicted on millions of his fellow beings.

A striking example of this formalistic attitude was to be provided during the trial. One evening, in accordance with the procedure that the defense must be shown in advance all the exhibits which we intended using, a preview was given in the courtroom of some films that were to be introduced in support of evidence. Some depicted shattering scenes of helpless victims being loaded into trains like cattle; others, which had been shot surreptitiously inside the camps, showed all the ghastly details of mass slaughter. There were scenes of naked men, women and children being lined up before Nazi execution squads. As the soldiers fired, one wave of writhing bodies after another fell into the deep, open common grave that the victims themselves had dug beforehand.

Finally came scenes of the liberation of the camps by the Allied troops, showing thousands of bodies being shoveled into mass graves by bulldozers as a measure against possible epidemic infection. They were pictures of unspeakable horror.

The courtroom was almost empty at the time. The judges were not present, nor was the general public admitted. But counsel for the defense, Dr. Robert Servatius, and the accused were in their usual places.

Suddenly, in the middle of the showing, Eichmann, who had been watching the film calmly and unperturbed, never lowering his gaze nor missing a scene, started an agitated argument with his guards. Everyone was under the impression that he wished to communicate to his counsel an objection to the veracity or genuineness of the pictures being shown at that particular juncture.

But the reason for his disturbance was totally different. He had noticed some people sitting in the seats reserved for the public and had been told they were newspapermen; he was protesting against having been brought into the courtroom in slacks and a sweater, instead of the dark blue suit he had been given for the trial.

I doubt whether he ever entered the hall without first adjusting his tie into a neat knot or smoothing his hair. Nor did he ever omit a courteous greeting to his lawyer.

For him, these external niceties were indubitably all-important. He must appear in the public eye at his best.

Sometimes he provided a droll illustration of the way his mechanistic mind operated. One morning he was given by mistake six slices of bread for breakfast, instead of the usual two. He ate all six. When the guard asked him whether he would like to have six slices in the future, he replied, "Oh, no. Two are quite enough. But when you give me six, I have to eat them."

His mask and self-control were so impressive that it was only in such matters as his eating habits, minor though they might have seemed, that we were occasionally vouchsafed a glimpse of how the accumulation of evidence was affecting him. During the pretrial interrogation, he was questioned about a secret Berlin meeting in 1939 at which sixteen high-ranking Nazis came together to arrange for the concentration of all Polish Jews in ghettos near railroad junctions, where they could be made slave laborers and prepared for the "Final Solution."

Apparently Eichmann was not aware at this stage that we had evidence which would pinpoint his attendance at that conference. He denied he had ever been there. But when he was shown a document proving that he was in fact one of the sixteen high-ranking Nazis present, he at once agreed it was a fact. But that day, instead of consuming everything placed before him, he asked to be excused from having any lunch or dinner.

He was fanatically hostile to religion. Once, under my cross-examination, he admitted that he became so infuriated at seeing his wife reading a Bible that on two occasions he snatched the book from her hands and tore it to pieces. He refused to take the oath on the Bible during the trial, saying he did not belong to any church. To the Rev. William Hull, a Christian Protestant clergyman who visited him in prison to try to reconcile him to religious belief through reading the Bible, he said, "I am not interested in Jewish stories." Neither his devout wife, who came from Buenos Aires to visit him in prison before his execution, nor the Rev. Mr. and Mrs. Hull, who called on him thirteen times in all, could persuade him to make his peace with the Church. He remained steadfast to the Nazi concept of God, which was represented by the powers of Nature and reflected in the biological world. There was no room for morality, Jewish or Christian, in the order he believed in.

Might was right; power was virtue; the greatest sin was weakness. "To obey is the highest command. Obedience was my ideal in life," he proclaimed.

To these precepts he remained faithful to the end. He died as he lived—a pagan, a polished, finished and unalloyed product of the Nazi system.

*

Adolf Eichmann's career in the Nazi Party, which he joined at the age of twenty-six years in 1932, and in the SS Corps later, was revealed in more or less intimate detail some four years before he was brought to trial in Jerusalem.

It was 1957. The war had been over twelve years. He had successfully eluded the pursuers who sought him all over the world and was living with his family, with which he had been reunited in Argentina. He felt safe there under the assumed name of Ricardo Klement.

One day he was persuaded by some cronies who belonged to a group named "*Kameradenwerk*" to talk. "*Kameradenwerk*" was active in equipping escaped Nazis with false papers, providing them with jobs, maintaining contact with neo-Nazi bodies throughout the world and issuing a fascist, virulently anti-Semitic periodical called *Der Weg* (*The Way*). The regular contributors to *Der Weg* were its editor, Eberhard Fritzsche, a former leader of the Hitler Youth in Argentina, and Willem Antonius Maria Sassen, a Dutch Nazi journalist.

For some time *Der Weg* had been engaged in a campaign to refute what the group called "the lie about the six millions." The paper maintained it was all a calumny, that in reality no gas ovens or crematoria had existed in Hitler's Europe, that no Jews had ever been destroyed there but had all survived the war and were cheating the world with a hoax about alleged genocide, so as to press their demands for a Jewish state and for the payment of reparations by Germany.

In truth, the argument went, the Jews were kept in camps during the war so that the Reich could keep an eye on them and compel them to work a little.

Eichmann was commissioned to prepare a "detailed account" that would prove that the Jewish losses in the war were small and in great part due to Allied air raids. This was incorporated in a document he composed at the time and later submitted to the court by the prosecution.

But Willem Sassen remained unsatisfied. As he later revealed in an interview (*La Razon*, September 12, 1960), he wanted to know more about the "Final Solution," especially about the persons involved. "Let us write a book together to counter the enemy propaganda," he suggested to Eichmann, who was to supply "the facts." It was agreed that the source of the information was not to be revealed as long as Eichmann lived.

Eichmann consented and talked. Their conversations were tape-recorded and then transcribed. Eichmann later made handwritten corrections and remarks on the transcript. Altogether they used sixty-seven tapes which, transcribed, covered 659 typewritten pages. Some edited sections from this transcript were published in the American magazine *Life* and in other periodicals. The editors of *Life* stated that their researches confirmed the complete authenticity of the document. So, incidentally, did our own extensive research.

The Israeli prosecution had secured the document but was able to use only part in evidence, as will be shown in a later chapter. The entire document has yet to be published.

The Eichmann-Sassen talks were conducted in a friendly, uninhibited atmosphere.

The book they were preparing had to deal both with the facts of the Final Solution and with its justification. The main thesis was that the Jewish problem had been of the utmost importance for Germany, but it was the Jews themselves who had worked the thing up to the point of an alternative: "Either the German people will live or the Jews; there is no room for both." It was international Jewry that, in its devilish perversion, in order to present a claim for statehood later on, had provoked naïve and single-minded Germany to destroy the Jews. It was a diabolically clever Jewish scheme, with the assistance of certain secret services, for Jewry "to get its own territory after two thousand years of homelessness. They were willing to sacrifice their own blood to secure their national existence." This is Eichmann's conclusion, following a fourteen-line summary of four thousand years of Jewish history and an elaboration on the prophecy of Isaiah, "who always showed his people their mission." "That," he said, "was why Kastner told me in Budapest that it was so difficult to be a Jew."

In other words, the Jews were instrumental in their own slaughter. World Jewry, with Zionism first and foremost, chose Europe as the theater of war.

"The battlefields of this war were the destruction camps."

Sometimes Sassen proved to be a severe cross-examiner, and Eichmann would fly into a rage; he often concealed from his interlocutor some of the horrors he later admitted in court to be true recitals. He deliberately besmirched some Jewish personalities; he blamed other people for his worst crimes. From time to time he said, "We had better omit this from the book" or "You'd better publish this whole part only after my death." But his inner world, his character, his emotions, his likes and dislikes and, above all, his attitude toward the job he had done during the war were all brought sharply into focus.

When first given charge of Jewish affairs at Security Service (SD) headquarters, he did not take on the job "like a senseless ox." On the contrary. "It gave me uncommon joy, I found it fascinating to have to deal with these matters." At that time he had thought in terms of a political solution, a separation between the Germans and the Jews in line with the Nazi Party program. Later, when the physical liquidations were ordered, "my job was to catch these enemies and transport them to their destination. . . ."

Sassen wanted more information about individual cases. Eichmann replied that "of course, it was also part of the duties of my department to decide whether to send a particular Jew to a concentration camp," but, he stressed, this was not his main concern. The main idea was to solve the entire Jewish problem once and for all. "I lived in this stuff, otherwise I would have remained only an assistant, a cog, something soulless. . . ."

Then the "Final Solution" was ordered in the form of physical extermination. Eichmann was required to free Europe from its "unwanted guests."

"I thought it over," he told Sassen, "and when I realized the necessity for it, I carried it through with all the fanaticism that an old Nazi would expect of himself and that my superiors undoubtedly expected of me. They found me, according to their experience, to be the right man in the right place."

"This I say today, in 1957, to my own disadvantage," he continued. "I could make it easy for myself. I could now claim it was an order I had to carry out because of my oath of allegiance. But that would be just a cheap excuse, which I am not prepared to give."

The Jewish press referred to him as the "Czar of the Jews," he recalled. "But the Jews were actually right in saying that I was working relentlessly to kindle the fire wherever there was a sign of opposition. I was not just a recipient of orders. Had I been that, I would have been an imbecile. I was an idealist."

There was nothing personal in it, he emphasized. "Personally I never had any bad experience with a Jew. . . . The enemy was not persecuted individually. It was a matter of a political solution."

"For this," he declared, "I worked 100 percent . . . in giving orders I was certainly not lukewarm."

Time and again Eichmann stressed that he had nothing to regret. He would not behave like other top Nazis, who crawled on their stomachs and expressed repentance: "It is against my convictions to say even now that we were wrong at the time."

He told Sassen: "To be frank with you, had we killed all of them, the 10.3 million, I would be happy and say, All right; we managed to destroy an enemy."

(He was alluding to a figure that the Nazi statistician Korherr had fixed as the Jewish total to be comprised in the holocaust.)

Many Jews remained alive, Eichmann concluded. Perhaps he had not exerted himself hard enough after all; perhaps there had been too many obstacles to overcome. "But these things had better be omitted from the book."

*

The Sassen manuscript was not the only source of information in our possession about Eichmann's inner attitude. It was also mirrored in other evidence.

Rudolf Hoess was the Commandant of the Auschwitz camp—"the death factory," as it was commonly called. About a year after Germany's collapse, in 1946, he was arrested by the British military police and interrogated by Field Security, then handed over to the American authorities and taken to Nuremberg. He gave evidence as a witness at the trial of Ernst Kaltenbrunner, chief of the *Reichsicherheitshauptamt* (the RSHA), the Reich Security Head Office. Later he was turned over to the Polish authorities and imprisoned in Cracow.

After his preliminary interrogation Hoess wrote an autobiography. Eichmann figured prominently both in his Nuremberg statements and in this book. Nobody envied him the job of commanding Auschwitz, Hoess said, and nobody wanted to exchange places with him, not even the tough types of the Gestapo. When he had his moments of weakness or doubt, he used to call in Eichmann. He stated: "I had many detailed discussions with him on all matters connected with the Final Solution."

Yet even when quite close together, and the drink had been flowing freely, so that Eichmann was at his most expansive, "he showed himself to be completely obsessed with the idea of destroying every single Jew he could lay hands on" maintaining:

Without pity and in cold blood we must complete this extermination as rapidly as possible. Any compromise, even the slightest, would have to be paid for bitterly at a later date.

After such inspiring talk, delivered with such vigor and determination, Hoess was able naturally to bury any inner anxieties he had felt.

The admiration between the two men was mutual. Eichmann spoke to Sassen about Hoess as a man to be admired, both for his outward appearance and for his qualities of tranquillity and devotion. "He did his difficult and onerous job because it was absolutely essential according to his convictions for the blood of the race to which he belonged," he said. "Hoess was no bulldog, no uncomplicated, brutal commandant of a concentration camp, but a man accustomed to judge for himself and account to himself for what he did."

Other testimony on Eichmann came from Dieter Wisliceny, an SS captain and his erstwhile superior, whom the eager, ambitious junior officer eventually caught up with and passed on the ladder of promotion. But they were on extremely friendly terms and worked together for a number of years.

Giving evidence at Nuremberg before being handed over to the Czechoslovak authorities for trial, Wisliceny, while describing Eichmann as "a coward at heart," said of him that "his character and personality were important factors in carrying out measures against the Jews. . . . Eichmann was very cynical in his attitude toward the Jewish question. He gave no indication of any human feeling toward these people. He was not immoral; he was amoral and completely ice-cold in his attitude."

The same motif occurred in the evidence of the Protestant Dean, Dr. Heinrich Karl Grueber, of West Berlin, one of the few Germans with the courage to help Jews under Hitler, who came to face Eichmann from the witness box in Jerusalem. Dr. Grueber stated:

"He was like a piece of ice or marble. Nothing ever touched his heart. Whenever I came to plead with him on behalf of a Jew or a Jewish cause, the answer was always negative. . . . Once he tried to dissuade me from my endeavors for the Jews, saying that it would not do me any good."

It didn't. Dr. Grueber was arrested on Eichmann's orders and sent to Sachsenhausen concentration camp.

Ten years before the trial, Dr. Bernhard Loesener, a senior official in the Nazi Ministry of the Interior, wrote of him in these terms:

"Of all the people I knew, Eichmann . . . was the strongest personification of satanic principles."

Such, then, was the man who was to be judged by a Jewish court, in the first Jewish state to come into existence in almost two thousand years.

It remained only to clarify his role in the holocaust of European Jewry, and for that, of course, the holocaust itself had to be described.

This book is largely based on what came out in the course of the trial and on the evidence presented there. The proceedings put the historical facts on record by the best-known process for eliciting truth, through evidence on oath, in open court, subject to cross-examination and documentary corroboration.

The chapter of history unfolded in Jerusalem is recent in time and decisive in importance, but is already, I fear, fading from the minds of men. This book may, I hope, bridge the gap.

CHAPTER 2

The Pathology of Hatred and Its Organization

Eichmann's historically unique career took place in Germany. It was there that one of the strongest currents in the life of the nation was militant anti-Semitism—a fierce, deliberately fanned hatred of the Jewish people.

Under the Nazi regime this hatred came to be channeled and manipulated through a complex of highly efficient state organizations.

The hatred itself was no novelty. Living among the Gentiles, the Jews clung to a different religion and to different customs. Yet it was not solely a question of the dislike that human beings feel, perhaps naturally, for the unlike. There was an added source of venom in the relationship Christianity bears to Judaism.

The rejection of Jesus by his own people, and the subsequent survival of the Jewish community after the establishment of the Church, could be explained in the Christian religion only as part of the great struggle between God and Satan. In rejecting Jesus, and in continuing to reject him down the ages, the role of the Jews was understood by the Christian doctrine as that of satanic agent, and so the grotesque charge of deicide was a natural form for religious fanaticism to take. Throughout the Middle Ages this charge kept fanning the flames of enmity. Social and economic distress kept adding fuel. The mere presence of the Jew in a community was a convenient explanation for many misfortunes. In time he became a handy scapegoat for all shortcomings—whether it was the outbreak of epidemics in the Middle Ages, when he was accused of poisoning wells, or economic depression in modern times, when he was accused of pauperizing the masses.

Yet in the German-speaking countries anti-Semitism was much more. There it had been for centuries an important factor in intellectual and political life. During the Dark Ages these lands were the classical centers of oppression. In modern times they became breeding places for Jew-baiting based on ideological motivations. There anti-Semitism was not only practiced, as human wickedness often is; it was also preached from rostrums and proclaimed from pulpits as a virtuous cause and a national goal.

Even religious reform played on anti-Semitism. Martin Luther himself denounced the Jews as "thirsty bloodhounds and murderers of Christendom," who stole children to cool their tempers with Christian blood. In the nineteenth century loathing for the Jews was very fashionable in German intellectual quarters. Important names were associated with it. Friedrich Hegel, the philosopher, regarded the Old Testament, the creation of the Jewish genius, as the embodiment of "a demon of hatred," in opposition to Hellenic beauty and virtue. Bruno Bauer denounced Jewry as the expression of "Asiatic lust and egoism." A political scientist, Heinrich von Treitschke, kept repeating that "the Jews are our misfortune." Friedrich Delitzsch, the orientalist, developed a religious motivation for Jew hatred.

Other members of the German intelligentsia were more practical in their approach. The Heidelberg professor Jacob Fries simply demanded that the Jews be wiped off the map. "Do not negotiate with bacilli but destroy them. Jews are cancer-germs in our life," preached the novelist Paul Boetticher (Paul de Lagarde). An active "*Antisemiten Liga*" was founded by intellectuals in Berlin in 1879. Its promoter, the writer Wilhelm Marr, announced that since "Semitism" is the exact antinomy of "Germanism," the Jews must be uprooted as "destroyers of culture" and disintegrators of mankind.

Nowhere else in the world did so many writers and thinkers conform with an ideology of hate.

On the German political scene anti-Semitism was for years a welcome and widely used propaganda stunt. At a period of national struggle it was convenient to have on the spot "a stranger" whom one could blame for all one's own shortcomings. "The Germans lack all notion of their own viciousness," wrote Nietzsche, who had a profound knowledge of his people. The nationalistic slogans of "Let us have colonies!," "We need living space!" went well with the cry: "Out with the Jews!"

On top of all that was piled a hatred based on racial theories. The Jew was to be discriminated against and later destroyed, not for what he believed in or for what he represented or for crimes he had allegedly committed. He was abhorred for the fact of his birth and for his mere existence as a Jew, irrespective of what he stood for.

Racist theoreticians flourished in Germany. One of the foremost was Eugen Duehring, who claimed that the Jews were the worst specimen of the Semitic race, and preached that Christianity, being the religion of the Aryan peoples, should dissociate itself from the Old Testament.

Even more outspoken was Houston Stewart Chamberlain. This son of an Irish admiral had a strange influence over the shaping of European history. Twice in one generation his teachings stimulated the German people to go to war against his own homeland. Kaiser Wilhelm wrote to him: "You wield your pen; I my tongue and my broadsword."

Chamberlain abandoned his native England for his adopted Germany, and left his first wife to marry Richard Wagner's daughter. He idolized his father-in-law ("the sun of my life"). He was neurotic to the point of hallucinations. ("I am driven on by demons.") He produced a book, *The Foundations of the Nineteenth Century,* which he thought contained the master key to all problems of history and civilization. The secret, he believed, lay in purity of race; he went on to explain all history in the light of this revelation. It was the "moral Teuton" alone who had made all the important contributions to culture. Therefore the value of any nation was in direct proportion to the quantity of its pure Teutonic blood. The Jews were "aliens" to civilization and their influence was "disruptive." Christ could not have been a Jew, as was "proved" by his Galilean origin and his difficulty in pronouncing Aramaic gutturals; so he must have been an Aryan. "Whoever claims that Christ was a Jew is either ignorant or a liar." The Aryan was distinguished by his bright and splendid complexion, expressing spiritual elation, while the Jew had inherited a round head and a beaked nose. The Jews were "a negative bastard race," who even lacked a true religion.

At the end of the nineteenth century the German Chancellor von Caprivi summed up anti-Semitism in his country with the words: "The movement now introduced in Germany is already widely beyond the welfare of the state. Passions have been evoked that may become impossible to channel."

*

The air of Germany was therefore densely contaminated with hostility long before the appearance of Hitler, and must have strongly influenced his makeup. He described in detail the moment when his nationalistic senses became "receptive" to his fathomless hate. These were the days of his hardship and frustration in Vienna, between 1909 and 1913, when he was watching political trends in various parties, and accumulating observations and ideas that he was, later, to put first on record and then into practice. He eagerly absorbed anti-Semitic literature, available in Vienna in great quantities.

Hitler accepted it all as gospel truth. He was smitten by both Wagner and Chamberlain. Through Wagner he learned of Arthur Gobineau, a French writer who preached that the mental and physical abilities of any human being were determined solely by his racial affiliation. All that counted was purity of blood. A nation is "spoiled" by absorbing foreign blood. Thus the Germans, "the race of princes, became contaminated and were on their way to decay because they permitted intermarriage with other races."

These were the "revelations" that Hitler later repeated almost word for word in his own book. He now began to see the Jews wherever he went. "The more I saw them, the more strikingly and clearly they stood out as a different people from the other citizens. . . . The odor of these people in caftans often used to make me feel ill."

Then his mind, never quite normal in sexual matters, made a stupendous "discovery": the Jew was responsible for prostitution and the white-slave traffic.

As has been recently established, Hitler had been strongly influenced by the racial preachings of a strange religious sectarian, Lenz von Liebensfeld, whose periodical *Ostara* he had devoutly collected and eagerly devoured. *Ostara* was constantly clamoring over the "imminent dangers threatening the blond woman" from the rich and "treacherous dark Jew," with his suggestive eyes and beguiling smile.

At that time, Hitler recalled, he really began to hate the Jews. It was for him a time of the greatest spiritual upheaval, he said. "From being a softhearted cosmopolitan I became an out-and-out anti-Semite."

His inner revolution crystallized into a desire to obliterate two thousand years of "Jewish" civilization and "rationalism" and to revert to a mankind guided by instincts. "It is true we are barbarians," he said. "We come to rejuvenate the world." The Jew was a living symbol of the past, which had to be brushed aside, among other miscreations of history, to make way for the coming millennium of the German Reich.

Beautiful, easygoing Vienna was destined to become both the breeding ground of Hitler's burning urge to destroy the Jews and the laboratory, where his disciple—another Adolf—acquired the first practical knowledge of how to bring it about.

His burning hatred of the Jew Hitler was to bear with him throughout his life. In *Mein Kampf* it appears and reappears in many shapes and forms. He sought the Jew in every conceivable gutter and attributed to him every imaginable filth. He had nightmare visions of hundreds of thousands of German girls "seduced by repulsive, crooked-legged Jewish bastards." The Jews had no civilization of their own, and therefore were bent on destroying all other civilizations. For this purpose they dominated the press, high finance and the trade unions. They even assumed the air of liberals when it served their purpose. They corrupted literature and the arts. They were cheating the world in pretending that they had national aspirations for a Jewish state; in fact, they had not the slightest intention to build such a state or live in it. All they wanted was to swindle and to dominate the world. There and then he declared war against them, promising himself to employ every weapon that the human spirit and will could furnish, "leaving to fate to decide in whose favor the balance should fall."

He was relentless even when fate finally showed its hand. In the last days of the Reich, when he realized that the game was lost, when he saw his empire in rubble and the thunder of Soviet cannon could be clearly heard in the bunker of his Berlin Chancellery office, he wrote in his testament: "Above all, I enjoin the government and the people to uphold the racial laws to the limit and mercilessly to resist international Jewry, the poisoner of all nations." Over six million Jews had already been exterminated by his orders. Yet even in his last hours he was not satisfied.

In *Mein Kampf* Hitler laid down in advance, with an astonishing similarity to what he later put into effect, his ideas of how he would reach power, the kind of government he would set up and the policies he would pursue.

Decadent democracy would be replaced by the *Fuehrerprinzip* (leadership principle), which was "consistent with the laws of nature." There is one who commands; all others must follow. Bourgeois simpletons sitting on office stools in various ministries babbling about social ideas and the wishes of the workers would be removed. Germany would annex the rich territories of Eastern Europe, which she needed as *Lebensraum* (living space). The state would be a racial unity. The master race, the Germans, would set out ultimately to dominate the world.

Hitler wrote of the importance of physically terrorizing the individual and the masses. "Intimidation in workshops and in factories, in assembly halls and at mass demonstrations, will always meet with success." The Aryan master would be merciless, like Nature herself, and trample on his opponent. He would preserve culture by subjugating all lower races.

Hitler thus denied the existence of a common denominator for humanity. According to him, there is no duty between man and man. In place of the injunction, "Thou shalt love thy neighbor as thyself," he said, "Crush him that is unlike yourself"; for the ideal of human brotherhood he substituted the principle of master and servant. Jewry and all it stood for was obviously the very antithesis of this creed.

Yet in his heart of hearts Hitler knew that the whole business of race was humbug. "I know perfectly well," he told an intimate associate, Hermann Rauschning, "that in the scientific sense there is no such thing as race. As a politician I need a conception which enables the order which has hitherto existed on a historic basis to be abolished and an entirely new order enforced and given an intellectual basis. And for this purpose the conception of race serves me well."

Hitler's uncanny instinct did not deceive him. The masses were willing to listen to his flood of invective and eagerly absorbed it all: the racial self-glorification and the nationalistic bombast, the world-domination boasts and the white-hot anti-Semitism. The sower found a tilled and ready soil. His message sounded familiar after so much theoretical and practical indoctrination in hatred, and in Germany it needed no revolution to find supporters.

The Nazis held democracy in contempt for "having betrayed the invincible army" of the Kaiser, while the German democrats lacked the courage of their convictions. They too were anxious to preserve the "honor of the Wehrmacht," which they were rebuilding both openly and secretly, and they never disclosed to the nation that it was the generals, not the politicians, who pressed for an immediate armistice in 1918.

*

The admiration of power and belief in the destiny of Germany to dominate the world had for a long time been part of the German people's heritage. Fichte and Hegel had developed the idea of the absolute superiority of the state. Peace corrupts nations, it was said, but war purifies them. Treitschke proclaimed war as the highest political and moral virtue. The hope for lasting peace he regarded as a sure sign of decay. Quotations from Nietzsche were absorbed half-baked by the Nazis. They were intoxicated by such slogans as "the will to power," "the transvaluation of all values" and "the lord of the earth."

The Nazis linked "the will to power" closely with "the will to hate." Germany had long cultivated a whole range of gratuitous enemies of her own choice. Poland was as "the natural enemy," France "the traditional enemy," England "the principal enemy," Russia "the inevitable enemy." But the Nazis needed now "an eternal enemy" inside the camp. "The new order" had produced a "new idol" to worship and needed a tangible devil to abhor. The State replaced God, the Fuehrer became the Son through whom the Deity addresses the people. The Jew was the Devil in this cosmogony. He was the source of all disasters. This fitted in with the crude conception of Jew-Satan; consequently, because of him Germany had lost World War I; he had treacherously stabbed the army in the back; he had brought about the hateful Versailles Treaty; he was responsible for unemployment. It was only natural that a Nazi anthem should read: "When Jewish blood spurts from the knife, then all goes doubly well." Moreover the Jew was a defenseless scapegoat. He had nothing to hit back with.

The far-flung anti-Semitic propaganda campaign was varied according to the circles it was directed at. Julius Streicher catered to the dregs of society, whom he delighted with obscene and pornographic pictures of bowlegged Jews and vile stories about the Jewish arsonist, the Jewish poisoner, the Jewish race-defiler. Alfred Rosenberg supplied the upper classes with "scientific" explanations of the disruptive powers in Jewry. He supplemented Chamberlain's *Foundations of the Nineteenth Century* with his own *Myth of the Twentieth Century*, a seven-hundred-page concoction of disconnected paragraphs that was accepted as first-class scholarship. Goebbels told the workers that the Jews were "capitalist bloodsuckers"; when he addressed bourgeois circles he called the Jews "dirty radicals and Communists." So everybody had a "legitimate" reason to hate the Jew. The record was played on either side, according to need.

Thus the six hundred thousand Jews of Germany, less than one percent of the population, were inflated into a national danger, which became the cornerstone of the whole Nazi propaganda.

It is not surprising, perhaps, that the German masses swallowed the drivel of Nazi dogma. What was, however, astonishing was the almost complete surrender of the German universities. In many other countries the institutions of learning were the outstanding, often also the last, bastions of democracy. In Germany they were among the first to acclaim dictatorship.

For years intellectuals had helped to corrode the national spirit. Without resource to the crudest expressions of the Nazi propagandists, they provided, in effect, a "perfumed National Socialism." They propagated violently nationalistic ideas and preached "the myth of nationhood" and the absolute supremacy of the state. They extolled the idea of a new, powerful spirit, which would brush away all conventional thinking, make a quick end to liberal nonsense and, by ruthless force, bring about the new social order. When Hitler appeared on the horizon, all these circles quickly decided that he could fit in with their idea of the redeemer.

They quoted Goethe's *Faust* as authority for the duality of the German soul, which divorced erudition from daily behavior. On this authority they were content to leave the German intellectual as they found him: quoting by heart from Plato and enthralled by Wagner's music in his spare time, and in office hours unflinchingly engaging in murder, torture and deceit.

German educators and professors saw no reason to heal this dangerous breach. Actually they perceived no breach and were happy with this product of the national culture.

The complete failure of the German schools of learning to prevent a return to the jungle was not the first in that country's history. No one is better qualified to testify on this subject than a German refugee professor, Wilhelm Roepke of Marburg University, a thinker of world renown.

"The professor was always subserviently helpful to the Government, whether by justifying Bismarck's policy of protective duties, by providing legal justifications for an unbridled submarine campaign, or, finally, by burning incense to National Socialism," Roepke wrote. "These are only some of the final stages of spiritual treason, which show the unforgivable guilt that many German universities bear for having paved the way of the National Socialist hordes." The German professors "were all too ready to whitewash the attacks on culture, right and morality and to swallow, nay, often to applaud, the most absurd theories."

In the absence of intellectual opposition Hitler made the most of Teutonic subservience. Everybody rallied round him. He carried with him people like Philipp Lenard of Heidelberg University, a Nobel Prize winner, who undertook to produce a "German physics" as opposed to the Jewish science of Einstein; Wilhelm Mueller, of the Aachen Technical High School, who proclaimed the failure of the Jewish plot to pollute science; and Johannes Stark, another Nobel Prize winner, who acclaimed Hitler and his colleagues as a heaven-sent gift from times long past, when races were purer, men greater and minds less led astray. Few German scientists were dismissed from office for disloyalty to the regime, though there were illustrious names among them. Some of these, like Jaspers, remained in Germany and held their peace, never actively opposing the regime. The overwhelming majority of the leading intellectuals took public vows to support the new order. "It was a scene of prostitution that has stained the honorable history of German learning."

After the war some of these venerable university teachers offered humble apologies for their silence, inaction and dissimulation. Various reasons and many excuses were offered. The fact remains, however, that the bulk of the German intellectuals went along with the Nazis in 1933, sought leading positions and publicly upheld the ideology of the new power. They were, at most, passive onlookers, struck with "blindness to the misfortunes of others, lack of imagination of the heart and inner indifference toward the witnessed evil" till it touched them personally.

Goebbels could now, in true medieval fashion, burn in public the books of noted writers and scholars "for their subversive influence on German thought and home," while inflamed and rejoicing students consigned to the fire the masterpieces of Jack London, Upton Sinclair, Helen Keller, Sigmund Freud, Emile Zola and others, along with the works of German masters like Jakob Wassermann, Stefan Zweig, Erich Maria Remarque or Thomas Mann. Goebbels proclaimed that the Germans would from now on live in the illumination of these flames. The overwhelming majority of them did.

In the perfect pose of a fanatical book-burner, Goebbels pointed to Hitler's *Mein Kampf* as the source of all wisdom.

*

By the time *Mein Kampf* was written, in 1924-25, Hitler had several years of struggle behind him. The German Army, secretly reborn immediately after World War I, had engaged him as a regimental education officer charged with combating pacifism, socialism and reform. On behalf of the army he became familiar with right-wing circles in Bavaria, eventually acquiring the title of *Führer* (leader).

Hitler had a remarkable gift for appealing to the masses; he could play on their deepest emotions and skillfully provide an outlet for the repressed desires of the mob. Burning with a sense of mission, he was obsessed by a boundless faith in his own powers.

He gathered a strange assortment of people around him: Hermann Goering, the frustrated aviation ace of World War I, later to become President of the Reichstag, the creator and head of the Luftwaffe and the dictator of the German economy; Julius Streicher, the sexually depraved pornographer, who had distinguished himself by blackmailing the husbands of his mistresses; Alfred Rosenberg, the Russian-trained architect, who was to shape the Nazi ideology; Joseph Goebbels, ambitious and avid for power, a gifted orator wielding a trenchant pen; Ernst Roehm, an army captain, for whom soldiering was life itself, who was later the Commander of the SA, the party's storm troops for street skirmishes and secret murders.

These were some of the people with whom Hitler embarked on "the conquest of a democracy" that he despised, "by democratic means" that he loathed.

The architects of the machinery responsible for most of the subsequent atrocities were comparative late-comers. These were Heinrich Himmler and Reinhard Heydrich.

Himmler was among Hitler's partners in the Munich *Putsch;* for a while he devoted most of his attention to his poultry farm and fertilizers, but was recalled by Hitler in 1929. It is not easy to size up this man; he was "one of those terrifying human beings foreign to normal human behavior," a romantic mystic, a believer in astrology and an animal lover. ("How can you find any pleasure in shooting at some innocent, defenseless deer? It's pure murder," he told Felix Kersten, his personal physician and masseur.) Seemingly mild and resembling a schoolteacher in appearance, he was the terror of a continent, an unflinching exterminator of human beings. To his Fuehrer he was *"der treue Heinrich"* ("the loyal Heinrich"), to his subordinates an admired leader ("I still respect and admire him," said Eichmann in Argentina twelve years after Germany's collapse). To Europe he was the bearer of unspeakable tortures.

Heydrich, according to his biographer, Charles Wighton, was one of the most extraordinary human characters of the twentieth century: "History may prove that he was the most demonic of all." "I never knew a cooler dog," said Eichmann of his erstwhile chief. He was cashiered from the navy for refusing to marry a girl he had compromised; later he became the uncrowned king of the night clubs in prewar Berlin. He was also a daring pilot: he would insist on joining the Luftwaffe in dangerous assignments, to the dismay of top Nazis, who never understood why he craved active service. In the occupied countries he became known as the "hangman of Europe."

There was something he had to live down: a strong rumor in top Nazi circles that he had a Jewish grandmother. "Such people could still be used so long as they were kept well in hand and for that purpose his non-Aryan origins were extremely useful," Himmler told Kersten. From Heydrich's personal dossier it appears that the gossip had been investigated and his Aryan descent proved. (Eichmann told Sassen he had never heard of Heydrich's Jewish origin and would not believe it.) But the slur was more than enough to make Heydrich doubly zealous in proving his absolute loyalty to the Fuehrer's ideas.

Heydrich started by terrorizing all opponents among his own people. His ambition was boundless. His god was not even the state, but power, which he sought for its own sake. To make himself indispensable he complied blindly with all Hitler's schemes. "He was the hidden pivot around which the Nazi regime revolved, the puppet master of the Third Reich," his subordinate Schellenberg said of him. Hitler described him during his lifetime as "highly gifted but highly dangerous," and eulogized him after his death as "the man with the iron heart."

The team of Heydrich-Himmler produced between them the machinery to implement Hitler's threats and promises on the home front, to keep the country quiet and to impose a permanent terror on the occupied areas.

It was composed of two organizations that were soon to become notorious —the SS (*Schutzstaffel*) and the SD (*Sicherheitsdienst*).

*

The SA (*Sturmabteilung*) was the popular army of the Nazi Party. It engaged in fierce fights with Socialists and Communists and in clashes with the police of the Republic. Its slogan was: "Possession of the streets is the key to power in the State." It was an unruly mob with strong revolutionary tendencies, fed on the so-called "socialist" principles of the National Socialist movement. Nationalization of property, confiscation and distribution of private wealth—this was its program. Hitler let them nurse their ideals while secretly maintaining contact with high finance and heavy industry. During the struggle for power he needed the brawling, strong and adventurous boys of the SA, and he was careful not to disillusion them. When they mutinied in Berlin, smashing up the headquarters of the party, yelling for their pay, Hitler rushed personally to the scene, imposed a tax on the party for the benefit of the SA, made a round of the beer halls, appeased the rebellious, appealed to the doubtful and showered promises on all, till he finally succeeded, in the course of the night, in re-establishing his authority.

But Hitler knew the SA would never be the blind instrument of obedience and servility he would need once he came to power. It was good enough for the years of the uphill efforts, but a crack instrument had to be prepared for the years of power. The small SS organization, counting no more than 280 men, was earmarked for this role. The SS had initially been meant to be the Fuehrer's personal guard, but when Himmler took it over in 1929 both he and Hitler had far broader aims. The SS was to forge far ahead of its rival, the SA. Nothing suited Heinrich Himmler better than to become the Reichsfuehrer SS, the commander of an order of knighthood, through which the Fuehrer would dominate the party, the state and—later—the whole world.

Himmler started building up the SS. He took in only men on whose blind obedience he could count. "*Meine Ehre heisst Treue*" ("Loyalty is my honor") was inscribed on the troopers' belts. Their badge was a skull and crossbones, to remind them of their duty of *Kadavergehorsam,* literally: "the obedience of a corpse."

Himmler soon realized he needed an efficient intelligence service, too, and was just wondering whom to entrust with the job when Heydrich, in search of a job, called on him at his poultry farm in June, 1931. Himmler asked the former naval officer to draft within twenty minutes a proposal for an espionage setup. Heydrich devised a plan that impressed Himmler. He told his caller to report to work immediately. Thus the SD, the *elite corps* of the SS, was launched.

Heydrich very soon turned it into a mammoth espionage and intelligence network, which grew until it comprised 100,000 confidential agents, graded according to the credibility of the information supplied and the permanence of their employment. There were confidential agents (*V-Leute*), ordinary agents (*A-Leute*), informers (*Z-Leute*), casual employees (*H-Leute*) and doubtful informants (*U-Leute*). The SD accepted and paid for any information about people's private lives, their hobbies and weaknesses, domestic troubles and love affairs, desires and secrets, income and expenditure. Anything that could be used for blackmail was welcome. Heydrich believed in knowing as much as possible about as many people as possible. His "Salon Kitty," a brothel all of whose girls were on the SD payroll, proved to be a veritable mine of information. The "Salon" was for exclusive guests only, with microphones installed in each bedchamber. Foreign diplomats and dignitaries, including the Italian Foreign Minister, Count Ciano, were frequent visitors. So was Ribbentrop.

But Heydrich was never satisfied with intelligence work alone. He wanted executive powers. Immediately after the Nazi takeover he was prodding Himmler to lay hands on the German police.

The organization of the police under the Nazis was a strange tangle of overlapping and confusion. This was partly the result of the dualism of party and state institutions, which, though merged, never gave up their birthmarks. There was also another dualism: pre-Nazi Germany had been a federation of states, the two most important being Prussia and Bavaria, each of which had a different police setup. Complete unification was a lengthy process.

Moreover it is still an open question whether part of the confusion was not due to a cunning and deliberate blurring of departmental boundaries, which always enabled a strong-willed official to extend his powers. It also helped to obliterate footprints, should anyone be called to account for his criminal acts. "Behind the apparently iron front of Teutonic organization there was a sort of willed chaos. . . . The general impression created is of a system knocked together in an *ad hoc* manner by the members of a ruling caste intent on reinsuring themselves," wrote Crankshaw, an acknowledged authority.

This "organized chaos" later gave Eichmann, too, latitude for his activities and a range of powers much exceeding the ordinary authority of a divisional head. At his trial he attempted to exploit to the hilt this state of affairs, shrinking to the unassuming office and role of a small bureaucrat, who, as is "clearly shown by the official designation of his department," simply "could not" have been in charge of the gigantic enterprise of the Final Solution.

The first to take over the Prussian police, in February, 1933, was Goering. Its core was now its political department in Berlin, the Secret State Police, better known as the Gestapo. It soon became a den of thieves and murderers. "It was so usual for the members of the Gestapo to arrest one another," Gisevius, an important figure in it, said after the war, "that we scarcely took notice of such incidents, unless we happened to come across a more detailed example of such an arrest by way of the hospital or the morgue."

Himmler, having first installed himself as the Chief of the Bavarian Police, with Heydrich as his main assistant, now coveted the job in Berlin. They put up the Dachau concentration camp for political prisoners, which soon became the training depot for future top personnel in the camps, recruited from among the SD old-timers. Skillfully exploiting the internal maze of intrigue that soon enveloped Goering and his cronies, the Himmler-Heydrich team finally succeeded in ousting him from the police. On April 10, 1934, Goering delivered the Gestapo to Himmler; two weeks later Heydrich was appointed Deputy of the Gestapo. Order was soon restored.

Both in Prussia and in Bavaria the Nazis took over the existing police force and all its cadres. Only a handful of officers were forced to leave. Almost everyone stayed on to serve the new masters. In the Bavarian police they discovered a man who was to prove his mettle under the Nazis. His name was Heinrich Mueller.

With the police well under control, the time was ripe for a showdown with the SA. Its commander, Roehm, was making himself a nuisance by voicing the constant resentments of his men. There had been no socialization; the political and personal pay-off they had been promised was constantly being delayed. Had they fought for this bourgeois government of Hitler, with the Ruhr magnates and business bosses behind it? Hitler realized that the street fighters had outlived their usefulness.

Tension between the Wehrmacht (the German Army) and the SA had been smoldering for years; now it mounted to fever pitch. A suggested compromise was torpedoed by a forged document produced by Heydrich, which "proved" that the SA was to be armed with heavy weapons. Hitler was now pressed on all sides for action, and finally gave his consent to the "Night of the Long Knives." Roehm and his senior officers were summarily executed by the SD, with Heydrich personally in charge of the lists of people to be shot or arrested. The purge started on June 29, 1934, and, for good measure, also included some other "enemies" of the movement, till Hitler ordered it stopped on July 2.

Two years of consolidation followed. The *Totenkopfverbaende* (Death's-head Units) were expanded. These were the terror troops of the concentration camps. The SS and the SD were kept intact as party outfits. In 1936, when Himmler was appointed Chief of the German Police, he divided it into the Order branch, the *Ordnungspolizei* (Orpo) under Daluege, and the Security Police (Sipo) under Heydrich, who had under him both the Gestapo and the SD. The final union of the party and state organs had to wait till after the outbreak of the war, when Himmler was finally able to bring under one roof the various bodies he commanded.

In September, 1939, the RSHA (the Reich Security Head Office) was created under Heydrich. It included various offices. One was Amt (Bureau)

III, Home Intelligence, the original SD, now entrusted to Dr. Otto Ohlendorf, economist. Amt V was the Criminal Police, under Arthur Nebe. Amt VI got Foreign Intelligence, under Heinz Yost. Amt VII was established later and entrusted to another university man, Professor Six. It dealt with "ideological" matters, and later also with "scientific research and evaluation."

The Gestapo became Amt IV, under Heinrich Mueller, who now joined the party and was given the rank of SS major general (Gruppenfuehrer). Mueller was and remained to the last "the man behind the scenes." Though he devised and executed all major Gestapo operations, he always remained in the background. Inscrutable in private contacts, he was a hard and silent worker. His "specialties" were Communists and saboteurs. After the war he disappeared as swiftly as he had always acted. His last known appearance was at the Fuehrer's bunker, two days before it fell, when it had become a genuine madhouse. Mueller came to investigate a charge of treason; having done his job he disappeared without a trace.

Not surprisingly, Jewish affairs ultimately became the exclusive province of the Gestapo, whose task was, officially, "combat against adversaries" (*Gegnerbekaempfung*).

The Gestapo also had an "Emigration and Deportations Department," officially charged with "Jewish affairs." It was headed by someone who had become a specialist in this field, and was an obvious choice for the job.

His name was Adolf Eichmann.

CHAPTER

3

The Beginnings of a Man and Bureaucrat

To assess the complex character of this dark-souled man, and to gain some comprehension of the forces that motivated him after he became a Nazi, it would be instructive to examine, if only in outline, the circumstances of his early upbringing and middle years until the apogee of his power. It is a story told at times in his own words.

Eichmann's early life was conventional enough. He was born in 1906 in Solingen, Germany, the eldest of five children. His parents, Adolf Karl Eichmann and Maria nee Schefferling, both Protestants, moved with their family to Linz in Austria when he was eight years old. Though not very diligent, young Adolf managed to get on at school and later spent four years in high school. But at his father's insistence—"and much to the annoyance of my teachers," he related—he was sent to a technical high school, where once again he failed to excel at his studies. He wrote a poem that was greatly enjoyed when declaimed aloud at a class ball, but this seemed to be his outstanding achievement.

One of his vivid memories of this time was that his mathematics teacher Brant, who allowed his students great latitude, used to tell them stories about World War I.

He had, moreover, the same history teacher, Dr. Leopold Poetsch, as Adolf Hitler had had in Linz. Germany's Fuehrer paid a warm tribute to this man: "He was decisive for my whole later life. . . . He used our budding national fanaticism as a means for educating us. . . . There we sat, often aflame with enthusiasm, sometimes moved to tears."

Eichmann Senior was at that time the commercial manager of the Linz electric works. At home the atmosphere was strictly patriarchal: Father gave the orders and expected rigid compliance. He was religious and gave his children a pious Protestant doctrinal education. He went to church every

Sunday. "It was owing to [my] father's influence that I left the Church as late as 1937, long after all my comrades had done so," the son later recalled. He was then thirty-one years old, and had been an active Nazi some five years.

Maria Eichmann died when he was ten; his father soon remarried. The second wife too was a devout Protestant. Under her wing he used to read the Bible and mark with red pencil the passages that interested him most—the descriptions of battles and wars.

"The years of my youth were quite sunny," he recalled. "We were seven children at home, among them one sister. I used to engage a lot in sport. My old man insisted that I take a course in fencing and jiujitsu. My best friend at the time," he added to Sassen's surprise, "was a Jew from Tyrol. His name was Harry Selbar. He used to come to our home and I used to visit him. His older brother impressed me. I used to walk in Linz with Harry even when I already wore the Nazi party emblem, as after all we grew up together, so to speak."

The impact of the Nazi ideology quickly brushed aside old associations. "Since 1932 I lost all contact with Selbar," Eichmann concluded.

Thus Eichmann himself precludes any possible speculation about "a broken home" or "an unhappy childhood" which might have accounted for his later development. Nor were there any "early bad experiences" with Jews which might have been responsible for the implacable Jew-hatred of his later years. If any explanation of his future attitude is sought in the home atmosphere, it lies elsewhere. "My old man always had an open ear for nationalistic ideas; on these he was quite outspoken," Eichmann recalled. As was usual in many middle-class circles, they were rendering to Caesar more than to God. Religious though the home atmosphere had been, it was deeply steeped in nationalism, but it was German nationalism. The genial trait of enjoying life, so typical of many Austrians, was held in contempt. In contrast the proverbial Germanic virtues of discipline, industry and thrift were held up as a model of behavior. Even more marked was the general feeling of bewildered frustration at having lost World War I. It was the offspring of self-pity, envy and a longing for revenge.

Though too young to have served in World War I, young Eichmann joined the Union of Front Fighters; he was highly flattered by the society of senior ex-officers, all handsomely bemedaled, who on occasion paraded proudly through the streets of Linz. He was overjoyed to march in their ranks or to join them at rifle-shooting exercises.

Though in his opinion "the Nazi Party in Linz at the time consisted mainly of frustrated people or half-wits," Eichmann took a deep interest in it and, even before joining the party, he admired it sufficiently to break off his engagement to a girl who was critical of the "marching SA idiots."

Some time after leaving school, he was able through "Uncle Fritz," his stepmother's cousin, to get a job with the Socony Vacuum Company as a traveling representative. Uncle Fritz enjoyed a certain social status: he was the president of the Austrian Automobile Club and maintained good relations with the local Socony Vacuum people.

Later, Eichmann had more to say about his putative uncle:

"Imagine: one day he came to see me in Berlin, in 1943, with a very good-looking girl, telling me she was his daughter from his first marriage. I didn't know her. Then Uncle Fritz revealed that his first wife, Dora, had been a Jewess. He had married her whilst a struggling law student. . . . He wanted me to help her (his daughter), the half-Jewess, to get to Switzerland. . . . I met them at the hotel at the evening. We had a few drinks and a good time, and she left for Switzerland. I had to repay him for what he had done for me."

During the interrogation and trial Eichmann repeatedly spoke of his "Jewish relationship," which, he said, made it impossible for him to have been anti-Semitic. But in talking to Sassen, he waxed wrathful over Uncle Fritz:

"In 1945, I heard that Fritz saw my children and said, 'Here are the children of that swine.' I then told my wife: 'The days when we could lay these people out prostrate are over now, but the day will certainly come when I shall personally kill this man with my own hand!' "

Employment with Socony Oil gave Eichmann the opportunity to move around, enjoy life, make friends. He had some love affairs during this period; he described them in detail to Sassen. They are recorded on tapes marked in his handwriting: "This tape is for information only."

Some incidents he found amusing. When he asked the grandfather of one of his girl friends for permission to marry her, after they had been engaged for over two years, a political discussion ensued and Eichmann defended his nationalist views. The argument grew so heated that he banged his fist on the table. "Naturally, they showed me the door," he said with a laugh.

He was never at a loss for girls. At an inn in St. Nicolai on the upper Danube he was served by little Fanny Baeck. To impress the girl, he attempted to swim across the Danube, but a strong current prevented him. A friendship ensued until one Sunday, when the family went to church, he took her to a neighboring woodland, "where we celebrated our common interest in our own way." They were surprised by the girl's sister, who rushed to her father in bitter complaint. Everyone made a loud fuss, so Eichmann formally asked to marry Fanny. But her sister continued to be sour.

"So I became offended and told the little one: 'Unless your sister apologizes by 8 o'clock this evening, I shall never enter this house again.' "

He was relieved at the girl's failure to apologize; taking formal leave, he withdrew and boarded a river boat for Linz. He remembered that the family's big dog followed him and he had to pay a fine, because dogs were not allowed on these boats. Then Fanny came to interview "the old man," but Eichmann asked his father to put her off "unless it should transpire that there were more serious consequences of the relationship." There were none and the affair was ended.

From then on Eichmann's relations with women remained practical and generally shallow. He was successful in establishing contacts, used women freely and kept up simultaneous affairs, both during his three formal engagements as well as after his marriage. He would extricate himself from an affair simply by getting up and leaving. But there was one boundary he never overstepped: all his love affairs were confined to Aryan women.

Some of these associations caused trouble. A young and gay widow friend in Vienna, during the prewar years, was the owner of a farm she was anxious to get rid of. Eichmann saw to it that the Jewish community acquired the farm for a sizable sum, to be used as a training depot for prospective pioneers in Palestine. The matter was discovered and an investigation was ordered, but Eichmann's personal friend Dr. Stahlecker, the Commandant of the Viennese Gestapo, hushed the matter up. Some years later, in Budapest, he fell under the spell of the dashing, beautiful young divorcee Ingrid von Ihne, whom he eventually brought over to Austria when the advance of the Russians made Hungary too hot. Though the relationship with the socialite von Ihne tickled his pride, he looked for a simpler and more comfortable contact. This he found in the person of a Viennese girl, then in Budapest, Margit Kutschera, who was popular with some top Nazis in the Hungarian capital.

The woman Eichmann married, Vera Liebl, came from Bohemia. He met her on one of his travels, during his early days of struggle, and ultimately proposed. They got married in 1936. The relationship, very warm at first, cooled off gradually. Mrs. Eichmann took little interest in her husband's work and felt most comfortable in her own family circle. Their home remained for some time in Prague. Eichmann was thankful to his wife for giving birth to three boys while they were in Europe and to a fourth after they were reunited in Argentina. For his children he had a great deal of affection, which he displayed in his own way by instilling discipline into them.

In later life he used to speak of the old times with a nostalgic note. He recalled that one day in 1932 a family friend, Boleck, invited Eichmann's father and himself to a meeting of the Nazi Party. There a man spoke about nationalist movements in Germany whose members were being attacked and killed by "traitors and fatherland-sellers" because of their patriotic aspirations. Already strongly under the spell of Nazi propaganda, Eichmann become aroused and approached Dr. Ernst Kaltenbrunner, an old friend, who was in the place, sitting in a corner.

Before he could say a word, Kaltenbrunner, a veteran Nazi, told him: "You belong to us!" He made Eichmann sign a membership application on the spot.

Twenty-five years later Eichmann was to tell Sassen: "I still remember how glad and proud I was at that moment."

It was, indeed, a moment that decided his own fate and that of many others.

While talking in whispers to Kaltenbrunner during the meeting, Eichmann mentioned his encounter with the Linz "Schlaraffia Club," a jocular name for "idlers," an association of people who, in Freemason fashion, liked to meet for a drink and a jest. Eichmann was told that no Jews were admitted to the club. "This impressed me favorably," he recalled.

He became a full member of the party and of the SS and an active propagandist. He went to work wearing the party emblem on his lapel. But his heart was not in Austria—it was in Germany, where great things were afoot. Led by another ex-Austrian, who had left his country for Germany, the Nazis were storming their way to power. Eichmann felt an itch for a uniform and a longing for full-time service.

Fate played into his hands when, about Whitsuntide, 1933, he was dismissed by Socony in a company move to reduce its staff. Mendaciously he told his father that the company had engaged a new Jewish inspector, who had dismissed him for belonging to the Nazi Party.

He went straight to Kaltenbrunner, who told him to go to Germany, where Boleck was training an SS brigade made up of Austrians. Armed with a passport issued by the German Consul, Eichmann lost no time in joining Boleck.

"We'd better make a soldier of you," Boleck told him.

A year's service followed in the army and in the SS training depots at Lechfeld and Dachau. The drill was hard and at times almost beyond endurance. Later he used to display with pride the scars on his elbows, the visible consequences of exercises crawling through barbed-wire fences. It was there that he acquired the power to master his body and the ability to control his emotions. These were also his military years, the memory of which he cherished, as did most Germans. Military service was supposed to wash away the drawbacks of his birth: that he was not altogether the ideal Prussian type, that he was not quite blond and only almost blue-eyed. Along with other high-ranking Nazis he had to live down such obvious deficiencies by an overwhelming display of loyalty and devotion.

Opposite the training depot was the notorious concentration camp, a prototype of the camps he was to become closely associated with less than ten years later.

This was the school of terror, violence and horror in which the future Nazi minions were hardened. Its first commander, Theodor Eicke, laid down its principles:

"Prisoners are enemies of the State.

"Orders have to be obeyed whatever their import.

"Tolerance means weakness."

Eichmann joined the exclusive SD, the Security Service of the SS. He was given the rank of Scharfuehrer (sergeant). In the beginning of 1935 he was assigned to the Jewish Department, where he met some of his future close collaborators, such as Wisliceny and Dannecker. For the next ten years this was to be his whole life.

He began teaching himself Hebrew and Yiddish after his application for a grant of fees for tuition from a rabbi was turned down. "Don't they trust me enough to allow me contact with a Jew?" he grumbled. Soon he was proficient enough to read a Yiddish newspaper.

He was put up for an SS commission in 1937, backed by his superior, Wisliceny, who praised his "comprehensive knowledge of the organizational methods and ideology of Jewry, the enemy," and by SS Major Six, head of the office (later a defense witness at the trial).

Eichmann's elevation to an officer's commission coincided with an SD decision to take over Jewish affairs more directly, in line with the extension of its activity to other parts of the world. Ordered to be present at a Nuremberg party rally, attended by a hundred foreign contributors to Julius Streicher's vitriolic Jew-baiting paper *Der Stuermer*, Eichmann was proud to establish contact with and enlist an American to do "real intelligence work" on Jewish organizations in the U.S.A.

Immediately afterward he was sent to the Middle East to look over the situation there, and especially to report on Palestine. His report, written jointly with Herbert Hagen, another member of the mission, was strongly anti-Jewish and anti-Zionist. Palestine was presented as "an economic chaos" in which Jews cheated each other because they had no Gentiles to deceive.

Eichmann was well launched.

CHAPTER 4

Overture to Destruction: Eichmann Wins His Spurs

From the day Hitler took power, on January 30, 1933, Jews were officially considered enemies of the state. Thousands were arrested almost immediately. Rabbis, community leaders and merchants disappeared into concentration camps. "I remember the first dreadful scenes," testified Mr. Benno Cohen at Eichmann's trial. Mr. Cohen is today a member of Israel's Knesset (Parliament); at that time he was a lawyer in Berlin and the president of the local Zionist organization. "Some people returned from the camps beaten and completely broken. Women were constantly getting notifications from the camps: 'Your husband has died of a heart attack. The ashes are sent herewith. Postage is three and a half marks.'"

On April 1, 1933, a boycott day was proclaimed throughout the Reich. The Brownshirts marked every Jewish business or office with a Shield of David and with slogans like "Danger!" or "One-Way Road to Jerusalem." German girls who had Jewish boy friends were marched through the streets wearing placards reading: "I am a swine. I have contacts with Jews." A shower of enactments soon excluded the Jews from public office and the professions of law and medicine, expelled them from the press and banned them from films and theaters.

On September 15, 1935, at the annual party rally in Nuremberg Hitler announced the racial decrees (named after the city), giving effect to his long-established belief that Jews were not German citizens but aliens. They were deprived of citizenship and given the second-degree status of "subjects." German-Jewish intermarriage or sexual relationship was forbidden. Jews were forbidden to employ Aryan domestics under the age of forty-five.

In unanimously approving the Nuremberg edicts the Reichstag declared itself "imbued with the consciousness that the purity of German blood is essential to the continued existence of the German people and animated by the inflexible resolve to secure the future of the German nation for all times."

To be stigmatized as a Jew meant immediate economic disaster. Many people of doubtful origin started frantic researches into their ancestry. A new profession came into being, that of "family researchers," who helped to "discover" that one's grandfather or grandmother had been born of extra-marital relations with a non-Jew. People would then go to court to claim "reclassification."

Many Germans carried matters much further than the laws required. Jews were often denied entrance to shops, even for the purchase of food. Pharmacies would not sell them medicines. Hotels denied them a night's lodging. At the entrance to many towns signboards appeared: "Jews not wanted here." At road curves posters read: "Drive carefully. Jews–75 kms or over." For the duration of the Olympic Games in 1936 some of the signs were removed, for the benefit of foreign visitors.

Germany was in effect expelling its Jews. A great wave of emigrants left the country in the first years of the new regime in spite of severe limitations on the transfer of property abroad. Then the restrictions were tightened still further. On top of high taxation of emigrants, strict currency regulations were enforced. On the other hand, few prospective countries of entry allowed the pauperized refugees in. The outside world was, generally, not prepared to accept them (see Chapter 12). A tragic, vicious circle of frustrated efforts to leave Nazi Europe was initiated, in a world that was a perfect picture of "a planet without a visa."

It was, however, in Hitler's homeland itself, some five years after his assumption of power, that the biggest organized, systematic and direct drive to expel Jews was launched. Underestimated at the time, even by the Jews, it was in many ways an ominous precursor of far more sinister developments.

It was in Austria that Eichmann won his spurs.

*

With the forcible annexation of Austria (the *Anschluss*) on March 13, 1938, the SD decided to take a more active hand in driving out the Jews. Its chief, Heydrich, promised the elated Fuehrer that his original homeland, which he had now "led back to the Reich," would soon be cleared of Jews. The Austrian SS, who had long been champing at the bit, were allowed a free hand; the result was an orgy of violence. Thousands of opponents were immediately arrested. The more important prisoners were detained in the cellars of Hotel Metropol, the new Gestapo headquarters, from which Heydrich conducted operations and where he held the last Austrian Chancellor, Dr. Schuschnigg, and Baron Louis von Rothschild. For others a new detention camp was provided in Mauthausen, since both Dachau and Buchenwald were brimming over.

Eichmann was called in immediately, and arrived in Vienna four days after the *Anschluss.*

He was now an officer, an expert on Jewish affairs, and had been a rising star in the SD ever since his Palestine assignment in 1937. His manner had meanwhile changed accordingly, as his personality began expanding with new responsibilities. He was now quite accustomed to addressing Jews in the abusive, humiliating manner characteristic of him in his prime. His change in manner had been consummated as the Nazi policy on Jews took shape.

"I did not recognize the man," said Dr. Franz Eliezer Meyer, who knew him in 1936 and early 1937 when Eichmann officially attended Jewish meetings to take notes. His cool, usually civil demeanor had led everyone to take him for a typical bureaucrat, pedantic but otherwise inoffensive. "Now we faced a ruler of life and death who spoke with arrogance and rudeness," said Dr. Meyer.

He had shouted obscenities at Dr. Stahl, head of the Jewish community in Berlin: "You old sack of dung, you've been out of a concentration camp too long."

The SD had decided on the expulsion of the Jews, and thought that the best way to prepare the ground was by systematic terror.

Thousands of Jews were kidnaped in the streets and forced to clean the SS latrines or to remove the Schuschnigg government signs from the sidewalks. Testifying at the trial, Moritz Fleischmann, who had been active in Jewish life in Vienna, told that one day, when he was surreptitiously entering the office building of the Jewish community, he was detained by an SS man. "He gave me a bucket of boiling water and told me to scrub the sidewalks. I soon found out that the bucket was full of strong acid, which burnt my hands; they swelled up." Fleischmann saw the SS men lead out Chief Rabbi Taglicht, a dignified man of seventy, in his rabbinical gown and his prayer shawl; when the rabbi knelt down to scrub the pavement with the Viennese mob around him, sneering, jeering and applauding, the sentry turned to him: "How do you like it now?" To which the Chief Rabbi Taglicht quietly replied: "If the Lord likes it, I am his servant."

Fleischmann said that Jews "were rounded up like dogs" and thrown into cars which took them to Dachau. Soon their relatives were receiving the well-known notifications that "ashes were available against the payment of postage." The reign of terror resulted in many suicides.

With the terrain sufficiently prepared by violence, the SD was now ready for the expulsion of the whole Jewish community. Eichmann was assigned to the job. Though still a member of the Intelligence branch, he was attached to the Viennese Gestapo Chief Stahlecker.

Eichmann watched the Gestapo at work on the Jews for several days, then came up with a plan for a swift and total expulsion of the Jews from Austria. It needed, he argued, not only external oppression but also pressure from the inside. The Jewish leaders themselves must assist in the emigration.

Eichmann's plan was simple and ingenious. The SD would re-establish

Jewish communal life and reopen the requisitioned Jewish autonomous institutions. But these would function only for the purpose of securing the departure of their people. The Jews would be allowed to run their affairs, under proper supervision, of course, but only as long as prescribed emigration quotas were filled. The alternatives to cooperation by the Jews were the Dachau and Mauthausen concentration camps.

He knew that the local Jewish functionaries saw no future for their people inside the country and were more than willing to explore all avenues for emigration. He also knew that they preferred an organized and orderly exit to the hopeless and frustrating wandering of frightened people among the endless queues outside foreign consulates in a vain search for visas, often ending with the desperate suicide of a whole family.

The Gestapo would thus assume supreme control over Jewish life and secure the cooperation of the Jewish officials. For the sake of appearances Eichmann preferred the establishment of a special authority to be called "the Central Office for Jewish Emigration" (*Zentralstelle fuer Juedische Auswanderung*).

Heydrich approved the scheme at once and put Eichmann in charge.

*

He threw himself into the work with his usual eagerness. The closed and ransacked offices of the Jewish community were reopened. Some Jewish functionaries were released from concentration camps. He told them it was his job to clear Vienna and Austria of Jews. He said he would require complete obedience and unlimited cooperation in the interests of the community itself. Any resistance would be, in any case, brutally crushed, he added.

He installed himself as the ruler of the community by several devices. All its funds were frozen and could be released by him alone. He ordered the functionaries to bring up for his decision all major matters; he soon controlled institutional life. He prescribed the number of classes at schools, the strength of personnel in hospitals, the quotas of inmates at old-age homes and institutes for the blind, even the administration of the archives, the public library, the cemetery and the burial arrangements. All were now run "by orders."

Another device was the constantly overhanging threat of deportation to the concentration camps and the trickle of releases he would procure from time to time.

Eichmann would receive the functionaries of the community for an audience, listen to their problems and issue his instructions, which they were obliged to reduce to writing and provide him with the original. Emigration matters and the latest census of driven-out Jews were always the first and most important items on the agenda.

To incivility and vulgarity he added a new feature, which was to play a major part in his activities from now on: deception. He admitted during the trial that he deceived Jewish leaders systematically. His vulgar talk was intended partly to intimidate them, partly to impress them with his sincerity. "I'm frank with you, be frank with me," he told Jewish representatives.

He soon found out that things went much easier when he mingled his threats with vague promises that he never meant to keep. He also discovered that Jews were immensely impressed by interest in their cultural and national aspirations and that because of their inborn optimism they were easily taken in by false assurances about their future.

Deception was, of course, an established practice in German psychological warfare. It had been used with excellent results both at home and abroad. For a long time before Hitler the Germans had been taught that objective truth does not exist, since truth consists merely in what can be "put over" and good propaganda can be relied upon to make up for any exposed lie.

But with Jews it went much further and deeper. Deception was perfected into an art and became one of the main instruments of the system. It was carried on in the concentration camps and the ghettos later on, and brought to an extreme of guile and knavery. People at the gates of the gas chambers were deceived by being told that they were about to undergo "disinfection" before being sent further on for "resettlement" to do "productive work."

Eichmann was the first to introduce the method and later to perfect it. On meeting the representatives of Vienna Jewry, he told them a cock-and-bull story about being born in Sarona, near Tel Aviv, and knowing Yiddish and Hebrew, to show that they could not really cheat him.

"We exchanged astonished looks," testified Moritz Fleischmann, "when Eichmann proceeded to cite by heart a whole page of Adolf Boehm's book on the history of Zionism." Boehm himself, who was among the Jewish leaders present, was quite taken aback.

"They believed it about my birthplace in a Templar colony in Palestine, and after I used some Hebrew stock phrases they also believed I knew the language well," Eichmann informed Wisliceny laughingly. Thus began the rumor, later circulated in whispers in the ghettos and camps, about a legendary, all-powerful but ever-invisible Nazi officer who decided the fate of the Jews, who mixed among them as a spy but whose identity remained a riddle.

In Vienna he developed an approach that later became standard for the treatment of Jewish functionaries. He ordered the imprisoned director of the Jewish community office, Dr. Joseph Loewenherz, to be brought up. Then, at the first available excuse he slapped him in the face, saying immediately that it was his intention to rehabilitate Jewish lives and asking Loewenherz to prepare a plan for the organization of the Jewish community and for the promotion of Jewish emigration from Austria. He made it quite clear that cooperation with him was the only way to survival, both for the Jewish masses, for the functionaries themselves and for the members of their families.

"Poor Loewenherz had to deal with Eichmann," Fleischmann recalled.

"Every talk was a renewed humiliation." Eichmann later boasted of his "humane and correct" attitude toward the Jewish leaders. "I was not like my deputy Guenther, who would not let a Jew get nearer to him than three steps," he said. "I maintained the contact with them as was due to an opponent. Like a gentleman."

(We wanted Loewenherz to give evidence at the trial about these "gentlemanly" ways, or at least to answer a prepared questionnaire. He was a sick man and lived in New York when the preparations for the trial were in progress. Our consul paid him a visit. Loewenherz was very agitated and promised to answer the questions in the near future. He never did. The excitement of recalling Eichmann's rule in Vienna was too much for him; it brought on a heart attack. Three days later he died.)

Eichmann had worked out a procedure to simplify the expulsion process. He made all authorities concerned with emigration refer their agents to his own headquarters, at the requisitioned Rothschild Palace in Prince Eugen Street.

"It all went like on an assembly line," he repeatedly boasted. So it did. A Jew would enter the office of the *Zentralstelle;* he was still somebody, having a job or a shop, an apartment to live in, some property or cash in the bank, his child still registered at school. As he proceeded from window to window he was stripped of all these things one by one. When he finally left the building he was jobless, his property had been requisitioned, his child crossed off the school roll and his apartment taken away. All he had now was a passport with the letter "J," valid for two weeks. It was his task to find a foreign visa. He was expressly told that if he were to be found in Austria after the passport expired, it would still be valid but only for a single, one-way journey: to a concentration camp!

Eichmann felt he had found the proper way to deal with the Jews: first, to unleash unbridled bloodletting and barbarity, causing as much and as widespread suffering as possible; then, before they could recover from the shock, to invite their leaders to cooperate with the authorities " to alleviate further hardship." The immediate and ostensible goal of this cooperation was always consistent with the good of the community. In the case of Austria it promoted emigration, which the Jews desired in any case. Moreover, it secured the discontinuation of the horrors, even if only for a while. It was quite natural that most Jewish functionaries considered it their duty to lend a hand.

Thus Eichmann laid down in Vienna the cornerstone for a system which was later developed and brought to perfection throughout occupied Europe, by using the Jewish spokesmen themselves as unwitting tools.

An added touch of deception on Eichmann's part was a display of interest in Jewish internal affairs. He wrote to his friend: "Tomorrow I shall again inspect the offices of the Jewish community and of the Zionists. This I do at least once a week. I have them [the Jewish leaders] completely in my hand. They don't dare to make a step without me."

Concurrently with his display of interest in Zionism and Jewish affairs, Eichmann minced no words about the nature of his mission or what he intended to do to rid Austria of its Jewish inhabitants. The mixture of vague promises and small favors to the community with harsh, brutal words became typical of the methods deliberately applied to bewilder the Jewish leaders.

His power grew as rapidly as his rise in rank. From second lieutenant in 1937 his promotion became a yearly affair. By the beginning of 1939 his superiors rated him a "recognized specialist" in his sphere, energetic and impulsive, one who handled organizational and other tasks extremely well. By 1941 he had attained the rank of SS Obersturmbannfuehrer, lieutenant colonel, which he retained to the end.

Arrogance grew with expanding power. Not only Jews but even Nazis in high positions felt the force of his personality. Once he waged a furious telephone argument with the all-powerful Chief of the SS Staff, General Karl Wolff. The latter insisted that the life of a certain Jew be spared. Eichmann was just as insistent that it would not be. As the argument grew more heated, Wolff shouted into the instrument: "Do you realize you're talking to a general of the SS?" Eichmann replied: "And do *you* realize you're talking to Lieutenant Colonel of the Gestapo Adolf Eichmann?"

Wolff hung up on him. Eichmann was so enraged that he challenged the other to a duel. It was only on the personal intervention of Himmler, Chief of the SS, that the duel was called off.

Another target for his arrogance was the Secretary of State for the Ministry of Interior, Wilhelm Stuckart. Having accidentally found in a file what Stuckart had written about "Eichmann's gypsy methods," he went at once to the Gestapo Chief Mueller asking "to have Stuckart before the pistol." He demanded a duel. But Mueller did not want trouble and pacified him.

*

The establishment of the *Zentralstelle* in Vienna was actually a novelty. Up to then every authority had taken a bite at Jewish affairs from its own angle, whether as a propaganda stunt, in which Goebbels and the regional party leaders (the gauleiters) were mainly interested, or for the purpose of getting hold of Jewish money, which Goering and Schacht, the President of the Reichsbank, were after, or from the viewpoint of racial laws and complete segregation, which was uppermost in the minds of Hitler and Streicher. No concerted, over-all effort in Jewish matters had ever been made. Now it became known among the leadership that Heydrich had produced a basic scheme, which was being carried out in Vienna.

Eichmann soon received some important visitors. The Ministry for the Interior sent out a representative to look over the Center; an official from the Propaganda Ministry paid a call, and—what was most important—the Ministry for Economic Affairs made an inspection. They all liked what they saw. Here was a way to expel Jews and at the same time rob them of their property. Favorable reports were dispatched to Berlin and soon resulted in an important appointment. On January 24, 1939, Goering nominated Heydrich head of the Central Office for Jewish Emigration *for the whole Reich.* Wohltat, of the Economic Office Ministry, was to work with him, since the financial aspect was, of course, not to be forgotten. Goering's directive specified the rules according to which the new office would operate. They were all modeled on Eichmann's work in Vienna; his methods thus became the order of the day.

Jewish leaders from Berlin were ordered by the Gestapo to visit the *Zentralstelle* in preparation for the installation of the system in Germany. They were aghast. "It was terrible, terrible," testified Dr. Meyer at the trial. "Like a factory . . . A man was just passed on like an inanimate object in an automat. In Berlin it was not like that at the time. We could still argue, at least, with the authorities. Eichmann asked what we thought of it. At that time we still thought we could tell him 'No,' and we said that this was unthinkable in Berlin. . . . Then he assailed us."

"I had to be everywhere and to deal with everything," Eichmann recalled. "Heydrich said I was acting like a small prime minister. Anyway, I could fix a special rate of exchange for a person, which even the Reichsbank could not do. . . . I would appear suddenly in places where nobody expected me. My subordinates treated me with such respect that the Jews thought I was really a kind of a king."

Foreign currency was one of his main concerns, since without it nobody was admitted to foreign countries. He made the Reichsbank provide it in return for exorbitant payment in German money. Rich Jews had to pay enormously high rates of exchange, and the difference was used for the acquisition of foreign currency for the poor. A fund for emigration was created under his orders; he sent Jewish leaders abroad to collect donations for it. They got almost ten million dollars from Jewish bodies. Migration turned into good business for Germany. When the hundred-thousandth pauperized Jewish emigrant left Austria, Heydrich came in person to Vienna to congratulate his protégé.

Eichmann was intoxicated by his success. He was positive he had found the right way of dealing with the matter, which would provide the ultimate answer to the Jewish problem. So he coined the phrase that was to become the code name for an unspeakable crime, a cover for the systematic murder of six million human beings. He called it the "Final Solution." All his files bore this designation.

"I suggested these words," he told Sassen. "At that time I meant by this the elimination of the Jews, their marching out of the German nation. Later . . . these harmless words were used as a camouflage for the killing."

He traveled extensively in the Rothschilds' requisitioned black limousine. "I used it for my travels, in the course of which I visited many of the SD branches in Austria to provide them with 'injections' for the Final Solution," Eichmann recalled later.

While Eichmann was merrily kicking the Jews out of Austria and robbing them under the guise of providing "exit permits," other Nazi agencies were requisitioning Jewish treasures of art and jewelry. Ransom was openly required for the release and emigration of the richer people.

In the meantime, the British Prime Minister, Neville Chamberlain, and his French colleague, Édouard Daladier, had paid their respects to Hitler at Munich. With the surrender of the Western powers to Nazi extortion and the sacrifice of Czechoslovakia, there seemed no limit to what the leaders of Germany would permit themselves. Churchill was among the few who described the Munich pact as it really was: "a total unmitigated defeat." For Hitler it was the green light to go ahead. The repercussions on the Jewish scene were immediate.

*

Heydrich had to cast about for ways to get rid of the poor Jews who could not get entry permits to other countries. He learned that the Polish Government had passed a law under which many thousands of its Jewish nationals, residing permanently in Germany, would be deprived of their nationality. The law was to take effect on October 30, 1938. A day before the deadline all Jews of Polish nationality were rounded up in Germany.

Among them were Zindel Shmuel Grynszpan and his family. In his evidence he told the court that after twenty-seven years' residence in Hannover he was ordered to leave immediately. About six hundred people, old and young, were assembled in a building, and on Saturday, October 29, they were marched to the railway station. The streets were black with people, shouting and yelling, "Out with the Jews!" At the station they were ordered to board a train. "We were told by the police that we would return soon, and need not take anything with us, only our passports." The train headed for the Polish border. Other trains loaded with Jews from all parts of Germany were speeding to the assembly point. Altogether fifteen thousand men, women and children arrived. "When we approached the frontier," Zindel Grynszpan said, "we were told to give up all the cash we had on us. Each was allowed to keep ten marks. 'You did not bring in more, you won't take out more,' we were told. Then, after a personal search, the people were marched into no-man's land toward the Polish frontier. The SS men were cracking their whips. Anyone who lingered was whipped; blood was spilt on the road. They tore away the few personal belongings we had with us. I fell, and my son pleaded with me to run, or else we should all die. Thus we reached the Polish border." The Polish sentries were taken by surprise and started shooting. Finally, the frontier roadblock was lifted. The refugees, who had not eaten or drunk for two days, poured into the small town of Zbonszyn. The Poles put them in a closed camp.

Thus the first Nazi deportation, the forerunner of those to follow, was successfully carried out, in the eyes of the whole world.

Zindel Grynszpan wrote to his son Herszel, a young lad of seventeen, then on a visit to an uncle in Paris, telling of the family's plight. Herszel decided to take revenge. On November 7 he called at the German Embassy and asked to see the Ambassador, but Count von Welczek was away. A Counselor of the Legation, Ernst vom Rath, passed by. Herszel drew the revolver he had brought with him and fired twice. Vom Rath was fatally wounded and succumbed two days later. Herszel was arrested. Upon the collapse of France he fell into the hands of the Germans, who were about to try him on the charge of murder. A charge sheet was drafted in preparation of a show trial of an international character. An alleged homosexual impulse was hinted at. Thus the boy's heroic deed was to be besmirched. (It was a favorite trick of Heydrich's to trump up sexual charges; he used it with great success against von Fritsch, the Commander in Chief of the Wehrmacht.) The President of the People's Court wrote to the Gestapo inquiring whether international personalities were involved in Grynszpan's act. Grynszpan was transferred to Sachsenhausen camp, where Eichmann interrogated him. This was the last time he is known to have been seen alive.

On November 9, 1938, Hitler celebrated in Munich, together with cronies, the usual anniversary of the *Bierhalle* plot of 1923, when he first attempted to grasp power. Reminiscences and talk lasted traditionally till late at night. This time it was arranged that he should leave the table early. After he had gone, Goebbels revealed that "spontaneous" reprisals against the German Jews for vom Rath's "heroic" death were already in progress. The night that followed has gone down in history as the "Night of Broken Glass" (*Kristallnacht*).

The Nazi Party now staged a full-size pogrom throughout the Reich. Heydrich teletyped instructions to all local police offices not to interfere and to all SD branches to take an active part in the "demonstrations." Synagogues were ordered to be burned, provided there was no danger of the fire spreading to surrounding buildings. Permission was given to demolish, but not loot, Jewish businesses and private apartments. As many Jews, "particularly rich ones," as the prisons could accommodate were to be arrested and immediately transferred to concentration camps.

Eichmann was immediately alerted in Vienna.

A night of violence and horror followed. Places of worship, some of them centuries old, went up in flames, including the famous synagogues of Cologne, Frankfurt, Breslau, Nuremberg and Berlin. Next day they were still burning. Even ceremonial halls in cemeteries were set on fire.

"I could not believe my eyes," testified Dr. Benno Cohen, "when I saw the Berlin synagogue burning. The fire brigade was there, but did not lift a finger. They were instructed to be on the spot only for the protection of the nearby Aryan houses. Jews were rushing into the burning building and saving the Holy Scrolls while the hilarious crowd all around jeered at them."

Jewish houses were broken into. Jews were thrown out of moving trains and buses; some women were raped. Thousands were beaten up; some were drowned; those attempting to escape were shot. The SD offices all over the country dutifully reported the heroic deeds perpetrated by a "nation's boiling soul" (*kochende Volksseele*). Two days later Heydrich made the first stocktaking: 191 synagogues burnt down, a further 76 totally demolished, 11 community centers and cemetery chapels pulled down, 815 Jewish places of business demolished, 29 big stores destroyed, and finally 36 Jews killed and 36 seriously injured. "The figures are probably much higher," Heydrich wrote to Goering, with the reports still coming in. He was right; next day he learned that several thousand business places had been destroyed.

The Nazi rapists had broken the Nuremberg Laws, which forbade sexual intercourse with Jewish women; they were consequently expelled from the party and placed on trial. But proceedings for murder were discontinued or only minor punishments imposed, since "everybody realized that it was an organized political party activity, whether this was openly admitted or not," reported the head of the party court, Walter Buch.

This happened in peacetime, almost a year before the war started, again with the whole world looking on.

On Hitler's orders Goering now summoned a top-level ministerial meeting to plan over-all measures against the Jews. Verbatim minutes were kept. As the economic boss of Germany, Goering also had to save from bankruptcy a number of insurance companies, which were flooded with claims for damages to property, amounting to 25 million marks (over 8 million dollars); damage to window glass alone amounted to 6 million marks. Goering was in a recriminatory mood: "You should rather have killed two hundred Jews and caused less material damage," he snapped at Heydrich. "Where are we going to get the foreign currency to replace all these windows?"

They went on to discuss the general Jewish problem. For Goering it was mainly an economic matter; his idea was to throw the Jew completely out of business. It was there and then decided to transfer all Jewish property, shares and business into Aryan hands. In compensation the Jews would get unmarketable government bonds. The insurance problem was settled simply: the insurance companies would pay over part of the compensation to the treasury; the Jews would get nothing, but would be ordered to repair the damage.

Goebbels suggested that the burnt or damaged synagogues should be torn down by the Jews themselves and the space used for parking; it was so ruled. Jews would travel in special compartments in trains and not be allowed into cinemas, theaters and places of entertainment together with Aryans, Goebbels continued. Goering asked: "What if the train is full?" Goebbels supplied the answer: "Well then, we will throw the Jew into the toilet and let him stay there throughout the journey."

"Jews should not be permitted to hunt in forests," suggested Goebbels. "Well, we shall give them a piece of the forest and see to it that various beasts that look damned like Jews—such as the elk with his crooked nose—get in there and establish themselves," rejoined Goering.

This was the officially recorded talk of the German top leadership.

Heydrich brought them down to earth. "By eliminating the Jew from the economy you have not solved the basic problem of getting him out of Germany," he reminded the assembled ministers. "We have in Austria a Central Office for Emigration, which has so far succeeded in driving fifty thousand Jews out of the country, while in the same period only nineteen thousand left the old Reich territory," he boasted. "This was done with the cooperation of the Ministry for the Economy by streamlining the operation." He proceeded to explain Eichmann's methods in detail.

"But this costs foreign currency," objected Goering. "At the Jews' expense," Heydrich explained. Goering cheered up and beamed his consent.

Heydrich went on to suggest the institution of a distinctive badge for every Jew. Goering, always sartorially minded, interrupted: "A uniform." "A badge," continued Heydrich quietly. "It is necessary and helpful as a police measure." From the police point of view, however, he strongly opposed Goering's suggestion for the establishment of ghettos. "We could not control a ghetto where Jews congregate exclusively with Jews," Heydrich said.

Before the meeting broke up, Goering had an idea: "Gentlemen, what do you say if I find a legal formula to make the Jews pay a collective fine of, say, a billion marks in expiation for their base criminal acts, etc.? That will hit them where it hurts. The swine won't commit another murder so soon. And, in general, I must say: I wouldn't like to be a Jew in Germany now."

Eichmann was in Vienna when his work was so highly praised at the Ministers' Conference. Of course he was quick to realize the potentialities of the *Krristallnacht* pogroms. Jewish doctors, lawyers and officials were rounded up. "We were taken to the police," recalled Fleischmann. "The mob was yelling all along the streets. Then we were taken to a half-demolished Jewish school and herded, three hundred people, into one classroom. Many were only injured, as I was, but others were seriously wounded. We stood there, the water from the walls running down on us. . . . We were there from 7 P.M. till 1 A.M. Then we were driven out into a courtyard. At 10 A.M. next morning Eichmann arrived. He was full of wrath. He said that the Jews were not disappearing from Vienna quickly enough and that he would know now what to do and what measures to take." Of course everyone was completely terrorized.

Fleischmann was released four days later, after signing an undertaking that on pain of death he would not reveal where he had been or what he had seen.

Twenty-three years later these events were still strongly impressed on his mind. He gave his evidence in a clear, strong voice, with close attention to detail. He was the only survivor of the group of six Jewish functionaries who had first met Eichmann in Vienna.

Like many other prosecution witnesses, Fleischmann was not cross-examined by the defense; this meant they did not challenge a word of the evidence.

Following the pogroms, Eichmann's pressure continued, and even increased. Whenever the number of emigrants dropped, even for a while, he would threaten that the "November days will be repeated." When cross-examined on this Eichmann said: "That was a joke between me and Dr. Loewenherz." Loewenherz seems to have lacked a sense of humor. In the extensive report, prepared in 1945 by the Jewish Community of Vienna for the Nuremberg trials, Dr. Loewenherz (who confirmed its authenticity) is quoted as follows: "Only owing to my repeated assurances that our desire to emigrate was as strong as ever, but that despite all our efforts the possibilities were limited and, above all, could not be automatically assured, did I succeed in persuading Eichmann to abstain from the measures he had indicated."

*

Heydrich had won his battle: from now on Jewish affairs were a police matter, and the Jews were thus in his hands. It is true that he still had to operate within the framework of the Ministry of the Interior, because of jurisdictional formalities, but there was no question about his being in charge. Jewish affairs were now to be handled this way to the end, when expulsion-plus-robbery was abandoned in favor of more radical measures.

Eichmann was entrusted with the actual day-to-day work of the Central Emigration Office, with Mueller acting as director.

Eichmann summoned the leaders of the Jewish institutions in Berlin. Jewish emigration in Berlin was now to be conducted on the pattern of the Viennese office, which they had already been ordered to inspect. "By the way," he asked, "how did you dare, despite my orders, to speak to the Jews of Vienna and even incite them against us?" Dr. Stahl, the chairman of the Jewish community, rose: "We said a word of comfort to our brothers in Vienna. It was only natural. We have been under this rule longer than they and we had to console them. As to emigration, we are as interested as you, but there are difficulties in getting visas." Eichmann was furious and shouted his usual threats. "You have been too long out of the concentration camp" was his often repeated phrase. A senior officer (probably Mueller) who was present, never uttering a word, whispered something into his ear. Eichmann said more calmly: "The conference is suspended; wait outside." After half an hour he called the representatives in, announced that the Central Office for Jewish Emigration would go into operation in Berlin and that they must supply "quotas of passports." They replied that they could not undertake to do this; in any case, they would act only as representatives of the Jewish institutions and be responsible only to them, not as agents of the Gestapo.

Eichmann controlled himself with difficulty, warning the Jewish leaders that they would have to comply; he dismissed them peremptorily with the words: "By tomorrow morning you will have to tell me that you will cooperate and who your representative will be." Next day Dr. Eppstein, deputizing for the chairman, went to see Mueller and handed over a statement that the Jews would assist in emigration but would do so only on behalf of their own organizations, not as agents for the Gestapo. "This we had to do," Dr. Benno Cohen said at the trial. "War was in the air, and we too wanted the Jews to get out." Mueller accepted the statement without comment. The incident was considered closed, but not before Eichmann had achieved a personal satisfaction. He made Dr. Stahl write to Dr. Loewenherz saying that he was not justified in criticizing the Jews of Vienna for the way they conducted the work of emigration. At the next meeting with the Viennese representatives Eichmann delivered "the apology" in person.

Soon he had to see to the establishment of yet another office for driving out the Jews. Czechoslovakia, which had been left to her fate at Munich and forced to give up the Sudetenland, had to surrender the last of her nominal sovereignty. The puppet President Hácha was summoned to Berlin, presented with a four-hour ultimatum and told that any resistance would be broken by brute force. "If the Czechs do not give in, Prague will lie in ruins in two hours," Goering said, in the course of "the conference." Hácha and his Foreign Minister gave in; Hitler took the Czech people "under the protection of the Reich." The Protectorate of Bohemia and Moravia was created; Czechoslovakia was wiped off the map.

Czechoslovakia had a sizable and old-established Jewish population. In their talks with Czech leaders, Hitler and Ribbentrop said that they attached the greatest importance to the Jewish problem. They both told Dr. Chvalkovski, the Czech Foreign Minister, that Germany would not give guarantees to a state that did not "eliminate" the Jews. Heydrich sent Eichmann to Prague; another branch office for Jewish emigration promptly came into being with Hans Guenther in everyday charge. Stahlecker was transferred from Vienna and appointed Gestapo Chief (BdS) of the Protectorate. He was a great help. "They ordered several Jewish officials of the community offices to work at the Central Emigration Office," recalled Walli Zimet, herself one of them. At the entrance to the building an SS man was stationed whose duties included the beating up of callers. Then they had to state their professions and recite three times: "I was a Jewish lawyer (or doctor or journalist), thief and rogue," before being allowed inside. The assembly-line system was copied. A prospective emigrant had to give up all his property and assign it to the authorities. When all the formalities were finally settled he was referred to Anton Burger of the SD, who threw in a last farewell by imposing a personal duty of twenty, fifty or even a hundred thousand crowns. Anybody who could do so would borrow the money, pay up and leave the country.

Very soon familiar methods of pressure were applied here, too. Synagogues went up in flames and mass arrests were effected. Eichmann was constantly pressing Jewish functionaries for even higher emigration figures. "When we knew he was about to come, the whole building was terrified. Guenther would ask the Jewish community to send round as many people as possible, to behave as prospective emigrants, even with no documents and with empty file-covers, just so that Eichmann should see that there was a great commotion and be satisfied at having seen many people on the emigration route."

Eichmann was now virtually in charge of all three offices. In Vienna it was all right, he said later. In Prague, too, in spite of all the difficulties, he somehow managed to get the Jews out. In Berlin itself matters were more troublesome. Somehow it did not work. Other central authorities did not cooperate properly, he complained. This was not the only time Eichmann had found that his methods and measures were more impressive in foreign capitals than at home.

To some of the Viennese and Prague Jewish leaders he was more approachable, though this had nothing to do with official contacts, in which he was as hard as ever. One day he stopped all further releases from Dachau and Buchenwald until five hundred Jews emigrated daily from Vienna. On another occasion he issued an order by telephone for a Jewish refugee home there to be cleared immediately, adding that everyone found inside would be deported to Buchenwald.

In a sense, I think, Eichmann considered his days in Vienna the happiest in his life. It was here that he got his first independent assignment. He had developed new methods and had scored notable successes in a field that everybody thought of supreme importance. He was mentioned and praised to the highest authorities as the man who had finally done something practical to rid Germany of the Jews. Moreover, it was there that he first tasted the flavor of absolute power over men and reveled in the sight of a civilian's lowly bent back. His achievements with the Viennese Jews were the stock-in-trade for his future career. It was on them that he practiced his tricks, and in a way he always retained a soft spot for them, as a scientist may have for his first guinea pigs. When, years later, some of them were exterminated on the direct orders of his deputy Rolf Guenther he was even sorry about it. ("But don't put this into your book," he told Sassen, "since Guenther is still alive.")

The later stages of his career, when he was engaged in much greater tasks, were, after all, less gratifying. For one thing they did not carry promotions, since a lieutenant colonel was good enough for the butchery job. Second, the bloodshed had to be organized in strict secrecy and from behind closed doors. No more open praises and mentions in dispatches for Adolf Eichmann, no longer—until his Hungarian period—could he even boast of his achievements. He could not openly reap the glory of having cleared a place of Jews by dispatching all of them to the gas ovens, as a military commander could for conquering new territory, since his job was strictly confidential. And there were far fewer contacts now with timid civilians, whom he always liked to see cringing before him.

In retrospect the Viennese days were definitely the best.

As Eichmann was busy running the Central Office for Jewish Emigration with its three branches, the Reich was nearing war. Hitler preferred to gain one conquest after another without firing a shot. So far the means he had employed were intimidation, subversion, false promises and assurances of "peace in our time." Now he decided to use a new card in the game: the Jews. He always believed in the gratuitous image, inflated beyond all proportion, that he himself had created of the Jews' importance in the Western world. The idea of using the Jews as hostages in his campaign of extortion was not new. "A day will come," he once said to a close circle of friends, "when Jews will be Germany's best protection. They will be the pledge that will guarantee that the foreign powers would let Germany go her way in peace. When this stage is reached, there will be nothing left to take away from them but their precious Jewish lives."

In the midst of the crisis that developed immediately after the brief honeymoon of Munich, Hitler appeared before the Reichstag on January 30, 1939, the sixth anniversary of his seizure of power. In a long speech reviewing his achievements and proclaiming, as usual, his "peaceful intentions," he had this to say:

"And one thing I would wish to say on this day, which is probably memorable not only for us Germans. In the course of my life I have often been a prophet and I have often been laughed at. It was the Jews in the first place who during my struggle for power laughed at my prophecies, that I would one day assume the leadership of the German State and of the whole nation, and then bring the Jewish problem, as well as many others, to a solution. I believe that in the meantime that pealing laughter of Jews in Germany has stuck in their throats.

"Today I wish to be a prophet once more. Should international Jewry, inside and outside Europe, succeed once more in plunging the nations into war, the result will not be the bolshevization of the earth and through it the victory of Jewry, but the annihilation of the Jewish race in Europe."

Many of Hitler's prophecies did come true for a while, but were later completely belied. The Reich that was to last for a millennium was shattered. The "master nation" was defeated by the "racially degenerate" Slavs of Soviet Russia and the "plutocratic degenerates" of the Western democracies. Germany itself was divided. The rich fields of the Ukraine, promised to it "forever" by the Fuehrer, were restored to their owners.

Yet one "prophecy" Hitler did fulfill. When his blackmail failed and his threats proved of no avail, he brought about the war and the annihilation of European Jewry.

Czechoslovakia and the free city of Memel were his last bloodless conquests. After the British and French guarantees were given to Poland it was obvious that any further pressing of territorial demands would lead to an armed conflict.

At a conference with his generals on May 23, 1939, Hitler told them that further successes would definitely require a war. The claim to Danzig would be only the pretext, he said. The main idea was to expand eastward. Having secured Russia's noninterference by the Ribbentrop-Molotov Pact, he summoned his leading generals again on August 25 and gave them a last general review, explaining why this was the proper time to go to war and exhorting them to be hard and brutal. "I shall give a propagandist reason for starting the war—never mind whether plausible or not. The victor will not be asked afterward whether he spoke the truth or not. In starting and waging a war it is not right that matters, but victory."

Somebody mentioned the possibility of another Munich. "I am really afraid," Hitler said, "that some *Schweinehund* will make a last-minute proposal for mediation."

The propaganda stunt was supplied by Heydrich. Foreign and local correspondents were shown the bodies of a few criminals removed from prison, who had been dressed up in Polish uniforms, shot and placed at the entrance to the Gleiwitz radio station, near the border. This was the "corpus delicti" to prove a "Polish attack" on a German station, which was allegedly overpowered. A Gestapo man called Naujocks testified at Nuremberg that it was he who had brought over an SD man to read a strongly worded announcement in Polish and German. Several hours after "the incident" the German Army was pushing into Poland "to punish the aggressor." World War II had begun.

PART II

*

The Crime

CHAPTER 5

Deportation into Ghettos

It was the war that enabled the Nazis to make a really "principled" application of their racial theories. Extreme solutions were now possible.

The Nazis had schemes aimed generally at "subhuman" peoples like the Gypsies and the Slavs, especially Russians and Poles. But the Jews came first. They were the only people doomed to perish completely while the war was on.

The process of destruction was applied in stages. The marking of the Jews with the yellow badge was a necessary preparatory measure. The succeeding stages were:

1. the local concentration of European Jews, in most places their "ghettoization"
2. the murder of individual Jews in the ex-Soviet areas, by units known as the *Einsatzgruppen*
3. the application of the "Final Solution," involving the roundup of all accessible European Jews for deportation to certain designated areas
4. the creation of the death camps, for the systematic massacre of all Jews

This program did not leap into existence full-blown. Though there was a sort of natural logic in it that we now see led inexorably toward the Final Solution, it is difficult to say whether the actual idea of the death camps had been present in Hitler's mind since his accession to power; in any case, it was the cover of the war and the nonretaliation on the part of the free world that made him realize its practicability and induced him to put it into effect.

From my own point of view as prosecutor, these historical considerations, while of course deadly in their fascination, were of special interest insofar as they enabled me to determine the precise role played by Eichmann. He readily admitted that he was the central authority for marking the Jews with the yellow badge. But this was only a small part of his activity. It was up to me to demonstrate the true function he performed in all other stages of destruction.

The immediate stimulus for the ghettoization of the Jews came about through the two and a half million "additional Jews" the Germans found on the Polish territory they controlled after their destruction of the Polish Army.

This had taken only about ten days after the German military machine had begun its onslaught. For the first time the world had witnessed a modern blitzkrieg, with a devastating attack from the air followed by the swift and widely spread blows of an armored fist. Even the gallantry of the Polish soldiers and the loyalty of the citizenry could not withstand the swarms of Stukas that completely dominated the skies, coordinated with a mighty thrust of rolling steel on land.

Poland was woefully unprepared for such warfare, as was indeed every country but Germany at the time. It soon gave in. The Russians then converged from the east, implementing their secret agreement of two weeks before for the bisection of Poland.

The "additional Jews" presented new problems; new methods had to be tried out. The crack operation units sent by Heydrich to Poland in the wake of the German Army had been entrusted with "security problems," but their first job was, in fact, dealing with the Jews.

At the trial Ada Lichtman told the story of what happened to her own town, Wieliczka, near Cracow.

When the Germans entered the place they rounded up all Jewish men, told them to undress and to run about naked in the streets. "Anybody who stopped for air got stabbed in the back with a bayonet. Almost everybody returned home bleeding. My father too."

Several days later it got worse. On September 12, 1939, a new SS unit arrived in town. "They ordered all Jewish males out. They gathered them all in the market place and told them to keep their hands on their necks. Then they picked out thirty-two Jews. They also took along four Poles, among them a college teacher, a priest and an officer. All these were marched into the market place and ordered to shout: 'We are traitors.' Then they were loaded on a truck. I ran with another girl after the truck," continued the witness, "till we reached a small forest. There we found all the men lying on the ground, in groups of five. The four Poles were lying in a separate group. They did not move. I bent down over my father and kissed him. He was dead. All these men had been shot."

Ada Lichtman thought it was a bloodthirsty local commander who had ordered the atrocities. So she escaped to the town of Mielec. She found that the horrors went on there too. "Bearded Jews were ordered to shave. When they refused, the Nazis 'shaved' them with a penknife or a bayonet, cutting out pieces of flesh." The girl escaped farther east, but it was the same everywhere. "In Dubinka the Germans gathered twenty orthodox Jews, told them to put on their prayer shawls and phylacteries, to sing religious hymns and to raise hands to heaven. Then some German officers poured gasoline on them and burned them alive. I saw it all with my own eyes. . . . An old man was holding a child in his arms. He was told by the Germans to put the child down. He pleaded with them that the child couldn't walk. They shot the old man on the spot. I can still hear the child shouting: 'Shoot me first, not grandfather.' Then they shot the child too."

With small variations, according to the ingenuity of the people in charge, this went on in all occupied Poland. "In Sanok the first thing the Germans did was to put the synagogue on fire," testified Jacob Gurfein. "A Jew was rescuing the Holy Scrolls. They threw him into the fire. Then they searched for Jews allegedly suspected of Communism. When they did not find them they took others with similar names and shot them."

This was an initial terrorizing bloodletting, a prelude to further steps.

The German Army was not happy with the "excesses" of the crack units. Lieutenant Colonel Lahousen of the Military Intelligence reported that many soldiers were "disturbed" to see young men exercising their courage on defenseless civilians instead of fighting at the front.

Heydrich called a halt to the shootings and instead ordered the establishment of courts-martial for the local population. He wanted only such verdicts as would *not* impose the death penalty reported to him.

He further ordered the establishment of ghettos for Jews with "Councils of Elders" at their heads. "This originated with me," said Eichmann to Sassen. The practical experience which he gained in Vienna was now put to wider use.

Dieter Wisliceny, too, said that initially Eichmann's main interest in Polish Jewry was the establishment of the ghettos and the Councils of Elders. Heydrich, who was originally opposed to ghettoization, accepted Eichmann's method and invited him to a secret briefing session of the high-ranking officers where this was decided upon.

Heydrich announced there and then that the newly occupied Polish area would be divided into a section adjoining Germany, which would be directly annexed to the Reich, and a "foreign-speaking" province, which would be governed by a special commissioner. The "German" area must be cleared of all Jews. Polish manual laborers might remain a while to serve the Germans who would settle there; other Poles would be deported.

For the treatment of Jews he had special directives: all of them would be massed in the towns *in preparation for further removal.* They would have to disappear from the countryside. All German Jews would likewise be deported to the Polish towns.

All this was in its main outlines agreed on by the Supreme Command of the Wehrmacht.

Following the conference, Heydrich issued urgent detailed instructions to the crack units. All recipients were exhorted to maintain the strictest secrecy with regard to the *ultimate goal* of the measures against the Jews. The short-term directives were to concentrate the Jews immediately in the towns, especially near railway junctions. A Jewish Council of Elders was to be established in every community. Its members were to be held personally responsible, "in the fullest sense," for the transmission and exact execution of all instructions.

All Jewish businesses would be taken over by Aryans, the order continued. Industries or trades of economic value or importance for the war effort would be carried on by non-Jews. Heydrich asked for current reports as well as for a detailed review of the industries and businesses controlled by Jews.

*

Eichmann's pretrial examination on this key document was carefully thought out. He was first shown Heydrich's directives and invited to comment. Professing complete ignorance, he said that only now, having seen this document in the Israeli prison, did he realize how ghettos came into being. "I know only this: that I had nothing to do with it." Now it had all become clear to him, he said. He had also found out now that the "Final Solution" had already been in the minds of the higher leadership as early as 1939—and it had not matured, "as he had always thought," two years later, at the outbreak of the Russo-German war. This was "a basic regulation," he said, adding cautiously, "but I had nothing to do with it. . . . I came in later and found the whole thing there, including the Councils of Elders."

It was only then that his interrogator, Chief Inspector Less, showed him a copy of the official minutes of the September 21 conference (which we discovered) where he appeared on the attendance list. Eichmann was visibly shaken. At first he mumbled for several minutes; then he said: "It obviously can no longer be doubted that I was at the meeting, as I am listed here."

In court he realized how serious the matter was; he retracted his admission, maintaining now that he could not have been present at the briefing session, since he did not receive his transfer to Berlin until October. This was the first time he had branded an official document of his government as untrue. Other instances followed later. Such denial tactics were hardly novel. The records of Nuremberg and other war criminal trials are bespattered with disavowals of documents, orders and even of signatures. The more damaging the evidence, the more fervent the repudiation.

Eichmann was therefore obviously the initiator of the ghettoization measure that proved to be a crushing instrument in the Nazi fight against Jewry. Once they had the Jews cooped up and isolated in the ghettos all the rest was much easier. The ghetto proved to be a decisive step in the annihilation process. Eichmann had good reasons for his efforts to dissociate himself from it when on trial.

At the time of the events he had considered the ghettos an important transitory stage. In autumn and winter of 1939 he believed, as most Germans did, that the phony war in France would soon be over, now that Poland was gone and there was nothing the West could fight for. Hitler had launched a peace offensive. "If England and France reconcile themselves to the fact that Poland can't rise again, they can have peace within two weeks," he told the Swedish mediator Dahlerus. It was generally mooted that a semiautonomous Polish province would be created, under German protection of course, as a concession by the Fuehrer to the West.

Now Eichmann had an idea. Before peace negotiations started let the Jewish problem be solved through a *fait accompli* by dumping the Jews not just into ghettos, big or small, but into something different—a territorial concentration near the demarcation line between the Reich and Soviet Russia. The projected Polish province was in any case to be a kind of buffer state between these two; why not have a Jewish one as well? He needed someone to back him up, and found a staunch supporter in Stahlecker. "He knew I was not talking rubbish," he said. So they both proceeded deep into Poland until they reached the Soviet demarcation line. South of the town of Radom they reached the river San, in the lower Polish plateau. They decided that the region just across the river called Nisko was "the place." All that was necessary would be to carve out a small area for the Jews at this spot, and remove the local population. It seemed so simple that they reported immediately to Berlin.

Heydrich, to whom they submitted their plan, realized the possibilities that a reservoir of Jews under his supreme authority could offer. At least it was worth trying out. So he gave his approval even without clearing the details higher up; for the time being he had a free hand in Poland anyway. The country was in a state bordering on chaos. With the cessation of hostilities millions were wandering on the roads, either returning home or fleeing to and from the Russian zone; entire divisions of disbanded Polish soldiers were moving around; nobody would pay much attention if Jews were thrown into this confusion, to create the nucleus of a reservoir.

Eichmann knew he had to work fast. He started with communities where he already had a grip on Jewish affairs and where by trickery, intimidation or persuasion he could talk the Jewish representatives into believing that his scheme would be for the good of the Jews themselves.

The first deportees came from Czechoslovakia. Max Burger told the court about a shipment of a thousand Jews who arrived in Poland from Morawská Ostrawa in locked railway compartments. They were ordered to bring along building materials. Eichmann awaited them at the Nisko railway station. With him were some of the Jewish functionaries of Prague and Vienna: Edelstein, Murmelstein, Storfer and Friedmann.

Eichmann addressed the arrivals; "Here, six or seven kilometers from this place, across the San, the Fuehrer has promised a new homeland to the Jews. There are no apartments or houses; if you will build them, you will have a roof overhead. There is no water. The wells are infected with cholera, typhoid and dysentery. If you drill and find water, you will have it. Once you cross the river you will never come back."

The belongings of the deportees and the building materials were loaded onto wagons, pushed by the Jews themselves. At last they reached the indicated place. "Now build barracks for the SS guard," they were ordered. This was the first structure they put up.

The next day all those who were considered "unfit for the colonization project"—about two hundred people—were ordered out of the camp. They were marched several kilometers with their baggage and then ordered to continue eastward into Russia, and never to come back to the camp. Anyone who showed his face there would be shot, they were told. They scattered in the woods; some reached Lublin, others crossed into Russia.

Those who stayed behind were put to work. More Jews arrived from Austria and Czechoslovakia. An unusually heavy winter set in. The SS guards took whatever they pleased from the belongings of the arrivals, "to cover the expenses of the guards." The "settlers" had to buy food from the local farmers, and were told to continue building. Jewish organizations learned of their plight and money was sent from abroad. All "settlers" were under constant supervision; nobody could leave the area without permission.

Soon Eichmann was given another assignment through which he could enlarge his scheme. He was put in charge of one of the great population movements of modern times.

*

On October 7, with the Polish war over, Hitler declared that the "consequences of the Versailles Treaty were obliterated." Germans who had been forced to live abroad could now settle in the homeland, from which "all alien and undesirable elements would be removed." Himmler was entrusted with the duty of "consolidating the German people" and was authorized to effect such changes of population as might be necessary. Occupied Poland was especially recommended for this purpose, as Heydrich had already revealed to his high officers. Himmler ruled that all Jews must be removed from those ex-Polish areas which were incorporated into the Reich. This also affected some of the Poles, especially those who were particularly unfriendly.

Himmler called in Heydrich to do the job, and Heydrich put his usual assistant in charge. Eichmann took over. A new department, under him, designated IV-D-4, dealing with deportations and emigration, was created in the RSHA.

Soon a real wandering of peoples developed across Poland. Eichmann drove Jews and Poles into the ungermanized part of Poland, called the General Government, while bringing *Volksdeutsche* (ethnic Germans) from Volhynia, central Poland, the Baltic States and Rumania into the evacuated homes and farms. The deported Jews he dispatched into the area round Lublin, not far from "his" Nisko. He now had an old friend there, an Austrian who was in charge of the local SS and police. His name was Odilo Globocnik; he had fled to Germany in 1933 after having murdered a Jewish jeweler. After the *Anschluss* he was promoted for his services to Gauleiter of

Vienna. In this office he was found guilty of corruption but was soon forgiven; he was exactly the man the SS needed in the heart of Poland: a ruffian and drunkard, who combined brutality with dynamic energy and a complete absence of moral restraint. He was close to the leaders' hearts; Himmler called him "my dear old Globus." He too was later to play a decisive role in the tragedy of European Jewry. For the moment he was quite content to have transports of Jews delivered to his door. In any case, he did not care in the least what was to happen to them; if Heydrich and Eichmann wanted to have a Jewish concentration in the Lublin area, that was all right with him.

Hans Frank was appointed to take charge of the General Government. He was one of Hitler's early cronies; he had joined the party immediately after completing his law studies. An able and energetic lawyer, he was one of the Nazi intellectuals, the legal adviser of the party. Then he became Minister of Justice in Bavaria and in this capacity told jurists that independence of the law did not exist in Germany. "Ask yourself how the Fuehrer would decide your problem—that is your law." The forty-two-volume journal containing his speeches and the minutes of his conferences and meetings during his governor generalship in Poland was produced at Nuremberg. It is a unique relic of the Nazi era, revealing the barbarity and ruthlessness of a highly intelligent and well-read man who was ready to descend as low as necessary in the service of his Fuehrer. He was told in very vague terms that by February, 1940, about a million Jews would be packed into the area between the San and the Vistula. At the time he did not demur.

People were transported in locked wagons in the particularly severe winter of 1939–40. The journey often lasted as long as eight days, the human cargo not being allowed to alight. The representative at the receiving end in the General Government reported one hundred cases of freezing to death in a single transport. Frank described in his diary how the trains rolled in, "fully laden with people, as often as not laden with corpses." Trying to put this area assigned to him into some order, he began to grumble.

To streamline the operation, Heydrich called a meeting of all concerned on January 30, 1940. A Minister of the Reich, the Austrian quisling Arthur Seyss-Inquart, was there in his new capacity as Frank's deputy. So were all the senior SS and police officers of the occupied areas and a nine-man delegation from the RSHA. Eichmann was there, of course, with his deputy Guenther, and his assistants, Dannecker and Rajakowitsch. Altogether there were forty-three participants.

Heydrich promised to coordinate the evacuations with the authorities of the General Government. The new department, IV-D-4, under Eichmann, would see to it; it would deal centrally with all matters, including the repatriation of "ethnic Germans." But he announced that the evacuations would go on, and repeated, for Seyss-Inquart's information, the projected figures for the immediate future: 190,000 Jews, Poles and Gypsies. He rejected all suggestions to put a brake on what they called "the mass movements."

In the annexed areas the German press was triumphantly announcing that one town after another had become "*judenrein*" (clear of Jews), and the progress of the settlement of ethnic Germans in the territory was proudly reported. Ley, the Minister of Labor, announced at a meeting in Lódz: "We need this land and we shall keep it. Perhaps this is harsh, but life is always harsh. In fifty years this will be a flourishing German country, with not a Pole or a Jew in it. We Germans believe in a higher right and a higher race. With this right we came to Poland."

By the same right they deported the Jews of Stettin and Schneidemuehl, which were not even in ex-Polish territories, when the Jewish apartments there were needed by the authorities. A detailed report was drafted at the time by the Polish-Jewish Aid Society, in cooperation with the Quakers and the Red Cross. The Danish newspaper *Politiken* carried the full story by its Stettin correspondent in its issue of February 17, 1940. As the first wartime deportations from the Reich itself, they attracted attention.

The Jews were rounded up by the SS between 3 and 4 A.M. Women, children, the aged—all were herded to the Stettin railway station and told they were to be taken to Poland. One piece of hand luggage was allowed per person. Included were ex-servicemen, who had fought for Germany in World War I, even some who had won the Iron Cross, the highest award for bravery. To a question whether housing would be available for them in Poland, an SS man replied: "You will be unloaded in the open fields and you will take care of yourselves."

The SS were as good as their word. The deportees were brought to the vicinity of Lublin and ordered to march some twenty to thirty kilometers in the snow, at 22 degrees below freezing. The march lasted over fourteen hours; seventy-two people were left on the road to freeze to death. Among them was a woman, found with a three-year-old baby in her arms, both frozen to death, the mother's last movement being to protect the child with her clothing. A five-year-old girl was found with a piece of cardboard attached, carrying her name: Renate Alexander. The girl was on a visit to relatives in Stettin. She was later brought to the Lublin hospital, where both hands and both legs were amputated. All the surviving deportees had arrived penniless and were slowly dying, the report concluded.

But the property the deportees had left behind was well taken care of. Goering arrived on the scene to establish an organization to which all the property of expelled Jews was to be transferred. With typical Nazi perversity it was named "The Trusteeship Office–East" (*Treuhandstelle-Ost*). Eichmann gave assistance to the new office; a joint conference decided that in future the deportees would be searched for valuables or money exceeding one hundred Polish zloty (about twenty dollars), which each was allowed to keep. In fact, they were not even allowed that much; the General Government authorities later requested that those in charge of the evacuation should permit the deportees to keep on them at least twenty zloty each.

Finally Hans Frank put his foot down. He was not particularly sensitive to the sufferings of Jews or Poles, but he was ambitious and quick-tempered. He wanted the General Government to become, under him, a model of a conquered country, where native slaves would toil for their masters with unrestricted obedience. The incessant flow of people into his region played havoc with his plans for stabilization. He ruled the General Government on behalf of the Fuehrer himself; hence his wish had to be the law of the land. His contempt for Himmler and his chilly hatred of Heydrich were of long standing; he resolved not to let them "reign" in his domain.

He again brought up the question of the deportations before Hitler, this time threatening to resign. The Fuehrer, who was also approached by his Foreign Minister, Joachim von Ribbentrop, on the unfavorable publicity the deportations were receiving in foreign capitals, ordered Goering—his usual mouthpiece in Jewish affairs—to call a halt. A directive stopping further deportations without Frank's consent was issued in March, 1940.

*

The Nisko project also had to be abandoned. Some representatives of the camp reached Cracow and sought contact with the Governor General. They were never received in audience, but when Frank learned the particulars of the SS design of a Jewish reservoir under the control of the Gestapo inside his territory, he became furious and ordered the immediate return of the deportees. About a third of them made their way back to Austria and Czechoslovakia. To cover up the failure of his scheme, Eichmann ordered that they be registered by the police as "returning from vocational training."

When Eichmann visited Cracow at the time, Streckenbach, the local Gestapo chief, told him over a glass of brandy that Frank had a good mind to order Eichmann's arrest if he continued with his machinations.

This was an unforgivable affront. Himmler and Heydrich were already undermining Frank's position with Hitler; they now intensified their campaign. They made Frank's position impossible by keeping control over his Secretary for Security, the Senior SS and Police Leader Krueger, and all police personnel. They stopped calling on him when they visited the General Government and openly defied his wishes. They and their subordinates, including Eichmann, consistently meddled in his domain. Eichmann even continued his deportations, especially from the Warthe Province, in the central part of the annexed territories. On various excuses he was driving out from there "only" a thousand families per week, a long time after Goering had issued the stop directive.

For three more years the Gestapo maintained their "state within a state" in Frank's Poland; twice again they made him tender his resignation. The story of Frank's conflict with the SS covers hundreds of pages in his diary. At long last, after four years of struggle, he won his battle and established himself as undisputed authority in Poland.

As far as the Jews were concerned this made no difference at all. Frank was as much their hater as the SS, but he wanted to exterminate them on his own orders and by his own methods. In any case, by the time the SS were ousted from authority in Poland no Jews were left. Frank kept his post to the end; along with other major war criminals he came to the dock at Nuremberg, and eventually to the gallows.

Eichmann had a deep grudge against Frank. "Just imagine," he told Sassen, "what we could have done with the Nisko plan. There was the district of Lublin. I wanted to have the whole of it. I wanted the town of Radom as the capital of this Jewish territory, which would have stretched over the entire district."

Eichmann's personal dream of becoming the "Protector" or at least the "Deputy Protector" of a Jewish area, and so to assume for once a territorial authority such as Heydrich later achieved in Prague, had been frustrated by Frank's intransigence. It was unpardonable.

At the police investigation and in court, Eichmann was less "imperialistic" in describing the Nisko project. It was to be, he said, an autonomous "preparatory Jewish state" (*Judenvorstaat*), from which further emigration would be possible. "It was meant as a possible temporary solution for some time, so that meanwhile there would be no fire under our fingernails."

After the Nisko project has been abandoned the Nazi "specialists" analyzed its potentialities. Professor Peter Heinz Seraphim, the author of a popular Nazi encyclopedia on anti-Semitism, said in a lecture in March, 1941, that the Lublin District could in any case hardly have contained several million Jews. The scheme was faulty since it would have allowed further contacts between Europeans and Jews. This in itself was fatal. Consequently Professor Seraphim thought there was only one solution: the Jews must leave Europe.

In fact, Eichmann applied himself to such a project, which again coincided with the military developments and with renewed hopes for an early peace.

After a brief campaign France had been brought to her knees. On June 22, 1940, Hitler had ordered the French representatives to appear before him in the Forest of Compiègne in the armistice railway carriage, preserved by the French as an historic relic, where the Germans had capitulated to Marshal Foch twenty-two years before. This was the hour of Hitler's great triumph: France, the traditional enemy, had been beaten.

Peace talks were again in the air in Germany, where nobody believed that England would go on fighting alone. Hitler daily awaited news of England's capitulation. He said he "could not conceive of anyone in England still seriously believing in victory."

Again Heydrich did not let the grass grow under his feet. Among the possible spoils of the war were the French possessions overseas. This opened new vistas for activity in Jewish matters.

*

Three days after the Compiègne armistice Heydrich instructed Eichmann to prepare a letter to Ribbentrop. With Germany now controlling areas populated by three and a half million Jews, new solutions must be sought, he wrote. Emigration would not do, and a "territorial final solution" would be necessary. Eichmann unearthed a plan he had been interested in more than three years before—the Madagascar scheme. This huge French island in the tropics (today the Malagasi Republic), was at the time a popular choice for the suggested settlement of "superfluous" Jews. The idea was first entertained by the Polish Government, which in 1937 even dispatched a research group to the island to explore its possibilities. The report was entirely negative. But the Nazis took it up anyway. Goering mentioned Madagascar as a possible dumping depot for Jews at the Ministers' Conference of November, 1938. Rosenberg wrote about it in 1939, and Frank announced in 1940 that colossal relief would soon be felt in the General Government when the Jews had been transported "piece by piece" (*Stueck um Stueck*) to Madagascar. The Foreign Office, prompted by Heydrich and Eichmann, prepared a blueprint under which the French would cede the island to Germany, which would establish naval and air bases on the coastal strip. The island itself would serve as a Jewish settlement area.

Eichmann studied the project, consulted various agencies and finally came up with his own detailed scheme. This he described in court as "his great effort to provide a place where Jews could live among their own folk and be glad to get a piece of land beneath their feet." The idea, he claimed, he got from Zionist writings, especially those of Herzl and Boehm.

The project he had submitted at the time held out no such rosy prospects. It provided for the removal of the island's local population and the deportation of a million Jews per year to the place, over a period of four years. They would be completely isolated from the rest of the world and live in a police state. No provision was made for economic facilities. It was merely said that the Jews of the West would have to cover the transport costs of the deportees, whose property was to be confiscated by the Reich. They would be put to work to drain swamps and build roads. The administration would be in the hands of the Security Office.

But nothing ever materialized. No peace treaty was signed with France, Madagascar was never ceded to the Germans, and the British Navy later landed on the island. Historians differ as to whether the Nazis had at any time seriously considered the plan as a practical possibility or whether it was just empty talk to cover sinister future steps. Hitler mentioned it, obviously for camouflage purposes, as late as July, 1942, when he knew perfectly well that the whole scheme had long been abandoned. The project sounds highly impractical, unless it was meant as an annihilation measure without the actual spilling of people's blood.

With its abandonment, there was nothing to do but await Hitler's pleasure in Jewish matters.

Local leaders grew impatient. Hans Frank was again pressed to admit large numbers of Jews into the General Government. Baldur von Schirach, the Reichstatthalter of Vienna, said he had fifty thousand Jews in the city whom he wanted to get rid of immediately; and Erich Koch, the Oberpraesident of East Prussia, announced that he had to unload his Jews and Poles on Frank. Only with great difficulty could Frank avert a serious new influx of deportees. The ghettos that had been established in the big cities of Poland were overflowing with people; hunger and disease were rife.

The Heydrich-Eichmann scheme for immediate ghettoization was carried out quite independently of the Nisko and Madagascar reveries. But putting millions of people in ghettos was a process that had to be adapted to local needs and to practical considerations. In smaller places with predominantly Jewish populations, a whole town would sometimes become a ghetto; elsewhere a few communities would be thrown together to form a larger concentration.

Hundreds of thousands of Jews were soon ordered from the countryside into the bigger towns. A bewildering shower of anti-Jewish regulations followed, starting with the imposition of the yellow badge in 1939 and with confiscatory measures ordering Jews to deposit all their money in banks, simultaneously blocking accounts and restricting withdrawals. Jewish businesses were then expropriated and placed in the hands of German "trustees." Jewish houses were requisitioned, and all property was registered, including not only valuables and jewelry, but even household articles. Food rations for Jews were much smaller than for Poles. Hunger made its appearance in Jewish homes.

A new horror took shape when kidnapings for labor started. Jews, regardless of age, would be stopped in the streets or in public places, ordered to leave buses or streetcars and marched into labor columns. German formations would suddenly appear, cordon off streets and start shooting and rounding up Jews. Some of them never returned, others came back after a time. A man could never know when, if ever, he would see his home again. This was usually a renewed occasion for cutting off Jewish beards, sometimes plucking out the hair like feathers from a slaughtered fowl. In many cases a Jew's beard was set on fire; if he turned into a torch, so much the worse for him.

The Polish mob was encouraged to plunder Jewish property. Dr. Emanuel Ringelblum, the historian of the Warsaw ghetto, recorded on March 28,

1940, that for six days on end Jewish apartments and shops were broken into. Jews defended their property; skirmishes developed that were filmed by the Germans. "Often the filming team arrived before the mob," Ludwik Landau, the gifted chronicler of the Polish underground, recorded in his diary for the same day. A Polish policeman would order a Jew to open his shop, then tell the mob to take away whatever they wished, while the German police calmly looked on.

"Their purpose is clear," recorded Landau. "They wish to incite enmity between the Jews and the Poles, to compel the Jews to turn for protection to the Germans, who will appear before the world as appeasers and protectors of order."

"At first we had to face laws and regulations aimed at humiliating and suppressing us, and exposing us to hunger," said a survivor. "Still we thought we would somehow be able to circumvent the decrees and survive. Then we realized that we were considered outside the law."

The street continued to be a constant source of danger. Germans would whip Jews simply for pleasure. Women would be dragged off by their hair. Sometimes a shooting squad would enter a Jewish quarter and start firing in all directions for no other reason than to inflict terror. A group of SS men driving at gunpoint a band of beaten, bleeding Jews, bareheaded, weary to death, dragging their feet with the utmost difficulty, was a common sight.

People were afraid of the street; if possible they stayed at home. When hunger drove them out, they used to move along the walls of houses or close to fences, so as to be able to escape at the first sign of danger. In many places they were forbidden the use of sidewalks; these were "for Aryans only."

It was at this stage that the Germans usually enforced ghettoization. In different places various ruses, adapted to local conditions, were officially used to make the Jews go into the ghettos. In Warsaw it was said that the establishment of the ghetto would "guard the non-Jewish population from the spread of disease prevalent among the infected refugees and protect the Jews from Polish excesses." In Lódz "better and more concentrated possibilities of employment" were offered as an inducement. In other places it was imposed as "a punishment" for alleged shooting on German soldiers; generally it was said to be a measure to separate the Jews from the non-Jewish world. "In principle the General Government was the first to implement the severance of Jews," the local authorities boasted.

The ghetto site was invariably the slum area of the town. It was tightly packed, with no open spaces, and was separated from the non-Jewish part either by a wall, as in Warsaw, or by a barbed-wire fence as in Lódz and Tarnopol. The Jew could leave the guarded ghetto only for work or by written permit; no non-Jew was allowed to enter except by special authorization. Unauthorized movement was punished by instant shooting. Posters were often placed outside the ghettos, warning strangers of "epidemics." Mail from outside was returned with the stamp: *"Seuchengebiet"* ("Infected Area").

*

One of the biggest ghettos was set up in Lódz, the second largest town in prewar Poland, with a substantial Jewish population. It was the center of the country's textile industry and was at one time nicknamed "the Polish Manchester." Now it was named Litzmannstadt and incorporated into the Warthe Province and so annexed by the Reich. Many thousands of Jews there were skilled workers and experts, and the Germans realized the potential of its Jewish labor. In the order establishing the ghetto, the Regierungspraesident Uebelhoer had said: "This is of course, a temporary measure. I shall later decide at what time and by what methods the ghetto, and together with it the city of Lódz, shall be cleansed of Jews. In any case our final aim is to burn out this plague-boil completely."

The worst area of the town, Baluty, was apportioned to the Jews, who were ordered to vacate all other quarters, street by street, till they were all inside. Then, in May, 1940, the ghetto was fenced round and cut off from the rest of the world.

"At that time there were 203,000 Jews in Lódz," Henryk Ross, an employee of the ghetto administration, recalled. "Six to eight people were herded into one room." The allotment of food was cut down from month to month. Each person received a loaf of bread as a week's ration. Potato peels were a cherished delicacy. "I saw families with children that would all die during a single night of hunger and cold." Altogether over 120,000 Jews died of hunger within the four years of the ghetto's existence, continued Ross.

Eichmann was, of course, fully informed of what went on. His man in Posen, SS Major Hoeppner, reported to him regularly; one of the written reports has survived. On July 16, 1941, Hoeppner warned Eichmann of the great danger of epidemics in the starving Lódz ghetto. "The Jews are not getting food and it is seriously to be considered whether it will not be more humane to settle it with them through a quick working medium, especially with those who are unable to work. This will be pleasanter than watching them starve to death."

Yet Eichmann undertook to push into Litzmannstadt another twenty thousand Jews and five thousand Gypsies from the Reich. The city administration was truly alarmed. In a detailed memorandum the German Mayor pointed out that there were no free quarters in the ghetto, except in the factories working for the Wehrmacht. For lack of fuel the ghetto inmates had already torn down doors, windows and floors to feed stoves, it was said, and with no further supplies available there would be no possibility of feeding even the existing ghetto population. This was bound to endanger the army's supplies in any case. Consequently there was no room whatsoever for additional inmates. The report was sent to Himmler via Regierungspraesident Uebelhoer. The latter's "concern" for the Jews is easily explained. The danger of epidemics because of the human overpopulation and lack of proper medical care had always loomed over the ghetto. Disease might easily spread to the Germans themselves. Moreover, Uebelhoer was making a solid profit on every living and working Jew; for each of them he received from the Labor Ministry 6 marks per day, while paying out to the Jew himself 0.8 mark. He was not eager actually to kill the goose that was laying golden eggs.

Eichmann went to have a look at matters on the spot. He came back without having seen either Uebelhoer or Mayor Ventzki, but reported that the local authorities had given their consent to further deportations. Uebelhoer, on hearing this, almost exploded. He sent a long telegram to Himmler accusing Eichmann of lying and double-crossing (with the "gypsy-like manners of horse-traders"), again pleading that no more deportees be sent in. Himmler, though first tending to be conciliatory, replied with hauteur, reminding Uebelhoer he was addressing a superior. Swallowing his pride, Uebelhoer rushed to Berlin to see Heydrich. A heated exchange followed. "Uebelhoer told me," Heydrich reported to Himmler, "that he would complain against Eichmann to the Reichsfuehrer, whereupon I replied that I was responsible for him and the complaint should be brought against me."

Eichmann had his way. German Jews and Gypsies were deported to the Litzmannstadt ghetto; within two weeks the full quota of 25,000 deportees was dumped there.

In setting up the ghetto in Warsaw the Germans found that they could easily play the Jews against the Poles by making them argue with each other over which streets and buildings should be included in the ghetto. This was to be the largest ghetto in Europe. At one time it held half a million prisoners and its establishment naturally took some time.

"The whole population is on the move, from and into the prescribed areas," Landau recorded in his diary on August 22, 1940. The movement was intensified toward the end of the month, quarter by quarter, to the accompaniment of extortion and robbery. Each day brought a new shower of regulations as to ghetto boundaries and a new crop of rumors about its ultimate site. "Nobody knows where to stay for sure," recorded Landau in September. "The Jewish community office has no information and is utterly helpless. In certain areas both Christians and Jews are moving. The whole population is in a state of great tension." In October the area was finally delineated. Soon it was walled up and isolated.

Zivia Lubetkin Zuckerman recalled: "On the Day of Atonement 1940 we heard the announcement over the radio that the final order to set up a Jewish quarter was issued. The order said that since epidemics spread among the Jews, in order to safeguard the health of the Aryans, the Jews, who were germ-carriers, must leave the mixed quarters and move to a Jewish area. Since the lives of the Jews up to that time were disorganized and disrupted, their concentration in certain streets and in separate areas would enable them to live more quietly and enjoy cultural and social autonomy. . . . So the Jews were forced into an area that was hardly enough for the 150,000 people who lived there before, and now they pushed into it another 300,000 people. For several days one could see scenes of Jews with their families, pushing handcarts loaded with packages and luggage, moving from their houses, trying to take with them the little property they could save, not knowing where to go or what would be their fate. Several days and nights they remained on the streets. . . . Other Jews took them in. On the average eight people were living in one room. . . . One day with no warning . . . the Jews found the gates of the ghetto closed and guarded by German and Polish policemen. Till then there had been a possibility . . . of getting over to the Aryan side, for work or for business. Now that was all finished. Actually the ghetto, with its hundreds of thousands of Jews, turned out to be one big jail, where the Jews received 125 grams of bread per day, one kilogram of jam per month, sometimes a little soap substitute, and a little coal-waste for cooking and heating. Worst of all—in this big jail there were no rules. . . . The Germans could come into the ghetto to plunder, to kill, to torture, to take people to forced labor, to do as they pleased."

The same thing repeated itself hundreds of times over in other places. In Cracow, after the size of the Jewish population in the newly established capital of the General Government had been reduced by the expulsion of some sixty thousand Jews, the remaining thirteen thousand were crammed into the Podgórze area. "It was behind the Vistula," testified Rivka Kuper. "This was one of the poorest areas. The streets allocated to us consisted of old, dilapidated houses. Three or four families were forced to move into one apartment of a room and kitchen. Epidemics spread quickly, especially among the children. It was almost impossible to observe sanitary regulations in spite of all the doctors' efforts and for all the social workers' assistance."

Eichmann would inspect the bigger ghettos from time to time. It was among his duties to see that the Jews remained cooped up in the big jails. When the German Ambassador in Bucharest learned that Jews were being smuggled out by their youth organizations from the ghettos in Poland to neighboring Rumania, he immediately alerted Eichmann.

By autumn of 1941, within two years after the Heydrich-Eichmann directive on ghettoization, Jewry in the General Government was all behind the walls, and made ready for the next move. This followed soon, when the war moved further eastward and its flames reached into the densely Jewish areas of Eastern Poland and the Soviet Union.

CHAPTER 6

A Slaughterhouse on Wheels: The "Einsatzgruppen"

As I have indicated, however, the ghettoization of the Jews was merely the first stage in the comprehensive Nazi program of annihilation. The next stage was the remarkable institution of the "*Einsatzgruppen*," a unique war machine that was an adjunct to the Wehrmacht as it rolled over the vast plains of Poland and Russia.

The *Einsatzgruppen*—a word that may be translated as "Operational Units"—were used with striking effectiveness in the systematic murder of the Jews that partly paralleled and partly followed their ghettoization. But though systematic, the murders perpetrated by the *Einsatzgruppen* were limited to occupied Soviet Russia, and affected principally those Jews who were sent there from Germany in order to be exterminated.

The wholesale murders of the *Einsatzgruppen* preceded the final stage of the Nazi program—the death camps.

At a conference in Prague on October 10, 1941, Eichmann was asked how to get rid of fifty thousand Jews quickly. He came out with the reply that it would be best to send them to "the camps of SS Brigadiers Nebe and Rasch." In cross-examination I asked him how he had known there was any room in these camps. He answered that he was in constant touch with Nebe and Rasch by letter and cable. "The number of deportees and the date of deportation were settled by common consent."

"You knew these people were about to be killed shortly?" I asked. "Yes, that is true," was Eichmann's reply.

Nebe and Rasch were the commanders of two newly established *Einsatzgruppen,* hand-picked by the Gestapo to crush civilian resistance in the occupied areas of the Soviet Union, and to shoot as quickly as possible every Jewish man, woman and child they encountered there.

"This will be a war of annihilation," Hitler told his generals when the planning of the Russian offensive, under the code name "Operation Barbarossa," was completed. "The Commissars are the bearers of ideology directly opposed to National Socialism. Therefore the Commissars will be liquidated."

Thus the famous "Commissars' Order" came into being. It was the cover for wholesale murder.

The German High Command relayed the directive in simple terms. "Resistance will be punished not by legal prosecution but through ruthless measures by the occupying forces, for the eradication of any inclination to resist," ordered the Commander in Chief of the Armed Forces, Field Marshal Keitel.

As the orders went down the echelon, their meaning became clearer. Field Marshal von Brauchitsch, the Commander in Chief of the Army, ordered that the *Einsatzgruppen* were to have all powers to deal with civilians in the occupied area. They were placed under the control of the RSHA in Berlin, and were allowed complete freedom of action up to the front line.

Then *Einsatzgruppen* commanders were briefed at special sessions, with Eichmann present. Their orders were simple. "The Jewish population is to be totally exterminated, and all Jewish children murdered," it was relayed by Dr. Otto Ohlendorf, Commander of *Einsatzgruppe* D. Walter Blume, Commander of Unit 7, disclosed the reason for the action as given during the briefing session. "The Jews of the East are the mainstay of Bolshevism and therefore, according to the Fuehrer's wish, must be exterminated."

The old bogey of Communist Jew, not in use for two years since the Russian-Soviet *rapprochement,* was disinterred, this time as justification for outright murder. The directive said: "Kill all Jews!"

Other duties of the Operational Units included fighting partisans and destroying top Bolsheviks and "political enemies."

With his usual cunning Hitler had combined several objectives. The mass killings were to mesmerize the civilian population of Soviet Russia and browbeat it into submission. He believed that once the "degenerate Slavs" realized the futility of opposition to the "German masters," who did not hesitate to resort to extreme measures, they would lay down their arms and stop fighting. He obviously also wanted the whole army, some of whose chiefs had so far remained aloof from National Socialism, to become his irredeemable partners in crime. Trusting to the lowest human instincts, he wanted them to become bound to him by complicity in mass murder. Furthermore, here was the chance to solve part of the Jewish problem finally and for all time. He had made up his mind long ago that in the new order he was about to establish there would be a new demographic composition of humanity in which the Jews had no place. Other "undesirable" races would follow later. "We will remove millions of people of inferior races that breed like vermin," he once said to Rauschning.

There was still one doubt in his mind, and so far this had kept him from murdering Jews wholesale: What would the world say? How would it react? But to this he provided a reply: "When Barbarossa commences, the world will hold its breath and make no comment."

He was right. The massacres that now overtook Eastern Europe and Jewry evoked no real rescue reaction, though the news soon burst on the world (see Chapter 12).

Four *Einsatzgruppen,* each of battalion strength, went into action under the direct command of Heydrich, the Chief of the RSHA, seconded by Mueller, the Gestapo Chief. They were commanded in the field by, among others, two University professors, a lecturer, several doctors of law, a physician, a banker, an opera singer and an ex-priest.

*

When I was looking for possible survivors of the *Einsatzgruppen* executions to give evidence at Eichmann's trial, Avraham Aviel, a municipal official of Tel Aviv, came to see me. "You will not find many," he told me quietly. Aviel was born in a little village, Dogliszow, near Grodno, in the part of eastern Poland occupied by the Soviets. When the Germans entered in June, 1941, they immediately expelled all the Jews to the neighboring town. This procedure was usually followed in rural settlements, to facilitate killing in larger batches.

"Meanwhile," Aviel proceeded with his evidence in court, "we were held in a closed ghetto and put to work. . . . Then a group of Jews was picked out one day. Most of them were young, strong people, about one hundred. They were given spades. I remember these spades, with long handles for digging. Equipped with these tools, the people were ordered to march. . . . My father was in that group. . . . We knew that the moment father was left alone he would try to escape, and so he did, as we later found out. Half an hour later we heard shots. Then they took a second group, which included my brother Pinchas. We thought that once outside the town there would perhaps be an opportunity to escape. If not, we figured it was better to be shot in the back while fleeing. But there was some hope that father had managed to escape, because we knew what his way of thinking was. A few days before, he had given my little brother the outfit of a shepherd. My brother looked like an Aryan. He was blond. We thought he would disguise himself as a peasant boy. He managed to leave the ghetto but was later captured by White Russians and Poles who wanted to find out whether he was a Jew. They took off his pants and, seeing he was indeed a Jew, they returned him to the ghetto. Then we realized that everything was sealed off, that even a little boy could not leave. Our desire was that at least one of us should survive. . . . When the Germans came, equipped with automatic weapons, as if marching out to the front, I left the house and I saw a large group pushed from the edge of the ghetto in the same direction in which the groups with the spades had been going. At that moment a number of Germans entered our house. One of them stood at the entrance, blocking it, and the others went through, searching and driving out our people. Whoever passed through the entrance got a blow with a truncheon. . . . I tried to find out where my family was. I saw my mother, brother and uncle. Then we marched together. We were about one thousand people. My mother walked in the center—I and my brother at her sides. Mother told us to say a prayer, *Shma Yisrael,** and die as Jews. I repeated the words after her, but I had inner resistance. We were brought to the market place in the middle of the town, were told to kneel, heads down. Whoever did not do so was either shot right through the head or severely beaten. I was shorter than the others, so I could raise my head without being discovered, and I saw in front of me a long trench about thirty yards long. We were led to that trench. Machine-gun bursts were heard and people would fall into the trench. I saw a Jewish girl struggle. She refused to undress. They hit her and then she was shot too. All were shot—children, women, family after family. At this moment I noticed a group of Jews who were digging those graves and noticed my brother Pinchas among them.

"I took leave of my mother and started jumping over the heads of people who were sitting next to me, and thus—I don't know how, it was a miracle really . . . I managed to reach the edge of the road and they apparently did not notice me. Right next to me I found Zelig, the carpenter from our town—he had been employed by the Gestapo and had a labor card, a special document saying that he had to be spared. At that moment he was approached by a German who stuck the revolver into his neck. He held out his labor card. The German shot him and his face darkened, but he still spoke for a second. He said, 'I have a card.' He was shot again and fell. At that moment a German came up to me and asked, 'Who are you? What are you doing here?' I had a labor card saying I had been a locksmith. I said I was a good locksmith and blacksmith and he left me alone. I lay down and crawled in the direction of my brother. My mother was shot then, together with all the other Jews near the trench. My brother Yekutiel was shot on that day too. Only later did I learn that I was the only one from the group who, for some reason, managed to escape and survive. The shooting went on. There were a few people left over from other groups. We were taken off by the Germans in the direction of the town. We were about 90–100. We did not know what would befall us. We were returned to the deserted ghetto. We knew that no one was home but we still went into the house where we had lived. We took a prayer book and left the house again. Next day the survivors were ordered by the Germans to present themselves for work. I had to work as a locksmith. . . . I could not bear to see the faces of the men who had shot our loved ones and decided to escape. I went into the woods."

While wandering in the woods, Aviel found other Jews. Spontaneously

* The Jewish profession of faith: "Hear, O Israel; the Lord our God is one God."

they formed small groups. "Our first action was to attack a Gestapo outpost not far from my village. . . . We had a few arms we had purchased from the peasants. Then escaped Russian prisoners of war joined us. We fought later with the partisans." This is how Avraham Aviel survived.

Rivka Yoselewska was another witness to the shootings. Only four days before testifying she suffered a heart attack. When Chief Inspector Michael Goldman of the Israeli Police visited her for interrogation she almost fainted. Her family asked us to excuse her, but I was sorry to miss her evidence. We agreed that she would make an effort to come to court. She appeared a few days later and told a story that heightened the nightmarishness of the trial.

Mrs. Yoselewska described the day disaster befell her little town, Zagorodski, near Pinsk, in eastern Poland. She well remembered the autumn day in 1941. Her father had just returned from a clandestine prayer meeting in a cellar. The German occupation authorities forbade Jews to get together even for prayer, but people nevertheless prayed in secret. This was the day of the new moon, according to the Jewish calendar, and her father extended to the family the traditional blessing for a happy month. Scarcely were the words out of his mouth before pandemonium broke loose. The Jewish quarter in which Mrs. Yoselewska lived was suddenly surrounded by hundreds of SS men, who with shouts and whiplashes ordered all Jews out of their homes. They were chased like animals to the central square of the town, where they were kept until the next morning, without food or water. Then, when they were exhausted by fear and fatigue, all were marched outside the town. They reached a huge ditch and were told to stop and undress.

"Even when I saw the naked people who had arrived before us, I still did not believe they would kill us, I hoped it would be just torture," she said. Taking off her clothes, she stood there clinging to her six-year-old daughter. Her mother, her grandmother and her sister were all nearby. Her hopes were in vain. The SS men started shooting the Jews one by one, firing point-blank into the back of each victim's head, then kicking the body into the open pit. Yoselewska saw her father and mother disappear into the ditch. Then the Germans approached her grandmother, who was holding two little girls in her arms, comforting them and pointing to heaven, where they would soon meet all their beloved ones. In a moment all three were shot. "Then I saw my sister embrace a girl friend; the two of them tried to cover their nakedness with each other's bodies, pleading with a uniformed SS man to spare their young lives. In reply they were both shot and went down.

"As I stood there paralyzed with horror," continued Mrs. Yoselewska, "my little daughter, Malka, was wrung from my arms and killed."

At that particular moment, she said, she felt nothing more. The German who shot her missed his aim, and the bullet merely grazed her head. She only felt a booted leg kicking her into the ditch to bleed to death or die of suffocation.

Later she regained consciousness. "I felt I was choking and desperately needed air," she said, "and so I lifted myself from among the bodies, many of which were still alive and were biting at me and pulling me down. By then the shooting was over and the Germans were gone." She had only leaden skies above her head and an endless grave under her feet.

"I fell down, scratching my nails into the thin layer of earth covering the bodies, begging to be admitted back to my family. Blood was oozing from the grave; whenever I pass a spring now I remember the red fountain."

She sat there in a daze for three days, waiting for death to come. People passing by thought she was a ghost or a madwoman, and hurried on. Finally a farmer, more courageous than the others, approached her, gave her clothing and food, and led her away into the forest. There she was looked after by partisan fighters, whom she joined. Her wounds healed; she managed to survive the war. She is married now in Israel and has two children.

Her story shattered the courtroom. Her words were simple and direct, her tone quiet and restrained. She spoke for almost an hour and a half; loud sobbing was heard from the audience, and tears flowed freely from many eyes. A stony silence fell upon the courtroom when I turned Mrs. Yoselewska over to the defense counsel for cross-examination. He rose to announce that he had no questions.

We were able to produce the affidavit of a German who had witnessed the executions, Hermann Friedrich Graebe, who was employed during the war as a civilian engineer in a building firm. His sworn statement had been produced before at the International Military Tribunal of Nuremberg. At one time I intended to summon him to give evidence, but the defense counsel agreed to the submission of his affidavit without calling him as a witness.

Graebe had seen the *Einsatzgruppen* in action near Rowno. He heard from one of his assistants that the Jews were being shot just near their office, and he went to see for himself. "I saw a big earth ditch, some thirty meters long and forty meters deep," he said. "Before it were several lorries from which people were being driven out by Ukrainian militiamen under the command of an SS man. The people who had got off the trucks—men, women and children of all ages—had to undress upon the order of the SS man, who carried a riding or dog-whip, and put down their clothing in fixed places. I saw a heap of shoes of about 800 to 1,000 pairs, great piles of underlinen and clothing. Without screaming or weeping, these people undressed, stood around in family groups, kissed each other, said farewell and waited for a sign from another SS man, who stood near the pit, also with a whip in his hand. . . .

"No complaints or pleas for mercy were heard. A family of about eight persons passed by—a man and a woman, both about fifty, with their children of about one, eight and ten and two grown-up daughters of twenty and twenty-four. An old woman with snow-white hair was holding a one-year-old child in her arms, singing to it and tickling it. The child was cooing with delight. The couple were looking on with tears in their eyes. The father was holding the hand of the ten-year-old boy and speaking to him softly; the boy was fighting back his tears. The father pointed toward the sky, stroked his head and seemed to explain something to him. At that moment the SS man at the pit shouted something to his comrade. The latter counted off about twenty persons and instructed them to go behind the pit. Among them was the family I mentioned. A girl, slim, with black hair, pointed to herself as she passed by me and said 'Twenty-three years.' . . . People were closely wedged together and lying on top of each other so that only their heads were visible. All had blood pouring from them. Some of the people shot were still moving."

It was considered a privilege to be shot on the spot; sometimes it was a mercy begged for. Feinstein, a Jew from Memel, recognized his neighbor in the firing squad and shouted to him: "*Gustav, schiess gut!*" ("Gustav, aim well!") After every execution the squad members had a smoke, usually a drink and a friendly chat. Everything was done with proverbial orderliness. When the District Commissioner of the Sluck area requested the *Einsatzgruppe* to postpone other executions for a few days, to enable the Jews to complete the work they were doing in the workshops, he was told that was impossible under the timetable. "We have only two days for Sluck. In these two days the town of Sluck must become free of Jews." In Riga a column of Jews that had been marched from the ghetto to the execution site was returned by a nonchalant sergeant who, having looked at his watch, said: "It is one minute after twelve. The action for today is over."

Eichmann went to inspect the *Einsatzgruppen* at work. Near Minsk he saw the young troopers shooting into a pit already full of writhing bodies: "I can still see," he said in his interrogation, "a woman with a child. She was shot and then the baby in her arms. His brains splattered all around, also over my leather overcoat."

*

The army cooperated fully. "The attitude of the army requires special notice," reported Group C from the Kiev area. The same group reported from Tarnopol they were "glad to notice so much hostility toward the Jews in the armed forces." The other groups sent in similar reports. Dr. Stahlecker, Eichmann's old friend, now the commander of Group A, reported "very good, almost cordial relations" with the army commander in his area. Dr. Ohlendorf, the commander of Group D, described his relations with the Wehrmacht as "excellent."

The army command had one reservation: that soldiers should not "gaze curiously at such procedures." It forbade the "distribution of photographs and the spreading of reports about such events." These, it was ruled, "will be regarded as a subversion of decency and discipline in the army and will be punished strictly." Some pictures were reported to have fallen into the hands of Hungarian and Slovak officers and to have been smuggled out to America; this was considered "very embarrassing."

Nor did the local population present difficulties at first. "Almost every local man here considers it necessary, if he can turn it to his profit, to accuse before the German police his friends and relatives of having been Communists," stated one of the commanders in his report. The Germans encouraged a "profit approach." Part of the Jewish loot was distributed among the local people, all of whom "gave their approval to the measure," reported Group C after its gigantic slaughter of Babi Yar near Kiev. "We are deluged with denunciations received from all parts of the population," reported Group C, specifying the important help they got even from leading members of the Communist bodies in detecting the Komsomol units assigned to do sabotage work. Group D reported from the Crimea that "the population is hostile to the Jews, and in some cases they supply Jews to the commandos for liquidation. The '*starostas*' (village elders) asked for permission to kill the Jews themselves."

Many local "volunteers" were enlisted into auxiliary units, especially in the Baltic States and in the Ukraine, and were immediately put "to work." They were most helpful: being acquainted with the area, they knew the places Jews could hide and the people who would offer them refuge, they spoke the local language and could be relied upon to transmit and carry out all orders. On the whole they were "most reliable," as Dr. Stahlecker put it. They soon became the terror of the Jewish population and the Germans would detail to them the dirtiest jobs, such as shooting the children ("1,107 Jewish adults were shot by the Commando and 531 juveniles by the Ukrainians"), beating people to death with clubs or dragging them from hideouts. Their salaries were often paid from the loot of Jewish money, and they became financially interested in the "success" of their actions.

Some ethnic Germans who had lived for ages in eastern Poland and in Russia wholeheartedly welcomed the slaughter. "We were downright frightened by their bloodthirstiness," said a group commander.

In the southern Ukraine the population was reported to have "accepted with thanks the solution of the Jewish problem but could not be moved to more active steps. . . . They felt anxiety at the possible return of the Soviets. To allay their fear psychosis . . . the Commandos made the Jews march through towns under appropriate guard before they were shot." The spectacle of defenseless people, beaten and hounded, being dragged to execution, among them women and children, was a calculated measure of psychological warfare.

In other places the instigation to anti-Jewish excesses was more successful. "After some encouragement from the Security Police the local population engaged in a self-cleaning process," reported Dr. Stahlecker from Lithuania. He was referring to the awful pogroms in Kaunas in the course of which the Lithuanian "partisans" killed or tortured to death some six thousand Jews within the first days of the German occupation. But the spirit of pogroms spent itself. Stahlecker found it "essential to establish a provable fact that the liberated population took of its own accord most severe measures against their Bolshevik and Jewish enemies." He was astonished that the action did not last longer and that he met with no understanding response in Esthonia and with only limited success in Latvia, where "only" five hundred Jews were "rendered harmless through pogroms." But he did find there many volunteers to assist in executions elsewhere.

There is one report of a local man siding with the Jews. Senitsa Werszowsky, the Mayor of Kremenchug, was reported to have been shot for "attempting to protect the Jews."

*

Yet after some time difficulties were reported. The Germans found out that the slaughter was seriously interfering with economic needs. "The complete elimination of Jews is not practical, at least not at this time, because of the important share of the Jews in handicrafts," wrote Dr. Stahlecker. "Some trades are manned exclusively by Jews and the Jewish artisans are irreplaceable for important war effort works. . . . Even in industries the immediate removal of all Jews from the process is impossible." The armament inspector for the Ukraine wrote to his headquarters: "If we shoot the Jews, let the war prisoners die out, expose the urban population to starvation and are about to lose part of the rural population next year owing to hunger, the question is: Who is going to produce anything in this area?"

The solution was to put the Jews to work for a while. This called for the establishment of ghettos in the bigger cities. In Kaunas, after the first big massacre, a Jewish committee was ordered to appear before the authorities and was told that for the creation of "normal relations," and as the "only possibility of avoiding further pogroms," the establishment of a Jewish ghetto was essential. A similar development was reported from the Ukraine, where *Einsatzgruppe* C "had to exclude for the time being the more expert Jewish laborers from the executions." However, in order to placate the RSHA for the delay Stahlecker sent in on January 31, 1942, a map of the area under his jurisdiction where the places completely cleared of Jews were neatly marked with coffins.

Gebietskommissar Wilhelm Kube, in charge of the civilian administration in White Russia, was aroused by some reports of executions in his area. Kube was an old-fashioned Nazi himself, actually one of the founders of the party. After a period of disfavor he had been reinstated into public service through Himmler's intervention. Yet he summoned up enough courage to protest against some of the measures he encountered. "Expert laborers must be spared in any case," he wrote to his superior, Hinrich Lohse, the Reichskommissar for Ostland. "With these methods we will not achieve peace and order in White Russia. To bury alive seriously wounded people, who crawl out of their graves, is such a bottomless piece of vileness [*eine so bodenlose Schweinerei*] that it ought to be reported to the Reichsmarschall [Goering]."

In a private letter to Lohse he wrote he saw in the Minsk ghetto Jews deported from Germany who held high military distinctions during World War I.

> They will probably die or freeze to death in the next few weeks. . . . I am certainly hard and prepared to assist in solving the Jewish problem, but these people who belong to our cultural sphere [*Kulturkreis*] are often quite different from the bestial native hordes. . . . I ask you, out of consideration for the Reich and for our party, to issue unequivocal instructions to carry out what is necessary in the most humane way.

Lohse inquired in Berlin whether it was to be understood that all Jews in the Ostland were to be liquidated, and was this to take place regardless of age, sex and economic considerations?

He was soon told to mind his own business. The Ministry for the Eastern Territories coolly replied to Lohse's query. "It is assumed that in the meantime clarity has been achieved on the question in a series of conferences that were held. As a matter of principle, economic interests shall not be considered in regulating the problem. Any questions that may come up have to be cleared directly with the Senior SS and Police Leader." Put simply, Lohse was told that the Jews were a police matter and that he had better not make a fool of himself.

The Ministry itself was rebuffed by Heydrich. In an attempt to restore some order into the area devastated by the *Einsatzgruppen,* the Ministry had issued a blueprint for the administration of the territory under its jurisdiction, called the "Brown Portfolio." It was circulated among various offices for comments. Heydrich's reaction was sharp.

"On Jewish matters," he wrote, "the central authority is the police, and I would ask you to redraft your directions on the Jewish problem according to the version settled by the RSHA. The officer in charge is SS Sturmbannfuehrer Eichmann." Eichmann's "amended version" followed soon: "All measures for the removal of Jewry will have to be taken without regard to economic considerations," and not as had been proposed by the Ministry. Eichmann further laid down that "the Jewish problem must be solved immediately, and not, as had been suggested, through a step-by-step removal from trade . . . and transfer to agriculture." All Jews in the East, including those deported from the Reich, had to be treated "by the same measures that apply to the solution of the Jewish problem throughout Europe," and not merely subjected to "strong restrictive steps." Eichmann obviously had the last say in the matter.

*

The *Einsatzgruppen* shooting squads provided an opportunity for getting rid of some German Jews, who were made ready for the last push. All records of the Gestapo were destroyed before Germany's collapse, but we were able to unearth one that we presented at the trial and which showed for the first time how the process worked. It was the Jewish file of the Duesseldorf police. It nailed down Eichmann's guilt on this point.

It begins with an order to several Gestapo offices throughout the Reich, including the one in Duesseldorf, to round up, detain and transport fifty thousand Jews, to confiscate and seal their apartments, to search them bodily and to leave each his watch and wedding ring. The Duesseldorf police soon reported to Eichmann that the order had been carried out. The local "crop" was 1,007 people. A detailed breakdown by age (from six years upward), profession and sex was attached. Every five deportees were neatly recorded by four vertical lines and one oblique.

The captain in charge of the transport submitted a nine-page report. The loading took place on December 11, 1941; there were some troubles: a man attempted to commit suicide, a woman hid in the station lavatory, a child died en route. The guards suffered much discomfort when the heating apparatus in their compartment broke down; it was below freezing. It was too bad that he, the captain, had to allow Jews to draw water at a few stations during the four days' journey from Duesseldorf to Riga. This imposed too heavy a burden on the guards, but they were compensated by the good treatment of the German Red Cross nurses, who served the guards with barley broth and beef at Shavli station. At the same station the light was cut off in the deportees' cars.

We were unable to produce in court any survivor of the Duesseldorf deportees, but we had one of the fifty thousand in the witness box. Leona Neumann was sent out from Vienna to Riga in January, 1942, together with fifteen hundred people. The guards had it easier this time. The deportees' cars were all sealed. During the six-day journey no one was allowed to get in or out. "We knocked down the ice formed on the carriage windows to get some moisture," she testified. Many froze to death. Many were too exhausted to get out on arrival and were shot. Only about a thousand reached the Riga ghetto.

The *Einsatzgruppe* promptly reported the arrival of the deportees to Eichmann. "Everything was ready in Riga and Minsk to accept the Jews from the Reich. These deportees have a complete misconception of their future," the report read. "They appear to take seriously what they were told at home about pioneering tasks awaiting them in the East. . . . Many brought along agricultural tools." To put an end to all this nonsense, executions started. Leona Neumann and nine other deportees were saved when they were assigned to a labor unit.

Surviving Jews were put to work during the lull that followed the first wave of executions. But not for very long; in the summer of 1942 the *Einsatzgruppen* launched their second stage of operations: liquidating the remnants, the small ghettos and the communities that had been by-passed earlier. Lists were now prepared of the "absolutely essential Jews"; all others were shot or poisoned in gas vans sent down to "relieve" the shooting squads. The trucks were camouflaged to look like peasants' huts, into which the victims were lured. Yet their secret leaked out quickly; the local population called them "death vans." Sometimes a whole ghetto, like that of Janów, was set on fire and burnt down with all its inhabitants.

The obsessive character of this whole anti-Jewish program is noteworthy. At the height of a most destructive war—a war, moreover, on two fronts, a long-time nightmare of the German armies—the destruction of the Jews took precedence over all war needs. War industries in entire regions lacked manpower at this time and had been abandoned. Leather and metal factories were shut down; workshops stood empty. Yet with single-mindedness and zeal the Nazis put their anti-Jewish program into effect.

Indeed, the ruthlessness and sadism of the killers even increased. The Nazis were taking out on the Jews the failure of their plans to break Russian resistance. An SS man would now sink his fist into the belly of a pregnant woman and throw her alive into a grave. Victims of shootings would be left wounded for a whole night, dragging themselves bleeding to the neighboring villages where they were rounded up and shot again.

Gebietskommissar Kube was subdued. He duly reported that together with the "technically very able" commander of the local *Einsatz*, SS Lieutenant Colonel Dr. Strauch, they liquidated 55,000 Jews in Minsk, 16,000 in Lida and 8,000 in Slonim, "without affecting labor requirements."

Still Kube soon fell into new difficulties. The Ministry of Foreign Affairs complained he had disclosed to Italian officials who visited Minsk that the packages they saw were the belongings of deported Jews, and he even went so far as to show them a gas van in which Jews were being killed. "The fascists were deeply shaken," concluded the report. Afterward Kube had a serious altercation with Strauch when the latter arrested seventy Jews Kube employed directly. In the heat of the debate Kube stated, according to Strauch's immediate complaint, that "our procedure was unworthy of a German and of the Germany of Kant and Goethe. He said my men literally satisfied their lust during these executions. I protested energetically and emphasized that we, in addition to having to perform this nasty job, were also made the target of mud-slinging." When several months later Kube was killed by a woman of his household, Himmler said his death was a blessing for Germany and that anyway he was heading for a concentration camp.

The *Einsatzgruppen* inquired in Berlin whether foreign nationality was life-saving for Jews. Eichmann's department issued instructions directing them to include in the "over-all measures" Jews of sixteen different nationalities, but to hold off for the time being with regard to "other foreign Jews." The department later ruled that Jewish nationals of ten other countries (including neutrals like Switzerland and Turkey, and Germany's allies like

Italy) should be moved from the *Einsatzgruppen* area to the Buchenwald and Ravensbrueck concentration camps, "until grounds of foreign policy permit them to be sent back to the East."

Soon other problems arose. The Ministry for the Eastern Territories wanted to know who, after all, was to be treated as a Jew. The question was of importance, as the *Einsatzgruppen,* almost without screening, were shooting anybody "reported" to be Jewish. It was found out that they also "conveyed to the Final Solution" Crimean Tartars and some Moslems. So the Ministry summoned a large-scale conference, with seventeen representatives of six other ministries and of the army, to decide on the matter. Eichmann was represented by his man, SS Major Suhr. Problems concerning the due treatment of *Mischlinge* and the impracticability in the area of the Nuremberg Laws were discussed at length. Finally the conference resolved that any person belonging to the Jewish community, or generally reported to be Jewish, or whom all circumstances indicated to be Jewish, would be treated as such, with the important proviso that cases of doubt would be decided by the civilian administration. Heydrich immediately demurred; the Security Police must have a say in the "doubtful" cases, he declared. "Jewish matters are our responsibility," added Himmler, refusing "to tie my hands by silly definitions."

How the "doubtful" cases were actually dealt with is grimly illustrated by the case of a woman the fight for whose life we were able to reproduce from salvaged Nazi documents.

Jenni Cozzi, a Jewess born in Latvia, was married to an Italian high officer with whom she had lived abroad. After her husband's death she came to stay for a while with her family in her native Riga. Here the war caught up with her; the Nazis imprisoned her in the Riga ghetto. The Italian authorities, approached by the colleagues of her late husband, requested her release and return to Italy. The matter was referred to Eichmann's department as were all Jewish matters. His deputy, Rolf Guenther, wrote to the German Foreign Office that he could not accede to the request, as "the Jewess Cozzi will certainly use her knowledge of events in the Riga ghetto for spreading anti-German atrocity propaganda. Please ask the Italian Consul-General in Danzig to refrain from supporting the case of the Jewess Cozzi." But for the Italians it was a matter of a "debt of honor" to a deceased officer. So the Italian Embassy in Berlin took the matter up. Eichmann was again approached and now entered into the picture in person, writing to his Foreign Office that the request for the release of the Jewess Cozzi and her return to Italy was "unjustifiable" (*"nicht vertretbar"*). "Please cause the Italian Embassy to abandon the further support for Cozzi," he wrote. The Ambassador, however, proved impervious to the argument that Cozzi was only a Jewess and requested the allied government of Germany to enable her to return to the country of her citizenship. Eichmann was again timidly approached by his Foreign Office with the request to reconsider his decision or else to provide "persuasive arguments" against Mrs. Cozzi "which would be appreciated even by the Italians."

At this stage an unprecedented event happened. The Italian Fascist Party intervened on behalf of Jenni Cozzi with their sister Nazi Party. Still Eichmann said: "No." Then, when Mussolini's government was overthrown, Eichmann wrote to his Foreign Office that in view of "the changed political conditions in Italy" he would refrain from dealing with the matter further. "I took the necessary steps," he added, "to ensure that the Jewess Cozzi should remain in the Riga concentration camp until further orders."

The story of the *Einsatzgruppen* is related in their "achievement reports" with "cold factuality," as it was called in the judgment of the Nuremberg Military Tribunal, which says:

> The story was written as the events it narrates occurred, and it was authored by the doers of the deeds. It was written in the terse exact language which military discipline requires and which precision of reporting dictates. . . . Every subkommando leader was instructed to inform his Kommando leader of developments and activities in his field of operation, every Kommando leader in turn accounted to the *Einsatzgruppe* leader, and the *Einsatzgruppe* leader by wireless and by mail reported to the RSHA in Berlin.

A special unit was set up at the RSHA to ensure that specially selected addresses should get all detailed *Einsatzgruppen* reports. SS Lieutenant Colonel Gustav Nosske testified in Nuremberg that he had been in charge of this unit, which, among its other duties, had to see to it that Eichmann received full information about the "Jewish actions" and that these reports reached him promptly in his secluded and secret office. From behind his desk at Kurfuerstenstrasse 116 in Berlin, Eichmann could tick off one Jewish community after the other. From time to time, he would make "summaries of the reports" and present them to Heydrich and Mueller for further instructions.

The reports would simply state, for instance, that 23,600 Jews of Kamenets Podolsk were executed in the three last days of August, 1941, or that 33,771 Jews of Kiev were massacred on the twenty-ninth and thirtieth of September, 1941. Sometimes they would send in periodical reports totaling the activity to date: Group A reported on October 15, 1941, a total of 18,430 Jews and 3,387 Communist functionaries executed. Group D reported on December 12, 1941, that, having shot a further 2,190 Jews and 19 Communist functionaries, its sum total of executions "rose to 54,696." Group B reported on November 3, 1941, that it had "so far liquidated about 80,000 people."

The reports regularly contain accompanying items telling of measures to "confiscate" Jewish property: cash, valuables, cattle, furniture, clothing, footwear, watches and personal effects. As the Nuremberg judgment in the *Einsatzgruppen* case says, "Even in the dread and grim business of mass slaughter a definite profit was rung up on the Nazi cash register."

It has been estimated, on the basis of a thorough study of all reports, that the number of Jews killed in the *Einsatzgruppen* campaign totaled about 1,400,000.

Yet even this was soon to be surpassed. A plan was being worked out and put into effect for the killing of every single Jewish individual caught up in the Nazi dragnets.

The greatest blood bath in history was soon to flood an entire continent.

CHAPTER 7

The Final Solution

Both the proliferating ghettos and the murderous *Einsatzgruppen*, while remarkably effective, were nevertheless felt to be inadequate as methods of coping with the "Jewish question."

In accordance with Hitler's "total" view of life a more systematic, principled and revolutionary means of settling that question had to be found.

It was found, and given the appropriately terse name of the "Final Solution." This phrase was, in fact, "copyrighted" by Eichmann, as he indicated in his conversations with Sassen.

This "solution" was, of course, a synonym for mass slaughter: it involved the concentration of the victims in immense abattoirs and the administrative arrangements for getting them there—in other words, mass deportations and death camps.

Midsummer of 1941 saw a rising tension in the Jewish Section Department IV-B-4 (which had developed out of IV-D-4) of the Gestapo. With Russian Jewry being annihilated by shooting, the question was what the decision would be on the rest of Jewry under the Nazi heel. It was obvious that emigration was no answer. For months Eichmann kept informing various authorities that "in view of the undoubtedly coming final solution" further emigration of Jews though still possible was of no primary interest. Even the title of his department was changed in March, 1941. The "emigration" was dropped; it read simply: "Jewish affairs and deportations."

The Madagascar daydream exploded. Everybody was holding his breath: what would the Fuehrer do? Would he come out again with a simple and obvious answer, leaving everybody gasping at his genius as so often in the past? He did. After a trial period of a month's wholesale killing of Jews behind the Russian front without any immediate retaliation from the free world, it seemed quite safe to proceed.

Hitler ordered the killing of all Jews in the Reich and the pillage of their property.

Officially, the order took the form of a directive by Goering to Heydrich, the Head of the Reich's Security office. It read:

In supplementing the task assigned to you on January 24, 1939, to bring the Jewish problem to a possibly satisfactory solution through emigration and evacuation in accordance with circumstances obtaining at the time, I hereby commission you to make all necessary preparation, in the organizational, material and financial sense, to bring about a total solution of the Jewish problem in the German sphere of influence in Europe.

Wherever other government agencies are concerned, they are to be called upon to cooperate. I further commission you to submit to me as soon as possible an over-all plan concerning the organizational, substantive and financial measures for the execution of the desired final solution of the Jewish problem.

There are many significant features in this directive. Hitler, who gave the order, again spoke on Jewish matters through Goering. It was only natural to place it all officially in Heydrich's hands. For years the Jews had been in his domain. Heydrich, though now very powerful, and soon to be appointed Protector of Bohemia and Moravia, replacing the "weak" von Neurath, was anxious to be delegated this new responsibility, which would give him enormous additional powers. The actual work would be done, in any case, by his faithful, "competent department chief," Adolf Eichmann.

Heydrich's appointment automatically involved Himmler with all his powerful SS offices—particularly the Head Office for Economy and Administration (*Wirtschafts und Verwaltungs Hauptamt*), which took care of the looting of Jewish property. So it was finally decided that the directive would go straight to Heydrich personally. In the same way, Heydrich appointed Adolf Eichmann to be "the competent authority" for "the actual execution of the Final Solution of the Jewish problem," thereby automatically switching in the whole machinery of the Gestapo.

*

Goering's directive was couched in general terms, according to the prevailing rules of *Tarnung* (camouflage), without spelling out its import. But everyone knew what it involved. The "circumstances obtaining at the time" when expelling Jews was the main object, no longer existed. The "Final Solution" now meant physical extirpation.

The previous order: "Drive them out and rob them!" was replaced by: "Kill them all and loot their property!"

When Goering was examined on this document at the Nuremberg Trials by the American Chief Prosecutor, Justice Jackson, the Reichsmarschall succeeded in misleading his interrogator. As the Jewish subject approached, Goering's nervousness mounted. He even placed in front of him a card on which he had inscribed self-hypnotic instructions. On one side he had written in red: "Slow, make a pause," and on the other: "Quiet, keep calm."

Jackson asked: "Then it was you, was it not, who signed, on July 31, 1941, a decree asking Himmler and Heydrich to make the plans for the complete solution of the Jewish question?" Goering: "No, that is not correct."

Jackson was surprised. He started reading the document into the record, with Goering repeatedly interrupting on the ground of alleged mistranslation. He provided a translation of his own, substituting there and then the words "total solution" for "final solution." The court seemed to accept Goering's "explanations."

Here an astonishing thing happened. Jackson did not realize that the technical term "Final Solution" appeared in the next paragraph of the very document he held in his hand. He was thoroughly disgusted both with the inaccuracy of the translation he had to rely on and with Goering's evasive tactics. He dropped the subject altogether and passed to other matters.

The incident upset Jackson so much that he went to see the American judges, Justices Biddle and Parker, in chambers, complained of their attitude toward him and announced his intention of resigning from the trial and going home. They had great difficulty in mollifying him.

It was only then that Goering felt at ease and boasted: "This is how I brilliantly outmaneuvered Jackson. No lawyer could have handled such a document better."

This is the more remarkable because Goering, though here and there denouncing Hitler's policy, went a long way in accepting responsibility for many of the decisions that led the Third Reich to war, fully aware of the gravity of the admission and of the weight the tribunal attached to the charge of conspiracy to wage war. His general attitude was expressed in his reply to the Soviet prosecutor, Rudenko: "I stand by my Fuehrer now, in bad days, as I stood by him in good times." Yet even he recoiled from the order for the Final Solution and took refuge in an obvious lie, denying all knowledge of what had happened to the Jews and disclaiming any complicity.

Goering kept repeating that if he had only known what was going on he would never have supported mass murder. "I assure you we never for a moment had such things in mind," he told Gilbert, the prison psychologist. "I only thought we would eliminate Jews from positions in big business and government."

This, of course, was utterly false, as were the absurd protestations and denials of some of the others accused. Kaltenbrunner, Heydrich's successor as head of the RSHA, also maintained that he never knew what was going on. "I had nothing to do with the executions," he declared in court. And to Gilbert: "I never gave orders and never executed them. You have no idea how secret these things were kept even from me. Because of the press propaganda I was labeled 'the gas chamber specialist.' "

They all denied their complicity in mass murder; it was too much to bear in bright daylight. Only those few Nazis who openly expressed contrition, like the ex-Governor of Poland, Hans Frank, and the Nazi Minister of Munitions, Albert Speer, or those who were actually caught red-handed, admitted these charges. Even notorious and open instigators of the slaughter of Jews, like Julius Streicher and Alfred Rosenberg, maintained before the tribunal that they were always opposed to the killings. Everyone put the blame on Hitler, Himmler, Heydrich and Eichmann.

*

It was Eichmann who drafted Goering's historic directive. "Doesn't it bear the initials of my department?" he asked the astonished Sassen. "But this is an order from Goering to Heydrich," Sassen protested. "That may be so," replied Eichmann, "but I dictated it. These are my words. We had prepared the letter and submitted it to Goering for signature."

Apparently he also kept another order signed by Himmler, which, in a moment of intimate talk, he took out of his safe and showed to his friend Dieter Wisliceny, under the seal of absolute secrecy. It was addressed to Heydrich and to Gluecks, the Chief Inspector of the Concentration Camps, dated April, 1942, charging the two men with the execution of Hitler's order for the biological destruction of the Jews, except for those capable of working in the munition factories. "Eichmann told me that within the RSHA he was personally responsible for the execution of this order," Wisliceny said in his testimony in Nuremberg.

In all probability Wisliceny was telling the truth, though this second order was never found. In April, 1942, at the height of the deportations, Himmler may well have issued a directive specifying the respective responsibilities of the RSHA and the Head Office for Economy and Administration. In any case, even according to this version Himmler was relying on Hitler's order. Generally, nobody needed to get such orders in writing and nobody cared. Surprisingly, however, one man did. It was Odilo Globocnik. "He wanted to have it in black and white," recalled Eichmann, adding that it was strange because nobody else had asked for such things.

Once the order for extermination was out, feverish efforts were started to find the best way in implementation. The *Einsatzgruppen* had been engaged in direct shooting, but this method gave rise to many misgivings. The shooting squads became addicted to alcohol. Some of them grumbled that they found it difficult to fire on children. Eichmann himself complained that these people would quickly turn into sadists. The Ministry for the Eastern Territories, where the executions took place, maintained that the system was not "elegant."

On a visit to Minsk, Himmler expressed a desire to see it for himself. SS Major General Nebe, Commander of *Einsatzgruppe* B, obliged. Watching one wave of human beings after another fall under the volleys of rifle fire, Himmler grew nervous. Two women did not die immediately, and Himmler shouted that they should stop torturing them. When it was over, SS General von dem Bach-Zelewski addressed him: "Reichsfuehrer, there were only a hundred here." "What do you mean by that?" snapped Himmler. "Look at the eyes of the men of the Commando," replied von dem Bach, "observe how badly shattered they are. These men are through with their nerves for the rest of their lives. We are raising neurotics or savages here."

Himmler was visibly shaken. He addressed the assembled *Einsatzkommandos,* telling them that he understood how repulsive this duty was, but their consciences should not suffer. It was all being done as a necessity for a fighting nation. "Look at nature," he said. "Creatures that are too tired to fight go under." He repeated Hitler's favorite parallel between biological phenomena and moral actions. "A bug or a rat has a right to live, as a thistle has a right to grow. Yet men exterminate vermin and weed out thistles. This is in self-defense, otherwise vermin will kill men and thistles will destroy the crop."

Following the speech Himmler asked Nebe to consider "more humane ways than shooting." Nebe suggested the use of dynamite. Von dem Bach objected, but Himmler decided to try it out. The results were lamentable.

*

When it came to admitting all these things, Eichmann, too, disclaimed responsibility. In facing the court, he, too, condemned the slaughter, stigmatizing it as one of the gravest crimes in the history of mankind. But only three years earlier he had given vent to an obscene oath when Sassen suggested that at heart Eichmann might have been against the murders. "Who told you so?" he shouted. "When I saw our own victims after the big air raids I always thought that the Fuehrer was right. If so many Germans were killed, it was good at least that the enemy was also taught a lesson." Sassen tried to argue that in point of time the air raids took place after the extermination had begun, but Eichmann was adamant.

It was quite obvious to me that at the time Eichmann had fully identified himself with the new "radical method," as he called it. Like other leading Nazis he considered the slaughter absolutely necessary. True, when Heydrich first informed him of the Fuehrer's decision, it left him speechless for a while. Then he thought it over. The Fuehrer was right, of course, as usual. It was the right thing to do, he mused, in fact the only right thing. It involved, of course, new and onerous duties. Not very pleasant at times, but great things always require a sacrifice. He was proud to be right in the middle of it. He knew he was making history; it gave him a feeling of elation that future generations would regard him among the benefactors of mankind for having "freed the world of a pest."

True, the killing of people, even of Jews, was still *formally* forbidden. Since the action was bound to remain strictly secret it could not ever become "legalized," and would remain "outside the norm of authority." But who cared? It was not the law or the individual's conscience that had to be consulted but only "what was good for Germany."

So he decided to apply himself to the fulfillment of his life's destiny with all the zeal and devotion he could muster.

In any case, nothing less could have been enough to keep him in his position for the next four years.

*

The killings by the *Einsatzgruppen* led to all sorts of difficulties, some of them due to administrative rivalry: the Wehrmacht, for instance, sent out its own killing parties against the civilian population. In addition, faulty screening sometimes resulted in some of the "wrong people" being herded before the firing squads.

Worst of all, news of the butchery soon spread all over the country. In spite of strict orders to keep them secret, the mass operations were bound to become common knowledge. This resulted in the escape of Jews from the areas near the front, many of them joining the partisans or fleeing deep into Russia. It also turned out that the swiftly advancing *Einsatzgruppen* left behind them, in spite of the efficiency of their paramilitary machine, large pockets of Jews it was impossible to catch. "In the bigger cities more Jews returned after each shooting than were originally there," complained the Commander of *Einsatzgruppe* C.

It was also obvious that in Central and Western Europe the immediate and abrupt removal of all Jews from the workshops and factories was found to dislocate production even more seriously than in Soviet Russia. Things had to be planned in advance.

All these difficulties called for a new method, with two objects in mind: to find a way that would relieve the *Einsatzgruppen,* at least partly, of the direct job of shooting, and temporarily to harness able-bodied Jews for the war effort.

Eichmann was sent out to inspect Globocnik's installations in the Lublin area. Experiments were being carried out there in killing people with exhaust gas from the Diesel motor of a submarine. The latest innovation in use at the time was mobile gas vans, first employed in the Chelmno (Kulm) extermination camp. Eichmann had a look at them too. "The Jews had to undress," he described the process in his pretrial police investigation. "A lorry arrived, covered on all sides, with the doors opening in the front. The car came to a certain roadblock. There the naked Jews were forced to get in. The doors were locked and the car drove away. . . . It reached a long ditch; the doors were opened and the men, dead or dying, were thrown out. . . . I saw a man there in civilian clothes holding a pair of pliers in his hand and removing gold teeth from the mouths of the corpses."

Poison gas had already been in use in Germany for some time. The Nazis had a scheme for killing the mentally insane which they called mercy killing or euthanasia; apparently they could hardly wait for the smoke screen of war to put it into effect. By an order dated September 1, 1939—the very day war broke out—Hitler authorized the Chief of his Chancellery, Buehler, and his private physician, Dr. Brandt, to administer "mercy killing" to incurable persons. The order was implemented by Brack, of Hitler's Chancellery, who employed for the purpose an officer of the Stuttgart police, Kriminalkommissar Wirth. It was Wirth's job to carry out the killing by using carbon monoxide gas. He was later transferred to the Lublin camps and placed under the orders of Globocnik.

Others, too, were seeking a "cleaner" way to dispose of the Jews. Among them was Dr. Erhard Wetzel, a senior official of the Ministry for the Eastern Territories. He reported on October 25, 1941, that after consultations with Brack and Eichmann the three of them had decided to use poison gas for killing Jews. Brack had promised to assist by putting up the installations required and by sending his expert, Dr. Kallmeyer, to Riga. It was decided, Wetzel added, to use "the Brack method" on the "unfit" Jews in the East. It was only a while later that Wetzel's superior, the Commissioner for the East, forbade all officials of his Ministry to take any part in the execution of Jews, "this being the exclusive duty of the Security Police."

Hoess, the Commandant of Auschwitz, was engaged in experiments of his own in search of a method of quick mass killings. In the summer of 1941 he was summoned by Himmler, who told him that the Fuehrer had ordered the killing of the Jews and that the SS would carry out the order. In Himmler's opinion, the existing extermination methods in the East were inadequate for this large-scale operation, and Auschwitz had therefore been earmarked for the purpose, because of its geographical location and the ease with which it could be camouflaged. Hoess was also told that he had been personally entrusted with the task, which called for supreme devotion. Himmler added a significant statement: "You will learn further details from SS Lieutenant Colonel Eichmann of the RSHA, who will call on you in the immediate future."

Hoess recalled in his autobiography that shortly afterward Eichmann came to see him in Auschwitz and disclosed the plans for the operation, which had to cover deportees from numerous countries. They discussed possible ways and means, and agreed that all the killing would be done by gassing. "Eichmann told me about the method of killing people with exhaust gases in trucks, which had been previously used in the East," Hoess wrote. But this was inadequate for the masses of people who were due to arrive in Auschwitz. "The use of carbon monoxide, as was done with mental patients in some places in the Reich, will necessitate too many buildings," he added; so this method too was discarded. The matter was left unresolved, and Eichmann decided to try and find a gas that was readily available and would not require special installation for its use.

At the end of November, 1941, Hoess continued, he was summoned to a conference in Berlin attended by all Eichmann's assistants. It appeared that Eichmann had not yet discovered a suitable kind of gas. But while Hoess was away his assistant tried out "Cyclon B" gas on Russian prisoners of war; he found that it dispatched the victims instantly. Eichmann was immediately notified and rushed to Auschwitz. After a thorough discussion and inspection on the spot the two men decided to employ this method for the mass extermination.

At a later stage a dispute developed on the respective merits of the "Cyclon B" and "exhaust gas" systems. Wirth regarded Hoess as his "untalented pupil," while Hoess was able to point to the greater speed and certainty of his method. Eichmann's department preferred the "Cyclon B" and contacted an expert to assist them in getting it and introducing it throughout the camps. His name was Kurt Gerstein. He was an engineer who had had some trouble with the Gestapo in the prewar years. He had spoken out somewhat freely about some of the Nazi measures and been interrogated and even detained for a while as a result. When one of his relatives died suddenly in a lunatic asylum, he decided to find out for himself the truth about the alleged exterminations. So he volunteered to join the sanitation department of the SS. Soon after he had taken up his post, Rolf Guenther, Eichmann's deputy, called on him and asked for 100 kilograms of poison gas to be supplied immediately to Eichmann's headquarters at Kurfuerstenstrasse 116. "Nobody should know about it and you will have to accompany the transport personally" were Guenther's instructions. He further requested Gerstein to proceed immediately to the Belzec camp to carry out an inspection and to make the necessary arrangements for improving the methods of killing they were using there.

Gerstein went to Bełżec, where for the first time he saw the whole destruction process. The shock was terrific; he decided he must do something about it immediately. The opportunity came soon. On the train back to Berlin, he encountered an acquaintance, Baron von Otter, Councilor of the Swedish Legation. They secluded themselves in a separate compartment and Gerstein, bursting with indignation, gave the Swedish diplomat a detailed account of what he had seen in the camp, producing the orders for the supply of poison gas he had on him. "You must promise me that you will pass on this information to Stockholm immediately," pleaded Gerstein. Von Otter promised and kept his word. The news was transmitted to Sweden.

At the beginning of 1944 Guenther again approached Gerstein asking for an enormous quantity of poison gas for unspecified purposes. In April, 1945, Gerstein proceeded to Rottweil, which had recently been occupied by the

French. There he borrowed a typewriter from a priest and wrote out a full report on what he knew about the camps. Next day he encountered two Allied officers, one British and one American, with whom he deposited the document and to whom he made a full statement. He was arrested by the French occupying authorities; on July 7, 1945, he hanged himself in prison in Paris.

*

While searching for the most efficient way of killing the victims, Eichmann had to solve some other preparatory matters.

First, the rounding up of the Jews had to be extended and streamlined. A distinctive badge, which would facilitate the process enormously, had already been discussed at the November, 1938, meeting, under Goering's presidency. The introduction of the yellow badge, which took place in Poland shortly after the occupation, was delayed in Germany itself. Goebbels, always in search of opportunities to take a hand in Jewish affairs and realizing the full psychological effect of marking the Jews, approached Hitler and obtained the Fuehrer's consent to introduce the badge throughout the Reich. The Gestapo took it up from there, with Eichmann in charge. He first approached the Foreign Office, asking whether they had any objection to the imposition of the badge on Jews of foreign nationalities. Before Ribbentrop had a chance to reply, the first decree, signed by Heydrich, was out, instructing all Jews of German nationality, from the age of six upward, to wear a yellow Star of David attached to their clothing on the left-hand side. Two Secret Police regulations, both dated September 15, 1941, were issued by Eichmann's department to all Gestapo offices in the Reich ordering that offenders against the new regulation would not be tried but taken into "protective custody." This meant a concentration camp.

It became Eichmann's responsibility to see to the enforcement of the yellow badge regulation throughout the Reich and in all the occupied provinces.

With the problem of identifying the Jews disposed of, the Nazis had to devise a "legal" way of stealing Jewish property. Here, again, a law and a Secret Police measure were employed. For some time, since the beginning of 1941, they had been discussing a more convenient system of getting hold of the property of deported Jews. At an interministerial conference, at which Eichmann was faithfully represented by his legal adviser, Dr. Rajakowitsch, and the German Home Office by Dr. Hans Globke, it was suggested that a Jew who settled abroad permanently should automatically forfeit his citizenship and his property be confiscated by the Reich. Furthermore, a Jew who stayed abroad "under circumstances showing that he is not there temporarily only" would be considered to have left permanently. This was now finally enacted and became publicly known as "Regulation 11." Eichmann's department ruled secretly that Jews deported to the East would "settle there permanently." No one was more competent than Eichmann in making sure of their failure to return.

Public opinion in Germany was being conditioned for the large-scale deportations that were shortly to take place in the Reich. On November 16, 1941, Goebbels wrote an article saying:

> The guilt of world Jewry for the outbreak of this war has been proved so conclusively that no words need be lost on this subject. The Jews wanted their war and now they have it. . . . Jewry is now suffering a fate which, though hard, is more than deserved. No compassion and certainly no sorrow is called for. In this historic conflict every Jew is our enemy.

A decision had now to be made whether any further emigration of Jews should be allowed at all. This was a matter of great import, so Mueller and Eichmann went to see Himmler about it. The Reichsfuehrer received them at his front headquarters in Kiev. It was the end of October, 1941. Eichmann reported on the recent emigration figures and on the very limited possibilities for the further departure of Jews. Doubts were raised whether it was worthwhile to let out the few Jews who could get foreign entry permits since they would certainly spread the news of what was being done to the Jews in Nazi-occupied Europe. Then and there Himmler ordered the stopping of all emigration permits to Jews, unless especially authorized in individual cases where particular German interests were involved. Thus all exits were blocked and the curtain was rung down on European Jewry. It was doomed.

Every widening of the war theater extended the Nazi annihilation activity. The war with Poland produced the "Final Solution" schemes and their preparation; the entrance into war against Soviet Russia sealed the fate of Soviet Jewry; the imminent war with the United States was the signal for total destruction.

When the practical preparations were finally completed, Heydrich faced a last knotty problem: how to nail down all the Nazi authorities in obedience to his leadership in the work of extermination. Heydrich decided it was high time to have a conference with all would-be pretenders to the title of "Commander of the Final Solution." He was especially concerned about the conditions in Poland, where Hans Frank's cooperation, or at least tacit consent, was imperative. The district party leaders (gauleiters) were trying to play a lone hand and had to be controlled. The Foreign Office, for its part, showed too much free will; it had to be curbed. This was even more important now that Heydrich could not give his personal attention to Jewish affairs and had to leave their control largely to Eichmann.

Heydrich was now officiating in the Hradcani palace of the Bohemian kings, in his new capacity of Deputy Protector of Bohemia and Moravia. So he decided to take off some time from his busy schedule in Prague, to summon a high-level conference of Permanent Secretaries of State to settle matters once and for all. He instructed Eichmann to invite each dignitary personally and to add a personal touch to every invitation. "You had better add that the matter is of extraordinary importance and that we should achieve a common view by all the government agencies involved," he told Eichmann.

The meeting was first called for December 9, 1941, but because of America's entry into the war the day before, it was postponed to January 20, 1942. On that day fifteen high-ranking officials assembled for a conference and luncheon in the fashionable Wannsee suburb of Berlin, in the building of the German branch of Interpol.

All the invitees duly appeared. Dr. Buehler, the head of Frank's government, came from Cracow. Dr. Meyer and Dr. Leibbrandt represented Rosenberg's Ministry for Eastern Territories; Dr. Stuckart, the Permanent Secretary, attended for the Ministry of the Interior; Dr. Freisler, the Permanent Secretary for the Ministry of Justice; Under Secretary Luther represented the Foreign Office, and brought along a written brief of instructions. Colonel Klopfer (today a practicing attorney in West Germany) appeared for the Party Head Office. Goering was represented by his Secretary of State Neumann, of the Four-Years-Plan Office; Kritzinger represented Hitler's Main Office. The commanders of police in the General Government and the Eastern Territories were there; so was the director of the Ministry for Race and Settlement. The RSHA was officially represented by Mueller and Eichmann. Rolf Guenther was there as Eichmann's aide, to assist in preparing the minutes.

Heydrich opened the conference. He spoke from a draft prepared by Eichmann reminding the assembled officials of his appointment as plenipotentiary for the Final Solution in Europe. It was important that there should be clarity in matters of central importance, he said, and to forestall any possible argument added: "The responsibility for carrying out the Final Solution, regardless of geographical boundaries, lies with the Reichsfuehrer SS [Chief of the Security Police and of SD]." He then proceeded to inform the Secretaries of State of steps that had already been taken "in a legal way" by the Central Office for Jewish Emigration for the removal of Jews from the German *Lebensraum*. The "legal way"—further emigration—was now stopped, Heydrich continued, and in its place "the evacuation of Jews to the East has been adopted as a further possibility for the solution of the problem." He said that some operations had been undertaken as "preliminary measures," though they were of practical importance. (He was evidently referring to the activity of the *Einsatzgruppen*.) In the Final Solution Germany had to deal with eleven million Jews, he said, listing the countries affected, which, somewhat optimistically, included England, Portugal, Turkey, Sweden, Spain and the whole of the U.S.S.R., as well as all occupied countries and all German satellites.

Heydrich went on: "In the course of the final solution the Jews will be brought to the East to be used for labor. They will be put to work in big columns, the sexes apart, in road-building, whereby no doubt a large part will fall out through natural causes. The surviving remnant will have to be 'treated specially,' because they will undoubtedly be the part possessed of more resistance and, being the product of natural selection, would, if set free, constitute the natural reserve for the re-creation of Jewry, as history has proved."

Eichmann was using here almost verbatim, in the draft he had prepared for Heydrich, a passage from a book he had read, which, he said, had influenced him greatly: Kastein's *Eine Geschichte der Juden*.

The idea was obvious: The Jews would be moved eastward; the able-bodied would be spared for a while to work and be liquidated later. "For this purpose Europe will be combed from West to East," Heydrich continued. Should problems arise in the occupied or satellite countries, the Foreign Office was requested to maintain contact with "the authorized department head" of the Security Police.

A lively discussion followed, dealing mainly with mixed marriages and their offspring, the "half-breeds" or *Mischlinge*. These were treated as hybrids (*Zwischenrasse*): half their blood was Aryan, hence valuable and pure; the other half was Jewish, hence polluted and inferior. They belonged neither here nor there. A part of their being deserved survival while the other part called for extinction. So the "experts" tried to calculate exactly what proportion of Jewish ancestry could be considered as having been sufficiently watered down by Aryan blood to be acceptable.

They evolved complicated tables, in some cases depending on such criteria as "a particularly undesirable appearance" (*besonders unguenstiges Erscheinungsbild*), which would mark a *Mischling* as a Jew and seal his doom.

Some of the top Nazis considered the half-Jew as an even more serious adversary than a full one since in addition to Jewish traits he also possessed "leadership qualities," as a consequence of his Aryan blood. Among those who took the most uncompromising view were Eichmann and Reischauer of the Party Head Office. They advocated the treatment of all *Mischlinge* as full Jews.

At Wannsee it was suggested that the *Mischlinge* be allowed to stay in Germany, provided they submit to sterilization "to avoid any further offspring." Mixed-marriage cases were then discussed at length. Finally both matters were deferred for further consideration.

Nobody raised any problems as to the killing of the Jews themselves. They all acclaimed the idea of physical annihilation and bowed to Heydrich's authority, queueing up to be the first to serve. On behalf of the General Government Buehler asked to be first in the line to "finally solve" the problem of the Jews, "as we have already begun it." The Jews created a "potential danger of epidemics" in his area and must be removed. Most of his 2.5 million Jews were not fit for work anyway, he said. He ended with the acknowledgment that "the solution of the Jewish problem in the General Government is of course within the province of the Chief of the Security Police and the SD, and his steps will be supported by the authority of the General Government."

Finally, the "various possibilities for a solution" were discussed. At the trial, when asked what this meant, Eichmann said they debated different methods of killing. The participants were then served drinks and took luncheon together. The Final Solution conference was over.

Heydrich, Mueller and Eichmann stayed behind for a "fireside talk." It had all gone like a dream. There had been no opposition to Heydrich's authority and no questioning; technical objections, so frequent at high-level Nazi conferences, had not been raised; Frank had been defeated and, through his representative, had had to accept Heydrich's leadership; so had the gauleiters, for whom the Party Head Office spoke. The Foreign Office had barely a word to say.

Heydrich was elated. This mood he still reflected a month later, writing to the Foreign Office that he "noted with joy" the complete agreement of all authorities concerned on the actual basis of the Final Solution. He asked the Foreign Office to get in touch now with "his department head" for all organizational, technical and material requirements.

This "department head" was specified by name. He was Eichmann.

Eichmann was encouraged by the unreserved approval that all these assembled, highly placed leaders had given the Final Solution. He was actually a little surprised himself at the reassuring effect this had on him; it evoked in him a sort of "Pontius Pilate feeling." It was they, the "Popes of the State," in fact, who had sentenced the Jews to die. He himself, Adolf Eichmann, son of a church warden, would have no blood on his hands. Not that he particularly cared; still, it was a nice thought.

Eichmann referred to the Wannsee meeting as the "Enabling Conference." This was derived from the name given at the time to the law, passed by the Reichstag in 1933, that gave Hitler absolute power in the Third Reich (*Ermaechtigungsgesetz*). Now everyone agreed that Heydrich was the unquestioned authority in all Jewish affairs, with Eichmann his powerful executive arm.

The conference had been held in strictest secrecy; even the top men in the Foreign Service were not informed.

Some of the participants in the conference were examined at Nuremberg by Dr. Robert M. W. Kempner, Deputy Chief Counsel for the U.S., who was first to discover the Wannsee minutes after the war. None of those interrogated was able to remember a thing. Stuckart did not know why the conference had been held; he had learned of the liquidation of the Jews only after the war. Klopfer did not know whether he had stayed at the conference till the end, but he was sure that while he was there nobody had spoken about killing people. Leibbrandt remembered only that he had once been invited by Heydrich to a luncheon where "all sorts of matters" were discussed, including "the whole war in the East." Kritzinger admitted he had heard "some stories" about the deportation of Jews from someone who had spoken to a police official just back from the East. Only later had he, the Director General of Hitler's office, also received some official reports. Neumann was quite sure he had never been at Wannsee; he had never heard of Jewish deportations and privately had always helped Jews.

Kempner recalls that so great was Neumann's fear of admitting that he had even sat at one table with Eichmann under Heydrich's presidency that he even failed to take credit for what he had suggested at Wannsee—that Jewish expert laborers should not be deported immediately.

In the wake of the conference the liquidation of the Jews proceeded with extreme speed. Germany was now engaged in a life-and-death struggle with both the West and the East, and had to strain all her resources, manpower and transport to feed the military machine. Yet, though every engine was precious for the war effort, every able-bodied man was irreplaceable at the front and every rifle indispensable for the fighting, enough means of locomotion, manpower and army equipment could still be spared to fight the Jews.

CHAPTER

8

The Great Deporter I: Germany and Occupied Europe

The concept of deportation, while intellectually simple enough, in fact represented a vastly complicated administrative problem. How could millions of people be rounded up and transported, in a war where rolling stock was at a premium, to abattoirs whose existence had to be camouflaged in some way so as not to alert the victims?

It was the very complexity of the administrative apparatus that was to enable Eichmann to base his defense on the obscurity of his bureaucratic function. During the trial, of course, it became clear that Eichmann's role was paramount, but his whole approach was to pretend to be a mere cog in a vast machine, and the labyrinthine intricacy of the Nazi deportation apparatus gave him an opportunity to dissemble his real role.

Once the decision had been taken on the extermination program, the existing network of concentration camps had to be modified; some of the camps were to become the abattoirs, some of them remained partially slave-labor camps. The immense work of deportation, for all the variety of forms it took, was aimed at the abattoirs, which thus often became a bottleneck because of the very pace of destruction.

It was Eichmann's job to coordinate, concentrate and expedite the complex administration of the ramified program of deportations. He did this with single-minded zeal.

*

The Wannsee Conference of January 20, 1942, marked the final submission of the German Government to the authority of the Gestapo in Jewish affairs. Eichmann, as the "competent authority" for the Final Solution, was vested with enormous powers. But it was only in greater Germany, including Austria and the Protectorate (now the *Grossreich*) that he could issue direct orders to all district police centers. In the occupied and satellite states of

Europe he had to conduct his affairs through intermediaries. The German hierarchy there presented an assortment peculiar to the authoritarian Nazi state-party system at war. In occupied France, in Belgium, in Greece and in Serbia there were military commanders taking orders from the Wehrmacht. In Poland there was a general governor and in Holland a protector, both directly responsible to Hitler. In the satellite countries there were the ambassadors and plenipotentiaries, who had to be approached through the Foreign Office. Then there were Senior SS and Police Leaders, the regional representatives of Reichsfuehrer Himmler in European capitals, nominally subordinate to the senior German representative on the spot but quite independent in all security matters. In the occupied zones there were, further, the Security Police commanders (BdS) and the ordinary police commanders (BdO) in charge of the daily policing of their areas, usually operating with locally recruited forces. In the unoccupied countries there were often also "police attachés" to the German embassies.

On the whole, the German authorities abroad presented an incongruous network of institutions and personalities that had to be cut through. Eichmann needed his own men, and he would usually send someone from his departmental staff to be attached to the local embassy or to the BdS as "an adviser on Jewish affairs." The advisers, though formally on the staffs of the offices abroad, would in fact be subject directly to Eichmann and accountable to him. These men were his extended arm. He would summon them from time to time for individual or collective conferences or briefings, and they would rush to his Berlin headquarters whenever they got into local trouble or needed an immediate decision. Eichmann, though not an easy master ("He was brutal to his subordinates and without interest in their personal welfare," his close collaborator, Dieter Wisliceny, said of him), was ready to rally round to get his men off the hook, if it was for the good of the service.

He would turn up unexpectedly in Paris, The Hague, Bratislava or Brussels to have a look at things on the spot and constantly prod his men into more vigorous action. He worked out a fixed formula of procedure. This started with standardized anti-Jewish legislation for degrading the Jews and making the rest of the population keep their distance from the "pariahs." The yellow badge was introduced everywhere. Then Jews would be ejected from the country's economy, at a pace depending on local conditions. A process of confiscating property would be set in motion, beginning with seemingly innocuous "registration" and progressing rapidly to total seizure. Jewish owners would be replaced by others, who would thus acquire a vested interest in never seeing the return of the rightful proprietors. Finally, the Jew himself, isolated, humiliated and stripped of his possessions, was taken on his last journey eastward.

To see this through was the task of each of Eichmann's men throughout occupied Europe. The same pattern was applied wherever a victorious swastika flag was hoisted—from the frozen subarctic regions of northern Norway to the sun-bathed Aegean islands of the Greek archipelago, from the rugged slopes of the Caucasus to the lofty peaks of the Pyrenees.

"Our job was to detain, concentrate, load, convoy and transport the Jews to the camps," Eichmann succinctly described his department's work in one of his Sassen talks.

Though the multistage process was the same everywhere, there were important local variants where regional needs and obstacles had to be taken into account. It was not a simple matter to uproot a population established for centuries in the life of a country. In Germany proper this had been effected gradually during the prewar years. Everywhere else the process was peremptorily imposed and constituted a colossal burden on the strained wartime economy. Moreover, in some parts of occupied Europe there was a measure of resistance to the wholesale destruction of Jewry.

*

To counteract the economic difficulties, the Nazis held out to foreign countries the alluring bait of looted Jewish property. Here, they said, was a unique chance of both getting rid of the Jew, "the parasitic consumer," and getting rich at his expense. To the fascist and anti-Semitic leaders who rose to power under the Germans, this argument had a strong appeal. But even where local vassals supported all anti-Jewish measures it was easier to talk them into starting with recent arrivals, the refugees and the foreign nationals, who were not yet deeply integrated into the economy. Their disappearance would not create an irreplaceable vacuum or stir up too many inquiries.

Eichmann usually agreed to begin with such Jews, to break the ice at the point of least resistance. With regard to "foreign Jews" the problem arose which country would inherit their property. As a further incentive to deportations Eichmann evolved the "territorial principle"; this meant that the country expelling a Jew automatically acquired all his possessions, whatever his nationality may have been. Germany magnanimously took the lead, waiving all "its own" claims to the property of German Jews living in other countries and deported from there.

In exchange for the benefits so lavishly showered on her friends, Germany sometimes requested a modest per capita payment in cash for every deported Jew, as a contribution toward the cost of his "transportation and maintenance in the East." This was Eichmann's idea. Though most countries refused to pay, in some instances he was successful.

But after a time some of the local rulers became troublesome. "At first they would throw us their Jews without hindrance. Everything seemed to proceed smoothly. Then suddenly these damned difficulties set in," Eichmann complained. Not all the collaborators were wholehearted supporters of the "New Order." Some sat in on the game as long as they were on the winning side. They all kept a watchful eye on the latest developments at the front; their enthusiasm for destroying Jews was closely linked to the location of the German pennants on the war map.

They would also pester the German Foreign Office for "exceptions" for Jewish individuals or groups they wanted to spare for one reason or another. Eichmann would impatiently brush all such requests aside; he resisted any deviation from the finality of the Final Solution in favor of an individual, whatever the political argument his Foreign Office might timidly advance.

At the end, even Himmler, whom he adored, found it difficult to curb him when a halt was called to the killings.

But sometimes there were certain limits before which even Eichmann's juggernaut had to stop. The German Foreign Office insisted that nationals of the belligerents, the neutrals and some of the Axis states be excluded from the general anti-Jewish measures, as long as this was considered necessary for the Reich's foreign policy.

On the whole, however, the Foreign Office did not present a serious obstacle. Eichmann would resort to cheating its functionaries when necessary, as he finally admitted in court, but generally there was no need for it. They were willing enough to do his bidding. He would have to goad them from time to time, but there were no disagreements in principle; cooperation was perfect. The Foreign Office often used the existence of Jews in satellite states as an excuse for interference in their affairs; then Eichmann would become automatically involved. It also kept him informed of reports that leaked out and were published in the foreign press about anti-Jewish atrocities. Eichmann for his part would alert the Foreign Office to any manifestation of Jewish influence in a foreign country, even if it was only the appearance of Prince Eugene of Sweden at a charitable function for Jewish refugee children.

*

The problems left undecided at Wannsee were taken up. Two further interministerial meetings, which historians refer to as "the second and third Final Solution conferences," were held, this time at Eichmann's headquarters. In attendance again were representatives of the Reich Chancellery, the General Government, the Ministry of Justice, the Ministry of the Interior, the Four-Year-Plan Office, the Foreign Ministry, the Eastern Territories Ministry, the Party Head Office and the SS itself. Eichmann presided over one of the conferences, and probably over the other as well.

The problem of the *Mischlinge* was thrashed out for the hundredth time. A compromise suggestion of the State Secretary for the Interior, Wilhelm Stuckart, was examined, that all *Mischlinge*—there were 125,000 of them in the Reich's territory alone—should be left alive, but subjected to sterilization. "We must meet the other side halfway," Stuckart told his subordinate, Loesener. In this way Stuckart wished to have his cake and eat it; the leadership qualities of the half-Aryan would be preserved for Germany as long as he lived, but he would not spread further the inferior qualities of his Jewish heritage. On the sterilization issue they looked for a simple and quick device that could be used during the war, without putting too much strain on the hospitals.

Practical experiments with radiation and other methods were carried out in the concentration camps. Prisoners were forced to have their genitals X-rayed. Men were then put under observation for signs of remaining virility and finally subjected to the removal of testicles. Women, mostly young girls, were mutilated after irradiation by the forcible removal of ovaries. The mutilated organs were then further examined and explored. Himmler took a great personal interest in these experiments, looking for a method that he intended to apply en masse to "Russians, Poles and Jews," to secure "the ultimate victory of Germany" by utilizing these peoples' labor power while ensuring their subsequent gradual disappearance. Eichmann's office was requested to keep in close touch with the investigations in the camps.

The second Final Solution conference was skeptical about the sterilization of *Mischlinge*. "This would still leave too many administrative problems" in respect to a "third race," even if they survived only for a short time. It was recommended that sterilization should be the exception; normally the *Mischlinge* would be sent away.

The third conference received reports that wholesale sterilization during the war was a practical possibility. "In view of this the proposal to sterilize all *Mischlinge* is agreed upon."

Another recurring problem taken up by the additional Final Solution conferences was the 28,000 mixed marriages in the territory of Greater Germany. At Wannsee Stuckart had advocated legislation invalidating such marriages, followed by the deportation of the Jewish spouse. A compulsory divorce by the courts seemed to be the right procedure. But some misgivings were expressed. "What would the Vatican say to this?" asked one Ministry. The Ministry of Justice was not enthusiastic about a procedure under which the courts would automatically pronounce a divorce once the Gestapo certified a spouse as Jewish.

After consideration the third Final Solution conference decided there was no alternative to enforced divorces "since clear legal rules must prevail." Nobody could be spared.

Eichmann showed his hand again: No exceptions.

The various agreed-upon proposals were referred to thirteen different offices and were finally submitted to Hitler for decision. Here, however, a new factor intervened. The armed forces had a stake in the question since *Mischlinge* who were treated as full Germans served in the army. They were subject to discrimination and handicaps (no service medals or military distinctions), but still they were part of the Wehrmacht. It would certainly be disastrous for their morale if, while on leave, they had to stay in a home marked with a humiliating stigma or found the home gone altogether and one or both of their parents deported. The matter assumed such proportions that the High Command took it up with Hitler, who decided to defer for a while the measures against *Mischlinge* and their parents.

Though the Wehrmacht prevailed in the question of *Mischlinge* and partners in mixed marriages, who were on the whole saved, all other suggested "exemptions"—for the bearers of the highest military distinctions in World War I or for the aged—were successfully resisted. All these people were deported, either to Poland or to Theresienstadt, the softened version of transit to a death camp, and their possessions were confiscated.

Robbery continued to accompany murder. The organized seizure of Jewish private and communal property was in itself an enormous organizational feat. Eichmann had his lawyers, Hunsche, Rajakowitsch and Suhr, assist in the "legal" implementation of the process, in which, as he put it, his department IV-B-4 "was most heavily involved."

He also had to plan and to carry out the transport of the doomed people. It was a gigantic effort. Even getting the trains was a notable achievement in wartime. In addition, transports had to be coordinated, bombed-out lines detoured, trucks exploited to their maximum capacity, and the flow of people to the camps adjusted to prevent overflows and bottlenecks. Most important of all, Jews had to be loaded on the trucks, after they had been marked, screened, torn away from homes, detained and convoyed.

Higher-ranking officials could not match Eichmann's achievements. One day he was called to the Fuehrer's Chancellery office, to meet Colonel Brack, who was in charge of killing the insane. "Could you relinquish some of your trains for us?" Brack asked. "I thought then," Eichmann told Sassen, "here I am in the most important place of the Reich, from where all I did was being watched, day and night, and here this chap asks me for a few trains because he wishes to heat the stove with some idiots. . . . Why don't you yourself order the Minister of Transport to give you trains? I had to fight hard for them."

Let us now briefly follow the trails left throughout Europe by Eichmann's relentless and strenuous work as "the great forwarding agent of death," the nickname he earned from one of the leading personalities of the RSHA.

*

In Germany matters were fairly simple. Eichmann first notified all police offices in the Reich that mass evacuation of Jews was to follow, regulated by two factors: the availability of reception space in the camps in the East and transport facilities at home. He further issued exact directives for the seizure of Jewish property.

At the trial we submitted for the first time the complete local Gestapo files, the only ones so far known to have escaped the deliberate destruction of all archives. They reflect perfectly the precision of the German bureaucratic machine, famous for its efficiency whatever the commodity or process it was dealing with.

Upon receipt of orders from Eichmann's department within a week the Gestapo secured accurate lists of the Jews to whom the deportation directives applied. Next came Eichmann's instructions "for the personal seizure of the deported people, their transport and the transfer of their property to the state." With attention to minute detail, they specified what articles the deportee could carry in the one suitcase which was allowed per capita in addition to fifty marks in cash. The local police awaited a further signal from Eichmann's transport officer as to when the train would be available for their contingent. Once this was received, immediate detention and concentration of the deportees followed, confiscation orders served, apartments locked and the keys taken away. Detailed reports were sent back to Eichmann. It all worked with clocklike accuracy.

"I was deported from Wuerzburg," testified Mordechai Ansbacher. "A day or two before the deportations, people were concentrated in the local central theater and in a large café. . . . People from the countryside were transferred to the local hospital. . . . Everybody was under strict control; we could not even move from one room to another. . . . People sat on their suitcases; they were not allowed to move without permission, not even to the lavatories."

"There was usually no way to escape deportation otherwise than by suicide," testified Mrs. Hildegard Henschel, the widow of the last chairman of the Jewish community in Berlin. "There were in fact about twelve hundred suicides in Berlin alone when the deportations started," she said. German Jewry was less resistant to the suicide urge than the communities farther east.

"The inspection of the deportees' property was called 'the sluice' [*Die Schleuse*]," Mrs. Henschel continued. "The Gestapo would throw out any item they disapproved of. The guards were always SS men armed with riding whips. The community tried to assist the deportees and alleviate suffering by providing a hot meal on the spot. People were loaded in bitter cold. . . . My husband would be called from time to time to the local Gestapo Office. Then he would leave his watch, ring and wallet on the office table. This was an agreed sign between us. Whenever I called and his secretary told me he was out and these things were on his table, I knew he had gone out and might never return."

Rolf Guenther personally made selections from the two or three thousand employees of the Berlin community office whose labor cards constituted a temporary protection against deportation. "People were assembled in the big ceremonial hall of the Jewish community building and told to go either to one side, which meant deportation, or to the other side, which meant they would be left over," continued Mrs. Henschel. "They were told that if those marked as deportees did not appear at the appointed places, others, who were marked as hostages, would suffer. . . . Of twenty such hostages eight were once shot for nonappearance of the people marked for expulsion."

Final roundups followed in Berlin in February, 1943. About eight thousand Jews were suddenly arrested at home or at work and concentrated in a huge Concert Hall and other places. "Parents arrested at work were frantic about what would happen to their children. . . . Women were looking for their husbands. . . . Finally all people were moved," Mrs. Henschel recalled.

This was the end of the centuries-old Berlin community, the cradle of Jewish enlightenment and the springboard of so many outstanding Jewish scholars and leaders.

A similar fate befell all other communities in Germany, Austria and the Protectorate. Property was looted and people were deported. Total deportations from Vienna into the General Government were planned and prepared by Eichmann early in 1941, but he did not have his way until sometime later, when the killing centers were established in the East. In the Protectorate the same system was applied as in Germany. "In Prague Jews were concentrated in specified places. There were 'recorders,' whose duty was to register the property in the empty flat," testified Ernst Recht. "According to this list the different items would be brought to the Transport Department, where I worked. The process was supervised by SS officers and other ranks. Sometimes we needed eighty to a hundred trucks per day, all coming and going, with articles from the Jewish apartments."

Special care was given to objects of art in the possession of Jews. Eichmann had that well in mind from the beginning. The Gestapo competed with other authorities in the Reich to keep such morsels for their own use, and was constantly skimming the loot. They even invited the deportees, who were in any case being deprived of their property, "to donate" as much as 25 percent of their confiscated cash to a special "account," which was put at the disposal of Eichmann's department.

Jewish public property—schools, hospitals, charitable institutions, community buildings—was all taken over on Eichmann's orders and transferred to the Reich.

Organized German Jewry ceased to exist.

*

At Wannsee it had been decided "to comb Europe from West to East" for Jews. France was among the first areas to which the process was applied.

SS Captain Theodor Dannecker was Eichmann's first emissary in Paris. The French authorities were cooperative. France was undergoing its deepest historic crisis. In exhange for his surrender Marshal Pétain retained some authority in both the occupied and "unoccupied" parts of France, which he ruled from Vichy with the traitor Pierre Laval as his Prime Minister. They soon had a Commissioner for Jewish Affairs, and a special unit, *Police des*

Questions Juives (PQJ), to take care of the Jews. Racial legislation followed, throwing the Jews out of public service and the professions. Their businesses were "aryanized." Some forty thousand unfortunate Jewish refugees from Poland, Germany, Austria or Belgium, mostly penniless, who placed their trust in France as a traditional asylum for the persecuted, were detained in the camps of Pithiviers, Beaune la Rolande and Drancy.

By the end of 1941 a roundup of "Jewish intellectuals," even those with French citizenship, was effected.

At Compiègne camp Eichmann's emissary held a thousand Jewish hostages arrested in Paris for an alleged attack on German military personnel, as well as another five thousand Jews who had "a police record." Eichmann planned to deport all these and asked his Foreign Office if there were any objections. There were none.

Eichmann then issued detailed instructions to SS Colonel Knochen, the Security Police Commander in Paris, on the compostion of the transport, the cargo allowed per person, and ordered the contingent to proceed. The first deportation train left France on March 27, 1942. At the last moment the camp authorities were in doubt whether thirty-four Yugoslav citizens were "eligible" for deportation. An urgent query was signaled to Eichmann, who ruled that they were. The destination prescribed by Eichmann was Auschwitz.

Things kept moving according to pattern. Eichmann ordered that preparations be made for more deportations. He further directed that the yellow badge be introduced. This was soon imposed throughout occupied France. In June, 1942, Eichmann ruled that a hundred thousand Jews should be "moved" from France, the French paying for transport, equipment and fourteen days' food. The pace was too slow, so Eichmann himself turned up in Paris. He refused to listen to excuses and issued written instructions for a "great move," which, for safety's sake, he made Dannecker acknowledge in writing. A definite train timetable of deportations was laid down.

But Dannecker could not keep to the schedule and had to leave one train out. Eichmann immediately rang up from Berlin. He did not get Dannecker, so he spoke to his deputy, Roethke, who explained that in Bordeaux they could not find more than 150 stateless Jews and did not have the chance to assemble enough other deportees. Eichmann retorted that this was a matter of prestige, that he had great difficulty in getting trains, that nothing of this kind had ever happened to him before, that the position was most shameful, and he would not even know how to explain it. He would have to consider "whether France should not be left out altogether as a deportation country." The trembling Roethke took in the whole harangue and put it all in writing. He managed to get out a plea to Eichmann not to implement his threat, promised that all other trains would leave on time and pointed out it was not their fault.

To placate Eichmann, Roethke could soon point to the large-scale arrests effected in Paris a week later: 12,884 Jews were detained, including 4,051 children. Laval actually encouraged the Germans to arrest and deport stateless and foreign Jewish children whose parents had been detained. Pastor Marc Boegner pleaded with him to leave them out. "They must stay with their parents," snapped Laval. "But they were already separated from the parents," said the pastor. "They were not separated," Laval retorted. "I tell you they were," insisted the well-informed pastor. "What will you do with the children?" Laval asked. "French families will adopt them," replied the pastor. "No, I don't want that. Not one of them must remain in France," was Laval's final word.

The children were soon taken to Drancy camp, where Professor Wellers was detained. He later testified:

"They arrived in buses, under the guard of the French police. The live cargo was quickly unloaded. . . . The children were frightened. . . . I was among the few who had access to them. . . . Some were barely two or three years old, they did not even know their names and we could not identify them. We put little discs on them bearing the names we gave them. . . . They were all in rags and terribly dirty. They had sores all over their bodies, and all suffered from diarrhea. They could not even get down to the lavatories. . . . We had four groups of detainees to clean them and take care of them. At nights we were not allowed to stay with them. . . . They were crying, waking each other up and calling for their mothers. . . . It was awful. . . . René Blum, the brother of France's ex-Premier, was with me. One day we saw a boy perhaps seven or eight years old. He was in tatters, though it was obvious his clothes had once been of good quality; he had only one shoe. But he seemed very gay. René Blum, a tall man, bent down and asked the boy's name. He said, 'My name is Jacques Stern.' About his parents he said that his father had worked in an office and his mother played the piano. 'She plays well,' said the youngster. He asked whether he would soon leave the camp and join his parents. We always used to tell the children that they would soon be reunited with their parents, though we knew it was a lie. . . . We told him that in two or three days he would join his mother. Then he took from inside his torn coat a piece of the army dry biscuit which the children were given, and said: 'I've kept this; I'll give it to Mother.' René Blum was about to caress him when suddenly the boy, who a moment ago had been carefree and gay, burst into terrible loud sobbing. We left the room in silence. . . . . All four thousand children were soon sent away."

This was done on direct orders from Berlin. "Eichmann has decided the children will go with the next transports to the General Government," noted Dannecker, and three weeks later reported to IV-B-4 the execution of this order. The children were sent out in the general transport to Auschwitz.

The transports kept rolling, each carrying about a thousand people.

Cabled instructions came regularly from Eichmann's Berlin office, specifying the train numbers, departure times and the names of the convoy officers responsible. His men in France dutifully reported to him the departure of transports. Some trains, on Eichmann's instructions, were directed to Auschwitz, others were sent to Chelm, the railway station from which the trains were directed to the nonselection death camps in the Lublin area.

I asked Eichmann in cross-examination: "These people went straight to liquidation?" "I was never there," was the reply, "but it is quite possible. I don't want to deny it."

On August 28, 1942, Eichmann ruled that all stateless Jews must be deported from France by the end of the year. But the Vichy police were slowly tiring of the job. "Many of them told me in secret that they conducted the searches with deliberate negligence, so that some Jews could escape," testified Professor Wellers. "In the hilly regions Jews are escaping to the mountains during the raids and the French policemen are getting tired of climbing," Roethke complained. Fearing that he would soon run short of stateless Jews, he added: "The French must now be told to hand over all naturalized Jews; otherwise we will carry out the great raids ourselves and send out every yellow-badge bearer."

But Helmut Knochen, the Security Commander in Paris, addressed himself directly to Mueller, the Gestapo Chief, maintaining that France should not be antagonized at the moment. Had Laval been promised political gains, he would also have "swallowed" the total anti-Jewish measures. In the circumstances Knochen urged discretion. Roethke, on his part, was blindly following Eichmann's instructions and packed a train with Jews of French nationality. The French police refused to provide guards, and Roethke had to apply to the Wehrmacht for assistance.

In the long run this was impracticable, so Roethke went to see Laval about the promised "denaturalization" of Jews which the government had already approved. Thus French Jews would become stateless and subject to the earlier deportation decrees. Laval made it clear that Pétain would not sign this law. The old Marshal had displayed the other side of his mysterious nature; he had debased himself a great deal, but he stopped short of the last leap. Without his signature there was no law, and Laval made it clear to Roethke that he could not, in the circumstances, place the French police at the disposal of the arresting parties. "If we do it with our own forces, Laval said, he could not stop us," Roethke reported. By this time the total number of Jews deported from France was well over fifty thousand.

Alois Brunner, one of Eichmann's trusted assistants and highly praised by him ("one of my best"), was now put in charge of the Drancy camp. "A complete change set in when he arrived," testified Professor Wellers. "He sent away from inside the camp all the employees, the doctors and even the two Red Cross nurses, who had been with us for a year, and ordered the

French police to guard the camp only from the outside. Inside he brought in SS men. They intimidated and terrorized the prisoners. They had a peculiarly vicious torture, called 'the top.' They would stick a low pole into the ground and order a prisoner to put his right hand on the pole and his left on his back, and to circle around with his head bent down. With whiplashes they would make people run around quickly. After ten such circles people used to fall in a faint. . . . They would shoot at people to intimidate them. . . . Brunner was a big strong man, with an evil face and vicious eyes. His lips were thick and moist. His favorite pastime was lashing people. . . . He introduced another innovation. He kept in the camp ten people with their wives and children, as a special unit. Every day they received two or three addresses of Jews living in Paris, and were ordered to bring them to Drancy. So he used Jews against Jews. . . . We called them 'missionaries.' For five months he was constantly threatening these wretches that if they failed to do his bidding they would be sent away with their families. Ultimately they were all deported. It was one of them who was ordered to fetch my wife and children."

The Drancy camp kept feeding the deportation trains. The Germans finally made one last attempt to seize all remaining Jews without the assistance of the French police. The order was issued by Knochen on April 14, 1944. But most of the Jews were already in hiding by that time and many evaded the dragnet. Less than two months later the Allies landed in Normandy, and a great part of the Jewish population of France was saved.

Of 300,000 French Jews about two-thirds survived the war. Roethke alone had reported seventy-five deportation trains of about a thousand people each. If France was comparatively less affected than other countries, this was due to a great extent to the asylum offered by the Italians in the part of France occupied by them and to the courage and humanity of many Frenchmen who helped the Jews.

In France, as elsewhere, Eichmann applied himself to the "small fry" with no lesser zeal than to matters of principle. He insisted on a special report when René Blum was deported from Drancy to Auschwitz. When he learned "very confidentially" that a Jew, Max Gollub, was about to acquire the nationality of a South American state and thus claim passage to Switzerland, he cabled an order for Gollub's immediate arrest and deportation. He would not accede to the request of the Rumanian authorities to allow the seventy-one-year-old attorney Rosenthal, in view of his past services, to stay in Paris. "Any exception will create a precedent which would impede the dejudaization measures," he replied. His own man, Roethke, suggested making an exception in the case of Abraham Weiss, who had invented a light invisible from above that was very useful in the black-out, and sending the man to Bergen-Belsen instead of to Auschwitz. Eichmann ruled that "as the patent of the Jew Weiss has been already transferred to the Reich's Patent Office, there was no further interest in his affair and he should be dealt with in accordance with the general measures." So Roethke instructed the Drancy camp to deport Weiss. The instruction bears a handwritten addition: "Leaves with next transport," and beneath it: "Settled 19.1.44."

*

In neighboring countries Eichmann ran across different problems.

Belgium, like France, was under military occupation, but there was almost no civilian authority. King Leopold III surrendered on May 27, 1940, but stayed in his country, formally "a prisoner." The army of occupation had its own problems and did not place Jewish affairs first on the list of priorities. They dutifully effected the registration of Jews and were not overworried when they arrived at a figure of only 42,000 while in fact there were more, even after a mass escape to France. Then the army promulgated the usual anti-Jewish laws and confiscatory measures, and took over Jewish property, but for a while did not press matters further.

When in March, 1942, Eichmann ordered the introduction of the yellow badge throughout the Western area of occupation, he received a report that the head of the Military Administration, SS General Reeder, "saw no direct necessity for it," and would not act unless so ordered by his superiors. Eichmann was asked to see into the matter, which he did; the badge was duly introduced in Belgium within three months.

At a conference of his "experts" in June, 1942, Eichmann ruled that Belgium's quota for the near future was to be ten thousand deportees. The military authorities pointed out that deportations would cause unrest and bring about economic difficulties should Jews of Belgian origin also be deported. There is "too little understanding of Jewish matters here," they complained. Eichmann saw no reason for sparing Belgian Jews, though his quota was soon filled. He went to Belgium to deal with the difficulties on the spot. The detention and deportation figures rose immediately. Jews were now kidnaped on the streets, sought out in their hiding places and forcibly removed. Informers were offered prizes for information leading to the discovery of hideouts. It worked.

For lack of transport thousands were awaiting their deportation in the "transit" camps of Breendonck and Malines. The official Belgium Government report describes the arrival of the train.

"When they arrived in Malines, the doors were opened and a terrible sight was revealed. Thick fumes and a disgusting odor escaped, and out of the doors, forced open by the pressure from within, they poured, like fish spilling out of a fishing boat one of whose sides had been removed—a horrible conglomeration of bloated, reddened and bluish bodies, their eyes protruding from their sockets and clothes soaked in sweat and excrement.

Nine corpses were removed from the trucks, eighty unconscious people were removed to the infirmary."

In the other camp hundreds of people were executed on the spot. The Jews were ordered to dance around the corpses, singing: "We shall never forget Breendonck, the paradise of Jews."

But it was only after the Gestapo had its own personnel in sufficient strength to rely on that they went out for a really big raid. On Friday night, September 3, 1943, with the active aid of the Flemish Nazis, they struck at Antwerp, where most of the surviving Jews were hiding. Thousands, including Belgian subjects, were rounded up and deported. This was in breach of express promises given by the officer in command, General von Falkenhausen, to Queen Elisabeth and to Cardinal van Roey.

The total crop Eichmann reaped in Belgium was about 25,000 people, who perished in the camps. The aryanization of Jewish property was almost total.

But he was not altogether happy. Summing up to Sassen, he said discontentedly: "It was a very meager affair in Belgium" (*"Es war eine sehr magere Sache in Belgien"*).

Daring acts of the Belgian underground were responsible for saving many Jewish lives. They were more successful than the neighboring Dutch, though not for the lack of the latters' wholehearted trying.

*

Holland was placed under a "civilian" government. After the Queen and the Cabinet had left, Hitler proclaimed that the country would be governed by a High Commissioner and appointed Arthur Seyss-Inquart, the Austro-Nazi, to the post. The new ruler, hitherto Hans Frank's deputy in Poland, in his inauguration address declared that Germany had no imperialistic designs on the Netherlands and did not wish to force its political convictions on the Dutch people. Clearly, the Germans intended to use Holland as a springboard for the invasion of Britain; they had a strong interest in keeping the country calm.

Whatever their designs vis-à-vis the Dutch, there was no doubt as to their intentions toward the Jews of Holland. They had to be destroyed.

Seyss-Inquart had four commissioners general, through whom he ruled the country. Three of them were Austrians, like himself. Among them was the Senior SS and Police Leader, Hanns Albin Rauter. He announced at a public function: "I will gladly pledge my soul in heaven for what I have undertaken here against the Jews. He who has discovered the meaning of Jewry as a race and nation cannot do otherwise than we have done."

The Commander of the Security Police (BdS) in Holland was SS Major General Wilhelm Harster, who set up the new "Green Police," manned by Dutchmen. They carried out raids and roundups, broke strikes, carried out executions and reprisal murders, and soon became a byword for terror. When Harster was replaced in 1943 by SS Brigadier Erich Naumann, a commander of an *Einsatzgruppe,* terror rose to even greater heights.

Eichmann had little to worry about with these men to do the job on the spot.

The first steps taken in Holland were the routine anti-Jewish measures. But in February, 1941, the Dutch Fascist Party (NSB) raided the Jewish quarters in Amsterdam. The Jews organized defensive Action Groups (*Knokloegen*) and struck back with what primitive weapons they had. A few NSB followers were wounded, and one was killed. Rauter, in the medieval tradition of the ritual murder stories, reported to Himmler that a Jew had bitten through the man's jugular vein and sucked his blood. In reprisal the police arrested four hundred young Jews, who were first humiliated in public and then sent to Mauthausen. The Dutch proclaimed a sympathy strike, which started in streetcars and spread to shops, offices, factories and shipyards. The Germans proclaimed a state of siege, and the SS went out into the streets, killing seven people and wounding many more. The strike was broken, and over a hundred ringleaders arrested. The Germans now established a Jewish Council and Eichmann sent over Edelstein from Prague to acquaint the local Jews with the functions of such a body. But Edelstein told the people the truth. "He was a true and loyal Jew," Dr. Melkman testified. "He told us the Germans intended to kill us all, and that we were in grave danger."

Then Eichmann set up in Amsterdam a "Center for Jewish Emigration." This was a fake, for there was no possibility of emigration by that time. It still fooled the Jews, as Eichmann knew it would. "The name itself aroused many hopes in our hearts," Dr. Melkman testified. "We thought they would help us to leave Holland. Afterward we found out that its head was Aus der Fuenten, the main organizer of Jewish deportations. . . . Later we had more examples of the Nazi system of deception."

The initial deportation quota of forty thousand Jews which Eichmann had prescribed was soon filled. Every week one or two trains, each loaded with 1,200-2,000 persons, left for Auschwitz or Sobibór.

Westerbork was the transit camp for deportations. "Every week, on the night between Monday and Tuesday, at 3 A.M. the hut was hermetically closed. Nobody was allowed to enter or leave, and the head of the block read out the lists of people for the next transport," Dr. Melkman testified. "These were alphabetical lists; sometimes there was an additional list, also alphabetical. I must say that of all the awful things I lived through in camps, murders and whippings and many other matters, this left the strongest impression. Every week, on Tuesday, at three o'clock, before dawn, in complete stillness and darkness, to wait till they reached a letter in the alphabet and one knew then whether he, his family, his friends, were included in the death sentence. This went on week after week. . . . Ever since I've been allergic to Tuesdays."

With the "ordinary" work so well taken care of, Eichmann could apply himself to the special problems that arose.

It was known that many Jews were in hiding, like the family of the well-known Anne Frank. Eichmann repeatedly pressed the authorities during his visits to Holland to increase the prizes for informers, "which will certainly increase the monthly output of arrests."

"My wife and I worked in the children's home of Westerbork," said Dr. Melkman. "From time to time the Germans would bring in children whose hiding places had been revealed. . . . I remember a case of a boy. His family name was Van Dam. He was about ten, and had been hiding for a year in a narrow room. He was forbidden to talk and walk so that the neighbors should not hear him. When he came to us he whispered. We told him he could speak up. When he finally understood, he started running about the courtyard, unable to stop himself. All the time he was shouting aloud that for a year he had been forbidden to speak or walk. . . . Three days later he was sent to Auschwitz."

Eichmann was truly alarmed when he learned that the Jewish Council had succeeded in securing foreign passports and entry permits to Ecuador, Haiti, Honduras, Palestine and Paraguay for some Jews detained or about to be detained in Westerbork. He requested an immediate stoppage of correspondence for the Westerbork prisoners, other than a monthly postcard in German, confined to a personal greeting. He ordered all incoming and outgoing mail to be forwarded to his department for distribution. He further directed that the passports should not be delivered at all and that the postal authorities in Switzerland, where the passports were mailed, should be told, if they inquired, that "the mail must have been lost through enemy action." All foreign passports sent from abroad to rescue Jews were fake (*Schwindelpaesse*), he said, and the bearers must be sent to Auschwitz. He was so much concerned with the incident that he delegated a member of his staff, SS Captain Moes, as a special investigator.

The NSB Fascist Party in Holland had had a few Jewish members before the war, and asked that these five or six people, now excluded from the party, be allowed to emigrate. Eichmann refused "on principle," but promised to send them out last when people would have got so used to the idea of deportations that they would make no trouble. He also agreed that converted Jews should be the last to be deported.

Finally, outside those who were in hiding, only six thousand Jews, employed on munitions in the Vught camp, remained in Holland. According to Rauter, "the army absolutely needed them." He asked Berlin to leave them there. All this Rauter included in his general review of the successful anti-Jewish campaign in Holland. Himmler himself made no other comment than to mark it with the words "Very good." A similar request to spare the Vught camp Jews was made by Eichmann's office in The Hague.

But for Eichmann this was unthinkable. "It is out of the question that several thousand Jews should remain in a country made free of Jews," his department ruled. "The Vught camp Jews could work for the armament industry in the East," it added. "Similar applications from Greece and France had all been rejected." Within a few months they brought the number of Jews employed at Vught down to 2,500. Eichmann finally insisted that these too should be sent out to Auschwitz, and so they were.

He rushed to The Hague in November, 1943, upon hearing that Seyss-Inquart intended to exempt from deportation a few Jewish experts in the diamond industry and was about to refer the matter to the discretion of the local authorities of Amsterdam. "It is preposterous [*widersinnig*]," Eichmann said, "at this advanced stage, to let other agencies deal with a matter that is a police-security affair." He had his way again: the Jews were deported.

Finally, in January, 1944, the Arms and Munitions Office of The Hague asked for the release of seven Jews, specified by name, for particularly important jobs. But Eichmann's office said no, "in view of the prompt total clearing of all Jews from the Netherlands" ("*Unverzuegliche voellige Entjudung der Niederlande*").

Confiscation and seizure of Jewish property was conducted on a gigantic scale. The requisitioned and aryanized bank of Lipman and Rosenthal was in charge of collecting Jewish valuables, money, jewelry and securities. Eichmann's man Dr. Rajakowitsch was sent out to assist. Another agency, the *Einsatzstabl* Rosenberg, dealt with the loot throughout the Western occupied areas. They were given formal access to all apartments of deported Jews, and were later able to report having secured "the contents of 71,619 Jewish apartments in France, Belgium and Holland and having sent to thirty-four towns throughout Germany, furniture, household articles, clothing and other specified articles, in 735 good trains composed altogether of 29,436 cars." The entire German population became the recipient of the loot.

Eichmann's men showed the utmost brutality in confiscating public property. They cleared the Jewish hospital at Apeldoorn, on Eichmann's direct orders, by piling naked patients, most of them mental cases, into a train and sending them out to Auschwitz.

On individual cases Eichmann was adamant, as usual. A Dutch Jew named Andreas Michaelis, who lived in Zeist, was married to a non-Jewish woman. She had refused to leave him. She was Swiss by origin and her father, Jean Barmann, was an influential pro-German in Switzerland. The German Foreign Office held that it was "politically most desirable" to leave Michaelis out. But Eichmann simply said he would not do it. A similar fate awaited the Foreign Office's intervention for Caroline Simmons of Amsterdam, the mistress of the Italian Professor Guarnieri. Eichmann's final reaction to the recommendation for an exit permit was an instruction to his office in The Hague to send the woman "to the East." This meant Auschwitz.

But in view of the prevailing shortage of foreign currency he agreed "to consider on an individual basis, in spite of heavy political misgivings," applications for emigration in return for a heavy ransom of at least 100,000 Swiss francs (about $25,000).

However, in the case of Professor E. H. Meyers, of Leyden University, he would not agree to his departure, because "the man is an intellectual"; so even the offered ransom of 150,000 Swiss francs was refused, since it would mean the possible survival of an outstanding Jew.

The efforts to save Professor Meyers were described by his Dutch lawyer, Mrs. van Taalingen-Dols, in her affidavit and diary, *The Struggle for a Man's Life.* Having enlisted support from the highest local quarters, including an SS agency, she was admitted to "the holy of holies," the headquarters of IV-B-4, at Kurfuerstenstrasse 116 in Berlin. This in itself was a great achievement, on which she was warmly congratulated. Eichmann, "the supreme chief of Jewish affairs . . . and an extremely influential person," as she recorded at the time in her diary, "was away." His deputy, Guenther, received her and agreed, as a special exception, to deport Professor Meyers to Theresienstadt instead of "to the East," which in fact was done.

Altogether there were 115 ransom applications; 34 were approved, for a total payment of over a million dollars.

In July, 1944, the final report from Holland was that the Jewish problem in the Netherlands *"can be considered solved"*: 119,500 Jews had been deported and a further 2,591 were awaiting deportation in transit camps.

Eichmann had every reason to be satisfied with the over-all result, which was achieved after a supreme effort. Years later he told Sassen:

"In Holland the deportations started magnificently [*es war eine Pracht*]. Then difficulties cropped up one on top of the other. It is indescribable how many difficulties were made on all sides. We had to fight to get more. . . . Then again a group would arrive with ten or fifteen thousand . . . and so it went on."

His "fight" in Holland had resulted in the almost total annihilation of Dutch Jewry.

*

The process of "combing Europe" spread in all directions. It soon reached the northern areas of German occupation, Denmark and Norway, with similar results.

With its satellites and allies in Central and Southern Europe, Germany scored varying degrees of success on the Jewish front.

Slovakia was treated by Hitler with relative favor, to prove that timely and tactful falling in line with the "New Order" might secure survival and comparative well-being even for "degenerate" Slavs. Since the Slovaks had broken their alliance with the abandoned Czechs even before the war, they were allowed by Hitler a certain degree of autonomy under the fascist, clerical and anti-Semitic People's Party, headed by Father Josef Tiso. In August, 1940, these people undertook to establish a "National Socialist and Catholic" state.

The same month Dieter Wisliceny arrived in Bratislava as Eichmann's emissary. His first duty was, as he put it himself, "to aid and advise the Slovak Government in matters concerning the Jewish problem." He toured Jewish labor camps in Upper Silesia with senior Slovak officials to demonstrate the potentialities of the treatment of Jews "in the German fashion." He showed them how the machinery worked in Prague and Vienna. Soon afterward a Jewish Code (*Zidovsky Kodex*) was introduced, which was in some respects more far-reaching than the Nuremberg Laws.

Wisliceny submitted to the Slovaks his detailed plan, which was soon put into effect, for the confiscation and "aryanization" of Jewish property. Then he insisted, on Eichmann's instructions, on getting "20,000 able-bodied Jews for a labor assignment in Germany." The Slovaks suggested that "on religious grounds" the members of the deportees' families would have to be sent along, so that families would not be disrupted.

At the time, shortly after the Wannsee Conference, the pretense of "deportation for labor" was still being maintained. An offer of a category of Jews in addition to what he had officially asked for, made Eichmann uneasy. He proceeded to Bratislava, settled everything discreetly and gave his oral consent to the suggested enlargement of the consignments.

Wisliceny made all the usual arrangements. A Jewish central body was set up. Its head bore the title of "*Starosta*" or "*Judenaelteste*." "The first to occupy the office was Heinrich Schwartz. He was elected by the Jewish bodies and enjoyed their confidence. The Slovaks arrested and tortured him, and after some time he managed to escape to Hungary," testified Dr. Abeles, at the time head of the Welfare Department of the Bratislava community. "His successor, Arpad Sebestyan, was appointed directly by the Slovaks, without consulting the Jewish organizations."

The deportations started in March, 1942. By June about 52,000 Slovak Jews had been transferred, through local transit camps, into the Lublin area and into Auschwitz.

Eichmann learned that some Slovak leaders were inquisitive about the fate of the deportees, so he went off to Bratislava to see them. "I told them in simple terms and without mincing words that all efforts must be made to remove the last Jews from the area. . . . I knew Mach long before he was Minister of the Interior and could speak to him in a different manner than the official German Ambassador Ludin. . . . I threatened the Ambassador too and told him the Reichsfuehrer wanted it all done immediately," Eichmann summed up his Bratislava visit to Sassen.

Mach gave a state banquet in Eichmann's honor. During a bowling game which followed the official function Mach was called to the telephone and was told of the attempt on Heydrich's life. Eichmann canceled all further engagements and left for Prague immediately.

To allay the suspicions of some members of the Slovak Cabinet, Eichmann conceived a new idea. He dispatched the Nazi journalist Fritz Fialla "to visit" Auschwitz, accompanied by Wisliceny. Fialla (active today in Germany as a journalist) produced, as instructed, enthusiastic articles for his German paper *Der Grenzbote,* which appeared in Bratislava, mentioning by name people he had spoken to in Auschwitz, all of whom "had declared that they were being treated in a most humane manner" and had only regretted that the other Jews of Europe were not there. "I saw only laughing faces around me in Auschwitz," Fialla wrote. The articles were published in October, 1942, in Slovakia and in France, accompanied by pictures of "the happy settlers."

Mail suddenly arrived too. There were thousands of letters and postcards, all signed by deportees from the camps in Poland, all saying: "We are working, we are well!"

"These people were forced to write letters to their friends saying they were well," testified Rudolf Hoess, the Commandant of Auschwitz, at his trial in Cracow. "There were Gestapo people around who dictated the versions, inspected the letters and had them forwarded." Sometimes the writers were permitted to live for a while; as often as not they were dead even before the mail was delivered.

Eichmann pointed to the letters and articles as conclusive evidence "to counter the horror tales spread in Slovakia about the fate of deported Jews." But the Slovaks were still suspicious and wanted their own delegation to inspect the camps. For the time being they suspended further deportations.

Wisliceny used this lull for a "small" extortion on the side. He entered into negotiations with the Jewish Rescue Committee for a "Europa plan," under which the Germans would stop deporting European Jews in return for a payment of two to three million dollars. Wisliceny said he could do nothing with regard to Polish Jewry, which was lost. But he could "treat the rest of European Jewry in a spirit of self-restraint." A Jewish committee calling itself "the working group" was founded, under the leadership of Rabbi Michael Dov Weissmandel. They worked in great secrecy. "We took it seriously," said Dr. Abeles. "We wrote to the Jewish Agency representative in Istanbul and the representative of the American Joint Distribution Committee in Geneva. The matter was relayed to London." A first installment of about fifty thousand dollars was paid out to Wisliceny.

The "working group" also looked after refugees, sent its emissaries to the labor camps, established workshops to train people to make them "essential" to the country's economy, and supported deportees in the camps in Slovakia and the General Government. Gizi Fleischmann, a noble, idealistic woman in her forties and a veteran Zionist leader, became the nerve center of the whole underground activity. Although suffering from serious heart trouble, she transferred to somebody else her emigration certificate to Palestine, which would have enabled her to join her two daughters, whom she had sent on earlier. "My place is here," she said, and stayed on in Bratislava to make use of her contacts in Slovakia and abroad. She was secretly relaying to the outside world the truth about the ghettos and camps. Eichmann's man, Alois Brunner, finally found her out after five years of activity, and had her deported to Auschwitz with the specific instructions: "R.U." ("*Rueckkehr unerwuenscht*—Return undesirable"). This was the code word for immediate execution without screening. Upon her arrival in Auschwitz her name was called out at the platform. "Farewell, Jewish children," she managed to say to her friends before being led away, never to be heard of again.

In August, 1944, a partisan revolt broke out in the country, with the hope of joining the rapidly advancing Red Army. A state of war was proclaimed throughout Slovakia; the Germans marched in. Wisliceny was urgently called for by Ambassador Ludin, but Eichmann preferred to put Brunner in charge. Transit camps were reactivated, especially Sered. Mass deportations followed. "Brunner dealt personally with every transport," testified Adolf Rosenberg, himself a Sered prisoner.

By December the Germans got about ten thousand additional Jews. Thousands more were executed by the *Einsatzgruppe* that crushed the rebellion.

Slovakia was plagued by the Nazis almost to the very end. Brunner was active till the last days of March, 1945, and helped to raise the total number of Jews deported from Slovakia to about 71,000.

Eichmann had had his way again. "For me the political horizon was the important thing, not getting some 18,000 shabby [*lumpige*] Jews more," he told Sassen about the later part of the Slovak operation.

*

Fascist Italy was a close ally. Her association with Nazi Germany finally had its effect on the country, where for decades there had been little anti-Semitism and Jews had attained high offices in the public service, from Prime Minister downward. In 1938 the Fascist Grand Council heard Mussolini's "Aryan Manifesto," and approved edicts that were a somewhat softened version of the Nuremberg legislation. King Victor Emmanuel had to contersign these laws and expressed his pity for the Jews. "There are twenty thousand spineless people in Italy who are moved by the fate of the Jews," snapped the Duce. "I am one of them," replied the King simply.

Later the Jews were thrown out of the professions, yet they somehow managed. "We adjusted ourselves," Dr. Hulda Campigniano testified. "My father, a university professor, was removed from the university together with ninety-four other professors. He moved to Jerusalem. I went to teach in a Jewish school. My brother had to give up his position at the University of Florence . . . but physically we were unhurt."

Nor did the Italians agree to allow Jews in their various areas of occupation, in Southern France, Yugoslavia and Greece, to be deported. This caused much bitterness among Eichmann's men in these countries; complaints poured into his headquarters. The Germans were shocked when the Italian Fourth Army liberated two or three hundred Jews already arrested for deportation by the French police in the Italian zone. The alarm was also raised from Zagreb that the Italians were interfering with the deportations from Croatia. They had installed Jews in a hotel, "and were assisting good-looking Jewish girls and wealthy Jewish men to avoid being sent away." Wisliceny had troubles in pursuing escaping Jews into Italian-occupied Athens. The Italians requested that he reduce the number of his visits to their zone, hinting that one day he might find himself in jail there.

This created an impossible situation for the Germans. Not only were Jews in the Italian areas getting protection, but various puppet governments, like those of France, Bulgaria, Rumania and Slovakia, were pointing to the Italian attitude as an excuse for their own slowdown on anti-Jewish measures. The Foreign Office was constantly pestered by Eichmann; finally Ribbentrop decided to act.

In preparation for a visit to Rome in February, 1943, he had requested the SS Command to pass on to him immediately all its requests on Jewish matters. Counselor von Hahn wrote to Eichmann asking for a "concretization" of the SS wishes. Eichmann's reply was forwarded the same day, both in writing and by telephone. He requested that all Jews be removed from the South of France. Outrage was expressed that a donation of three million francs from the Jews of Nice for relief of bombed-out civilians had been received and acknowledged with gratitude by the Italians. Italy was asked to stop sabotaging German measures and, as a partner in the Axis, "to join in the total European measures." Ribbentrop took the matter up with the Duce, who said that his generals had "a different mentality in these affairs," but promised to look into it personally. He had now appointed Lo Spinoso a police commander of the rank of a general to be Commissioner for Jewish affairs in the South of France. A special police unit was put at his disposal.

Yet matters did not seem to improve. Eichmann invited Lo Spinoso to a meeting in Paris, but the reply was that the Italians saw no point in it.

Roethke found out that Lo Spinoso was under the strong influence of a Jew—a bank director called Donati, who financed the maintenance of two thousand Jewish refugees in the spas of the Côte d'Azur. The Gestapo laid a trap to have Donati kidnaped from Nice and brought to Marseille, but he eluded them and proceeded to Rome. "His detention is of extreme importance," concluded Roethke in his report to Eichmann.

The Italians were willing to make a concession with regard to their zone in Greece. They would intern the Jews there, they suggested, and put them on an island or transport them to Italy. Eichmann replied that this would not do. "Only the measures which are being taken in the German zone can be considered sufficient, which means transfer to the East," he laid down.

The Italians did not give in yet, but soon an event happened which reversed the scales. On July 24, 1943, Mussolini had to yield to the Fascist Grand Council, which deposed him. The Allies landed in southern Italy and on September 8, 1943, the new head of government, Marshal Badoglio, announced Italy's surrender. The immediate German reaction was to seize all northern Italy, including Rome. Three days later, SS Lieutenant Colonel Otto Skorzeny, the special duties man of the RSHA, raided the mountaintop hotel where Mussolini was detained, packed him into a plane and flew him to Rome. On September 15 Mussolini, by the grace of Hitler, announced the establishment of the Italian Social Republic. He was now a mere shadow of his old pompous self. The area nominally under his jurisdiction was virtually governed by the Germans.

Eichmann now dispatched Theodor Dannecker to Rome, with orders to carry out urgent raids on the eight thousand Jews of the city, and bring them to northern Italy for "liquidation." Thereafter Dannecker had to proceed throughout the country and arrest its Jews, "step by step from the front line northwards.'"

"In September, 1943, things changed radically," testified Dr. Campigniano. "The Germans entered town after town and the first thing they did was to secure a list of the local Jews. . . . I was in Florence. . . . There was a panic among the Jews, but they did not really understand the danger. My brother went from house to house to urge people to escape into the villages or hide in monasteries. . . . He organized an aid committee with the assistance of a priest. . . . We had heard of the extermination process and the gas chambers, but somehow people did not believe it would happen here; they thought the Germans would just enforce the discrimination to which we had become used under the Fascists." The first arrests started in Florence by the end of the month. The Italian deportees were soon sent to Auschwitz and to other destruction camps.

With Rumania, another ally in Southern Europe, the Nazis experienced even more ups and downs.

Rumania had a long Jew-baiting record. Its leader ("The Conducator"), Ion Antonescu, was praised by Hitler as "more radical in Jewish matters" than the Germans themselves. Moreover, having joined in the anti-Russian campaign, the Rumanians staged the biggest single slaughter of the war, by shooting sixty thousand Jews in the Odessa region. But then the bloodthirst was quenched. The Rumanians kept amassing their Jews in the newly conquered territory between the Dniester and the Bug rivers, but stopped killing them. They were willing that the Germans should do it for them, especially as *Einsatzgruppe* D was active nearby. So they kept pushing the Jews across the Bug.

But this interfered with Eichmann's timetable and offended his sense of orderliness. He asked the Foreign Office to prevail upon Rumania to stop the "illegal transports of Jews," or, he threatened, "I would have to take police measures."

The ominous warning was carried out. "It was obvious," Eichmann said later, "that if these Jews were illegally marched off, the security authorities in the East settled the matter in their own way through their units." "You mean they were liquidated?" he was asked in the pretrial inquiry. "Yes," was his reply. Twenty-eight thousand Jews, the target of Eichmann's darkly predicted "police measures," were killed.

One of Eichmann's men, Gustav Richter, had been sent to Bucharest as "adviser on Jewish affairs," but hitherto had been active mainly in guiding the Rumanians in preparatory steps and teaching them, to their astonishment, that there was a "legal" way to rob Jews of their property; now he was told by Eichmann to prepare the deportations in the German-prescribed fashion. This meant sending them to the camps in Poland. *Einsatzgruppe* shootings were strictly reserved for certain parts of Jewry; it was obviously "illegal" to use them for others. (This was a typically German attitude. One of the camp survivors told me he was present when the commandant, upon scrutinizing the list of persons executed that day and finding a man who according to his classification should not yet have been killed, severely rebuked his deputy, saying, "Now see what you have done, you have killed an innocent man.")

A great "legal" deportation from Rumania was planned for September 10, 1942. The Foreign Office was notified by Eichmann that at first only people fit for work would be moved. In the notification addressed to Himmler, however, he disclosed that people unfit for labor would also be included and "specially treated" in the Lublin camps. The second message too was somehow relayed to the embassy in Bucharest. The Ambassador, von Killinger, realized that he was being told only part of the truth. In an outburst of indignation, he wrote he "was not at all surprised that Mr. Eichmann did not find it necessary to maintain contacts with the Foreign Office, as the methods of the gentlemen of the SS are only too well known."

Eichmann was amused by Killinger's outburst. "He should be excused," said Eichmann to Sassen, "as he was generally foolish. . . . Mr. Killinger was sitting in Bucharest and did not know how the cards were being played at home. He could not know that at least once a week the competent department chief of the Foreign Office would turn up in my antechamber and apply for an interview with me. . . . And while written memos were coming and going, matters were really settled by people who talked things over. . . . Richter complained several times that Killinger was padlocking his mouth, so I told him that whenever he had a problem or was dealing with more basic matters, he should take a plane or the next train and come to me to report."

But the big deportation ran into a snag after all. The date fixed for the great drive passed, and nothing happened. On September 11 Eichmann's department phoned anxiously from Berlin to inquire; Richter had nothing to report. The necessary trains for transporting Jews to the Bełżec camp via Lwów, in cattle cars at the rate of two thousand every second day, were allocated. Still the Rumanians made no move.

There were several reasons for this change of attitude. The first and foremost was money. Bribery and corruption on official and unofficial levels had long been proverbially characteristic of the Rumanian regime. Everything and everyone had a price. Jews were now pumping big money into the pockets of influential people to get a reprieve; leading Rumanians realized that they were much better off with the threat of deportation hanging over the heads of the Jews than if they were actually sent away. Richter was indignant. He published articles in the Rumanian press against "the Jew slaves," but that was all he could do. Furthermore, the outstanding leader of Rumanian Jewry, Dr. Filderman, and the Chief Rabbi, Dr. Alexander Shafran, were knocking on every door. Dr. Shafran found willing ears from the Orthodox Metropolitan, Monsignor Balan, the Papal Nuncio, Monsignor Cassulo, and the Queen Mother. They all spoke to people in authority and helped to bring matters to a temporary standstill.

Richter went to see Mihail Antonescu, the Deputy Prime Minister, who "was most embarrassed" and could not explain why the Rumanians were first so willing to push Jews wildly across the Bug to face the firing squads, but had now become so reluctant to send them out in orderly fashion "to the resettlement destination in the General Government." Soon the Germans learned that the Rumanians were generally wavering on the "radical solution" and were even considering letting the Jews leave for Palestine in return for 200,000 lei ($1,340) per immigrant, "thus killing two birds with one stone." This was serious. Killinger, swallowing his pride, suggested that Eichmann should come to Bucharest in January, 1943, "in view of the turn of the events." Eichmann knew better. Killinger was just looking for an excuse to pass the buck, so Eichmann wrote back that he was too busy in Berlin. But he did instruct Richter to carry on a relentless campaign against Jewish emigration.

Hearing that five thousand Jewish children were about to leave for Palestine on board a Turkish ship from Constanza, Eichmann's department asked for all possible "immediate steps," both in Turkey and elsewhere, to frustrate their departure. Eichmann was willing to make one concession: he would let the children go if they were exchanged for Germans interned abroad, at the rate of one child to four Germans of military service age. It was later added that the children would in no case be permitted to proceed to Palestine, as "the German Government would not lend its support to dislodge the noble and courageous Arabs from their homeland." Eichmann added a somber warning: the negotiations must be rapidly concluded, for soon there would not be five thousand Jewish children left in the Eastern area of occupation.

The Germans were still hoping, at this time, that their Rumanian ally would come to his senses and continue the work so well begun. But the Rumanians, who had lost all hope of winning the war, were already beating a retreat on Jewish matters. They were the first to join the campaign and the first to deflect. The Conducator ordered the retransfer of Jews from Transnistria, and some time later Mihail Antonescu prepared imaginary minutes of a conference which was never held, and which were obviously meant to serve as an alibi to be used after the war to prove that he had always been in favor of free Jewish emigration from Rumania. When the Russians knocked Rumania out of the war, there remained some 400,000 Jewish survivors, about half the country's original Jewish population.

*

In principle, Bulgaria had aligned herself with her ally. In practice, however, there was a tradition of liberalism in the country that was not easily gainsaid. Though the Jews had already lost jobs and were subject to curfew at nights, part of their property had been taken away and the yellow badge introduced, still the yellow-badge rule was not too rigorously enforced at first. There were no badges since the supply of electric current had been cut off in the plant that produced them on the ground of "power economy."

Never a wholehearted vassal of the Axis, King Boris was mainly intent on regaining territory lost by Bulgaria in the course of previous Balkan conflicts. Nor was he unrewarded; large slices of Thrace and Macedonia were handed over to him by the Fuehrer "forever." In exchange Bulgaria joined in the war against the Allies, policed the Balkans for Germany, kept a watch over Turkey and allowed her territory to be used by the Germans against other Balkan neighbors. But she did not declare war on her Slav brothers or even break relations with the Soviets. She also kept its constitution, which involved a form of parliamentary rule.

The Germans realized they had to proceed slowly. The Foreign Office asked for an "adviser on Jewish affairs." Wisliceny, who was much in demand, was busy at the time in Slovakia, so IV-B-4 delegated Dannecker instead, with the rank of Deputy Police Attaché.

Dannecker started with the usual point of least resistance—"the foreign Jews"; Bulgaria, too, had some of them in her recently acquired territories. The Bulgarians had agreed to have them deported, and it was left to Dannecker to settle the details. After several meetings with local politicians, for each of which Eichmann briefed him specially over the telephone, he put the whole arrangement on record.

Bulgaria has the distinction of being the only country that signed a written contract "to supply Jews to Germany," undertook to pay for their transport, and stipulated that she would never and under no circumstances request their return. Dates of departure from different areas were fixed, and a screening system was agreed upon, with exact specifications for the consignment and delivery of bills of lading. Jews were transported like cattle. The transaction affected twenty thousand people from secluded, mountainous areas, where they had been living for generations. A historian gives a vivid description: "In lambskin caps and brightly colored shawls they boarded the boxcars frightened and bewildered, to end their journey, after many days, on a lonely siding in Eastern Poland, where the whips of the pitiless Ukrainian guards goaded them to the fatal bathhouse."

Before Dannecker attached his signature to the agreement as "the German plenipotentiary," he received Eichmann's express approval over the telephone, but only after he had told his boss about the secret, unwritten deal he had struck with Alexander Beleff, a fascist anti-Semitic leader who had been appointed Commissioner for Jewish Affairs. As there were actually only about fourteen thousand Jews in the areas to which the agreement applied, Beleff, to fill the quota, would also supply six thousand Jews from Bulgaria proper, including "influential Jews," namely, "those who are rich or who have good connections in high circles."

Yet here Beleff was due for a surprise. Bulgarian political leaders, headed by Pesheff, the deputy speaker of the Sobranje, the Bulgarian Parliament, together with forty-two other members, petitioned the Prime Minister "in the name of the prestige and morals of the Bulgarian people, to abstain from any measure not absolutely necessary." Pesheff even introduced a vote of censure in the Sobranje. It was defeated, and he himself was consequently dismissed from office, but the effort was not altogether wasted. "At a hint from the highest authority"—presumably the King—the deportations from Bulgaria proper were stopped, and the people already arrested, in preparation for dispatch, were released.

The Bulgarians were willing to use Jewish labor potential to the hilt. Jews were concentrated in labor camps, and twenty thousand were moved from Sofia. Eichmann's office instructed the Foreign Ministry to tell the Bulgarians in no uncertain terms that this was just the first required step, that ultimately the Jews of Bulgaria would have to be moved to the East.

But this was as far as the Bulgarians would go. King Boris' mysterious death immediately on his return from a visit to Hitler on August 25, 1943, made matters even more difficult for the Germans. No more Jews left Bulgaria for Germany.

In Bulgaria, too, Eichmann conducted a vigorous campaign against Jewish emigration. Every piece of information about an intended refugee ship was pursued, reported and relentlessly blocked.

In neighboring Yugoslavia the Nazis had it easier.

*

After a brief campaign in spring 1941, Yugoslavia was crushed and dismembered. Serbia was put under military occupation and given a puppet government; Croatia was declared an independent kingdom; slices of the country went to Hungary and to Bulgaria; the Italians grabbed a part; another part was incorporated into the Reich.

Arrests of Jews soon followed. Benzler, the German Plenipotentiary in Belgrade, inquired what to do with them and whether he could move them to Rumania. The Foreign Office replied that this would not do; Jews should be put into camps. Benzler cabled back that this was impossible, as the country was infested with rebels and Jews might escape from the camps. He wanted "a quick and draconic solution," and inquired whether transportation to the General Government or Russia was possible.

Rademacher, the head of the relevant department, was told to contact Eichmann. On Benzler's original letter Rademacher noted: "Eichmann says no possibility of reception in Russia and General Government. Even German Jews cannot be disposed of there. Eichmann proposes shooting. [*Eichmann schlaegt Erschiessen vor*]."

That was on September 13, 1941, before the destruction machinery of the Final Solution was ready for full use.

Rademacher was questioned in Nuremberg on this document, and said: "I still remember talking on the telephone to RSHA, and writing down the main words of Eichmann's reply. . . . When I questioned him again, he simply said: 'Kill by shooting' and hung up."

So the Jews of Belgrade were shot on the spot. Two of Eichmann's men, SS Major Suhr and SS Lieutenant Stuschka, went there with Rademacher. Upon their return Rademacher submitted a detailed report. They found the problem concerned "only 4,000 Jewish males, 3,500 of whom will be shot by the end of the week," he said. "A further 20,000 Jews (women, children and aged people) will be moved temporarily to an island on the Danube."

Berlin provided an official excuse for the murders: reprisals.

The Chief of Staff of the Military Government, Turner, described the operation in a letter to his friend:

> That the devil is loose here you probably know. . . . I had 2,000 Jews and Gypsies shot during the last eight days in accordance with the quota of 1:100 for bestially murdered German soldiers, and another 2,200, again almost exclusively Jews, will be shot in the next eight days. This is not a pretty business. The Jewish question solves itself most quickly this way.

It was an *Einsatzgruppe* under the command of Colonel Dr. Wilhelm Fuchs that did the shootings. The directives for the measures against Jews came from Eichmann, he said. "In addition to shooting there were gas vans. . . . These were used exclusively for Jews, in accordance with instructions received from the Security Police in Berlin," testified SS General August Meisner, at his trial in Belgrade.

The annihilation of Serbian Jewry was almost complete. Eichmann had no deportation problems there. The Jews were killed partly on the spot, as he had ruled. The others were not moved to an island but transferred to the camps in neighboring Croatia.

Croatia was a fascist state established by Germany and Italy in part of Yugoslavia, under the leadership of Ante Pavelic, a terrorist who had been hiding for years in Italy. After the wholesale introduction of Nazi legislation and the imposition of huge "fines," the Croatians herded thousands of Jews into several camps. Evidence of some of them has survived only through the tales of horror told by the local population; not a single prisoner escaped with his life.

Jasenovac was set up as a death camp for Yugoslav partisans, but about twenty thousand Jews from all parts of the country perished there too.

After matters had been "settled," Eichmann sent down to Zagreb SS Captain Franz Abromeit. It was soon settled that the Croatian authorities would pay thirty marks for every deported Jew. This was cheap; Slovakia paid 500 marks and Bulgaria 350. A system of cooperation developed under which the Croatians supplied police forces for the detention of Jews and their transportation to local camps. From there Abromeit took them to Germany.

In early April, 1944, it was reported to Berlin that "by and large the Jewish problem in Croatia is solved." A considerable number of people had escaped to the mountains to join Tito's partisans, who had established a strong foothold in part of the country and carried on the liberation campaign.

*

Greece had bravely repelled the Italian onslaught of October, 1940, but succumbed to the Nazi blitz six months later. Mussolini now helped himself to most of the Greek mainland and the archipelago. Bulgaria was rewarded for her assistance by two slices in the east and the south. Germany occupied a narrow strip directly facing Turkey, with Salonika in its center, which was placed under military rule.

For the Jews this meant the end of their ancient community, which lived in Salonika long before the destruction of the Temple in 70 A.D. In the year 50, the Apostle Paul visited them in an attempt to find supporters for the new creed. The community had survived the long convulsions of the Byzantine Empire, the stormy years of Crusader rule, the frequent Moslem invasions, the long Turkish occupation and finally the Greek national rebirth. It had been torn by wars and repeatedly racked by fire and rapine, but it held its ground, strong and industrious. In the later Middle Ages it was considerably reinforced by Jews expelled from the Iberian peninsula. Throughout the ages, the Jewish community gave the city many of its outstanding merchants and industrialists; it even produced stevedores in such numbers that its port for a long time lay virtually idle on Saturdays, when the Jewish laborers did not come to work.

But Jewish Salonika, which had existed since antiquity, did not survive the four years of Hitler's rule. It was crushed in 1943—within four months.

Prostrated by its two wars, Greece had starved since the early days of the German invasion; it was the hungriest country in Europe. The Jews were immediately exposed to added suffering. "Every day they had something new on us," testified Itzhak Nehama. "Then, one day, on July 11, 1942, they ordered all male Jews between the ages of eighteen to forty-five to assemble the next day, on Saturday, in the very large Liberation Square. . . . About nine thousand turned up."

We had some pictures of this scene, which were found in Germany after the war. They were shown to Mr. Nehama, who said: "Yes, that is the place, these are the people. . . . They ordered us to do exercises for hours. We were standing under the strong sun, in our Sabbath clothes. Whoever did not perform as the SS man wanted would be beaten up till he fainted. Then water would be poured on him and he was ordered back. . . . It lasted from 8 A.M. till 2:30 P.M. There were German women on all the balconies around the place taking pictures. Whenever a Jew fainted and collapsed the women would applaud."

In one of the pictures the witness identified himself. "This is me," he shouted, excitedly, "bending my knees after six hours of exercises and all beaten up. . . I was ill several weeks after that. Four days I was almost unconscious. . . . Then we had to report for work in a labor camp. . . . We had no stamina left after the war and the hungry people were dying at work."

This was the right time for Eichmann to step in directly. In January, 1943, Eichmann delegated Guenther to Salonika to "negotiate on Jewish affairs." A few days later he was replaced by Dieter Wisliceny, who had arrived from Bratislava. Eichmann's instruction to him was "to effect the removal of Jews from the area of Salonika, it being estimated that he will need six to eight weeks for the performance of his duties."

Actually it took Wisliceny somewhat longer to deport the sixty thousand Jews of the city. Within a month Wisliceny had them all in a ghetto and, from the age of five upward, marked with the yellow badge. Life in the ghetto, and especially in the Baron Hirsch transit camp, once a hostel for poor Jews, was appalling. "It was full of dirt and lice. . . . When we were told we were going to Poland to settle near Cracow, to form our own community there, I said we would go. . . . We were even given Polish money in exchange for our Greek drachmas. People were told to take their umbrellas with them, because it was raining and snowing there. . . . Had I really known what actually awaited us, I would have preferred to die on the spot. . . . We were sent to Auschwitz."

The deportations began on March 15, 1943. The Jews went eastward, almost willingly boarding the trains, to escape the desperate conditions at home, fooled by the German temptations and believing their own rabbi, Dr. Koretz, who relayed to them the "resettlement near Cracow" story that he had been told by the Germans. In July it was almost over. Wisliceny reported the deportations and the amount of the victims' property looted in drachmas and foreign currency.

Soon afterward, with Mussolini's downfall, Italy's rule in occupied Greece came to an end; the Germans occupied Athens and the islands. The SS came in for the kill; General Juergen Stroop, who had just crushed the Warsaw ghetto revolt, appeared on the scene. But many Jews now went into hiding and dispersed among the islands. Of the expected eight thousand victims, the Germans caught only twelve hundred people, starved and weary to death—"probably the least interesting contingent"—they reported from Athens. Jews were tracked down by the armed forces in the various Dodecanese islands and put on old barges driven into the sea by German sailors, who, having opened the vent-holes, took to the lifeboats and left the Jews to their fate on the open sea.

*

It was only natural that the uprooting of non-Jews from their homes should also be entrusted from time to time to the successful deportation department of the Gestapo. In April, 1941, Hitler ordered that newly acquired southeastern Yugoslavia be cleared of Slovenes. Eichmann was chosen for the assignment, and succeeded within less than three months in rooting out thirteen thousand Slovenes and dumping them farther south. Thousands of them were found a year and a half later wandering in Bosnia and were moved to Poland. Eichmann was put in further charge when Himmler ordered the clearance of the Zamość area, between Lublin and Lwów, of its Polish inhabitants. "The Poles, in distinction from Jews, are to be allowed to die naturally," was the ruling. "Priests should normally be sent to a concentration camp and not to the 'pension villages,'" ruled Eichmann's office. Small Polish children were trained for "germanization" and placed in special camps; old people were moved for resettlement in "pension villages" to localities vacated by Jews. Other Poles were either transferred for work in Germany or sent to labor camps.

The usual deportation scenes followed. Polish children either died en route or developed severe frostbite. People were suffocated in transport and their bodies had to be removed from the wagons. The operation was originally planned to affect 140,000 people, but its scope was later reduced.

Gypsies were another specialty of Eichmann. He had pushed five thousand of them into Litzmannstadt in the autumn of 1941. Later they were rounded up by ordinary Criminal Police, but it was Eichmann's responsibility to have them transported to Auschwitz in large numbers. There, many died in terrible epidemics; they were finally exterminated.

Another example of Eichmann's activity was the case of the children from the Czech village of Lidice. The village itself was destroyed on June 5, 1942, in savage retribution for the assassination in Prague of Reinhard Heydrich by Czech patriots. All the men of Lidice were executed on the spot. The women were sent to the Ravensbrueck concentration camp; the children were sent in two transports to Litzmannstadt. Sixteen of them were considered fit for "germanization" and were removed to a special institution to obliterate the traces of their origin. The remaining ninety-three children were dumped on SS Lieutenant Colonel Hermann Krumey, who was in charge of the population resettlement office in Litzmannstadt. Krumey was notified that the children would stay under his care only temporarily. "Assuming that the children will get the special treatment, I notified department IV-B-4," he wrote. He had good reasons for this assumption, as the children, among them infants of under two years, arrived without any luggage, with instructions that "there was no need to take special care of them." It was obvious that the children were sentenced to die. Eichmann had a telephone talk with Krumey on the subject, and Krumey was finally instructed by IV-B-4 to deliver the children to the local Gestapo, "who got further instructions."

These children were never heard of again.

*

Heydrich's death called for further hecatombs: Jewish hostages were taken to Berlin; 152 of them were executed. But this was just a small part of the funeral rites. It was decided to link his name with the operation of destroying the Jewish population of the General Government and the seizure of their property. Odilo Globocnik was in immediate charge of implementing "Action Reinhard" in his camps.

"Action Reinhard" involved the final evacuation of all Jews to Globocnik's extermination centers, without any "quotas" and without regard for their manpower potential. It also involved the theft of all their possessions. Their real estate, money and valuables were taken away before expulsion. Their private belongings the Jews were told to carry with them on their "resettlement" and were cautioned "to keep an eye on them" en route. This was a pure camouflage measure. On arrival at "destination" all bundles were immediately taken away. With the exception of those in three or four big ghettos where the local authorities wrangled for a while with the SS for the further utilization of some Jews for slave labor, all others were packed on trains and carried to the camps. The technical limitations of transport and camp capacity were the only restrictions.

Brack, Hitler's specialist in euthanasia murders, detailed some of his men "for special duty . . . on the Jewish activity which must be concluded as rapidly as possible." A terrific strain was placed on the railway administration in July, 1942, to secure daily trains for the Treblinka and Bełżec camps. Himmler's chief of staff acknowledged this with special thanks, writing that "5,000 men of the chosen people are now being sent daily to Treblinka," and asked for even greater efforts.

The big German summer offensive of 1942 had just reached its peak: the Fourth Panzer Army was approaching the Volga River; von Kleist's tanks were penetrating deep into the Caucasus and regrouping for a final assault on the Grozny oil field; the Sixth Army was rapidly advancing along the Don River; the German forces were dangerously extended and exposed to a Russian flanking countermovement. Every available means of transportation was absolutely imperative for the troops and for the advancing front, especially in view of Hitler's fateful decision to take both the Caucasus and Stalingrad simultaneously. Yet the request for further efforts to promote "Action Reinhard" was attended to. At a high-level conference held at RSHA on September 26–28, 1942, it was decided to assign to it from then on eight trains per day for the General Government alone, and to add many more trucks to the two hundred large wagons available.

Thus the war effort and the destruction of Jews were treated as equally important. They were twin objects of the German supreme struggle, neither being subordinated to the other. War needs were no excuse for sparing Jews or for reducing the scale of their extermination. Similarly, the all-out drive to stamp out the Jews was no reason to slow down the advancing armies. Both goals were to be attained simultaneously.

Apart from the technical problems involved there was nothing to stop the operation. There were in the General Government no Polish groups whose wishes interested the occupying authorities. Any local opposition to the destruction of the Jews, insofar as it existed at all, was therefore no impediment. An opposing Pole was treated much the same as the Jew; and in any case opposition to killing Jews was very slight. Many Polish circles supported it wholeheartedly. So it was only the local needs of the authorities themselves which kept the Jews working for a while as slaves.

With "Action Reinhard" thus in good hands, Eichmann could tackle special problems related to the liquidation of the big ghettos in the East. In December, 1942, it was decided to reduce considerably the Bialystok ghetto, and Eichmann delegated Guenther to do the job. The local administration's pleas for a delay, motivated by the important services that Jews were performing for the army, were brushed aside; early in February, 1943, Guenther got his ten thousand Jews dispatched to Auschwitz.

The Litzmannstadt ghetto was finally the largest left in the East. Its slave-driving boss, Hans Biebow, making a fortune out of the horrible abuse of men, maneuvered the partial survival of the ghetto so that it could go on working for his enterprises. In these efforts he was actively supported by the regional administration. Eichmann was delegated to represent the Chief of the RSHA, Kaltenbrunner, at a conference to decide the fate of the ghetto. He was obviously opposed to its survival, and had Dr. Max Horn, the chief accountant of OSTI, on his side. OSTI was the company established by the Economic Office of the SS (WVHA) to exploit the labor force of the camps and increase their productive capacity. For reasons entirely different from Eichmann's, Horn was also in favor of liquidating the ghetto, which, according to him, "was disguising its losses." While Eichmann, however, wished all survivors to be deported and destroyed, Horn wanted the ghetto as a whole to stay, to be turned into an ordinary concentration camp, and then come under the WVHA. In a concentration camp the Jews would not get even the pittance they were "paid" in the ghetto. He needed it badly at the time, for OSTI's manpower had been virtually destroyed in the course of the November, 1943, executions. As a compromise, the ghetto was meanwhile reduced by further deportations and Himmler's opinion was solicited. Himmler ruled that the ghetto should be liquidated, but the local Governor Greiser, "who had been considering the ghetto as his domain," requested from the WVHA "compensation" in the amount of eighteen to twenty million marks for its machinery and installations.

At a Himmler-Greiser meeting the SS gave in for a while. As a compromise it was agreed that the ghetto would be "gradually reduced."

On the whole, by spring of 1944 Eichmann had every reason to be highly satisfied with the results achieved. Eastern Jewry, "the biological potential of the nation," as he called it, was gone. In the West he had put his hand on as many Jews as he could possibly hope for at the time. The Jews in hiding ("the submerged," or "U-boats," as they were called) could be relied upon to come to the surface in the end, through starvation or denunciation. As decided at Wannsee, the Final Solution had swept inexorably over virtually all of Europe that was under German domination.

CHAPTER

9

The Great Deporter II: Hungary

All, that is, except Hungary. An Axis satellite, it was not a wholehearted ally, even though Hungarian soldiers fought on the Russian front, supplying at times about a third of the non-German cannon fodder that Hitler was consuming. Some of its leaders were wavering in their belief in the ultimate victory of the Axis. After the German debacle at Stalingrad, Prime Minister Kállay even put out cautious feelers for a separate peace.

Eichmann's handling of the "Jewish problem" in Hungary illustrates in a peculiarly pure form both his bureaucratic efficiency, built on his total European experience, and the Nazi obsession with the Jews. For the chief action against the Jews of Hungary was undertaken when the German forces were in headlong retreat from the East.

In the trial I concentrated a good deal of attention on Eichmann's behavior in Hungary; it was highly instructive.

Anti-Semitism had slowly subsided in Hungary in the stormy aftermath of the short-lived 1919 revolution. The universities were still closed to most Jews; yet some of them played a part in political life, were members of the Upper Chamber and reached high positions in administration and business.

Nazi influence made itself felt immediately upon the *rapprochement* with Germany. In 1938 the first anti-Jewish law appeared, "for the restoration of social equilibrium." In 1941, on the establishment of a comradeship-in-arms with Germany, the Nuremberg legislation was introduced—in some instances, especially where half-Jews were concerned, even more severely than in Germany itself. At the same time deportations began. The government rounded up "Eastern Jews," of ex-Polish, Rumanian or Czech nationality, and pushed them into the recently overrun territories of eastern Poland. Police Leader Jeckeln undertook "to complete the liquidation of those Jews by September 1." He kept his word. The Jews were massacred by *Einsatzgruppe* C at Kamenets Podolsk and in the nearby towns. Only a few fled and reached Budapest to tell the tale.

Moreover, Hungarian Jews were mobilized for "auxiliary services," which in practice meant merciless slave labor in mine-clearing, river diversion and construction work for the armed forces. Any encounter between the Germans and the Jewish labor units was a cause for renewed outbursts. Eichmann's deputy, Guenther, complained of the Jewish laborers, "many of them ex-lawyers, industrialists and other intellectuals," who were permitted to buy hot meals at the Hegyeshalom railway station buffet, "where German officials are also forced to have their meals." Guenther asked his Foreign Office to intervene to have the Jews removed from this place, as the German customs and railway officials should not be offended by compulsory contact with Jews. The Foreign Office, of its own accord, informed the Gestapo that a Jew had had the insolence to accost a German police sergeant near Stanislawów with the words: "I am a Jew, but you can do nothing to me since I am a Hungarian soldier."

About fifty thousand Jews were employed in these "labor" camps, and more than half of them died of the strain, but that was as far as the Hungarian authorities would go for the moment. They embarked on a policy of economic restrictions on the Jews, but complete "aryanization" was difficult. A German businessman reported that the Hungarians had neither the capital nor the brains to replace all the Jews in business. German firms even met with a quiet Jewish boycott. The army economy officer reported to his command that the Jewish firm of Tungsram had declined to accept further German orders for pipes because of the alleged need to export to neutral countries.

On the whole, Hungary was the only country within the German sphere of influence where great numbers of Jews lived in comparative safety.

Obviously this was a situation that the Nazis could not tolerate for long. To placate them the Hungarian Government announced that it would remove Jews from all positions of influence and after the war deport all 800,000 of them. The Jews were accordingly driven out of agricultural holdings, and a special war tax was imposed on them. There were prospects that the Hungarians would deliver up their "foreign" Jews to Germany; Eichmann was consulted. In a reply dated September 25, 1942, he warned: "Experience has proved a partial action requires no less effort in preparation and execution than a total measure against all the Jews of a country." He was therefore against the expulsion only of the foreign Jews, who had fled to Hungary, because that would mean "putting into motion the whole evacuation apparatus" without really solving the Jewish problem in Hungary. "We had better wait till Hungary is ready to include all its Jews in the necessary measures," he concluded.

This, Hungary was not willing to do at the moment. The German Foreign Office increased its pressure. The pro-Nazis in Hungary, the Arrow Cross Party, embarrassed the government by pressure from within. But Kállay was firm. "The imprisonment of Jews in labor camps and ghettos would not be legal," he told them, "and the government did not consider it fitting at present to introduce legislation to this effect." Finally Under Secretary Luther wrote to Sztojay, the Hungarian Ambassador in Berlin, on January 16, 1943: "We are very much concerned that a country which was friendly to us should give shelter in the middle of Europe to about a million Jews. In the long run we will not be able to tolerate the danger without taking steps."

But Germany was not then in a position to "take steps" against an ally. Two weeks later von Paulus surrendered at Stalingrad.

It was decided to take the bull by the horns in a different fashion. Regent Horthy was summoned to meet Hitler and Ribbentrop in the Klessheim Castle, and was treated to one of the Fuehrer's notorious harangues, which, while covering the entire political situation, gave special prominence to the Jewish question. Horthy retorted that he had virtually deprived the Jews of all means of livelihood and did not know what else to do with them. "It is impossible, after all, to liquidate them or beat them to death." This really aroused Hitler's anger and evoked a tirade:

"In Poland this state of affairs has been cleared up thoroughly. If the Jews there did not wish to work, they were shot. If they could not work, they had to decay [*verkommen*]. They had to be treated like tuberculosis bacilli, with which a healthy body may become infected. This was not so cruel if one remembered that even innocent creatures like hares and deer have to be killed to prevent damage. Why should the beasts who wanted to bring us Bolshevism be spared? Nations that did not rid themselves of Jews perished. One of the most famous examples was the decline of the Persians, once so proud, continuing today a pitiful existence as Armenians."

Yet Horthy was convinced neither by Hitler's uniquely frank admission to a foreign statesman of the atrocities in Poland nor by his display of crass historical ignorance. Two days after the conference, on April 19, 1943, the very day the Warsaw ghetto revolt started, Himmler was informed that the Hungarians hesitated to deliver the Jews and preferred to give them good treatment.

The pressure continued in all directions. Ribbentrop found in Sztojay a sympathetic listener and a willing collaborator. The Ambassador warned his government that its stand on Jewish matters was the only obstacle to really intimate Hungarian-German relations. "They mark out Jewry as a more dangerous and greater enemy than any other adversary," he wrote; this was "a matter of life and death for Germany." Kállay instructed his Ambassador to placate the Germans and ask them not to misconstrue his intentions, but repeated that he would not send the Jews for "resettlement" unless he knew where they were going and was sure they would be given "a chance to exist."

Veesenmayer, the German roving Ambassador, was sent on December 10, 1943, to examine the position on the spot. He came out with a virulent anti-Hungarian report advocating strong measures to secure "the Hungarian outpost," harness the country completely to Germany's economic needs, and "take a firm grip on the Jewish problem, which is now on the order of the day. The clearing up of this problem is a prerequisite of Hungary's complete integration into Germany's fight for its security and survival."

But Germany was not so resolute in retreat as in victory. It was not till March, 1944, that the RSHA was ordered to draw up a list of an acceptable Hungarian Cabinet in case of the collapse of Kállay's government.

At the same time Eichmann was dispatched in great secrecy to Mauthausen to prepare a special commando. Himmler's order was: "Send down to Hungary the master in person." His directive to Eichmann was simple: "Comb the country from East to West; send all the Jews to Auschwitz as quickly as possible. Begin with the eastern provinces, which the Russians are approaching. See to it that nothing like the Warsaw ghetto revolt is repeated in any way." That much Eichmann admitted in court, adding: "The Hungarian gendarmery wanted, surely on grounds of convenience, to clear Budapest first, and I had to negotiate with Endre on that. . . . My orders were to begin not with Budapest but with the eastern part, to proceed from east to west."

In Mauthausen Eichmann assembled all his trusted henchmen, who had carried out the deportations throughout Europe and, their tasks completed, were now virtually unemployed. He had with him Krumey, Wisliceny, Dannecker, Burger, Hunsche, Abromeit, Novak, Seidl and all his personal assistants. Only Rolf Guenther stayed at Kurfuerstenstrasse 116 in Berlin, to keep the office running.

Rudolf Hoess was ordered back to Auschwitz to prepare the camp for its great new task. Finally, when everything was ready, Horthy was again summoned to the Klessheim Castle, ostensibly "to discuss the withdrawal of Hungarian troops from Russia." Upon his arrival Hitler presented him point-blank with a choice between a complete German occupation and a German-appointed Cabinet. Horthy chose the second alternative and sped back to Budapest, where he arrived on March 19, 1944. On the same day SS Standartenfuehrer Dr. Edmund Veesenmayer arrived to announce his appointment as "Plenipotentiary of the Reich in Budapest in charge of forming the new Government." Also on the same day, "the master" and his whole outfit, a military column a mile long, now called "*Sondereinsatzkommando Eichmann*" (Special Operation Group Eichmann), reached the capital to solve "the life-and-death issue for the Third Reich."

They had to move fast; Russian patrols had already reached the head of the Jablonica Pass in the Carpathians, the historic invaders' pathway from the East, leading straight to the plains of Hungary.

*

The day after the appearance of "Special Operation Group Eichmann" in Hungary, Jewish community leaders were summoned to appear before

Eichmann's men. "We asked the Hungarian authorities whether we should go there," Pinchas Freudiger, head of the Budapest Orthodox community, testified. "The Prime Minister's office promised a reply through the police; the police said we must comply with all German requests. They would not interfere." The Jewish representatives decided to attend the meeting.

Three German uniformed officers, Krumey, Wisliceny and Hunsche, accompanied by a civilian, a girl typist and a soldier, received them. The soldier immediately pointed a pistol at the assembled fifteen Jewish representatives. Eichmann was employing his usually successful technique of confusing people by simultaneously terrorizing and appeasing them.

Krumey said: "From this moment onward all the affairs of Hungarian Jewry are transferred to the competence of the SS. There will be some economic restrictions, but this will be all—no more than the necessities of the war require. Religious and cultural activities may continue. We will see to order and peace. Everything will be all right. Let me have the names of the leaders of all Jewish communities in Hungary. You will attend a further meeting of Jewish leaders tomorrow at the Astoria Hotel."

The general tone of the speech was quite reassuring.

At the conclusion of the meeting written instructions were issued ordering the submission of all Jewish matters to the Gestapo, IV-B-4. Jews were forbidden to leave Budapest without a permit; a Jewish Central Council, "a negotiating partner vis-à-vis the German authorities," was to be established immediately as the only authorized body of Budapest Jews. It was to maintain a round-the-clock telephone service to receive and record all communications. Any atmosphere of panic should be prevented.

The next day a bigger meeting, with over forty Jewish representatives, was summoned. Wisliceny was the main speaker, generally along the same lines as Krumey the day before. The Jewish leaders inquired about the numerous arrests that were taking place among Jews prominent in industry, business and the professions, and the wholesale seizures of Jews on trains and at railway stations. "Well, don't you know, there is a war on and hostages are being taken," replied Wisliceny innocently. "Nothing will happen to them if you behave yourselves. As for the arrests on the railroads—the Jews should not move around. Tell them to stay where they are."

The request to form the Central Council immediately was strenuously pressed. The Jews of Budapest again beseeched the Hungarian Government for assistance arguing that there was nothing in local laws about a *Judenrat*. The reply they received was: "Do as the Germans ask."

Horthy had settled it with his Regency Council, and told them that he had been accused of sacrificing the fatherland by not letting the Germans massacre the Jews. He added that, faced with the alternative, he had surrendered the Jews rather than have the Germans occupy Hungary. Kállay now sought refuge in the Turkish Embassy, and Veesenmayer dictated his choice of the Hungarian Government: Sztojay became Prime Minister, Andor Jaros, a notorious pro-Nazi, Minister of the Interior, with two known Jew-baiters as under secretaries; Lászlo Endre was put in charge of Jewish affairs and Lászlo Baky took over the gendarmery; Lieutenant Colonel Lászlo Ferenczy was to be responsible for deportations. The three "Lászlos" soon became Eichmann's personal friends and chief assistants. Baky was ordered to place the gendarmery entirely at Eichmann's disposal.

The Jewish Council was ultimately formed; Eichmann now appeared on the scene in person. On March 31, 1944, he summoned its first members: Samuel Stern, Dr. Ernö Boda, Dr. Ernö Petö, Dr. Janos Gabor, Dr. Karl Wilhelm and Freudiger. His main task, he said, was to raise the output of the war industries. The Jews would have to work; then no harm whatsoever would befall them. He asked the council "to cooperate" and provide volunteers. If not, he would take people by force. "I am not an adherent of violence, because I value manpower, but any opposition will be broken. If you think of joining the partisans or applying their methods, I shall have you mercilessly slaughtered. After the war the Jews will be free; all the Jewish measures will, anyway, be abandoned, and the Germans will again be good-natured as before. You tell me if anyone harms you and I will protect you; but I warn you not to try to mislead me. I know all about Jews. I have been dealing with Jewish affairs since 1934; I know Hebrew better than you do. I will visit your museum soon, because I am interested in Jewish cultural affairs. You can trust me and talk freely to me—as you see, I am quite frank with you. If the Jews behave quietly and work, you will be able to keep all your community institutions. I want you to develop your own school system and give me a list of the necessary requirements for buildings and other technical matters. In my experience, where Jews opposed us there were executions. This is war."

As a war measure, Jews would have to wear yellow badges "from five o'clock this afternoon," he said. "You had better contact a textile factory right away." When the members of the Council said they had to consult the groups they represented, he told them it was high time to get rid of their liberal habits. "You have to order, not to ask. I give you power to impose taxes. Take money from the converts; they are the richest. I'll treat them as Jews, anyway. I'll make every Jew subscribe to the existing Jewish newspaper, which will be another source of income." His parting shot was: "Tell me if anybody harms you."

The Jewish leaders were bewildered. However ominous Eichmann's threats, his general attitude was not that of a murderer. He had talked about schools and cultural institutions; he had given his word of honor to protect the Jews; all he wanted them to do was work. That in itself was not so terrible. True, they had heard of what had happened in Poland and other places, but perhaps the Jews there had not responded to an appeal for quiet behavior, they told themselves. They had little choice, they persuaded themselves. The Hungarians would not interfere, and the Jews were neither physically nor mentally prepared for any real resistance.

Even before the Germans had entered, Otto Komoly, the dynamic leader of the Zionist Organization, had sounded the Jewish war veterans on the possibility of organized resistance. It was turned down.

Nobody suggested physical opposition or mass escape. "Let us try it out and see what happens" was their conclusion. Eichmann's camouflage maneuvers had worked again. Before the Jewish representatives realized what was happening they were hopelessly enmeshed in his dragnet. Treachery and camouflage achieved the first major objectives: no repetition of the Warsaw ghetto revolt, no mass escapes.

In cross-examination Eichmann admitted the correctness of the minutes of the March 31 meeting. He also admitted that soon after the day of his "frank" talk and lavish promises of protection he had dispatched his transport specialist, Franz Novak, to Vienna to settle with the railway authorities the last technical details for the deportation of the Hungarian Jews to Auschwitz.

*

Now everything began moving feverishly. A series of orders was issued by the Hungarian authorities. Jews were forbidden to leave their apartments or keep telephones, radios and private motor vehicles. Their bank accounts were frozen, their valuables confiscated, their food rations reduced. They were expelled from the professions and the civil service; their shops, warehouses and offices were closed. These orders followed one another in such rapid succession that Veesenmayer was able to report on April 7, "Unusual speed under local conditions." He gave credit where it was due, adding that this result was brought about through the personal contact and influence of Eichmann's unit with Endre.

All this happened within the first few weeks and kept the Jewish Council busy. The *Sondereinsatzkommando* was showering it with demands: five hundred vacant apartments to be supplied immediately, following an Allied air raid on Budapest; labor units to be sent to build shelters and antiaircraft installations for the SS buildings; goods to be supplied. A demand for one thousand vacant apartments followed. The ghettoization and deportations started. Schools, community buildings, synagogues were requisitioned.

On April 4 a meeting was held at the Hungarian Ministry of the Interior, with Baky in the chair. High-ranking representatives of the army and Ferenczy were present, with Krumey, Wisliceny and Hunsche for the German side. Baky produced a plan for purging the country of the Jews and transporting them, irrespective of sex or age, to concentration camps. They were to be rounded up by the local police or gendarmery, under the guidance of the German Security Police, "which will be on the spot as an advisory body, and special importance must be attached to achieving undisturbed cooperation with them." The roundup was to be carried out by districts; the scheme was to be kept in strict secrecy till put into effect. Then Eichmann gave his approval, and the instructions were immediately promulgated. The Hungarian Council of Ministers gave its formal assent some time later, when the whole thing was already an accomplished fact agreed upon between Eichmann and Baky.

The Jewish Council could no longer reach Eichmann so easily. They submitted a written request to be permitted to send out delegates to the provinces, from which grave complaints were received, to relieve some of the suffering. Eichmann declared there was no need. The situation in the ghettos was no worse than that of German soldiers on maneuvers, he said. When the Council petitioned the Hungarian authorities, they were told that Jews were getting what they deserved; should they persist in their allegations, they would meet the fate of ordinary rumormongers. On the few occasions when the Council members obtained personal access to Eichmann, he would shout down all complaints with outright denials: "You are starting again with the propaganda stories. . . . I have ordered ghettoization in all the boundary regions of Hungary. This affects 300,000 Jews. I won't leave 300,000 enemies loose so near the border," he yelled. When asked why these orders applied to a town about 180 miles behind the front, he said it had been proclaimed "a military zone." "Ask your Hungarians for explanations on this," he roared. "Jews will have to remain in the ghettos and live there."

How ghettoization had been enforced was told by several witnesses. Dr. Martin Földi experienced the process in Užhorod. "The ghetto was established at a brick factory. It could have housed perhaps two thousand people with difficulty. We were fourteen thousand. The sanitation conditions were indescribable. There were no latrines. We improvised something in the open that was awful and had a depressing and demoralizing effect. A German Gestapo officer told me: 'You live here like swine. Shortly you will be sent to Germany, where you will work and live normally with your families.' "

Eichmann visited the larger ghettos on an extensive tour. He was hailed by the local press, which carried his picture and described his activities.

The dreadful conditions in the ghettos were reflected in the alarming reports the Hungarian authorities themselves received. In Nyiregyháza less than one spare meter of living space was allowed per person. Food was running out. In Munkács the Jews were located in sheds without side walls. Epidemics were threatening. The same was reported from Kassa, Kisvárda, Mátészalka, Užhorod and other places. But on his return from the inspection of the ghettos Eichmann expressed "complete satisfaction," and Endre said that the Jews "are getting some air at last. They live in the ghettos like in sanatoria."

Once he had the Jews inside the ghettos, Eichmann proceeded to Auschwitz, to find out whether the camp was really, as he put it, in a position "to stomach" (*zu verkraften*) the numbers of Jews about to arrive. He had given instructions on technical arrangements, including the disposal of the bodies, and was angry that his earlier request for the construction of another railway side line had not been carried out. He accompanied the first transport of Hungarian deportees in person.

The deportations were coupled with most cruel tortures to extract money and valuables. Wives were beaten before husbands, children before parents, to make them "confess" where their jewelry was hidden. Rubber truncheons, electric current, brutal flogging of soles and palms, sticking needles under the nails, were favorite devices of the Hungarian gendarmery under the general direction of Krumey and Wisliceny. From Kassa it was reported how the eighty-four-year-old mother of a distinguished citizen had been taken from the operating table while having her foot amputated and thrown straight into a wagon. This maltreatment so embittered her son that he whipped out a revolver to shoot himself. The weapon was knocked aside, but it fired and blew off half his face. He was thrown into the truck, unbandaged, after his mother.

The great deportations started in the middle of May, 1944. Eichmann, Wisliceny, Endre and Baky held a small celebration to mark the event. The deportations were carried out with staggering speed; sometimes as many as five trains, loaded with fourteen thousand people, arrived in Auschwitz on a single day. Upon the "advice" of Eichmann's representative, a hundred persons were loaded in a car. "Pack them in like herrings" was the instruction issued after a joint German-Hungarian consultation in Munkács. "It was a voyage of horrors," testified Zeev Sapir, a Munkács deportee. "We prepared some water before we left, but the SS men poured it out. . . . Women fainted; children were crying for water. After three days we arrived at a place where we saw high chimneys and smelt a strange stench. One of the prisoners told us we would soon go up there, pointing to the chimney. We were in Auschwitz."

When Eichmann was approached about the inhuman transport conditions, he said that there were many children among the deportees, and children did not need much air or occupy much space. "Stop bothering me with horror stories about deaths in the transports," said Hunsche when approached by Kastner. "I followed the matter up," he continued. "Here are the reports. There are no more than fifty to sixty dying en route in any single transport."

A campaign of deception continued from Auschwitz itself. "We were given a postcard and a pencil and told to write to members of our families. I wrote to my sister in Budapest. An SS man or Kapo dictated it. The text was approximately: 'I am all right, and am working.' We were told to write that we were in Waldsee . . . that is a summer resort in Austria," testified Martin Földi. The postcards bore no stamps or postmarks. "They arrived at the Gestapo and were dispatched from there," testified Freudiger. "I looked at one of the postcards through a magnifying glass and noticed that the writer had written 'Auschwitz,' which was crossed out and Waldsee written on top. I went to Krumey and showed it to him, he said: 'Freudiger, you are a clever man. You don't have to notice everything.' It was obvious they wanted Jewish families to get handwritten soothing messages."

In some instances, as in Munkács, resistance was offered. People said they would not board the trains in such appalling conditions. The recalcitrants were shot on the spot. There was no trouble with the others.

The pace of the deportations was so rapid that it brought Hoess to Budapest to inquire what Eichmann meant sending him many more people than Auschwitz could destroy in a day. Eichmann insisted he must work at high speed. They finally agreed on a schedule of two trains one day and three the next.

On July 11, 1944, Veesenmayer summed up the final total figures: 437,402 Jews deported. About the same time Ferenczy reported: "The country is now clear of Jews, with the exception of Budapest and the army working units."

*

In despair the Jews addressed themselves to the Hungarian people through an illegal pamphlet, reminding them that their ancestors had been living with the Christian population of Hungary for a thousand years.

> Not a word did we utter when we were deprived of our possessions, when we lost our human dignity and our honor as citizens. But now it is a question of our naked lives. . . . We must reveal to the Christian people of Hungary the fact that for several weeks now many hundreds of thousands of Hungarian Jews have been deported under tragic and cruel circumstances unmatched in the history of the world. . . . We address our entreaty to the Christian people of Hungary . . . who cannot permit the horrible death of innocent people.

Petitions were addressed to members of the government, to the Prime Minister and finally to the Regent himself, setting out all the deportation figures and appealing to his sense of justice.

What followed was a curfew order imposed on the Jews of Budapest allowing them to leave their houses only between 2 and 5 P.M. Preparations for the last big deportations were in full swing.

Plans for a great final knockout (*eine eintaetige Grossaktion*) to round up the 400,000 Jews of the capital in one day had been laid down by Eichmann much earlier, to take place in the middle of July. All the police and gendarmery units were to be brought from the provinces; all the cadets of the police and army training depots were to join in; all the postmen and chimney sweepers of Budapest were to be mobilized to act as pilots and guides. To facilitate their task, the houses where Jews lived were to be marked with a yellow star. Buses and other public transport were planned to be used during the gigantic round-up exclusively for the concentration of Jews, who were to be detained on an island on the Danube, near Budapest, and from there dispatched to Auschwitz within a few weeks. It was all worked out by Eichmann to the last detail and reported to Berlin.

The German Foreign Office had its apprehensions about such a colossal operation. "It is bound to produce strong reactions abroad," they cabled their embassy in Budapest. "You must produce some grounds for it, like finding explosives in Jewish institutions and synagogues, acts of sabotage, or assaults on policemen." Veesenmayer's reply was cool: so far there had been no repercussions from abroad about the evacuations from Hungary. As for the propaganda suggestion, he pointed out politely that Berlin did not know what it was talking about. All Jewish synagogues were already under strict control, all Jewish property had been confiscated, and the Jews had a very limited liberty of movement. So please abstain from any steps and leave the matter to us, he concluded.

When all was ready for the great round-up, a hitch occurred. Horthy suddenly got cold feet and called a halt to further deportations. Sztojay regretfully told Veesenmayer that this was due to the pressure being exerted on Hungary from all sides. The King of Sweden had protested against the deportations. So had the Pope, the Swiss and Turkish governments, and various personalities from Spain and from Hungary itself. "Why do you single us out," asked Sztojay, "when there are Jews still living unmolested in Rumania and Slovakia?" Veesenmayer reported that in his opinion the Prime Minister and his Cabinet were particularly impressed by an intercepted message stating that a list of war criminals containing seventy names "is now being compiled by the Western Powers." (It was actually a request sent by Dr. Kastner to London, via Bern, which fell into the hands of the Hungarian counterespionage.) The bombardments of Budapest, the Allied landing in France and the deterioration on the Western front, all had their obvious effects, Veesenmayer added.

Horthy issued warrants of arrest against Endre and Baky but had them reinstated upon Veesenmayer's vigorous protest. Hitler was now seriously aroused. He instructed his plenipotentiary to tell Horthy that he regarded the dismissal of the Sztojay Cabinet and the arrest of the state secretaries dealing with Jewish matters as a breach of faith, which would result in an immediate military occupation of Hungary. "The Fuehrer expects that the measures against the Jews of Budapest will now be set in motion without any further delay, with the exceptions conceded by the Reich authorities to the Hungarian Government at the suggestion of Veesenmayer." There must be no delay; otherwise the Fuehrer's agreement to even these "concessions" would be revoked.

The exceptions conceded to and accepted by the Fuehrer were 8,700 Jewish families and a thousand Jewish children under the age of ten, whom the Hungarians wished to let out, while the Germans haggled, saying that the original number had been only a total of seven thousand people. Anyway, for the first and only time since the annihilation directive, Hitler had authorized the mass departure into safety of thousands of Jewish families. In exchange he demanded all the remaining Jews of Budapest.

But there was one man on the scene who did not want even this trickle to escape, and who ventured to do what German field marshals seldom dared: he questioned and defied Hitler's order, and announced that he would appeal to the Fuehrer to reconsider his position. That man was Eichmann.

Veesenmayer reported on July 25, 1944:

> The head of the local Special Jewish Operations Unit of the SD, SS Lieutenant-Colonel Eichmann, has taken the position that, as far as he knows, in no circumstances does the SS Reichsfuehrer [Himmler] agree to the emigration of Hungarian Jews to Palestine. The Jews in question are without exception important biological material, many of them veteran Zionists, whose emigration to Palestine is most undesirable. Having regard to the Fuehrer's decision, of which he has been informed, he is about to submit the matter to the Reichsfuehrer SS and, if necessary, *to seek a new decision from the Fuehrer*. [My italics.]

Anyway, Veesenmayer added, Eichmann intended "to carry out the expected expulsion of the Jews from Budapest once it is proceeded with, with the utmost suddenness and with such speed that they will be driven out before anyone has had a chance to obtain a travel document or visa to a foreign country." Should anyone in spite of all efforts get out to the West, Eichmann would stop him and have him sent back by taking appropriate measures on French territory.

(In his evidence Eichmann attempted to explain away this document by saying that Veesenmayer had "erred" in the report, and anyway, he said, he did not have the Fuehrer's order in writing before him.)

When his mission was near its successful completion, the news of Horthy's intervention to stop the deportations sent Eichmann into a thundering rage. "In all my long experience such a thing has never happened before," he roared. "This can't be tolerated!" Upon encountering Dr. Janos Gabor of the Council he yelled at him, "I'll show you what it means to interfere in my affairs. How dare you!" He flew to Berlin but could get no support and was told to return to Budapest and await further orders.

He decided to get his Jews anyway.

*

An obvious choice was the Kistarcsa detention camp, some seventeen kilometers from Budapest, where many Jews were detained as hostages or on alleged suspicion. There was a special hut for the "Gestapo detainees, interned on the orders of the *Sondereinsatzkommando Eichmann*." Among them was the Jewish hospital's staff, arrested on the false charge of having operated a wireless transmitter, a group of engineers and executives from the coal mines, accused of sabotage, and hundreds of others. The Jewish Council kept a special employee, Dr. Alexander Brody, to take care of the prisoners and supply them with food. Istvan Vasdenyei was the Hungarian commander of the camp. Novak, Hunsche and other members of Eichmann's Commando were frequent visitors and had full authority. No release could be given without their order. Even Brody's admission card had to be countersigned by Krumey. "There were frequent deportations from Kistarcsa before," testified Brody, "but at the beginning of July the Regent stopped further deportations. . . . I was greatly surprised when Vasdenyei told me there would be a deportation of fifteen hundred Jews from Kistarcsa on the 14th and that a train had been ordered. I proceeded immediately to the Jewish Council to tell them."

"When we received the news," testified Freudiger, "we tried to contact Horthy. Finally we succeeded, through his son." On July 14 Wisliceny entered Kistarcsa and ordered fifteen hundred Jews to be deported. "We were packed into cars meant for the transportation of animals. . . . After traveling for some time in one direction we felt the train going back and in the evening we were back in Kistarcsa," testified Mrs. Elisheva Szenes. The alerted Regent had ordered the train to be stopped; it had been overtaken by the Hungarian police at Havan station and returned to Kistarcsa, despite the vigorous protests of the SD guards.

Eichmann was furious. "This was a duel between him and Horthy," people said; Eichmann had lost the first round.

Some days later the whole Jewish Council was ordered to appear at the Hotel Majestic on the Schwabenberg, the seat of Eichmann's Commando. "Everyone was nervous, because we had never been told to come all together," testified Freudiger. "When we arrived, one was missing. 'Send a car to fetch him,' we were told. He finally arrived at about 10 A.M. I asked Hunsche what was the matter, why we had been summoned. He told me to wait. I asked to be allowed to telephone the office, but he said he would do it for us. At about two o'clock he started talking about organizing Jewish life in Hungary, as if there were still Jews. This lasted an hour . . . then we were told to wait again. . . . At 6 P.M. I told him we had to go home, but he did not allow us. At 7 the telephone on his table rang . . . all we heard was that he said: 'Good, very good.' Then he sent us home."

But at Kistarcsa something else was happening that day. It was told by Dr. Brody. "The SS arrived in many lorries under Novak's command. They ordered that no one must leave the office or use the telephone and announced that the fifteen hundred people returned on the 14th were to be deported again. 'Eichmann will not suffer,' he said, 'that anybody should overrule his orders—not even the Regent.' People were ordered to get out. The SS threw them with great brutality into the lorries. Some had crutches, others were in invalid chairs. They were ordered by the SS to leave all these things behind as they would not be needing them any more. They sent old people of over eighty—I remember the widow of Sandor Fleissig, a member of the Upper Chamber and the head of the stock exchange, a completely helpless woman. Then they said: 'Brody, who has caused us enough unpleasantness, should go too.' Thereupon Vasdenyei nodded to his clerk, who smuggled me out. . . . I hurriedly took the train and ran to the office of the Jewish Council. I was astonished to find none of the members there. . . . I was told that Eichmann had ordered them all to come to his office that morning. . . . Only later at night did I speak to them over the telephone and learned that they had not been allowed to get out all day."

So Eichmann had won his duel, after all. By summoning the members of the Council he kept them all day long from contacting Horthy again. When Hunsche got the telephone call it was to announce that the train had crossed the Hungarian border and was speeding toward Auschwitz. That was the meaning of his words, "Good, very good." He saw Freudiger next day and asked him laughingly: "Are you still so nervous, or have you calmed yourselves now?" And Wisliceny added: "Did you really think Eichmann would let that old fool Horthy slap him in the face like that by sending back his train?"

At SS Budapest headquarters it became known that Eichmann had got his train out "by a trick." His prestige was restored, but Horthy was now accused of a breach of faith by the Red Cross, which he had personally promised to stop the deportations. The Hungarian legation in Bern was instructed to explain that the German authorities had done it without the knowledge of the Hungarian Government. "We have protested most sharply to the German Government on this."

In court Eichmann "did not remember" the incident; all he knew was that a train was once turned back. Anyway, he said, he could not understand how all this had happened. "We had no lorries in Budapest!" But he admitted the Hungarian gendarmery had them, so the riddle was solved.

"The master" was now moving heaven and earth to achieve two ends: to get all the Jews of Budapest to Auschwitz and to prevent the Hungarians from letting any of them out. He wrote to his deputy, Guenther, that the German Embassy in Budapest was not vigorous enough in resisting the Hungarian suggestions for emigration of Jews to Palestine. "It is necessary," he wrote, "to see to it that the Embassy receives clear instructions to oppose it." He appealed to Himmler, as he announced he would, on the "conceded exceptions of Hitler"; in accordance with Eichmann's request, Hitler canceled the exit permits.

*

Eichmann meanwhile had successfully blocked any rescue of Jews by Hungarians. He was now busy with several schemes of his own, to enable certain Jews to leave Hungary in return for heavy ransoms payable to the Germans.

Requests for money to save lives were not new in occupied Europe. There had been a few cases in Holland; Wisliceny had negotiated some in Slovakia. In Hungary it worked in different directions. Soon after the occupation the family of Baron Weiss was given free passage to Portugal in exchange for transferring to the SS control over their huge steel combine and their agricultural holdings, which included a large island on the Danube. Baron von Oppenheim was allowed to leave after handing over his stud farms to the SS. Other possibilities were explored.

Personally, Eichmann did not favor these dealings. "Now I have to go to Minister Jaros and tell him of this dirty business [*diese Schweinerei*] of letting the Weiss family out," he said. Yet when Geschke, the regional commanding officer of the Security Police, told Eichmann that money was needed in Budapest for local needs, he decided that the Jews would supply it.

He sent Wisliceny and Krumey to enter into money deals with Jewish representatives. As Freudiger was well aware, Wisliceny had been given money before in Slovakia by the "working group" of Rabbi Weissmandel and Gizi Fleischmann. The Jewish leaders there believed it was he who had secured them a reprieve from deportation. In Budapest Wisliceny sought contact with Freudiger and delivered a message from Rabbi Weissmandel, recommending the continuation of the negotiations. After Freudiger had read it, Wisliceny immediately destroyed the letter. "I am at your disposal," said Freudiger. "All the money you will get from abroad you will deliver to us," said Wisliceny. "To 'us' or to 'me'?" asked Freudiger. "None of your business," snapped Wisliceny.

The Hungarians were jealously watching the German extortions. They were willing to let the Germans have the Jews, but insisted on being the sole inheritors of their property. "A virtual contest developed between the Hungarians and the Germans for the theft of Jewish property," Joel Brand put it.

The talks about the emigration of Jews were soon taken over by another Jewish body, the Committee for Assistance and Rescue (*Vaadat Ezra Vehatzala*), whose members were Otto Komoly, Dr. Israel Kastner, Samuel Springman and Joel Brand, and which had been active for some time in Zionist quarters. Their job was to assist refugees. They acquired arms, equipped people with forged documents and smuggled them over the border. Now a new possibility of activity opened before them.

Soon after the occupation Brand established contact with Wisliceny. Kastner participated in the talks. Wisliceny renewed the offer he had made in Slovakia, and requested two million dollars, promising to further a scheme for the emigration of 100,000 Jews. He solemnly promised that there would be no ghettoization or deportations. "We undertook to pay it in ten monthly installments, assuming that in the meantime the war would be over," Joel Brand testified. The first installment of three million pengö as a token of goodwill was paid within a few weeks, with funds provided by the Jewish Council. Kastner now requested that a group of six hundred young pioneers be allowed to proceed to Palestine.

Then there was talk of a children's transport, to which, however, the Germans objected, because "it would be too obvious to the Hungarians." The Jews began compiling lists of people active in public life and of those who would pay for their inclusion; the money was to serve for further bribes.

Kastner wanted some people from the provincial areas that were most threatened at the time to be included. Finally, after stormy scenes, in the course of which Eichmann would fall into fits of rage, several hundred Jews from Cluj and other ghettos were also directed to Budapest. A year after the war he wrote in his report that he felt at the time as if he were playing roulette with Eichmann for human lives, asking himself: "Shall we be naïve losers, like so many others before us in occupied Europe? Not only would the millions we paid be foolish madness, but the loser in this game is also called a traitor." Little did he know then that ten years later a fanatical group of young Israelis, inflamed by what had happened at certain judicial proceedings over his activity in Budapest, would consider him both a loser and a traitor, and shoot him dead at the entrance to his house in Tel Aviv.

While these negotiations were being carried on, a new figure appeared on the scene: a shrewd merchant who had risen rapidly in the service of the SS, first as a horse buyer under SS General Fegelein, brother-in-law of Hitler's mistress, Eva Braun, and later as head of the economic staff of the Waffen SS in Budapest. His name was Kurt Becher. He negotiated the Manfred Weiss and Oppenheim deals, and it was he who now, together with Walter Schellenberg, the SS counterintelligence chief, proposed to Himmler to negotiate through the Jews of Hungary a deal to let Jews out for a ransom to be supplied from abroad. Becher, who had to equip the Waffen SS in Hungary, took the deal at its face value. Himmler and Schellenberg were interested in the political implications of the move, first and foremost as a means of contacting the Western powers on matters within their province. Himmler, who considered the war lost, was anxious to whitewash himself somehow and to pave the way to becoming an acceptable negotiator on behalf of Germany. An added touch to the proposal was to ask the Western powers for equipment, which would be used "against the Russians only." It was decided to let Eichmann handle the matter in Budapest. He was told to ask the Jews for ten thousand trucks to be supplied by the West in exchange for a million lives.

Becher returned to Budapest to act as the man behind the scenes, with Himmler's instructions still ringing in his ears: "You may promise the Jews what they want. What we shall keep—we shall see."

It was then, on April 25, that Joel Brand was summoned to appear before Eichmann at the Majestic Hotel. Behind him stood Kurt Becher in civilian clothes. " 'You know who I am,' Eichmann bellowed at me," testified Brand, imitating Eichmann's yell. " 'I carried out the actions in Europe, in Poland, in Czechoslovakia; now it is Hungary's turn. You belong to the Joint and the Jewish Agency. Blood for goods [*Blut gegen Ware*]. What do you want: fertile women, working men, children, old people? Speak up." Brand was, of course, completely flabbergasted; he started stammering. He said he had no goods; perhaps he could find money. "We don't need money or Hungarian goods," bawled Eichmann. "You go abroad and make contact with your people. Where do you want to go: Switzerland or Turkey?" Brand chose Turkey.

They met twice more; Eichmann specified his requirements and outlined the details. An agent of the German counterespionage, Bandi Grosz, came on the scene, urging Brand to accept the mission.

"A million Jews for ten thousand trucks, that is cheap," said Eichmann. "So they must be factory-new trucks, with all the proper accessories and equipment. Your wife and children will, of course, remain here; I want to make sure you will return. Bandi Grosz will go with you to see what you cook up in Istanbul." He warned Brand that it was all a close secret, especially vis-à-vis the Hungarians. "You must leave soon. I won't be able to wait. Today I start deporting. I'll keep the people a week or two somewhere and then I'll send them on" was Eichmann's final warning.

On May 18 Brand and Grosz arrived in Istanbul, where they were detained for a while. In prison Grosz let out the secret that as far as he was concerned the deal went much further than met the eye. It was to serve as a cover for sounding out the Allies on peace.

Finally Brand was allowed to proceed in the direction of Palestine, but after he crossed the Syrian border he was arrested in Aleppo by the British authorities, who permitted him a long talk with Moshe Sharett (then Shertok), of the Jewish Agency. After that the British transported Brand to Cairo, where they detained him despite his frantic objections, on the ground that he was an "enemy alien."

Eichmann was not aware of Brand's peregrinations, but he was not unhappy about Brand's failure to return. When Mrs. Brand came to see him, he told her: "Cable your husband that if he does not come back at once I'll put the mills of Auschwitz in motion. . . . My hands are now free." Mrs. Brand testified: "He was angry that a Jew had escaped him, but not that the deal had not materialized. . . . He was glad it was off."

Wisliceny said the same: "I knew Eichmann's mind. His idea was to carry on the deportations in such a manner that the negotiations ordered by Himmler would in any case be frustrated by an accomplished fact."

Kastner, who took over the negotiations after Brand's departure, had to find daily excuses for the delay in getting a reply. Such negotiations took time, he explained; it must be because there was no negative reply that Brand had not returned; the Allies could not so easily reach agreement on such a matter. He said that the continued deportations were a hindrance to the successful conclusion of the deal.

On June 9 Eichmann told Kastner: "If there is no affirmative reply from Istanbul within three days, I'll set the mills of Auschwitz in full operation." This was, of course, empty talk; the "mills" were already in full swing.

The authorship of the deal and Eichmann's attitude toward it were discussed at length between him and Sassen. "Such an idea about the ten thousand trucks would never even have crossed my mind," he told the Dutchman. "I would not even have thought of it." And again: "I always preferred to see the enemy dead than alive. But when I got Himmler's order to equip two SS divisions with ten thousand trucks, then let a million Jews go to hell . . . In the last resort I would have promised them even two million, because I would have squeezed out everything possible from the bargain." In cross-examination in court Eichmann admitted the "general correctness" of this passage, but he now had an entirely new interpretation. It was he who had proposed the bargain, he said, and it was he who got it approved by higher authorities. The Western Allies alone were to blame for its failure.

In prison Eichmann had read Brand's book on the failure of his mission, and had adjusted his version to Brand's. He particularly stressed one aspect of the deal: his alleged promise "to supply" 100,000 Jews as an "advance" upon Brand's return with an affirmative reply. While it is true that Brand later wrote so in his books, this part of "the deal" is missing from Mr. Sharett's exhaustive and detailed report of his conversation with Brand in Aleppo, written immediately after the meeting. The court found as a fact that Brand had erred in ascribing this item of "the offer" to Eichmann, though Brand no doubt believed at the time that he would be able to achieve it, if he were permitted to go back to Budapest instead of being kept for months on end in Cairo, while Hungarian Jews were being deported to Auschwitz at the rate of twelve thousand per day.

In court Eichmann was positive of his exclusive authorship of "the deal," though during the police investigation he had said twice that he could not remember who had initiated the idea: Becher, Himmler, himself or someone else. In cross-examination he admitted finally that he had never considered the transaction as a "rescue venture."

"So your heart was not in it?" I asked him in conclusion. "I never claimed otherwise," he replied. "It was prompted by material considerations."

The whole matter was kept secret from the Foreign Office and the embassy in Budapest. More than two months after Brand had gone, Ribbentrop urgently inquired of Veesenmayer whether he knew what on earth the British meant by stating over London radio that Germany was doing business with Jewish blood and asking for trucks in exchange for Hungarian Jews. Veesenmayer stammered in reply that several weeks before the Jew

Brand had been sent out to Turkey to acquire "some goods that the Germans lacked." "I learn from the legation's adviser, Grell," he added, "that the negotiations in Turkey are off to a good start and that the Reuter's message transmitted over the radio is actually only a camouflage maneuver for the benefit of the Russians."

That was exactly what Kastner had been telling Eichmann all along in his attempts to explain away Brand's failure to return. On July 20, 1944, the London *Times* carried the news under the caption: "*A Monstrous Offer—German Blackmail—Bartering Jews for Munitions.*" It was reported that 400,000 Hungarian Jews had already been liquidated, and now the Germans were blackmailing the Allies. The German offer seemed to be simply a fantastic attempt to sow suspicion among the Allies, the *Times* concluded.

*

Simultaneously with "the deal," secret preparations were made for the final deportation of all Budapest Jews. Detachments of Hungarian gendarmery were arriving in the capital in great strength. Eichmann had ordered the brick works at Bekasmegyer, from where earlier deportations were made, to be prepared again. It was rumored everywhere that the final move was close.

The Jewish Council approached the Red Cross representatives and at their suggestion submitted another memorandum to the Hungarian Government. "The press reports about Jews deported to Germany are tendentious and misleading and serve only to reassure the public and set their minds at ease," they wrote. "In fact the deportees are being gassed in the Birkenau and Auschwitz death camps." The Jews were perfectly willing to work inside the country, even to perform the most arduous labor, they declared, but they asked that the threat of deportation that hung over the heads of their children and themselves be lifted.

In any case, the Hungarians must have had little doubt about what had really happened to the Jews already deported. Whenever they asked the Germans to send back specified individuals who under Hungarian laws "did not count as Jews" and had been dispatched "in error," they were told by Horst Grell of the embassy in Budapest that these persons "were already integrated into German economic life in a manner which made their withdrawal completely impracticable," and "their return would present insurmountable problems."

The negotiations for the Budapest deportations were still proceeding. Veesenmayer exerted official pressure, while Eichmann worked through his contact men. The Hungarians requested "a written assurance" that the Jews deported from Budapest would not be burnt at Auschwitz. The Germans replied that they would be glad if "the Jews to be employed for labor service in the Reich could be supplied with clothing to make their accommodation as comfortable as possible."

A dramatic fight followed. Under further pressure the Hungarian Government agreed to recommend to Horthy that the final deportations should take place. Jaros, the Minister of the Interior, suggested August 25 as " the day," but under pressure from Eichmann it was predated for the twentieth. Veesenmayer reported that Eichmann was taking into account the possibility of Jewish armed resistance. On August 18 Eichmann had the President and two members of the Jewish Council arrested, and an SS parade was staged on the streets of Budapest, with armored cars, tanks and guns, to show that they had adequate forces for dealing with any emergency. On the same day he got Horthy to give his consent to a "limited deportation of Jews from Budapest" to begin on August 25. The tension among the Jews of Budapest rose to high pitch. But on the night of August 23 something happened that changed the whole situation. The Russians broke through the German-Rumanian defenses in Moldavia. Next day King Michael of Rumania told the Germans he would have to conclude a separate armistice; he asked them to leave. The royal palace in Bucharest was bombed by the Germans within an hour; repercussions in the Balkan States were instantaneous. Horthy threw Sztojay out of office and appointed General Geza Lakatos to replace him. Then he dispatched Ferenczy to Eichmann to tell him there would be no deportations next day, and requested Veesenmayer to withdraw Eichmann's Commando unit from Budapest.

Eichmann was mad with rage, as usual when his plans were thwarted. He used violent language to Ferenczy, sent out Wisliceny by air to Berlin to see Himmler, and in his frenzy submitted what for a Gestapo man must have been a virtual ultimatum: he suggested that if no immediate steps were taken he might well be recalled from Budapest. It was now all a matter of touch and go. Becher cabled Himmler reminding him of the "goods for blood" negotiations. Everyone was holding his breath waiting for what would follow within the next few hours. But Berlin was now too weak to react immediately. Wisliceny came back empty-handed, and Becher was instructed to go ahead with the negotiations for the deal. At 3 A.M. Berlin cabled that the deportations were to be discontinued. Over Eichmann's head this directive was addressed to Winkelmann, the Senior SS and Police Chief.

Wisliceny called in Kastner next day and told him with a big smile: "You have won; the *Sonderkommando* is leaving."

Eichmann was still hoping for a change. It was first settled with the new Hungarian authorities that the deportations would take place after all, beginning on September 2. This came to naught, but Eichmann was still hopeful, plying between Berlin and Budapest. His Commando was finally dissolved on September 29. To compensate him for the disappointment Himmler awarded him an Iron Cross, second class.

But "the master" had a hunch that the last good word had not yet been said. He first undertook a temporary assignment in Rumania, then stayed for a while at a castle, near the Austrian border, as the guest of his friend

Lászlo Endre, and finally accepted Becher's hospitality in the countryside. Generally he hung around not far from Budapest, waiting for another opportunity to strike at his quarry. He got it soon enough.

On October 14, 1944, with the Red Army marching on Budapest, Horthy went on the air to announce that Hungary was pulling out of the war. This time the Germans were ready for them. The 24th Panzer Division was sent out to Budapest. With it entered SS Lieutenant General von dem Bach-Zelewski, the antipartisan fighter and more recently the suppressor of the Polish revolt in Warsaw, and SS Lieutenant Colonel Otto Skorzeny, the famous kidnaper of Mussolini. Skorzeny lured out Horthy's son to an alleged meeting with Tito's partisans and had him flown, wrapped in a blanket, to Mauthausen. Horthy himself was presented with a twenty-four-hour ultimatum. On hearing that his son was in German hands he collapsed and gave in. A new government was appointed, this time of the Nazi Arrow Cross Party, Szálasi became Prime Minister and Vajna Gabor Minister of the Interior. The Jews were delivered over to the mercy of the Germans. Next day, on October 17, 1944, Eichmann arrived in Budapest.

"I am back, you see," he told Kastner, whom he had ordered to appear before him. "Our arm is still long enough to reach you. The Jews of Budapest will be deported, this time on foot. We need the trains for other purposes."

He went to work immediately. In the early morning of October 18 Veesenmayer stated that Eichmann would take urgent steps for the deportation and immediate ghettoization of the Jews. Several hours later he could already report that Eichmann had reached full agreement with the new Hungarian administration. Fifty thousand Jews would soon be marched out of Budapest. "As I learn in great secrecy, Eichmann intends later to send fifty thousand more," reported the plenipotentiary. The other Jews would not be put in labor camps. Ribbentrop was delighted with these reports. He wrote back that the new setup in Hungary was to be fully exploited and measures taken "to proceed against the Jews with the utmost severity."

At dawn on October 20 loud hammering was heard on the doors of the houses designated with yellow stars. "All Jews were ordered to be ready within an hour, fully equipped for a three-day march. The Arrow Cross men pulled all people out of their apartments into the courtyards. Heavy rain was falling. Men, women and children, old and young, were kept there till SS groups arrived. Then they were told to run along the streets. The thoroughfares were full of people, like rushing ants. They were employed in digging trenches on the outskirts of Kispest; within a few days the labor force numbered 35,000 people. Hundreds were dying daily of exhaustion. "The premises of the Jewish Council were like Dante's inferno; some two thousand miserable invalids and many children torn away from their parents had to be accommodated there, so that in every room these unfortunate people lay packed close on the floor. Moreover, during the two hours a day allowed the Jewish population for moving around, thousands of people came to the Council Office asking for help or food, or because they were anxious about their relatives."

In November the march began. "There were grandmothers and small children among us," testified Aviva Fleischmann. "We walked the whole day under the supervision of the Arrow Cross men. They were often shooting or throwing hand grenades; they said they were killing deserters and frightening others. . . . After the first day many fell; those who could not move on were shot or left to die on the spot. . . . We got no food, only some dirty water in the evenings, which they called soup. . . . We stopped for the night whenever it got too dark to proceed. . . . Sometimes just in the open . . . It was very cold at nights. Finally, after marching eight days, those who were still walking reached Hegyeshalom. . . . Two days later we were put across the Austrian border and placed in a camp. . . . Almost everybody had typhoid fever. We were put into barracks full of lice. People were dying by the thousands. People had dysentery, without minimal hygienic conditions. Three times a week we got a piece of bread. We were not allowed to go outside. . . . Children were born in the barracks. They would die within an hour or so, bitten by lice. Once the SS Lagerfuehrer placed a woman who was about to give birth on the floor under a big spotlight, saying he wanted to see how a human being comes into the world."

The International Red Cross people reported:

> Wherever we went, throughout the length of the highway, we witnessed horrible scenes. The deportees marched in endless lines, ragged, starved, and exhausted, including old people who could hardly drag themselves along. The gendarmes drove them on with rifle butts, truncheons and whips. They had to cover 30 kilometres daily. . . . We prepared 4,000 metres of narrow-gauge film for the Nuncio; every square testifies to the horrible suffering and the terrible treatment meted out to groups of the capital's Jewry who, under the Szálasi decree, were handed over to the Germans as "loan Jews."

This was too much for some Germans, who now, on the eve of collapse, were eager to disassociate themselves ostentatiously from too open brutality. SS General Hans Juettner, head of the SS Operational Head Office, saw "the shattering marching columns" while on an inspection tour and spoke about it to Winkelmann, who said he was helpless; Eichmann alone was responsible. Having missed Eichmann in Budapest, Juettner sent in a critical report to Himmler. Becher said the march was "clear murder." Yet it went on. On November 12 Veesenmayer reported "on the basis of information supplied by Eichmann 27,000 people of both sexes had already been marched off, and 40,000 would follow." Szálasi, who had proclaimed himself "leader of the nation," was approached by neutral representatives and the Papal Nuncio, who submitted memoranda setting out the atrocities of the march and calling for the suspension of further deportations. Szálasi ruled that Hungarian Jews would continue "to be lent to the German Government as fit for work, this being for the welfare of the Hungarian nation," (adding, however, that women should be removed only by transport vehicles) "and I do not wish to discuss the subject with anyone any more." The "vehicle ruling" worried the Germans. "If we cannot continue with the foot trek we shall not be able to go on with transports at all," Veesenmayer reported to Berlin.

Eichmann managed to wangle a few trains from Vienna to go on with his deporting. When he had no more trains he again set people on foot, meeting Hungarian protests with sheer arrogance. "Eichmann came to see me several times," Vajna Gabor, the Arrow Cross Minister for the Interior declared. "I knew he was Himmler's emissary, with special backing from Kaltenbrunner. They both told me so. He was not only energetic but also entirely arrogant, maintaining he had German might behind him. He declared the Germans would take over all Jewish deportations."

It was finally Himmler who intervened. In November he ordered the stoppage of all further extermination in the camps. Now more frantic than ever in his search for even a flimsy alibi, Himmler summoned Eichmann to Berlin and reminded him in Becher's presence that it was he, Himmler, who had founded the RSHA and that it was Eichmann's duty to obey him. "If you have killed Jews till now and I order you here to spare them, I wish to hear from you whether you will carry out this order or not." Eichmann went white and was petrified. He managed to utter: "Yes, Reichsfuehrer." Himmler dismissed him after a few minutes.

Becher realized that Eichmann had better be pacified. The relations between Hitler and Himmler were already strained on account of "the deal." Kaltenbrunner had gone to Hitler complaining of it as of "a matter most gravely damaging the Reich's prestige"; this step, he said, "had severely undermined Himmler's position." Becher, who was heavily implicated in the transaction, both openly and behind the scenes, was seriously frightened and begged Himmler, almost on his knees, to award Eichmann a high decoration. And so it happened that Eichmann now received, barely two months after his previous award, the "Cross of War Merits, First Class with Swords." This mollified him a great deal.

The *Fussmarsch* was off, but Eichmann was still engaged in ghettoization in Budapest. Armed resistance by the Jews flared up in several places. This was broken at the cost of several casualties on both the German and the Jewish sides. The Arrow Cross men developed a technique of carrying off Jews and torturing them for ransom. The streets of Budapest were strewn with Jewish bodies. Many others were thrown into the Danube. Children, especially the many orphans, were dying by the thousands. The International Red Cross found six thousand of them, aged two to fourteen, famished, ragged, diseased, in several buildings provided by the Red Cross. "Their bodies were eaten by filth and scabies, their rags were infested with lice. Huddled up in fear and infinite misery, they made inarticulate sounds. They had not eaten for days and there had been nobody to look after them."

These were the final death touches of Eichmann in Budapest. On Christmas Eve, 1944, when a further Russian advance was reported, he hurriedly left Budapest, where he had caused so much misery and suffering. He did not stay to see the enforcement of the decree he had prevailed upon Vajna Gabor to promulgate: the final removal of all Jewish children into the ghetto, which took place on Christmas Day.

More than ten years later, in the calm of his Argentine seclusion, Eichmann reverted to his last weeks in Budapest. He well remembered his mood and motives. He told Sassen: "I was responsible for the march, I admit it. . . . You see, when the Allies had bombed out the railway sections, especially the Györ junction, as well as many others on the Budapest-Vienna line, I wanted to show these Allies my hand, as it were to tell them: 'Nothing will help; even if you bomb and destroy, I still have a way to the Reich.' So I moved them on foot from Budapest to the border of Lower Austria. I had an order, of course, from the Chief of the Security Police and the SD. I could not do it without an order. But it was my suggestion. . . . There were, of course, difficulties on all sides . . . but finally Winkelmann congratulated me on the elegant performance. So did Veesenmayer. So did Endre. We even had a drink on it. For the first time in my life I drank mare's-milk alcohol."

So the master had proved his mettle after all, in Hungary as everywhere else. He had done all that was humanly possible to carry out his initial assignment, "to finish the job quickly and with heedless sharpness and in the shortest time to clear Hungary of Jews."

It is true that at the last moment the development of the war saved from his clutches a small part of Hungarian Jewry. When Budapest was finally liberated by a rapid move of the Red Army on January 17, 1945, there were still some 100,000 Jews in the city. It was the only ghetto that had escaped total annihilation.

But Eichmann was not to blame.

CHAPTER 10

The Death Camps

The Nazi concentration camps had been an instrument of terror since the inception of the Third Reich. They were designed not only to isolate opponents but actually to break them. The camps grew from year to year in size and numbers under a system in which security detention "unlimited in time" was possible without appeal or recourse to the courts. After a while, the camps became an essential part of what Professor Eugen Kogon called the "SS State," which commanded its own army and presided over a huge industrial potential, with mammoth production centers run by slave labor. As a side line they were used to mutilate prisoners and to experiment on human beings as guinea pigs, in order to try out Himmler's medical fantasies for strengthening "Germandom" and weeding out undesirable races.

It was the SS that initiated the camps and whose men were in charge throughout. They imposed a system of calculated and streamlined torture on a rising scale of intensity, beginning with the lash, through electric shocks, the crushing of sexual organs, burning with a soldering torch, hanging by the armpits, asphyxiation by plunging the victim's head into cold water and reviving him by artificial respiration. More refined methods were left to the ingenuity of the man on the spot.

As I have indicated, it was with the decision on the Final Solution that some of the concentration camps, used since 1933 as a method of political terrorization, were transformed into abattoirs. Some attempts at camouflage were made, partly to avoid alarming the Jews and other potential victims, partly in order to conceal the entire operation from the world at large. It was the death camps that were to prove to be Hitler's most significant change in the map of Europe.

A non-Jew might find a way out of the camp. His case could be "cleared" by the local Gestapo that had detained him, or he might be considered to have been so thoroughly broken as to be no longer dangerous. He might find refuge in the fold of his tormentors by falling in line with National Socialism and giving tangible or ostensible expression to his allegiance. Often a promise to abstain from politics was enough. But, from 1941 onward, the Jew was doomed. Once he crossed the gate of the barbed-wire enclosure with the word "*Jude*" in the "Reasons for Detention" column of his dispatch document, he was never released. He might occasionally be moved from one camp to another, if he could be better utilized in the new place or if he had to be destroyed there. Then his last ounce of energy would be squeezed out of him and he would be put to work under conditions that were bound ultimately to break a human body. Finally, when he became so visibly emaciated and exhausted that no further benefit could be expected of him, he would be ordered "to the right" by the slight, nonchalant finger movement of the SS doctor, presiding over a monstrous selection roll call of thousands, the fate of each prisoner being decided in a fraction of a second. "To the left" meant a temporary respite; "to the right," the gas chambers. "There is no way out for you from here except through those chimneys," the SS guards would tell Jewish prisoners.

These were the "regular" camps into which "opponents" of whatever creed or nationality were thrown. There were other camps, "for Jews only." Some of these were the "*Julags*," the Jewish transitional labor camps in the General Government. Others were annihilation camps in which the Jews were destroyed on arrival. Then there were some that were supposed to be "transit" camps. In these, the Gestapo Department for Jewish Affairs, IV-B-4, left a special imprint not only of its general directive powers but also of its methods of handling everyday matters. Two of them deserve a closer look.

One was a fortress town north of Prague, used a century and a half before by the Empress Maria Theresa as an outpost on the bank of the river Eger, and named after her. The other was in a village next to Belsen, northeast of Hannover. Both were held out to the Jews as havens of safety; in ghettos and camps both were looked to as distant but available sanctuaries of rescue; both were, in fact, instruments of destruction.

As early as October 10, 1941, Theresienstadt had been suggested to Heydrich as a transit camp for the immediate deportation of the Jews of Bohemia and Moravia. Heydrich, then the newly appointed "Protector" of the territory, had assumed office on September 27. The next day a state of emergency was proclaimed and a rule of terror started. A few days later Heydrich brought Eichmann over to Prague. They decided, among other things, to clear the old fort town of Theresienstadt of its military personnel and all civilians, let the Czech evacuees occupy vacated Jewish apartments and prepare the place as a Jewish assembly depot. "After further deportations to the East from this temporary camp, in which the Jews will in any case be heavily decimated, the whole area will be built up and developed into an exemplary German settlement," read the minutes of the conference. Shortly afterward, however, the place was given an additional assignment: it became part and parcel of a deception campaign. At that time the "deportations to the East" were still ostensibly meant only as "a labor effort." Elderly people could not very well have been included without throwing all pretense to the winds. There were also some misgivings about deporting Jews who held World War I military distinctions, though Hitler claimed "the swine got their distinctions fraudulently in any case." And so it was decided to send all these people, too, to Theresienstadt. On January 19, 1942, Eichmann thoroughly inspected the place and issued detailed instructions for its administration. Next day Heydrich announced at Wannsee that Theresienstadt was to be a ghetto for "old and privileged Jews."

At a conference with police chiefs Eichmann was more explicit. He told them that "for the sake of placating the elderly people they should be told that they would be moved in the course of the summer or autumn to Theresienstadt, which was earmarked as the ghetto for the aged. This is being done as a face-saving device for the outside," he said.

In internal documents Theresienstadt was referred to as "the propaganda camp." Eichmann called it simply "a signboard."

This was the camp shown to the Red Cross inspectors or to foreign visitors whom it was thought necessary "to convince" that all the horror stories about the killings of Jews were merely vicious enemy propaganda.

"Whenever these visitors arrived," testified Mordechai Ansbacher, "the whole ghetto would be turned upside down. . . . Certain areas were under absolute curfew and people living there all had to remain indoors. Generally, only those who still preserved a more or less human appearance were allowed to move about outside. . . . A beautification process would be on. Some places had to be cleaned and made shipshape. Some houses were painted on the outside and large signboards put up, saying: 'Central Synagogue,' 'Ghetto Theatre.' . . . They even prepared teams of children as if for football games. . . . They had a children's club for such occasions, where ice-skating was installed and to which ponies were brought. They put children into small beds with an engraved heart on them, as in a veritable palace. . . . They held rehearsals with children and gave them food, which was ferociously devoured. They had therefore to repeat the rehearsals, for we kept sending them new children each time, so that as many as possible should eat well for once."

To keep up the pretense and make a profit on the side, the Gestapo would "sell" prospective deportees apartments in Theresienstadt. The newcomers arrived brandishing "title" documents, but they were lucky if they were allocated a plank in an attic of the old fort or a piece of floor in an army hut. "Two weeks after our arrival half of my group were dead. The hunger was awful. . . . There was no water. . . . Hygiene was nonexistent. . . . Hungry people fought for potato peelings soaked in dirt. . . . Our transportation, including garbage disposal, was done in dead-wagons. . . . People would storm these wagons for a scrap of food. . . . Sometimes these were very distinguished persons, professional men, millionaires or former businessmen. . . . Those of us who worked at carting had to be severe with these people, because eating the terribly dirty scraps of food or swallowing uncooked, filthy potato peel would bring on disease—in many cases certain death." The death rate was appalling: in October, 1942, a record month, the figure was over three thousand. The crematorium was active day and night.

Into this place, where less than ten thousand people had lived before, people were now streaming from all over Europe, mainly from Prague, Vienna, Berlin, Brno and Frankfurt.

Soon the roll of prisoners swelled to sixty thousand; the congestion was relieved by transports to the East. "Theresienstadt was an assembly deportation camp rather than a ghetto," its former commander, SS Captain Dr. Siegfried Seidl, said. Altogether, out of some 141,000 people who passed through its gates, about 33,500 met their deaths on the spot, and over 88,000 were deported to the East.

Inside the camp death penalties were imposed for such offenses as "breach of censorship regulations." Sixteen Jews were hanged for this crime in March, 1942, when Eichmann, the man in supreme command, declared it a capital offense. "But I wrote only to my grandmother," protested one of the convicts before his execution.

This was the place about which Himmler, in search of an opportunity to whitewash himself, and with the usual Nazi capacity for convincing himself that the past could be retroactively changed just by wishing it so, said to Dr. Norbert Masur several weeks before the German debacle: "Theresienstadt is not a camp in the ordinary sense of the word, but a town inhabited by Jews and governed by them, in which every manner of work is to be done. This type of camp was designed by me and by my friend Heydrich, and so we intended all camps to be."

Bearing children in Theresienstadt was strictly outlawed. Childbirth was visited with immediate deportation for father, mother and child. A doctor who did not immediately report a pregnancy was regarded as an accomplice.

In February, 1945, on the eve of liberation, with the Allied armies converging from both sides, an order was issued to rebuild the old underground passages of the fortress, hermetically close all window slots and prepare gastight rooms. High prefabricated towers were rushed to the place. "Then we knew it was intended to build gas chambers," Adolf Engelstein testified. "The Commandant, to whom we spoke about it, said it wouldn't be so bad as all that. The next day he flogged Erich Cohen, a technician, for half an hour, saying he had passed on the rumor about the gas chambers. . . . But the works were stopped." The disclosure foiled Eichmann's preparations for a last act of liquidating the survivors.

*

Then there was the Bergen-Belsen foreigners' camp, which was established in the summer of 1943. The German Foreign Office decided then to proceed with a scheme of exchanging Allied nationals trapped in Germany by the war for German nationals abroad. They wrote to Eichmann on March 2, 1943, asking him to set aside thirty thousand Jews "of British, U.S., Dutch, Belgian, French, Norwegian and Soviet nationalities" (Poland was significantly omitted), to be kept in reserve for an exchange. A reminder followed six weeks later. The RSHA was obviously not overenthusiastic about the whole matter, but they were finally told by Himmler to cooperate, provided they could keep these Jews on their own terms. This alarmed the Foreign Office man, von Thadden, who learned from a senior RSHA official under what conditions the Gestapo intended to "preserve" these people in the Bergen-Belsen concentration camp. "The Jews won't be worked so hard that they will actually die, but they will be treated very severely indeed," von Thadden related, asking his superior to intervene but pleading with him not to reveal the name of his RSHA informant.

Not that the Foreign Office in general or von Thadden in particular was very concerned about the fate of Jews. The reason for their sudden interest is apparent from the message sent to Eichmann, telling him that to keep these Jews under such conditions and in an ordinary concentration camp would completely miss the point, as they would either not be available for exchange or be only too well equipped with atrocity stories to support a propaganda campaign abroad.

Eichmann, however, remained true to his methods. In apparent compliance with the request from above he kept the "exchange Jews" in what he officially called a "sojourn camp" (*Aufenthaltslager*), which was in effect as destructive as the death camps.

"In time it got worse and worse," testified Dr. Josef Melkman, "till it became so appalling that the camp deserved its terrible and shocking reputation. . . . Tens of thousands were placed in a camp built for several thousands. The sanitary conditions were indescribable. There was one lavatory, always out of order, for a hut of four hundred people. The Germans would cut off the water. Weiss, the *Lageraelteste,* would ask a plumber to connect the taps at night and close them again early mornings so that they should not notice we had water at night. . . . From time to time we would get what they called 'soup.' Then they almost cut off the food supply altogether. . . . Dead people lay outside on the paths of the camp. . . . Women fought in the gutters for food refuse. . . . There were fourteen cases of cannibalism in the camp. . . . 'Bring me as many dead Jews as possible,' the camp commandant, Josef Kramer, would tell the head Kapo."

The Red Cross asked for permission to visit the camp, which was officially registered as a center for alien enemies and hence under their protection. Eichmann stalled for time and finally refused, saying: "A typhoid epidemic has broken out there, which is being combated by the medical authorities with all the means at their disposal."

The Gestapo crowded into the camp many more prisoners than the

Foreign Office had asked for; on the day of liberation it still contained some 52,000 inmates. Dr. Mordechai Chen, then a captain in the British Army Medical Corps, entered Bergen-Belsen eighteen days after its liberation. He saw walking skeletons, which had lost any resemblance to human beings. "They moved around devoid of any human look. They collided with each other, walked forward or backward, without any emotional reaction or change of stare. . . . Heaps of corpses were all around. I knew that ordinary human beings would hardly believe such things had ever existed, and I was sure that in ten years certainly nobody would believe it, and we ourselves might not believe that we had ever seen it. That is why I asked a BBC correspondent I met there to give me some pictures which he took in the camp." Dr. Chen submitted these pictures to the court.

Of the liberated prisoners, some 27,000 died of exhaustion and undernourishment during the first few weeks after liberation, in spite of all efforts to save them. "People were actually dying while we were inspecting the camp," concluded Dr. Chen.

How vicious and deliberate the tortures had been was vividly described by Dr. Hadassa Bimko Rosensaft, one of the main witnesses at the Belsen trial. She had been deported to Bergen-Belsen after fifteen months' imprisonment in Auschwitz and put to work in the women's hospital. "The treatment of the internees by the SS is hard to describe," she said. "Blows rained down, and at roll call we had to stand about for hours and hours in snow or rain, in heat or cold. The standing alone exhausted us entirely. If anybody moved during the roll call, the whole block to which he belonged had to stand for hours and sometimes to kneel down, even with their arms raised high. If anyone was late for roll call, the whole camp had to stand on parade for many hours, and he, the culprit, was beaten so badly that he sometimes died of it. . . . We had the feeling that Belsen was becoming a second Auschwitz. . . . We received very small quantities of medicines. We had 2,200 patients in the hospital and, in addition, 15,000 sick women in camp, but for a whole week we received only 300 aspirin tablets. Three or four days before the British troops entered the camp, the SS men put white armlets on their arms. Suddenly we got two more rooms for our dispensary, and then we discovered that there were enormous stores full of medicines and instruments. . . . I knew nothing of their existence until shortly before the British came."

In the General Government, to which some of the recently overrun eastern parts of ex-Poland were now annexed, the ghettos soon gave way to huge labor camps. The purpose was now to squeeze the last ounce of strength and energy from the able-bodied Jews, while sending all others to destruction. Killing through labor received an official and written blessing. The Nazi Minister of Justice, von Thierack, agreed with Himmler that "asocial elements will be removed from the ordinary machinery of justice and delivered to the Reichsfuehrer SS for destruction by labor." This applied to all Jews, Gypsies, Russians or Ukrainians who were interned in camps; these people, once interned, were to be liquidated. They had no recourse to the courts and were to be dealt with in all penal matters by the Reichsfuehrer SS.

Finally even a law was promulgated under which the police alone were competent to deal with criminal offenses by the Jews.

This marked the formal and final abdication of law in Germany.

How it worked in practice was illustrated by orders of execution classified by the code words "special treatment of Jews" (*Sonderbehandlung von Juden*). Jewish shirkers were "sentenced" to be hanged. Himmler had "to approve" the sentences. His approvals were transmitted by Eichmann to a local Gestapo, with a direction for public hanging of the condemned Jews "in the presence of the members of their race." The due execution of the order was reported back to Eichmann.

Some witnesses at the trial told the story of the Jewish labor camps (*Julags*), where the Jews were subjected to the "duty of work."

Dr. Leon Wells, today of New Jersey, a distinguished scientist in optometry and a holder of international prizes, was at the time in Lwów, in the eastern part of the General Government. "On March 2, 1942, I was taken to the Janowska Camp at the outskirts of Lwów," he recalled. "It is a completely sandy spot. A few barracks were put up there and our work consisted first of the completely useless carrying of stones back and forth." The commander was SS Lieutenant Colonel Fritz Gebauer. "We did not have the minimal conditions for life. We could not get any water. We used to get a liter per day—coffee water—for drinking and washing. The order was to keep clean [*sauber*]. On the day I arrived, six people were taken out of our group; it was said they 'looked sick' and it was 'to our good' that they be put out of barracks. Outside they were not allowed to move. The temperature was below freezing point and next morning all six were frozen lying down where they had been put out. . . . A week later SS Second Lieutenant Willhaus joined the camp. At this time a shooting competition was begun between Gebauer and Willhaus; they would shoot out of their windows at the people marching back and forth loaded with stones, aiming at the tip of a nose or a finger. The injured people were 'no good' any more (*Kaput*) and they would finish them off with a shot."

Typhoid fever spread through the camps, but sick people pretended to be all right. The whole idea was to move around, even with typhus and pneumonia, so that nobody should notice you were sick. The sick were exterminated immediately.

A similar story was told about the Plaszów camp on the outskirts of Cracow. Moshe Beisky, today a judge in Tel Aviv, told the court the story of his youth in the "labor" camp. "At the beginning of January we were two thousand people. Those who left the camp for work outside were heavily guarded at first. Then the guards were reduced, as there was no more apprehension of escapes. The reason was simple; if anybody escaped, his whole group or most of it was shot. The groups consisted of seventy to ninety people. We were loading coals. Reveille was at 4:30 A.M. . . . The work was beyond human endurance. Any failure to complete it was met with the severest punishments, usually the killing of an individual or a group. Those returning from work were searched. If anything was found on them, especially food, which we sometimes managed to get outside, the punishment was from twenty-five to one hundred whiplashes on the naked body. . . . I once received twenty-five strokes and a certain part of my body was crushed completely. For weeks I could not walk but had to go to work all the same. . . . We were living in huts. There were wooden bunks in three stories there. No bedding; each had a blanket to spread on the planks. There were 250-300 people in a hut. . . .

"There were duties within the camp that were performed by women only. Their work consisted of carrying stones from the quarry below. . . . At the end of the trains, there were long ropes to which Jewish and Polish women were harnessed at both ends. These they pulled up the steep road from the quarry, for a distance of two and a half kilometers, under all weather conditions, for twelve hours a day. The women, like all of us, wore wooden clogs which would stick in the snow and the mud. And so one could see a picture—which I cannot describe, and I do not know if others could describe it either—of women walking, staggering and pulling, all day long."

Yitzhak Zuckerman, later the deputy commander of the Warsaw ghetto revolt, described the labor camp of Kampinos near Warsaw: "We were taken before dawn, a few hundred Jews, a weak group. Men who had not had anything to eat for a long time. When we arrived we had to work on diverting rivers and draining swamps. So we used to work for ten to twelve hours, standing in the water almost up to our necks. Then we were taken back to sleep in the same clothes. It was cold. Extremely cold. The following morning again, scanty food, a beverage they called coffee and 120 or 150 grams of bread. I need hardly add that after two years in the Warsaw ghetto, these Jews who were brought to work filled the Kampinos cemetery within the first few weeks."

Sometimes the terror was almost unbelievable. The Jewish child was a special object of venom. Noah Zabludowicz said: "Once I saw an SS officer in Ciechanów politely asking a Jewish mother in the street to let him try to appease her crying baby. With incredulity in her eyes and with trembling hands the woman delivered the infant, whereupon the Nazi smashed the baby's small head on the sharp edge of the curbstone. The mother did not even have time to cry out. At that moment I thought God had hidden his face from the human race."

Sometimes, but not often, there was an unexpected ending to all brutality. Dr. Jacob Buzminsky, now a Tel Aviv doctor, testified that once he saw an SS man whipping a Jewish boy, giving him eighty lashes. Usually fifty were enough to kill a child, but the boy was still alive. The SS man then told him that if he was able to run, he would spare his life. The youngster got up and ran away.

"Do you see this boy now in the courtroom?" I asked the witness. "Yes," he replied. Everybody craned his neck toward the entrance to the gallery expecting the boy to appear, but the witness pointed to the man sitting next to me at the prosecution desk—Chief Inspector Michael Goldmann, of the Israel Police. After his escape from his tormentor, Goldmann had later been sent to Auschwitz, survived the war and joined the police; his assistance in collecting evidence was important.

Dr. Bużminsky also had other stories to tell, some of them among the most terrible to be heard at the trial. On one occasion he remembered seeing an SS officer accost a woman who had come too near a fence separating the ghetto from the non-Jewish part of the town. She was carrying an emaciated infant about a year old, and when the SS officer drew his pistol to shoot her, the woman fell on her knees and pleaded with him to spare the child. "Shoot only me!" she begged. The officer snatched the infant away, shot the woman twice, and then, putting the child's leg under his boot, tore the baby in two, like a rag. The bleeding mother crawled to her baby and, as her blood mingled with the child's, she died.

The Jews, immured in the ghettos, felt they were abandoned by the whole world. They faced a catastrophe for which they were even less prepared than the nations of the world had been prepared for the Nazi military onslaught. The instinctive defenses of the wandering Jew, which traditionally had alerted him to approaching storms, had been deadened by a century and a half of emancipation. He was now drawing on the historic experiences of his forefathers in a frenzied fight for survival.

*

There were other camps in which the Nazis employed more direct methods to push Jews over the brink than just exposing them to disease and starvation. For several years trains would make their way across Europe from north, east, west and south, to converge on a few small stations in Poland. A cryptic directive from Eichmann's office, setting out the destination of a transport as *"Richtung Cholm"* ("Direction Cholm") or *"Izbica,"* would automatically settle the destinies of two or three thousand human beings. They would be carried, packed like sardines, all the way from the starting point to a relay station near Lublin, and from there sent on to one of the neighboring camps under the jurisdiction of Odilo Globocnik, the SS and Police Commandant of the area, or to Majdanek, which came under the Economic Office of the SS.

Before the war this was a quiet, rural neighborhood with no particular claim to fame or notoriety. The town of Lublin, some centuries ago an important road juncture, had been outdistanced by more prosperous centers.

Traces of its once historic role in both Polish and Jewish history were to be seen in a picturesque sixteenth-century cathedral, an archbishop's palace and a large elongated building, which had once been a famous center of Talmudic studies and Jewish self-government. Otherwise the town led a peaceful, provincial existence and the villages around were typical of the East European pastoral countryside.

For almost three years this area was transformed into one of Europe's busiest transportation centers, with trains following each other in close succession, arriving day and night at small stations now jolted out of their customary slumber. German, Dutch, French, Belgian, Italian, Yugoslav and even Greek engines and cars, never seen there before, came in a never-ending flow, in addition to an endless chain of local trains. On arrival the trains were full to bursting point of men, women and children. For the engine drivers this was the end of the road. After discharging their cargo they would go no further and reverse the trains.

This was the end of the road for the passengers too; they did not take the return journey; nor did any others fill their places. The return cargo consisted only of the clothing, shoes and underwear of those who had arrived there a short time before. For at Sobibór, Bełżec and Treblinka, where the trains unloaded, people were instantly exterminated, like candles snuffed out by a wind, and their clothing and baggage were shipped back. Occasionally there was a suitcase or two as well, secured with wax seals, for they contained the gold teeth and wedding rings of the arrivals, now to be deposited in the gold department of the Reichsbank. Sometimes, too, a few corded bales would be placed in the otherwise empty wagons. These contained women's hair, for which the frugal Reich authorities still had a use as filling material for mattresses and other purposes.

The killing procedure was merely the last phase of a process, and was as standardized as all the other Final Solution measures. It operated, almost uniformly, in the same manner in all the camps, with the usual German efficiency, accuracy and thrift. The normal mechanism of terror tempered with deception was applied to the end. This saved manpower and enabled relatively small crews to service large transports.

The arriving wagons would be opened by German or Ukrainian SS guards with deafening shouts of "All out! Quick, quick!" Dazed and half-insensible with the suffocation they had endured on their appalling journey, the people would be pushed out, driven on with whiplashes. While the bewildered arrivals were trying to find out what was going on, a uniformed SS officer would address them over loudspeakers, repeating the same speech to every new contingent. He told them that they would all now proceed to work on land, and it would be good for the Jews to feel for once they were doing something productive. Men would have to work while the women would keep house, or go out to work as well—at their own choice—while the children would go to school. Now everybody must proceed for disinfection and a shower. Time was short, so everyone should arrange his effects neatly and deposit them properly, so as to get them back on his return. Valuables and money must be handed in separately.

While the SS man was talking, the camp orchestra would play a gay march or tango, the music mingling with the soothing tones of the man in authority.

The thousands on the platform were utterly perplexed. All around them they could see multilingual notices: "To eastbound trains," "Proceed to the platform" "To the bathroom" "To disinfection installations," "To cash deposit." The railway station looked like any other rural terminal, with high lanterns, a large clock and well-attended flowerpots of colorful geraniums in bloom. Everything looked perfectly peaceful and normal, except for an inexplicable stench of charred flesh and a heavy overhanging smoke. But before they had a chance to collect their wits, the SS guard would again go into action, as soon as the officer's brief address was over. Whiplashes were again heard all around, as the guards forced the multitude into a quick run along the barbed-wire fences, adorned all the way with arrows pointing "To the baths."

Once inside the compound, men were ordered to one side and women to the other, while old people and invalids were ordered to proceed along a road marked with a Red Cross sign and the inscription: *"Lazarett"* ("Military Hospital"). Inside the compound everyone was ordered to undress and deposit his belongings. Women were directed to "barbers," who, with rapid cuts, sheared off their hair into potato sacks. A smiling SS man would be standing there, telling them in an ingratiating voice: "No harm will befall you. All you have to do is to breathe in deeply. This strengthens the lungs. Inhaling is a necessary means of disinfection." The rest of the process was described by Dr. Kurt Gerstein, who saw it all at Bełżec:

"For a number of men there still flickers a lingering hope, sufficient to make them march without resistance to the death chambers. The majority know with certainty what is to be their fate. The horrible, all-pervading stench reveals the truth. Then they climb some small steps and behold the reality. Silent mothers hold their babies to their breasts, naked; there are many children of all ages. They hesitate, but nevertheless proceed toward the death chambers, most of them without a word, pushed by those behind, chased by the whips of the SS men. A woman of about forty curses the chief of the murderers, crying that the blood of her children will be on his head. Wirth, an SS officer, himself strikes her across the face with five lashes of the whip and she disappears into the gas chamber. Many pray. . . . The SS men squeeze people into the chambers. 'Fill them up well,' orders Wirth. The naked people stand on each other's feet. About seven to eight hundred people in an area of about a hundred square yards. The doors close, the rest of the transport stands waiting, naked. . . . In the winter, too, they stand waiting, naked. But the Diesel engine is not functioning . . . fifty minutes pass by; seventy minutes, The people in the death chambers remain standing. Their weeping is heard. SS Sturmbannfuehrer Professor Dr. Pfannenstiel, lecturer in hygiene at Marburg University, remarks: 'Just like in a synagogue.' . . . Only after two hours and forty-nine minutes does the Diesel finally begin to work. Twenty-five minutes pass by. Many have already died, as can be seen through the small window. Twenty-eight minutes later a few are still alive. After thirty-two minutes all are dead. . . . Jewish workers open the doors on the other side. . . . The dead, having nowhere to fall, stand like pillars of basalt. Even in death, families may be seen standing pressed together, clutching hands. It is only with difficulty that the bodies are separated in order to clear the place for the next load. The blue corpses, covered with sweat and urine . . . babies and bodies of children, are thrown out. But there is no time! A couple of workers are busy with the mouths of the dead, opening them with iron pegs; 'With gold to the left—without gold to the right,' is the order. Others search in the private parts of the bodies for gold and diamonds. . . . Wirth points to a full preserves tin and exclaims, 'Lift it up, and see how much gold there is.' "

The invalids and the aged, removed to the *"Lazarett,"* have been shot in the meantime before the open pits. It was considered more efficient not to let them hamper the smooth flow of people into the gas chambers.

High-ranking SS officers, including Himmler himself, would come on inspection visits from time to time, reaching the compound through the entrance reserved for SS personnel which bore the inscription: "Entrance to the Jewish State." From there they could see the doors of the gas chamber, covered with synagogue curtains and bearing the Hebrew inscription: "This is the gate of the Lord into which the righteous shall enter."

The same procedure was followed in the Chelmno (Kulm) camp, reserved for the Warthe Province Jews, mainly from Litzmannstadt—only there the "disinfection installations" were mobile, and SS men would hand out towels and cakes of soap for use in the "showers," which were installed on vans. As soon as enough people were packed inside, the doors would be locked and exhaust gases be pumped into the hermetically closed compartment. The van would move off in the direction of the nearby forest, where the dead bodies were thrown out.

*

Once in a while a rebellious transport would arrive in the death camps. "There were hundreds, maybe more, SS guards who convoyed the train. The cars were broken. The people inside were half dead. An awful sight. Dead, alive, wounded, all mingled together. . . . They resisted. They did not move. . . . The Germans were shooting all the time. . . . Some of the people fell. The others were driven into the compound. SS Officer Miete shouted in a horrible voice 'Quiet!' He deafened the others somewhat. He said: 'I know well you want to die, but nothing will help you. You will have to go on living and working. Move on!' Somehow his trick succeeded. Some people started moving. . . . The Germans shot, on the way, more people than were killed inside in the gas chambers," testified a survivor.

Kalman Teigman recalled a train that arrived from Grodno. "The people did not undress, not even when they were beaten. The Ukrainians and the SS men shot into them. Still they did not undress. Suddenly one of the prisoners threw a hand grenade and a severely wounded Ukrainian was carried out. At last the Germans broke their resistance and drove the people into the barbed-wire passage. Most of them were pushed into the gas chambers in their clothing."

Occasionally one of the SS crew would approach an incoming contingent, point a finger at several young, healthy-looking arrivals, and order them to step out. Sometimes the Germans would screen a contingent for carpenters, locksmiths, tailors, shoemakers or other artisans. These were employed to do the work inside the camp and keep the place clean, to sort out the victims' belongings, carry the bodies to the crematorium, or bury them where there was no cremation. Some of them were "barbers," shearing off women's hair; others were "dentists," pulling out gold teeth from the corpses' mouths. They were the "service crews" of the camps, poor wretches whose life was one long stretch of hell. Now and then they were fettered when working outside. Most of them attempted suicide the first night after the horrors they saw on arrival. Many succeeded.

"They made me a dentist," testified Abraham Lindwasser. "I could not stand it, so I tried to hang myself. I was already swinging on my belt when a bearded Jew—I don't know his name—took me down and reproached me. Though the job was dreadful, he said, I must take hold of myself and to see to it that someone at least should survive it all, to describe later what was going on here. Physically the work was not heavy, he added, I should be able to stand it and help others."

These people, of whom there were several hundred in each camp, soon became objects of "sport" for the SS personnel in their spare time. They would be ordered to put mice inside their pants, which were tightly bound below, and stand motionless at attention, with the rodents crawling on their bodies. The slightest movement was met with a whiplash. The SS men would shoot at bottles placed on prisoners' heads. They would order them to walk on a plank under the roof of the hut, at a height of seven meters. Anyone who fell was "an enemy parachutist" and would get twenty-five lashes, or a savage dog would be set on him.

They kept dogs specially trained to assault human beings. A popular name for these ferocious beasts in the camps was "Bary." At the order: "Jew" or "Bary, man, attack dog!" the animal, huge as a calf, would assault its victim, literally tearing him to pieces. "People felt helpless before the dog. They would surrender to the beast," said a survivor.

Sometimes a prisoner would have to work on the dead body of a person he recognized. "I was 'a dentist' in Treblinka, till one day I recognized the body of my sister. . . . I could not touch her; I could not go on. . . . I asked the Kapo in charge, a Jew, to transfer me to teeth-cleaning, which he did. . . . Every week we sent out from Treblinka two suitcases with eight to ten kilograms of gold."

Michael Podchlevnik had a similar "encounter" at Kulm. "I was in the group that was in charge of burials. After several days I recognized among the bodies my wife and two children. I lay down beside them and asked to be shot. An SS man struck me twice and pushed me on, saying: 'You are still strong, you can work.' . . . That night I tried to hang myself, but my friends took me down. . . . Three days later I escaped jumping from the truck on which we were being taken from work."

This was one of the very few successful individual escapes from these camps.

The victims used to help and encourage each other. "With every new transport we wept. . . . At first we thought the world had come to an end, when we saw the transports arriving daily with people from all over the world. They came from France and Holland, dressed up as for a visit. . . . It went on day after day. Later, somehow—it's difficult to explain—somehow we got used to it. . . . We started thinking of escape or revolt. This gave us hope. . . . The people from the transports would shout: 'Avenge us! . . Save yourselves!' Every one of us had gone through so much already that if he had stayed alive so far he hoped he might perhaps live through it."

*

Auschwitz-Birkenau was the peak of all horror. Initially designated as the place of destruction of European Jewry, it soon spread out over a "sphere of interests" (*Interessengebiet*) that covered over fifteen square miles of territory between the rivers Vistula and Sola. Eight villages and a town were evacuated to accommodate a colossal industrial complex, comprising Krupp's Union armament plants, I.G. Farbenindustrie's Buna synthetic petrol and rubber works, chemical and metal factories, gas works and railway repair shops, besides quarries and hydraulic, agricultural and timber enterprises. It serviced, apart from the "mother encampment," thirty-nine ramifications, scattered all over Silesia.

But its main output was death. Three and a half million people were liquidated there in the three years of its activity.

On arrival at Auschwitz, a prisoner would have a number tattooed on his arm if he was to be left alive for a while to work. His number became the name under which he would henceforth be known. The uniformed Germans were his omnipotent gods. The Kapos and "*Blockaelteste*," whom the SS appointed from among the prisoners were powerful authorities. An inmate was a speck of dust, which existed only so long as one of these superior beings did not care to brush it off. His total insignificance was made clear from the moment of his arrival. "Here you are allowed to do only what you are told to do. Whatever you are not ordered to do is strictly forbidden and severely punishable," they were told. They would be drilled for hours on end to take their caps off before every SS man, whom they were allowed to pass only in military tempo, bareheaded, and not closer than six paces with arms stiff and held tightly to the body.

Then they made the immediate acquaintance of the punishment system, and were given a garment, which soon became stinking and vermin-covered, and wooden clogs. The cap was all-important: it served both for saluting and for dishing out food, and its color, in addition to other signs, disclosed the prisoner's standing in the hierarchy. So did the whip carried by everyone in authority. It was soon apparent to the new arrival that in order to be "somebody" on this planet it was necessary to be sadistically cruel. Thus a man could rise to be a "*Stubenaelteste,*" responsible for a room, and get an extra dish of soup. He could go further and become the "*Blockschreiber,*" the clerk responsible for counting the prisoners, or even the "*Blockaelteste,*" responsible for the whole block. A "*Lageraelteste*" was the head prisoner. At work some prisoners were "Kapos," the labor foremen, who had complete power of life and death over every inmate. These were often recruited from among habitual criminals.

But these rules concerned only those who had passed the first selection screening at the railway siding on arrival and were considered fit for work. All others were sent straight to one of the four crematoria, which together comprised forty-six ovens and could handle over five hundred bodies per hour. These people were not accounted for in the camp's registration office. Only a prisoner who was to live for a while and got his tattooed number was "recognized" in the record of arrivals. When he was later sent to be gassed, his card would be removed and stamped with the letters "S.B."—"*Sonderbehandlung*" ("Special Treatment"). If he was shot, hanged or whipped to death, or if he died of hunger, the record stated that he had succumbed to pneumonia, heart failure or dysentery. According to the register no one in the camp had ever come to an unnatural end there.

But even these records once led to embarrassment because of bureaucratic efficiency. The Bureaus of Vital Statistics in Germany used to exchange data. One day a letter came from the Oldenburg bureau suggesting that there must be some mistake in the data of the Auschwitz bureau, which showed so many deaths for such a small place. Ten days later the Thueringen bureau wrote that the Auschwitz registration office in its inexperience must have ascribed to one year all the deaths that had occurred there since 1870, when the bureaus were first established in Germany, as otherwise the large numbers were inexplicable. This, it was pointed out, was not the correct procedure. The Auschwitz office chief was alarmed, but he found a solution for the problem. He simply adopted a code for registrations by which every 180 deaths were recorded as one in the statistical forms that were sent out.

Much has been written by survivors about what came to pass in this Gehenna; perhaps the most vivid description was given by the author Yehiel Dinur, who writes under the nom de plume of K. Zetnik (the slang name for a concentration camp prisoner). "Why do you use this pseudonym?" I asked the man, who had just revealed his true name to the public for the first time. "It is no pen name," he replied. "I do not regard myself as a writer of literature. My writings are the chronicles of the planet Auschwitz. I was there for about two years. Time does not run there as it does here on earth. Every fraction of a second there passes on a different scale of time. The inhabitants of this planet had no names; they had no parents; they were not born there and they did not beget children. They breathed according to different laws of nature. They did not live nor did they die according to the laws of this world. Their name was 'Number . . . Katzetnik.' "

"Was this their clothing?" I asked him, producing his own prisoner's garb, which he now puts on whenever he starts writing a new chapter in the annals of that planet, in an agony of seclusion and hunger.

"Yes," he replied. "This is the garb of the planet called Auschwitz. And I believe with all my heart that I should continue to bear this name K. Zetnik, so long as the world has not been roused, after this crucifixion of a nation, to wipe out this evil, as it was once roused after the crucifixion of one person. I believe with all my heart that just as in astrology the stars influence our destiny, so does this planet of ashes, Auschwitz, stand in opposition to our planet earth, and influences it."

He managed to say a few more sentences. He believed that he, who had "dropped from that planet," was alive only thanks to the oath he had sworn to his comrades there, which had endowed him with supernatural powers of survival. "They always went away from me, they left me, and in the look in their eyes was this injunction. . . . For almost two years they went from me, always leaving me behind. I can see them, they are gazing at me, I see them . . ." That was as far as he got. He rose, wavered back and forth on the witness stand, and collapsed on the floor. He was carried to hospital, where it took him several days to recover from the shock. I did not dare to put him on the stand again.

*

Auschwitz was under strict instructions to differentiate between the "*Transportjuden*" ("Transport Jews"), destined for immediate or early destruction, and *Schutzhaeftlinge* ("detained prisoners"), Jews or others, who had been sent to a concentration camp for criminal offenses, such as using a public telephone or being caught outside during curfew hours. These prisoners had to serve their sentence in the camp, and consequently they were not subject to the "right-left" finger-movement selections. In effect, "the criminals" were better off than the innocent, for they were not supposed to be gassed till they had served their full sentence.

"The selections were the weekly terror," recalled Esther Goldstein. "All women had to parade naked before Dr. Mengele. Everyone straightened her back and pinched her cheeks to appear fresh and strong. Those who looked weak were sent at once to the crematoria."

"We were two thousand boys assembled on Yom Kippur—the Day of Atonement—on the central football grounds of the SS," testified Joseph Kleinman, who was a boy of fourteen at the time. "Suddenly a visible spasm passed through us all, as if we had been struck by an electric shock. It was Dr. Mengele, 'the angel of death,' who had appeared on his bicycle. . . . Mengele got up onto a platform . . . scanned the field, and pointed to a very lean and sunburnt boy of about fourteen who was standing in the first row. 'How old are you?' he asked. The boy answered shiveringly that he was eighteen. "I will show you," Mengele shouted. He called for a hammer, nails and a piece of wood, and pointed to a place on the goal-post at the height of one of the taller boys, where he wanted the plank to be fixed. 'Pass beneath it!' he shouted. . . . We saw immediately that the short boys were being ordered to one side, and we knew that this meant death. . . . I was in despair, because even taller boys than I had not managed to touch the protruding plank with their heads. 'Do something,' whispered my brother, who was standing next to me. . . . I saw a few stones nearby and put them into my shoes. I gained an additional inch, but could not stand on them, and I was about to take the stones out. My brother stopped me. . . . We tore up his cap and I pushed the pieces in between the stones. . . . Then the small boys who had not passed mingled with the others. 'This is sabotage!' shouted Mengele, and started the whole thing all over again. Finally I infiltrated between the tall boys. . . . About a thousand were supposed to have reached the required height. . . . The others were kept for two days in closed huts and then sent off to be gassed."

The date had been deliberately chosen, for on the Day of Atonement Jews recite a famous prayer describing the Lord, the shepherd, who passes his flock under his rod to decide who will live and who will die. "It was obvious that Mengele wanted to show us that it was he and no one else who passed us under the rod," said Kleinman.

Jewish holidays were generally favorite days for Nazi outrages, because of the added flavor of hitting at the Jew on his day of festivity. This was a well-known extra touch of brutality throughout Nazi rule. In Auschwitz they called it "the Goebbels calendar," which meant that Jewish Sabbaths and days of rest were marked on the Nazi schedule for emptying entire blocks, clearing infirmaries and sending their inmates together with the "Muselmans," to the crematoria.

A "Muselman" was a patented product, "made in Germany." This was a skeleton on bloated legs, still moving but liable to collapse any moment. Even when sitting still he would rock slightly, for his sense of balance was gone. From a distance he somewhat resembled a praying Moslem; hence the nickname. "This was the last stage of a prisoner's undernourishment," testified Dr. Aharon Beilin, a doctor in Auschwitz. "The first symptoms were psychological. He started to talk about food. There were two taboo subjects in Auschwitz: the crematoria and food. . . . Very quickly he would pass to the next stage, he would lose interest in his environment, would stop reacting to orders, not be able to control his orifices, and discharge his bowels where he stood. . . . Soon the 'Corpses' Unit' (*Leichenkommando*) would collect him together with the cadavers."

Life in Auschwitz was a rapid disintegration of mind and body. People were placed in conditions under which they were bound to become dehumanized. Civilized habits and human values were sucked out; the vacuum was filled with the two basic reactions of hunger and fear. People ceased to be disgusted by anybody or horrified at anything; their whole existence was a chain of prolonged horrors. They were reduced to animal responses. First and foremost they were constantly looking for food. Everyone was famished. "A wolfhound belonging to the SS Blockfuehrer was leashed behind our block," testified Gedalya Ben-Zvi. "There was always plenty of food in his dish, much more and better food than we got. My brother-in-law evolved a system of stealing the food: while he teased the beast with a stick, I would snatch the dish away. But later the dog learned the trick and did not move when teased."

A well-known psychiatrist, himself a prisoner, wrote:

> I spent some time in a hut for typhus patients, who ran very high temperatures and were often delirious, many of them moribund. After one of them had just died, I watched without any emotional upset the scene that followed, which was repeated over and over again, with each death. One by one the prisoners approached the still warm body. One grabbed the remains of a messy meal of potatoes; another decided that the corpse's wooden shoes were an improvement on his own, and exchanged them. A third man did the same with the dead man's coat, and another was glad to be able to secure some—just imagine!—genuine string. All this I watched with unconcern.

The struggle for existence was carried on to the last. The outcome sometimes depended on a pure accident. Nahum Hoch was sixteen at the time and, being tall, he had passed the "rod selection" of Yom Kippur, 1944. Several days later, on the festival of the Rejoicing of the Law, he was assembled with about a thousand other children in Blocks 11 and 13. "We were told to march in fives. . . . When we saw we were heading for the crematorium we refused to go. They shot at our legs and so drove us forward. . . . There were SS men with machine guns. We were brought to crematorium 3. . . . We halted at the door, but they again shot at our legs and forced us to get in. . . . We found ourselves in a large hall like a bathhouse. There were pegs all around the walls, with consecutive numbers. They told us to undress and hang up our clothing; we refused. So they started shooting inside the building. They told us to memorize the peg numbers so as to collect our things on the way out of the bath, but we knew this was all a pretense. We threw our things on the floor. . . . Some of us were already petrified as we stood there. Many like myself were reciting the prayer for the dying. . . . They pushed us into a small corridor and from there to a completely dark room. When we were inside they locked the doors behind us. It was then that I first heard the quiet desperate weeping. After some time—I don't know whether it was seconds or minutes—the door was opened again and we were told to get back to where we had left our clothes. . . . An SS officer looked at us . . . ordered a few to perform some exercises, to run to the wall and back again, and finally picked out fifty of the stronger boys. . . . The other children, seeing this selection, all ran to our side, but the officer forced them back, and placed a chain of SS men between us, the chosen group, and the others. . . . He ordered the others inside again and told us to pick up any clothes we wanted and get dressed. . . . We were taken outside, to the railway station, to unload potatoes. I never saw any of the nine hundred boys again."

Nahum Hoch and his group of fifty had been taken out of the gas chamber an instant before the fatal pellets were about to dissolve into death fumes, only because of a momentary shortage of manpower for unloading an unannounced transport of potatoes.

The human mechanism of self-preservation reacted to suffering by blunting human emotions. People could work on corpses without being revolted, could cover roads with human ashes (to prevent slipping) without becoming nauseated.

Daytime at the camp was fraught with danger from every SS man and Kapo, who were constantly whipping the ragged, filthy, lice-ridden slave laborers. At night they lay on wooden planks, tightly packed, ten or twelve on a shelf. If anyone wanted to turn over or to get up, he had to disturb eleven other people. Between daylight and nightfall there were the roll calls, twice a day, when masses of people froze into a solid numb block of terrified humanity.

When word came of the approach of Russian troops, the order for a march westward was given in Auschwitz and all its subsidiaries in the neighborhood. On the day of the order, January 7, 1945, the 54,651 prisoners were started on the trek, without food, without transport. People fell out all along the snow-covered roads. The SS dispensed a "mercy bullet" to any weary prisoner. "On some days there were as many as five hundred shootings," testified Dr. Beilin. "We spent the nights in stables or just in the open. . . . These were people who had already gone through everything, and now liberation was close. . . . Once they put us for the night into a very long underground excavation and locked the entrance. . . . We were suffocating but they did not open up to our shouting and knocking. . . . The next day there were a thousand dead among us. . . . An army unit passed by when the door was finally opened up at six in the morning and its commander, a lieutenant, shouted at our guards, pointing to an inscription at the entrance: 'How dare you put people into a place where it says: "Entry forbidden, danger!"?' The guard commander replied: 'Lieutenant, those are only Jews,' to which the officer said: 'In that case it is all right.' The place was a uranium mine."

The human wrecks of Auschwitz were finally deposited in numerous camps inside Germany, where a number lived until liberation day and after. None of them will ever be the same again, for all their rehabilitation and seeming readjustment. "I am afraid of my dreams," "I hate memories," they would often say. "In the camps we were afraid of death; after the liberation we became scared of life," Dr. Hadassa Rosensaft told me.

The huge stores of the prisoners' personal effects and their luggage were taken from Auschwitz into Germany and distributed all over the Reich at the rate of twenty carloads per week. The size of these stores (which they called "Canada") can be judged by the leftovers not entirely consumed by the retreating Germans, who set them on fire. The official statement mentions, among many other items, 348,820 men's suits, 836,255 women's dresses and 38,000 pairs of men's shoes.

This was the SS factory of destruction: a steady flow of human material was provided for it by the Lieutenant Colonel who headed the Jewish Department of the Gestapo.

CHAPTER 11

Under the Heel

Such, then, were the broad outlines of Hitler's monstrous enterprise. In deploying the complex and ramified data illustrating it within the framework of a case in law I had to make every effort to restrain my personal emotions as far as possible and to present the naked facts.

A natural question, which was bound to come to mind, was: Why was there no more open resistance? In other words, how did these millions of victims meet their fate, and why?

The chapter of history in which Eichmann's career took shape was so fantastic, so grotesque, so nightmarish, that in order even to begin to understand it I felt it was necessary to look at the other side of the picture.

How did the Jews and their fellow victims conduct themselves under the heel of the SS state?

*

"You were fifteen thousand prisoners, facing tens, even hundreds, of policemen. Why did you not attack them? Why didn't you revolt?"

Dr. Moshe Beisky was in the witness box when I threw this question at him. Today Dr. Beisky is a magistrate in Tel Aviv, a loved and respected citizen. He had been telling the court what he had gone through as a youngster of nineteen when the war broke out; he had just been describing the horrors of an execution at the Plaszów "labor" camp, near Cracow.

I knew of Judge Beisky's acts of personal courage and exemplary behavior in the resistance movement. He refused a chance to escape from the agony of Plaszów, saying that collective punishment, almost certainly by hanging, would be imposed on his entire block of two hundred people. He was the right man to explain the relative passivity of the prisoners, if it is possible to give any explanation of human behavior in hell. I did not tell Judge Beisky in advance that I was going to ask the question; I wanted to get his spontaneous reaction.

My question struck him like a blow between the eyes. A grimace of pain distorted his intelligent features. The strong, sturdy man, who an hour before had declined the court's offer to allow him to sit while testifying, and had almost dispassionately unfolded hair-raising scenes of horror, now asked for permission to be seated.

I was sorry to have to do this to him. "Why did you not at least warn me beforehand?" he reproached me later. My excuse was the reply he gave to my question. It came unprepared and in parts disorganized; it was delivered in a hushed, sometimes inaudible voice; but it was the most convincing piece of human truth I have ever heard on the subject. In his answer Dr. Beisky brought the trial to a new moral peak.

"It did not start with this. It began with something else," he said. "Jewry already had behind it three years of suppression, but here we were still working. The Germans had told us they needed manpower. We thought: Who knows? Perhaps? . . . It was obvious that if anyone started the slightest open opposition, all these armed guards around us would immediately open fire. . . . I confess that I am unable, after eighteen years, to recreate the feeling of terror. It no longer exists in me, and in any case I don't think it can ever be expressed in words. It is a dreadful thing to stand opposite a machine gun and to watch a boy being hanged. . . . Then there was still the hope that this war was bound to end one day. Should we endanger all fifteen thousand men? . . .

"I can't really transplant to the court all the conditions we were living under, but I will give you perhaps an example to illustrate this inexplicable reality. We had an engineer in our camp, a man called Grinberg. We all loved him dearly. He was in charge of putting up huts in the camp. Since the work could never be done so quickly as demanded, he was constantly maltreated. He would get twenty-five lashes, fifty lashes, or just ordinary blows with the fist. They set dogs on him. I never saw him without open wounds or with his head unbandaged. He pleaded daily to the camp commandant: 'Shoot me,' . . . but he never commited suicide, though it was easy. His wife and daughter were in the camp and he knew what would happen to them if he did. He endured a hundred varieties of hell. He was finally killed; so was his wife. But his daughter survived; she is now living in Jerusalem, I believe. . . ."

Judge Beisky then turned weary eyes on me. "And once we had escaped, where could we go? Next to us was a Polish camp. There were only one thousand prisoners there, but they were also being shot daily and were treated almost as we were. Why did they not escape or revolt? Their houses were round the corner. But still I do not remember any acts of rebellion or escape by the Poles."

Judge Beisky's comparison with the non-Jewish population of Europe is valid and deserves closer attention, for though the Jews were the first and heaviest, they were certainly not the only victims of Nazi rule. As we know now, every Jew was doomed to die during the war, while other nations were doomed "only" to slave labor and decimation to make room for the Germans, or to help establish their reign of terror. But the actual methods of extermination used were similar. In these there was no discrimination. "The Poles did not even leave us enough lamp posts in this blessed area of culture," Hans Frank, the Governor General of Poland, told a gleeful audience of Nazi leaders in Lwów, "to hang two Poles on every lamp post, as they say abroad we are doing."

*

The individual Gentile in occupied Europe was never sure of his life or liberty. He could be taken as a hostage for acts of sabotage and executed for any act of resistance, or he could suddenly vanish under the *Nacht und Nebel* (Night and Fog) decree of December 7, 1941, which provided for the detention and isolation of influential people in the occupied areas, to the despair of their families and friends. This was regarded by the German Army as "an enhanced deterrent measure." The SD was in charge of the operation, and soon filled the concentration camps with hundreds of thousands of Allied nationals.

If an individual was spared this experience, he might easily be one of the seven million forced laborers, rounded up, torn away from their families and shipped to Germany to slave in its factories, mines or fields, under the scheme of Fritz Sauckel, the Minister of Labor. "Exploit them to the maximum and spend on them the lowest conceivable minimum," he told the German employers.

The Poles were the first and among the severest sufferers, stung by the humiliating treatment of the Nazis, who did not accord their country the semblance of an autonomous political status, not even a protectorate. "This land will forever be an annex of the German empire, devoid of any identity of its own," said Frank. The German Minister of Justice declared: "This is our experimental ground for the rule of the world." The Poles, sustained by the national tradition of a fight for freedom over a century and a half, braced themselves for resistance. Forty thousand Polish hostages were taken in 1940; most of them never returned from the camps and forests to which they were deported. From summer 1943 on, acts of sabotage spread, especially in Warsaw. The Germans kidnaped passers-by in the streets, announcing that they would hang ten Poles for every German or German agent attacked. Public executions were a regular daily sight. Ludwik Landau, the observant chronicler of events for the underground Armja Krajowa (Home Army), recorded in his diary on October 19, 1943:

> The blood-red deeds of terror do not stop. Today's news is again of the shooting of eleven persons—I do not know why this "uneven" number. They are allegedly the scapegoats for a German shot yesterday at the Gdańsk railway station. Yesterday they announced the taking of new hostages to complete the number.

Today, to keep the imprint fresh, there were more kidnapings in the center of town. In the afternoon, at about 4:30, when masses of people were rushing home and the trams were full, police cars took up positions near Marszalkowska Street, at cross roads and near Savior's Square. At a certain moment all traffic was stopped and all passers-by were rounded up. Two trams were emptied, people were even dragged from the houses, till all the cars were filled. What will happen to them now? They hold already more hostages than necessary, even with the present intense "turn-over." They are apparently filling up again the emptied Pawiak prison . . . where they are now said to be holding five thousand prisoners. . . .

"People's reactions? Everybody talks of the executions with horror, and describes how the victims were brought in chains, how they were ordered to form two rows, one standing, one kneeling, and publicly mowed with machine gun fire . . . how other victims were told to lie face down on the pavement and shot in the back of the heads. Some people put down candles, sacred pictures and flowers there, and passers-by bared their heads, not heeding the nearby German guards. Beyond such gestures, there is obviously no other manifestation of resistance, *because there can be none. Horror rules.* [My italics.]

Only those who actually carried firearms had some sense of security. A revolver or a hand grenade made people feel equal to the oppressor, and served as a substitute for their lost independence. "He who had no part in the anti-Nazi underground," a veteran fighter wrote, "will never understand what the possession of firearms meant at that time. . . . Mere knowledge that, when necessary, you would be able to use your gun added security and inner strength."

If he had nothing to defend himself with, the individual felt completely helpless; it was a popular saying in the ghettos that "with empty hands you can accomplish nothing."

A Polish officer described his emotions when he watched some of his fellow prisoners of war, "moving like shadows," being led out to execution: "I looked on when they were ordered to the roll call, with a shower of whiplashes and kicks. We, their officers, watched it all, as we had previously watched a Polish boy being tortured or Polish women being slapped on the face. We officers, strong able-bodied men, who had been trained for and entrusted with the defense of our people, we saw it all—and we realized how valueless were our medals, our ribbons and our uniforms, when we no longer had arms."

Hostages were ruthlessly shot by the thousands; public announcements proclaimed their execution, "after trial," until the system worked. Frank informed his government on December 14, 1943, that, "while we had about two hundred Germans killed in June the number went down following the measures we took, and it is now no more than ten, twenty or thirty casualties per month. We shall therefore certainly proceed with our method."

Day after day Landau continued to record the mass shootings of hostages, including women; this "made a stupendous impression; people became so enraged that they could no longer contain themselves, and even said aloud in the streets that there should be some vengeance."

Meanwhile life went on. There were few Christmas shoppers, but queues formed in front of some of the stores.

In the summer of 1944 the Polish underground, encouraged by the appearance of the Soviet Army on the far bank of the Vistula, proclaimed an open revolt in Warsaw. This was crushed, after heavy fighting. The surviving rebels, thousands of them, fell into German hands and were massacred the *Einsatzgruppen* way. "The doomed people had to dig a long ditch. Then they were placed in groups of twenty-five facing this ditch—they had no shirts on them only trousers—and were killed, each with a pistol shot in the neck. After one group was executed another was brought along. No one shouted, asked for mercy or resisted"—was recorded by an eyewitness.

Poles were now forced into trace-effacing units and ordered to burn heaps of bodies all around Warsaw. The prisoners witnessed mass executions of their brave compatriots and the systematic liquidation of their comrades in suffering in the macabre units. Some of them recorded reminiscences. "This is now the end, I thought," recorded a Polish forced laborer in the unit called *Verbrennungs-Kommando Warschau* (Burning Commando, Warsaw) when kneeling and about to be shot. "Suddenly I was swept by a blind and desperate urge: a desire to live at all costs. To survive. I looked bluntly at those kneeling before me. . . . Who will shield whom when the shooting begins, I wondered. Suddenly I heard steps. A few German words fell, short and sharp like whiplashes and then a vile, torturing silence. 'Get up' was heard as from inside a mist."

Large-scale executions of civilians were the order of the day throughout occupied Europe, but most severely in the Eastern and Southern areas. On the slightest provocation the machinery of retaliation went into action. General Boehme ordered his units in Serbia to avenge the blood of the Germans, which flowed here in 1914 through the treachery of the Serbs." He told them that they must strike most severely at the whole population."

They did, and the brave Yugoslavs were led to the execution sites exactly like the Poles and the Jews, or like the officers' corps of two Italian divisions, nearly five hundred officers of the line, shot in September–October, 1943, when they rejected the Germans' ultimatum to disarm after Badoglio's *coup d'état*.

The taking of civilian hostages was described in the Hostage Case at Nuremberg:

The pattern of terror and intimidation was simple. After the Germans had entered a village, all the inhabitants—old men, women, and young children alike—were summoned to the central square or market place. From a sound truck a German officer would announce to the assemblage that there were partisan bands operating in the vicinity. The Germans wanted information concerning the size, location, and leadership of those bands, the number of men missing from the village, and the names of strangers presently living in the village. Unless the inhabitants came forward voluntarily with the desired information, other and more drastic steps would be taken to procure it. When there were no volunteers, priests, school teachers, small shopkeepers, or farmers—sometimes just every third, fifth, or tenth man—were called out of ranks and loaded in lorries for shipment to the division's hostage camp at some distant central collecting point. Whether to save one's husband, father, or son by revealing that a neighbor's brother had joined the bands or was absent from the village was a difficult choice for those who remained. Sometimes men or women weakened. More often they just stood there—some passive, others weeping, all hating.

But it was worse in the Soviet Union.

Under the "Commissars' Order" Communist activities and political "commissars" were executed. Ohlendorf, the Commander of *Einsatzgruppe* D, testified that they were liquidated in the same way as the Jews.

The Germans were being rapidly indoctrinated with the belief that the Russians, too, were *Untermenschen* (subhuman). Hitler himself had proclaimed that "the enemy consists not of soldiers but to a large extent only of beasts." The *Einsatzgruppen* commanders therefore treated almost every literate Russian prisoner of war as a "Communist activist," to be hunted down, identified and shot. Other Soviet prisoners of war—almost five million of them—were exposed to slow death by starvation and disease.

The Germans soon adopted their usual methods for dealing with the problem of "unnecessary people." After inspecting P.O.W. camps the generals would record: "All 20,000 prisoners are doomed to die here . . . a ghastly picture"; or: "Prisoners of war are dying of hunger here a hundred a day"; in the Pskov camp General Kuechler recorded a death rate of a thousand per week.

But "purge" by "natural causes" was not enough. Lieutenant General Hermann Reinecke, in charge of Prisoner-of-War Affairs at Army Headquarters, ruled that "the Bolshevik soldier has lost all claim to be treated as an honorable opponent under the Geneva Convention." So regular shootings of Soviet prisoners of war began. In various camps about three-quarters of the prisoners were liquidated. One man, Wilhelm Schubert, admitted to having taken part, personally, in the execution of thirteen thousand Soviet prisoners of war. The methods were "usual." An eyewitness related: "The prisoners of war were brought in parties. . . . The ditches were prepared and they were told to crawl into them. They despondently complied. About 150 people crept into every ditch. . . . When everybody was in, they were shot with machine guns."

The massacres continued till the end of 1942. Official German records reveal that *close to a million Russian prisoners of war were directly exterminated by shooting*. After a time the captured Soviet General, Andrei Vlasov, was permitted to organize his traitorous units; these either fought at the Germans' side or served them as auxiliaries. Vlasov's "Army of Liberation" reached the staggering figure of 160 battalions consisting of Soviet prisoners of war and deserters. For a greater part of them this must have been a means of escaping the massacres and the awful slow death of the P.O.W. camps, where close to two million Soviet prisoners died of starvation and disease. Of the captured five million Soviet prisoners of war only a little over one million survived the war in this status, almost all of them as slave laborers.

To all these appalling massacres there is no record of opposition that I know of, with one sad and pathetic exception. It reached us from the notes of a German Court of Inquiry, concerning the escape of several wounded Russian prisoners of war near Zhitomir, where SS Captain Killbach was ordered to apply "the special treatment" to forty-eight prisoners. He had assigned only three SS men to the job, but, as he later explained, these were veterans of "the special treatment," since they had acquired much experience in massacres at Kiev and other places; so he thought that with the aid of a Ukrainian driver they would be able to manage forty-eight disabled Russians. There was no difficulty in finishing off those of the victims who were legless, but while SS Staff Sergeant Fritz Knopf was shooting these in a ditch, he heard a commotion behind him; it appeared that the other prisoners had overpowered the two SS men, seized their arms, killed the driver and were now shooting in his direction. The hero was frightened when a bullet hit the ground near him; he testified before the court that, being sure he was hit, he ran away, but still managed to shoot six of the prisoners who were trying to escape.

Dr. Eugene Alexandrovich Kivelisha, a physician and a Soviet prisoner of war, described before the International Military Tribunal how he had marched in a column of five thousand prisoners, on their way to a P.O.W. camp:

"One of the prisoners stepped five or six meters out of the column, and without warning was killed by a German soldier shooting with a tommy gun. Several of his comrades rushed up to help him . . . but they too were immediately fired on without warning. Some of them were wounded and two were killed. . . . Almost any transfer from one camp to another was accompanied by the same kind of shootings and murders. . . . Once, during one of our transfers, a group of women and children attempted to give us bread and water . . . but the Germans would not allow them to come anywhere near us. Then one woman sent a little girl, about five years old, evidently her daughter, to the prisoners' column. This little child came quite close to the place where I had passed, and when she was five or six steps away from the column she was killed by a German soldier."

Dr. Kivelisha also gave a brief description of the treatment inside the camp on a normal day:

"The German guards, all armed with clubs as well as rifles and automatic guns, beat up all the prisoners of war within range of their blows for the purpose of maintaining order. The Germans would often intentionally set down a small barrel of soup among a great number of hungry men and once again, to restore order, they would beat up the innocent people with laughter, oaths, insults, and threats."

The Soviet prisoners of war were not the only Allied soldiers treated in this way. Countless acts of savagery were perpetrated against British, American and Canadian fliers, who baled out and were shot "while attempting to escape." Commando fighters were exterminated under Hitler's "Commando Decree" of October 18, 1942. Others were simply shot if "there was no possibility of escorting them," or when it suited the local commander. There were notorious massacres, including the shooting of the British Norfolk battalion near the hamlet of Paradis, opposite the Channel ports, in May, 1940; the execution of Norwegian sailors in July, 1943; the 129 American soldiers murdered near Saint-Vith over a year later; and the execution of paratroopers from the special Air Service Regiment in September, 1944. "All the prisoners were taken to a selected spot in the surrounding country, made to dig their own graves, and then shot."

Not one of them turned on an SS man to strike the executioner with his spade a moment before the inevitable shooting started. They were all paralyzed with terror.

The men who were thus led to death in both East and West were the flower of Allied youth, brave fighters, in the prime of their lives, all trained for battle. Many of them held high war distinctions. Yet they all behaved exactly like Engineer Grinberg in Plaszów and millions of his fellow Jews, though the prisoners of war had no "collective responsibility" hanging over their heads, nor would the members of their families pay instantly with their lives for any act of disobedience on their part.

Yet it did not even occur to anyone to suggest that the prisoners of war died like cowards and went "like sheep to the slaughter." Nor did anybody speculate on the "innate desire for death" that "must" have animated the Jews and led them subconsciously to cooperate in their own destruction as a psychoanalyst has "discovered in the case of the Jews." The comrades-in-arms of the massacred prisoners of war, people of the same stock, upbringing and mentality, ultimately pushed back the Germans, utterly defeated them, and crushed the mightiest war machine ever known.

It may be noted that the Germans themselves made docile and disciplined prisoners of war. When they fell into the hands of Russian partisan fighters, they usually had only one request: not to be delivered to the avenging Jewish partisan units. Otherwise they made no trouble. If they happened to fall into the hands of the Jewish fighters, they readily disavowed the "accursed" Hitler, who "alone was responsible for all the world's misfortunes." They often claimed to be of Jewish ancestry.

*

How did the Jews themselves react? Variously, to be sure, though of course there was not room for a great variety of reaction.

Until the German attack on Russia, Jewish pro-Communist elements in the ghettos followed the official Soviet line; they kept propagandizing for complete cooperation with the German occupation forces. In Russia itself the first wave of executions in the wake of the Nazi advance caught the Jews entirely by surprise. They were stunned with horror. During the two years of the Soviet-German *rapprochement* the population in Russia was getting from its press and radio only the most favorable comments on the Nazi ally. A German intelligence officer in White Russia reported in great surprise that "the Jews here are remarkably ill-informed about our attitude toward them. They do not know how Jews are treated in Germany or for that matter in Warsaw, which after all is not so far away. They even ask questions whether we in Germany make any distinction between Jews and other citizens. . . . They believe we shall leave them in peace if they mind their own business and work diligently."

After a while acts of Jewish resistance were encountered. Stahlecker reported he met with some in Kaunas. In Zagare a group of Jews in revolt broke out from the ghetto. "The greater part of them was found by a big search party and was shot," said the Nazi report.

> At the execution of all Zagare Jews that followed, some of them, while marching to the site, assaulted, at an agreed on sign, the *Einsatzkommando* men. Those who were not properly searched before by the Lithuanian guards, drew hidden pistols and knives shouting: "Long live Stalin" and "Down with Hitler," wounding seven of the police crew. The resistance was broken instantly. 150 were shot on the spot and the others were transported to the execution site without further incident.

There were many individual acts of bravery, like that of Zadok Slapoberskis of Kedainiai, who bit into the throat of an SS man, causing him to bleed to death, or of Abraham Weintraub of Mielnica who, after being shot, literally sprang from the grave and, with a last powerful effort, hit the SS officer and broke his teeth. In other cases Jews would at least spit into a German's face or slap him, or shout a last defiant cry: "Our blood will be avenged!" "You are too cowardly to look us in the face and shoot us from behind," shouted girls near Skawina. "You are heroes to kill defenseless people! What heroes will you be when you lose the war!" was the last voice that resounded in the woods of Biala Podlaska, before execution volleys were fired. "Your end is near!" shouted the naked Jews in Skalat on the brink of an open pit.

The doomed people spoke to and encouraged each other. Jews in Dombrowa exchanged wishes that their death might be accepted as a forgiveness for the house of Israel and as a sign of a nearing national redemption. They fell into an ecstasy, joined hands and went into a dance. The Germans were dumfounded for a while and then started shooting wildly. They were so infuriated that they slashed the bodies of the shot people with bayonets.

A rabbi or a spiritual leader would often address the community. Some of the speeches were recorded by survivors: "We are suffering the worst fate of all Jewish generations," said Rabbi Nachum of Kowel. "In a few minutes we will fall into this open grave, and nobody will even know where we were buried nor recite a prayer for us. And we so much yearn to live. . . . In this moment let us unite in the supreme wish to sacrifice to the glory of God even our desire to have somebody to pray for us. Let us face the Germans with joy for sanctifying the Lord's name." Then Joseph Avrech, a teacher, spoke: "We erected here an edifice of culture and learning that is now being destroyed. My heart breaks when I see this magnificent youth, so full of beauty, wisdom and belief, being brought to slaughter." Turning now to the Germans he said: "The Jews are eternal. Our people will see your defeat which is near. What a pity that we here won't be able to see it." A shot from the pistol of Manthei, the local Police commander, silenced the rest of the speech.

Rabbi Daniel Mowsowic of Kelmé quietly and unhurriedly reminded his community of the acts of martyrdom suffered by Jews throughout their history. "Let us sanctify the name of the Lord and sing: '*Ashreinu ma tov helkenu,*' ['We are happy with our lot']." When the Jews were singing with elation, he turned to the *Einsatzgruppe* commander saying: "I have finished, you can begin now."

The executioners themselves were often astonished by the dignified way Jews met their deaths. SS Colonel Blobel of *Einsatzgruppe* C, who was later in charge of another macabre Nazi activity, found a "psychological" explanation. "The Jews apparently do not appreciate human life," he said at his trial. "That is the only reason why they could march to death so quietly. Our men on the spot were more tense than the victims."

In the areas threatened by the advancing Germans, Jews who had now heard what was going on in the occupied zones started a hurried escape. They were often tracked down by the Wehrmacht or the local collaborator units and destroyed. The *Einsatzgruppen* were now reporting that Jews were escaping deeper into Russia, once they had been "warned by the excesses."

Jewish resistance stiffened; sporadic revolts took place. The first was in the small town of Nieśwież, south of Wilno. On July 18, 1942, when the ghetto was about to be liquidated, the youth, who had been preparing for some time, struck with all they had: mainly locally produced sulphuric acid, which they threw in the Germans' faces. They also had one machine gun, stolen in small parts, a piece at a time, by girls working in the arms-cleaning depot of the local police. They set the ghetto on fire and attacked. The fighting lasted till late into the night. All of them fell, except a few who escaped to the neighboring villages. The same happened in Kleck, almost at the same time, under the leadership of Moses Fisz.

Then followed Lachwa in Eastern Poland, under the command of Yitzhak Rochczyn. For some time he had been preparing the youth of the village for an open fight. "Ours is no life anyway," he used to say. "Better die fighting." Their efforts to get firearms failed, so they went into action on September 3, 1942, with axes, hammers and poles. Rochczyn was the first to charge an SS man with an ax and split his head open. A policeman's bullet hit him, killing him on the spot, but the other boys charged, killed some Germans and Ukrainians, grabbed their guns and opened fire. The stunned *Einsatz* recoiled; in the commotion some four hundred Jews escaped into the marshes. The Germans rallied and opened up a deadly fire in all directions. The strains of the national anthem "*Hatikva*" rose over the salvos.

The Jews of Tuczyń, a town in Volhynia, were told by the vice-president of the Jewish Council, Mayer Gimenfeld, that they should set fire to their houses "so as not to let the Nazis inherit us." "Anyone who has no petrol should come to me, and I'll give him a bottle," he said. When evening came the whole ghetto was in flames. The Germans started shooting, covering the ground with hundreds of bodies, but under cover of night many escaped into the non-Jewish areas. Next morning they were discovered by the local population; many were robbed by the peasants and either killed with axes or delivered to the Gestapo for the promised reward.

In Minsk-Mazowiecki resistance came from the artisans, headed by Henoch Gortenkranc, a tailor, and Menashe Grinberg, a house painter. They had some arms, acquired with money supplied by the Jewish Council, but Gortenkranc preferred to charge a policeman with his tailor's scissors. The Jews barricaded themselves in a school and fought to the finish. There were further fights in Krzemieniec, Lida, Miory, Slonim, Nowogródek, Luck, Braslaw, Glebokie, Zdolbunów, Adamów, Kobryń and numerous other places.

All these were the forerunners of a more coordinated resistance movement, which later spread all through Poland.

Reading the reports of these spontaneous, uncoordinated and widely spread acts of heroism one felt deeply ashamed of the harsh criticism leveled by the youth of Israel at the victims. By no means did they "go like sheep to the slaughter." Nor did they lack courage or human dignity.

Whenever resistance was encountered, the *Einsatzgruppen* reported that they were taking "especially sharp and total measures." The crushing of the smallest opposition was immediate and complete. Very few survived the acts of rebellion. In many places the story of the Jewish resistance had been collected from the German reports or from the tales of the non-Jewish population, as no Jew remained alive to put it on record. Many accounts, of course, never reached a recording historian.

It must be recalled that the Nazi policy of camouflage was eminently successful, perhaps because of the somewhat optimistic rationalism characteristic of so many Jews. The systematic Nazi disavowal of their real objectives coincided with a rationalist inability to believe in them.

In the camps themselves the idea of a revolt or mass escape used to ripen slowly, especially after the advent of a few prisoners with organizational ability or military training. In Treblinka it was a certain Dr. Choronżycki of Warsaw, assisted by a Czech Jew, Captain Zelo Bloch, who accumulated the first hand grenades. The news of the Warsaw ghetto uprising reached the camp and filled people with new faith.

After weeks of preparations Choronżycki was caught by the SS Lieutenant Kurt Franz with money on him, which he had prepared for the use of the insurgents after their escape. The doctor knew this would give him away. He assaulted Franz, cut his face with a surgeon's scalpel and instantly swallowed the poison that all the plotters carried on them for use if caught, to avoid interrogation and torture. All the efforts of the Germans to save him for torture were of no avail. They could only avenge themselves by mutilating his dead body.

But this was just the beginning. New people joined the plot: Galewski of Lódz, Dr. Leitner of Wegrów. It was noted that among the plotters was Rudolf Masaryk of Prague, a non-Jew, a relative of the great Tomáš G. Masaryk, who had followed his Jewish wife to the death camp. By a clever trick they obtained a duplicate key to the local armory. A date for the revolt was fixed and all preparations were made as carefully as possible. A plan was worked out; it included killing some of the SS men, setting the camp on fire and liberating the Polish prisoners in the nearby punitive camp for a joint escape. Two hours before the prearranged time the arms were being distributed to various points, when at the last moment two of the plotters were caught. It was imperative to start immediately, ahead of time. The signal was given by throwing a hand grenade at an SS man. Immediately the armory was stormed and in a few moments two hundred prisoners were armed. The gas chamber, the railway station and the guards' quarters were soon in flames. The barbed-wire fence was pulled down and people began to stream out. Unfortunately, however, not all the telephone wires had been cut; German reinforcements were alerted and began converging on the escaping prisoners. Hundreds were tracked down before they could reach the safety of the forests, and killed in encounters with the pursuing Germans, who themselves suffered heavy casualties. A few escaped. This was the handful of people who told the world about Treblinka and its revolt of August 2, 1943.

In the Sobibór camp the plans for revolt took shape on the arrival of a Jewish sea captain from Holland, whose exact name none of the survivors could recall. The idea was to set the camp on fire and escape in the resulting confusion. The captain talked one of the Ukrainian guards into supporting the plot, but somehow the Germans found it out, and the captain was immediately put to torture in public. "Tell us who conspired with you," they insisted. "Nobody. I was the only one who wanted to escape," was his reply. "Then we will behead all the men in your block before your eyes," they said. "You will do what you want anyway," he was heard to reply weakly. Block No. 3 was ordered to step out; all its inmates were beheaded. The captain was the last.

The initiative was taken over by a Soviet prisoner of war, a Jew from Rostov, Alexander (Sasha) Pechorsky. Sasha evolved a plan for liquidating the command of the camp one by one, relying on the proverbial German punctuality. The operation was carried out on October 14, 1943. The tailors, shoemakers and storekeepers among the prisoners were told to suggest appointments for SS officers in the workshops at definite hours, at fifteen-minute intervals. The Germans had just ordered new uniforms and boots for the winter season, and they were invited for "measurements." Each turned up at the appointed time and was greeted with an ax blow on the head. Within half an hour the command of the revolt, which included two Polish Jews, Salomon Leitman and Leon Feldhaendler, had several revolvers, taken from the SS officers. Everything proceeded according to plan. With the password "Hurrah" the central machine-gun post was seized and Sasha gave the order to force the armory. It was broken into by the prisoners, who started to pour out of the camp under heavy fire from the Ukrainian guards, commanded by two SS officers who had no "measurement" appointments.

A hot pursuit followed. Of the three hundred who succeeded in escaping, about a hundred survived to cross into the partisan area and join fighting units. Thirty-odd men lived through the war to hold a Sobibór reunion meeting in Lublin. Most of them are in Israel today; three came forward to tell their story in court.

Soon after the revolts both the Sobibór and Treblinka camps were liquidated. The Nazis simply could not bring themselves to rebuild them and continue the work of death on the spot where life had suddenly flared up. An extermination camp once breached had become useless. They were afraid that if a camp and its secrets were revealed to the world, it would certainly become the target for Allied bombing. Unfortunately, no Allied government ever entertained such ideas; the RSHA's anxieties were quite baseless.

The revolts marked the end of "Action Reinhard." Globocnik's last act was the final liquidation of the Majdanek, Trawniki and surrounding labor posts in Lublin and vicinity. These were combined "labor-destruction" camps. Globocnik had all surviving Jews, eighteen thousand of them, shot at Majdanek on November 2 and 3, 1943.

All further activities were thereafter centralized in the "regular" camps, mainly in the one which in any case had been the cardinal center of annihilation: Auschwitz.

*

The fact that people could manage to preserve even a hibernating semblance of a human soul in a destruction camp casts a new light on the incredible creature called man. But many of the prisoners achieved even more. They stayed human, were capable of feeling, self-sacrifice, mutual help. "In this hell of Auschwitz, some of us stayed alive because there was also friendship and solidarity. . . . We would carry typhoid-stricken, feverish people on our backs to the place of work, because if they stayed behind, they would be killed instantly," testified Raya Kagan. "We smuggled into the camp goods from the stores though it was a very serious matter to be found out at the body search. . . . We smuggled in vitamins, clothing and toothpaste, which was used as a spread on the dry bread," testified Gedalya Ben-Zvi.

There were some Kapos and *Blockaelteste* who behaved humanly. Some prisoners were asked by friends to volunteer for the job to be in a position alleviate suffering. Vera Alexander, today an art critic, was one. I put her on the stand.

"One day I was asked by Katia Singer, the *Rapportschreiberin,* to become the *Blockaelteste* of Block 3. I said I could not do it. She asked me to, saying we needed good people in such positions. . . . I agreed. There were ways of assisting people. First of all to see that everybody got the little that was allotted to him without it being grabbed by stronger prisoners. There were cases when I could hide in the block women who had been condemned to death at a selection and smuggle them back into a labor unit; or conceal sick women so that they could escape. . . . Once I tried to save a small girl whom her mother had somehow brought into the block. I hid the child for several weeks in the block, but somehow the notorious Irma Grese came to know of it. SS men arrived and fetched the little girl. . . . They threw her alive into the fire. The same night the mother 'went to the wires.'" "Going to the wires," in Auschwitz slang, meant committing suicide by throwing oneself onto the high-tension barbed-wire fence running around the camp.

Sometimes lives were risked for other purposes. "Once I saw an SS officer approaching our block. . . . He ordered a boy of fourteen down from the shelf and started whipping him. . . . There was nothing unusual about that, but this boy did not shout or cry or moan. We counted the lashes. He got twenty, thirty, but did not utter a word. We had never seen anything like it. After forty lashes the SS man turned the boy round and hit him on the face, the legs—but still he was silent. After fifty lashes the beating was over. We helped the boy to get up and inquired what he had done and why he had been whipped. He said: 'It was all worthwhile; I smuggled out some prayer books to my friends, so that they could pray.'"

Rivka Kuper, the Cracow underground fighter, said: "On arrival in Auschwitz we found friends and asked them to find some candles for us. . . . It was Friday night. In complete darkness we put up the two small pieces of wax we got as Sabbath candles, and started singing Sabbath songs in a subdued tone. Suddenly stifled weeping was heard all around. Jewish women who had been there for months had surrounded our group. . . . Later we always, somehow, found pieces of candle for Friday night."

Even in the dreaded "Punishment Block" No. 11 of Auschwitz, where prisoners were given "correctional treatment" and suspects were held for examination by the Gestapo, to be shot at "the black wall" after interrogation, Jews would gather for prayers. Josef Rosensaft, who after his liberation at Bergen-Belsen became famous for his leadership of the camp, was kept in this block in the infamous "Cell 21," where the prisoners were kept in closed shafts into which they had to crawl from below, and where they could just barely stand in complete darkness together with two or three others tightly pressed together, without any possibility of movement. Rosensaft was being "interrogated" there on his escape from the camp. How he survived eleven months of incarceration in a place where the prisoner's span of endurance was a week or two is again a riddle of nature.

"On the New Year and the Day of Atonement we held our prayers in the block," Rosensaft recalled. "I remember well reading of the Law there."

Professor Wdowinski, now of the New York New School for Social Research and onetime leader of the Revisionist units in the Warsaw ghetto revolt, was detained in the labor camp near Lublin. "We managed to bake *matzot* (unleavened bread) for Passover. We had two rabbis with us and we baked it in an oven near where we worked, smuggling the *matzot* out on our bodies. Two men were caught, Rabbi Stockhammer and a certain doctor, and received a dreadful beating on their naked bodies as a punishment."

There were countless personal acts of bravery and devotion. A woman from a Polish transport refused to undress before the sadist Schillinger, whose hobby was to choke Jews while they were eating. When Schillinger lifted his whip, the woman took out a concealed revolver and shot him on the spot.

Auschwitz, too, had its rebellious transports. Once a train arrived from nearby Bendzin-Sosnowiec under heavy SS guard. "Those people must have tried to jump out of the train and been shot, because many of them were hanging half out of the windows. . . . An SS officer shouted that today there would be no selections. . . . Everybody was to go to the crematorium. . . . Usually they sorted out about 150-200 people of a transport for work in the camp. . . . When the doors of the wagons were opened it was an awful sight. People who were still living actually poured out. Inside the train were heaps of bodies. The half-living stumbled over each other and fell onto the platform, to the great merriment of the SS guards. A girl of perhaps ten years old got up from among the dead, I don't know how, and began to walk. An SS man 'pitied' her and shot her. . . . Then we were ordered inside to take out the bodies," testified Gedalya Ben-Zvi.

Escapes were rare and extremely difficult. One day in the summer of 1944, all Gestapo stations throughout the Reich were alerted: Mala Zimetbaum, a Jewish girl of twenty, a deportee from Belgium, had escaped. Mala was actually the right-hand assistant of the dreaded SS woman Dreksler. Two years she had waited for this day, when she stole an SS uniform, removed some key documents and made for Slovakia in the company of a Pole who volunteered to help her "to reveal to the world" the existence of hell on earth.

They both reached Slovakia and were about to proceed across the border, when a patrol at a customs house decided to check on the strange couple in SS uniforms. A push at her sleeve revealed the tattooed Auschwitz number on her hand.

They were returned to Auschwitz. The Pole was submitted to the "seesaw" torture, which actually broke his limbs apart. Then he was hanged. Mala's interrogation lasted longer. The Gestapo wanted to know who helped them. Mala did not speak. One day a fellow prisoner, Raya Kagan, managed to sneak into her cell. "Mala, how are you?" she asked in a terrified whisper. Completely composed, Mala replied: "I am still fine."

The scene of her hanging had to serve as an exemplary measure. A huge roll call was ordered, and the SS Oberaufseherin Maria Mandel warned the thousands of prisoners of the end of escape attempts. Mala stood there, completely quiet. Suddenly she turned pale. With a hidden razor blade she had cut her wrist veins. The SS executioner approached her and with a blood-dripping hand she slapped her face. The saga of Auschwitz has it that she said: "I fall a heroine and you will die as a dog."

She was instantly removed and at nighttime her body was transferred to the crematorium. Her name became the legend of Auschwitz.

Slowly an underground movement developed; it comprised people of many creeds and countries. Its members helped people and saved lives whenever possible, trying to occupy key positions in the camp's hierarchy. They also prepared a military revolt, and were dependent on the cooperation of the Jewish girls employed in munition works for the supply of explosives. The girls were under the strictest control, but still they got out the supplies. "We used to smuggle out the explosives in small quantities from Birkenau to Auschwitz almost every day," testified Israel Gutman. Sometime later the *Sonderkommando* boys, who worked at the crematoria and were completely isolated from the rest of the camp, sent in word that they intended to revolt. "The command of the underground had their own calculations and asked us to stop it," said Gutman. But the *Sonderkommando* did revolt all the same, on October 6, 1944. They killed some of the SS men and their German Kapo, and exploded Crematorium No. 3 with dynamite, which four girls had smuggled out on their bodies.

There was a great commotion when the crematorium was seen to be on fire. "This was not the usual flame, which sometimes shot up from the chimney to a height of four meters. The crematorium itself was on fire," testified the painter, Yehuda Bakon. The SS men left their offices and all ran in the direction of the fire. A state of emergency was proclaimed and the *Sonderkommando* members who had succeeded in breaking through and dispersing inside the camp were rounded up one by one. "At the registration office we were told to fill out ninety-six death certificates certifying 'Shot in the attempt to escape' for those Jews. Most of them were from Grodno and Greece, and some Russians too," testified Raya Kagan.

An immediate inquiry was initiated, but results were achieved only after a spy was planted in the "union" factory. Four girls, Elen, Tosia, Regina and Rosa—two of them from Warsaw and two from Bendzin—were arrested. They readily admitted their part in the plot but refused to disclose any further names. All the beating and tortures did not make them talk. An employee of the "political department" saw Rosa Robota once after the tortures. She was broken, shattered and dazed from the beating. Her clothes were torn and her breast was bare.

The underground movement was alarmed lest Rosa should talk. But she put them at ease. She asked for someone to see her, and they managed to smuggle in Noah Zabludowicz, as an electrician who had come to make repairs. She was a raw, bleeding piece of flesh, Zabludowicz recalled. "But she managed to say that we had nothing to fear, and should carry on. She knew she must die, but no one else was in danger. Then she was hanged with the other girls at a roll-call. Their last word was 'Revenge!' " testified Israel Gutman.

This was about the time when Himmler had ordered the gas murders to be stopped. The Russians were coming close. Auschwitz was full of rumors, hopes and fears. Work was still going on, with long columns of prisoners marching to the usual command: *"Links, zwei, drei, vier, links"* ("Left, two, three, four, left"), on which the underground composed a poem, in Polish:

> Barbarians and monsters,
> The last trace of you we will expunge!
> And on your graves a mighty sphinx
> Will call forever: *"Links, links, links!"*

*

Yet all these acts of resistance and heroism were only one side of the picture. It was how the outposts, so to speak, of the community reacted to extreme and immediate situations.

How did the community as a whole behave? What was life like behind the ghetto walls?

Here I think a glance at what the Nazis destroyed is imperative.

In the period between the two world wars East European Jewry presented a picture of a vigorous society striving for the implementation of two international undertakings, both backed by the peace treaties: the assurance of rights for cultural and national minorities and the Balfour Declarations. The first imposed on the new states in Eastern and Southern Europe the duty of permitting the free development of the five million Jews who lived there; under the terms of the other, Great Britain undertook to enable the Jews to establish a National Home in Palestine.

While striving to achieve these political aims the Jewish communities were also developing communal organizations. They made an important contribution to the scientific and cultural achievements of the countries in which they lived. Professor Salo Baron of Columbia University, an authority on Jewish history, gave evidence at the trial on the general features of Jewish life in Europe on the eve of the holocaust. He vividly described the extraordinary vitality and powers of adaptation displayed by these communities, which produced—in almost no time—a ramified network of their own schools, hospitals and old-age homes, side by side with impressive cultural, religious, scientific and journalistic activities. Over eight hundred Jewish periodicals and newspapers appeared in Europe. Schools of learning flourished. Youth movements, imbued with national and social ideals, embraced most of the younger generation.

The Jews were attuned to the intellectual challenges of modern times. They were able to shoulder, simultaneously, many burdens at home and abroad. They produced thirty-four Nobel Prize winners in half a century. Yet they were entirely unprepared, physically or mentally, to face a total onslaught. They were used to the excesses of backward elements, against which they had learned to defend themselves, and which were usually suppressed by sometimes willing, sometimes reluctant authorities. They were trained in fighting anti-Semitism and exposing its lies and prejudices. The instinct of self-preservation led them to look for political solutions, but not to preparations for warding off imminent physical danger. Moreover, they lacked an over-all, central authority. Factional division was rife. Zionism, though a central power in Jewish life, was not the only movement on the scene and had to face competition from ultrareligious, ultraradical and assimilationist quarters. The Zionists themselves suffered from internal strife; politically they were mainly engaged in a conflict with Great Britain over the carrying out of the Palestine Mandate; emotionally and physically they were involved in the huge enterprise of building the Jewish-State-in-the-making. And all this was in addition to their active engagement in day-to-day activities in their own communities. Busy with these responsibilities, the Jews did not perceive in time from where the immediate danger to their survival was to emerge.

Inspired leaders and thinkers had premonitions. Chaim Weizmann, President of the World Zionist Organization, demanded in 1936 the exit of six million Jews (the exact number!) from Eastern Europe. They had no security and they must go, he pleaded before a British Royal Commission. The philosopher Henri Bergson wrote in his will that he had refrained from leaving the Jewish faith because the menace of an anti-Semitic upheaval made him wish "to stay among the persecuted of tomorrow."

Yet no one imagined anything approaching the horrors that actually took place. There were few illusions as to the hardships involved under the Nazi occupation, especially after the shock of the first massacres, but these were interpreted as a mere "bloodletting," a sacrifice to anti-Semitic propaganda. The halt that was called to the first murders seemed to uphold this view. The leadership used the lull that followed to apply itself to the relief of immediately pressing needs.

At first escape was possible, as the Soviet boundary was left virtually open for a while. "Only a few Jews availed themselves of this opportunity," writes Dr. M. Lenski. "Many of those who fled returned to Warsaw from Russia after a few months." Most of them refused to become homeless refugees. Others longed to rejoin wives, children or parents who had remained behind. The homes they had left exercised a strong attraction. Even the pauper wanted to stay in his own room. "Jews go on living even under the Germans," they argued, "so why should we run away? There will be time enough for that."

A characteristic line of thought which had accompanied Jews throughout their wanderings was that the individual had fewer chances than the collective group. Keeping together offered a better opportunity of thwarting an oppressor's designs than meeting them singlehanded. "Mr. Israel" was better protected inside "the House of Israel." The Jew flocked instinctively for protection to his own folk. This experience, valid for previous waves of persecutions, was responsible for Jews clinging together now, staying in places where they knew each other, where they had non-Jewish neighbors and friends they thought they could rely on. They refused to wander abroad into the unknown.

In various communities the possibility of mass escape was considered by the leadership. "We are afraid that when the first batch of fifty Jews finds a way to leave the country illegally, [the Germans] will immediately order a hundred thousand to do the same," Dr. Emanuel Ringelblum, a historian and a striking figure of Warsaw Jewry, noted in his diary on December 25, 1939. So the policy was "Wait and see," trying in the meantime to alleviate the suffering as much as possible. Everybody was "sure" that the war would be over soon.

The communities set up self-aid organizations, as in Warsaw where over one-third of the Jewish urban population were in urgent need of a roof over their heads, a hot meal and a necessary garment. Public kitchens were established, housing provided and warm clothing distributed.

Psychologically, the primary element of efficiency in the Nazi treatment of the Jews was guile. Immediately after the war a survivor from Lwów wrote:

There was not a single instance, not even when the last remnants of Polish Jewry were led to their death, in which the Germans openly unmasked and said: "We have come to murder the Jews!" On the contrary, with the infinite slyness of swindlers they repeatedly declared their only purpose was to put a barrier between the bulk of the Jews and the Aryans, to separate the "noble" mentality of the Gentiles from the "destructive" influences of Jewry. They declared that they would not harm us there, and we believed their smooth talk. Could anyone conceive that in the twentieth century it was possible to kill, annihilate and efface a nation for no wrong committed, including women, children, young and old, for no reason and with no necessity of war?

In different ways and phrases the same feelings were echoed everywhere. A leader of the Warsaw ghetto revolt, Zivia Lubetkin Zuckerman, put it in almost the same words in her evidence: "We just could not imagine that a nation would in this century pass a death sentence on a whole people. We kept asking ourselves: 'They humiliate us, they suppress us, but do they really intend to kill us all?' We did not believe it."

"At first they did not even believe the stories of the survivors of shooting operations," testified Dr. Dvorjetski. "I was a doctor in Vilna. One day I saw in the streets a woman barefoot, her hair disheveled. She gave the impression of being out of her mind. I took her into my room and she said: 'I come from Ponar.' 'From the labor camp at Ponar?' I asked. 'There is no labor camp, they kill Jews there,' she said." The woman told him the horrible story of the shootings and described her miraculous escape from the dead pit when she was hit only in the arm. The doctor did not believe her, but when he dressed her wounds he found creeping ants—ants from the woods.

"I went out and told people what I had heard about Ponar. 'Doctor,' they said to me, 'are you too a panic-monger? Instead of giving us a word of consolation you tell us nightmares!'"

People could not bring themselves to believe that the Germans, still remembered from World War I as "liberators" from Czarist oppression, coming from one of the most civilized countries in the world, could be capable of such horrors. Any news of it was met with incredulity or at most ascribed to the savagery of a local commander.

"After all, this is Europe, not the jungle," people argued. "They can't kill us all."

By a subterfuge, SS General Stahlecker induced the Jews of Kaunas to enter the ghetto after a blood bath by incited Lithuanians. We are in a position to follow the method in the recorded notes of a survivor. L. Garfunkel, a member of the delegation to the General, wrote:

> He [the General] announced that the Lithuanians refuse to live with the Jews, who are all Communists. Therefore we have to move to the ghetto, where we shall be secure. . . . "It is for your own good. You will be safe there and run your own affairs," said the SS officer. "Since you blame the Lithuanians for this, we would like to discuss the matter with them," said the Jewish delegation. "That is out of the question," was the reply. "You have nothing to consult them about."

A meeting of Jewish community leaders was called. People thought that perhaps it would really be better to live among their own folk now rather than together with the cruel Lithuanians. In a depressed though not despiring mood, the Jews decided to accept it and elected a committee to assist in the transfer to the ghetto. Garfuenkel continues:

> Little did they know what hell the Nazis had in store for them by imprisoning them in the ghetto. Nobody realized the hidden intention of the Germans. Everybody thought that this was a measure of isolation, to debase us and embitter our lives. But their real intentions were to keep us together like chickens in a hen roost, to take out for slaughter as many as were needed. They cheated us with glib talk, promising to maintain order, and viciously lured us into the trap without opposition.

*

The central authority in the ghetto was the Jewish Council (*Aeltestenrat* or *Judenrat*), as provided in the directive based on Eichmann's experience in Vienna. It was a body appointed by the Germans to represent the Jews and transmit the orders of the authorities. The individual Jew, unlike his Gentile neighbor, had no access to the authorities or to general public services. He could not obtain a ration card for food, a roof overhead, a place of employment, schooling for his children or a bed in a hospital except through the Council, which had to set up all services from scratch and to provide them to the public. The Council was given the power to impose taxes, set up a police force and, generally, to exercise authority inside the ghetto.

In many instances people considered themselves honor-bound to accept office on the Council. In the initial stages the work consisted entirely of relief and welfare activities, which were desperately needed by the population. Even so there were no illusions as to what it meant to be a kind of buffer between the merciless SS and the suffering community. "Yet, hard as it is, somebody must do it" was a convincing argument.

Others had to be persuaded. The minutes of the meeting at which the head of the Kaunas Council was elected have been preserved. After some discussion, a popular physician, Dr. Elhanan Elkes, was proposed. He refused, whereupon Rabbi Schmukler said: "How awful is our condition that instead of offering our beloved Dr. Elkes the honorable position of head of the Kaunas community we ask him to assume the humiliating office of 'Jewish Elder' to represent us before the Germans. But you should know, dear Dr. Elkes, that only vis-à-vis the Germans will you be the Jewish Elder. For us you will be our head, elected at our most tragic hour, when we all bleed and the sword is overhead. This is a crushing burden, but it involves a great right and privilege. You are not free to evade it: lead us, protect us; you will be with us and we will be with you, till the day of redemption comes." Loud sobs were heard. Dr. Elkes stood up, pale and speechless for a moment, and finally said he would make the sacrifice imposed on him by a cruel fate. A feeling of relief swept the assembly. "Dr. Elkes' devoted work during the three years of the ghetto's existence proved to the Jews that they had made no mistake in electing him when they were on the brink of disaster."

The type of the Jewish "interceder" (*shtadlan*), who speaks the language of the authorities, faithfully represents his brethren, and like Biblical Mordecai, "seeketh the welfare of his people," is well known in Jewish history. Underneath his outer garments the *shtadlan* used to wear the traditional Jewish grave clothes, for he might not return alive from his errand of mercy. The type of the medieval Jewish "go-between" reappeared in the modern ghettos of Europe.

Many members of the Councils soon paid with their lives for any "disobedience." Dr. Joseph Parnas in Lwów was shot for refusing to compile lists of people for deportations. "I can supply you with furniture, rugs, coffee and brandy, but I won't give you Jews," he said. His successor, Dr. Landsberg, and members of his Council were hanged in retaliation for an attempt made by a Jew on the life of a German. The third Jewish Council of Lwów was soon liquidated too and the ghetto turned into a "work camp" (*Julag*) under direct German command. In some instances, as in Lechatov, the Nazis liquidated eight successive Jewish Councils. The head of the Zloczów Council was shot when he refused to cooperate in a locally invented form of viciousness: he had been asked to sign a document attesting to the need for executions owing to the spread of infection. Dr. Brawer of the Grodno ghetto was shot "on suspicion of disloyalty." Markus Horowitz, "the protector of the Kolomyja ghetto," as he was called by his community, committed suicide with his sister when requested to cooperate in deportations.

Often the execution of the chairman of a Council was marked by special cruelty, as in Stanislawów, where Mordechai Goldstein was ordered to choose the rope with which he was to be hanged. As he was a corpulent man, the rope gave way, and the Ukrainian militia finished him off with rifle butts.

All members of the Jewish Council at Bereza Kartuska committed suicide after a night's conference, since they refused to carry out the Gestapo's order of assembling Jews "for transport to work in the East." In Mlawa the whole Jewish Council was hanged for "not carrying out orders." They had to wait at the execution site for an hour with the ropes around their necks, till the executioner knocked the stools from beneath their feet.

The list is long and varied. In Zduńska Wola the head of the Jewish Councils, Dr. Jacob Lemberg, was asked to compile a list of ten Jews about to be executed as reprisals. Otherwise he, his wife and his two children would be hanged. "These four names you mentioned are the only names you will get through me," he replied. Hans Biebow, the tyrant of the Litzmannstadt ghetto, had his shot. In Pružana the Gestapo surprised a contact man of the underground in the Jewish Council office. Two members of the Council were shot on the spot, the others refused to disclose the names of the underground members. Next day they were deported together with a transport of 2,500 people. Within one month, the whole community was deported to the camps.

In the hundreds of memorial books of the destroyed communities there are reports of similar acts.

Sometimes, especially in the early stages, a resolute stand against the Nazis was of some avail. When the Jews of Siauliai (Shavli) were ordered to deliver fifty Jews "at the prison house" next day as a collective punishment for the smuggling of foodstuffs into the ghetto, the Council declared that if the whole community was to blame, they would bear the consequences, and the members of the Jewish Council would surrender themselves. The local Gestapo commander said he had to get fifty Jews and did not care where they came from. An assembly of the community was held; it lasted all night. Some suggested that they should decide by lot who would be handed over; others proposed to call for volunteers. Finally, it was unanimously decided that every one of those assembled would place himself at the disposal of the head of the Council to be surrendered. Everyone was aware that this meant immediate death by shooting. The head of the Council, Mendel Leibowič, was requested to make a last attempt at negotiations with a view to the substitution of a fine for the death sentence. When he entered the offices of the Gestapo early in the morning, together with Aharon Katz, the secretary, the preparations for the execution of the fifty Jews were in full sight. After an hour they returned with tears of joy in their eyes; fifty lives had been saved in exchange for twenty thousand marks. People embraced each other and wept openly.

The Jewish Councils could at first alleviate suffering and reduce the scope of vicious orders, but they were soon placed in an invidious, often impossible position. They quickly found out that it was useless to appeal to German compassion, humanity or even reason. There was only a limited number of possibilities open to them in dealing with the Germans: to try to convince them that killing Jews was against their own interests, to play one German authority against the other, to bribe them or to give up all hope and prepare for the last fight.

But whatever course a Jewish Council took vis-à-vis the Germans—often combining various measures at different times, often secretly cooperating with the underground—they had only one course open toward the Jewish population if they were to stay in office and do the little good they believed they were doing; they had to ask the Jews to comply with the German decrees. In some cases this also meant supplying lists of "nonworking" Jews for deportation. If they refused to do this, they were shot—and often replaced with utterly terrified and browbeaten people.

In the ghettos where the old Jewish leadership continued to function, bringing with it into this hell a tradition of service and an established credit with the public, the Jewish leaders generally continued to enjoy the confidence of their brethren. In other places a tragic rift developed that led to tension, bitterness and estrangement. Some individuals regarded their own activity on the Council or its institutions, and their blind obedience to the Germans, as a life insurance policy, though this was a futile hope. They were executed or deported along with the others.

There was more to it. The belief of Jews in the ultimate defeat of Hitler never wavered, not even at the darkest hours and in the most oppressed ghettos. Therefore their foremost desire was expressed in the Yiddish word "*ueberleben*"—"to survive!" This was the most deeply rooted drive of all: to endure, to hold out, to live through it.

The Council pointed to a possible way of survival for at least a part of the population, by making the ghettos work. Their reckoning was simple: there was a war on, the Germans would not needlessly destroy badly needed manpower. There might be a chance to stave off disaster should the Germans be persuaded to keep Jewish labor power alive. "Work will save blood" was the slogan of the official leadership of the ghetto.

The reasoning was not devoid of factual basis. Jewish skilled labor was irreplaceable in trade and industry. "Only a handful of Poles are useful here; the real experts are Jews. They are mostly the former owners of the enterprises or the engineers," the army commander of the Przemyśl area wrote to headquarters. Goering, while ruling on August 14, 1941, that the Jews no longer had any place in the German-occupied areas, made an exception in favor of "labor formations."

These exceptions, applied even by the *Einsatzgruppen*, were made full use of by the authorities on the spot, especially when they were further persuaded with bribes. Hans Frank bitterly complained in December, 1942, of the chaotic administrative duplication in the Reich, "where we now have many authorities all rigorously fighting each other." One authority asked the General Government to produce war materials, while the other was removing Jewish labor, said Frank. The deportations of Jews fit for work had already caused the greatest difficulties in the building projects, he told his subordinates. Now he received an order to remove the Jews from the armament industry as well. Rudolf Hoess recorded that Eichmann, on the other hand, was a determined opponent of "selecting Jews fit for work"; he believed that this was "a constant danger to the Final Solution and would enable the Jews to survive."

The Jewish leaders were aware of these differences inside the Nazi camp between the advocates of immediate killing and those who favored temporarily using Jews for labor. "We know we are doomed, but we have got a respite of execution from the hangman. . . . That is why we wish to gain time and try every possible way so that people should remain alive," wrote Garfunkel in Kaunas. The idea was to mark time.

"We have only one purpose," Barasz, the head of the Bialystok Council, declared at one of its meetings: "to remain alive till the end of the war. For that purpose we have to prove we are useful. This will strengthen those Germans who are for us. . . . Industry in the ghetto has proven its usefulness. It is impressive." When Barasz got an important production order, he was elated. "We are about to produce boots. This will secure the further existence of the ghetto."

Barasz had to defend himself against the argument that the victorious Allies would later on frown upon such behavior. "They won't hold it against us," he told the underground fighters. At the Council meeting he expressed the same idea in veiled terms. "A new administration, if it comes, will not condemn us."

The first objective was, therefore, to impress upon the Germans that the Jews were working; to this effect bombastic pronouncements and proclamations were published. "We must prove to the Germans that we are useful and we have to increase our output. Thus we will also increase the numbers employed from 14,000 to 16,000; in this lies our survival," read a proclamation issued in the ghetto of Wilno. Yet obviously their hearts were not in the task of strengthening the Nazi war potential. There were acts of sabotage in workshops at Wilno, Czestochowa and other places. "We work as on half-holidays [*Hol-Hamoed*]," wrote a Jewish prisoner in the Lwów labor camp. The password P.P. (*pracuj powoli* [work slowly]) is gaining popularity here," recorded Jacob Poznański in the ghetto of Lódz. "Often we merely pretend to be working. There are ways and means of stalling for time and of sabotage." The same was heard in all the ghettos. "We won't work for the murderers," shouted the Jews in Bialystok, Lódz, Warsaw. "Then we won't survive," replied the Councils.

The ghetto population were especially distrustful of, and in many instances despised, the Jewish police. The very fact that Jews were wearing uniforms was abhorrent in itself. "Uniforms were reminiscent of the Gestapo, of the Ukrainian units and the Lithuanian Ipatinga, the Ponar murderers."

At first the functions of the police were quite harmless: to guard the streets, to direct and accompany labor units, and to secure order in public offices. After a while additional duties were imposed on them which demanded more toughness, ruthlessness and the use of force: to enforce obedience and effect arrests. Their general idea was that order and discipline were absolutely necessary in such times. "We have had enough parties, factions and debates in the past; now is the time for a coordinated effort" was the slogan of the Jewish police.

Many of their officers had had little previous contact with Jewish affairs. One of them later wrote under the pen name Jan Mabolt:

> It was a difficult and tortuous way for many of us, who were not acquainted with the language and spirit of our people and whose roots were in Polish culture, till we achieved full and complete participation in the life of the Jewish masses. . . . It is easy to condemn these people or deride them. . . . It is so easy, but so superficial. They were going through a process of inner conflict between their education and their habits on the one hand, and their desire to be active Jews, brothers in feeling and deed to the rest of their people, on the other.

Of course most of the first recruits left. Many of the others were executed by the Germans after each deportation, as they were no longer needed. In Stanislawów, after an "action," two policemen were hanged on each lamp post all along Belweder Street; the non-Jewish population was allowed to visit the ghetto for the occasion to have a look at the bodies. Other people now joined the police, many of them deliberately recruited by the Germans from the lower elements of Jewish society, and elevated to positions of power. In many instances a past criminal record or a sadistic deviation was welcomed by the Germans as a recommendation for the appointment. These people often became corrupt, vicious and cruel; they were obviously traitors. They stayed in office longer than others, at any rate long enough to inflict much suffering and evoke much bitterness. They were the most conspicuous and most talked-about types. When the underground started to consolidate its position, some of the Jewish police were the first obstacle they encountered; a clash was inevitable. Some of those had to be removed and were shot before the underground could go into action. But many of the Jewish police were loyal, good people, crushed by the realities of the Nazi hell. Almost all of them perished.

Jacob Gens was the Commandant of the Wilno ghetto police, and later the head of the ghetto Council. He was offered safe asylum by the family and friends of his non-Jewish wife. He refused, but sent his wife away, saying: "Let her save herself, if she can. I'll stay with my people inside the ghetto." When his policemen were asked for the first time to round up Jews in a neighboring village, he sent them out to do it. Instead of arresting one thousand five hundred, as requested, they captured eight hundred, mostly aged people. "I'll talk to you frankly," he told an outraged assembly of Jews in Wilno. "It is true that Jews have sent their brethren to death. When the Germans asked us to give them the old and the young, we gave them only the aged people. . . . They wanted the children, so as to cut down the size of the ghetto immediately. But we saved those who had to be saved. Those whose days were numbered in any case have gone. They are a sacrifice for our future. . . . I dirtied my hands, because I had to. These are the hardest times our nation has ever endured in all history. We can't afford to be sentimental. Let us save what can be saved. Had we been on the scene when the Germans destroyed all the Jews of the villages of Kimlishek and Bistritz, we could have saved some there."

"We did not know yet whether to curse him or bless him," Ruzka Korchak, an underground fighter, wrote. "How can you serve the Germans? You are traitors," argued some. Gens answered them: "You, the Jewish intelligentsia, will emerge from the ghetto clean and alive and with a clear conscience. But this is because I, if I stay alive, will be soiled with blood on my hands. Then I shall surrender myself to a Jewish court. In order to save a remnant I had to send Jews to death, to wallow in mud, so that others might live and remain blameless. If I don't supply the Germans with a thousand Jews, when they ask for them, they will come themselves and fetch two thousand."

The Germans called him "the proud Jew." Yet the Jews could not forgive his contacts with the Germans and his compliance with their orders. "It is true that I meet, even drink with them," he confided to a friend. "Today, over a glass of wine, I saved Borgranski's life. I have to save the young and the intelligent. They will continue the nation's life."

A heartbreaking tragedy developed when the Germans found out and arrested the leader of the underground, Izik Wittenberg. His men assaulted the Gestapo and liberated him. Gens relayed the message he got from the Gestapo: if Wittenberg is not delivered within six hours, the ghetto will be destroyed. Gens summoned the whole population. "What will it be," he asked them, "you or Wittenberg?"

"No description can depict what took place inside the ghetto," recalled Abba Kovner. "We, the members of the command, went to Wittenberg in his place of concealment. . . . Somebody volunteered to give himself up by impersonating Wittenberg. . . Gens said they will see through it. . . . I told the commander: 'Look, there are Jews below whom we shall have to fight to reach the enemy. Give an order and we shall fight.' Wittenberg said he would not do it. He gave me his gun, appointed me to replace him, went out and made his way to the Gestapo to surrender himself."

There are reports, however, that Gens secretly supported the partisans, that he visited them in the woods and supplied them with money. For two years the Wilno ghetto continued to exist. It bled, it suffered, it lost most of its Jews, but it was there.

When the ghetto outlived its usefulness, the Germans arrested Gens on the charge of not betraying the underground movements. He was secretly forewarned by a Gestapo man and advised to escape. His reply was: "If I, the head of the ghetto, escape, thousands of Jews will pay for it with their lives." He summoned the Jewish police, told them what he had to expect, and went to the Gestapo office, where he was executed immediately.

In Shavli Jacob Gens's brother was the chief of the Jewish police. He was ordered one day by the Gestapo to round up all the Jewish children under thirteen "for removal to an orphanage in Kaunas." Nobody believed the "orphanage story," and the Jewish police refused. "If you don't do it I'll have my Ukrainian SS do it," replied SS Major Forster of the Gestapo. The SS stormed the ghetto. "There was no corner from which they did not drag out our poor hidden children. They behaved like beasts, they pulled the children by the hair, dragged them on the ground, threw them naked into cars. . . . Screams of despairing parents and children pierced the air." It was then that the Jewish police were requested by the Jews themselves to join in the operation. "They had to take part in the awful task but they also helped to save some of our children and at least did not let the deportees be beaten up. Many of the policemen were themselves beaten for this, yet they continued to expose themselves and to help," recorded Yerushalmi on November 5, 1943.

A particularly afflicted ghetto was that of Litzmannstadt. It existed longest and it survived, crippled and bleeding, till September, 1944, when it was finally liquidated. The price for this "almost" survival was so much misery and humiliation on the one hand, and such an almost total submission to the Germans on the other, that the man responsible for the ghetto leadership, Mordechai Chaim Rumkowski, has gone down in history with no luster. When the Germans installed him as omnipotent ruler of the ghetto, he had already been a controversial figure, with almost no record of public life. His unquestioned acceptance of their orders, his collaboration with their deportation schemes, his lust for power, his personal ambitions, his odious behavior in personal affairs, and his often ridiculous attempts to install himself as "benevolent" ruler of the ghetto made him an object of contempt and hostility for many. "He is our greatest disaster," recorded a ghetto prisoner in his diary as early as February 7, 1941.

The ghetto prisoners hated him almost as much as they did the Nazis, possibly more. "He rages, he tortures people," another ghetto inmate recorded. Merin, the head of the Bendzin-Sosnowiec and surrounding ghettos, complained bitterly that it was Rumkowski who "taught the Germans how to exploit a ghetto." In his utterances Rumkowski used always the first person singular: "I have so many factories, I got flour from the Germans, I produce, I establish schools, I save you."

Yet even he was not unanimously condemned. At a highly secret meeting held in the ghetto at the end of 1942, to discuss sabotage in the workshops, his name was put on a "list of war criminals." But the opinions of the old-time Jewish leaders as to his personality were divided. The writer Zelikowicz said that he wished the oppression had not come through Jewish hands. "The Germans would have done it anyway, but it is bitter to see your own people as their tools," he cried. The poet Joachimowicz said: "But the Jewish police are our brothers; even if they delude themselves that they will survive, they will be with us in the same grave." The leftist leaders strongly condemned them: "They are sadists and traitors," shouted Skrzepicki and Feifel. The journalist Rosenstein countered: "There is no second man in Lódz who could have led this ship of the ghetto but Rumkowski." The ex-chairman of the artisans' association, Freund, said: "I don't believe in Rumkowski's proclamations, but let us have one thing clear: had it not been for him there would be no Jews in Lódz today. Rumkowski brought us a respite. It is neither he nor the ghetto police who are to blame. The Germans sentenced us to death and the world forgot us. That is why we have to use every maneuver to try and stay alive."

Even Rumkowski's severest critics admitted that he took special care of children. "You have to give him his due. He took an interest not only in schoolchildren but also in others . . . especially orphans, who had no one to look after them. . . . There he really proved his love and devotion to the child, taking care of them with all he had, never sparing efforts or means."

When the final liquidation came, Rumkowski voluntarily boarded the train for the extermination camp.

Czestochowa, in southern Poland, was a typical ghetto. Its sixty thousand people and its leaders strongly believed in the "rescue through work" policy. When Nathan Eck told them that labor had not saved the Jews of Warsaw, and that the workshop employees, too, had been affected by the mass deportations, they argued that if the annihilation decree was not of general application, they hoped their community had a chance to survive if it went on working. Otherwise there was in any case nothing they could do. "We will have to be on our guard for signs of danger," they decided after a grave debate, "but we believe that those Jews who work have a better chance."

This was another Jewish Council against which no one leveled any charges. "I heard nothing about them but good," recorded Eck.

There were not many outstanding personalities among those on whom the crushing burden of leading the Councils devolved. Very few of them, like Rumkowski of Lódz, or Benjamin Murmelstein, of Vienna, turned into submissive tools in the German extermination machinery. But many others made an almost superhuman attempt to rise to the needs of the hour. They all faced decisions for which they had no precedents to guide them. Many were imbued with a deep sense of duty, often a sense of mission. They clung to the "rescue through work" policy, which they believed to be the only solution; they followed it so tenaciously that in some cases they almost did not notice when they crossed the thin and sometimes indiscernible demarcation line between serving Jewish interests and becoming unwitting tools in

German hands. Even then many of them wholeheartedly believed that they could still save Jewish lives. The larger the community for which they were responsible, the more overwhelming was the responsibility and the more marked the desire to respond to the challenge of bewildering events. Almost all of them perished with their people.

Warsaw housed the greatest concentration of Jews in Europe; its Council was faced with gigantic tasks. Its appointed head, Adam Czerniakow, said at a public Jewish meeting: "I find myself in a post that I did not assume on my own initiative and that I cannot divest myself of. I am not independent and I do only what is possible. Everyone can testify that I work hard, from early morning till late at night. Since I was assigned to my post I have only once interrupted my work for two days, and you know which two days I have in mind [he was alluding to the two days he spent under arrest]. I am afraid of nothing. Don't think that I am driven to do things because I am scared. What have I to fear? Death? One dies only once, of this I am always aware, and this we must all remember."

When requested to sign deportation orders for "resettlement to the East," Czerniakow, now realizing that this meant an extermination camp, swallowed the contents of a vial of potassium cyanide. "I cannot act otherwise," he wrote in a farewell letter to his wife. On a second piece of paper, found near his body, were scribbled the words: "Ten thousand for tomorrow, then seven thousand each time."

The Warsaw ghetto was at the time seething with life and activity. House committees for social welfare were set up by the indefatigable Ringelblum. The inhabitants of a house would elect a committee and these would join in electing a "quarter committee." The committees took care of individuals in need, organized performances for the long hours of the night curfew and set up public kitchens, Rachel Auerbach, Ringelblum's assistant and friend, said in court. "We did it as a mutual aid project. We collected taxes through the house committees to keep people going, to give at least a little soup to every person. . . . In the kitchens we held concerts, artistic activities and lectures." The house committees provided an address to which a man in need could turn.

Widespread social aid activity called *Juedische Soziale Selbsthilfe* was conducted throughout the General Government. After a while they had to give up the use of the abbreviation JSS when the Lwów Gestapo claimed that this could be misinterpreted as "Jewish SS." They developed a unique work of relief based on mutual aid, with links with Jewish relief organizations abroad. Because of these and their Red Cross contacts, they were permitted for a while to function within the framework of the several social aid Societies in the General Government. Even so they had to fight for the right to move among the isolated ghettos and to distribute among as many people as possible the piteously insufficient means they had. Yet a piece of bread, supplied in time, often literally meant the saving of a human being.

Their problems were enormous. Footgear had to be furnished to children who could not even reach relief centers for lack of shoes. As leather was, of course, unavailable to them, they produced and distributed wooden sandals. Medicines were urgently needed in the disease-stricken ghettos and camps. Many drugs supplied from abroad were confiscated by the Germans as "*Mangelware*" (unavailable commodities). Yet even simple medicines were in acute demand. In the whole Warsaw ghetto there were ten pharmacies for half a million people. The German health services openly declared at the Krynica conference of doctors held in October, 1941, that they would let the Jews die out in the ghettos rather than allow epidemics to spread. "The Jews will have either to die out or starve to death," declared Dr. Walbaum.

The roof caved in on the social aid workers every day, yet they continued their work. Even buying straw for mattresses for refugees presented a problem in the conditions of wartime Poland. Establishing kitchens, aiding the sick, taking care of the children were enormous tasks in the poverty-stricken ghettos. They required every family that cooked a meal to give a dish to the poor. Often there were heart-warming examples of brotherly love on the part of people who would come to the relief centers and share with needy people the little they had left, refusing even to give their names. "I am an unknown soldier," said one such volunteer who came every day to one of the Warsaw centers, loaded with bread, clothing and bedding.

By the order of December 1, 1942, the General Government authorities ordered the immediate dissolution of all Jewish self-aid groups, as "all further social aid measures for the Jews were placed in the hands of the SS and the police." A limited permission was later issued to send food to the camps. It seems, however, that the Germans were often the main beneficiaries of these transports.

Calls for relief came from all the communities. From the parts annexed to Germany, like Bendzin and other places, reports of their great efforts were sent abroad. These included vocational training, with a double aim in mind: providing a better chance of survival in the present and preparing pioneers for eventual settlement in Palestine.

The Jewish communities in Slovakia set up training courses and workshops in the transit camps and for refugees from the neighboring ex-Polish towns. From small beginnings this developed into a ramified and highly qualified vocational training system.

There was a sudden flare-up of spiritual activity in all the ghettos. It was the bright, dramatic flicker of an immense effort on the brink of disaster, deriving its inspiration from suffering. There were thousands of writers, poets, actors and journalists in Warsaw. "We organized lectures, courses and schools. Then a series of publications and journals. All this we had to do underground because it was forbidden."

In Theresienstadt, for instance, the astonishing thing was the degree to which the youth carried on cultural activities under the direction of the young and inspired Fredi Hirsch. "We all loved him dearly," testified

Mordechai Ansbacher at the trial. "Then there was Fritzi Zucker, the wife of the deputy chairman of the '*Judenrat*.' She gave us her time, educating the children day and night, to strengthen us, and teach us to love our neighbors. . . . This was very difficult, because everybody was intent on looking after himself. Everybody was hungry. . . . Still we used to eat collectively on Saturdays and on holidays. . . . This raised our morale. . . . Fredi Hirsch sent us to the old people, to feed them and to read to them from the Bible or from the literature. The old people were very moved by this. . . . Most of them were sick and fragile. Often they actually died while a boy or girl was reading to them. . . . We used to sing Hebrew and Zionist songs, though this was punishable. . . . We even had illegal schools for children under sixteen, though this too was strictly forbidden."

University professors immured in the ghettos organized postgraduate courses and continued their research work in improvised laboratories. Special attention was paid to the fight against epidemics and to the relief of the "starvation disease" that soon afflicted the ghettos.

Books were illegally written and printed. Lending libraries were put into operation where bookshops were forbidden. In the Warsaw ghetto performances were given by a symphony orchestra and a choir. This the Germans permitted, providing no music by German composers was played. "The Warsaw ghetto is now a great musical center," said conductor Dawidowicz, proud to have musicians from Austria and Germany, as well as Poland, under his baton. Under various pretexts music-loving Poles would surreptitiously and at grave risk attend the illegal ghetto concerts. Five theaters gave performances, with pickets outside to direct people to the right places and warn the artists and the public should the German police approach.

In Wilno there was at first some opposition to theatrical performances. "No theater in a cemetery!" said a poster. But later everybody accepted the idea and enjoyed the experience. The Lódz ghetto also had its regular cultural activity. Its theater, symphony orchestra and art exhibitions attracted scores of thousands of spectators and listeners. Even a "Ghetto Encyclopedia" was initiated. Also, musical education was pursued and extensive research into Jewish national music was carried on there. Incredible as it sounds, secret cultural activity went on even at the horrible Janowska camp at Lwów. Literary evenings were organized, at which prisoners read recently composed poems. Ways were found to copy these pieces, some of which survived. Even the Jewish sanitary unit at Lwów continued its self-education to the last.

Bards of the ghetto appeared, first and foremost the great poet Yitzhak Katznelson. "My inspiration comes from the young men and women of the pioneer movements," he used to say. In hunger and misery he composed his poem "Job" and later his great work "The Song of the Murdered Jewish People." Other writers composed satirical poems and rhymes, which soon circulated throughout the ghetto.

A flood of journals, pamphlets and publications appeared. There were hundreds of them, in print, in hectograph, typewritten, often copied by hand and distributed from house to house, issued by various youth movements and cultural organizations.

Religious institutions were reactivated. Services were held, usually in hiding. The Germans ordered that Jewish holidays were to be ordinary working days, but they were always observed. People fasted on the Day of Atonement, though they had to work as usual. Other religious rites were widely observed. In many quarters there was an upsurge of religious feeling; the rabbis' sermons tragically reflected the grim reality. Rabbi Kalman Shapira's sermons in the Schultz workshops in Warsaw, where he was made to work as a tailor, have been preserved. "It is very difficult for us, for the suffering is unbearable," he said at a Sabbath service. "When so many of us are being killed, slaughtered and burned daily, only because they are Jews, then we who remain must face this ordeal with utter self-sacrifice and strengthen our spirits and our faith in the Lord. . . . The children are the first to suffer at the hands of our enemies. . . . It is a wonder how the world continues to exist when it is filled with the weeping of these children. . . . These innocent children, pure as angels, killed only because they belong to the house of Israel, they are more sacred even than the angels."

Rabbis who were placed by the Council in charge of workshops to save their lives would quickly turn these places into schools of learning, where gifted people gathered to study the Talmud and skilled laborers increased their output to cover up the deficiency of the "nonworkers." Guards would be placed outside the workshops to warn of an approaching German search unit; at a given signal books would be hidden and a general appearance of a working group maintained. This was usually coupled with a well-concealed synagogue. The nonscholarly workers, especially the younger ones, were given lessons in Judaism from time to time. It once happened in such a synagogue in the Litzmannstadt ghetto that while the youngsters and some of the older people were chanting the songs customary before the Sabbath evening service, the commotion of searches and roundups was heard outside. After a few minutes' silence they continued in subdued tones: "Though I walk through the valley of the shadow of death, I fear no evil." This they repeated several times "with great devotion," giving the words the interpretation attached to them for ages by "the sanctifiers of the Lord in the various sites of oppression and execution."

Rabbis stayed with their communities and often gave the example of a dignified death. Before the final liquidation of the Warsaw ghetto, local high authorities of the Roman Catholic Church finally decided to do something for the Jews and offered asylum to three of the last rabbis of Warsaw and their families. This was a supreme test of character for the last remnants of the once world-famous Warsaw rabbinate: Rabbi Menachem Zemba, Rabbi Shimshon Sztokhauer and Rabbi David Szapiro. When the secret offer was made, they held a brief consultation. "We know," said one of them, "that we can't help our community in any way. But at least we can stay with them and this consolation we owe to them." They declined the offer.

Rabbi Zvi Yečheskiel Michelson, dean of the Warsaw rabbinate, deliberately remained at home while a large roundup was on. He did not go out as the Germans ordered, but put on his praying shawl and phylacteries and stayed inside. He preferred to be shot on the spot, hoping that thus his body would be thrown into one of the wagons that accompanied the roundup and find a last resting place in the Jewish cemetery. So he willingly opened the door to the search party, but when the Germans saw the tall old man, with his long silver-white beard, they became uneasy. One of them mumbled, according to the Jewish policeman who accompanied the search: "This must be Moses in person." They slammed the door shut and left the aged rabbi alone. He must have decided then that staying with his people in their last moments was even more important than being buried in a Jewish cemetery. He rose, went down to the courtyard and joined the marching ranks of Jews toward the "*Umschlag*," from which the people were sent to Treblinka.

*

The Jews were cut off from the rest of the world. They had no newspapers or radios, and depended on rumors for information. The few people who listened surreptitiously to the Allied transmitters used to spread the reports, which in the ghettos were always optimistic. They announced that the Germans were losing campaigns, that Hitler was ill, that peace was close at hand, that there was going to be an exchange of European Jews for Americans of German origin, or that Roosevelt and Churchill had decided to take the Jews under their protection. Nobody knew how these "rumors of good news" sprouted.

One day somebody brought to the Warsaw Jewish Council the news—"which everybody knows already"—that America and England had announced all surviving Jews to be their nationals. Immediately a "correction" followed: they were to be declared Palestinian nationals and placed under British protection. Some of the sharpest minds of the Warsaw ghetto debated and analyzed the "news." Dr. Yitzhak Shipper, sociologist, lawyer and politician, declared that it was a legally sound proposition, politically feasible, even probable, and well founded in precedents. So everybody agreed that the story was true and "proved" that the Jewish leaders outside had finally awakened the world's conscience. Dr. Stein, of the Jewish Seminary, said it must have been the appeals of great Jewish scientists that had influenced Churchill and Roosevelt. Rabbi Menachem Zemba said it was probably the rabbis who had moved the world. Only the famous historian, Professor Meyer Balaban, had his doubts: "I don't believe in the conscience of the world; in any case, I will not live to see it." The conclusion of these learned men was that it was not so important how the rescue had been brought about. "The fact is that redemption is close at last."

Finally, when the rumors were cruelly belied, the disillusioned Jews invented a mocking nickname for their origin: they all emanated, it was said, from the telegraphic agency YWA (*"Yiden Willen Azoi"*—"Jews want it that way").

*

Soon the ghetto developed its way of life and its slang. No one rang the bell; only the Gestapo did that; a visitor was expected to knock at the door. A man starving to death was called "an obituary face"; a man who rationed out his food to last till the next distribution was called a "calendar man." "Fire" was the warning for approaching search parties. One who escaped deportation was described as "taken down from the fork." The question "What is the score today?" meant: "How many German planes have been shot down by the Allies in aerial combat?"

They knew that we would be interested one day in knowing how they lived and what went on in their minds.

> The world will ask what the people of Musa Dagh in Warshaw Ghetto thought of when they understood that death would not spare them. Though we are all condemned to death, we have not lost the image of man. Our brains go on working, just as before the war. The serious Jewish reader is greatly interested in war literature. Memoirs of Lloyd George and all the great novels of World War I are intensely read. . . . Comparisons are made with the present times, and on the basis of insignificant indications conjectures are advanced about the approaching hour of the defeat of the "unconquered" German Army.

Thus Ringelblum noted in his diary in June, 1942.

The urge to write, to record, to leave a mark, a sign, a story, was overwhelming. People started writing memoirs and diaries in the ghettos, in prison, in the camps. "Write and record [*Schreibts und verschreibts*]" was the directive given by the famous Jewish historian Simon Dubnow to his disciples in Riga. Ringelblum used to record every piece of news, even rumors and anecdotes, and set up clandestine archives for which he recruited volunteers from all walks of life, asking them to chronicle and perpetuate events. He extended the work of his institution, which for conspiratorial purposes he called *"Oneg Shabbat"* ("Pleasure of the Sabbath"), to cover individual events in Warsaw and in the provinces. Israel Lichtenstein, one of Ringelblum's assistants, wrote in his testament, which he buried together with other material: "I plunged with fervor and joy into the work of helping to gather material for the archives. I was designated to watch over them till the end. . . . I have hidden them. . . . Oh, I hid them well. . . . May they be preserved!"

"Perhaps we are the only passengers left on a sinking boat?" wrote Rachel

Auerbach. "It may even happen that no evidence will remain to tell of our catastrophe. . . . At least our descriptions will be left over as our witnesses." Some archives were unearthed and survived the people who collected them. They are an authentic source of knowledge about what happened.

Another urge of the ghetto prisoners was to find a hiding place. Escape was no longer possible, so they built underground shelters which they named "bunkers," or improvised other hideouts where they could take shelter while a roundup was on. Sometimes, as in the case of Anne Frank's family in Amsterdam, this became a permanent refuge. In most places it had to serve as a temporary shelter, with a well-concealed entrance, a ventilation system, a water supply and sometimes even gas and electricity. It is hardly possible to imagine the ingenuity and the work required to dig out and construct such subterranean nests. The work had to be done at night, so that no one on the surface would be aware of the activity below. The bunkers were large and small, sometimes they were even built in two or three stories. "Our ghetto architecture" was the bitter name the Jews used for these efforts. In Wilno they named the shelters "*malinas*." Every house had a hideout, in the cellars, under water wells, beneath the lavatory or under a storage chamber. There was a whole network of *malinas*, with passages connecting one with the other. For months, even for years, there were two ghettos in existence: one above and an underground city beneath."

The Warsaw ghetto revolt was carried on from such bunkers for several weeks. In his report on the liquidation of the Jews in Galicia, SS Major General Katzmann repeatedly speaks of the concealed "bunkers." In the town of Rohatyn he found hideouts called "Stalingrad," "Sevastopol" and "Leningrad," camouflaged from above by a seemingly natural garden. "It was all done in a workmanlike manner," he wrote. In Lwów he could not find all the "catacombs," so he simply dynamited every suspicious-looking place, adding a treatment with flame-throwers for good measure.

The building of concealed shelters was linked with the widespread belief in the ghettos that the deportations were a single, onetime campaign of bloodletting, which was ordered everywhere, but once over would not be repeated. It was, therefore, all-important not to be in sight when the searches and roundups were on. The Germans on their part supported the "single purge" theory. They would promise on their "word of honor" that the "last" deportation was irrevocably the end of the affair, and that the remaining Jews would be left in peace. "The Gestapo men told us that the Fuehrer needed all the remaining Jews for work and had given orders not to deport any more. They said there would be no more shootings, no more executions." The promise was kept only till the next "action," but it was useful in luring Jews out of their hiding places. People used to talk of those ghettos from which deportations had already been carried out as "safe." "The disease is over there," they would say. Nathan Eck, at the time a refugee from Warsaw, was considering escape from Czestochowa, in which he had found refuge and which had not yet been "affected," to the Bendzin ghetto, where it was "over." He writes:

> We assumed that the enemy had decided to kill many hundreds of thousands of Jews, maybe millions, and that the murder would not pass over any community. Even this conclusion was maddening enough, and many people rejected it. But the possibility of a devilish scheme to destroy us all, to the last man, did not occur in September 1942 even to the greatest pessimist.

This belief led even people who had succeeded in escaping from the deportation trains, execution sites or camps to return to the ghettos from which they had been deported, considering them to be "safe" now.

The coveted guarantee of safety was a document. The best was usually an Aryan descent certificate, which enabled its holder to remain outside the ghetto. For those inside it was usually a labor card, which testified that the holder was employed; it was tantamount to the right to live for the bearer and his family. Those who had no cards were "illegal"; by law they ought to have been deported and had to hide. They literally starved or froze to death.

The cards were of various kinds. There were "good," high-grade cards, especially such as bore the confirmation of the Security Police, or the cards of the Wehrmacht workshops. Others were considered less valuable. From time to time the Germans would annul all previous cards, issuing new ones, in constantly decreasing numbers. A deliberate, constant, kaleidoscopic change of documents went on, in order to keep the Jews perplexed and always chasing the "latest" labor card. It goes without saying that there was a lot of corruption; whoever could afford it purchased a "good" document. The liquidator of Galician Jewry, Katzmann, angrily reported that the Wehrmacht was issuing labor certificates to "Jewish parasites," which of course sabotaged the SS measures of deportations. He found cases where a Jew had accumulated as many as ten or twenty different "protective" documents.

At first there were cards with or without photographs; then a ruling was issued that a card without a photograph provided no protection, so everyone had to get a new card. Then it was announced that a white card was needed, signed by the district office and countersigned by the employee, to testify that the bearer was a "specialist." Then yellow cards were issued. These were called "life-cards" because the Germans promised that their bearers would remain alive. Members of the family received at first blue and later green cards, which were later exchanged for pink and violet cards. Later they changed the card system and issued "ghetto passports." Finally they issued pieces of metal to be worn on the neck. "We called them 'dog numbers,'" recalled a survivor. A man who got a card could affix the names of two children, no more, and his wife or mother, but not both. He had to choose which of the two was to live. "I remember a case of a man coming up to his mother and saying: 'Mother, what shall I do? You led me to my marriage canopy, but now I can take only you or my wife.' And the mother replied: 'The Book of Genesis orders a man to leave his parents and cleave to his wife. . . . I give up my life for your wife.' Then she blessed her daughter-in-law and the children and went away. . . . That was my mother."

*

The courage and endurance of the Jewish woman in the ghetto were unbelievable. Her fate was often more cruel than her husband's. Often she remained alone with the children when he was detained or deported. She had to work like a man, and also to keep up the home inside the inferno. Many women volunteered for social work. "There are house committees where the management is exclusively in the hands of women," Ringelblum recorded in Warsaw. Dr. Aharon Peretz, a gynecologist in Kaunas, recorded:

> In fateful hours the Jewish woman held out with more courage than the man. She was not carried away by undue self-confidence, but she did not sink to the depths of despair either. She was too much absorbed with daily worries to take notice of passing whims. . . . As a doctor I witnessed some of the women's most difficult moments and always admired afresh their greatness and strength. . . . Because of the extreme tension, the worry and the hard labor, many of them developed pathological processes—about eighty per cent lost their monthly cycle. . . . Unwittingly they would reach advanced stages of pregnancy. . . . By an order of July 1942 pregnancy in the Kaunas ghetto was punishable with death to the father, the mother and the infant. . . . We had to start making abortions by the hundreds. . . . Yet there were many women who refused an abortion, for all the danger involved, and with great courage awaited the day of giving birth. One day an intelligent woman called on me. She was pregnant. She asked whether she could postpone the abortion for some time. Her reason was that the Casablanca Conference was taking place at the time and she hoped for a political change.

The greatest tragedy of all was that of the children of the ghetto. They grew up before their time, almost overnight. A survivor said in court: "We were astonished that three- or four-year-old children could understand the tragedy of the situation. They kept silent when necessary. They knew all the hideouts. When we were about to apply a sedative injection, such a small boy would say: 'It is not necessary, I'll keep still.' We were astounded by their behavior."

In Warsaw there were over 100,000 Jewish children. Most of them were thrown into the streets. They were the little breadwinners. They dug under the walls, hid near the ghetto gates, crawled through barbed wire on their way to the Aryan side to bring back some food—a piece of bread or a few potatoes, which they got by begging on the other side. "With their hard-earned treasure they would crawl back through breaks or chinks in the ghetto barrier. Parents would sit at home all day, nervously awaiting the return of their only breadwinner. In tears they would gulp the food brought at such great risk." Had it not been for the smuggling of food, which was punishable with instant death, the ghetto prisoners would not have survived even until the deportations.

Children took over commerce. They peddled goods, sold and bought foodstuffs, traded in foreign currency. Hundreds of them died daily of hunger. At first the sight of a child curled up on the pavement, dead of hunger, caused great excitement. Then people got used to it. "At least 75 percent of the children were in urgent need of social relief," said Dr. Adolf Berman, former director of the CENTOS children institutions, which rendered aid to many of the homeless little ones, running over thirty orphanages in Warsaw alone.

A stupendous educational effort was undertaken in the ghettos. Teaching, apart from vocational training, was forbidden. By using kitchens for children as a cover, a conspiratorial network of schools, primary and secondary, religious and secular, was established. They had regular colleges, where the attendance of pupils was recorded, conferences held with parents, graduation examinations held and diplomas awarded—all illegally. The Jewish Council of Wilno instituted compulsory education. Children even had holiday performances and their own theaters. "We parents trembled when they appeared on the stage, dressed up as butterflies or angels. We did not dare to look into each other's face, conscious of what might be in store for these children tomorrow."

In the Litzmannstadt ghetto twenty thousand children attended the primary schools. For several hours at least they could sit in clean rooms and forget for a while the darkness and despair of the life outside. For a time private courses and secondary education were also organized. When this was prohibited by the Nazis, teaching went on clandestinely in the workshops and factories, where the teachers were officially designated as "labor inspecors."

There are confirmed reports of unbelievable acts of cruelty by the Germans toward little children in the ghettos. Some were tossed in the air and caught on the bayonet point, others were shot at simply for fun or thrown alive into rivers. There were special "children actions," in which these "enemies of the Reich" were dragged to the boxcars.

Orphanages were emptied. Teachers and educators accompanied their wards of their own free will. "I remember the famous educator, Janusz Korczak, and his last march at the head of the procession of children. There were two children at his side; they went in pairs. The head inspector of the institution, Mrs. Stefania Belczycka was with the small children. . . . Korczak was offered his freedom, but he refused; he said he would stay. He was worried that some of the children who were suddenly awakened did not have time to put on their shoes when they were ordered to get up in the middle of the night and get downstairs immediately."

In spite of the dreadful realities there were few suicides among Polish Jews. People acquired poison, but used it only as a last resort to escape torture. "There are fewer suicides today in the ghetto than before the war," recorded a survivor in his diary. "There is a widespread belief that suicide means submission and despair, that it is a sort of desertion. Nobody wants to desert. Everyone has one thought and one wish: to hold out and survive."

People always hoped that at least some of them would survive to tell the story. "For a while an upholsterer lived with us," a survivor said. "On his departure, the upholsterer made the following speech: 'We are now living through such times that you have to live and you must wish to live despite anything and everything. Previously when you were forced to move from one apartment to another that did not quite meet your needs or measure up to your standards, you were apt to throw yourself out of the window. . . . But now it is different. . . . Nothing can force a Jew to lay hands upon himself. . . . He wants to live to see what things will look like later.' "

"This determination to cling to life was the first manifestation of the passive resistance to the Germans that the bulk of the population put up," Ringelblum recorded in his diary. But a more active form of resistance steadily grew and gathered momentum in the ghettos. At first these movements were almost completely isolated from one another, but they developed almost simultaneously in many places and soon became a dominating factor.

The youth movements, especially the Zionist youth movements, became the centers of an underground conspiracy. "We wanted to live, and this desire brought us to the way of fighting, though it led to certain death," Gusta Dawidson-Drenger recorded in her diary, which was written in Cracow prison on scraps of toilet paper.

The youth movements maintained their clandestine activity even before the active resistance took shape. "We wanted to preserve a human and Jewish image, to develop the sense of Jewish honor, to be able to withstand persecution and debasement. This was the youth that, when it finally realized we were facing annihilation, seized arms," said Zivia Lubetkin Zuckerman.

The realization that this time it was not just another campaign of anti-Semitic oppression but a scheme for their complete and total extermination suddenly struck the young pioneers, most of them in their early twenties, like lightning. "If you ask me," said Zivia Lubetkin, "whether we were wiser or more courageous than the others, I answer: 'No.' It was our pioneering education that made us look unafraid at Jewish fate as it was. The youth sized up the events properly because of its outlook and personal training; there is no other explanation. There were many wise and heroic people in Warsaw who did not perceive it."

Yet it was not easy to come forward in public, tear down all illusions about the "deportations for labor," and tell people plainly that their relatives deported for "work in the East" were all dead, that nobody had a chance of survival. The first to come out openly was the Wilno underground, as early as January 1, 1942. It issued a pamphlet saying:

> He that has left the ghetto gates will not return. . . . Throw away your illusions. Your children and husbands are no more. Ponar is not a labor camp. Everyone was shot there. Hitler is plotting to annihilate all the Jews of Europe. . . . We won't go like sheep to the slaughter. True, we are weak and defenseless, but the only answer to the murderers is to fight. Better fall like free fighters than continue living by the grace of the murderers.

They had heartbreaking tasks ahead. In spite of all the evidence, people would not believe that the civilized and cultured Germans had turned into cold-blooded murderers. It was not easy to instill the spirit of a fighting underground into people who out of dejection and despair would say that in any case the struggle was of no avail. "Can our fight be more than just a mere symbol?" they asked. The reply of the young underground fighters was confident. "There was a sense and purpose in an early death if it was for something higher than life itself," as Abba Kovner, a leader of the Wilno underground, put it in his evidence in court. "Any revolt will undermine German strength and dislocate their organization. Let our people only know that they have nothing to risk. Then they will escape in great multitudes. Not singly, but in masses, onto railway stations, to the roads, to flood the country . . . Of course this will turn into a blood bath, but there is nothing to lose. . . . This spark will kindle the smoldering fire of resistance in Europe and turn it into a great purifying flame," said Shimon Drenger.

In Kaunas a definite plan to defend the ghetto was prepared by the underground. As soon as the German units entered to round up people for deportations, everybody was to rally at predetermined assembly points. The fighting units would engage the Germans with whatever weapons they had—axes, knives, pistols—and set buildings on fire, while the population would storm the fences and escape into neighboring woods.

The complete history of the Jewish resistance movement to the Nazis remains to be written. It will reveal a desperate effort to unify all Jewish factions into one fighting body; it will tell a story of unbelievable ingenuity in the acquisition of firearms and disclose the burning sense of duty these young people felt toward Jewish history. In some places they swept the Jewish Councils over to their side, or established tacit or express coordination with them. In other places, where the Councils did not want to listen to any possibility but a "rescue through labor" policy, they had to hide their activity from both the Jewish police and the Gestapo. They had no military training, no resources, and no standing in the community, no central authority on the inside—not even a government-in-exile on the outside. They could not promise a hope of survival, as the Council did; all they could give was the hope of an honorable death. They had nothing to offer to broken, terrorized, exhausted and starving people but the faith that it was worthwhile making a great last effort. How they succeeded in achieving what they did is a miracle.

One of the most important functions of the underground was to establish contact between the ghettos and coordinate their efforts. Yitzhak Zuckerman, Zivia's husband, deputy commander of the Warsaw ghetto revolt, used to tour the country regularly; he had some "Aryan" documents for the purpose.

But it was easier to maintain contact through girls who looked Aryan. "We traveled between the ghettos to find people we were told to meet, to tell them that deportation meant death, and that there could be no rescue if people went voluntarily to the trains," said Rivka Kuper, widow of the heroic leader of the Cracow underground, Dolek Liebeskind. "We had our contact points all over. We forged documents and so helped people to move."

Some of the veteran members of the youth movements who had already secured forged papers and were in hiding outside the ghettos were told to move back inside. An encounter is recorded between one of them, Lisa Magun, who met a friend in a Wilno ghetto street. The friend was astonished: "You, Lisa, with your Aryan face and your good documents, you are back? This is madness." "Who knows what is madness and what is wisdom?" was Lisa's reply. She started a year's work of incessant travels between ghettos. When she finally fell into the hands of the Gestapo, she smuggled out a letter to Abba Kovner, saying: "I am tranquil, because I know what I have to die for." All the frantic efforts of the underground to save her were futile.

"I was a courier between the underground in Cracow and in Warsaw," Hela Rufeisen told the court. "Then I went to other places, like Rzeszów and Lwów. My job was to transfer documents and explosives. Twice I fell into the hands of the Gestapo, but succeeded in disposing of the things I carried. Once I escaped and was wounded when they shot at me, but I entered the Warsaw ghetto and later took part in the revolt."

Gusta Dawidson-Drenger recorded in her diary:

> Anyone who saw Hela on the train, speaking with such charm to her neighbors on right and left, or passing along the platforms, all smiling and attractive, might have thought she was going to visit a fiancé, proceeding on a vacation, or even black-marketing. Nobody would have imagined that this girl was responsible for a whole platoon of our people, their nourishment and their safety. . . . Under the sports jacket hanging nonchalantly over her shoulder were two pistols. A third was in her bag.

Such girl couriers established a new type of heroine. They volunteered for the most dangerous assignments. "They accept the most difficult missions and discharge them without the least complaint or even a moment's hesitation," Ringelblum recorded in his diary. "They are constantly exposed to the greatest danger. They are ready to take tremendous risks just on the strength of their 'Aryan' appearance and the scarves with which they cover their heads." This was true of all of them; of Mina Liebeskind, Gusta Drenger, Gola Mirer, Tosia Altman, Haike Grossman, Witka Kempner, the sisters Sara and Rosa Silber, and dozens of others.

The movement grew, and in spite of unspeakable terrors soon spread into many places. A steady triangle was established between Warsaw, Wilno and Bialystok, which radiated its inspiration all over occupied Poland.

One of their problems was whether to fight inside the ghetto or break out and join the partisans. "In the eastern part," said Yitzhak Zuckerman, "where the forests and the marshes were near, there was a big Jewish partisan movement. Some twenty thousand Jews were fighting in White Russia and the Ukraine. But for us it was a matter of principle to fight inside the ghettos everywhere, and not only where the forests were too far away. We, the young and the strong, could not leave the ghetto and let the aged and the sick be carried out to Treblinka." Abba Kovner told the same story. The Soviet partisan commander in the Wilno area pressed him to send out the youth to fight in the woods. "I explained to him and to the higher command that our aim was to give a fighting reply to the murder in the ghettos, for the sake of our honor and our people. It was not a matter of saving our lives. . . . We were living among our people, with our mothers, sisters and brothers, and we had to save either them or their honor. We did not want, until the very last moment, to take out of the ghetto the little arms and the few young men we had, and leave them alone."

They had to decide when the fighting should start. Each additional day allowed for better preparations, but was fraught with new dangers. Active members were being constantly arrested and deported in the general round-ups. Some members of the command maintained that the fighting should start only when the worst came to the worst. Others were all for immediate combat. "We knew that the delay might destroy us, and we resolved that this was now the limit. Not another Jew would be deported. Even then there were people who told us that we were precipitately assuming responsibility before Jewish history for the fate of the Jews."

There were places where the underground refused to wait. Dolek Liebeskind in Cracow was burning with the desire to fight and take revenge. "There was no weakness in him. He did not believe in any other way. . . . 'Nobody can escape,' he would repeat. 'Let us die honorably. Let us, a few, create a legend of heroism.'" On December 22, 1942, when the streets of Cracow were full of German Christmas shoppers and army clubs and cafés were crowded, they struck at the main meeting places of the SS officers. The fighters entered in German uniform and attacked with hand grenades and small-arms fire. Others attacked and disarmed Gestapo men on the streets, distributed leaflets and waved Zionist and Polish flags on the bridges of the Vistula. The Germans were taken completely by surprise. Many were killed and wounded.

The authorities were stunned. A Jewish attack on senior officers in Cracow, Frank's headquarters, under the nose of the SS command, was unbelievable. Hitler himself, then at the height of the winter campaign, requested immediate explanations. Heinrich Mueller reported that the Jewish terrorists Adolf (Dolek) Liebeskind and Yehuda Tenenbaum had been killed after a lively exchange of fire with the Gestapo, and a hiding place of firearms, money and ammunition had been discovered.

The fall of some of the leaders was not the end of the affair in Cracow. Their work went on. Soon, however, arrests followed. Usually no underground fighter let himself be arrested without fighting for his life. Escapes from both the women's and the men's prisons were organized on March 15, 1943. Gusta and her husband Shimon escaped, met and continued their underground activity, editing the illegal *Fighting Pioneer,* until they were arrested and executed several months later.

In Bialystok the commander was Mordechai Tenenbaum-Tamaroff, a fearless fighter, who risked his life hundreds of times. The revolt was his whole life. In January, 1943, he heard of the first Warsaw uprising and, not receiving a reply to his queries, believed they had all fallen. He thought he was now all alone, the last to lead Jews into battle, and he felt a crushing responsibility for the future of his community.

At the beginning of February, 1943, he received the news that the Bialystok ghetto was about to be liquidated. The signal for general preparedness had been given, and Tenenbaum recorded in his diary: "I now go to the big conference, where it will be decided how we shall begin; but first a bath, a shave and a cup of tea . . . there is panic outside, but we are tranquil." And later in the day: "All is ready, but devil take it, we need 30 wire-springs. All the other parts are there. Each spring—a hand grenade. We are short of 30. I can't get such wires in the whole ghetto." Later in the day: "The action has been postponed. A miracle has happened. Tomorrow everybody goes to work." And later again:

No reply from Warshaw to my cables. I shall go crazy. . . . Zivia, Yitzhak, all the people . . . whom I lived with for six months and whom I loved, are they all gone? We won't confer together any more, laugh and suffer together. . . . And Tema—[his beloved, to whom he had assigned the most dangerous duties] I am afraid to think of it, but my heart tells me she is no more. . . . And here they don't begin the action that will put an end to all this. . . . I shall send cables out every day to all the addresses I have, and if it is true [that the Warsaw underground is gone], I shall complete all preparations earlier. In a month everything will be done and ready.

But the next day the Jews of Bialystok were not permitted to go to work after all. The panic grew: "They [the Germans] want people to deport," Tenenbaum recorded in his diary. "The atmosphere is electric. People jump at every word. The shadow of death approaches, between a mountain of despair and a spark of hope." He went to see Barasz, the chairman of the Council, privately.

"They asked us for 17,600 Jews," said Barasz. Then they brought the number down to three transports of 2,100 each. They will take only the unemployed. The "good" Germans say they will not allow more than one transport to be taken because this sabotages the labor effort. How nice of them! Barasz believes they will take all three transports, day after day. . . . The conference. Barasz imparts the main information. I tell them that if the "action" is of this size, we won't react. We sacrifice 6,300 Jews to save the other 35,000. . . . The military situation at the front is now such that a radical change may take place any day . . . and we are not ready yet.

Several days later he recorded: "Nonsensical optimistic 'news': Barasz was told that the ghettos of Bialystok and Lódz will remain intact till the end of the war. Silly and empty talk."

On his writings he inscribed, before burying them: "Greetings to the 'researcher' who will bring them out into the daylight again." To his sister, in Palestine, he wrote a long letter, telling of their mother's and Tema's deaths, informing her of the annihilation camps and of the delay in starting the revolt.

Had we already thrown our homemade hand grenades, no Jew would now be alive here. But we will throw them. People here look at me, somewhat ashamed, somewhat entreating: "Perhaps not yet, perhaps some other time." . . . How much people yearn to live. . . . If I really wanted it, I could, at the cost of my honor and against my will, see you again. But I don't want it.

On August 15, 1943, he led his people in battle. The Germans had to use artillery and a plane to crush the revolt of a few hundred boy and girl fighters. The fighting went on for several days. The outcome was, of course, inevitable. With a few exceptions, they all fell fighting.

That much was clear in all the ghettos: once the underground went into action, it would spell the doom of everybody. It was difficult to take the responsibility to precipitate the end.

In Czestochowa they produced the first homemade hand grenades in February, 1943. "We trembled with joy," they said. They imposed a tax on the ghetto to support the resistance, but before they had a chance to use their weapons, some of the most experienced members were arrested and executed when a Polish driver they hired delivered them to the Gestapo. Finally, on June 25, 1943, they went into open action. After several hours of fierce fighting they all fell. The ghetto was blown up. A group that tried to escape was betrayed by their Polish guide. They were captured and, after an exchange of fire, were shot on the spot.

In Wilno they sabotaged railways, tank repair workshops and munition plants. They had to smuggle the explosives into the ghetto and smuggle out the saboteurs with the stuff on them. "The German railway was sabotaged in Lithuania not by the Poles, the Russians or the Lithuanians but by the Jewish women fighters, who did not even have a base to return to, and had to find ways to get back to the ghetto." After a brief, fierce encounter with the Germans, the underground fighters of Wilno joined the partisans.

In Kaunas the Jewish resistance, with the active assistance of the Council, developed a ramified and widespread organization, the story of which has only recently been told, revealing glorious acts of bravery in the Commando operations inside the ghetto and in the ranks of the partisans which the resisters were steadily joining.

In Riga the Jewish police actively assisted the underground. "The resistance movement grew steadily," testified Eliezer Kerstadt. "We slowly accumulated arms. . . . The SD somehow got to know of it. While searching a place, they found, to our misfortune, lists of the active members. Three hundred members of the underground were arrested and executed."

In many other places, like Lwów, Brody and Przemyśl, the resistance was liquidated by the Germans through mishaps, searches, denunciations or general deportations, before they had a chance to act. Katzmann reported finding numerous caches of arms in Jewish hiding places.

But the great saga of Jewish resistance, which became a glorious symbol, is the story of the Warsaw ghetto revolt. It was the only uprising in occupied Europe that broke out with no relieving forces to count upon, no retreat to hide in and no chance of success, other than the saving of human dignity.

The epic of the young heroes who engaged the Germans for over a month and afterward continued to fight for weeks from the smoldering ruins and rubble, is well known. Much has been written and said about it; much still remains to be told. It certainly needs no detailed repetition in this brief glance into the ghettos, which can give no more than an outline of the main features.

It started on August 20, 1942, when the resistance set buildings on fire at night to mark the blacked-out city for Russian bombers. In the resulting confusion the first few pistols were smuggled in. Then came the dreadful September "selection" at "The Pot," the corner of Mila and Gesia streets, which lasted six days. Those who were ordered to the left, to Stawki, went to the deportation wagons; to the right was the road of survival. About 100,000 Jews were deported, including a considerable part of the Jewish police. When all was over, sixty thousand Jews remained in Warsaw out of half a million, mainly the young and strong whom the Germans considered still able to do some work. "We were ashamed to have remained alive," said

Yitzhak Zuckerman. "Two members of the command fell. Our people said this was the moment for a last act of despair, to put the whole ghetto on fire and die with it. It was a most dramatic and decisive moment in the life of the underground. I opposed the proposal and did not gain much popularity. My view was that since we had remained alive it would be senseless to give away our lives so cheaply. If we could gain a few days or months they should be used for getting arms and training."

Frantic efforts were continued to get more firearms. On January, 18, 1943, the underground struck and the first German victims fell. A fierce exchange of fire ensued. The Jews fought to the last round of ammunition. Mordechai Anilewicz, the commander, was the only one of his group of thirty to stay alive. When there was no ammunition left in his rifle, he snatched one from a German and made his escape with his fists. Skirmishes continued next day.

The Germans were taken by surprise. They never expected a Jewish rebellion. The poet Yitzhak Katzenelson wrote:

> They did not know, they did not believe.
> The Jews are shooting—
> I heard an ugly voice in a corrupt mouth,
> before he breathed his last, unclean breath,
> Not his normal shout I heard,
> Only a horrified cry: "Is it possible?"

Katznelson entered the bunker of the underground saying: "I am happy to die amidst fighting pioneers. We will take with us into our graves the awareness that the Jewish people will endure eternally."

The January uprising was a turning point. The Germans retreated. Himmler himself was alerted and, after inspecting the ghetto, ordered it to be razed to the ground, "because Warsaw will never quiet down and its criminal deeds will never end as long as the ghetto stands. It is necessary that the dwelling space for 500,000 subhumans, which will never be of any use to the Germans anyway, should completely disappear."

The Gestapo sent their contact man to the Council to appease them, to promise more food, establishment of kindergartens, assuring everybody that the people who remained were productive and would most certainly not be deported. Anyway there was no reason for panic, as the deportations were only for labor. They used the German industrialist Toebbens as an emissary to deny the "malicious" rumors that the deported Jews were being killed. The underground replied with a manifesto: "Jews! Don't believe the lies spread by those who are working for the Gestapo. . . . The time has come to fight. No Jew will mount the transport wagon! If you can't fight, hide!" The Council finally replied to the Germans that they no longer had any authority over the ghetto.

On April 19, 1943, on the eve of Passover, the Germans entered the ghetto.

The attacking force was headed by Juergen Stroop, forty-eight-year-old Major General of the Waffen SS, a veteran of the campaigns in Poland and Russia, a soldier of wide experience. He had at his disposal one reinforced armored battalion, one cavalry battalion, three German police battalions, Ukrainian and Polish auxiliary police units, artillery equipment and sapper demolition squads. Facing him was the twenty-four-year-old Mordechai Anilewicz, whom the underground had appointed as its commander. He had at his disposal about a thousand youngsters, armed with three light machine guns, a few hundred revolvers, eighty rifles, a few thousand hand grenades and explosives.

Zuckerman, the deputy commander, was over on the Aryan side of Warsaw in search of firearms when the revolt started. Five days later Anilewicz smuggled out a letter to him, saying:

> Our most daring expectations were surpassed: The Germans withdrew from the ghetto. . . . We attacked the Germans and inflicted heavy losses on them. Our losses, on the other hand, were on the whole light. Even this is an achievement. . . . We are forced by circumstances to take recourse to guerrilla fighting. . . . Tonight our groups are starting out . . . to scout the area and seize arms. . . . We need hand grenades and rifles. . . . Individuals perhaps will survive. Sooner or later all the others must fall. In all the bunkers of our members there is not enough air to light a candle. . . . Perhaps we shall see each other again. The main thing is: the dream of my life has come true. I saw a Jewish fighting defense in Warsaw ghetto in all its greatness and splendor.

"We were happy and laughing," said Zivia Lubetkin Zuckerman. "We knew, we felt, then that the end of the Germans was near. We knew they would defeat us, of course, but we knew they would pay dearly for it. . . . It is difficult to describe it. . . . When we threw our grenades and saw German blood on the streets of Warsaw, after they had been flooded with so much Jewish blood and tears, a great joy possessed us. . . . They, the great fighters, were fleeing from our primitive homemade grenades. . . . Of course they came back. . . . They had ammunition, water and bread . . . all the things we lacked. . . . They came with heavy artillery and tanks. . . . Using Molotov cocktails we set a tank on fire. . . . They left hundreds of dead and wounded there. . . . In the ghetto people were embracing and kissing each other, although everyone knew it was almost certain he would fall. Rabbi Meyzel put his hand on my head and said . . . 'Bless you, it will be good to die now. We should have done it earlier.'"

The fighting was conducted mainly from the cellars. The bunker of the command at Mila 18 was a great underground structure with wide ramifications. Each cave was named after one of the destruction camps. The heat inside "Treblinka bunker" was unbearable. Everyone was swimming in his own and other people's sweat. An incessant flow of fighters from other bunkers made the food situation simply disastrous.

The unequal fighting continued from house to house. At night the fighters emerged to get food and strike at the German positions. Street fighting developed, in the course of which many more Germans fell. Stroop sent out daily reports to his impatient superiors, explaining the inordinate length of the operation by the

> stubbornness of the Jewish bandits, who show a high resistance power. . . . In many instances bunkers were breached from which people had not emerged since the beginning of the fighting. . . . In many cases they finally lacked the strength to come out. . . . They are shooting to the last round of ammunition. . . . Some of them appear in the streets wearing German uniforms. . . . We are relentlessly using all our forces and energies by night and day.

"We are now approaching the core of the resistance," he reported on April 27. Four days later he wrote: "Many gang leaders and obvious bandits were caught today. . . . Nobody leaves a hiding place, even after discovery, otherwise than through force."

High German quarters were deeply disturbed. On May 1, Goebbels recorded in his diary: "Exceedingly serious fights in Warsaw between the police and part of our Wehrmacht and the rebellious Jews."

On May 4, Stroop requested further aid from the army. Three days later he reported that he had located the central bunker of the command, which would soon be stormed. On May 8, 1943, the seat of the command at Mila 18 was forced by the Germans.

The 120 fighters did not respond to the request to surrender. The Germans threw in gas. The fighters got nearer to the entrances of the bunker and waited for the Germans with their weapons ready. But instead more gas was poured in. "Let us kill ourselves and not fall alive into their hands," suggested Arieh Wilner.

A macabre scene of suicides followed. Sometimes a revolver would not work and its bewildered holder would ask a friend to shoot him. While this went on somebody shouted that one of the several secret entrances to the bunker was undetected by the Germans. Only a handful left. All others, over a hundred fighters, fell. Among them was the heroic, handsome, ever-smiling commander, Mordechai Anilewicz.

Yet even now the fighting continued. On May 12 Stroop set fire to the ghetto. On May 15 he handed in his report on almost a month of fighting, beginning with the words: "There are no longer any Jewish habitations in Warsaw." Still the shooting went on for a few weeks more from among the ruins. As late as May 22 Goebbels noted: "The battle of the Warsaw ghetto continues. The Jews are still resisting."

Finally, in June, all was quiet. The ghetto was dead.

Only a handful of the fighters forced their way through the sewers to the Aryan side of Warsaw. Fifteen months later they fought again, this time in the ranks of the Polish underground, when Polish Warsaw revolted. The Soviet Army was then on the other side of the city across the Vistula.

Eichmann was sent out to the spot after the ghetto revolt to inspect the scene of the fighting, as he told Sassen: "Mueller told me to get out there to see for myself how far these things could go. . . . I was shown the nests of resistance, which had been taken only with concentrated charges. I was shown the scene of the great campaign. It was a hard fight. I seldom saw a place so destroyed as Warsaw." On another occasion he told Sassen: "Our losses were several thousand. . . . I never imagined that ghettoized Jews would be able to fight in such a manner."

CHAPTER

12

The Great Powers and the Little Man

I have tried to convey the flavor of life behind the ghetto walls, and to show the reaction of the Jewish people and of others to the unprecedented Nazi outburst of ferocity.

But the Jews, though the chief target of Nazi bestiality, were only one element on the world scene. Hitler had become the chief of state of an immensely powerful civilized country, a member of the concert of nations. He had expressed his views, his character and his mentality with such clamor both before and after he took power that the world had had ample time to form its opinion.

In order to situate Eichmann within his historic context it is essential to understand not only the behavior of his victims but the international reaction to Hitlerism.

After his advent to power Hitler repeatedly proclaimed his desire for peace, his rejection of the very idea of war and his assurances that he had no territorial claims whatsoever. He promised never to annex Austria, renounced forever all claims to Alsace-Lorraine, and swore to remain for all time unconditionally faithful to his nonagression pact with Poland.

All these solemn pronouncements, so different from the fiery propaganda of the Nazis during their struggle for power, might well have deluded a complacent world. Many naïve people sighed with relief, hoping that, with the responsibilities of government on his shoulders, and with the internal social and economic problems that he said he was going to tackle first, Hitler would leave the rest of the world in peace.

On the Jewish front, however, there was no room for any illusions. The Boycott Day of April 1, 1933, the racial laws of September 15, 1935, the *Kristallnacht* of November 9, 1938, marked a steady crescendo of tragedy. No one could have entertained any hope here, for the Nazis made no attempt to conceal their intentions. Nor was there any real secret about the mass arrests, the persecutions, the concentration camps and the declared aim: to get rid of the Jews at all costs. It was only the last stage of the Final Solution that was implemented behind the smoke screen of war operations, and even then the news soon leaked out.

How did the world respond to this unprecedented moral challenge?

For a while it pretended to have noticed nothing alarming. Germany continued to be an honored and much courted member of the family of nations, even while breaking its formal and ethical obligations one by one. The world still traded with Germany as before; the Olympic Games were held in Berlin in August, 1936, as if nothing were wrong. The Olympic Committee did not take action on the Nazis' crass, last-minute breach of promise in totally removing all German athletes of Jewish origin. The foreign sportsmen received a warm welcome; brilliant parties were thrown in their honor, with Goering, Goebbels and Ribbentrop playing the cordial hosts. Friendships were struck up, such as that between Deputy Fuehrer Hess and the Duke of Hamilton, to whose home in Scotland Hess flew on his peace mission several years later. Even the SS organ *Das Schwarze Korps* published "A Word to Our Guests," telling them they would be welcome whether they were liberals, Fascists or socialists, and only asking them not to interfere in Germany's internal affairs, "just as we do not criticize affairs in their respective countries."

The world was content to leave the Jewish question alone as Germany's internal affair. No foreign entanglements or international difficulties followed upon the virulent anti-Jewish measures in Germany. The diplomats of the Third Reich were put to no embarrassment on this score; its emissaries were received everywhere with full honors. Heydrich was elected head of Interpol (then called International Criminal Commission).

When the Jews started to stream out of Germany under the impact of the first Nazi blows, the League of Nations appointed James G. McDonald to the newly created post of High Commissioner for Refugees (Jewish and others). After over two years of impotent efforts to tackle the difficulties, he gave up. In his letter of resignation of December 27, 1935, he drew the world's attention to a "portentous fact which confronts the community of states, since more than half a million persons . . . are being crushed. . . . When domestic policies threaten the demoralization and exile of hundreds of thousands of human beings, considerations of diplomatic correctness must yield to those of common humanity." He urged organized mankind to bring pressure to bear upon Germany to stop creating refugees or to open its own doors to them.

Nothing of the kind was done. The Jews remained in the no-man's land of humanity.

Finally, after more than five years of inactivity, the Western world, under extreme pressure of public opinion, decided to act. An international conference on refugees was convened at Evian, Switzerland, by President

Franklin D. Roosevelt. In July, 1938, representatives of thirty-two countries listened for a week to lofty speeches; there was such a flow of loquacity that if words of compassion could produce a haven no Jewish tragedy would have taken place.

The delegates were all aware of the problem; the Chairman of the Conference, Myron C. Taylor, spoke of "the harrowing urgency of the situation," when men and women were being "uprooted from the homes where they have long been established," and declared on behalf of the United States that the continuation of the present situation would produce "catastrophic human suffering." He made an urgent plea for immediate international cooperation; so did Lord Winterton for Britain, and other delegates. But when it came to concrete proposals, it soon transpired that each country expected the others to shoulder the burden. Palestine—the only country where an existing Jewish population was clamoring for the admission of Jewish refugees in unlimited numbers—was excluded because of the well-known British policy. Santo Domingo, Alaska, British Guiana, Madagascar and Kenya were mentioned as possible areas of absorption. The participating countries, whose total population well exceeded 500 million people, were unable to take in half a million helpless wrecks, especially those who were penniless. One after the other delegates rose to declare how willing they were to help, but were, unfortunately, unable to. In order to avert the complete failure of the Conference, the ball was passed to an Intergovernmental Committee on Refugees, which established its seat in London with George Rublee, an American, as Director, "to improve the conditions of emigration." After some preliminary efforts he reported to the Secretary of State that he had found all doors locked against the immigrants, with new restrictions appearing almost daily everywhere.

From diplomatic contacts the Germans soon learned that America was not prepared to change the national quota system or increase the quotas, and in other places only Jews in possession of sufficient foreign exchange would be admitted. Ribbentrop heard from the French Foreign Minister, Georges Bonnet, that France's great interest in the Jewish problem was, in the first place, "not to receive any more Jews." With an air of commiseration and understanding, Ribbentrop replied: "We all wish to get rid of the Jews, but no country wishes to admit them."

Switzerland complained to Germany of the "mass crossings of the border by Jewish refugees," especially from Vienna. "Switzerland, which has as little use for these Jews as has Germany, will take measures to protect herself from being swamped by the Jews."

This was the reaction of the proverbial countries of asylum.

Not long afterward, Hitler publicly derided the democratic world, which "is oozing sympathy for the poor, tormented Jewish people, but remains hard and obdurate when it comes to helping them."

The reason for this attitude, and the concealment of even the little that was being done, was admitted by the British Prime Minister, Neville Chamberlain, at a top-level conference with his French colleague, Édouard Daladier. "One of the chief difficulties," he said, "was the serious danger of arousing anti-Semitic feeling in Great Britain." He therefore could not publicly admit that the United Kingdom had been for some time admitting five hundred Jewish immigrants per week, and that Australia was taking in a certain number "without any publicity."

This was exactly what the Nazis were aiming at: that the democratic leaders should be ashamed of publicly appearing to support the Jews. Later Goebbels recorded in his diary: "We are going to step up our anti-Semitic propaganda so that . . . no enemy statesman will dare to be seen at the side of a Jew without being immediately discredited by his own people as a stooge of the Jews."

In this field the Reich's Propaganda Minister attained a degree of success that surpassed all expectations. The politicians' fear of being stigmatized as "Jew-lovers" brought about a conspiracy of inactivity—and, for as long as was possible, of silence—on the plight of the Jews, which was later interrupted from time to time, under the strong pressure of public opinion, by ineffectual lip service. No doors were opened to the Jews and no refuge was offered.

*

The *Kristallnacht* pogroms on November 9, 1938, shook the world. The flames of the burning synagogues luridly illuminated the sufferings of the Jews; its first victims ominously foreshadowed the future. Pressed by the outraged press, the democracies decided "to act" once more. So six days later Roosevelt sharply denounced the outbreak and recalled the U.S. Ambassador "for report and consultation," and Chamberlain announced in Parliament on November 17 that Jews who had no means of support would be allowed to settle in . . . Tanganyika. But Rublee's tentative plan that each of the Evian countries declare its willingness to absorb 25,000 refugees was rejected by the countries concerned.

Roosevelt was fully aware of the increasing seriousness of the situation, as is shown by his almost prophetic pronouncement. "The fact must be faced that there exists in Central and Eastern Europe a religious group of some seven million persons for whom the economic and social future is exceedingly dark," he cabled to Myron Taylor on January 14, 1939.

In practice, however, the American Government looked to Portugal to let the Jews settle in Angola, and asked Mussolini whether he would not allow the Jews into his newly conquered province of Ethiopia. The Duce refused, saying that America was large and rich enough to settle Jewish refugees in its own territory "if it entertained such lively sympathy for the Jews."

The British Government, which was to approach the Lisbon authorities on the Angola project, refused to do so in view of the "sensitivity of Portuguese opinion" on colonial matters.

The Nazis watched it all and drew their own conclusions. Hitler told the South African Defense Minister, Pirow, that "Germany exports anti-Semitism," and consequently "the Jewish problem would now emerge everywhere. We shall solve it in the immediate future. . . . The Jews will disappear."

Rublee's main efforts were now directed to getting the Germans to release part of the immigrants' property, as only this made them eligible for entry visas to foreign countries. The Nazis were adamant and declared that they would continue to requisition Jewish property. But they came out with a counterproposal: that "International Jewry" should float a loan of a billion and a half marks to Germany to finance the exit of the Jews; the loan was to be repayable from increased exports of German goods. America called this, with understandable indignation, "barter for human misery," and refused to consider it.

The impasse could not be broken. The Germans would not allow the Jews to take out money, while other countries would not admit penniless immigrants; Rublee soon resigned his thankless post. With the annexation of Czechoslovakia on March 15, 1939, the refugees were altogether abandoned. They were victimized by unscrupulous travel bureaus and other corrupt agencies, which purported to have obtained the much-coveted entrance visas, but in fact simply dumped people across the frontiers on vermin-infested barges.

A typical example was a boatload of refugees packed on board the *St. Louis,* which sailed from Hamburg for Cuba. When the boat arrived in Havana, the nine hundred refugees were not permitted to land, for their visas were all void. The President of Cuba, Laredo Bru, ordered the ship to leave; for a while it wandered about in Caribbean waters. Then the President announced that he would allow the passengers to disembark against deposits of five hundred dollars each, but while this was being arranged the offer was rescinded, on the ground that the time limit had elapsed; the ship sailed back to Europe. Jewish welfare bodies submitted guarantees that the refugees would not become public charges and would eventually re-emigrate. Under this stipulation, and "provided this will not constitute a precedent for further shiploads," the wanderers were finally allowed to set foot, in various groups, in Britain, Holland, Belgium and France.

On May 17, 1939, while shiploads of refugees were wandering across the seven seas, seeking asylum as far away as Shanghai, Hong Kong and Singapore, the British Government published its "contribution" toward the alleviation of their sufferings in the form of a White Paper on its Palestine policy. It proclaimed that in the course of the next five years not more than 75,000 Jews would be allowed into Palestine; thereafter Jewish immigration would depend on Arab acquiescence. The British Navy was sent out to patrol the Mediterranean and imposed a blockade on the "illegal immigration" vessels bound for the shores of Palestine. Despair fell upon the abandoned Jews of Germany, Austria and Czechoslovakia. Soon they were engulfed by the gigantic world conflict, which immediately brought three million additional Jews under the Nazi heel, with many more to follow.

*

The news of the first massacres, executions and expulsions in occupied Poland soon reached America, but the United States did not change its own immigration policy. Roosevelt urged the Intergovernmental Committee on Refugees, which met in Washington on October 17, 1939, "to survey and study definitely and scientifically the geographical and economic problem of resettling several million people in new areas on the earth's surface." But "the most important of the colonization plans touched upon by the President was the Dominican Republic project." This was all America had to offer to the stampede of frantic people fleeing from the European death trap; nor did America's policy change when it was reported that 400,000 Jews were trying to escape to Spain but only those with visas permitting them to proceed further were allowed to enter the country.

At the time Germany was still committed to the policy of expelling the Jews; it remained so for at least two years. "Our interest continues to be in a great Jewish immigration, which we are interested in promoting by all means whatsoever," wrote the RSHA to the Foreign Office in October, 1939.

At the turn of the year Britain was subjected to the blitz. Canada and America announced their readiness to save the endangered children of Britain; a gigantic evacuation scheme was started. It was abandoned only after the sinking of a ship by submarines and upon Churchill's determined opposition.

At about that time *Pets Magazine*, appearing in Chicago, published in its issues of August and September, 1940, an urgent appeal to American dog-lovers "to furnish homes for refugee British dogs, if and when it was possible to get them over here." The idea was to evacuate the blitzed-out purebred dogs of Great Britain and bring them to safety. There was a picture of a puppy, entitled "I want a home," with the caption: "I was born three weeks ago. . . . I am homeless, hungry, weary of roaming the countryside," accompanied by a pathetic editorial. The appeal produced what the editors called "a most gratifying response." Several thousand Americans wrote back, saying that they were each ready to provide a haven for a refugee dog.

No one thought of anything similar for the Jews. No one even considered the possibility of putting refugees on any available ships calling at neutral Spain, returning in ballast to neutral ports or bound for waters proclaimed as American security zone. No doubt there would have been great difficulties involved in any such action, but no one seems to have even considered its feasibility during the two precious years when the exit doors were still open, America was still neutral and Germany was still courting it to stay so. But there were ways and means of saving non-Jews, even though the scarcity of shipping was immense. In 1942 the United States Government agreed to assist in transporting thousands of Polish children and their mothers, altogether ten thousand people, from the Soviet Union to some other country. It was planned to take them to South Africa. Some time later the Secretary of State, Cordell Hull, informed his British colleague that America was then spending about three million dollars for the transportation to Mexico of Polish refugees who had come out of Russia and were being assembled in Persia.

With regard to a suggestion to evacuate "60 or 70 thousand Jews threatened with extermination unless got out very urgently," Eden told Roosevelt and other top American statesmen that "the whole problem of the Jews in Europe is most difficult and we [the British] should move very cautiously about offering to take all Jews out of a country. *If we do so, then the Jews of the world will be wanting us to make similar offers in Poland and Germany. Hitler might well take us up on any such offer* and there simply are not enough ships and means of transportation in the world to handle them" (my italics). Eden pleaded with the Americans not to make too expansive promises in regard to the refugees.

The British were, therefore, not at all certain that it was "useless to make offers of asylum" since Hitler would in any case reject any appeal to let the Jews out, as the spokesman for the government said in the House of Lords. On the contrary, they were most apprehensive that he might very well agree.

The Nazis, on their part, were constantly probing how far they could go with the Jews without incurring some special, immediate retribution. As time went on and nothing much happened, they were reassured. But they still braced themselves for some counteraction on the part of the West, or at least for some vigorous reaction. "There will be repercussions in America," the occupation authorities in France warned when Jewish businesses there belonging to American citizens were forced like all other Jewish shops to put up the yellow badge. The American Government lodged a protest, to which the Germans did not reply. No further action was taken; that was where the matter was left. This was in November, 1940, over a year before America entered the war.

Gone were the days when the United States Congress in 1913 forced President Taft to abrogate the American commercial treaty with Czarist Russia for discriminating against Jews of American nationality by not allowing them to enter Russian territory.

For almost three years even the specific mention of Jewish suffering was taboo in Allied proclamations, so as to lend no support to Hitler's allegation that the democracies were fighting a "Jewish war." When the news of the *Einsatzgruppen* murders reached the West, Churchill poured all his powerful scorn on the "methodical, merciless butchery" which "surpasses anything that has been known since the darkest and most bestial ages of mankind." He confessed that he could not define the enormity of the horrors which he called "a crime without a name."

But the victims, at least, had a name. It was left out.

Sometime later, on January 13, 1942, an Inter-Allied Conference was held at St. James's Palace, London, at the invitation of the Polish Government-in-exile, with seventeen countries represented as participants or guests. Many speeches were delivered denouncing the tyranny of the Nazis and the deeds of their barbarian gangs. With the sole exception of Mr. Joseph Bech, the Luxembourg Minister of Foreign Affairs, who spoke of the deportation of "our monks, our priests, our Jews, our intellectuals," not one of the distinguished prime ministers, foreign secretaries and ambassadors even breathed the name of the main martyr. Nor were the crimes against the Jews even mentioned in the joint declaration proclaiming that the guilty would be handed over to justice.

In the same month of January, 1942, Roosevelt, having now officially joined the common struggle, addressed heartening messages to the peoples of Belgium, Czechoslovakia, Denmark, France, Greece, Yugoslavia, the Netherlands, Norway and Poland. The messages were broadcast to each of these countries in its own language. The President spoke of "the unprovoked murder, executions, imprisonments, tortures and starvation" inflicted by "the horde of German troops and Gestapo agents." He castigated Hitlerism for what it was, pledged America to fight to the end to smash the war lords and to liberate the enslaved people of Europe, and extended to the occupied nations words of encouragement. There was not a single word about the Jews.

Not that it was unknown in London, Washington and Moscow that the Jews were being singled out even among the subjugated nations for "special treatment." From December, 1939, onward, the British press carried partial reports on some of the massacres. *Die Zeit*, the German organ in London, reported the early deportations from Berlin; it even named Eichmann as the executioner of German Jewry. In his message to the *Jewish Chronicle* on its centenary, Prime Minister Churchill wrote: "None has suffered more cruelly than the Jew the unspeakable evil wrought on the bodies and spirits of men by Hitler and his vile regime. The Jew bore the brunt of the Nazis' first onslaught." But this knowledge was not for use in general pronouncements of policy. Even Churchill's message of good wishes on Balfour Declaration Day, promising that "better days will surely come for your suffering people," was sent to Dr. Chaim Weizmann, President of the Jewish Agency, with the request that "it be treated as private."

The Germans observed it all and were quick to draw their conclusions.

They had long realized that the notion that the Jews were so close to the hearts of the democratic leaders was all humbug. Now they found out that the world did not even care. Barely a week after the St. James's Palace Conference, on January 20, 1942, another conference was held. It was at Wannsee, Berlin, where the technique of the Final Solution was decided on.

A tragic symbol of the free world's attitude was the fate of the *Struma,* a small vessel of 180 tons used for the transport of animals on the Danube, which succeeded in eluding the vigilance of the Nazis and sailed from Rumania toward Palestine overburdened with a cargo of 769 Jewish refugees. After a perilous journey on the rough Black Sea, the ship anchored in Istanbul on December 16, 1941. The Turkish authorities did not allow the passengers to disembark. The Jewish Agency immediately requested permission for their entry to Palestine. The British Government took two months to "consider the matter," and on February 15, 1942, it announced that, "in view of the precarious supply position in Palestine," only children between the ages of eleven and sixteen would be admitted. With regard to the others there were also "security reasons" to be considered, it was said, for Nazi spies might have been planted among the refugees. The Jewish Agency pointed to the thousands of non-Jewish refugees—Greeks, Poles, Serbs, Frenchmen and others—who had found a sanctuary in Palestine. On the ridiculous "shortage of supply" excuse, the Agency declared that every Jewish home in Palestine would be opened to the refugees. It was willing to devote its entire immigration quota under the White Paper of 1939 to the rescue of these refugees. "It is unimaginable," the Jewish Agency wrote, "even on humanitarian grounds alone, that the gates of this country should be closed before Jews who escaped the horrors which befell Rumanian Jewry, and that they should be sent back for annihilation, while this country was welcoming, and justly so, non-Jewish refugees from enemy countries."

The people on board the vessel grew desperate. "Our conditions are awful here," they wrote from Istanbul to their relatives in Palestine. "Do what you can for us. We do hope that after all we will soon arrive at our final destination."

They soon did. Their destination was final, indeed.

When the British High Commissioner still refused to allow the refugees entry to Palestine, the Turkish authorities ordered the captain of the *Struma* to leave Istanbul Harbor, despite his protests that the ship was not seaworthy. The vessel was tugged out and sailed in the direction of Bulgaria. Two days later, on February 24, 1942, it sank in the Bosphorus. With the exception of one survivor, all its passengers and crew perished.

Angry questions were asked in the House of Lords. Lord Wedgwood openly charged the Palestine Administration with anti-Semitism and Lord Davis said that Hitler's cause had been served by this "stupid, callous and inhuman act," for no other reason, he said, than to curry favor with the Arab recalcitrants.

Lord Cranborne, for the government, dismissed all protests with the argument that the British must be impartial between Jew and Arab. "Any departure from such policy would at once raise wider issues," he declared. In view of the exigencies of war he asked for forbearance and discretion, as it would be injudicious, he said, to bring out these subjects at this moment.

In a private talk with Lord Cranborne, Weizmann pointed out, in reply to the "foreign agents" argument, that not a single spy had been found among the Jewish refugees previously admitted. "It was quite obvious that the Jewish Agency would not wish to fill Palestine with undesirables. This war meant much more to the Jews than to any other people." Lord Cranborne finally admitted that "he had not been greatly impressed by the argument that the refugees should not be admitted on the grounds of security."

Though the British had to give up the "planted spies" excuse for refusing to admit refugees, it was still kept in circulation by others. The American Under Secretary of State used it even in replying to an appeal by Eleanor Roosevelt, the President's wife, for refugees to be admitted to Africa or America. He wrote back saying that there was no shipping available for the purpose, and anyway it could not be done, as the Germans "undoubtedly" introduced subversive agents into any shipload of refugees, "such as that on board the *Struma*." In an internal memorandum, however, the State Department did not even list this as one of the six reasons for rejecting a plan advanced by Turkish quarters, to transport 300,000 Jews from Rumania to Syria and Palestine "for temporary cantonment." The memorandum concludes simply: "We are not ready to tackle the whole Jewish problem."

Finally, some Jewish personalities proceeded to break the conspiracy of silence. Following the *Struma* disaster, first alarms were sounded from Palestine, where the news of the Jewish plight was proclaimed after a day of national mourning. But there was no echo to the cry from Jerusalem, so the fight was carried to London.

On June 25, 1942, the *Daily Telegraph* carried a report supplied by Shmuel Zygelbojm, the Jewish member of the Polish National Council in exile, revealing what was earlier hinted at but never before expressly stated, namely, that the massacres of the Jews were all parts of a deliberate policy aimed at the total destruction of the Jewish population. Four days later the British Section of the World Jewish Congress convened a press conference and gave the evidence of the extermination of a million Jews. The BBC relayed the information and newspapers all over the world carried it. In New York a mass demonstration was held in Madison Square Garden on July 21, 1942. Roosevelt sent a message stating that "the American people will hold the perpetrators in strict accountability in a day of reckoning," and Churchill confirmed the story of mass butchery.

Indignation was expressed in protest meetings, editorial comments and radio broadcasts. Thousands of Jewish schoolchildren demonstrated in American cities. A day of mourning and prayer was proclaimed in New York. Prayers were held in churches and synagogues. New and more authentic information on the outrage was soon released. Dr. Stephen Wise quoted White House sources, saying that two million Jews had already been exterminated, and that the intention was to finish off the entire program, if possible, by the end of the year. Sidney Silverman, M.P., published similar information in London.

As the summer of 1942 waned, further news was received from Poland. Jan Karski (later of Georgetown University), a courageous emissary of the Polish underground, arrived in London, where he was received by several British Cabinet Ministers, including Eden, the Foreign Secretary. He told them of the situation in the Warsaw ghetto, and of the Bełżec destruction camp, which he had seen with his own eyes. Later he proceeded to America and was received by Roosevelt, who questioned him extensively on the German campaign against the Jews. Now everyone had an account from a non-Jewish eyewitness.

A demonstration of protest was held in the Royal Albert Hall in London, at which the Archbishop of Canterbury described the events in Europe as "so horrible that the imagination refuses to picture it"; Churchill sent a message saying that "the systematic cruelties to which the Jewish people had been exposed under the Nazi regine are the most terrible events of history and place an indelible stain upon all who perpetrate and instigate them." The Prime Minister had nothing to say on saving the victims of the crimes which disgraced Germany's reputation.

On December 17, 1942, Eden informed the House of Commons that Poland had been turned into the principal Nazi slaughterhouse for the Jews. He confirmed that "the number of victims of these bloody cruelties is reckoned in many hundreds of thousands of entirely innocent men, women and children," and that the Nazis "are now carrying into effect Hitler's oft repeated intention to exterminate the Jewish people in Europe." He reaffirmed the Allied resolution "to ensure that those responsible will not escape retribution." The House stood in silence as a tribute to the martyred Jews in Europe. Similar declarations on behalf of the Allies were published in Washington and in Moscow. Several months later both houses of Congress adopted a resolution condemning the atrocities committed on the Jews.

But there was not a word on rescuing at least part of the doomed people.

The ghastly picture of a nation doomed to death profoundly shocked the people of Britain, but all their leaders would do was to brandish once again the already familiar threat of retribution. The Archbishop of Canterbury wrote in a letter to the *Times*: "At least one might offer to receive here any Jews who are able to escape the clutches of the Nazis. . . . In comparison with the monstrous evil confronting us, the reasons for hesitation usually advanced by officials have an air of irrelevance." Major General Neill asked in a letter to the editor: "Why do we not make an effort to save at least a part?" Similar letters were written by Bernard Shaw, Gilbert Murray, Harold Nicolson, Lord Sankey and others. The Archbishop of York, in the course of a debate in the House of Lords, charged his people with "watching a deliberate, a cold-blooded massacre of a nation."

Still nothing was done.

Goebbels, having watched the Western press campaign for some time, felt reassured and recorded in his diary: "The question of Jewish persecution in Europe is being given top news priority by the English and the Americans and is being handled in high style. *Fundamentally, however, I believe both the English and the Americans are happy that we are exterminating the Jewish riffraff.*" (My italics.)

*

Public opinion now strongly demanded some action, and the democracies decided to show that something was being done: they held another conference on refugees. This one was called at the invitation of the British, who asked the Americans to participate in "a preliminary exploration" of the refugee problem. This was at the peak of the extermination campaign, when Jews were being gassed at an average rate of about fifteen thousand per day. It took the United States six weeks to accept. On the eve of the conference the Archbishop of Canterbury stressed the terrible urgency of the matter, and pleaded in the House of Lords that England should revise its scheme of entry visas. He suggested that British consuls in Spain, Portugal and Turkey be given blocks of unspecified visas to be used at their discretion for saving refugees. "We should open our doors irrespective of whether the German door is opened or shut," he declared. "My chief protest is against procrastination of any kind. At this moment we have upon us a tremendous responsibility. We stand at the bar of history, of humanity and of God." The Archbishop had the support of leading peers of all parties and religions for a resolution that was carried unanimously and that called for providing asylum in England to persons in danger of massacre.

A similar resolution, supported by 277 Members of Parliament, was tabled in the House of Commons.

Lord Cranborne answered for the government that "it would be a mistake to throw undue emphasis on the Jewish side of this question." Then, after repeating that the British Government "was willing to help, to the limits of our resources," he read a joint Anglo-American statement, saying that Britain and America agreed on "the practical steps which may be taken." It was declared that "particular reference had been made in this context to persecuted peoples in Eastern Europe," that "actual arrangements for relief and evacuation have already been made," and that both governments "have already agreed upon the necessity for urgent and immediate action."

In view of what has been since officially revealed about Eden's talks at the time in Washington with the highest American leaders, it can safely be asserted that the solemn Anglo-American statement was deliberately misleading. If anything was in fact agreed upon between the two great Western democracies, it was to abstain from any "urgent and immediate action." This was made clear when the much-heralded conference on refugees was finally held in Hamilton, Bermuda, on April 19, 1943.

Even before it started, Hull warned that America would not be able to help the refugees, in view of its immigration policy. Figures were officially published stating that during the last ten years over half a million entry visas to the United States had been issued. However, even the unquestionably loyal American Jewish Committee was bound to assert that these figures were "deceptive" and stated that at the most 165,000 Jews had entered the United States between 1933 and 1942.

The place of the conference had been chosen, said the American Jewish Committee, "in a spot inaccessible in war-time, difficult for the press to work in, and consequently shielded from the pressure of public opinion which might have been more concerned with action than with reasons for inaction."

Jewish relief bodies were not admitted to the conference. The deliberations, mostly *in camera,* lasted eleven days. The chairman, Harold Dodds, President of Princeton University, openly said that, under the circumstances, "the solution to the refugee problem is to win the war"; the British delegation expressed its belief that "there was little possibility of any immediate relief for millions of hopeless people in Europe."

The recommendations of the conference, which were submitted to both governments, remained secret.

Democratic Congressman Emanuel Celler, writing in the *Free World* of July, 1943, called the Bermuda Conference "a diplomatic mockery of compassionate sentiments and a betrayal of human interests and ideals." In a broadcast statement he said: "The problem cries for immediate solution and not for excuses. There are twenty-eight nations fighting Hitler and yet not one, including England and the United States, has said, 'We will take Hitler's victims.' "

The World Jewish Congress called the conference "a monument of moral callousness and inertia."

A spirited debate on the subject developed in the House of Commons. Eleanor R. Rathborn, M.P., the noble and inspiring chairman of the National Committee for Rescue from Nazi Terror, who had long chastised her government for its inactivity, again took the lead. She published a pamphlet entitled *Rescue the Perishing,* in which she outlined a practical scheme for providing refuge for those in danger. One by one, she listed and refuted the official arguments and submitted several practical and concrete rescue proposals.

"The inactivity of other countries will not excuse us," said Mr. Ridley,

M.P., and Colonel Cazalet, M.P., said that the argument that the admission of refugees would increase anti-Semitism was a victory for Goebbels.

The government was attacked from all sides of the House. Professor A. V. Hill, M.P. for Cambridge University, asked whether the Home Secretary, seeing a child drowning in a pond, would jump in to save him, or argue that he had saved other children already, or that the shipping position made it necessary to be careful of his trousers, or that it was essential first to call a conference of all those others who might equally well jump in—or perhaps he would say that some people do not like children anyway.

Professor Hill tried to dispel some of the smoke screen of the routine arguments. "Is transport really so difficult?" he asked. "Are not ships returning in ballast to this country and America from North Africa?"

Eden rose to reply for the government. He simply said that he would not raise false hopes, and did not believe that the rescue of more than a few was possible before victory was won. He did not refute any of the arguments and said nothing to answer the concrete and practical proposals of rescue which were advanced. Was there any valid reply to them, or was the true answer echoed in the reaction of Lord Moyne's entourage in Cairo to Joel Brand, who came from Budapest on a rescue mission: "Save a million Jews? What shall we do with them? Where should we put them?"

Great Britain had written off European Jewry.

Shmuel Zygelbojm in London could stand it no longer. He wrote a letter saying that the responsibility for the crimes fell in the first instance on the perpetrators, but indirectly on the whole of indifferent humanity. "Perhaps by my death I shall contribute to breaking down that indifference. . . . My life belongs to those mass graves of the Jews of Poland and I therefore give it to them." Having signed the letter he took his life.

A partial rescue effort failed for different reasons. The British Government, under strong pressure, announced its willingness to allow the entry into Palestine of five thousand Jewish children from Eastern Europe. The Germans agreed, provided that the children be exchanged for German nationals interned by the British. The British refused, however, maintaining that the scheme was not an enemy aliens' exchange, since the Jewish children were not British nationals. This was the end of the matter.

There were humanitarian voices in America, too. Senator William Langer thundered in the Senate: "By doing nothing we have acquiesced in what has taken place there." Representative Sommers said in the House he was "confused and disturbed" since America acted so promptly in offering protection for European works of art and was deliberating indefinitely on offering protection to human beings. Senator Gillette introduced a resolution on behalf of thirteen Senators of both parties calling for the establishment of a committee to save immediately the Jews of Europe from extinction. A similar resolution was introduced in the House by Representatives Baldwin and Rogers. Representative Emanuel Celler asked for designation of immediate sanctuaries and for a "revision and adjustment of immigration laws to war conditions." Mrs. Mercedes M. Randall, Chairman of the Women's International League for Peace and Freedom, in her pamphlet *The Voice of Thy Brother's Blood* acknowledged with shame, as a non-Jew, that in America the whole affair had been left entirely to some Jewish personalities. She proved that America could have saved at least half a million refugees more, even without increasing the immigration quotas, had it made a slight effort. "Shall we have to live out our lives with that terrible cry: 'Am I my brother's keeper?' " she asked in conclusion.

These were voices crying in the wilderness.

The typical reaction was that of Representative Hamilton Fish. Though shocked to the core by "the horrifying picture that a race was being exterminated without America taking action," all he advocated as a practical measure was "to address neutral nations to try to put an end to this murderous program."

It took five years of war before the President of the United States announced in a message to Congress on June 12, 1944 that America would now "manifest once again in a concrete way that our kind of world and not Hitler's will prevail." To save lives, America would bring to its shores one thousand refugees, mostly women and children, who had escaped to southern Italy. Even this colossal American contribution was begrudged. Senator Robert Reynolds, Chairman of the Senate Committee on Military Affairs, asked the Attorney General what authority the President had to act in violation of the immigration laws. Francis Biddle replied that these refugees constituted a burden to military operations in the Italian theater of war, and that they were being dealt with on a basis similar to that of "prisoners of war, and other Axis nationals who are admitted to this country temporarily and detained here outside but not in violation of the immigration laws."

The State Department for its part made an attempt to suppress further news of the events in Europe which was being regularly dispatched by Gerhard Riegner, the representative of the World Jewish Congress in Geneva, to Dr. Stephen Wise in New York, through the good offices of the American diplomatic service. The first batch of reports was withheld from publication for over two months till the State Department received their confirmation from the American legation in Bern. Under Secretary Sumner Wells then advised that the news be made public. But when Riegner kept reporting that Jews were being killed in Poland at the rate of several thousands per day in one district alone, the State Department reprimanded the U.S. Minister in Switzerland, Leland Harrison, for making the American diplomatic mail available "for the transmission of private messages." Harrison was ordered not to send back any more of Riegner's information—any more stories of atrocities which might provoke more mass meetings and more public protest.

The State Department was accused immediately after the war, in this context, of a calculated attempt "to shut off the public pressure by shutting off at the source the flow of information which nourished it." This grave charge was leveled by none other than Henry Morgenthau, Jr., the Secretary of the Treasury in Roosevelt's administration. His charges went even deeper. He said: "Officials dodged their grim responsibilities, procrastinated when concrete rescue schemes were placed before them. . . . I do not make these charges lightly. The Treasury's responsibility . . . gave us a front-row view of those eighteen terrible months of inefficiency, buck-passing, bureaucratic delay and, sometimes, what appeared to be calculated obstructionism. With sinking hearts we battled for action against the eternal stretching out of memoranda, committees, conferences—all devouring precious time while innocent people perished miserably in concentration camps and gas chambers."

Stephen Wise worked out a secret plan for smuggling out Jews in exchange for bribes to be deposited in Switzerland. Seventy thousand lives could have been saved. Roosevelt gave the plan his full support and Morgenthau backed it immediately. But the State Department now held matters up for months. The British Ministry of Economic Warfare was informed and wrote back saying that "the British Foreign Office is concerned with the difficulty of disposing of any considerable number of Jews should they be released from enemy territory."

Morgenthau called the reply from London "a satanic combination of British chill and diplomatic double talk, cold and correct, and adding up to a death sentence." Ultimately, according to Stephen Wise, nothing was done "owing to shocking delay and sabotage . . . for five full months after the license had been approved by the President of the United States, the Secretary of State and the Secretary of the Treasury." Wise, one of the staunchest supporters of the Roosevelt administration, sums up the episode: "Let history, therefore, record for all time that were it not for the State Department and Foreign Office bureaucratic bungling and callousness, thousands of lives might have been saved and the Jewish catastrophe partially averted."

The position was clear. While both America and England emphatically maintained their own barriers against any serious rescue attempts, America was prepared to explore schemes involving sanctuaries outside the United States. England, for its part, turned a deaf ear to such proposals too, since they might have resulted in pressure on the gates of Palestine. Between the two democracies, European Jewry was left to perish.

*

Immured behind ghetto walls, the Jews of occupied Europe could not understand the long and continued silence of the outside world despite the outrages perpetrated against them. The only explanation they could find was that the Nazis had somehow succeeded in keeping the Allies in the dark. Otherwise they found it inconceivable that they should just be given up without any attempt being made to save them. So they repeatedly made desperate efforts to smuggle the news out, "to let the world know." Secret transmitters were used, underground channels were exploited and every conceivable contact was utilized to pass on the message. They could never be sure of success. The prolonged silence from the outside was agonizing. Did the reports sent out at such great risks reach the outer world?

At long last, in the summer of 1942, the ghettos heard their plight described in the British broadcasts to which they listened clandestinely. Everyone was deeply moved. "London simply did not know what was happening in detail; hence the silence," Ringelblum recorded on June 25, 1942. "The news that the world has finally been deeply stirred by the account of the massacres in Poland has shaken us all to the very depths," he went on. Now people were confident that something would be done.

As the months passed by and no news of help came from the outside, while the deportations and the killings continued, the survivors grew desperate again. In October, 1942, two Jewish representatives met in great secrecy in Warsaw with Jan Karski, the Polish underground's emissary to the free world. "Tell the Allies the whole truth," they urged. "Threats of retribution after the war will not save the Jews. . . . Germany must be impressed by power and violence." The cities of Germany ought to be mercilessly bombed and at every bombardment leaflets dropped telling them that this was in reprisal for the crimes against the Jews. "Tell the Allied governments that they can't approach this war from a purely military standpoint. The democracies cannot calmly put up with the assertion that the Jewish people of Europe cannot be saved. . . . Offer the Germans an exchange . . . offer them money." Karski protested that it was incompatible with the strategy of war to offer the enemy money and give him back his soldiers to be used in the front lines.

"That's just it . . . that's what we are up against," the Jews replied. "Everybody tells us, 'This is contrary to the strategy of this war.' But strategy can be adjusted. . . . Let's adjust it to include the rescue of a fraction of the Jewish people. Why does the world let us die? Haven't we contributed our share to culture, to civilization? Why do they fight for all the others? Haven't we worked and fought and bled?"

The message from a dying people claiming the right to live was delivered in a few days. But the strategy of the war was not changed. Many devastating air raids were launched against German towns and production centers. The growing strength of the RAF inflicted on Germany a remorseless revenge for the partial "rubbing out" of British towns that Hitler had boasted of during the blitz. Churchill had promised the Nazis they would reap the whirlwind, and indeed they did. The raids had a serious effect on

CEDULA DE IDENTIDAD

No. 212.430

Firma del interesado

PULGAR DERECHO

I. D.

Prio. No. 389.071

Foto tomada 3-4 de 1952

Adolf Eichmann's false identity card in Argentina,
where he was known as Ricardo Klement

Fórm. 86

Certifico que don Ricardo Klement *que dice ser de estado* soltero *que lee y escribe* si *y cuya fotografía, impresión digito-pulgar derecha y firma figuran al dorso, es nacido el* 23 *de* Mayo *de* 1913 *en el pueblo de* Bolzano *Provincia de* .... *Nación* Alemania *que tiene 1 m.* .... *ctms. de estatura, el cutis de color* blanco *Cabello* rubio *Barba* afeit. *Nariz dorso* recto *Base* cajada *Boca* med. *Orejas* meds.

Mat. .... *Distrito* .... *Div.* ....

Observaciones: ....

Tucumán, Abril 3 *de 195*2

INVESTIGACIONES

AMADO JURI
JEFE DE POLICIA

The accused

Eichmann on trial.
Foreground, defense counsel,
Robert Servatius.
Left, Dieter Wechtenbruch,
assistant defense counsel

Gideon Hausner

Prosecution staff.
Left to right,
Hausner,
Jacob Baror,
Gabriel Bach,
Jacob Robinson

Abraham Selinger, commander of Bureau 06, at a press conference

Chief Inspector
Michael Goldmann
of the Israel police

Supreme Court Justice
Moshe Landau

Judge Benjamin Halevy

Judge Yitzhak Raveh

WITNESSES AT THE TRIAL

Heinrich Karl Grueber

Jacob Wernik

Michael A. Musmanno

Zivia Lubetkin Zuckerman

SPECTATORS AT THE TRIAL

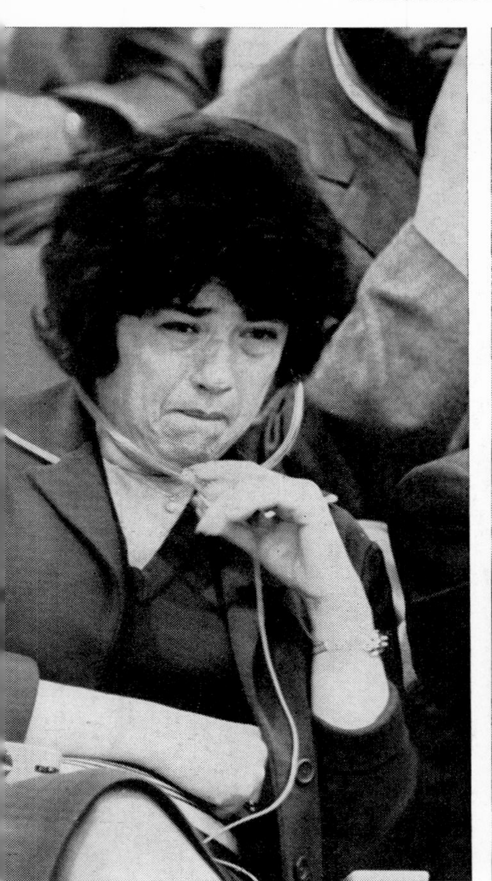

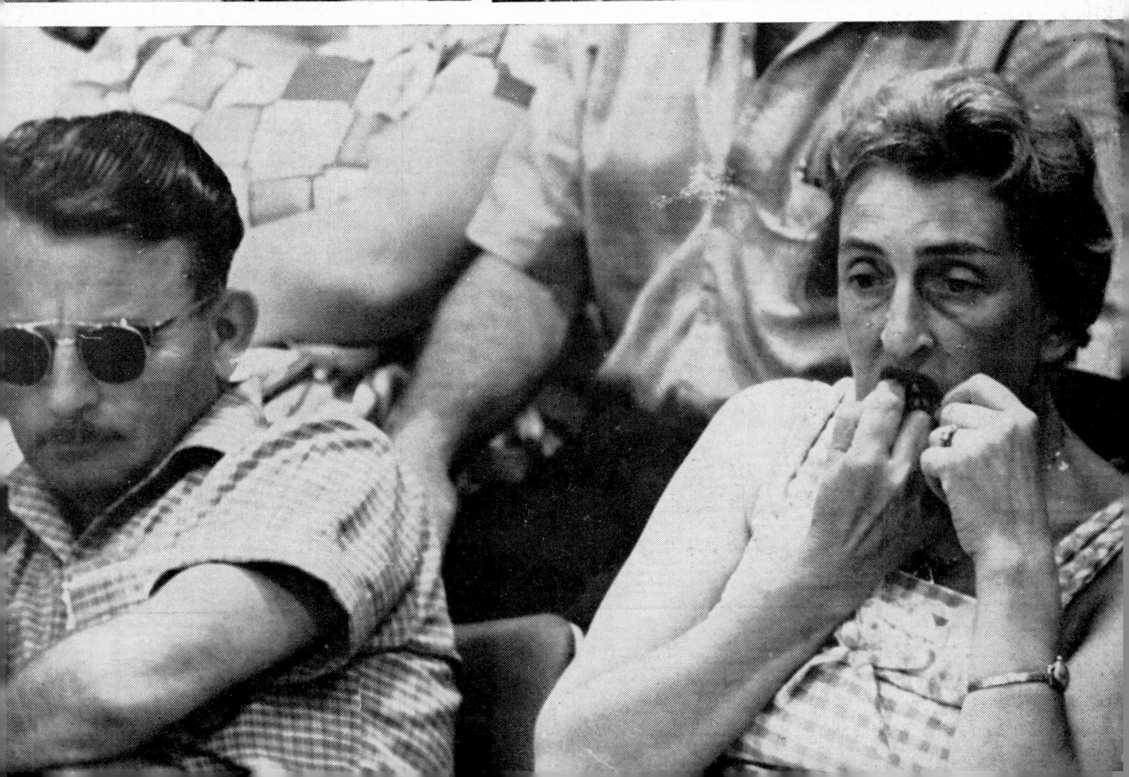

Courtroom scene

German morale, as is repeatedly indicated in Goebbels' diary. After a heavy raid on Dortmund Goebbels recorded that "people are gradually beginning to lose courage. . . . Morale is lower than ever before. . . . Hell like that is hard to bear." The raids were aimed primarily at industrial and military objectives. Yet some of them were unmistakably in the nature of war reprisals. But not for any of the destroyed ghettos.

It was remarkable that Kurt Gerstein, the anti-Nazi SS officer, in a whispered talk in a compartment of the Berlin express train with the Swedish diplomat von Otter (see page 91), advocated the same methods of bombing with leaflets as the two Jewish resistance fighters at their meeting with Jan Karski in the deserted, half-ruined house in a Warsaw suburb.

The absolute refusal to "adjust" war strategy to the call for measures to save Jewish lives was nowhere more cruelly demonstrated than in the obstinate rejection of the urgent Jewish request to bomb the extermination camps and attack the railway lines and junctions leading to them. There were good reasons for the Jewish requests: once an extermination center was exposed and prisoners succeeded in escaping from it, it was not used any more (see p. 188). It was not easy to improvise a substitute. The Jewish representatives therefore repeatedly urged this course in London, Washington and Moscow. "It would mean, in the first instance," wrote Weizmann in his urgent plea to bomb Auschwitz, "that the Allies waged war on the extermination of the victims of Nazi oppression. . . . Secondly, it would give the lie to the oft-repeated assertion of Nazi spokesmen that the Allies are not really so displeased with the work of the Nazis in ridding Europe of Jews. . . . Thirdly, it would give weight to the threats of reprisals." After almost two months of "careful consideration" the Foreign Office wrote that, to their regret, the Air Staff was compelled "in view of the very great technical difficulties involved to refrain from pursuing the proposal." When all this was first made public in the course of the Eichmann trial, there was widespread comment, and two Members of Parliament expressed their "anxiety and bewilderment," requesting the British Government to make public all the available documents. The Prime Minister promised to consider the request, but no disclosure was ever made. The picture became even more bewildering with the statement of Sir Arthur Harris, then Chief of Bomber Command, who was most emphatic that "Auschwitz had never been mentioned in any strategic directive." Sir Arthur, while skeptical of the practical value of such bombing, left no doubt as to its technical feasibility from bases in Italy. Similar objectives, he said, notably the Amiens prison, were bombed with pinpoint accuracy and great success. This was supported by Group Captain Leonard Cheshire, V.C. "We could have bombed Auschwitz accurately," he wrote.

Similar requests to destroy the extermination factories were submitted in Washington and received similar treatment. The Assistant Secretary of War, John J. McCloy, replied to Dr. Kubowitzki (Kubovi) that "such an operation could be executed only by the diversion of considerable air support essential to the success of our forces now engaged in decisive operations elsewhere." The saving of Jewish lives was, apparently, neither "essential" nor "decisive."

In fact, the industrial installations all around Auschwitz were bombed by the Allies several times, twice in broad daytime. Flying Fortresses of the American Air Force dropped leaflets saying that the place was next on the list to be bombed and warning civilians to leave it.

The death camp itself was left untouched.

*

There were other proposals, too. Early in 1944 the Jewish Agency submitted a scheme to the British authorities for the dropping of hundreds of Palestinian Jews by parachute into Hungary. In the considered view of British military circles, the plan would have been militarily advantageous to the Allies and might have been helpful in preventing the massacre in Hungary. But after it had been approved by all the military authorities concerned, and arrangements had been initialed to carry it out, the Foreign and Colonial Offices interfered and, for political reasons, instructed the military authorities to drop the scheme.

This was recorded by Weizmann in November, 1945, in preparation for giving evidence at the Nuremberg Trials. But the Nuremberg prosecution abandoned their earlier intention of calling him as a witness, and it was first made public at the Eichmann trial.

Ultimately, only thirty-two Palestinians, all veterans of the Hagana (the voluntary Jewish self-defense force in Palestine), including three women, out of the hundreds who volunteered and completed parachute training, were finally dropped by the British in Rumania, Bulgaria, Hungary, Italy, Slovakia, Austria and Yugoslavia. They were under strict instructions to fulfill all their military assignments before addressing themselves to Jewish matters. Unfortunately, they arrived too late and were too few to arouse the remaining splinters of Jewry to any large-scale revolt or rescue effort. But their mere appearance, even though some were soon captured and executed, had a tremendously heartening effect on the survivors, and they became the backbone of Jewish self-rescue activity.

The Jews of the free world found themselves under a double disability in their rescue attempts. First, they were under the curse of being eternally dependent on others. They had no autonomous organs, such as were available to even the smallest of the Allies. They did not sit on any of the international councils and had to rely on others in matters large or small. Even a triviality like getting an entrance visa to Turkey for the head of the Jewish Agency's Political Department had to be dealt with through the British diplomatic authorities. Any move the Jewish institutions took had to be approved by some foreign authority, which could always slam the door in their faces when their pressure became too insistent. Moreover, the Jews were loyal citizens of their countries and sensitive to the plea not to hamper the war effort by any "exaggerated" demands.

The Jewry of Palestine, about half a million strong, was locked in conflict with the British over the White Paper policy and had to keep a watchful eye on Arab brigands, quiescent at the moment after harrowing the Jewish settlements for three years. It had to divide its meager resources between the task of volunteering for the British forces and maintaining its own underground security organization. Still, when all is said and done, it seems inexcusable that the Jewish leaders allowed themselves to be browbeaten with the stock watchwords of "war necessity" or "put victory first," paraded before them by the Allied spokesmen, as if there were any inconsistency between defeating Hitler and saving some of his victims.

Dr. Nahum Goldmann admitted as much in public. "We are all guilty of not having gone to all lengths," he said. "We were overimpressed with the argument that the generals should be left in peace to fight the war."

It is certainly painful today to every surviving Jew to recall those awful years, when he was, after all, leading a normal life and attending to his daily joys and sorrows even while the terrible massacre was going on in Europe.

The Jews from inside the inferno had a message for their brothers, too, when they briefed Jan Karski in Warsaw on the eve of his departure for the free world. "Let them go to all the important English and American offices and agencies. Tell them not to leave until they have obtained guarantees that a way has been decided upon to save the Jews. Let them accept no food or drink, let them die a slow death while the world looks on. Let them die. This may shake the conscience of the world."

The message was delivered. When Zygelbojm received it in London, he started violently. "It is utterly impossible," he muttered. "They would never let me die a slow, lingering death. They would simply bring in two policemen and have me dragged away to an institution."

Drastic measures were considered in America. Some Jewish leaders, among them Goldmann, favored mass demonstrations and closure of shops and offices. Palestinian emissaries, especially Rabbi Meir Berlin and Leib Jaffe, called for immediate and dramatic steps. "We cannot accept the verdict that there is nothing we can do. How can this silence here be further maintained?" said Jaffe. But American Jewry, the largest and safest in the world, yielded to the tempting argument that the war effort must not be diverted by one iota.

Finally, some of the world leaders did not want to be bothered with Jewish affairs any more. "I cannot afford to see Dr. Weizmann," Churchill said, "for I have a sleepless night after each interview with him, which is bad for the war." So Weizmann had no alternative but to let Churchill sleep out his nights; he continued with his efforts in America. He told a huge meeting in Madison Square Garden on March 1, 1943, that "expressions of sympathy without accompanying attempts to launch acts of rescue become a hollow mockery in the ears of the dying." He asked for havens to be designated in the territories of the United Nations and the gates of Palestine to be opened. "Stop Hitler now" was the slogan. But there was no response.

The Jewish Agency had for some time been making its own aid and rescue efforts, especially through Turkey, where it kept an official, Chaim Barlas. After a while a delegation got there, representing various parties. Their difficulties were heartbreaking. They had to maintain underground contact with occupied Europe, to get Jews to gather clandestinely in groups at embarkation points on the vigilantly policed shores of Rumania and Bulgaria. They had to arrange for a ship to arrive at the spot in time, pass through the coastal mine belt, and make a quick dash through submarine-infested waters toward Turkey, from which the refugees would somehow proceed to Palestine. In order to get to the Jews of Europe it was necessary to send out special volunteers. Sometimes there was no choice but to bribe unsavory types to maintain contact with the ghettos. To get to and from the German-controlled ports of the Black Sea it was necessary to tempt captains and seamen with sums amounting to pirate's ransom. These methods might have been suitable for smuggling out an escaping individual; here they had to be used to evacuate large numbers, including women, children and babes in arms.

Under directions from the delegation, a few surviving members of the Jewish youth movements were smuggled out of ghettos and directed to frontier towns of the General Government, Rumania, Hungary and Bulgaria, to create an underground route of escape to the Black Sea. Hundreds of futile attempts had to be made before one succeeded, but soon the route was filled with people streaming through. The dropped Palestinian parachutists were vital links in the project.

Every ship was a new adventure for the Jewish Agency men in Turkey and involved seemingly insurmountable difficulties. They could never be sure of success till they actually saw the refugees arrive. Often, now, they were allowed to proceed to Palestine legally under the White Paper quota of entrance certificates. It had needed the *Struma* disaster to make the British give up their "food shortage" and "security risk" objections. But sometimes all the anxiously waiting rescuers would welcome were bloated bodies washed ashore from a refugee vessel torpedoed by a submarine. So much greater was their joy when they could embrace and accompany to freedom several hundred Jews disembarking from a ship that had broken through all barriers. "We preferred to risk a way of escape to life than let them take a sure way to death," wrote Menahem Bader, one of the few emissaries in Istanbul who has so far recorded his reminiscences. The whole rescue story is an epic tale of trial and error, of heartbreaking needs, frustrating failures and pitifully inadequate means for a colossal task. Yet tens of thousands of

Jews owe their lives to the handful of devoted rescue workers in Lisbon, Geneva, Stockholm and, mainly, Istanbul, who were out to thwart the Gestapo. Whether this was all the Jewish people, scattered, divided and disabled as it was, could do to ward off the greatest disaster in its history will continue to plague our national conscience.

There were also other organizations and agencies dealing with assistance and rescue; most of these were American Jewish philanthropic bodies, which by their very nature had to comply with accepted legal norms and were unable to go beyond routine methods, despite the unprecedented tragedy. Some Jewish representatives in neutral countries were so superpatriotic that they refused even to maintain contact with refugees who had arrived "illegally," and were adamant in their refusal to pay ransoms for Jewish lives otherwise than through official bank accounts.

In 1944, with the appearance of the public-spirited War Refugee Board representatives in various capitals, a new approach governed the rescue activities. American embassies were instructed to lend their support to these direct emissaries of President Roosevelt, and the word went round that America was now out to save what could still be found of European Jewry (see page 240). Five years earlier this might have meant the saving of millions of lives; now it could be no more than burrowing among the ruins in a search for survivors.

Even so, the Board lent power to these last-minute efforts, which were now backed by the full force of the United States Government. Its representatives were quick in cutting through red tape, and soon found out that unorthodox methods must be applied. From funds supplied predominantly by Jewish bodies, they assisted in the rescue activities of various underground movements and enabled private agencies fully to utilize their own resources. The Board found ways to transport some refugees from Spain to North Africa and to arrange for the granting of American visas to thousands of Jewish children in Switzerland, thus reassuring these countries that they would not be left alone in shouldering the burden. Moreover, entry permits to America, withheld for three years, were now given under the old unused quotas to people still in Germany; ultimately these saved many lives. It was arranged for citizenship of Latin-American countries to be accorded to many camp prisoners in Germany. This, though not a decisive measure, spared a number of people the horrors of deportation and kept them alive. By discreet use of funds, some untrodden avenues of escape from occupied Europe were marked out and put to use.

Whenever acting officially the War Refugee Board representatives attached to the American embassies had to adopt legal patterns, and many were the futile efforts spent on securing safe conduct from all belligerents for a vessel in the Black Sea. Unofficially, the dynamic workers of the Board found other ways and means, to which the brief final report of the last Executive Director, William O'Dwyer, bears evidence. They kept alive orphans hidden in convents and private homes by bribing officials to prevent deportation of the children; they moved some refugees, mainly non-Jews, from Baltic states to Sweden, and the energetic representative in Ankara, Ira A. Hirschmann, fought tooth and nail for every single refugee whose life he could save. One of his daring undiplomatic steps yielded immediate results. He simply told the Rumanian Ambassador to Turkey that the day of reckoning was approaching, and unless the Transnistrian camps were broken up the Rumanian ruling clique could expect no mercy from the Americans. A week later the two men met again on the neutral ground of the International Red Cross building in Ankara. Ambassador Crestianu agitatedly showed Hirschmann the cabled reply of the Rumanian Conducator, saying that there would be no more deportations of Jews and that the camps in Transnistria would be broken up immediately.

This, in itself, was probably the Board's biggest single rescue achievement. At the time there were still over forty thousand Jews in these Rumanian horror camps. Most important, however, was the growing conviction of the Germans that the Western world did perhaps care what happened to the Jews, and that their lives had, after all, a certain bargaining value. Himmler, feverishly attempting to establish contact with the West, was most interested when Becher reported on his meeting with Roswell D. McClelland, the War Refugee Board's representative in Switzerland. The contacts were later extended to Count Bernadotte in Sweden; a dramatic meeting was even arranged between Himmler and the Jew Norbert Masur of Stockholm. All this finally led to Himmler's order to the concentration camps' commanders to deliver the surviving inmates to the Allies alive. But this came on the eve of the collapse.

The War Refugee Board had first prompted Roosevelt to issue a new declaration against war criminals, this time explicitly naming the Jews among the victims of Nazi barbarism. The Board also drafted a statement to be issued by General Eisenhower, warning the Germans that his advancing army expected them to stop harming concentration camp prisoners. It was the Board, finally, that took seriously the gruesome offer of blood for goods brought by Joel Brand from Budapest.

Hirschmann was ordered by Roosevelt to see what could be done with this offer and to keep the door open for further negotiations. Obviously, the offer might involve serious traps for the Allies; the British immediately said they were against any further talks on the subject. Hirschmann was instructed to see Brand, then detained in Cairo. Lord Moyne was anxious to persuade Hirschmann to proceed to London for talks there without seeing Brand. But Hirschmann was insistent. His interview with the emissary from Budapest lasted several hours, and resulted in an immediate favorable report to Washington, where Edward Stettinius was now the Secretary of State. "We will not give the Germans trucks; this is out of the question," he told Nahum Goldmann, who came to see him. But he was ready to negotiate further on the other things the Germans wanted: tea, coffee, goods. "The offer comes from high up," Stettinius said, "and the Germans must be made to think we take it seriously."

The matter was referred to the highest quarters. It was finally Churchill himself who ruled in a message to Eden: "This persecution of Jews in Hungary is probably the greatest and most horrible crime ever committed in the whole history of the world. . . . There should therefore, in my opinion, be no negotiations of any kind on the subject. Declarations should be made in public, that everyone connected with it will be hunted down and put to death."

Weizmann's pressing request that Brand be sent back or that Menahem Bader be allowed to proceed to Budapest with the reply that negotiations were in progress, even if only as delaying tactics to prevent such later measures as the notorious murderous foot trek, were all rejected by the War Cabinet.

Despite his desperate protests Brand was kept in Cairo; several days after Churchill's ruling the BBC and the London *Times* carried the news of his mission. The secret was revealed. The negotiations were off.

Eichmann recalled it all in his own way in his talks with Sassen: "The foreign countries could never pillorize us enough for our measures," he said, "but had they stretched out their arms even a little to take in the Jews not a single deportation train would have left for any concentration camp. . . . At the end we gave them another chance, when the Reichsfuehrer said: 'Take them away from us, but this time you will not get them for nothing; you will have to give us goods.' Again the foreign countries refused the offer. So, of course, the trains to the camps had to roll on."

*

The Protestant Church in Germany, to which the majority of the country's Christians adhered, was split between the old Evangelical group under a Nazi stooge, Bishop Mueller, and the Confessional Church, which was opposed to Hitlerian ideas, and many of whose pastors were imprisoned. But even they would stand up for the Jews in exceptional cases only. Among them was Landsbischof Wurm of Wuerttemberg who fearlessly told the Nazi authorities that he regarded the suffering brought on Germany by the Allied air raids as a due punishment for what had been done to the Jews. Another was the famous pastor Dr. Heinrich Grueber, who organized a whole bureau to assist Jews in hiding and to get them out of the country. When he was detained in a concentration camp, his work was carried on by his wife Margarette and by Pastor Werner Sylten, who was also ultimately arrested and deported to Dachau, where he died. With Grueber's bureau smashed in Berlin, the activity was taken over by Pastor Hermann Maas of

Heidelberg. The Nazis had him arrested, too, and even sentenced to death. But the death penalty was commuted and he lived long enough to be the first German invited to visit Israel.

Outside Germany, too, there were noble rescue actions by Lutheran pastors in Italy and by the Reformed Church pastors in Holland.

The old Metropolitan of the Greek Catholic Church in Lwów, Andrzej Szeptycki, strongly condemned his Ukrainian compatriots who took a part in the outrage and prohibited their attending religious services. To the orphaned son of the Chief Rabbi he said : "I want you to be a good Jew. . . . I am saving you for your people."

On the whole, however, these were only isolated sparks in the general darkness. The world awaited a fully authoritative word of guidance to the faithful, consolation to the victims and thunderous condemnation of the wicked. This was expected to come from the Vicar of Christ on earth—the Pope. Germany's leaders, for all their ruthlessness, were nervous too. Would they be excommunicated by Rome and have to institute a Nazi papacy?

But the expected word from Rome never came. Pius XI, who proclaimed that "in spirit we are all Semites," and who in 1937 issued his famous anti-Nazi encyclical *"Mit brennender Sorge"* ("With Burning Anxiety") against "pernicious errors and still more pernicious practices," died before the outbreak of the war.

His successor was made of different stuff. Pius XII's encyclical *"Summi Pontificatus"* was issued when the flames of war were already consuming Jewish dwellings, but there was nothing to indicate his attitude apart from general words of balm. As the massacres continued, many eyes were again turned to Rome. Jewish institutions supplied information on the events and Roosevelt's personal representative at the Vatican pointed out that "its silence was endangering its moral prestige and is undermining faith both in the Church and in the Holy Father himself." All the Holy See would say in reply was that in line with a policy of neutrality it could not protest against particular atrocities and had to limit itself to "condemning immoral acts in general." To the Berlin correspondent of the *Osservatore Romano* the Pope said that he could not bring millions of Catholic soldiers fighting in the German Army into a conflict of conscience.

The response of the German Catholic Church to the Nazi challenge presents generally a picture of moral collapse under the impact of primeval forces. The racial theories, diametrically opposed to Christian principles, were rarely condemned. Even Cardinal Faulhaber of Munich, who repudiated the racial doctrine and was strongly attacked by the Nazis, made it clear that he was not defending the Jews of his time.

The Catholics in Germany were mostly concerned with the "non-Aryan Christians," the converts and the *Mischlinge* rather than the Jews. The blood bath that followed left almost the entire German Catholic clergy cold. They had strong words of condemnation for "euthanasia," against which the

Bishop of Muenster, Count Galen, openly preached. But, even when opposing the system and denouncing its measures, they did not come out in defense of the Jews.

The Papal Nuncio in Germany, in a talk at the Foreign Ministry, "groped around" to the subject of shooting hostages, but quickly took a hint and refrained from tackling the question further. Gerstein was later peremptorily dismissed from the residence of the Nuncio in Berlin, to whose adviser he had told the news of Bełżec.

A solitary voice pierced this silence. The Provost of Hedwig Cathedral in Berlin, Bernard Lichtenberg, openly prayed for the Jews and for the concentration camp prisoners. He was sentenced to two years' imprisonment, was rearrested immediately on his release and died in 1943 on the way to Dachau concentration camp.

Among the captive populations some of the Princes of the Church spoke in a different style. Notable examples are the Nuncio Andreía Cassulo in Rumania, who openly intervened for the Jews. So did Cardinal van Roey in Belgium, Archbishop Saliège of Toulouse, France, and others. Archbishop de Jonge of Utrecht forbade collaboration in hunting down Jews and denounced the wrongs done them. The Bishop of Paris, Monsignor Chattel, for some time wore the yellow badge, as did his priests and nuns, to identify themselves with the suffering people. Above them all towered the noble Cardinal Roncalli (the future Pope John XXIII), who, as the Papal Nuncio in Ankara, made many efforts on behalf of the Jews and was a true lover of his fellow man.

Some cloisters were opened to hide Jews. Most notable were the abbeys in Italy, which gave refuge to three or four thousand Jews escaping the razzias. Underground fighters, abandoning the security of a convent near Wilno and taking leave of the Mother Superior, were told: "Go, my sons, to fight and I shall come after you. God is with us." The Jesuit Father Chaillet was arrested in Lyons for hiding eighty Jewish children.

There can be no doubt that the interventions of the Cardinals and the Nuncii in various capitals on behalf of the Jews had the consent of the Pope, but whenever directly approached for guidance, the Vatican was slow with remonstrances or even objections. To Marshal Pétain's inquiry on the anti-Jewish legislation pressed on occupied France by the Germans, the reply transmitted by Léon Bérard, Vichy's Ambassador to the Holy See, was that "the Church does not necessarily condemn every measure taken against the Jewish race." Removal of the Jews from public office and the imposition of "peculiarity of dress" were "not unknown to the Church," Bérard wrote, and the Holy See would therefore not pick a quarrel with the French Government over the proposed *Statut des Juifs,* provided there was no obstacle to intermarriage and the liquidation of Jewish interests in business was "charitably" performed.

Little wonder that Pierre Laval, the Vichy Prime Minister, had no patience with his own priests who seemed to be literally more Catholic than the Pope in their defense of the Jews. He simply told them that he would not tolerate their interference in French internal matters by siding with the Jews and put some of them in jail.

The Pope's ambivalence was again clearly demonstrated in Slovakia, a satellite presided over by a Catholic priest, Josef Tiso, whom Pius XII welcomed as "a dear son." The Vatican regarded Slovakia with special favor. The Pope blessed the country's ambassador, Sidor, in his own language, which was unprecedented. Slovakia was also the Vatican's special charge. When deportations of Jews began from there, the Holy See, always in possession of firsthand information, told the Bratislava authorities that the Jews were not being "resettled" in the East, as was officially announced by the Germans, but were being annihilated there. Slovakian authorities replied that the Jews were being "mobilized for labor" in the East, like the 120,000 Slovakians sent to work in the Reich. The Vatican let it go at that. In 1943 Bratislava announced the renewal of the deportations. The Vatican was now approached by Jewish institutions through Monsignor Roncalli, who without the slightest hesitation undertook to interfere. Two further notes were sent from Rome to Bratislava; this time the deportations were stopped. In 1944, when Roncalli became aware of the German mopping-up operations on Slovakian Jewry, he intervened again, and even wanted to proceed to Rome to plead with the Pope. He was told that "the Holy See had already taken all necessary steps." In Rome Sidor was this time given a rather lukewarm *note verbale* on the subject; Bratislava replied that the Jews were being deported by the Germans as a military measure.

The Germans were uneasily watching the Holy See. Goebbels bared his teeth when he heard that the Pope was urging Spain to stay out of the war. "He gives expression to his enmity to the Axis. . . . After the war we shall have to see to it that . . . such attempts at interference are made impossible."

Then other news reached the Nazi Propaganda Minister. "I hear on all sides that one could come to some terms with the present Pope. He has expressed partly very wise views and is not so opposed to National Socialism as might be gathered from the utterances of some of his bishops." Later still when the Vatican refused outright to identify itself with the war aims of the Allies, Goebbels' conclusion was: "This would indicate that the Pope is possibly closer to us than is generally assumed."

A further test for the Vatican was the great razzia on the Jews of Rome during the night of October 16–17, 1943, following Mussolini's overthrow. Weizsaecker, now the Nazi Ambassador to the Vatican, cabled home that the College of Cardinals was shocked, since the Jews had been hunted down "under the windows of the Pope." Pressure was being brought "to force the Pope out of his reserved attitude," he continued, especially as French bishops had adopted a clear and condemnatory stand on similar occasions.

Weizsaecker advised that an announcement that the arrested Jews would not be deported might mitigate the expected strong reaction. The head of the German Church in Rome, Bishop Hudal, was even more alarmed. He demanded that the local army commander, General Stahell, call an immediate halt to the arrests, "in the interests of hitherto good relationships between the Vatican and the German Military Command," since otherwise "the Pope will have to take a stand favorable to the propaganda of the enemy."

After a few uneasy days, the alarm proved to have been unnecessary. Weizsaecker could report that the Pope "had not allowed himself to be drawn into any demonstrative censure against the deportations of the Jews of Rome. . . . He has in this touchy matter done everything in order not to burden relations with the German Government and German agencies in Rome." Weizsaecker went on to say that, although the Vatican's organ, *Osservatore Romano,* carried a communiqué on the "charitable activity of the Pope," it was "so richly embroidered and unclear that very few people will read into it a special allusion to the Jewish question," and the whole matter could now be considered closed. The allusion to "the charitable activity" apparently referred to the asylum given to a few dozen refugees in the Vatican itself. This time it was not only the Supreme Pontiff who failed to raise his voice. In his capacity as Bishop of Rome, the Pope kept silent when over twelve hundred men, women and children were forcibly seized from his city and most of them dispatched to Auschwitz—for destruction, as he well knew.

In the conversations between Eichmann and Sassen, the latter showed some interest in the reaction of the Catholic Church. They were discussing Slovakia at the time, which was governed by a Catholic priest. "The Roman Catholic Church?" asked Eichmann. "I never received any solid protests from them, certainly not to an extent that would warrant my attention."

In the debate that has recently broken out again, various reasons have been offered for the Vatican's silence. The present Pope, Paul VI, has come out in the open to defend his predecessor, who while still alive never answered the charge of silence leveled against him years before his death. Whether the reason for Pius XII's silence and inactivity was practical, political or personal, history must record that in an hour of direst need on the part of oppressed mankind the Pope stood aside.

A member of the underground in Warsaw recorded in his diary:

> The world keeps quiet. The world knows what is going on here and still keeps quiet. The Representative of God in Rome, the defenders of the good cause in London and Washington, they all keep quiet. . . . The voice of protest now rings out not from the countries of freedom but from where it is most difficult to speak out and to act—from the depths of captivity.

This was true. There were some people on the defeated continent of Europe who stood up for a murdered nation. They were few, unorganized and weak. They were the common people, who had no voice in formulating the Allied war aims or proclaiming the Four Freedoms promised for liberated mankind. Nor did they issue pious declarations. Instead, they went out to save lives, at the constant risk of their own. It was not often that they could accomplish much, and well they knew it, but still they persisted for months and years. The reason they did so was stated simply by Jan Campert, the poet of the Dutch resistance: "For the heart could not behave otherwise."

There were two small countries that thwarted almost completely the Nazi designs. One was Finland, which had been attacked by Russia in 1939 and which two years later joined Germany in its war against the Soviets. The military alliance was even cemented by courtesy visits of Hitler to Helsinki and of Marshal Mannerheim to Berlin. Still, dependent as it had become on Germany and completely surrounded by German forces, Finland refused to give up its two thousand Jews "for resettlement." "We are an honest people," declared Witting, the Finnish Foreign Minister. "We would much rather die with the Jews than give them up."

Himmler was furious. "The Finns will have to choose between hunger and delivering up their Jews," he said, before proceeding to Helsinki for talks. Still, he did not get the Jews of Finland after all.

But there was a painful price that this small and isolated Jewish community had to pay. The Jews, being full citizens with full rights and duties, were of course also mobilized in the Finnish Army, and consequently found themselves fighting on Hitler's side.

Another, different, rescue story was written by the people of Denmark, whose country was overrun by the Germans in April, 1940. The Nazis proclaimed that this Nordic country would be an "Exemplary Protectorate." It was intended to keep it as window dressing to impress what were considered "hesitant" countries, and show them that life inside the "New Order" could be bearable, even profitable. Consequently the King and his government were allowed to stay in power. Understandably, the occupying forces demanded some concessions in return, starting with the appointment of a pro-German Prime Minister and going on to continuous inroads on Denmark's economy and declining autonomy. Indirectly, of course, the Germans controlled major matters from behind the scenes.

The Danes, though enjoying a unique and privileged position among the overrun countries, were not taken in by the Nazi game, even when they were allowed the unprecedented privilege of holding free parliamentary elections in March, 1943. The response of the people was to give about 2 percent of the votes to the Danish Nazi Party and overwhelming support to the democratic coalition. Acts of sabotage spread throughout the country and in August, 1943, martial law was proclaimed. The government and

Parliament were dissolved, the King became a virtual prisoner, and the Germans assumed direct control. The time seemed ripe for tackling the Danish Jews, who had so long been spared the horrors of Nazi occupation.

By the end of September the news of an impending deportation leaked out, causing much alarm. King Christian X sent an official warning to the Plenipotentiary of the Reich, Werner Best, telling him that any measures against "the Jewish citizens of my country" were "bound to produce the gravest results."

The Danish people took matters into their own hands. People approached their Jewish neighbors and friends, even entirely unknown Jews, telling them: "We know what is going to happen; if you need a place of hiding, you can rely on us." Many people received more than one offer. Within three days Danish Jews were hiding among Christian friends and when the Gestapo called on their houses, according to addresses they had seized a month earlier from the Jewish community, there was nobody in. All the raid yielded was about 470 persons, who were found at home, among them Chief Rabbi Friediger. These were deported to Theresienstadt.

But the Jews were still in Denmark, and it was no small feat to hide and finally remove them. The Germans instituted immediate searches; it required all the ingenuity of an outraged people, and all the fervor and zeal of the now fully mobilized Danish underground, to do the job. Everyone who was approached lent a hand. A typical reaction was the reply of a Copenhagen cab driver, who was asked to assist in transporting people. "But, of course," he said. "What these green uniforms did today is sheer swinishness. I don't know much about the Jews, but to hunt down people as if they were rats is against my morals and my religion. I am at your disposal day and night."

The whole Danish nation, men and women, was gripped with the ambition not to let the Germans get the Jews. It was an unbelievable effort, even as an organizational feat, to escape the vigilance of the Gestapo, to find all the necessary fishing boats, to lead the Jews secretly to the shores and to ferry them across to Sweden.

Students and Boy Scouts were the main leaders of the wonderful rescue. Money was collected to pay for the passage and the Danish police would surround an area on the seashore at night, as if in search of saboteurs, but actually to block the way to outsiders while the Jews were embarking and the boats were leaving, testified David Melchior, one of the rescued people. In many cases ambulances were used to carry people to the embarkation points. The whole population was united, as never before, behind the underground rescue movement.

This "small Dunkirk" operation lasted several weeks, with unbelievably few mishaps. In one case the Germans received information about a Jewish hiding place, and one Dane was killed in the shooting that followed. Sometimes the passage had to be delayed for a night or two; otherwise it met with complete success. When the month of October was over, Danish Jewry, about eight thousand people, was safe across the waters of Oresund, with the Swedish Government and people magnanimously offering them a warm welcome and a safe refuge.

When the news of the failure reached Berlin, Eichmann went white with fury. "I will ask for the heads of the saboteurs," he raged.

In fact, he soon arrived in Copenhagen to have a look at things on the spot. The Reich's plenipotentiary blamed the army for failure to allocate manpower for the house-to-house searches, but found consolation in the fact that the country was, after all, now purged of the Jews.

But the Danes were now requesting the return from Theresienstadt of those who, under the German general instructions, should not have been deported in the first place, the *Mischlinge,* the very old people and the mixed-marriage couples. Moreover, they insisted on sending parcels to the deportees and visiting them. Their unceasing pressure and interest ultimately resulted in a relatively very high percentage of survivals among the Danish deportees to Theresienstadt.

The Danes were not alone in their magnanimity. The Norwegian underground transported eight hundred Jews across the country to safety in Sweden under exceptionally perilous circumstances. The French resistance sent over many Jewish children to Switzerland though, unfortunately, not all of them were granted asylum there. In other places, where a neutral refuge was not close at hand, Jews could be rescued only by hiding them inside the country, with a constant risk of detection by the Gestapo, by its local supporters or simply by people greedy for the prizes given to informers. Every life saved had to be fought for. The rescuer had to avoid receiving callers at home and led a double life under imminent and constant danger for the whole household. It was no trifling matter to hide Jews in hunger-stricken Europe, to share with them meager food rations, to sneak into their place of shelter and stealthily remove their refuse, sometimes even to bury the dead beneath the floor boards and then clandestinely remove the accumulated debris. Still such people were found, very few in numbers but very great in spirit. They were the anonymous, unrewarded and unmedaled heroes of humanity, struggling to preserve the image of man.

The motives for the rescue work varied. Sometimes the self-sacrifice sprang from strong religious belief as in the case of Catharina Burger, the schoolmistress of Haarlem, Holland, who kept Jewish children in her house, managed to hide and feed them, and insisted that they celebrate the approach of the Sabbath every Friday night to keep up their morale. Then there was Bronislawa Czajkowski, the devout Polish peasant woman, who with her husband and son hid two Jewish families in their stable for almost three years. She went so far as to bake a kind of unleavened bread for them on Passover. One day her son Andrzej learned that in a neighboring village the Gestapo had wiped out two Polish families and set their houses on fire for hiding Jews. The boy was, naturally, frightened and told the Jews in hiding that they would have to go, but Bronislawa rushed in, saying that if they left she would go with them.

In other cases the effort was motivated by pure and simple humanity. Edward Chacza, a Polish miner, turned his house in Baranowicze into a permanent hiding place for Jews escaping from the neighboring ghettos. "It was a natural thing to do," he said after the war. He was imprisoned for months by the Gestapo, who found him out, but even under torture he did not disclose the place to which he had removed "his" Jews a moment before his arrest. Two Jewish orphan sisters said after the war about their Belgian savior, Marie Lodzyk, who had hidden them for five years: "She did it because she loved human beings and wanted to help them. She was a true mother to us."

"I never liked the Jews," declared Wasyl Lopatynski, the Ukrainian Mayor of the small town of Kosów, "but I cannot stand Nazi brutality." So he hid seven Jews in his house after the local ghetto was liquidated; his wife treated them as her own children for two years till they were liberated.

For others, helping Jews was their way of fighting the Nazis. Dr. Giuseppe Moreali, an anti-Fascist, took care of the stream of refugees passing through his village, Nonantola, in northern Italy. He was constantly supplying forged documents to people he had never met before, enabling them to escape to Switzerland. Suzette Spaak had under her permanent charge hundreds of Jewish children hidden in Paris. "I'll do anything to defeat the Nazis; this is part of the job," she used to say. From a happy, contented mother and wife, she turned into a fearless underground worker; all day she rushed around Paris in the guise of a society lady, providing people with documents, finding hospitalization for sick Jews and, above all, arranging to feed her young wards. Many of them survived the war owing to her work, but she did not. The Gestapo caught up with her; she was shot.

Sometimes it was a loyal maid or house companion who hid her former employers, now completely dependent on her. Sometimes the rescue would begin with an offer of shelter as a business proposition and then continue as a humanitarian act. For example, there was Ezio Giorgetti, who took on a group of thirty-eight Jewish refugees in his hotel in Balaria. After they had no money left to pay for their keep, he became their provider, kept them at his own expense and at terrific risks, until he got them to safety.

Usually the rescuers refused any financial reward, even after the war. "We did not do it for payment," said Alphonse and Emilie Consette of Belgium, whom a thankful family wanted to reward. "You will need your jewels yourselves now," said Kleopatra Pawlowska to a group of Jews she had hidden in her Warsaw apartment for three years, handing over the package she had kept for them, when they parted after the war, and refusing to accept any remuneration.

A postman, Fernand Siplet, in Bois de Villiers, Belgium, warned a hiding Jewish family that there was a lot of talk among the neighbors about them and volunteered to transfer them to a safer place. He brought them to the house of Léon Florant, a pensioned invalid. The refugees were given the large bedroom in the house and were treated with utmost kindness.

They were kept there two and a half years, and survived.

There were rescuers in Germany itself who hid Jews and supplied them with false documents. Emma Richter hid a Jewish woman in her small shop in Berlin, and kept others alive in Theresienstadt with regular parcels. Anonymous threats and the inscription "Jew-lover," which appeared on her door, did not deter her. There were German political prisoners in the camps who used their positions in the camp hierarchy to assign Jews to "vital" employments, which saved them from the gas chambers. Ludwig Woerl, an imprisoned Social-Democrat, filled the hospital at Auschwitz, of which he was the *Lageraelteste,* with Jewish doctors.

In the occupied areas there was the exceptional case of Oscar Schindler, a German in charge of a factory that employed Jewish slave laborers from the Plaszów camp, near Cracow. He managed to keep them alive, to protect them from the Gestapo and even to bring over hundreds of members of their families who had been deported to other camps. When the Russian front drew closer and they faced the horrors of deportation, he transferred all his workers, about a thousand people, to Bruenlitz in Sudetenland, where he re-established his factory and where the prisoners were finally liberated.

In the Wehrmacht there were a very few isolated instances of help for the Jews. Foremost among them was the case of Sergeant Anton Schmidt, who cooperated with the Jewish underground in Wilno and Bialystok, supplied them with forged documents and allowed them to use German Army transport. He was detected by the Gestapo, brought before a court-martial and executed.

SS Lieutenant Schwarz of the Sobibór destruction camp was another notable exception. He was visibly embarrassed when he encountered the first "transport," and soon afterward sneaked into the prisoners' huts saying: "I had no idea where I was being sent. I can't stand it and I have applied for transfer. Now I leave you." After handshakes and an exchange of good wishes he was gone. "He became a legend: a human SS man."

Poland was swept at the time by violent anti-Jewish propaganda, to which the local population was often quite responsive. When the Warsaw ghetto was on fire during its glorious revolt a common reaction of the surrounding Poles was: "They're getting well cooked." There were many Poles who, while determined to oppose Hitler, were happy to be rid of the Jews and actively cooperated with the invaders in hunting them down. Such Jew-haters constantly spied on neighbors suspected of hiding Jews, denouncing them and bringing down police search parties on the slightest pretext. As often as not, they would finish off the escaping refugees on the spot, even foregoing the prize in bread and bacon handed out for every Jew discovered. Still, there were other Poles as well. A handful of liberal Catholics established a Council for Assistance to the Jews. They organized and coordinated widespread rescue activities, especially for children, cared for the sick and smuggled people out from the ghettos to the Aryan side of the towns. Wladyslaw Bartoszewski, a journalist, was one of its leaders. To neutralize Nazi teachings, the Council appealed to other instincts. One of its widely distributed publications was written by Marja Kann, a Girl Scout leader, who wrote in a pamphlet called *In the Eyes of the World:* "In a few years a child when seeing a funeral will ask his mother whether it was a man who died or just a Jew. This is what the heart of the Polish mother should be afraid of."

One of the most devoted workers of the Council for Assistance to the Jews was Wladyslawa Choms, better known as "the Angel of Lwów." A small, slender, good-looking woman, she made it her mission to hide Jews and smuggle them out of the country. She kept Jewish children in sixty Polish homes, convents and other institutions. The sewage canals of Lwów were her regular line of contact with the ghetto, which she provided with food, parcels and arms. Through the sewers she got out those children whose mothers risked parting with them. She expressed a desire to live in Israel among the people she rescued; she is now living in Haifa.

A church organist, Ignacy Ostjanowski of Czernezica in southern Poland, hid twenty Jews in the cellar of his church when the ghetto was liquidated. He placed another group in a barn. His son Czeslaw used to bring both groups their food, calling on them with the greeting: "The sun will rise again soon."

The group hiding in the church came to a bad end. One of them ventured outside, was seen by the Gestapo and shot at. He retreated to his hiding place, but the trail of blood led the Germans to them. All, with the exception of one survivor, were captured and shot. Ostjanowski did not give up the other group. "I go to pray and you do the same in your language," he told them.

The Ukrainians, who learned after the war that he had hidden Jews, were still so saturated with anti-Semitism that they set his house on fire. The people he rescued brought him to Israel, where he is now living with them.

In Holland assistance to people in hiding became one of the principal aims of the underground. They had a special organization, LO, to help *onderduikers* (the divers). It was the largest body of the resistance. The placing of "divers" with appropriate hosts was systematically carried on, with regional *beurs* (exchange offices) to coordinate the work and to exchange information on techniques. The underground press published "Ten Commandments for Divers," advising the hiding people to help their hosts with the housework but generally to remain as unobtrusive as possible. They were given professional advice on how to maintain their emotional stability.

There were Dutch enthusiasts who abandoned their jobs, neglected their families and became saviors of human lives. Joop Westerweel and his wife

Will were an outstanding example. They placed their three small children with foster families to be free for the job. "He who loveth his son or daughter more than me is not worthy of me," Joop quoted from St. Matthew when deciding on this step. The Westerweels became the center of a group that organized a whole network of hideouts and little by little smuggled out the inmates of Jewish orphanages, bringing the children and their instructors across France to Spain.

After a year of incessant dangers Will was arrested. She survived the Gestapo torturers and fifteen months of jail and concentration camp. Joop, though well aware of the ever-tightening ring of the Gestapo, continued with the work of rescue. He now constantly had to change his identity. Finally he got arrested trying to smuggle out two Jewish girls from Eindhoven. He had in his possession the identity documents of a professional smuggler who had a very black record with the Gestapo. But the Nazis soon discovered his true identity. Five months of torture followed. All the attempts of his friends to release him were in vain. "You know I shall never betray you," he wrote in a message which he smuggled out to them. "I am a very ordinary person, so please don't idealize me," he added. "I have just to pass these difficult days. If my fate is doomed, I shall go as a man."

When led to execution Joop Westerweel loudly recited a song of freedom that he loved.

One of his daughters, now married, lives with us in Israel.

A remarkable and outstanding feat was performed by Charles Coward, a recaptured British prisoner of war, interned in a penal camp near Auschwitz. When he found out what was going on in the nearby death factory, he persuaded all his fellow prisoners of war to give up their chocolate and cigarettes, with which he bribed the German guards to put several corpses from time to time near the ditches where the Jewish prisoners were employed. For each corpse one Jew could jump over the ditch and escape while the bribed guards looked away, and the camp records still tallied.

In Budapest there were two foreign diplomats who threw protocol to the winds to save human lives. The Swiss Consul General, Carl Lutz, put Jews under his country's protection on any pretext, thus shielding them from deportation. The second was the Swedish Attaché, Raoul Wallenberg, who distributed passports left and right to anyone who had relatives in Sweden or even business contacts with his country. He put thousands of Jews, especially children, into what he called "the internationally protected zone" of thirty houses in Budapest, which he proclaimed to be under his country's protection.

When the terrible foot trek of November was under way, Wallenberg followed it with truckloads of food, clothing and medicines. He removed from the marching columns everyone who could for any reason be declared Swedish, and encouraged the local peasants to supply water and hot meals to the women and children. Eichmann was furious. "I shall kill the Jew-dog

Wallenberg," he threatened. The Swedish Government protested to Berlin, which replied that this could not have been meant seriously. "In any case, the interference of the Swedish legation in Jewish matters was illegal," said the German Foreign Ministry.

The incidents here related are only a few fragments of a great human saga, which is being pieced together by the Jewish Martyrs' and Heroes' Memorial Authority, Yad Vashem. It is from their archives that most of the material I have quoted has been derived.

On the Mount of Memory, on the outskirts of Jerusalem, along the road leading from its main building to the Shrine of Commemoration, Yad Vashem has planted the Avenue of the Righteous Gentiles, each tree being marked with the name of one non-Jewish rescuer of Jews. A Dutch peasant, Johannes Bogaard, was recently honored with the planting of a tree to bear his name, in thankful recognition of his incredible feat. At various times, by his own efforts, he hid about three hundred Jews in his own and in neighboring villages. His father and brother were suspected, were arrested and executed in the Sachsenhausen camp; still Bogaard did not hand over the Jews who were in hiding.

The elderly peasant, now retired, but still full of vitality, threw a glance at the place allocated for the avenue, already greening with several scores of saplings. "All my life I have been planting trees," he said, "but this is more than just a tree. It is a symbol."

Johannes Bogaart was right. The Avenue of the Righteous Gentiles is a symbol of man's faith. One day, when people everywhere will come to recognize all their true heroes, this green belt on the peak of Zion's mountains will be a true and lasting monument to the spirit of the common man, who, in mankind's darkest hour, rose to new heights of humanity.

PART III

The Mills of Justice

CHAPTER 13

Escape and Capture

I have tried to give a rounded view of the Nazi butchery and of the reactions to it, both of the victims and of the Great Powers. The extraordinary masked personage I was prosecuting on behalf of the State of Israel and of the Jewish people had to be situated within a concrete historical context. Jews and Gentiles alike must learn, I felt, what womb had borne the monster. The man in the dock stood out brightly in a blinding beam of light, but in the darkness beyond were the victims, and beyond those victims was an immensely complicated administrative machine. The small audience in the courtroom and the unprecedentedly vast audience outside had to understand during the trial itself the complex chain of events which had brought Eichmann before them.

Now all this dark tangle of torture and bureaucracy lies behind us. The focus can be narrowed down to Eichmann's escape, capture and trial.

*

By December, 1944, the German power was crumbling rapidly. The whole of the Eastern front had collapsed, and the Russians, entrenched in East Prussia, had penetrated into Czechoslovakia and were gathering their forces for a further thrust across Poland. It was clear that they would soon be in control of the Balkans as well.

The Germans were still resisting on the Western front. They were pinning their hopes on a split between the Allies. It was unthinkable to them that the West would allow the Russians to penetrate so deeply into Europe, and they thought the longer the Western forces were delayed, the better the chances for a peace overture from them.

But here, too, Hitler's last gamble, the counteroffensive in the Ardennes, had crumbled, in spite of its military ingenuity and its initial success. Even the infiltration of Skorzeny's desperadoes in American Military Police uniforms behind the Allied lines in France was soon under control.

This was the background of Eichmann's hasty retreat from Budapest in

December, 1944. The good old times in Hungary, the cozy villa on Roses Hill, the two mistresses, the three cars and the seven servants were all a thing of the past. The estate in Bohemia with which Himmler had promised to reward him after the war looked like a distant dream as he proceeded along roads now full of omens of the approaching downfall. Soviet planes dominated the skies. Burnt cars, carcasses of horses and long columns of escaping refugees obstructed his passage. The ruins of the disintegrating Reich were everywhere to be seen.

Earlier in the war the prospect of a cease-fire had made Eichmann interested in a territorial concentration of Jews. Now, with defeat looming ahead, Eichmann spent most of his energies working for the destruction of every last Jew he could still lay his hands on.

But he was now going against the stream. Himmler had also seen the handwriting on the wall and had ordered the mass killing stopped. The deportations to the death camps were discontinued.

Eichmann saw no sense in this move, but there were subtle ways of circumventing the orders. When the SS commanders in Poland, for instance, were told by Himmler to evacuate the camps and march the inmates into Germany, Eichmann immediately issued "supplementary working instructions," saying that "if, in the course of the evacuation, the Jews should offer resistance or cause difficulties, they are to be most severely punished."

"Imagine! Some of the commanders were idiotic enough to misunderstand my clear intention," he raged to Wisliceny. But he consoled himself that many others had grasped his meaning and shot the Jews on the march.

He had every reason to feel depressed. Ever since 1941 Eichmann had taken the utmost pains to remain "the man behind the scenes"; he had never even allowed himself to be photographed. But his role in Hungary had catapulted him into notoriety. There he had had to come out into the open, where everybody could see him; Brand had even carried his name abroad. He knew his name was already prominent on the Allied war criminals list; he realized there was no retreat for him.

The RSHA headquarters had been bombed out; Kaltenbrunner with all office chiefs had moved to Eichmann's sanctuary at Kurfuerstenstrasse 116. He was hurt at their never inviting him to join them in the snack bar of the building. "Are they already keeping themselves at a distance from me, as if I were the blackest sheep in the flock?"

In the Wagnerian twilight of the gods that now descended on Germany, Hitler vacillated between hope and despair. "I have never learned the word 'capitulation,'" he would say one day to his generals. "You are not to conclude that I am even remotely considering the loss of the war." The next day he would say: "If the war is lost, the nation will also perish. There is no necessity to take . . . into consideration the basis which people will need . . . to continue with even a primitive existence. On the contrary, it will be better to destroy these things ourselves. . . . Those who will remain after the battle are only the inferior ones, for the good ones have been killed."

Eichmann reflected these moods of Hitler's. One day he would tell his subordinates that he was about to form a partisan commando in the mountains, to fight to the last or await a breach between the West and Russia. The next day he would say he had decided to commit suicide and had already provided poison for himself and his family.

Yet, while Hitler's last pronouncements were steeped in bitter disappointment over the failure of the war, Eichmann felt the elation of a man with a mission fulfilled. In *his* sector Germany had been victorious. Therefore, he did not have, like his Fuehrer, to bequeath an injunction to future generations to carry on with the work, predicting that "the seed that has been sown will one day grow to the glorious rebirth of the National Socialist movement." Eichmann could jubilantly talk to his men of an assignment accomplished. "I will jump with joy into my grave," he told them, "in the knowledge that I drag with me millions of Jews." Years later, of course, he wished he had never uttered these words, and he vigorously repudiated his hangman's bravado.

But despite his unflagging zeal in the destruction of his Jewish "enemies," Eichmann now also showed a normal prudence. A great part of his time was taken up with a comprehensive effort to efface the evidence of the crime. He saw to it that all central and local archives on Jewish matters were eradicated by fire and that not a single paper outlasted its writers. Had all office heads been as efficient and conscientious as he in carrying out the destruction-of-records order, no Nazi talebearing documentation would have been left to the world. Senior Gestapo officers were then being provided with false identity papers in the general scheme of "submerging" and disappearing in the army or among the civilian population. For a while Eichmann watched his colleagues, the Gestapo department chiefs, elbowing their way to the false-document clerks, but decided this was no good for him anyway; he was too deeply involved to escape that easily. So he dramatically pointed to his gun and told his chief Mueller, who was watching him, that this was the only identity document he wanted.

*

In April, 1945, Himmler ordered Eichmann to bring to safety a hundred notables from Theresienstadt. Though Eichmann never carried out the assignment, it led to a farewell visit to his family in Austria, where he had installed them. He provided his wife with poison to be taken by her and the children if the Russians caught up with them. He noticed that little Dieter did not immediately respond to his mother's call, so he slapped the boy hard. "I thought this was the best way to part with him, by implanting some discipline in him."

Then he went to see Kaltenbrunner at Altaussee, in the Austrian Alps, where the latter had retired with the treasures of the Reich Main Security Office.

The Chief of the RSHA was playing solitaire and sipping brandy. Eichmann announced his intention of going up into the mountains with a commando. Kaltenbrunner read his mind instantly. "That's good," he said. "You can't surrender. It will also be good for Himmler, who will be able to talk differently to Eisenhower knowing that Eichmann is in the mountains and won't surrender."

Kaltenbrunner thought Eichmann had to be out of sight before the Nazis could even hope to start talking to the Allies about an armistice.

Eichmann gathered his men, about 150 of the veteran Security Service staff, many from his department and some from counterintelligence, in a local hotel. He brought in ample supplies of provisions, paid for with foreign currency he had received in a box full of gold, jewels and money. ("I later found out that the foreign currency I got was forged . . . in the course of the big forgery scheme carried out by our counterintelligence," he told Sassen.)

He had to clear out of Altaussee, which was to be surrendered to the Americans without a fight. On his way higher up the mountains he picked up the Rumanian rebel Horia Sima and his "Cabinet," who had recently proclaimed themselves the "reconstructed Rumanian Government" and were carrying large bundles, which when the wrappings were peeled off proved to contain tightly packed rolls of money. "They looked after the money more carefully than after their bread," he recalled.

With this crew Eichmann kept on climbing. But it was clear that the escapade was ridiculous. This was no fighting outfit. The men under his command had been bureaucrats who had never seen service at the front. They were helpless; they could not even use their weapons. In any case, Germans were poor guerrilla fighters and discipline was soon relaxed. The wireless went out of order. On top of all this the local population, now awaiting the arrival of the Allies at any moment, were unmistakably uncomfortable about the mysterious intruders. Eichmann was relieved when Kaltenbrunner's messenger brought the order to stop all resistance. The war was over. Germany had surrendered unconditionally on May 7, 1945.

*

Eichmann's unit now awaited its inevitable capture by the Allied forces. But even his own men were too much concerned with their skins to tolerate his presence among them. It was his friend Anton Burger ("my faithful Burger") who told him: "We have discussed the matter among ourselves. You are wanted as a war criminal; we are not. If you leave us, you will be doing your comrades a great favor."

Eichmann told his men to save themselves as best they could, took leave of them and of Horia Sima, and was off.

The stay in the mountains had restored his confidence. He was sufficiently invigorated to meet the future. He knew his family had had no reason to take poison and remained alive. He was determined to devote all his skill and cunning to the effort to survive in spite of everything. His adjutant, Jaenisch, joined him in a trek into Germany. After covering a lot of ground on foot and by hitch-hiking, they were captured by an American unit not far from Ulm and became prisoners of war. Eichmann's name was now Adolf Karl Barth; he wore the uniform of an airman second class of the Luftwaffe.

He soon found out this disguise would not do, as the Americans were checking prisoners of war for the SS tattooed blood-group mark on the arm. So after some rest in the camp, and before they were screened, Eichmann and Jaenisch escaped. This was not too difficult, since the prisoner-of-war camps were loosely guarded. But they did not get far this time; by August, 1945, they were again in American hands. Now Eichmann gave his name and rank as SS Lieutenant Otto Eckmann of the 22nd Cavalry Division. He chose a name similar to his own in case someone who had known him before should unexpectedly address him within the hearing of a man in authority. "Eckmann" sounded enough like "Eichmann" not to make people suspicious. The Americans had to accept the prisoners' stories about themselves, as they all claimed that their documents had been destroyed "on orders."

Life was fairly easy at first at the Oberdachstetten camp. Lieutenant Eckmann volunteered for a labor group and tried to remain as inconspicuous as possible. He had no difficulty in hoodwinking the counterintelligence investigators. "I was just a shade cleverer than the interrogating officers," he chuckled to Sassen when recalling the incident. Months passed by; Lieutenant Eckmann was not molested.

The four victorious powers, America, Russia, Britain and France, were still acting in harmony. They announced their determination to hold war criminals accountable for their deeds. "We are engaged in the biggest manhunt in history," Eden said in the House of Commons. They were looking for a million men who figured in the war criminals list, he said, and announced they would comb every ruined cellar, every peasant yard and every prisoner-of-war camp in a relentless search. They had the whole Allied army free for the assignment.

Twenty-one of "the principal criminals," including Goering, Ribbentrop, Kaltenbrunner, Hans Frank and Keitel, were soon in Allied hands and preparations were on for a stupendous international war criminals trial, the first in history. A tribunal of eight of the conspicuous legal talents among the victorious Allies was convened in Nuremberg on November 20, 1945.

The grim indictment of the major war crimes was set forth. It was not long before Eichmann's name crept into the proceedings. On January 3, 1946, Wisliceny shocked the courtroom and the world with a description of the "Final Solution," evoking Goering's comment: "That Wisliceny is just a little swine who looks like a big one, because Eichmann is not here." The papers were full of new "discoveries" about the Final Solution which became a daily topic of conversation. Lieutenant Eckmann felt the ground getting too hot under his feet. He was thoroughly disgusted with Wisliceny's disloyalty and much alarmed by it. He decided it was time to disappear.

*

According to an officers' unwritten code, Eichmann approached Lieutenant Colonel Oppenback, the senior officer officially responsible for his group, disclosed his true identity and asked for "permission" to escape. "I have known your identity for a long time from your man Jaenisch," replied Oppenback. An officers' conference was summoned; everybody saw the point of Eichmann's fading out. He was granted approval and set off alone. This was two days after Wisliceny's testimony in Nuremberg.

He was eager to leave the American Zone; he made his way northward, heading for the Celle District. According to the forged papers he had received in the camp, his name was now Otto Heninger; he carried a recommendation from a fellow prisoner of war to the latter's brother in Kohlenbach, suggesting his employment as a forest ranger. There he joined a group of Germans from the Eastern Zone, now under Russian occupation, who preferred not to return home. The house they stayed in was called "the island," and they kept very much to themselves. Eichmann worked his way up to a small chicken farm; for a while the food shortage in Germany made this a good business.

Four years passed. His name was mentioned more and more in the postwar trials. The International Nuremberg Tribunal branded him unanimously as "the man in charge of the extermination program of the Jews." In the Doctors' Case, the *Einsatzgruppen* Case, the Concentration Camp Case and the Ministries Case, his name stood out prominently as the executor of the Final Solution. He was soon referred to by the prosecution as "the sinister figure." Some Jewish survivors were looking for him everywhere.

Eichmann stayed on in his retreat not far from the dreaded Bergen-Belsen camp till he thought it safe to venture across the ocean.

In Germany some ex-Nazi organizations had been formed under different guises, soon after the defeat. One of them was "the ODESSA" (*Organisation der SS Angehoerigen*—Association of SS Members), which had been established to smuggle out some of the most exposed suspects. Another body was *Die Spinne* (the Spider), which commanded excellent contacts in many circles, including foreign countries. Both organizations were financially assisted by legally established social welfare bodies, which as such were encouraged by the representatives of the Western Allies, who now with the Cold War in progress were wooing the Germans. Eichmann was not forgotten by his comrades. He was put in a group of four, which left on the established underground route for Austria and from there into Italy.

A monastery in Genoa was the meeting place of many escaped Nazis. There a Franciscan monk provided Eichmann with a refugee passport bearing the name of Ricardo Klement. On July 14, 1950, he obtained an Argentine visa; a month later he landed in Buenos Aires. In October he applied for an Argentine registration card, stating that he was a German national, born in Bolzano, Italy, a mechanic by profession. He obtained his identity documents in April, 1952, in the province of Tucumán, under his assumed name of Ricardo Klement. He was now employed as a labor organizer by the Capri construction, measurements and waterworks company, which sheltered many ex-Nazis. After a while he felt that the place was remote enough for his family to join him there; he contacted them, this time not through underground channels but directly.

Mrs. Vera Eichmann had been living since the end of the war with her three sons, Klaus, Horst and Dieter, most of the time in Austria. She told the children their father was dead. Now she said that "Uncle Ricardo, the cousin of their late father," who lived in Argentina, wished them to join him. Eichmann had urged her not to reveal the truth to the children, "who might talk." In 1952 the family was reunited in Argentina. The children, who had been small when parting from their father seven years earlier, did not recognize him. For the time being he remained "Uncle Ricardo" to them.

During the following years he held various posts: he managed a rabbit farm, worked for a juice extracts business; finally he joined the German automobile firm of Mercedes-Benz, to which he was openly introduced and openly recommended as "SS Lieutenant Colonel Adolf Eichmann, in retirement." His self-confidence grew. At first he would express his ideas only through marginal notes in books he was reading. On a page of *The Atom,* by Dr. Fritz Kahn, he wrote that he had found fresh confirmation of his attitude to the "National-Socialist belief in God," which he regretted he was unable to implant in his three sons. In a book by Gerhard Boldt, called *The Last Days of the Reichskanzlei,* he found doubts as to Hitler's leadership and perhaps a shade of disloyalty. Eichmann gave vent to his scorn in a plethora of insults and a shower of exclamation marks: "The author should be skinned alive! Buttocks with ears! His name is dirty pig! With such scoundrels we were bound to lose the war!" (When questioned on these marginal notes in his pretrial examination, Eichmann said that as long as he did not lend his books to anybody, which he had not done, his marginal remarks were his own affair and "should be of interest to no one.") "Uncle Ricardo" often spoke to his children about "their father." They must not believe the stories circulated about him. He had been besmirched as a war criminal, Uncle Ricardo said, but this was untrue. Their father was a loyal officer who had only done what he had been told and had never killed a single person.

A fourth son was born in 1956 and christened Ricardo Francisco, Ricardo after himself and Francisco after the Franciscan priest in Genoa who had provided the passport to Argentina. He was registered as born out of wedlock, Mr. Klement having acknowledged parenthood.

It was around this time that Eichmann became bold enough to talk more freely to Sassen, the Dutch ex-Nazi he had become friendly with, and some of his other friends about his wartime experiences, and they decided to write a book together (see Chapter 1).

The importance of the Sassen document lies not so much in the facts it covers as in its revelation of Eichmann's attitude toward current problems and especially his vitriolic, permanent and implacable hatred of the Jews, which accompanied him across the seas and was as vivid twelve years after the collapse as at the time when the machinery of the Final Solution was in full swing.

The talks and exchange of views between Eichmann and his friends covered 659 typewritten pages, the size of a long novel. During the police interrogation in Israel, Eichmann, not knowing whether we possessed the document or not, guardedly volunteered the statement that "about three years previously" he had gone into the subject of his activities "in great detail with Mildner and Sassen," in Argentina. "We analyzed everything minutely and reduced it to its rudiments," he said.

He felt he could talk freely to Sassen and company. "I am no longer being pursued. That much is clear," he told them.

*

But in this he was not entirely correct.

True, the official pursuit of him was over. On the lists of "wanted" persons of the United Nations War Crimes Commission the number had gone down from a million to several thousand. "We then looked for Eichmann most assiduously and if we had found him, we would have tried him," declared Telford Taylor, chief of counsel for the Nuremberg prosecution. But they did not find him, and with the courting of Germany that soon began on all sides no Allied government really cared.

But there were other trackers. These were camp survivors who, as soon as they could walk again after their agony, started searching for him. They found out that Burger was with him; they finally secured one of his rare pictures; they traced his family and his mistresses. They planted a housemaid in a family with which he was believed to maintain contact, as well as a "friend" in the Eichmann household itself, who used to take the children out for a walk or a row; they pursued every available scent. Once or twice they were actually on his heels, but his trail vanished again. Some of the information they received now appears to have been a red herring; after all, Eichmann was a professional, his trackers were amateurs. He skillfully avoided mistakes that could have betrayed him. He never contacted his wife at that time as he knew that she was bound to be watched. Above all he was an excellent actor and enjoyed an uncanny run of luck. His place in the Nuremberg dock remained empty.

The pursuers, Tuvia Friedmann in Vienna, Shimon Wiesenthal in Linz and their assistants, received alternately threatening letters and commercial offers to "sell" Eichmann to them. Though they still pursued every scrap of information, they were growing weary of their thankless job.

Gideon Rufer (Raphael) of the political department of the Jewish Agency arrived on the scene and took a hand in the direction of the operation. Rufer went to Nuremberg and got a full statement from Wisliceny, who volunteered to track Eichmann down. "We have other plans for you," replied Rufer. "What are those?" eagerly asked the exhilarated Nazi. Rufer did not reply. He drew a noose with his finger and pointed upward.

Wisliceny's guess that Eichmann was probably hiding in a prisoner-of-war camp was correct. But there the Jewish search parties had no jurisdiction. They alerted the Allied commanders to such a possibility and that was all they could do. Rufer soon had to leave for another assignment and left matters in the hands of his able successor Arthur Pier (Ben-Nathan). But at the end of 1946 Pier could only report to Rufer that he was "still pursuing the information brought from Nuremberg," but so far without success.

Soon Jewish endeavors all over the world were channeled into the political struggle for a state and, later, the fight for its independence and survival. The homeless and displaced refugees flocked to their new home, which was beset with enormous political and economic difficulties. The major Jewish effort was directed toward Israel. The trackers' ardor cooled.

From time to time reports appeared in the press that Eichmann had been "seen" in Kuwait, Egypt, Damascus. The sources of information were always doubtful and could not withstand even a cursory examination. Wiesenthal stayed in Linz, tracking down hundreds of other war criminals; Friedmann moved to Israel and continued to amass valuable documentary material and to collect evidence that he supplied to prosecution authorities in Germany and Austria. Eichmann was still uppermost in their minds. Friedmann kept bombarding the government and the Knesset with requests to do something about discovering Eichmann's whereabouts. Wiesenthal, on his part, was pursuing every piece of information. He noticed that the obituary announcing the death of Eichmann's father on February 5, 1960, was signed among other mourners by Vera Eichmann, née Liebl. This proved that her reported "second marriage" in Argentina was a fake, since she still called herself Eichmann.

At that time the Israeli Secret Service was already pursuing a clue passed on to them by our Ministry of Justice, which had received a strictly secret piece of information from a reliable and authoritative foreign source. It said that Adolf Eichmann was living in Buenos Aires.

The report had every semblance of truth. At the end of January, 1960, one of the Service's ablest investigators arrived in Argentina. As a child he had been miraculously saved from the Nazis but had lost his family, including his parents, at their hands.

After some preliminary difficulties he located the house into which the Klement family had recently moved in one of the Buenos Aires suburbs. There was no difficulty in identifying Mrs. Klement and her sons. But the crucial question was the identity of Ricardo Klement, the head of the family: who was he? To establish his identity beyond doubt was the investigator's job. The Israeli installed himself in a nearby place, watching the house and awaiting an opportunity to take a few telephotos of the man. Imperative as it was to make sure whether Ricardo Klement was really Adolf Eichmann, it was equally important, though most difficult for a single operator, to avoid leaving even the faintest trace and arousing the slightest suspicion. Eichmann's skill in last-moment disappearance was too well known. The mission of indirect identification had to be accomplished without any contacts with the man or his entourage.

Once the Israeli operator was almost caught. Having verified his suspicions about the household, he visited a lady in a nearby house, telling her that he represented a British sewing-machine factory that was interested in putting up a plant in the area. Would the lady consider selling her house for the purpose? The lady replied she would, for a proper price. "Do you know whether the neighbors would be willing, too?" asked the man, leading up to the subject of his inquiry. Without a second's thought the good woman jumped to the window and shouted at the top of her voice in the direction of the Klement house: "Señora Klement, would you sell your house for a sewing-machine factory?"

That same evening Eichmann heard the story from his wife. It aroused his suspicion. Who would put up a factory in that remote spot, which still awaited its turn for connection with the municipal water installation? It seemed strange. He pondered over the riddle for a while, but, as he later said, dismissed his fears and soon forgot all about the incident.

Never had the mission come closer to failure.

Finally an opportunity of taking the pictures presented itself when Ricardo Klement was busy in his garden on a Sunday morning. With these in his pocket the Israeli returned home.

A careful and discreet attempt was now made to have the pictures identified by people who were known to have seen Eichmann at one time or another. But many years had passed since their encounters with him; the persons questioned said the pictures were "very much like the man," but they could not be sure. This was obviously not enough. A police expert was called in to compare the pictures with an old photo of Eichmann; he reported that though he could not make a definite identification there were no counterindications whatsoever to these being pictures of the same person.

That was considered sufficient to justify further steps. In April, 1960, four Israeli volunteers arrived in Buenos Aires.

Klement's movements to and from the factory he worked for were now established. It was learned that he used to disembark from the bus that brought him from work at a certain station not far from his home. One evening, at about 8 P.M., two cars were waiting between the bus station and the house. Eichmann emerged from the bus and headed for home. He was accosted by one of the men, who clutched the hand Eichmann held in his pocket, grabbed him with the other hand, and brought him to the ground. Resistance lasted no longer than five seconds. He was soon put into a car, which carried him away. It was then established that "the hand in the pocket" was inoffensive; he had no arms on him and was simply reaching for his flashlight.

Inside the house to which he was taken Eichmann immediately confessed his identity. "I am in the hands of Israelis," he added. No reply was given, but he was asked in German whether he agreed to proceed to Israel to be tried for his deeds during the war. "I do not wish this but am prepared to stand trial in Argentina or in Germany," he said. No reply was given. Several hours passed. Eichmann told his guard he wanted to speak again to the man who had spoken to him before. He had thought it over and was obviously afraid of being liquidated on the spot. "All right," he told his previous interlocutor, "I am prepared to proceed to Israel to stand trial," he said. "Will you sign a declaration to this effect?" he was asked.

"Yes," was the reply.

In a dark room, lit only by the beam of a flashlight shining on a sheet of paper, Eichmann wrote the following:

> I, the undersigned, Adolf Eichmann, declare of my own free will that, since my true identity has been discovered, I realize that it is futile for me to attempt to go on evading justice. I state that I am prepared to travel to Israel to stand trial in that country before a competent court. I understand that I shall receive legal aid, and I shall endeavour to give a straightforward account of the facts of my last years of service in Germany so that a true picture of the facts may be passed on to future generations. I make this declaration of my own free will. I have been promised nothing, nor have any threats been made against me. I wish at last to achieve inner peace. As I am unable to remember all the details and may be confused about certain facts, I ask to be granted assistance in my endeavours to establish the truth by being given access to documents and evidence.
>
> Buenos Aires, May 1960 (*Signed*) ADOLF EICHMANN

It was already past midnight. "What date should I put, yesterday's or today's?" he asked. "Just leave it May, 1960," he was told. Ten days later he was in Israel.

Eichmann's capture reflected a certain ironical quirk of history.

Subtlety in the choice of means was never an outstanding German characteristic, but Eichmann had succeeded in outwitting the Jews. Many people had wondered how it was possible for "the clever nation" to have been so utterly outmaneuvered by Eichmann's cunning psychological warfare. On the other hand, violent methods were never, throughout their history, a typical reaction by Jews to acts of oppression. Yet Eichmann fell finally into the hands of Jewish trackers, who did not have to resort to physical force, but who were certainly backed by it. In Israel Eichmann expressed to his lawyer his appreciation of the deed, saying that he would never have expected Jews to be capable of accomplishing his abduction in such a manner.

CHAPTER 14

The Preparation of a Case

On May 23, 1960, the Prime Minister of Israel, Mr. David Ben-Gurion, informed a stunned Knesset that Eichmann had been found and brought to Israel, and would be put on trial for his share in the "Final Solution." The country was at a peak of excitement, which was widely reflected throughout the world.

In Israel the investigation of crime is in the hands of the police. Elsewhere war crimes have been handled by historians and lawyers, even at the initial pretrial stages. In this case, however, it was decided to leave it to the usual authorities—a decision that was never regretted. A special investigation bureau was set up by the police under Commander Abraham Selinger, with a staff of other German-speaking officers and men. Our police had five departments at the time. The new outfit was called "Bureau 06."

Eichmann was kept in an old police building, which was watched over by a special unit of Frontier Police. Double checks on entering and leaving the place, tough security precautions, including antiaircraft posts—all these made the place look like a secret headquarters. No chances were taken of possible attempts at escape or even rescue commando raids.

On May 29, 1960, the deputy chief of Bureau 06, Assistant Commander Ephraim Hofstaedter, addressed Eichmann in German as follows:

"I am told that you have expressed your readiness, and even an interest in giving your version of your part in the so-called Third Reich. Is this so?"

"It is so," replied Eichmann.

"It is clear to you that you are under no coercion whatsoever?" asked Hofstaedter.

"Yes," was the answer.

"Well," replied Hofstaedter, "in that case Chief Inspector Less will stay with you and will begin taking your statement right away. It is obvious that you will need certain documents for the purpose. Superintendent Less will make a list of these and we shall try, as far as possible, to supply you with them."

Thus started an investigation that continued for about eight months. Eichmann's statement was recorded on tape and transcribed on 3,564 type-written pages. Every page was submitted to him for his initialed corrections. To every complete transcript of a hearing he put his full signature.

In the initial stage of the interrogation Eichmann was nostalgically talkative about his early years, his childhood, family and school. In addition to the recorded investigation he set down in writing memoirs, notes, charts and observations on documents, which covered hundreds of pages. We had the impression that he believed his safety depended on keeping talking. When Superintendent Less would occasionally skip a day of interrogation, Eichmann would grow nervous and ask the guard for the reason. He was visibly relieved when the questioning was resumed.

As a prisoner he was exemplary; tidy and of fixed habits. "Even his slippers were never an inch removed from the place which he had chosen for them," an officer in charge said. He would rise whenever an officer entered his cell and would not sit down till told to.

On the whole he was, therefore, a garrulous prisoner; he revealed an astonishing memory. He could remember in the smallest detail books he had read in the twenties, the name of the German Consul who had given him a visa in Linz in 1933, the way the furniture had been placed in his first office, the names of all the persons he had come in contact with on a trip to Palestine and Egypt in 1937, and the price of a meal and a glass of beer at a military canteen he had visited twenty-five years before. "A roll was given there extra, without charge," he recalled.

It was only about Jewish matters that he had lapses of memory. He couldn't remember, either then or at the trial, what he had seen at the extermination camps. He couldn't remember when he had first ordered Jews to their deaths. And he couldn't remember why it had been necessary for him to bring to Poland orders to cover the killing of 750,000 human beings. Unfortunately for him, his earlier feats of memory had been so extraordinary that no one could seriously believe he was capable of such remarkable lapses.

After the first few sessions with Chief Inspector Less, Eichmann read into the record a written statement, saying among other things:

> I am prepared, unreservedly, to say everything I know of the events. Inwardly I have long been ready for such a general statement, only I did not know where fate would place me for making it. On January 7 I was told that I should face the Court within this year, and I was told I should not survive my 56th birthday. The first has taken place and the second, I think, is unavoidable.

(The fortuneteller who had thus foretold Eichmann's future was nearly right. He stood trial the following year; he was to live to the age of fifty-six and two months.)

> This knowledge alone makes me absolutely ready to say everything I know without any regard for my own person, which is not so important to me any more. Throughout my life—from kindergarten till May 8, 1945—I was used to discipline, which developed in the years of my SS membership into unconditional obedience, like that of a corpse [*Kadavergehorsam*]. . . . Disobedience would in any case have been of no avail. . . . In spite of all this I know I cannot wash my hands in innocence, because the fact that I was only and exclusively a carrier out of orders is today meaningless. Those who planned, decided, directed and ordered the things have escaped their responsbility, cheaply, by suicide. Others who belonged to this circle are either dead or not available. Although there is no blood on my hands I shall certainly be found guilty of participation in murder. Be that as it may, I am inwardly ready to expiate for the dark events and I know the death penalty awaits me. I do not ask for mercy because I am not entitled to it. Should it serve as a greater act of expiation, I would even be prepared to hang myself in public as a deterrent example for anti-Semites of all the countries on earth.

*

I myself had been completely involved in the Eichmann trial from the very beginning, having been appointed Attorney General of Israel two weeks before the Prime Minister's dramatic announcement. On first reading Eichmann's statement I was filled with mistrust. His Spenglerian version of an inevitable fate that had governed all his actions in the past, his present-day submission to an inexorable destiny and his desire for future expiation seemed to me remarkably spurious. I was convinced he had done his job not as a blind tool, but with passion. He was happy in his work; he loved it. This reaction to his deeds was surely a consequence of his scale of values, not of any predestination. Consequently I was not taken in by his sudden desire to "expiate his sins."

Future revelations lent full support to my distrust. Eichmann never acquiesced to his lot, or else he would not have doggedly fought for his life as he did, both in the subsequent interrogation and during the trial, nor would he have vehemently refused the exhortations of the Rev. William Hull to admit his moral guilt in writing. "I did nothing wrong," he told Mr. and Mrs. Hull, who came to see him at his own request and offered spiritual comfort. "My brother is a lawyer at Linz," Eichmann said. "He wrote me that on the evidence submitted there was only one verdict possible, and that I should be set free. Any other judgment would be illegal. . . . They would sit in court and have a wonderful time with such a paper. If I say now that I am sorry, they will pounce on that and say: 'Where there is sorrow there is guilt.' "

He was not, indeed, ever sorry for what he had done. "To my mind regrets do not help nor do they change matters. They cannot bring the dead to life. Repentance is a matter for small children," he replied when I pressed him in cross-examination. Surely where there is no inner sorrow for what one has done, any "expiation" is empty talk. What is there to atone for if there has been no wrong?

"Eichmann does not realize the possibility of a death sentence, and it might come as a severe shock to him if he should have to face it," said his lawyers. One of them even told me later: "When the time comes you will need six men to drag him to the gallows." I knew, therefore, that this was not a man who yielded to inevitable destiny.

The "confession" Eichmann purported to make was a clever piece of acting. There was much cunning in his offer to "hang himself" as a warning to anti-Semites. He knew how sensitive Jews were to this centuries-old hatred, and he hoped they would bask in the prospect of this repudiation coming from him. Whatever else may be said of Eichmann, he certainly had a profound insight into the weaknesses of his "opponents."

The part of the police interrogation that followed fully confirmed my disbelief in the sincerity of the "confession." Whenever he sensed danger, Eichmann would refrain from giving direct answers to Less's simple questions. He made full use of the possibilities inherent in the German language to becloud meaning with verbosity, and would admit only as much as he considered absolutely necessary. Of course, he did not know at the time whether the Sassen document had already been published; this uncertainty must have caused him a great deal of anxiety. He would repeatedly put out cautious feelers in this direction and, in the meantime, keep talking. He admitted what he thought could be proved in any case, mainly by things that he had read or that Sassen had brought to his attention three years before; everything else he would deny as much as possible.

Here are some typical examples:

LESS: You sent people to Auschwitz only?

EICHMANN: Auschwitz, and there was once a transport conference, though I, my God, never took part in any such conferences. It went somewhere else, so it seems to me, so it seems. But I don't know, did it go to Treblinka, into a ghetto, into one of the big ghettos? I really can't say now, Mr. Chief Inspector, I never had any contact with the Economic Office. This was Guenther's job, and I never took part in a transport conference. This was the assignment of Captain Novak, and several times, I think, Guenther was present. I never participated. . . .

LESS: And they were subordinate to you?

EICHMANN: Yes, they were subordinate to me. . . .

LESS: How many Jews did you send to Auschwitz for destruction?

EICHMANN: Here I would ask to be permitted to use, on this point if possible, to obtain for it, authentic source material, and it seems to me that one of the most important things would be to get the transport schemes which the Ministry of Transport had prepared at that time. Today—I can't say, first because I did not fix the schedule of the transport conferences, did not telephone, as I had already stated with your permission, and even if I had done so I would not have anything in my memory. I would have to name just a figure which would not be good to anybody.

LESS: How many Jews were gassed and killed there?

EICHMANN: Mr. Chief Inspector, I have read that Hoess stated he killed four million Jews. Personally I considered this figure exaggerated. If we talk of figures at all, whether it was one million, four million, or even a hundred, in principle it is all the same.

There followed an elaboration covering a whole page, with different conjectures and statistical experiments. Chief Inspector Less grew weary of all this and asked: "Didn't you speak to Hoess about the figure of Jews destroyed at Auschwitz?"

EICHMANN: Never, never. He told me once he had put up new structures there and could kill 10,000 people per day. So much I have in my memory. Whether I am imagining it today I do not know. I don't think I am imagining it. I can't bring to mind when he said it, how he said it, and how the surroundings looked. . . . Therefore I don't know any more. Maybe I read it somewhere and am imagining what I read. This too, is possible.

This was an example of a favorite technique of Eichmann. When questioned about a particular event, he would offer several "theoretical" possibilities of how the thing might have happened, including one close to the truth, and leave us the choice between them, saying he could not remember which was which.

About the Wannsee Conference, he said he merely had to send out the invitations, after Heydrich had told him how he wanted them to read, and had also to prepare data for Heydrich's speech.

"But why did they need little Eichmann there at all?" asked Less, thoroughly annoyed now with these evasions.

"I was the department head and had to be present, Mr. Chief Inspector," he replied. "I had no opportunity to make a speech there or distinguish myself, as these were Secretaries of State. In no case, after all, did I discuss such matters with a Secretary of State. . . ."

LESS: But why did Heydrich not just ask you to prepare the material? He could not very well ask you at the conference whether what he said was correct.

EICHMANN: No, he wanted this beforehand. I had to report to him exactly as I twice reported to him on emigration matters. The Wannsee Conference was the beginning of the killing process. Was it not?

Eichmann was again trying to sound Less out. His "professional" approach was obvious. He was an "old hand." Moreover he had had a full dress rehearsal about the whole investigation during the Sassen talks in 1957.

Less tried a different approach. "Did not your participation there mean that you had more prominence in the Final Solution than you have described here?"

"No, no, Mr. Chief Inspector, I would have confessed to it right away had it been so. . . . People knew me, I was a department head in the IV-B-4 office, and a department head of the Secret Security Police could never overstep the framework he was harnessed in. That was out of the question."

It soon became clear enough how Eichmann wanted to portray his particular function in the Final Solution machinery. He was a mere pipe or conduit through which orders and instructions were relayed, he said; whatever he received from above he passed on. He was not answerable for the orders of his superiors, over whom he had no control, nor for the execution of these orders lower down, which was the responsibility of other people.

"I never took part in deportations, not a single time. This was left to the authorities on the spot; as I said, the Security Police could not even have done it, as they had no personnel for it. I don't even know how they carried out the deportations down there. . . . If we discuss the example of Salonika, there were only a couple of Security Police people there. I don't know who carried it out. I don't know at all."

What possible guilt can you attach to a mere transmitter? he would imply. Of course, if under your current notions of jurisprudence you choose to call such an innocent role "complicity in murder," that's your affair.

At this stage he would not yet go so far as to brand an official German document as an outright forgery or to declare its contents to be "a regrettable mistake," as he later did. He would therefore admit, very grudgingly, a fact that Less could prove to him in black and white. Sometimes he would be taken aback by a document he had not imagined to be in our possession. He was dumbfounded when Less was able to show that he had taken part in the conference of September 21, 1939, and that he had thus been in on the "Final Solution" conspiracy from this early stage, after he had first categorically denied that he had known anything at all about this meeting. "Because of the stupidity of those fellows of the SS Economic Office, who have kept all the documents, these things have now got into the Jewish literature," Eichmann once complained to Sassen about the availability of some documentary proof.

At all costs he wanted to shorten the period in which he had dealt with deportations; so he first claimed that he had had nothing to do with the 1939-40 expulsions from the annexed Polish territories. He said that he had known nothing of Gestapo Department IV-D-4, which was set up at the time to deal with these matters. Less showed him a letter bearing the insignia of the department and signed by him. "This IV-D-4 here is, of course, a stenographic error," Eichmann said. "It should be IV-B-4, because IV-D-4 never existed."

Chief Inspector Less asked what the letters "RZ" on the letterhead signified. "Is it not your office of *Reichszentrale*, the Central Office for Emigration?"

Eichmann sensed danger. "I am slowly getting befogged," he said. "I must say—well, RZ? This is . . . this must have slipped my memory completely—but I can't even now believe it—I realized it myself now I—one could, one should, perhaps somehow follow the thing up. . . . I am myself confused, so, Mr. Chief Inspector, because I can't remember at all, I would not grant it yet—but please, this does not mean that, Heaven forbid, I deny—I would just—I become myself confused when I read it."

Less showed him another IV-D-4 document, and another, whereupon Eichmann admitted that the department "must have borne" the name IV-D-4 and that it was no "stenographic error," but as he had said before, he would have thought it improbable.

Less showed him the minutes of a meeting held on January 30, 1940, in Berlin, concerning the same deportations. Eichmann read it. Judging by the participants, he said, it was a "very high-level" conference (Heydrich, Seyss-Inquart, Krueger, Mueller, Best, Ohlendorf, and many others). "It is entirely strange to me," he said. Then Less handed him the continuation of the attendance list. "I see by my own name here that I took part in it, together with Guenther, Dannecker and Rajakowitsch. . . . Yes, it says here also that because of transport difficulties, all transport affairs had to be centrally handled; here I see it says that Department IV-D-4 will be set up to take up the steering of the evacuation work. . . . Maybe Rajakowitsch had his fingers in this pie, I would not deny it. I did not do it, it is entirely new to me. Of course, I could have read the document at the time, probably did read it, it is difficult to say after twenty years. But I must have entirely forgotten all about it."

Finally, when shown more and more documents, he had to admit not only that IV-D-4 existed but that he was its head, and that it later developed into IV-B-4, covering both Jewish affairs and deportations.

In this way the interrogation went on step by step.

While Superintendent Less was questioning Eichmann, Bureau 06 was collecting, sorting out and preparing the colossal array of documentary evidence from which the story of Eichmann's ten years' activity in seventeen different countries was pieced together. Thousands of instruments were scrutinized. Those that had any relevancy were examined, recorded and catalogued. They kept feeding Less with material for the further questioning of Eichmann. It was a great organizational and intellectual effort.

Though his name was frequently mentioned in the various postwar trials and occupied a central position in the history of the Final Solution, the complete case against Eichmann had never been prepared before.

Léon Poliakov, in his pioneering work of 1951, referred to him as "the master of life and death in the destiny of European Jews." In Gerald Reitlinger's comprehensive work of 1953 he was described as "the Great Inquisitor." Some time later Joseph Tenenbaum dubbed him "the Gestapo hangman, a fanatic and ruthless executor of the evil design."

He was often mentioned in a famous libel case that took place in Israel in 1954, in the course of which Dr. Kastner's contacts with him were closely scrutinized. Yet nobody had ever put together a complete documentary case against him, since once he had disappeared there was no occasion for it.

When Bureau 06 looked around for a first foothold for its investigations, they found a dossier on Eichmann in Tuvia Friedmann's Documentation Center in Haifa. There they obtained the first data on his life, a few records derived from his personal file at the SD, some documents on deportations signed by him, Wisliceny's statement, the Wannsee Conference protocol and a number of other key documents. It was something to start with.

The archives of Yad Vashem, the Martyrs' and Heroes' Memorial Authority for the commemoration of the Jewish holocaust, proved to be most helpful. They contain mimeographs of all the documents dealing with Jewish affairs out of the huge archives of the German Foreign Office, which were captured intact by the U.S. First Army in various hideouts in the Harz Mountains, a solid mass of 485 tons of paper, rescued just in time, as they were about to be consigned to the flames. This huge store of historic documents, going back to 1870, was for years dumped in a warehouse in Alexandria, Virginia, under the jurisdiction of the U.S. National Archives. The originals were soon returned to Germany, but copies were left in America, as well as at Whaddon Hall in England, in charge of the German War Documentation Project under joint American-British control. It was from there that Yad Vashem obtained in 1956, through a special emissary, microfilms of thousands of documents dealing with Jewish affairs, including two rolls of films containing the "Final Solution" dossier. It also obtained some copies of the Berlin Document Center Archives, which contained an especially rich catch—the personal dossiers of the SS Head Office.

The Yad Vashem documents bore the stamp of authenticity, as they were directly traceable to the official German archives. This was of prime importance. After the war scores of thousands of Nazi documents were photostated or simply copied and filed away in various documentation centers. There is little ground to doubt their genuineness, and they usually bear enough "birthmarks" to be given credit by an historian, but a court of law would never admit them in evidence unless their origin could be satisfactorily accounted for and traced to the official source. Through affidavits from Yad Vashem archivists and their British and American colleagues, we were in a position to prove that our documents were derived directly from the German Foreign Office records via the Allied Documentation Center.

Then there were thousands of other documents, which were in the briefs of the prosecution or defense at the postwar trials, but for one reason or another had been laid aside. Part of this wealth of documentation also found its way to the Yad Vashem archives. They presented a real problem. It was impossible to let go of an important document, but the amount of labor involved in tracing it to its source was sometimes enormous. With no catalogues and no indices available it was often like looking for a needle in a haystack.

With the hunt for documents going on, the same instrument would arrive from different sources under one of the numerous postwar documentation markings. "P.S." (Paris-Storey), for instance, was the sign for the documentation office run at the time in Paris by Colonel Storey; "L." stood for the London Centre; "N.O." signified the office that dealt with Nuremberg Organizations; and "N.G." for Nuremberg, Government; "N.I." for Nuremberg, Industrialists; "N.O.K.W." for Nuremberg, *Oberkommando der Wehrmacht;* "E.C." for Economic Case; and so forth.

The same document might have passed through different centers, or different parts of it might have been used, checked and marked by different documentation offices, resulting in a maddening variety, duplication and even triplication of markings.

To avoid confusion, Bureau 06 established a central registration card system, which catalogued every newly received instrument and marked it with its own consecutive number. This central registration system proved most helpful in piecing together Eichmann's life story. The detection work was often like the effort of assembling a gigantic jigsaw puzzle. The investigators had to fit it together, though there was no pattern to which they could look for guidance, and they could not know where the piece they held belonged, or even whether it belonged in the picture at all.

The 06 Bureau was soon divided into various geographical or regional sections, each dealing with one of the countries in which Eichmann had been active, with Hofstaedter, the deputy head of the Bureau, directing the incoming documents to one or more sections. If he thought the document had no relevance, he would mark it "E.E." (*Ein erech*—of no importance). The prosecution later managed to salvage some documents from Hofstaedter's very strict screening.

Police officers were turned into research students. The Bureau put in their hands some general reference works, and told them to get busy and start working. The standing order was always to look for the original of a document and never to be satisfied with a reproduction. The study of the Nazi hierarchies, especially those of the SS and the Gestapo, was placed, among other duties, in the able hands of Chief Inspector Reshef, a police officer by profession, a lawyer by education and an historian by heart.

They soon compiled a personal file on Eichmann and general files on the SS and the German Government agencies that were later of substantial importance to the prosecution.

Yad Vashem is the depository of copies from various documentation centers, including the important Centre de Documentation Juif Contemporain in Paris, which contains much vital information. Kibbutz Lohamei Hageta'ot (the ghetto fighters' settlement) has rich archives, which supplied important material. The published material of postwar trials, including the forty-two volumes of the International Military Tribunal, were combed for evidence. The fifteen bulky volumes of reports from the subsequent trials and other voluminous publications proved to be a mine of information on Eichmann and his department.

Commander Selinger went abroad to contact documentation centers in Holland, France, the United States and England, and met historians to ask their assistance. On the whole everyone was most helpful. The Iron Curtain countries did not admit him, but submitted valuable material through our embassies. The Polish Government even published two special documentary bulletins of their Commission for the Inquiry into Nazi Crimes, both dealing especially with Eichmann and containing important and hitherto unknown material. Yugoslavia sent in important documents and gave wholehearted assistance. Czechoslovakia helped us to obtain vital data. The only country that did not even reply to our request for assistance was Soviet Russia.

There was one country that we decided not to ask for help in the search for documents. This was Germany—both parts. The West German authorities, however, willingly responded to all our requests for special assistance in the authentication of proof we had ourselves obtained.

Bureau 06 was working under great strain. It was understaffed and the pressure of time was immense. I was being urged to start the trial soon, but was unable to begin until they had finished; so I had to pass the pressure on to them; at times this caused strained relations. I put two of my future trial assistants at their disposal. Assistant State Attorney Gabriel Bach was from its inception the adviser to the Bureau on legal matters and District Attorney Jacob Baror lent assistance, too. Bach spent weeks on end at Bureau 06 headquarters, a police station not far from Haifa; he gave them important guidance.

But it was the officers and men of Bureau 06 itself who had to carry out the investigation. At the end of December, 1960, they sent in the first of their final summaries, each dealing with events in a particular country, according to a fixed pattern of description. There were also some elaborations on particular problems. Altogether we got twenty-six such résumés—some, like Superintendent Schwenk's excellent work on Germany, consisting of about one hundred pages. Chief Inspector Reshef produced his material with textbook precision. Chief Inspector Goldmann's works on Poland and Soviet Russia were particularly helpful. We even got from Chief Inspector Dayan a glossary of the peculiar Nazi terminology. All others were most helpful, too.

On the whole the prosecution received as much assistance in documentation as it could possibly hope for.

As a result of Selinger's diligent and painstaking work, we managed to obtain some of our most important documents. His ability, thoroughness and unlimited devotion were a constant inspiration to his unit, and were ultimately responsible for its success.

At the trial itself we had a small unit of police officers to assist us in current matters. They were with us at the prosecution desk, each in his turn, when evidence was needed on the countries they had worked on, providing valuable and reliable aid. Later I held consultations with them and the heads of the Bureau on matters pertaining to cross-examination and the preparation of questionnaires for the examination of witnesses abroad.

Shortly before Bureau 06 was wound up I asked Dr. Robert M. W. Kempner, the former assistant U.S. Chief Counsel at Nuremberg and a renowned authority on Nazi documentation, to have a look at what we had, just to make sure that in our hurry we had not missed anything of special importance. It was gratifying to hear from him that our material surpassed by far that which was known to the prosecution authorities at Nuremberg.

CHAPTER 15

Some Prosecution Problems

From the moment Prime Minister David Ben-Gurion announced Eichmann's capture, Israel itself was on trial. The whole world seemed to be watching to see how we acquitted ourselves of the task we had undertaken. Enemies gleefully predicted a show trial; friends were worried that we might lose face; neutral observers were simply skeptical. This "trial" of the trial continued everywhere, throughout the proceedings in Jerusalem; for two years the Eichmann "syndrome" remained a major topic of international discussion.

It was the irony of fate that the Jews had to fight even for their right to try Eichmann, as they had had to fight so often in the past for rights accorded without question to others. It was maintained that we could be neither objective prosecutors nor impartial judges, that we were bent on staging an act of vengeance aimed at a small cog in the machinery of the Third Reich, whose importance we had deliberately inflated.

The "legality" of our law for the punishment of Nazis and their collaborators was challenged, though a dozen countries at least had promulgated similar enactments. It was maintained that we had passed this legislation especially to fit Eichmann's trial, though in truth we had had it in our statute book since 1950, ten years before his apprehension, and there was no attempt to amend it. Because of its retroactive validity a leading American journalist dubbed our statute "jungle law," completely forgetting that the occupied countries that fought Hitler had adopted similar legislation (for there was no other way to put the culprits on trial), and that the four major Allies, including America, had sat in judgment at Nuremberg and elsewhere under precisely such retroactive statutes.

The problem of jurisdiction, basically a legal issue, became the topic of a heated debate all over the world. Never before had a jurisdictional claim been the subject of a global controversy. The kidnaping aspect, essentially a political problem, was hopelessly mixed up with other points in the debate, which soon raged everywhere—legal, historical and emotional issues all playing their part. There were many understanding voices, but there were others, too.

Soon we were also brought to the bar of the United Nations Security Council by Argentina, where Eichmann was captured. It was alleged that the act of bringing Eichmann to justice in Israel constituted a threat to the world's peace.

Even after the Security Council had resolved the issue, essentially in our favor, the debate continued in some places. Later, Gallup Polls were held in America and in Europe: "Where should Eichmann be tried?" "Is the trial fair?" Hundreds of editorials and comments were written, some by jurists of high repute.*

The controversy seriously threatened to distort the image of the proceedings before they had even started. Not only might this situation frustrate our intention to provide a universally accepted record of the events through the trial, and thus also send forth a reminder and a warning from Jerusalem, but by the turn of events it was we who now found ourselves in the dock. The scales being tipped against us obviously had to be rectified if the trial was to be what we wished it.

Though it tremendously increased the responsibility entailed by the trial in any case, I decided to let the controversy run its course without taking any active part in it. My duty as public prosecutor was to speak to the court and, by persuading it, to persuade public opinion. Fully conscious of the odds involved in not countering immediately the arguments leveled against us, which for a time gathered momentum, I refused all invitations, some of which came from leading publications, to comment on matters being so widely discussed. I reserved my answer for the right place and the right time—in court.

It was obvious, however, that we faced a formidable task; we were bound to present an overwhelming legal case to sweep away all juridical doubts, and we had to offer an immaculate factual case to establish beyond a shadow of doubt the truth of our allegations. Only after clearing the ground of all skeptical objections and lingering doubts could we aspire to establish the complete structure of our accusation.

I aimed at reasoning with people and convincing them, and therefore decided to avoid, as much as possible, any emotional overflow. We had to handle all the material within the framework of a trial; we had to guard ourselves against being carried away by our feelings. It was a court of law we were facing, with the whole world as the audience. I therefore repeat-

* The impact of the trial is reflected in the unusual attention and extensive coverage it received. I have, therefore, thought it appropriate to give an indication of the public reactions to Eichmann's capture and trial, and to the judgment. To avoid breaking the flow of the narrative a small sampling of press and other reactions and the gist of the Security Council deliberations are given in an appendix.

edly pleaded with the witnesses to stick to facts, to avoid any demonstrations or outbursts, to stay calm and factual, even when this was excruciatingly difficult.

Later, with the court exerting its entire weight to secure a dignified conduct of the trial, our efforts resulted in much calmer proceedings and therefore also in a much fairer trial than could have been possible in many other places.

I assumed my new office as Attorney General of Israel when the controversy over Eichmann was already in full swing. I had to get acquainted with my general duties. A heavy pressure of work had piled up, too, and some other trials of public importance required the personal appearance of the Attorney General. An old security mishap had suddenly flared up and was referred to an investigating committee, whose findings were tossed over to me and called for further investigation, including some travel abroad.

All this kept me very busy during my first months in office, while the trial was approaching; I had no opportunity to prepare for it seriously. It was only in January, 1961, barely three months before the proceedings were due to begin, that I could give my undivided attention to the trial. Even this was made possible only by the generosity of the Minister of Justice Mr. Pinchas Rosen, who agreed to take over my daily duties in addition to his own.

The preparation of a war crime trial is a very long and involved process; there is an enormous mass of detail to be mastered. It is not like a criminal trial, where all you have to prove is what a particular individual did at a certain specified moment. Here you have to substantiate what a man was doing for years—in Eichmann's case the work of his lifetime. In the background you have, instead of a single criminal or, at most, a gang of accomplices, the whole complicated machinery of a state. Such trials were worked on and prepared in Germany and Poland for years.

In Israel people were anxious that we should begin with the trial as early as possible. It was too much of a nervous strain for the public to live very long in expectation of it. So I was asked time and again to speed up the groundwork and to keep the trial as short as possible. This, by the way, was the extent of my government's interference with the trial and with the way it was ultimately conducted.

I was soon consuming the Nuremberg Trials reports at the rate of a volume per day. I had to study Eichmann's extensive statement, and to master all the massive documentation—thousands of instruments, some of them containing many pages—amassed by Bureau 06, for I had to decide finally which documents would be submitted in court. On top of this I had to acquire a thorough knowledge of the Jewish publications on the catastrophe in Europe. I had also to prepare the opening statement and the complicated legal argument. All this called for a supreme effort. I retired to my favorite Sharon Hotel, near the seashore, with two carloads of books and files, working almost round the clock in complete isolation, with the hotel personnel going out of its way to see to my comfort. It was a desperate race with the calendar. Only by keeping strictly to the extensive daily quotas of work which I prescribed for myself was it possible to carry out the initial assignments. For relaxation I would watch, from time to time, the magnificent view of the Mediterranean, which rolled its majestic, foam-capped, winter waves right up to my windows. After six weeks of feverish work the first and most difficult stage was completed. I had a comprehensive knowledge of the facts and the draft of my opening address, which I wrote out in longhand. I could now return to Jerusalem to continue with my preparations and decide on numerous other matters which had to be dealt with.

*

First was the basic problem of how I should present our case. Bureau 06 had prepared a very good brief from a police point of view. It was all based on the Nazi documents. There is an obvious advantage in written proof; whatever it has to convey is there in black on white. There is no need to depend on the retentive memory of a witness, especially many years after the event. Nor can a document be browbeaten or broken down in cross-examination. It speaks in a steady voice; it may not cry out, but neither can it be silenced. There was therefore much good sense in Bureau 06's suggestion that the number of witnesses be kept very low.

This was the course adopted at the Nuremberg Trials—a few witnesses and films of concentration camp horrors, interspersed with piles of documents. It was all efficient and simple. But it was also one of the reasons why the proceedings there failed to reach the hearts of men.

In order merely to secure a conviction, it was obviously enough to let the archives speak; a fraction of them would have sufficed to get Eichmann sentenced ten times over. But I knew we needed more than a conviction; we needed a living record of a gigantic human and national disaster, though it could never be more than a feeble echo of the real events. I decided, after I had had the opportunity to go deeper into the matter, to call many more than the thirty-odd witnesses proposed by Bureau 06 as a mere supplement to the documents. I decided that the case would rest on two main pillars instead of one: both documents and oral evidence.

There was, in fact, much more to it than a desire for a complete record. I wanted our people at home to know as many of the facts of the great disaster as could be legitimately conveyed through these proceedings. It was imperative for the stability of our youth that they should learn the full truth of what had happened, for only through knowledge could understanding and reconciliation with the past be achieved. Our younger generation, absorbed as it was in the building and guarding of the new state, had far too little insight into events which ought to be a pivotal point in its education. The teen-agers of Israel, most of them born into statehood or during the struggle for it, had no real knowledge, and therefore no appreciation, of the way in which their own flesh and blood had perished. There was here a breach between the generations, a possible source of an abhorrence of the nation's yesterday. This could be removed only by factual enlightenment.

Then there was also the world at large, which had so lightly and happily forgotten the horrors that had occurred before its eyes, to such a degree that it even begrudged us the trial of their perpetrator. It was imperative, for its own good, that the world should be reminded, with as much detail as possible, of the gigantic human tragedy, which is an ineradicable part of a century with unlimited possibilities of both good and evil.

In any criminal proceedings the proof of guilt and the imposition of a penalty, though all-important, are not the exclusive objects. Every trial also has a correctional and educational aspect. It attracts people's attention, tells a story and conveys a moral. Much the more so in this exceptional case. It was mainly through the testimony of witnesses that the events could be reproduced in court, and thus conveyed to the people of Israel and to the world at large, in such a way that men would not recoil from the narrative as from scalding steam, and so that it would not remain the fantastic, unbelievable apparition that emerges from the Nazi documents. For the whole extent of the Jewish catastrophe surpasses human comprehension. Our perception and our senses are geared to limited experiences. There is a maximum volume of noise that a human ear can take in; any louder explosion leaves us deaf. There is just so much pain that our nerves can stand; any added torture drives us to take refuge in unconsciousness. There is a limited intensity of horrors that our minds can grasp; any further piling up of shocks fails to register—it makes us recoil and leaves us blank. We stop perceiving living creatures behind the mounting totals of victims; they turn into incomprehensible statistics.

It was beyond human powers, in short, to present the calamity in a way that would do justice to six million personal tragedies. The only way to concretize it was to call surviving witnesses, as many as the framework of the trial would allow, and to ask each of them to tell a tiny fragment of what he had seen and experienced. The story of a particular set of events, told by a single witness, is still tangible enough to be visualized. Put together, the various narratives of different people about diverse experiences would be concrete enough to be apprehended. In this way I hoped to superimpose on a phantom a dimension of reality.

It was obvious that we must immediately go in search of additional witnesses. For I wanted people to testify on the various stages of the destruction process from the beginning of the war, on the great Jewish centers and what had gone on in them, on the way the big communities had hoped to ward off the disaster and, finally, on the extermination camps themselves in their different phases. Above all, I wanted people who would tell what they had seen with their own eyes and what they had experienced on their own bodies.

This was less than two months before the trial was due to start. Bureau 06 was already being disbanded, and it was only with difficulty that I could get from the Inspector General of Police a small rear-guard group of three officers to assist me.

I asked Mrs. Victoria Ostrovski-Cohen, then Deputy District Attorney, of Tel Aviv to interview some of the people I chose as prospective witnesses. She is an energetic and experienced lawyer, somewhat hardened by some of the most difficult criminal cases in the country's biggest district, with which she had dealt with considerable ability. Yet after a while I noticed that she was beginning to show the strain of the assignment. So I took it over myself, together with Chief Inspector Michael Goldmann of the police, himself a survivor of the holocaust.

We read through hundreds of statements deposited at the department for oral testimony of Yad Vashem, the National Memorial Institute, headed by Rachel Auerbach, an historian, a survivor of the Warsaw ghetto and later one of our witnesses to the events there. She was most helpful in placing at our disposal her department's huge collection of statements and putting us in touch with prospective witnesses. After a preliminary sifting I would interview those who appeared less tongue-tied and finally pick out the people who would later give evidence in court.

This, however, could not be accomplished before the beginning of the trial and had to be continued even after the proceedings had started.

Many were the evenings my colleagues and I thus spent, while the trial was already in progress, talking to possible witnesses and taking down their statements, on returning to our rooms in the courthouse after a full two-session day in court. The building was quiet at such times, without the hum of newspapermen and visitors who filled the place in the daytime, as we would listen to the tragic story of yet another community, similar to what we had already heard hundreds of times and yet always new and shattering.

Soon after I started the interviews, I found that many of our witnesses were extremely reluctant to relate their experiences. In fact, the first reaction of some was: "Can't you find someone else? I don't know that I can do it!"

The reluctance to testify was partly due to a deliberate attempt to forget events that in any case came back often enough to plague them in their dreams; they did not want to recall them. But there was also a deeper reason: they were afraid they would not be believed. One witness told me: "When I was hiding out in Warsaw after the ghetto revolt, I thought I was the only Jew who had remained alive out of the millions of Jews in Poland. I knew I had to live to tell the world what had happened, after Hitler's defeat." And as this witness and the other emaciated survivors finally emerged from the forests, the camps and the hideouts, they felt a great urge to tell their stories. But when they started to pour out their hearts, and told tales so staggering that they were beyond comprehension, a listener would occasionally express some doubt, in word or gesture. More often than not this doubt existed only in the imagination of the narrator, but for many of these deeply wounded and sensitive people this was enough to make them take refuge in silence. They buried their dreadful knowledge deep in their hearts and never brought it up again.

Once we had persuaded someone that it was his duty to tell in court a part of what he had been through, we ran into another difficulty. Many people, once they agreed to tell their story, did not want to be limited. "If I talk, let me tell all about it—from beginning to end" was the typical reaction of a previously reluctant witness. People were concerned at having to limit their testimony to an hour or two. "How can I possibly tell what happened in so short a time?" they would ask. Basically, however, they were willing to help, and eventually we managed to get them to tell their stories piece by piece, in the way we wanted.

At my first encounters with prospective witnesses I immediately found that these were not the usual, familiar deponents, who after an effort to remember would be able to render an intelligent version of an experience, however shattering. A court lawyer learns by experience how to make a witness re-create comprehensibly a road accident in which he was run over or the scene of an assault on his person. There may, sometimes, be a traumatic moment that the witness has lived through which has been blacked out from his conscious memory, but this can be bridged over by the rest of his testimony. In this trial, however, the witnesses were required to relive a trauma that had lasted several years. At a pretrial conference they would sometimes stop conveying facts in an intelligible manner and begin speaking as if through a fog. The narrative, which had been precise and lucid up to this point, became detached and obscure. They found it difficult to describe in concrete terms phenomena from a different world. In order to establish a workable contact with such witnesses, and get through to them, it was necessary to overcome steep emotional barriers.

At times I experienced agonizing doubts as to my ability to convey to the court events so remote from my own experience. Although I was born in Poland, lived there till I was twelve and visited it before the war several times (my family had settled in Palestine in 1927) I had no personal experience of the Nazi horrors. Consequently I decided, shortly before the trial, to pay a visit to Kibbutz Lohamei Hagetha'ot (the ghetto fighters' village), a communal settlement north of Haifa, where many rebels and survivors of the ghettos had settled. There I talked with Zivia Lubetkin Zuckerman and Yitzhak Zuckerman, the leaders of the heroic Warsaw ghetto revolt. For hours I listened to this couple, who personify the tragedy of European Jewry and the rebirth of its few remnants. I told them of the points I hoped to make at the trial.

"What will you say about the Jewish Councils?" Yitzhak asked me. He is a tall, lean man in his middle forties with the look of an athlete, a small mustache and the smiling eyes of a kindly uncle, his back incurably injured from those days. He still remembered the bitter internal strife. "This is going to be the trial of the murderer, not of his victims," I replied. "But you will not be able to avoid the issue," Zivia said. This unpretentious woman, simple in her manners, has a very direct approach. Her eyes reflect a peculiar combination of the hardness of steel and the gentleness of velvet. "No," I replied, "and what we shall bring forth will be the truth. No embellishments." "That is good," said Yitzhak. "The whole truth must be told."

We went on to discuss the position of the leadership of the revolt.

"Was not the timing of your activity one of your most difficult decisions?" I asked.

"Yes," they told me. "Because we knew that once we went into action that would be the end of life in the ghetto."

We continued to discuss details. I did most of the talking now for I wanted to check with them my impressions and deductions.

At about 2 A.M. we felt exhausted. There was silence for a moment in the couple's small Kibbutz room. Suddenly Zivia remarked: "You know, you talk as if you were there with us."

I knew then that I had passed the test; I felt I would be able to handle those unusual witnesses—the survivors of a holocaust.

In direct contrast with the tongue-tied witnesses, there were others who came forward voluntarily, and even insisted on giving evidence. The latter I usually treated with caution, apprehending that they were overanxious to get the publicity attendant on their appearance at the trial. When the trial was under way, we were flooded with many offers to give evidence, but could not avail ourselves of the proposals that had arrived so late. In some cases it was a real loss. The well-known historian Jeno Livai was late in arriving from Hungary, and though he had many personal experiences to describe, the court refused our application to hear him after we had closed our case. When the trial was over a letter came from the Hungarian commander of the Kistarcsa camp, offering to come forward to testify on Eichmann's visits and the selections he had carried out there.

There were six or seven prospective witnesses I may have wronged by a "group" rejection. These were survivors who had, on one or more occasions, encountered high-ranking SS officers on inspection tours in the camps or in Gestapo offices. Having now seen Eichmann's picture in the press, these people had, independently of each other and in different places, come to the conclusion that the person they had seen at the time was Eichmann. There was no doubt whatsoever as to their honesty and integrity; they were convinced that their identification was correct. Moreover, inspections of the camps by high-ranking leaders like Himmler, Kaltenbrunner and others, were an established fact. Eichmann himself admitted his own visits to the

Auschwitz and Chelmno camps. It certainly stood to reason that he had gone to see what was happening in other camps too, and some of these witnesses may therefore have been right in their identification.

Yet, on the basis of forensic experience, I preferred to treat such testimony with caution. Subconscious projection of a personality encountered in distressing circumstances onto a widely publicized picture is not unknown in legal practice. How could we know for certain that this was not happening to them? Notwithstanding the strong protests of the people concerned, I preferred, for reasons of caution, to leave their evidence out with the exception of statements that had independent corroboration.

Thus I left in the evidence of Jacob Friedmann, an ex-prisoner in Majdanek, on Eichmann's visit to the camp in late autumn of 1942. It was also described by a man from Soviet Russia who wrote to me. This visit was further mentioned by Eichmann himself in his talks with Sassen. Friedmann recalled having seen Eichmann in Majdanek, where he appeared as the central figure of an inspection group. After Friedmann had been forced to attend the roll call of nine thousand prisoners, which had lasted throughout the night, the inspection group arrived, and he heard the "central figure" remark, pointing to the prisoners: "This whole heap must be removed." When Friedmann later retired, trembling, to his plank bed in his hut, he heard a prisoner from Slovakia say that he had seen that man before. It was Eichmann, he said.

Of course, we also had to be mindful of the possibility of mistakes by people who were now being called to relate events of sixteen or twenty years before. For this reason we preferred to call those who had given statements at Yad Vashem long ago, or who had put their reminiscences on record in published or unpublished works, since their memories could more easily be refreshed by their writings. Thus a number of authors who wrote books about their experiences were called to give evidence. We also found that writers were usually equipped with good powers of observation and carefully checked their facts before publishing them.

I wanted to tell what had happened in every area under the Nazis, and I wanted the story told by a broad cross-section of the people—professors, housewives, artisans, writers, farmers, merchants, doctors, officials and laborers. That is why we called such a mixed collection of individuals to the witness box. They came from all walks of life, just as the catastrophe struck the whole nation. I asked a plumber to give evidence on the events in Bialystok, an important Jewish center. After his statement was recorded, a well-known writer, a leader of the underground in the same place, volunteered to give evidence on the same events. By many standards the latter witness might have been preferable. But I wanted to have the plumber tell his story in his own simple words; so, finally, I kept him on the list and summoned him to court, regretfully foregoing the evidence of the author, as I could bring only one witness to testify to the fate of this community.

Naturally, we preferred local residents to people from abroad, as this saved both cost and effort. We summoned witnesses from abroad mainly to cover points on which we could not have found adequate evidence in Israel. All of them, with two exceptions, were Jewish.

These two witnesses were vital. One was a German pastor from Berlin, a man of deep faith, great courage and profound love of his fellow man. Dr. Heinrich Karl Grueber was a relatively unimportant clergyman in those days of the war, when the majority of the church closed their eyes to Hitler's barbarism and hailed him as the savior of Europe. Dr. Grueber did not. He hid people of Jewish origin, provided them with food and medicines, and organized an underground movement to smuggle them out. He had the unbelievable courage to go to Eichmann to plead for them. He proved that it was possible to have enough faith, humanity and courage to remain righteous even in the Hitlerite Sodom. Eventually Eichmann had him jailed. Grueber was sent to a concentration camp, where his teeth were knocked out and he developed heart disease. But he survived to come to Jerusalem and look Eichmann straight in the eye in our courtroom.

When the white-haired, sturdy clergyman of seventy, who spoke with a clear, boyish voice, stepped down from the witness box, it was obvious that his evidence was vital for putting the trial into a moral perspective. There were, after all, sparks of humanity even in Nazi Germany. It was all-important to know it, to sustain a belief in the morality of man.

Our second non-Jewish witness was an American man of law, a judge of the Supreme Court of Pennsylvania. He is a devout Catholic and insisted on receiving the Pope's blessing before proceeding to give evidence in Jerusalem. Michael Angelo Musmanno, whose Italian origin is clearly carved on his distinguished Roman face, was one of the American judges at Nuremberg. There he rendered world-famous decisions, combining highest judicial standards with deep moral convictions, couched in language of a beauty rarely equaled in legal records.

Judge Musmanno had also some interesting facts to relate. As an American Naval officer, he was charged by his military superiors, before he assumed his judicial post, with the conduct of an official investigation into the facts surrounding Hitler's disappearance. It was all-important to find out whether the Fuehrer was still alive, for if so the war was not really over till he was caught; and if he was dead it was imperative to make the Germans aware of it and stop awaiting a "return from Elba." In the course of Commander Musmanno's mission he had learned of the mass killings of Jews. The story had struck him like a thunderbolt. Ever since, at every interrogation he held, whether it was the questioning of Goering and his cronies or the examination of Hitler's admirals, generals, secretaries and bodyguards, even to the cook and the barber, he would always revert to the extermination of the Jews and inquire how and why and through whom it had been done. He kept hearing Eichmann's name repeated on all sides, as he later heard it time and again when he sat in judgment on some of the most infamous Nazi criminals.

*

Closely coupled with the choice of witnesses was the scope of the charge sheet, for evidence had to be adduced on the matters on which Eichmann was to be indicted. I had to decide whether it was to be a limited indictment, specifying particular acts on which we had more evidence than others, like the French, Dutch, Slovak and German deportations, or whether it should be an all-embracing charge encompassing all Eichmann's ramified activities, both direct and vicarious.

There were obvious advantages to a more restricted charge sheet. I could pick out and concentrate on those few instances where it could be easily shown that he acted more viciously and fanatically than was warranted even by the orders he had received, as in the Kistarcsa deportation or the destruction of last remnants of Dutch Jewry. Then his defense of superior orders would have immediately exploded, and he would be unquestionably convicted of murder. This would have undoubtedly simplified the legal argument. But then I would have had to limit my evidence to these incidents alone and thus miss the point of the trial: the covering of the whole Jewish disaster.

If I decided on a comprehensive charge sheet, imputing to Eichmann responsibility for all his widely ranging criminal activities and using particular instances as proof of his exceptional malice, the prosecution would not be fettered by details of dates, places and people affected. But there was a second side to the question. For we would then be bound in law to adduce a sufficiently comprehensive amount of proof to substantiate our wide and general allegations. Should we not be in a position to do so, the whole thing would boomerang, with the result of acquittal on a charge too widely framed and not adequately supported by evidence.

In fact, at the trial of the main war criminals before the International Military Tribunal, where the charges were of a general nature, some of the accused were acquitted on precisely such grounds.

In an ordinary case there is no great harm in losing or dropping one count in an indictment if there are other substantiated charges. But our case was different. Were Eichmann to be acquitted on a point or two, it might not make any real difference to the ultimate result, since there was ample proof on other major charges. But if he was cleared of some of our allegations, people would immediately deduce that he was only half as bad as we had painted him. Therefore the temptation to restrict the charge sheet was strong, especially insofar as the events in Eastern Europe were concerned.

We had succeeded in finding documentary evidence to link Eichmann with what had happened in Poland and Russia. But the Gestapo archives in the General Government and the *Einsatzgruppen* documentation have almost totally disappeared, with the notable exception of the "achievement reports," copies of which were accidentally filed in another archive and found there. The German Foreign Office was mainly concerned with foreign subjects in these territories, and therefore what had happened there was not recorded in their captured documents. There was still the evidence of the orders for slaughter, which Eichmann brought to Globocnik, and a tangible trail of his general activity and his specific acts in Warsaw, Riga, Minsk and southern Poland. But in quantity it was so much less than the wealth of documentation on his activity in Western Europe, which had been saved through the Foreign Office files and some salvaged Gestapo files from France and Holland, that I knew the court was bound to ask itself why this was so, and ultimately perhaps begin to wonder whether Eichmann could be charged with any real complicity in the butchery in the East and whether he could be held answerable for what went on there.

It was one of the most difficult decisions I had to take. After a great deal of thought, I decided that we would draft a comprehensive indictment, charging Eichmann with guilt for the Final Solution in all the occupied territories, including the Polish and Soviet areas. There were two reasons for my decision: First, he was the head of the Jewish Department of the RSHA and Heydrich's departmental chief charged with carrying out the Final Solution, "irrespective of geographical boundaries." So by the very nature of his position he was directly linked with what was done anywhere for the attainment of that object. This, coupled with the documentary evidence we possessed, would provide the factual proof of our allegations.

Moreover, his central position also carried a legal consequence, owing to the well-known principle of complicity in crime. Every man who counsels, aids or procures a criminal is guilty along with the actual perpetrator. This is valid for all criminal activity. Every member of an armed gang is in law as guilty of murder as the man who actually pulls the trigger that kills the bank cashier. This includes the driver who transported the gangsters and the confederate who remained outside on guard to prevent interference. It is a necessary and a just rule of law, which imputes to every active participant in a crime all the natural consequences of the joint venture. This principle of law should, I felt, be made applicable to the unprecedented charge we had to formulate.

For the "Final Solution" was an enormous criminal undertaking carried out in different places by a multitude of different people. They were all criminals. But while a man of the rank and file, who took part in a simple operation of rounding-up Jews for deportation, would be held criminally responsible for his own acts alone, a man who held a higher and more central post would be responsible for the acts of all the people whom he directed from his pivotal position. A local commander would thus be accountable for the crimes of the hundreds who acted at his bidding in his locality, while a district commander would be answerable for the acts of thousands of his accessories throughout the district. It stood to reason that Eichmann, the central staff officer of the venture's headquarters, was criminally answerable for all the millions of acts committed in pursuance of the criminal undertaking, even if he were to claim that some acts had "bypassed" him.

This was the way in which we could properly charge Eichmann as the central pillar of the whole wicked system, together with legions of perpetrators. For he was by no means alone in the gigantic enterprise; it involved almost the whole German administration. There were, of course, varying degrees of involvement, beginning with the issue of "certificates of descent" all through the expulsions and deportations, ending with the pouring of pale-blue crystals into tightly packed gas chambers. These were all parts of a coordinated effort of different government agencies in the service of an all-embracing criminal venture. It was "naïve to assume," as Eichmann said, that "there sat a single spider in a cobweb, who managed to catch everybody. . . . Every central agency had to deal with its own Jewish measures." In that he was right. There were several hundred highly placed officials who pulled the strings and directed different aspects of the enterprise. Scores of thousands had the administrative assignments of marking, detaining and herding Jews, distributing their looted property, crossing their names out of population registers, deleting them from food rationing lists or returning their mail with the inscription: "Left without leaving a forwarding address." Then there were the brigades of actual killers in the fields and camps. But the man who was the central figure of this colossal undertaking was legally an accomplice in all these crimes.

So I charged Eichmann "together with others" with the various crimes enumerated in our law of 1950 for the punishment of the Nazis and their collaborators. The first charge dealt with the ultimate murder of millions of Jews; the second with placing them, before they were killed, in living conditions calculated to bring about their physical destruction; the third with causing them grave physical and mental harm; the fourth with devising measures for the sterilization of Jews and the prevention of childbirth among them; the fifth with causing their enslavement, starvation and deportation. The sixth count in the indictment dealt with the general persecution of Jews on national, racial, religious and political grounds. The seventh point dealt with the spoliation of Jewish property by inhuman measures, involving compulsion, robbery, terrorism and violence. The eighth count of the indictment set forth that all these acts were, under our law, punishable war crimes.

Then came four points in the indictment dealing with the extermination of non-Jews. The ninth point charged Eichmann with having deported half a million Poles, the tenth with having deported fourteen thousand Slovenes, the eleventh with having sent to concentration camps tens of thousands of Gypsies, and the twelfth with having caused the deportation and murder of about one hundred Czech children from the village of Lidice.

The last three points charged Eichmann with membership in organizations declared to be criminal by the judgment of the International Military Tribunal of Nuremberg: the SD, the Gestapo and the SS.

Altogether there were, therefore, fifteen counts, all under Sections 1 and 3 of our Nazi and Nazi Collaborators (Punishment) Law, 1950. The first twelve of these charges carried the capital penalty as the maximum punishment.

As I read the draft of the charge sheet prepared by my assistant, Jacob Baror, according to the résumé of our prolonged consultations, I knew that I was opening the field for a full contest. Against such a general charge Eichmann would try to find shelter behind his superiors, and his own specific acts of fanatical viciousness would not be sufficiently spotlighted. It was, however, the only way I could unfold the whole extent of our national tragedy. Let Eichmann invoke his "superior orders." Their execution was in any case illegal, since they were contrary to the universal principles of ethics and the rules of civilization.

On February 21, 1961, I signed the charge sheet and sent my secretary to hand it in at the registry of the District Court of Jerusalem. It received a routine serial file number: 40/61.

*

In drafting the indictment we took into consideration the technique to which a German defense counsel is accustomed. Instead of our normal short formulation of particulars of offense, we drew up a more detailed outline of the general charges, stating immediately at the outset the capacity in which the accused acted, which entailed his criminal responsibility, and describing by way of illustrative particulars the acts for which we said he was accountable. This came somewhat closer to the continental usage, under which the whole case, with its documentation—sometimes even with reference books—is thrown into the charge sheet. We did this to facilitate the work of the Cologne lawyer, Dr. Robert Servatius, whom Eichmann had by then appointed to represent him.

The choice of a defense counsel was a matter that had been among our worries ever since Eichmann was brought to Israel. It was obvious that an Israeli lawyer would not do. He would not be able to establish that close and confidential relationship that must exist between a client and his attorney, and he might find himself under too great a strain as the result of a conflict between national emotions and defense counsel's professional duty. The Minister of Justice, Mr. Pinchas Rosen, made inquiries with a view to appointing a Swiss German-speaking lawyer or an American attorney who had acquired experience in defending war criminals before military courts in the

Far East. He even obtained a list of such American jurists. But before he could find anyone appropriate, some offers came in. A Wall Street firm in New York, a Scottish lawyer and a Chilean wrote to him offering their services. All these offers were submitted to Eichmann by Assistant State Attorney Gabriel Bach, but he decided to accept none of them. He entrusted his defense to Dr. Robert Servatius of Cologne, who had been recommended by his half-brother, himself a lawyer in Austria. Dr. Servatius had had considerable experience in defending war criminals before various courts. He had represented Fritz Sauckel, the Reich Commissioner for Labor, and the Leadership Corps of the Nazi Party before the International Military Tribunal. He had appeared for Dr. Karl Brandt in the famous Doctors' Case and for Paul Pleiger in the Ministries Case, the last and longest of the twelve "subsequent trials" of the Nuremberg Military Tribunal. In making his choice Eichmann said that this was one of the grounds of his decision. "I assume he has experience in these matters," he said, "and that I shall probably not have to tell him so much as to a novice; he would probably also be acquainted with the whole technical-bureaucratic procedure in the various ministries and central offices . . . since he must clearly have already become half a specialist in these matters."

From our point of view it was obviously preferable to have a lawyer chosen by Eichmann rather than one appointed from above to defend him, but there were still certain difficulties to overcome. First we wanted to know something about Dr. Servatius' background, since it was impossible to admit as counsel and, thereby, as an officer of the court, one with a Nazi past. Fortunately Dr. Servatius could produce proof that he had never been a member of the Nazi Party. From 1935 till his country's collapse he had served as an officer in the German Army. When I first encountered the rather heavy Rhinelander of sixty-one, who obviously cared little for politics and more for the pleasures of the table, I kept wondering what made him take on this strenuous assignment. He assured me he had volunteered for it only because he considered it his professional duty.

In order to enable Dr. Servatius to appear before our courts it was necessary to get the Knesset (the Israeli parliament) to pass a special law dispensing with the usual requirements of local professional qualifications and citizenship, which are the normal requisites for a lawyer's right of audience in our courts. When this was finally accomplished, we were informed that the Eichmann family had no money for lawyers' fees. Unless the Government of Israel supplied the funds, the accused would not be able to proceed with his defense. At about that time an abridged and cosmeticized version of the Sassen document was being published by *Life* magazine, which, it was assumed, must have resulted in a substantial income to Eichmann's family. There was, therefore, an understandable opposition on the part of many Israeli taxpayers to any financial involvement by the state in the costs of the defense.

Finally, however, the government made available the sum requested by

Dr. Servatius—$30,000. He told us he would repay the money if he succeeded in his claim against the German authorities—who, he thought, were obligated by law to cover the defense costs. He presented his claim to a German court, but without success.

Dr. Servatius called in to assist him a young legal luminary from Munich, Dieter Wechtenbruch, very bright, sharp and quick-minded, who ably supplemented his more experienced and more conservative senior.

On the whole, the prosecution staff was able to establish with the two defense attorneys a relationship which, without ever crossing the professional demarcation line between prosecution and defense, facilitated a workable arrangement to get our respective jobs done. We were mindful of the fact that the defense attorneys were not versed in local legislation. They had been briefed by a local lawyer to acquaint them with our procedure, but when they found that it is based on Anglo-Saxon principles, with which they were familiar, and after they had acquired a working knowledge of our legal framework, they looked to us to explain any particular argument we were advancing. Baror and Bach saw to it that Wechtenbruch was supplied with any information he asked for, and the Law Faculty of the Hebrew University placed its library at the defense counsel's disposal.

The defense refrained from delaying tactics, which are not unusual in big criminal cases. It concentrated on the main issues of the trial, abstained from petty technicalities and avoided crossing swords on matters that would have been of no real help to the accused.

It later became evident that Dr. Servatius was wisely refraining from any serious cross-examination of the witnesses from the concentration camps and ghettos, on the general parts of their narratives; he probed, instead, into any part of the testimony that might directly implicate his client.

On the relevant issues, such as the fight over the legal problems involved, we found our adversaries militant and resourceful. Dr. Servatius announced in advance that he was going to contest the legality of the trial, that he would raise all issues that were at stake in previous trials of war criminals and challenge our right to try Eichmann. All of this he eventually did, with considerable ability and thoroughness.

My assistants were few in number, but formed a team any attorney would be proud of. The oldest among us was Dr. Jacob Robinson, aged seventy-one, an international lawyer of standing who was an aide on Jewish affairs to Chief Prosecutor Jackson at Nuremberg. Before World War II he was Lithuania's representative at the League of Nations, and after Israel was established, the legal adviser to our delegation at the U.N. Dr. Robinson is, moreover, one of the most noted scholars on the history of the holocaust. I later adopted *in toto* his meticulous and highly learned blueprint on the problems of international law involved, and made it the central pillar of my argument on the subject. His considered and wise advice, and his unflinching personal friendliness, sustained us in many difficulties.

The youngest on our team of four was Gabriel Bach. German-born and

British-educated, Gabi, as everybody calls him at the Ministry, likes to tell the story of how humiliated he had felt at school in the first years of the Third Reich, when all the children were marching and parading, while he, the ostracized Jew, was banned from their company. Gabi kept his sense of humor and his composure throughout the full two years he worked on the case. I never saw him lose his temper. He was always completely dependable and had soon mastered all the details of the documentation. His great legal talent and his organized method of work were an enormous asset. He worked with Bureau 06 from its inception and established excellent relations with its staff. Several months later I called on the District Attorney of Tel Aviv, Jacob Baror, to join our team. He is Frankfurt-born and comes from a line of orthodox rabbis and leaders. A small, simple skullcap invariably adorns the back of his head, for he, too, is deeply religious. His burning eyes and small beard give his face the typical expression of a Jewish intellectual. I had in him a staunch assistant, effervescent, always bubbling with new ideas, unreservedly ready to pitch in on an additional assignment even when it meant a series of sleepless nights.

We were all German-speaking, which helped a great deal. Bach and Baror had to study in greater detail the part of the case I assigned to each of them to lead later on in court. Baror was allocated the evidence on Germany, the Protectorate, Theresienstadt, Bulgaria, Yugoslavia and Greece; Bach was responsible for the whole chapter of the West as well as for the evidence on Slovakia, Rumania and Hungary. I took over the whole of the East and the camps, in an attempt to relieve my associates of the most emotionally burdensome part. Dr. Robinson, unpretentious as usual, did not wish to lead any evidence throughout the hearings.

Zvi Terlo, the young Assistant State Attorney, very talented and eager for work, helped me out personally a great deal in various assignments, especially in the early and the last stages of the trial. Talking things over with him always helped to clear my thoughts. He was always keen to give a hand, but I soon had to send him back to regular duties.

Though I could fully rely on Bach and Baror to brief their witnesses, I had to be fully cognizant personally of all the statements and to become quickly acquainted with all the documents, to decide what we should put in and what we could omit.

Most difficult of all, we had to steel ourselves for the coming trial.

CHAPTER

16

The Opening Battle

The composition of the court was made known. Under the procedure governing the few offenses for which the maximum penalty is death (which do not include murder), a Supreme Court judge must preside over the proceedings. Justice Moshe Landau, forty-seven years old, the youngest member of Israel's highest tribunal, was designated. Born in Danzig and educated in London, he brought with him to the trial twenty years of judicial training, profound scholarship and sound practical wisdom. In judicial circles he is known never to concur in a colleague's opinion without going into the matter thoroughly himself. He is bald, with short bronze hair framing a thoughtful, sensitive face. An exterior of benign judicial decorum conceals a wealth of emotion, habitually restrained by a scrupulous objectivity.

His two colleagues were appointed by Dr. Benjamin Halevy, then President of the Jerusalem District Court and since elevated to the Supreme Court. One of them was Dr. Halevy himself, a graduate of Berlin University, a youthful fifty, with a grayish lock of hair often descending on his forehead. Soft-spoken, but unyielding where justice is concerned, he chooses his words carefully. He is quick-thinking and his alert eyes never lose sight of the slightest detail in the courtroom. He can descend on an attorney or witness with the swiftness and accuracy of a hawk. Judge Halevy has handled some of the most difficult and controversial cases in the country's history, one of his decisions having even caused a Cabinet crisis.

The third member of the bench, Dr. Yitzhak Raveh, of the Tel Aviv District Court, also acquired his legal training and degree at the University of Berlin. Like Judge Halevy, he was fifty, and had arrived in Palestine in 1933 with the first outbreak of Nazi excesses in Germany. When a trial is in progress, he often bends his head, with its thinning, reddish hair, and covers his large intelligent face with widely spread fingers. Sometimes, when least expected, he would interpose a pertinent question in mellow tones, or make a highly relevant point which had somehow escaped everyone else's attention. He is the thorough type of judge who is anxious for every word to sink into his mind. In his long black robe, he looks as if he were predestined for the bench.

The building in which the trial was to take place was Jerusalem's about-to-be-completed new cultural center for lectures and concerts. Some temporary adaptations were made for the judges' chambers, and the wings were converted for the accommodation of the defense and prosecution staffs, the accused and the court archives. The large hall beneath the courtroom, planned as the municipal library, was set aside for the press. The building reverted to its original purpose after the trial and, therefore, all internal arrangements were "for the duration" only. So was an unbreakable bullet-proof glass enclosure, reserved for the accused, which was erected on the right of the court, with glass walls facing the public but open toward the judges, who could thus observe him unobstructed even by a transparent partition.

There were good reasons for our precautions. Some Nazi circles were most anxious to silence Eichmann, who possessed a mine of information on many criminals still on the run. Suggestions that he should commit suicide were subtly made to him in letters and postcards. Some were artfully disguised, like a set of chess problems numbering fifty-five (Eichmann's exact age), all ending with a stalemate, which, as every chess player knows, is a position into which a player, overwhelmed by his opponent's superiority, has maneuvered himself and out of which he cannot get. This is considered to be a shameful result for the stronger party, who would have otherwise won the game. More directly suggestive was a postcard drawing Eichmann's attention "to its beautiful new stamps." Beneath them was glued half a sharp razor blade, well suited to cutting one's veins. A letter containing only the words "Courage, Courage" and the signature "Martin" was believed by handwriting experts to have been written by Martin Bormann, Hitler's deputy, who had disappeared in May, 1945.

We further learned that some neo-Nazi circles resented Eichmann's seeming "cooperation" with his interrogators and the course he had chosen for his defense. They had expected him to declare that he would not collaborate in the trial, and so prepare a build-up for a martyr's posture. Eichmann's fight for life and his self-depreciating attitude disgusted them and frustrated such a plan.

In view of the notable suicides by some of the top Nazis, from Hitler, Goering and Goebbels down to more recent and less widely known cases, we decided not to take any chances with Eichmann. The court building was carefully guarded. It was surrounded by a steel-mesh fence and admission was allowed to bearers of passes only. Once past the gate, the visitor was taken into one of a row of booths, where his pass was again inspected and he was politely searched. The press and important visitors were provided with portable transistor radios and earphones, through which they could receive a simultaneous translation of the court proceedings into four languages: Hebrew, English, French and German.

The simultaneous translations were recorded, transcribed and distributed daily among the foreign visitors and journalists. These records were obviously susceptible to error, as simultaneous translations are bound to be, and bore an appropriately cautionary notice; still, they were a help to foreign journalists in their daily reporting.

The official record of the court was taken both by complete tape recording of everything said in court and by shorthand. All that was said in a foreign language was subsequently translated into Hebrew, with the court itself overseeing the translator's accuracy.

The government invited foreign countries and central legal bodies to send observers, and some did. Western Germany sent out an official delegation, and Professor Peter Papadatos of the University of Athens came as an observer on behalf of the International Commission of Jurists.

When Eichmann was about to be transferred to Jerusalem, his earlier place of detention was shown to newspapermen, which put an end to the yarns published for months in some widely circulated magazines, including photos and illustrations, about an underground concrete shelter where the prisoner was held near an airport next to "a secret camp," and similar nonsense.

A month before the trial began the court had authorized the entire proceedings to be filmed for television purposes, so that the whole world could watch. While overruling Dr. Servatius' objections, the court ordered that the filming must not interfere with normal and proper trial procedure. Accordingly, only one company, Capital Cities Broadcasting Corporation, the first to apply, was given permission to film the proceedings by video-tape, after undertaking to provide material on demand to other networks.

With the help of tapes flown daily from Jerusalem, most networks reported the trial in detail. In America, especially in New York, substantial interest was sustained throughout the proceedings. Thus, during the entire trial, one-hour summaries prepared by leading correspondents were currently presented by the American Broadcasting Company once a week over sixty stations; in the New York area ABC gave commercially sponsored half-hour summaries five evenings a week. An offer by ABC to supply printed copies of the indictment evoked 24,000 replies.

British and West German television stations furnished similar services, and other countries made their arrangements with the film companies.

Hundreds of journalists arrived to report the trial, as well as world-famous historians and writers commissioned by newspapers or television and radio stations.

The audience included the notable historian Professor Hugh Trevor-Roper of Oxford; Professor Julius Stone of Sydney, a renowned authority on international law; the Earl of Birkenhead, representing the *Daily Telegraph;* Lord Russell, the author of many books on the Nazi period; and the Nuremberg prosecutor Brigadier General Telford Taylor. Joseph Kessel of the French Academy was there, together with well-known writers, like Irwin Shaw and Robert St. John. American newspapers sent out some ace reporters, two of whom, Robert S. Bird of the New York *Herald Tribune* and Homer Bigart of the *New York Times,* stayed with us throughout the trial. Patrick O'Donovan came to report for *The Observer;* there were also some outstanding German newspapermen.

The Government Press Office, never overstaffed, soon had its hands full of work. I appointed Mr. Gideon Hassid, Deputy State Attorney, to be our spokesman, together with Mr. David Landor, Director of the Press Office. They supplied the newspapermen with current information and relieved the prosecution of a public relations burden which we were unable to bear. Within the first four weeks of the trial it was covered by over five hundred special correspondents from abroad, and in the course of the trial some two hundred more correspondents came to watch and report. We were told at the time that the coverage far exceeded that given to major international events.

Special telecommunication services were made available in the court building in the large press hall, to which correspondents could retire to watch the proceedings on closed-circuit TV and listen on their transistor radios.

I was thankful that the Press Office took care of the news-hungry press so efficiently, so that I was free to do my job and had to see only the few journalists about whom the Foreign Ministry or the Press Office were insistent. I occasionally had to ask even these to excuse me because of the great pressure of work, although this sometimes evoked resentment.

The atmosphere in the country was one of tense expectation mingled with concern. In the air were Biblical phrases, which had foreshadowed the event over twenty-five centuries before: "The delivered shall come up on Mount Zion to judge the Mount of Esau." Though the approaching shadows of the past reopened many wounds, the people of Israel were united in a grim determination to see it through; they braced themselves for the coming ordeal.

The day the trial began many newspapers all over the globe carried such headlines as: "The eyes of the world are turned today to Jerusalem." Throughout the trial, indeed, our press provided the fullest possible coverage; papers carried almost verbatim reports of the proceedings, including full day-to-day commentaries by leading columnists.

Silent crowds would often gather outside the courtroom, quietly awaiting their turn for admission. Israel's leading personalities, including Cabinet Ministers, members of the Knesset, university professors, well-known writers and public figures, were among the regular spectators.

The country literally lived the trial, and public interest remained unabated even during the hotly contested election campaign that was going on at the time (the polling was held a day after the arguments in the case were closed).

The radio (we had no television) provided a very wide coverage, with the main features of the trial broadcast directly from the courtroom. People would often close their shops to listen; bus and taxi drivers were reported to have stopped their vehicles when the proceedings grew too moving. Schoolchildren brought transistor radios to school, and the teachers had to stop work from time to time to allow group listening. The proceedings could be heard in the public streets, for the radio voices emerged from every open window. It was an event that overshadowed everything else.

On April 11, 1961, a little before 9 A.M., Eichmann entered his glass cubicle, flanked by a policeman on either side and with a police officer in front. As he silently entered the packed courtroom there was an audible gasp. Hundreds of eyes concentrated on him in an effort to decipher the enigma of a mass murderer.

It was then that I laid eyes on him for the first time; there had been many opportunities to see him before, but I had preferred not to encounter him until it was absolutely necessary. But I knew a great deal about him. During the first weeks of his detention he had been a frightened prisoner. At the sound of steps in the jail corridor at night he would hurriedly cover himself up with his blanket. But once he convinced himself that we were not using Gestapo methods, he grew reassured. Contact with his lawyers helped to put him at ease.

We knew that he had mustered all his considerable will power not to show any weakness. He would seldom make a request. During the ten weeks that had passed between the date of his apprehension and the day when he was asked by Bach to choose a lawyer, he was not told anything about events in the outside world. He was given only novels to read. So he had no way of knowing that his presence in Israel had been publicly announced, that we had had an international dispute with Argentina over him, and that his apprehension was a matter of great interest all over the world; as far as he was concerned he might have been catapulted into outer space. But he had never asked to communicate with his family or inquired after news of them or anybody else. Such self-restraint must have required quite an effort.

I had of course seen many photographs of him before the trial and was quite familiar with his appearance, yet I almost felt like searching him for fangs and claws. For externally there was little to indicate his nature. The first unusual feature I noticed was a twitch around the mouth, when he lifted his lips; this gave his face a strange, almost grotesque expression. Only the narrowed eyes behind their glasses seemed to give one a hint of something formidable. Later, during my cross-examination in court, when he felt cornered on particularly slippery grounds, these eyes would light up with bottomless hatred. At one point my assistant tugged at my robe and whispered, "Did you notice his eyes? They frightened me!"

But such moments were brief; almost at once the fire disappeared and he reverted to his assumed gray, colorless style. His bearing as a Gestapo leader was gone; there was now no indication of his diabolical strength, and little to show his all-too-well-known viciousness, his arrogance and his power to do evil. "The prince of darkness is a gentleman," I recalled Shakespeare's words in *King Lear*. His appearance out of uniform, with no heel-clicking high boots, made him look as paltry and insignificant as all the top Nazis looked in the docks of a courtroom. Only closer inspection revealed his telltale hands, his thin, knife-like lips and that flicker of hatred in his eyes.

Only rarely did his power of self-control fail him. One day shouting was heard in the corridor leading to his detention cell on an upper floor of the court building. A moment later, as I was eventually told, the secretary of the defense attorney, Miss Liese Grude, rushed out of the room that had been allocated for Eichmann's meetings with his lawyer. Notebook still in hand, she ran along the corridor sobbing and shouting hysterically, "The Jews are right! He's a murderer! I don't want to see him again!"

It appeared that Eichmann had become impatient with his attorney's advice on some piece of evidence. His face had contorted with rage, his eyes lit up with animal fury, and he spoke so abusively that the young lady had become really frightened.

But these aspects of Eichmann's personality, while of course fascinating from a human point of view, were peripheral to my task as prosecutor. I had to keep myself sternly in hand and cope with the legal intricacies I could see Dr. Servatius was preparing for me.

Before Eichmann would plead one way or another to the charge, Dr. Servatius got to his feet to submit the preliminary objections in law. He argued that since the whole Jewish people was affected by the holocaust, Jewish judges could not be disinterested enough to avoid bias.

"It follows from the nature of this case," the defense counsel said, "that the accused must feel apprehension about the possibility of bias on the part of the judges. Not prejudice in the true sense of the word; it is enough if the accused had a justified fear on that account." Dr. Servatius added that "it was not an opinion expressed by an individual judge in a previous case that gave vent to such a fear." So the defense counsel did not challenge any particular judge for any personal reason. He simply objected to our judges collectively.

"The subject matter of this case is participation in events of a political character," defense counsel continued. "To this must be added the influence of the political press, which had already condemned the accused without hearing. This must have a decisive influence on the judges."

Then, he said, Israel's Nazi Punishment Law of 1950 was contrary to international law, as it was extraterritorial and retroactive. It made a man answerable for deeds he had committed outside the territory of Israel and even before it had ever become a state; moreover, it made him accountable after the event for deeds or acts that were quite "legal" at the time under the prevailing system. They were even more than legal, he said; they were acts of state, for the execution of which an individual cannot be made responsible. How can you declare today that these acts were a criminal offense then? he asked. Such an enactment, he argued, offended against the principles of international law, "which does not recognize the extension of state sovereignty to cases such as the present." The Nazi Punishment Law should be declared invalid, he said, and the court should refuse to sit in judgment under it.

This law smacked of revenge, he added, or of a desire to exact expiation, but the accused could not expiate for the injuries inflicted by his state. Only the state could make such amends, which in the case of the Federal Republic of Germany had taken the form of the reparations it was paying to the State of Israel. "Great material help has been extended to the State of Israel in consequence of previous persecutions," he stressed. Moreover, he said, Eichmann did not belong to the leadership group, and his functions in Germany had been grossly inflated by journalists.

Finally, Dr. Servatius dealt with the abduction of Eichmann, which he wanted to prove by two witnesses; one, he said, had taken part in the kidnaping, and the other, according to him, had piloted the plane that brought Eichmann from Argentina. Proof of the abduction, he argued, would deprive the court of jurisdiction. Then, on the conclusion of a brief oral argument, he submitted a very extensive written plea, comprising over a hundred closely typed pages, a copy of which he had delivered to me that morning.

Even a cursory perusal revealed a very learned work. It contained a frontal attack on the principle of law enunciated at Nuremberg and a broadside on the problem of territorial jurisdiction, with authorities quoted. Most of these arguments we had anticipated, but the approach to some of the problems was novel. This was a new and original attempt to upset in Jerusalem the precedents established since 1945.

According to our procedure, arguments in a criminal case are invariably conducted by oral pleading, but we did not insist on Dr. Servatius doing so, and tacitly agreed to this exception for the defense, which preferred to proceed along the lines customary in Germany.

For a moment I was tempted to ask for a similar relaxation in our favor, which would have simplified matters a great deal. But I thought it would be more fitting for us to plead in our courts in accordance with our standard procedure. Consequently, I stood up to reply to the defense by word of mouth. The answer lasted about four sessions.

At the conclusion of the first day, a friend, a senior government official, came to see me. He looked worried. I asked him what was on his mind. "How long will you take over the legal argument?" he inquired. I told him what my estimate was. He said: "Servatius spoke for three-quarters of an hour. People did not hear his written brief, and they will think his arguments are very strong if they need so long a reply. Besides, there are over five hundred journalists and observers here from abroad. Most of them won't stay for more than a week. They may not even see the beginning of the real trial. They are bored with the legal debate; think of what they will write home."

There was much truth in this, as the next day's headlines, both at home and abroad, proved. But this was a trial, not a show; it could not be helped.

*

First to be dealt with was the "fair trial" issue. A judge can be just, although he cannot be expected to be impartial toward crime, I argued. Any judge trying a traitor or a spy represents the "enemy" country in a way, and he is far from being neutral to the issue. Dr. Servatius wanted the trial to take place in Germany. It was a strange argument indeed that a judge could be disqualified because he was a fellow national of a murderer's victims, while his belonging to the nation of the murderer should be regarded as a qualifying feature. If there was a man in the world "neutral" toward genocide, it was he who should be disqualified as a judge, I maintained.

In reply to the argument of "expiation" through German reparations to Israel, I recalled that according to the agreement between the two countries the payment was not regarded as an atonement for the crimes; it was not even the return of part of the loot, but simply a contribution toward the resettlement of displaced survivors in Israel. There could be no amends for or forgetfulness of such crimes. We could only hope that future generations in Germany would be different from their predecessors, and that the children would not have to bear the sins of their fathers. Toward those who had actually perpetrated the extermination of a third of a nation, there could be no forgiveness, nor could pardon be bought by any compensation in the world.

On the abduction issue I pointed to an unbroken chain of American and English decisions, dating back over a hundred years, all showing that a court does not inquire into the circumstances under which a person has been brought before it; once he is physically present, the court will proceed to try him. Abduction across frontiers may become a political issue between the countries involved, but it is not a consideration for the court. In one of the numerous American precedents on the subject, when a man was forcibly detained aboard a Greek ship in the Bosporus and taken to the United States for trial, the United States Court of Appeal ruled:

The mere fact, if true, as stated by the defendant that he was kidnapped from the Hellenic authorities, would not give this Court power to examine such fact. The Court has no such power. . . . If either the Hellenic Republic or Turkey, by proper complaint, sought to vindicate its laws by protesting against the kidnapping of this defendant within its territory, it is reasonable to assume that the United States would enter into such negotiations with those countries as would secure justice for all concerned.

In a recent case the United States Supreme Court said:

This Court has never departed from the rule . . . that the power of a Court to try a person for crime is not impaired by the fact that he had been brought within the Court's jurisdiction by reason of a forcible abduction.

The British courts took the same view. Lord Chief Justice Goddard ruled in a well-known case:

If a person is arrested abroad and he is brought before a Court in this country charged with an offence which that Court has jurisdiction to hear, it is no answer for him to say . . . : "I was arrested contrary to the laws of the State of A or the State of B where I was actually arrested." He is in custody before the Court which has jurisdiction to try him.

There is no international tribunal that could deal with criminal complaints, I pointed out. The Permanent Court of International Justice at The Hague has no such jurisdiction. The Nuremberg and Tokyo tribunals had long ceased to exist. All the efforts of the small countries to set up an International Criminal Court had so far been unsuccessful because of the opposition of the great powers, in both West and East, who jealously guarded their judicial exclusivity. I was glad to be able to mention the appearances of my colleague on the prosecution, Dr. Jacob Robinson, in a different capacity, before the United Nations Committee on International Criminal Jurisdiction. This bore witness to Israel's efforts to secure the establishment of a court for the enforcement of international law. The matter had been on the agenda of the United Nations General Assembly since 1957, without getting any further.

I could have taken a short cut in replying to Dr. Servatius' challenge to the "legality" of our law, since our courts, like those of Britain, have no power to declare a statute unconstitutional or illegal. But it was important to show that the argument could also be answered on its merits. This I proceeded to do.

Territorial limitations on jurisdiction are not an accepted principle of international law, I explained. On the contrary, many countries claim jurisdiction for crimes against their nationals wherever committed.

The matter was once raised at the Permanent Court of International Justice at The Hague when France claimed that an officer of the French ship

Lotus had been unlawfully tried before a Turkish tribunal. It appeared that the *Lotus* had collided in the open sea with a Turkish steamer and cut it in two, eight Turkish citizens being drowned. The watch officer of the *Lotus* was arrested when he disembarked at Constantinople; proceedings were initiated against him under a Turkish enactment that makes any act injuring a Turkish national, wherever committed, an offense punishable under Turkish law. A dispute between France and Turkey ensued, which was referred by mutual consent to The Hague Court.

The tribunal ruled that the Turkish statute was in accordance with established principles of international law:

> Far from laying down a general prohibition to the effect that states may not extend the application of their laws to persons, property and acts outside their territory, it leaves them in this regard a wide measure of discretion. . . . Turkey, by instituting criminal proceedings in pursuance of Turkish law against Lieutenant Demos, officer of the watch on board the *Lotus* at the time of the collision, has not acted in conflict with the principles of international law.

There is ample authority for the proposition that states may legislate to punish foreigners for deeds committed abroad "if such deeds have consequences" within the legislating country. In fact, a number of countries have adopted this kind of legislation, among them Austria, Brazil, Denmark, Finland, Germany, Holland, Italy, the Soviet Union and Switzerland.

Where, if not in Israel, were the effects of the disappearance of European Jewry most strongly marked? I asked.

But there was more to the question than that, I continued. Some crimes have always been considered to strike at the welfare of humanity at large, for they are not limited to specific geographical units. Piracy is an example of an offense that may be committed in various places, on land, in ports and on the high seas. It transcends the boundaries between states, and affects so many communities that its due punishment is a matter of universal interest. It has always, therefore, been the law that a pirate can be tried by any country into whose hands he falls, for he is "an enemy of mankind at large."

The perpetrator of a crime against humanity is considered to be on a similar level. His offense is not aimed against a particular part of society; it is a crime against the human race. It is, therefore, within the power of any civilized state to try him; indeed, it is actually a duty of every sovereign power to act as a guardian of international peace and, in discharge of this duty, to put such offenders on trial before its courts.

Eichmann could, therefore, have been put on trial in any civilized country. At least eighteen different states were directly affected by his crimes, and each could have claimed the right to try him. But none had done so; they had all recognized Israel's prior claim. No country had asked for Eichmann's extradition, I informed the court. At the time of the trial there was no other country that claimed the right or assumed the duty to try

Adolf Eichmann. That duty, therefore, fell to our courts alone. It was our right, under the law; it was our obligation, as a member of civilized mankind.

The argument that Israel did not yet exist when the offenses were committed was highly technical. She could certainly, as a member of the family of nations, claim her right to a share in the universal jurisdiction over crimes against humanity. Moreover, the State of Israel had grown from the Jewish community in Palestine, which had been internationally recognized since 1917, under the Balfour Declaration and later under the Peace Treaty, which gave it the status of a "Jewish National Home." Palestinian Jews had fought under their own flag in World War II; postwar Israel had been recognized by the Western Allies as having been a cobelligerent and had been invited to join them in terminating the state of war with Western Germany.

In this context I recalled the precedent of a British Military Court at Singapore, which had tried a Japanese warrant officer for unlawfully killing American prisoners of war in the French territory of Indochina. The accused claimed that the British had no jurisdiction over him since he had committed no wrong against them or on their soil, but the jurisdiction of the court was upheld on the ground that the Allies had a common interest in punishing the perpetrators of offenses against each other's nationals, since "they were all engaged in a common struggle against a common enemy." How much stronger was Israel's right to try the exterminators of her own flesh and blood, who were more to us than mere "allies," who part company after the common struggle is over?

*

At the postwar trials defense counsel had often claimed that since the acts condemned by the Nuremberg principles had been "legal" under the law as it stood at the time of their perpetration, they could not be made illegal now by adopting retroactive prohibitions. Without a law, it had been argued, there could be no outlawry; without a prohibition, no crime; and without a defined crime, no punishment.

Dr. Servatius expounded these views at length in his written brief.

It is true that some jurists had accepted these arguments as plausible and orthodox principles. After the war some eminent lawyers had even urged the shooting of the Nazi leaders out of hand as "a bad lot"—or, at most, after a "drumhead court-martial." They had argued that law was not yet a suitable weapon against international lawlessness of the Nazi type.

Had it not been for the enormous range of the Nazi crimes and their cynical flouting of all principles, the legal doubts might have led the Allies to change their minds, notwithstanding all previous commitments. But when the full extent of Europe's martyrdom emerged into the light of day after the smoke of war had cleared, the leaders of the world felt that this was too much. To let the perpetrators of these atrocities find refuge in an inhuman "law" would be a greater evil than adapting old principles to the grim reality of the twentieth century.

The majority of lawyers had defended this view and had emphatically rejected the orthodox attitudes as dangerous formalism. They maintained that the fact that Hitler had created a pirate state and called crime by the name of virtue could not render his followers immune from personal responsibility. Otherwise we would arrive at the absurd result that a ruler merely had to be ruthless enough to abolish all moral prohibitions and create a legal vacuum, to enable his followers to commit the most heinous crimes with absolute impunity. If that was where formal justice led, then it was the wrong road. "*Summum-ius, summa iniuria,*" the Roman jurist said: "Rigid law is the denial of justice."

So the Allies decided that there would be a trial and that the law, too, along with the United Nations and the Security Council, should be forged into a weapon to protect mankind. A charter was signed in London on August 8, 1945, by the United States, Soviet Russia, Great Britain and France, laying down that individuals would be held responsible for crimes against peace, war crimes and crimes against humanity. An International Tribunal "for the just and prompt trial and punishment of the major war criminals of the European Axis" was set up, in which the four powers sat in judgment on twenty-two of the surviving Nazi war chiefs and the institutions that were pillars of the system. Twelve of the accused were sentenced to death and three to life imprisonment; four received jail sentences of ten to twenty years, and three were acquitted. The four occupying powers enacted Control Council Law No. 10, providing for "the prosecution of war criminals and similar offenders, other than those dealt with by the International Military Tribunal." This law called for the establishment of separate courts in each of the four zones of occupation, each power setting up its own tribunal. The period of international judicial cooperation was soon over, with a short-lived revival for the trial of Japanese war criminals.

The International Tribunal was "Military" in name only. Some of the greatest legal minds of the victorious nations were engaged, both on the bench and at the prosecution desk. In the American Zone of occupation professional judges also sat in many "subsequent trials" in Nuremberg and Dachau, before which 1,814 more war criminals were arraigned. Of these, 450 were sentenced to death.

Trials were also held in the British, French and Russian zones, and there were more trials in various countries occupied by the Nazis during the war.

In almost all these trials the plea of retroactive penal legislation was raised by the defense and rejected by the courts. The criminals knew, it was held, that they were acting "not only in defiance of well-established principles of International Law, but in complete disregard of the elementary dictates of humanity." Justice Michael M. Musmanno added in the *Einsatzgruppen* Case judgment:

> Humanity is the sovereignty which has been offended and a tribunal is convoked to determine why. This is not a new concept in the realm of morals, but it is an innovation in the empire of the law. Thus a lamp has been lighted in the dark and tenebrous atmosphere of the fields of the innocent dead. . . .
>
> But the jurisdiction of the Tribunal over the subject matter before it does not depend alone on this specific pronouncement of international law. As already indicated, all nations have held themselves bound to the rules or laws of war, which came into being through common recognition and acknowledgment. Without exception these rules universally condemn the wanton killing of noncombatants. In the main the defendants in this case are charged with murder. Certainly no one can claim with the slightest pretense at reasoning that there is any taint of *ex post factoism* in the law of murder.

All this was embedded in legal consciousness. Even reliance on the few dissenting views of those who still adhered to old principles could not brush aside the new pronouncements.

But Dr. Servatius in his written plea launched a clever outflanking attack. He surveyed the development of the new idea of law as a protection of mankind from Nuremberg onward. He pointed out that in fact the new rules had not been universally absorbed into the national law systems of the modern states; that even the Genocide Convention had failed to attract the necessary minimum of adherents—with such notable abstainers as the United States, Russia and Britain—that after the Universal Declaration on Human Rights the world powers could not yet agree on a universally binding convention for the protection of such basic rights. If that was so, he argued, and if the new principles had failed to promote worldwide confidence in a rule of law, why did we have to make inroads into accepted and well-tried principles, and what did we gain by abandoning them? Was it not better to revert to the accepted notions of "positive laws"? These might not purport to provide an answer to all the ailments of mankind, but at least they furnished a stable guide to lawmakers, who, unbridled by restraints, might be tempted to embark on arbitrary, rudderless schemes. Why not simply call the Nuremberg principles "the law of the victor," recognize them as revenge on the vanquished and revert to the old, well-trodden ways?

Though the criticism of post-Nuremberg developments was justified, the conclusions drawn were, to my mind, false. There was no reason to throw out the baby with the bath water. The principles were correct, even if their implementation was slow and inconsistent. I pointed to the absorption of the Nuremberg principles by the European Convention of Rome in 1950, and the 1951 Convention of Refugees (to which even the Vatican and Switzerland were parties) and by the International Law Commission of the United Nations. Should we despair of all the real progress that had been made and try to put the clock back?

In his written brief the defense counsel referred to the Nuremberg principles as "legalistic nihilism." "If this defense was accepted," I argued, "it would follow that under conditions of dictatorship such as existed in Nazi Germany there could be only one accused and that is Hitler." Here Judge Halevy interposed: "But he, too, since he was a head of state, could claim immunity?" "Yes," I answered, and cited a passage from the judgment of the American Tribunal which tried some of the officers of the SS Head Office for Economy and Administration:

> The Germans have become so accustomed to regimentation and government by decree that the protection of individual human rights by law was a forgotten idea. The fact that the people of Eastern territories were torn from their homes, families divided, property confiscated and the able-bodied herded into concentration camps . . . all this was complaisantly justified because a swollen tyrant in Berlin had scribbled "AH" on a piece of paper. And these are the men who now keep repeating *"nulla poena sine lege"* (no punishment without a legal prohibition).

I recalled that even had Eichmann been tried in Germany, as his counsel desired, his argument would have been no defense. Even under the law applicable under the Nazis it was no defense to a criminal charge for a subordinate to claim "superior orders" if according to his ideas and concepts the act enjoined upon him was wrongful.

The presiding judge interrupted: "What about this qualification of 'according to his concepts'?" "Yes," I replied, "let Adolf Eichmann therefore come forward, if he wants to, and prove to you that according to his ideas and concepts the rounding up of millions into concentration camps and gassing them there was not a wrongful act."

Dr. Servatius replied briefly. He said there was no legal vacuum involved in Eichmann's case, as a German court could still try him. It was true that Germany had not yet applied for his extradition, but it might still do so, for he was a German citizen. "The accused has a claim for protection by his state, a claim arising out of the inactivity of his government. He can still bring a complaint before the Administrative Court, and indeed he will do."

This was a surprising statement, for no such step had been taken by the defense up till then. Nor was it taken thereafter.

The court wished to know for certain what was Eichmann's nationality. "Is he a German citizen?" asked Judge Halevy. "Yes, indeed," replied Dr. Servatius. "Not an Austrian?" the judge continued. "No," replied the defense counsel. It was important to find out the country of Eichmann's nationality to know who could claim him. Germany never did. Before the trial started

Chancellor Adenauer, then on a visit to America, announced that his country had definitely no intention of making any such request.

Dr. Servatius reverted to the jurisdictional problem. "The cardinal feature is whether the accused was kidnaped from Argentina on the orders of the Government of Israel." The presiding judge wished to clear up the point:

"It is not clear to me why you attach such decisive importance to the distinction between kidnaping on the orders of the government or by private initiative." Dr. Servatius replied that if a state orders the commission of an act contrary to international law, it cannot afterward rely on it.

The presiding judge pressed the matter further: "If we assume that he was kidnaped by private initiative, would you then say the Israel Court was competent?"

Dr. Servatius was obviously embarrassed by this question. He finally replied: "To my way of thinking, the position is the same in both cases."

This disposed of the defense counsel's application for summoning alleged parties to "the forceful abduction" as witnesses, since he agreed that it made no difference at whose behest they had acted.

Principles relating to piracy or the slave traffic did not apply to Eichmann, Dr. Servatius claimed. "Those who perpetrated such acts are enemies of the human race, and every state is under obligation to do its best to see that they will not cause any further harm. . . . But humanity is under no danger from Eichmann. When Hitler's regime came to an end, he became a peace-loving citizen. It was his bad fortune that he was obliged to bow to the authority of that inhuman system, but he conquered himself and rose above the concepts of that government. He has become absolved from his oath."

The court announced its decision at the next regular session. On the question of disqualification, the court noted that the fear of bias was adduced "not against any one of the judges in particular, but against all three of them, on the grounds that they were members of the Jewish people and citizens of the State of Israel." To this the judges replied:

"The present trial is concerned with the responsibility of the accused for the actions enumerated in the indictment. In elucidating this question we will have no difficulty in maintaining the guarantees of which every accused person is assured according to our criminal procedure that every man is presumed to be innocent and that his case is tried on the basis of the evidence brought before the court. Those who sit in judgment are professional judges, accustomed to weighing evidence; they are carrying out their task in full view of the public; learned and experienced lawyers are conducting the accused's defense.

"As for the accused's apprehensions regarding the background to this trial, we can do no better than to repeat what is valid for every judicial system worthy of its name: that when a judge sits on the bench he does not cease to be flesh and blood with human emotions and urges. But he is bidden by the law to overcome those emotions and urges. If this were not so, no judge would ever be qualified to sit in judgment in a criminal case evoking strong disgust, such as a case of treason or murder, or other heinous offenses. It is true that the memory of the holocaust shocks every Jew to the core. But now that this case has been brought before us we are in duty bound to overcome these emotions too, whilst sitting in judgment. This duty we shall discharge. . . .

"After considering the arguments of learned counsel for the defense, the court, and each one of its members, regards itself as qualified to try this case."

The court also rejected Dr. Servatius' objections to the jurisdiction of the court on the grounds of the circumstances in which the accused had been brought to Israel from abroad; and to the validity of the Nazi Punishment Law, under which the accused had been indicted.

While the legal battle went on Eichmann remained almost motionless. Unmoved in his glass box, he watched the contesting lawyers and the court attendants carrying armloads of legal books adorned with markers. He looked, as one discerning observer remarked, almost like "a charity patient in hospital, already anesthetized and laid out on the operation table, while the learned doctors display their skill, point out symptoms, expound theories of health and illness to the students in the amphitheater and put forth their differing views."

The length of the legal arguments evoked varying comments. Some local commentators grew impatient. "The methodical approach to building up a watertight case for Israel's right to try Eichmann is not being followed by foreign newsmen," complained a leading local paper, usually level-headed.

Others were even more critical. "Hausner's argument could, according to experts, be studied at universities. But is this the way to open this trial?" Others went still further: "Why does the Attorney General have to be on the defensive? He specializes in killing climaxes. Do we need to cite a case from Idaho to prove that we are entitled to try Eichmann?"

Some correspondents complained of the "dryness of the proceedings" and the "endless explorations of underground passages of international law."

Others, however, were more charitable.

Professor Trevor-Roper remarked:

> I listened to those endless English and American precedents and heard the familiar domestic names of Coke, Blackstone and Dicey echoing somewhat strangely in this claim of an ancient oriental people against a modern German barbarism. I saw clearly that the Israeli Government, in spite of all the emotion which it does not fear to revive among the people, is resolved that the case against Eichmann shall rest, in its basis as in its conduct, not on a mere demand for retribution, however just, nor on moral claims, however irrefutable, but visibly and unmistakably on the established theory and practice of civilized states.

Many observers found, to their great surprise, that our view of the kidnaping issue and the validity of retroactive laws was "firmly embedded" in American and British legal principles and that American judges had tried war criminals precisely under such laws, S. L. A. Marshall wrote:

> Most of the way, as the State sets the foundation stone by stone, we hear American voices speaking to the tribunal through Mr. Hausner with such weight that if there is lingering doubt about the proprieties of the trial then our quarrel is with our own lawgivers.

Patrick O'Donovan showed a deep insight into my motives. He reported:

> To prove the legality of this trial is perhaps the essential work of the prosecution. . . . These elaborate preliminaries, meant for an audience that stretches far beyond the narrow frontiers of Israel to the whole civilized world, must be settled before the squalid and cruel details of the indictment can be faced. The trial has not bogged down, but it must justify itself before it can properly begin. . . . It is in fact an essential preliminary, without which the trial would be a waste of time and a disgrace.

The Earl of Birkenhead summed up his impressions:

> Many of us who have attended the early sessions of the trial have been surprised by the widespread belief that Eichmann could not be impartially tried by a Jewish court, and that the proceedings must therefore be unfair.
>
> How could this be when every word, every gesture in court is being scrutinized by 500 trained and suspicious men, while the attention of the whole world is focused upon it as through a burning glass?
>
> Indeed, far from being unfair, it is already evident that the Israeli Attorney General is leaning backwards in his determination to ensure that scrupulous justice is observed and the defense given every conceivable latitude.

Thus the long-winded argument had its reward not only in the court's decision, which was in our favor, but also at the bar of world public opinion. I knew that the legalism of my approach was bound to dull for the moment the drama of the proceedings. I could have cut my argument to about half its size, and in any other circumstances would have done so. But in this unique case it was my duty to show, for everyone to see, that we were on firm legal ground in all we did. The buttressing of our case with legal precedents was perhaps unexciting, but was certainly vital.

Moreover, since we were advancing the principles of international law an inch further, it was incumbent on us to prove that the additional layer that was being added to the structure in Jerusalem rested on well-established foundations. It was gratifying to note that the overwhelming majority of legal opinion fully endorsed our views. But this was only made known much later.

CHAPTER

17

The Case for the Prosecution

How does one speak for six million dead?

There was no precedent to guide me, nor could there have been. It was the first time in history that such a crime had been perpetrated, and the first time that a tribunal had been established to try it.

It was also the first time that a Jew would face one of his people's oppressors in court. Throughout the annals of their dispersion, milestoned with tears and blood, the Jews could either flee from a persecutor, beg him for mercy or try to bribe him. Now, as the result of the resurgence of the State of Israel, there would be a trial and the persecutor would face justice.

But what justice could be exacted for a third of a nation, tortured and extinguished?

I kept asking myself what the victims themselves would have wished me to say on their behalf, had they had the power to brief me as their spokesman, now that the roles were reversed and the persecuted had become the prosecutors. I knew that the demand for retribution had resounded in many of the last messages bequeathed by the dead. "Avenge our blood!" was scribbled on scraps of paper hidden in the sewing machines of the Chelmno camp, and scratched with fingernails on the walls of the gas chambers in Majdanek.

There was no way to implement this in the literal sense. The historic "vengeance" was Jewish survival itself, after the tremendous extremes to which the greatest military power on earth had gone to have us destroyed. After much heart-searching I felt that I should interpret the last will and testament of the departed as a demand to set a course for scrupulous fairness. For they had all been put to death though innocent of any crime. That their chief murderer should now receive a meticulously just trial was the only way they could be truly avenged.

This, I thought, would be the real vindication of their memory. I saw no other way.

*

With the preliminary legal points disposed of, I had to present the facts of the extermination, to pinpoint Eichmann's role in it and to prove that he was among the rulers of the system, not the insignificant underling he pretended to have been. This last was necessary to refute the defense that he had acted exclusively under superior orders, which I knew his counsel would present.

The presiding judge read over again the fifteen-point indictment to Eichmann; fifteen times the latter repeated the well-known formula adopted by the accused at Nuremberg: "In the sense of the indictment—not guilty."

"In what sense do you admit to being guilty, Herr Obersturmbannfuehrer?" I said to myself. As Justice Landau continued reading, my eyes wandered to the seven-armed Menorah, or candelabrum, the emblem of Israel, hanging high over the judges' chairs. It was impossible not to be carried away by associations. The Menorah was one of the sacred vessels of the Temple in Jerusalem. It was carried off by Titus nineteen centuries ago and brought to Rome as a trophy by his victorious legions. On the Emperor's arch of triumph it is carved out in stone over the engraved figures of the chained, bound captives of Judea. Now, under the authority of the Menorah, restored to dignity and honor, a central figure in the vilest persecution in Jewish history was standing trial in the reborn Jewish commonwealth, with the strictest observance of the rules of justice, openly for the world to see. Indeed, the wheel had come full circle. It was almost too difficult to believe. "When the Lord brought back those who returned to Zion, we were as in a dream. . . ."

Firm words broke my reverie. "The Attorney General may now proceed," said Justice Landau, turning to me with his usual benevolent expression.

I rose to deliver my opening address.

I had prepared the speech in advance. It had already been in print, translated into four languages, several days before the trial started. Still, I was not quite happy with the way it began; it was important to bring out, in the very first sentences, the whole import of the trial. And so, late in the preceding night, I had jotted down a few lines on a piece of paper. I woke my wife, who was a faithful collaborator, a severe critic and a loyal partner throughout the preparation of the trial and in all the further stages. "Yes, this is right," she said. It was from the same piece of paper that I read the opening sentences in court several hours later. The translators, who had the speech ready in their booths, barely had time to copy the passage, translate it and add it to the prepared text. This is how I began:

"As I stand here before you, Judges of Israel, to lead the prosecution of Adolf Eichmann, I do not stand alone. With me, in this place and at this hour, stand six million accusers. But they cannot rise to their feet and point an accusing finger toward the man who sits in the glass dock and cry: 'I accuse.' For their ashes were piled up in the hills of Auschwitz and in the fields of Treblinka, or washed away by the rivers of Poland; their graves are scattered over the length and breadth of Europe. Their blood cries out, but their voices are not heard. Therefore it falls to me to be their spokesman and to unfold in their name the awesome indictment."

Murder had been with the human race since the days when Cain killed Abel, I said. "But we have had to wait till this twentieth century to witness a new kind of murder: not the result of a momentary surge of passion or a mental black-out, but of a calculated decision and painstaking planning; not through the evil design of an individual, but through a mighty criminal conspiracy involving tens of thousands; not against one victim whom an assassin may have decided to destroy, but against an entire people."

I went on to describe the new kind of killer whom we would encounter in this trial—"the murderer behind the desk"—and proceeded to speak of the rise of anti-Semitism and racism, the role of the SS, the Security Service and the Gestapo in the program of annihilation. I briefly sketched Eichmann's life history and career. Next came a general description of the "Final Solution," which rose to a dreadful climax in the murder of a million and a half Jewish children, "whose blood was spilt like water throughout Europe, when they were separated by force from their mothers who tried to hide them, torn to pieces before their parents' eyes, their little heads smashed against the walls."

The story of the extermination in Poland followed, and the wholesale killings by the *Einsatzgruppen* in the areas governed by the Soviet Union. There, I knew, words could not describe the mass shooting of close to a million and four hundred thousand people before open pits. I cut short the address and read, instead, a lullaby composed at the time in the Wilno ghetto:

> Hush, my baby, hush, be silent!
> Here the graves are seen;
> They were planted by the butchers,
> Still they lie and green.
>
> Hush, my child; don't cry, my treasure;
> Weeping is in vain,
> For the enemy will never
> Understand our pain.
>
> For the ocean has its limits,
> Prisons have their walls around,
> But our suffering and torment
> Have no limit and no bound.

When I had finished reading there was silence for a moment; I simply could not go on. Fortunately it was almost 6 P.M., about time for the adjournment of the session. The presiding judge must have realized my predicament; he asked whether this was a convenient place to stop. I nodded thankfully.

Next day I reviewed the events in Northern, Western and Southern Europe, dwelling in greater detail on the story of Dutch Jewry and then proceeding to describe briefly the repetition of this "theme with variations" in other countries. I followed with Hungary, with Eichmann's feverish attempt to finish off his task, even leaving out some of the well-tried phases of the Final Solution process. Then the death camps were described.

The next chapter was a short review of "the world that has vanished." It was a brief description of our "Atlantis"—of the historic role of European Jewry, which bred so many of the giants of the spirit, and the part that had been played in Jewish life by the ancient communities now wiped out. The tragedy of the relationship between Jewry and Germany called for a few words. Despite centuries of persecution, the German Jews had displayed a special affection and devotion to their country, flocking with patriotic zeal to its colors in World War I and devoting their energies to its reconstruction in the twenties—though all this served merely to fan the wrath of the Nazis.

I devoted a few lines to the East European Jewish townlet, the *"shtetl,"* the home of millions of Jews, which I remember so well from childhood; each with its study center and lodging house, a reservoir of scholarship and love for Israel, where the Jewish spirit was nurtured till the last generation and the tradition of Jewish family life was preserved in the typical small home, a stronghold of piety, tradition and yearning for the coming of the Messiah—which was no more.

The last chapter was a brief review of our charges and the evidence which we intended to introduce. I ended with the words:

"Adolf Eichmann will enjoy a privilege he did not accord to even a single one of his victims. He will be able to defend himself before the court. His fate will be decided according to the law and the evidence, with the burden of proof resting upon the prosecution.

"And the judges of Israel will pronounce true and righteous judgment."

The delivery of the opening address took eight hours and lasted three sessions. Immediately afterward Chief Inspector Less went into the box to introduce Eichmann's voluminous statement, both in transcript and in seventy-six recorded tapes. A few selected passages were played in court. For the first time we heard Eichmann's voice, first proclaiming he was "only a minor transport officer" and then offering to hang himself in public "for expiation."

Eichmann listened intently to his own words. It was somewhat uncanny; there were two Eichmanns present. One was sitting there, tense, rigid and silent in his glass cubicle. The other, unseen, kept talking, prevaricating and explaining away his actions. Just as we were listening to his explanation of the annihilation methods in the Lublin camps, sirens were heard outside, calling for the two-minutes silence in memory of our heroes fallen in the War of Independence, which we always observe on the eve of Independence Day.

The whole statement, six volumes of it, was admitted in evidence, marked T/37.

We now began to adduce the oral evidence, starting with an authoritative presentation by Professor Salo Baron of Columbia University, who painted a comprehensive picture of the Jewish scene in the last generations, reviewing what we had had and what we had lost. Once we had this general outline on record we could proceed by a "searchlight system," concentrating on a few central Jewish communities and then moving the spotlight to other places, where it would stop for a while before progressing further. We used this technique since it was impossible to prove in detail the fate of over fifteen hundred Jewish centers and many thousands of Jewish localities that had been wiped out. Professor Baron's evidence filled in the gaps. He gave the court the general picture in each European state immediately after the catastrophe. We could then ask the court to infer that what had been proved in regard to the fate of one Jewish community had also befallen other Jews in the same country, for they were no longer there after the war and sentence of death had been pronounced upon them all. Professor Baron gave us the somber statistics of six to seven million Jews destroyed by the Nazis.

Then the eyewitnesses ushered in the Jewish people's modern Scroll of Lamentations. First was Zindel Shmuel Grynszpan, Herszel's father. A devout, bearded Jew, with the traditional skullcap on his head, he told in a tremulous voice the story of the first expulsion from Germany and his young son's courageous behavior in Paris. We then called the witnesses whose tales have been described in the previous chapters, starting with prewar events in Germany, Austria and Czechoslovakia.

Dr. Benno Cohen, the last chairman of the Zionist Organization in Berlin, depicted the earliest stages of the persecutions starting in 1933, when the Zionist organ *Die Juedische Rundschau* was still able to write: "Bear with pride the yellow star!" He went on to describe the tightening anti-Jewish measures: the expulsion of the Jews from the professions and from public life and the shower of anti-Semitic laws that soon followed. At that time Eichmann was still merely "keeping an eye" on Jewish life, as a junior Gestapo officer. Next came the story of Eichmann's first independent assignment in Austria and his spectacular success. The events of the *Kristallnacht,* the pregnant forerunner of all the further persecutions, were related. Moritz Fleischmann, the last surviving functionary of the Viennese Jewish community, came all the way from London to tell this story. As he relived in the witness box the shock of the first days of Nazi rule in Vienna, he cut an agonized figure, tortured by a meticulous memory. It still pained him physically to recall the days when the whole population, "fantastically inflamed," hailed the Nazi overlords and lent its support to the debasement and persecution of its Jewish compatriots.

Fleischmann's deeply furrowed face darkened when he recalled Eichmann's announcement to the six leaders of Viennese Jewry whom he had summoned that he would finally clear the whole of Austria of Jews "in the shortest possible way."

"Who said that?" asked District Attorney Baror, who was leading this part of the testimony.

"He, Eichmann," replied the witness.

"Do you remember his face?"

"Yes, though he was younger then and wore no spectacles."

"Younger than when?"

"Younger than today."

"Do you see him today?"

Fleischmann stopped for a moment, had a good look at Eichmann. There was complete silence in the court. Then Fleischmann said: "Yes, he is here opposite me. I do identify him."

Dr. David Meretz pictured the panicky flight of the Czech Jews after Eichmann installed himself in Prague in 1939. It was a Kafkaesque picture. The mental association increased when the name of Dr. Emil Kafka, one of the then leaders of the Prague Jewish community, was mentioned. "We were hopelessly trapped. The Gestapo was pressing for immediate exit and there was no place to go," said Dr. Meretz.

Then the prosecution witnesses plunged us into the war years and the mass persecutions in Poland. The narratives were so overwhelming, so shocking, that we almost stopped observing the witnesses and their individual mannerisms. What impressed itself on the mind was an anonymous cry; it could have been voiced by any one of the millions who had passed through that Gehenna. The survivors who appeared before us were almost closer to the dead than to the living, for each had only the merest chance to thank for his survival.

"We were marched toward the Soviet border," related Zvi Pechter, testifying to the first days of the occupation of Poland. "The Germans were killing people by the hour. . . . A boy of fifteen bent down to pick up a piece of bread, and he was shot on the spot by the commander of the march. . . . They were removing people from the columns and shooting them by the roadside. After three days, only about a hundred wounded and starving people, out of the two thousand who started the march, reached the bridge across the river Bug—the Soviet boundary. . . . They ordered us to march on to the bridge and cross into Russia. The Soviet guards did not let us in."

Then the organized and systematic extermination was pictured. I questioned the witnesses on the fate of individuals who had perished. Only then did the nameless and faceless dead come to life for a moment before our eyes, "vivid as a scream in the night," as one observer put it. After their agonies had been recorded, they returned, as it were, to their mass graves, and once more became only part of the incredible statistics of the holocaust.

Some of the stories of the witnesses sounded like an opium dream, yet they were true. Dr. Leon Wells told the story of the gruesome "Death Brigade 1005." It was organized in the middle of 1943, when the tide of war began to turn against the Nazis and it occurred to them that their crimes might be exposed when the mass graves in Eastern Europe fell into enemy hands. With this in mind they sent out a brigade under SS Colonel Paul Blobel to reopen all the graves, pile up the bodies and burn them. They pulverized the bones in grinding machines, dispersed the ashes and covered up the graves so as not to leave a trace; they even planted saplings on the spot.

Dr. Wells testified that the Nazis had exact records of each grave's location and the number of people in it. On one occasion he took part in a ghastly masquerade. He reached the grave where, thirteen months earlier, the slave-labor group he belonged to at the time had been shot and buried, while he had managed to escape. Caught once more, he now helped to open the grave. But only 181 bodies were found, instead of the 182 the records indicated. "We dug for three days in search of my own body," said Dr. Wells, "before we were ordered to give up and move on." If Dr. Wells had indicated that his was the body they were searching for, he would have certainly been shot on the spot—if only to make the records tally.

There was evidence, both by Hoess and by Wisliceny, that Eichmann had directed Blobel's activities, but in its final judgment the court gave Eichmann the benefit of the doubt on this score.

The story of Jewish Warsaw, its life, its fight for survival, its rebellion and fall, was depicted by the witnesses whose evidence has been summarized in previous chapters. "In July, 1942, the liquidation of the Warsaw ghetto had begun," testified Zivia Lubetkin. "One day the Germans announced by posters that it had been decided to transfer eastward those Jews who were unemployed and had no means of subsistence. All working people were exempt. At first people figured that only a small percentage would be deported, and maybe that those who were starving would really get work in the newly conquered German territories in the east. So everybody assembled in the huge square called the *'Umschlagplatz.'* In fact about 70,000–100,000 people were deported, as it later transpired, to the Treblinka death camp. Everybody was seeking employment to get a 'labor card,' which was a lifesaver. . . . Then one day in September, 1942, all Jews were ordered to assemble immediately in a few narrow streets."

We had another eyewitness description of this operation:

"The Germans are transporting the surviving Jews into 'The Pot,' between Zamenhoff, Stawki, Smocza and Gesia streets. A wooden gate blocks off the whole width of the pavement. Through this gate of life and death, the crowd passed slowly in single file. Each person has to submit to a thorough search. There is a line of young, alert SS men, on guard . . . revolvers hanging from their uniforms. 'Quicker, quicker!' they yell, accompanying their threats with lashes of the whip.

"The crowd marches on in endless line, through the gate of life and death. Pale and confused figures pass by, their eyes red with fear. Men help their wives, mothers clasp their little ones. Daughters carefully guide their old mothers. Families try to keep together and cling closely to each other. Each person holds firmly in his hands the 'work-card.' They hold on to this document desperately, for it is the only guarantee of their right to live, and—even more important—the right of their dear ones to live.

"Today is the great day. The weather is pleasant. The sun is shining brightly. Untersturmfuehrer Handtke wipes the sweat from his fat, red face. Then he wipes his neck and gets ready again for action. He lashes out again with the whip and strikes the terrified victims on their heads and faces and any other part of the body he can reach. An energetic and aggressive officer is showing the confused people which way to go.

"Left—toward Stawki—is the gate of death, leading to the train that will carry them off to Malkinia and Treblinka. This is the place marked out for the women, the old and the crippled.

"A gesture of the hand to the right—that is the way to Leszno, Karmelicka, and Nowolipki streets, the way to life. To the right go those from whose toil and sweat some profit can still be wrung."

By the end of 1942, barely sixty thousand remained of the Warsaw ghetto with its half-million Jews.

The searchlight of evidence moved swiftly to Bendzin, Lódz, Wilno, Bialystok, Kaunas and Riga. The same tale of depravity, torture and psychological warfare was reported from every corner of Nazi-occupied Europe. German skill in lies and chicanery was displayed everywhere. After every manhunt, in which thousands were sent to their deaths, a rumor was spread by the Nazis that the remaining Jews would be spared. Many, exhausted with hunger, misery and suffering, would venture out of their hiding places or return from the forests, only to be captured by their persecutors in the next manhunt.

The witnesses described the satanic character of the program: the deadening of men's senses by systematic terror and starvation; how they were slowly deprived of emotional and intellectual vigor and turned into terrified, lifeless robots.

"We were made to stand stark naked at the roll calls. Thousands were standing, sometimes throughout the night," related Judge Beisky.

"We were put to work for the SS disinfection unit in the ghetto of Riga," recalled Leona Neumann. "We were ten deportees from the Reich and ten Latvian Jews. The clothing of people already killed was sent to us for cleaning, disinfection and repair. It was later sent to German clothing stores. One day one of the local people cried out. He recognized the bloodstained coat of his little daughter who had been shot. . . . There were more such cases." But even such prisoners continued working, their shouts being silenced by the SS man's whip.

"One day all children were told to step aside," recalled Judge Beisky, when testifying on the horrors of the Plaszów "labor" camp. There was a great commotion in the camp. Mothers rushed forward, crying and shouting. They felt that their children were being sent away. Then two things happened at once. Machine guns were mounted and loaded for action. The other thing was the sounding of lullabies over the loudspeakers. . . . Thus the children were carried away to the tunes of lullabies and their mothers, half-paralyzed with fear and half-fooled, stopped in their tracks."

Dr. Aharon Peretz described similar scenes from the ghetto of Kaunas in Lithuania. "The climax of the horrors was 'the children's operation.' . . . It came at a relatively tranquil period. Suddenly automobiles entered the ghetto announcing that anyone appearing outside would be shot. Mothers somehow felt what it was about and started screaming, 'Children!' They rushed their children to the cellars. . . . The search lasted two days. During the first day I was together with seventeen children in the cellar. I gave them injections to make them sleep. Mothers brought their children from other houses and through the window I administered hypnotic injections to their children. . . . There were shattering scenes. The Germans entered all the courtyards in the ghetto and tore away every child they encountered. They tossed them into trucks, inside which music was playing. Mothers would approach the automobiles and plead with the Germans to give the children back. I saw one mother beseech the guards near the hospital. 'How many do you have there?' the German asked. 'Three,' said the mother. 'You may have one back,' said the German and climbed into the car with the mother. All three children looked at her and stretched out their little hands," continued Dr. Peretz. "All of them wanted to go with the mother; she did not know which child to select, looked from one to the other, and finally went away alone."

Dr. Peretz described the early period of occupation, which closely recalled the scenes in Warsaw. "One day they ordered everybody to a certain square. The Jewish Council was told that the Germans intend to select working people whose rations would be increased, and those who did not work would be sent elsewhere to be given better food. After the previous actions, we did not believe it, but it is in the nature of a human being to cling to hope for life. So 27,000 people assembled, not knowing what was in store for them. Then SS man Raucke appeared and began selecting people, sending them left and right. We noticed that he was directing to the left healthier and younger people with fewer children. . . . They were sent back to the ghetto, accompanied by the Jewish police. To the other side he was assigning elderly people, those who looked tired or who had more children. We finally suspected that this was a division of life and death. Thus did the Nazis reduce resistance, since everybody wished to live. . . . Hope still lingered that the others might live too, after all. Finally, about ten thousand people, those who were sent to the right, were all convoyed to an execution site."

The same story, with slight variations, was repeated from everywhere.

Then we followed the Germans farther into Soviet territory and heard of the unspeakable horrors of the *Einsatzgruppen*. Rivka Yoselewska and Avraham Aviel, whose testimony has been described earlier, submerged us even deeper into the tragedy, and made us feel that we must now be near the bottom of the inferno.

It was often excruciating merely to listen to one of these tales. Sometimes we felt as if our reactions were paralyzed, and we were benumbed. It was a story with an unending climax. Often I heard loud sobbing behind me in the courtroom. Sometimes there was a commotion, when the ushers removed a listener who had fainted. Newspaper reporters would rush out after an hour or two, explaining that they could not take it in without a pause.

The documents to be introduced were submitted together with the oral evidence to which they referred, so that one supplemented the other. Some sessions were devoted almost exclusively to documents, briefly analyzed as they were produced. Before I had completed the evidence on the events in Poland, we had entered over 370 prosecution exhibits, but the number was soon to increase fourfold. The documents were all-important, for it was through them that we were able to link Eichmann legally with the unrolling atrocities.

The court accepted almost all the instruments we offered in evidence, for we submitted only those that were relevant to the issue. We introduced not only the directly incriminating documents, but also others, which revealed the background and supported Eichmann's claim that many other agencies in the Reich were heavily implicated in the crimes.

In Israel, as in many other countries, it is part of the prosecution's duty to put the whole case before the court. Dr. Servatius, however, seemed to be surprised time and again when we produced such a document, and would say, in answer to the court's usual inquiry as to objections: "I have no objection whatsoever; this will be of assistance to the accused."

The prosecution team was thankful for the "documentation sessions," when all we had to deal with was instruments, steeped though they were in horror and suffering. It was still much easier to deal with them than to relive with the witnesses their incredible experiences as recounted on the stand. Moreover, I had to deal with most of the witnesses at least three times: once when reading their recorded statements, then when interviewing them before they were called to the stand, and lastly when leading them in open court. Many people were interviewed who were eventually not called to testify. On the whole, the preparation and handling of the witnesses was a difficult experience.

The strain finally began to tell on almost everyone connected with the case; people grew jumpy and exhausted.

With the weight of responsibility for the trial and with its nightmarish reality, it seemed that sooner or later we were bound to crack. As I was told afterward, there was some betting among foreign correspondents as to how long I would be able to stand it; the odds were heavily against me.

There were, in truth, evenings when I wondered whether I would be able to continue in the morning. My wife turned home into a relaxing refuge. She would always come with me to the courtroom, sitting right behind me; having her there was a constant encouragement.

Many people wrote that they were praying for my health and wishing me strength.

There was one incident that provided a slight relief from the tension. One day, as a result of a breakdown of the power supply in the area, the courtroom was suddenly plunged into darkness, with the exception of a tiny permanent light focused on Eichmann's dock, which was fueled by a storage battery provided for exactly such an emergency. It looked like an accusing finger directed at him. The session was adjourned when it turned out that a truck had hit a central current transmission post and that repairs would take some time. Dr. Servatius remarked, with dry humor, that this truck driver had provided the first break he had had for days.

Eichmann displayed no sign of being affected. He appeared daily in his glass cubicle with a load of books and an assortment of colored pencils that he would tidily arrange in front of him. He followed the evidence intently, feverishly writing notes, some of which he would from time to time ask the accompanying guard officer to deliver to Dr. Servatius. His eyes would watch the witnesses, observe the judges for their impressions, and look as far as the defense and prosecution tables. He almost never looked into the courtroom.

The attitude of the court was strict. It soon became obvious that in pursuance of their duty of overcoming their emotions, as they had announced in their first ruling, the judges were leaning backward in their determination to allow only the most closely relevant evidence to the prosecution. My argument was that once we had proved Eichmann's complicity in the crimes the behavior of his victims was obviously relevant. Even in an ordinary assault case, if you prove that a man pushed someone over a precipice, it is relevant to the charge to inform the court whether and how the victim resisted his assailant, or to show that he just rolled down the slope and broke his ribs. But the court generally considered the evidence on Jewish resistance to be extraneous to the charge, and we were soon engaged in heated arguments over different portions of this testimony. After part of it was heard, the presiding judge remarked, following the evidence of Abba Kovner on the Wilno ghetto and on the underground movement there, that "the testimony digressed quite far from the object of the trial," and that we should have asked the witness to abstain from speaking on "external elements which do not pertain to the trial." I replied that these matters were certainly relevant, as would become even clearer when I delivered my final address to the court on the legal problems of complicity in crime. The presiding judge replied that it was not the first time such evidence had been introduced, that the court had its own view about the trial according to the indictment, and that the prosecution should restrict itself to the court's rulings.

"You have got a hostile tribunal," one of the foreign correspondents jested as he passed me during the lunch recess that followed.

I did not go for lunch, however, that day, and asked Dr. Robinson to stay with me to talk matters over; the situation that had developed was serious. I believed that the court was adopting an all too severe line toward us. The truth on the revolts was important for its own sake, and also as an educational by-product of the trial for our own youth, who were constantly asking why there were no more revolts than they had heard of. Here was a chance to bring out the countless acts of heroism with which people were generally less acquainted. Of course, the enlightening aspect would not in itself validate the introduction of evidence that was inadmissible under the general rules. But my view was that those who fell in revolt against inhuman acts were, for the purposes of the trial, among the victims of the Final Solution. Eichmann was therefore answerable for them too, and we were entitled to unfold the full story of the resistance, which would reveal that there were uncoordinated underground nests in almost all the ghettos, though little was known of them. It would also show that any widespread and unified resistance movement was physically impossible in the isolated ghettos, contact between which was strictly forbidden.

On these issues we had already adduced evidence in the trial on larger resistance centers like Warsaw, Bialystok, Cracow, Wilno and Kaunas. I now wanted to bring out further and less-known incidents of active and widely scattered resistance to the *Einsatzgruppen* (see Chapter 11).

It was obvious, however, that any further attempt on our part to call this evidence would require a ruling from the court, with the strong probability of an adverse decision on its admissibility. In an ordinary case there is usually nothing disastrous in such a ruling, but here it might have widespread repercussions. It might even be falsely interpreted as indicating that the court doubted the full authenticity of the evidence on this point. Should

I place the court in such an invidious dilemma, even if I differed from its view on the legal issue involved? Usually I am all for arguing out an issue, but this seemed to be a time for discretion. So our further evidence on the resistance of the *Einsatzgruppen* victims had to be cut down.

*

The spotlight of evidence then moved to the witnesses on France, Denmark, Holland, Norway and other places. It was the turn of Professor Wellers, Werner Melchior, Dr. Josef Melkman, Hildegard Henschel and Hulda Campigniano to describe how the Nazi scourge swept occupied Europe, uprooting and leveling Jewish centers.

Here the more intricate and "refined" German methods were encountered, since they were dealing with countries for whose non-Jewish populations they had more respect than for the "semibarbarians" of Eastern Europe. The Jews deluded themselves that they would be spared, owing to their non-Jewish local connections. Gabi Bach led this evidence in court and submitted the voluminous documentation about these countries that had been found in the captured German archives. Entire sessions were now devoted to the documents.

Before the trial had begun, while settling the order of our evidence, I prepared alternative lists of key witnesses and other important supplementary, though less vital, proof, which would be omitted if the indispensable witnesses took up too much time. When the trial had been on its way for a month, about half the names on the first list had already been ticked off. So were many names on the other list. Within this first month we had already submitted eight hundred prosecution documents and called fifty prosecution witnesses.

Among these were Justice Musmanno and Dean Grueber. Their evidence added a great deal to the picture. It was as if the long-slumbering human conscience were speaking at last, expressing its grief and shame at what had happened. Moreover, each of these two witnesses undermined a large part of the expected defense. Dean Grueber proved Eichmann to have been a powerful figure who took independent decisions. The Dean was speaking of the occasions when he was admitted to Eichmann's office to plead for Jews. "I never had the impression that he had to consult his superiors on these matters. . . . The impression he imparted was that . . . it was he who took the decisions. . . . He always spoke in the first person, using the word 'I.' 'I order, I instruct, I cannot . . .' I do not remember that he ever said he would have to contact higher authority."

Dr. Servatius, who did very little cross-examination on the witnesses of the holocaust, rose to undermine the devastating effect of this evidence.

He adopted an interesting method: he read to the Dean excerpts from the Protestant German press, including the church organs that had hailed Hitler's rise to power, justified the anti-Jewish boycott and asserted that "nobody will be sorry if Jewish influence in German public life is reduced." Then came the question: "Don't you think that Eichmann could have gathered from such articles that he was doing the right thing, praised even by the church?"

The reply was clear. "There were many circles in the Protestant church that erred. . . . This church was always too respectful toward authority. We were subjects, rather than citizens. . . . Although there is still a long way to go from what was said in these papers and the things that were done later, I wish to say that I dissociate myself from them. I did so at the time too."

"But do you know that there was public support for Hitler on the part of learned people and university professors?" asked Dr. Servatius.

"Yes," Dean Grueber replied. "I know it well, that many who were adorned with academic titles fell in and accepted these things."

The defense had established its point, which in fact was not in dispute, that National Socialism had been widely acclaimed in Germany by all circles, including the overwhelming majority of the church.

The defense fared worse with Justice Musmanno. In Nuremberg he had heard everybody, including Goering, mentioning Eichmann as one of the few responsible for all that had happened to the Jews.

"Did not the Reichsmarschall try to whitewash himself and palm off his own responsibility onto a minor official?"

"He did not refer to Eichmann as a small official," replied Justice Musmanno. "On the contrary, he made it very clear that Eichmann was all-powerful on the question of the extermination of the Jews. He went into that at great length: that Eichmann had practically unlimited power to declare who was to be killed."

"Did he tell you that he had himself ordered Himmler and Heydrich on July 31, 1941, to bring about the final solution of the Jewish problem in Europe in the German sphere of influence?"

"I don't remember if he told me that, but of course it is true. But the instrumentality through which this program was to be carried out was Adolf Eichmann. He was the man to determine in what order, in what countries, the Jews were to die." Nor did Justice Musmanno yield on any other point. He told the court the story of General Karl Koller, on which the court later based on express finding. Koller, the last commander of the Luftwaffe, went to see Eichmann about the Jews among the Allied fliers who bailed out over Germany, all of whom Hitler had ordered to be executed in one of his last futile outbursts of rage.

Dr. Servatius cross-examined. "Was Koller a friend of the Jews?" "I don't know Koller's feelings," replied Justice Musmanno. "He made it very clear that he then looked upon the shooting of the Allied pilots, men in uniform, as sheer murder." Even Kaltenbrunner was prepared to give way, but Eichmann would not listen.

We called several witnesses to the events in Theresienstadt, in view of Eichmann's special authority there. A brief review followed of the main events in the Balkans and Slovakia. We usually released in advance information on the subject matter of the evidence to be introduced that day, and people who had come from the area concerned would flock into the courtroom, or to an adjoining hall where they could watch the proceedings on closed-circuit television and to listen to the story of "their" country. So we had a "Yugoslav day," a "Greek day," a "Czech day" and so forth. One could hear the language of the day's country spoken in the little buffet beneath the courtroom. "The events in the country from which I came were really no different from elsewhere," a visitor to the court told me. "But I know the people who were mentioned in evidence, I remember the streets that have been named. It is more real and more vivid to me than the events mentioned in the other parts of the evidence."

While the witnesses told their hair-raising stories, we never lost track of Eichmann himself. The documents, which were submitted by the hundreds, were signed by him, referred to him or in some way dealt with his share in the ghastly events.

There were several definite issues concerning him that we were particularly anxious to clear up. Was it true, for instance, that Eichmann was so strait-jacketed by his orders that he could not get out of his assignment? According to his pretrial statement, which he later repeated in court, he had applied several times for a transfer to another post, as he did not feel fit for his job after the annihilation had started. In his personal record at the SD headquarters, however, there was no trace of any written request. He claimed he had only applied orally.

We submitted Justice Musmanno's evidence to show that there was a way to get out of such blood-stained assignments. SS General Walter Schellenberg, who drafted the agreement between the Wehrmacht and the *Einsatzgruppen,* informed the American judge that "if a man could not get along with this type of order he would be sent back home." Justice Musmanno's tribunal, in fact, acquitted one of the accused, SS Master Sergeant Mathias Graf, who refused to accept the task of leading a squad of the *Einsatzgruppen.* Anyone reluctant to go ahead with the murders was free to volunteer for service at the front, according to affidavits from experts submitted in the *Einsatzgruppen* case. Dr. Servatius vigorously cross-examined Justice Musmanno, but all he elicited was the reply: "I sat seven months presiding over the trial of the *Einsatzgruppen,* and we took up case after case. I told you about Erwin Schulz, who refused to go along with his superior orders and asked that he might be released. And he was released by no one less than Heydrich. And not only was he released from carrying on these onerous, bloodthirsty deeds as a colonel, but later on he was even promoted to general. The same thing was true with Franz Six—a document was introduced along that line. The same was true with regard to Nosske."

We further proved that in October, 1943, Himmler spoke in Posen to high-ranking SS officers. We produced the text of the four-hour speech, in which he reiterated his idea that Germany's ruling destiny was the justification for treating other nations as slaves who would live as long as they served the Reich. He derided the "decadent" Allies, and extolled at length the heroism of the SS in destroying the Jews.

> This is an unwritten and never-to-be-written page of glory of our history, since we know how difficult it is to kill. . . . Once you have an order you have to carry it out. . . . If anyone thinks he cannot do it, he should say "I can't stand for it" and ask to be released. In most cases the order would be: "You have to do it anyway." Or one might reach the conclusion that: "The fellow is weak, his nerves are finished; well, he could be pensioned off."

This, Eichmann said in his testimony, applied perhaps to the highest officers, while the *Einsatzgruppen* dispensation might have been valid for the squads in the field. It never applied to him.

With Sassen he was more frank. Replying to the Dutch journalist's question whether he had ever attempted to disengage himself from his duties, Eichmann simply said: "No, never."

Nor did he favor the transfer of his subordinates to other posts. One of his men, Wisliceny, wrote: "Eichmann's guiding idea on staff policy was never to release anybody who had ever worked with him. . . . He would keep his men on his staff and would not release them though there might have been no immediate occupation for them."

Eichmann repeatedly told Mueller, the Gestapo chief, that the Gestapo was not acting with sufficient vigor against saboteurs and opponents at home. "We can only cleanse our stables if we put half a million Germans against the wall," he declared. Even the tough Gestapo chief was appalled, murmuring: "Yes, of course, Comrade Eichmann."

When I examined Eichmann on this point during the trial, he commented that he had recommended the execution of "only" 100,000 Germans.

We offered in evidence an affidavit by Dr. Hans Guenther Seraphim, of the University of Goettingen, who made a research study for the German courts on the possibility of obtaining a discharge from "emotionally onerous duties in the SS and getting a posting to the army." Dr. Seraphim's research fully supported our contentions. Later, we were strongly sustained on this issue from a quite unexpected quarter: some of the defense witnesses themselves.

Another problem that had to be cleared up was why Eichmann did not attain a higher rank. He told Sassen and his police interrogator in Israel that the rank of a departmental head was lieutenant colonel. "Had Mueller promoted me, that would have caused a palace revolution," he said. As long as "Jewish affairs" did not warrant more than a department at the Gestapo, he could not move higher up.

In December, 1944, when there was nothing much more to be done on "Jewish Affairs," he was promoted to a division chief with the rank of colonel, effective April, 1945. Everyone congratulated him. But by the time he was to collect his new insignia no one cared about high ranks any more. "The job was rotten and did not carry promotion," he told Sassen.

This, too, was later supported, though in a different way, by one of the defense witnesses.

We proved that in the extermination camps he enjoyed powers far transcending his official standing. Although Auschwitz came under the jurisdiction of the SS Economic Office, Eichmann had full authority over Jews sent there.

He brought to Hoess Himmler's instructions on the way Auschwitz was to be operated. On an official inspection in the summer of 1942 Himmler advised Hoess that "Eichmann's program will continue to be carried out and will be intensified month by month." When the process of destruction had got under way, "Eichmann arrived with a further order stating that gold teeth had to be removed from the corpses and hair cut from women." It is interesting that in his talks with Sassen, Eichmann recoiled from admitting the defilement of corpses. "I hear for the first time that gold teeth were removed. I would exclude the possibility that it ever happened," he said. In the pretrial interrogation he freely admitted that he actually saw it done.

It was of importance to note that at the trial of the heads of the Economic Office SS Lieutenant General Oswald Pohl and his subordinates were cleared of the charge of giving the order for killing, for this came from the RSHA, the judgment said.

Hoess's evidence strongly implicated Eichmann; we were anxious to have it corroborated. Professor Gustave M. Gilbert, of Long Island University, provided this corroboration. He gave evidence of his experiences as the prison psychologist at the Nuremberg Trials. He spoke to all the accused there, observing their reactions and keeping a record, which he later published. He made a special study of Rudolf Hoess, then detained at Nuremberg as a material witness, who knew that he was about to be extradited to Poland to stand trial there. Professor Gilbert described Hoess as completely apathetic. "He was resigned to his death; he had no interest whatsoever in falsifying any testimony. What he had already told me in his cell in Nuremberg, in our conversations, he repeated on the witness stand. It was all an automatic culmination of a career that was marked by death and must end in death, and he had no particular feelings about this—he just automatically wrote what he knew when asked."

Professor Gilbert supplied us with an interesting and entirely new piece of evidence. After Hoess had testified in Nuremberg on the destruction of two and a half million men, women and children, Goering dismissed it all as mere propaganda talk, because it was "technically impossible" to kill so many people within the time Hoess specified. The other top Nazis seemed to have been impressed with Goering's argument, and so Professor Gilbert gave Hoess a sheet of paper on which he wrote in German: "Goering wants to know how it was technically possible at all to destroy two and a half million people within three and a half years." Hoess gave his handwritten reply on the same page of prison stationery, setting out the main technical details of the extermination machinery, and making his calculation, which tallied with the figure he had mentioned. This single page is the "Final Solution" in a nutshell, and on it Eichmann's name appears in full prominence three times: once as the delivering authority, which sent the Jews to the camps; second, as the commanding authority, which issued instructions on the fate of the deportees; third, as the registering authority, which alone kept all statistical records of the annihilation. The original of this historic document, in Hoess's own handwriting, had been kept all these years by Professor Gilbert; it was now revealed for the first time and entered as a court exhibit.

I wanted to make sure that Hoess was not shifting his own blame onto Eichmann and asked Gilbert: "I take it that, as a psychologist, you certainly understand that sometimes there is a state of mind of the accused which tends to drag down other people, as it were, and incriminate them."

"Yes. It's one of the common guilt defenses."

"Would you say that Rudolf Hoess was in that particular state of mind when you were speaking to him?"

"No, definitely not. As I said before, he was a man who was just automatically telling the facts as he knew them. It apparently meant nothing to him that he had murdered millions of people; he had no hesitation in describing everything in detail; and without any attempt to share blame, or to attempt defense or anything, quite spontaneously—certainly not with any urging on my part. The name of Eichmann came into his statements again and again and again, and finally I realized that this man was a key figure in the extermination program."

A ghastly illustration of Eichmann's authority in the camps was the story of the supply of skeletons and skulls to the Strasbourg University "Institute of Ancestral Heredity" for research into "the activity and achievements of the Indo-Germanic race." The director of the Institute, Wolfram Sievers, informed Himmler's office that their anatomy specialist, Professor Hirth, required Jewish skeletons for this work. With Himmler's approval, Sievers applied to Gluecks, the Concentration Camps Inspector, to get "the goods" from the camps, but was referred by the latter to Eichmann. Eichmann asked for a direct request from Himmler's headquarters on the subject, which was duly procured. The still living people who were to provide the skeletons were then picked out at Auschwitz by an anthropologist, and Eichmann's department sent out 115 men and women—79 male Jews, 30 female Jews, 2 Poles and 4 of unidentified nationality—to be turned into skeletons at the

Natzweiler concentration camp for the use of Strasbourg University. The killing was done personally by none other than SS Captain Josef Kramer, the Commander of the notorious Bergen-Belsen camp. Professor Hirth supplied Kramer with poison gas and exact instructions on how to proceed. The bodies, which were then turned over to the scientists, were partly dismembered and partly preserved in alcohol. When the French took Strasbourg, they found these bodies and the dismembered parts, which they photographed and marked as "apparently Jewish." We produced in court the twenty-one macabre photographs they took.

*

After fifty sessions, we reached the chapter on Hungarian Jewry, which never believed that the disaster would sweep it away too. It all happened suddenly and proceeded with maddening speed; in the course of May and June, 1944, Eichmann managed to ship almost half a million Jews to Auschwitz. Fourteen witnesses unfolded the story of the last "island" of secure Jewry in Nazi-occupied Europe.

The shadow of another trial now fell over our courtroom, a trial held a few years before in Jerusalem, when the confidence of Hungarian Jewry and the tragedy of its leaders were partly exposed. It was a libel case against a man who had imputed collaboration and treason to Dr. Israel (Rezsö) Kastner, one of the leaders of Budapest Jewry. In the District Court Kastner was stigmatized for abominable conduct, but just before the delivery of the Appeal Court's judgment, which cleared his name and restored his honor, he was shot by a young fanatic.

The Hungarian community of Israel has remained divided on the Kastner issue. Some consider him a brave and heroic figure; others can neither forget nor forgive his contacts with Eichmann in Budapest and his failure to alert them in time in the provinces. "We boarded the train to Auschwitz never knowing what was in store for us" is their bitter complaint. "But Kastner and his friends knew. Why did they not alert us? Why did they soothe us?" This kept being repeated, even though the Supreme Court had found as a fact that after a certain date there was no physical possibility of passing on the information to the provinces.

One of the most level-headed men I know in our country who occupied a leading position in a responsible service, was among those who boarded the Auschwitz-bound train in the summer of 1944. I asked him why he did not escape or hide. He said: "Had I known what Auschwitz was, no power on earth could have made me get on that train. But there was no power on earth that could then have made me believe in the existence of an Auschwitz. Even when I was already inside the camp and a Polish Jew approached us, on arrival, pointing to the high chimneys and saying we would all go up there shortly, I was sure the man was demented." He added: "No one would have believed the warnings anyway, even had Kastner issued them."

There are many others, however, who never acquiesced in the Supreme Court's considered verdict exonerating Kastner and continue to blame the leaders of martyred Hungarian Jewry. I knew they were fairly active in an attempt to use our trial as a platform for reopening the whole issue. I had appealed to everyone to abstain from internal reckonings, since this was the trial of the exterminator and not of his victims. The issue was so heavily laden with emotions, however, that I could not be sure.

We had, therefore, to proceed very cautiously along this path. The Hungarian case was painstakingly prepared and every prospective witness was considered from all possible angles. My assistant, Gabi Bach, did most of the spadework; I told him that we would not call any witness who might use the platform for a pro-Kastner or anti-Kastner demonstration. Two witnesses were disqualified by this criterion. One came to me saying that he would now show the whole world that Kastner was one of the greatest Jews who ever lived; it was for that purpose, he said, that he had come from Europe to testify. He would also clear SS Colonel Kurt Becher of any charge. Although we might have otherwise called this man as a witness to supplement some aspects of the Budapest story, I refused to have him testify.

The man thereupon called a press conference to unburden himself of his outraged feelings against me.

Another witness we might otherwise have called was given up for the opposite reason. We knew that the man would not be able to overcome a vitriolic hostility toward some members of the Jewish Council, particularly Kastner, and that he would in all likelihood give vent to his feelings while testifying.

Bach discharged the delicate duty of leading the greater part of the evidence on Hungary with his usual tact; he managed to steer clear of highly explosive possibilities.

There were moments of great tension. During the evidence of Pinchas Freudiger, one of the leaders of the Orthodox community in Budapest, a spectator in the courtroom shouted at him in Hungarian: "You soothed us so that we should not run away while you were saving your families." An expression of sharp pain appeared on Freudiger's sober features. His little red beard quivered for a moment, but he did not reply. The presiding judge ordered the man to be removed from the courtroom and announced a recess.

The tragedy of the trapped Jewish leaders in occupied Europe emerged again in all its nakedness. What should Freudiger have done? How could he know that all was lost, and that the traditional means of keeping Jewry alive under persecution would not work this time? Is it not an understandable human weakness to care for one's own family? Who can say that he should have had the foresight to abandon all hope and alert the Jews with the cry: *"Sauve qui peut!"* Would it have helped?

It is inhuman and foolish from the comfort of an armchair to dispense ready-made prescriptions based on hindsight to these people on what they might have done.

Bach asked Freudiger whether he recognized Eichmann, whom he had encountered in Budapest. "In my memory," Freudiger said quietly, "there lives a uniformed Eichmann, wearing high jackboots, standing with his legs astride, his hand resting on his pistol, shouting at me from the heights of his master race. But this is he, here, opposite me."

Dr. Alexander Brody had come all the way from Brazil for the seventy-five minutes he spent in the witness box in Jerusalem. He saw the Kistarcsa deportation, for he was in the camp as an employee of the Jewish Council of Budapest to take care of the food supply. Eichmann's arrogance and zeal claimed fifteen hundred victims just to prove to the Regent of Hungary that his "stop-order" would not work. Brody witnessed both deportations and in a sad, nervous voice he told the story.

One of the prisoners on the Kistarcsa train was a man called Jacob Reich, who had been detained while visiting a friend in Budapest. From prison he smuggled out a letter to his wife, Margot, telling her not to worry about him. "I will see it through somehow," he wrote. "If you pass here opposite the building at 3 P.M. I shall be able to see you and you will see me." Then she learned that he had been moved to Kistarcsa, and several days later she received a postcard from her husband. Next to her name as addressee there was an addendum in her husband's handwriting: "Blessed be the hand that mails this card!" and beneath, in different handwriting: "Found soaked at the Karacsond railway station, and is being mailed." The postcard read: "Today is Wednesday afternoon. We have been packed and we are going. God bless you, my dear family. Father." Soon a letter arrived written on toilet paper, again with a blessing for the mailer. "We are going to Germany," wrote Jacob Reich. "Perhaps a second miracle will happen, like last Saturday's, and we will be turned back. I could not take anything with me. I shall suffer my fate somehow, and I do not want to make you sad, but I do wish to be with you. My dear children, look after Mother well. . . . From the goods train, with love, Father."

Margot Reich, a fragile, pallid, gray-haired woman, produced both letters and the postcard in court. She never heard from her husband again. All she knows is that he was last seen in Auschwitz.

Eichmann's Hungarian period, his last "great" chapter, was as packed with violence as the winter gales that strike when spring is near. It also produced a report of the writing-desk killer's personal participation in the murder of an individual Jew. We did not make it the subject of a specific charge—it would not do to single out this one Jewish boy from the six million victims—

but the incident was certainly indicative of Eichmann's attitude and so we introduced evidence on it.

Our witness, Abraham Gordon, was a boy of sixteen in April, 1944, when with hundreds of Jewish boys in Budapest he was ordered to report at the beautiful villa and hotel quarter of Schwabenberg, then occupied by the Gestapo and the headquarters of the Germany Military Mission. After a month of constructing army depots, Gordon was sent as one of a detachment of fifteen boys, to Roses Hill. At the entrance to a villa requisitioned from a Jewish industrialist by the name of Aschner, they were received by a stocky German in civilian clothes, who told them: "My name is Slavik, you had better beware of me." While the boys were being assigned to the work of digging trenches for air-raid defenses in the cherry orchard of the villa, their Jewish foreman whispered to them that this was the residence of the Gestapo leader Adolf Eichmann.

"I saw him several times there," said Gordon. "On one occasion he was sipping drinks on the terrace. . . . Another time he went down to the plantation during an air raid. . . . A few weeks later, while we were working, his driver, a soldier by the name of Teitel, taxed one of the working boys with stealing cherries. The boy was about sixteen, perhaps seventeen. His name was Solomon. Teitel came up to him and shouted: 'You stole cherries.' I can still see the scene vividly. Suddenly Slavik appeared in shorts, the upper part of his body naked, for it was a hot day. Eichmann came in sight on the veranda and beckoned to Slavik. They had a brief exchange of words. Slavik came back and then the boy was dragged away by him and Teitel. I can still hear his shouts: 'I didn't do it, I didn't do it!' They pushed the boy into the toolshed of the house. Slavik reappeared, circled the house and returned with Eichmann. They both entered the toolshed. Eichmann wore his uniform trousers and a shirt. It was a warm day. . . . Then we heard Solomon's screams, which lasted about fifteen minutes. Then there was a thud and silence. Eichmann came in sight out of the shed. He was somewhat disheveled; his shirt was sticking out. I saw stains. I thought they were bloodstains. . . . I am almost sure they were. . . . When he passed us, he muttered two words in German. I remember them. I shall never forget these words. He said: '*Uebriges Mistvolk*' [superfluous dung people]."

(This was a favorite expression of Eichmann's. Dr. Kastner reported him saying on the deportation of Jews: "I have to clear the provinces of the dung-Jews.")

Gordon continued slowly, with a marked effort to avoid any emotional outburst. "Immediately afterward Slavik came out of the shed and called for Teitel, who had left the shed earlier," he said. "They both entered the shed and dragged out the boy's lifeless body. They were holding him by his feet and tugging him. The boy showed no signs of life. His face was all bleeding and swollen; he was really torn to pieces, his limbs were as if torn apart.

They placed him near the back entrance. Teitel went away and brought the car. It was a military vehicle. We saw this car every day. It was an amphibious vehicle. They shoveled the boy's body into the back seat. Teitel returned about half an hour later. We were working in silence. Teitel approached us and said in Hungarian: 'I threw the stinking corpse into the Danube and your fate will be the same, so behave!' Teitel was a Schwabian, an ethnic German who lived in Hungary, and spoke the language. I never saw Solomon again," concluded Gordon.

Dr. Servatius elicited in cross-examination that Gordon had told the whole story to his elder brother the same day, "perhaps after an hour or so." But in Gordon's earlier statement it was recorded that this took place a year later. (The discrepancy was probably due to a spelling error: "*shana*" is a year in Hebrew while "*shaa*" is an hour.)

The defense immediately requested that Slavik be examined in the prison in Vienna, where he was then detained on the same charge. Slavik remembered having been Eichmann's major-domo. "Yes," he said, "we occupied the Aschners' villa in Budapest. It is true they had a Hungarian-born German chauffeur by the name of Teitel, who drove their car. It was an amphibious car."

"What happened to Teitel?"

"In June or July, 1944, Teitel murdered a Hungarian old lady. I heard that he was brought before an SS court and executed for that," said Slavik.

In its judgment the court, though expressing its "positive appreciation" of Gordon's evidence, refrained from arriving at a finding on the cherry orchard murder in the absence of corroboration as to the details.

*

Joel Brand, "the emissary for the dead," then gave evidence on the fantastic "blood for goods" deal. As he stood in the witness box imitating Eichmann's barking yell—"A million Jews for ten thousand trucks is cheap!" —I realized that the man was no more than a receptacle for memories. He had no present; his life had stopped long ago, probably in the Cairo prison, where he was kept by the British for months banging his head against the walls, shouting that he had to get back, for every day ten thousand Hungarian Jews were being sent to their deaths. It was there that Brand's soul had really died, though his body kept moving for twenty more years. All he could do was to keep telling the story of the mission that had fallen through. Even the Eichmann trial could not bring peace to his tormented mind; he succumbed three years later, soon after giving evidence in Germany against Krumey and Hunsche.

Following Brand's evidence, I submitted a series of documents from Dr. Weizmann's archives, then revealed for the first time. The tragedy of the Jewish people at that period, lacking all the instruments of power, without even a government in exile, frantically searching for ways to save the lives of its own flesh and blood, was vividly highlighted.

"The catastrophe is right on them," pleaded Weizmann with Anthony Eden. "We are consulting with Russia and America," replied the British Foreign Office. Weizmann pleaded: "Four crematoria are active daily in Auschwitz; send Brand back. Bomb the camps and the railway lines leading to them!" The Foreign Office replied that they would submit everything to the Cabinet and explore the possibilities with Stalin.

In fact, nothing was done. On October 30, 1944, when the tragedy was almost complete, the Prime Minister's private secretary, John Martin, wrote to Weizmann after a visit to Moscow: "We can assure you that both His Majesty's Government and the Soviet Government have in mind the danger of new persecution in Hungary and are doing what they can to avert it."

It was all empty talk. The greater part of Hungarian Jewry had by then perished in Auschwitz; others had been started on the dreadful march to the Austrian border.

"The whole world is now on trial" was the gist of reports that appeared in the press in various capitals.

At this stage I introduced the documents proving that the Arab leaders, the ex-Mufti of Jerusalem, Haj Amin al Husseini, the Iraqi rebel leader, Rashid Ali Gailani and others, had put pressure on the Nazis to dissuade them from allowing any possible departure of Jewish children to Palestine. The ex-Mufti found out that 270 of them had been smuggled out of Hungary and Rumania, in three rescue groups. "I should inform your Excellency," the ex-Mufti wrote Ribbentrop, "that the Arabs, the loyal friends of the Axis powers, feel hurt and offended when they observe this." He asked Germany "to torpedo all such further efforts." "The correct solution to their problem is that they be sent somewhere else, for instance to Poland," the spiritual leader suggested. "The Arab nation will appreciate this activity and will return friendship."

The ex-Mufti's ties with Eichmann were of long standing. At the beginning of 1942 Eichmann received him and his retinue at the department's headquarters and lectured to them on the Final Solution in Europe. The ex-Mufti was so strongly impressed that he immediately requested Himmler to designate someone on Eichmann's team to be his "personal adviser" on "finally solving" the Jewish problem also in Palestine, once the ex-Mufti was reinstated in his office by the victorious Axis. Eichmann welcomed the offer. "A priceless jewel . . . The biggest friend of the Arabs," recorded the ex-Mufti on Eichmann in his personal diary.

The personal ties between the two continued through the Mufti's nephew, who was later a caller on Eichmann at his office.

The ex-Mufti is no longer in power or in office, but he still enjoys a respected position in the Arab countries, which even in the face of the Jerusalem trial could not forbear displaying their implacable enmity.

The Arab press sent Eichmann such messages of encouragement as this in the Jerusalem *Times* (Jordan) of April 24, 1961:

"Find consolation in the fact that this trial will one day lead to the liquidation of the remaining six million."

On the other hand, *The Recorder* of Aden, May 14, 1961, claimed that all the figures of the holocaust were forged and the extermination story was all a lie.

After the Mufti episode the trial proceeded to the subject of the death camps, which took up four days, eight sessions. Since these were the places where the millions were actually exterminated, I found it imperative to bring out the story in some detail. Here, too, each witness was asked to describe only a small fraction of the reality in each of the five camps on which evidence was introduced. But the reality was not real any more. It seemed that the courtroom itself was now engulfed in the poisonous vapors of the crematoria. At times I could almost smell the lethal gases and the stench of burnt flesh. As the witnesses tonelessly gave their testimony, we relived the nightmare with them.

We moved as if in a trance; I doubt whether we were fully cognizant of all that was going on around us in those few days. When we stepped out of the court building, it seemed strange that the sun was shining, the air was pure, and people were going about their usual business. Inside was the image of a man-made hell.

Two witnesses testified *in camera* on the sterilization operations performed on their bodies in Auschwitz. These were "the practical experiments" with which Eichmann was kept "in close touch" as part of the over-all sterilization schemes discussed at the post-Wannsee conferences.

At one point I myself became in a sense a witness at the trial. There was one camp in Poland, Bełżec, that had no survivors, at least none we could locate. However, we knew that 600,000 Jews had been put to death there, and we had on hand a report by Dr. Kurt Gerstein, which gave a vivid description of the camp.

This Gerstein report had a certain history. Both his report and interrogation had been offered at Nuremberg by the prosecution, but owing to lack of proper authentication they had not been received in evidence. Though we were of course eager to submit the Gerstein statements, we could do so only after obtaining verification and authentication.

By clever and persistent research the officer in charge of the pretrial examination, Commander Abraham Selinger of the Israel Police, unearthed two ex-officers, one in Paris and one in Chadds Ford, Pennsylvania, who had questioned Gerstein in Rottweil. They both remembered the incident perfectly and were able to identify Gerstein's report and statement. Bach had Gerstein's widow examined in Germany to identify her husband's handwriting on the written statement. We further obtained the evidence of the priest Hecklinger, on whose typewriter the statement was typed. We obtained an official statement from the Swedish Foreign Office, confirming Gerstein's confidential talk with von Otter and the information he had given about Bełżec in 1942. Finally we got a French death certificate showing that Gerstein was dead. On the strength of all this supporting evidence, Gerstein's report was accepted by our court, and I read it out.

Thus it fell to me to tell the story of the death camp Bełżec, a place that I had never seen but that had become the burial ground for my uncles, aunts, cousins and boyhood friends who had lived in Lwów, the town where I was born and spent my early years.

Eichmann's involvement in the choice and supply of the poison gas became even clearer than before.

Finally our pilgrimage to the camps reached Auschwitz. The first attempt to describe it failed, when Yehiel Dinur fainted in the witness box (Chapter 10). "You relied on me and I failed you," the great writer wrote to me later, after he had recovered from the shock, which kept him bedridden for two weeks. I reassured him that the few sentences he had spoken on the "ash planet" stood for volumes. We had other witnesses on Auschwitz, on which we dwelt for three sessions. We accompanied the witnesses to roll calls before Dr. Mengele, followed the children to crematoria, in which they were sometimes allowed to play "outside business hours."

I finally decided to shorten this part of the evidence. In any case, words no longer conveyed their full meanings, and it looked as if in two or three more days of this we might lose control of our nerves and give way to hysteria.

Instead of more evidence I showed a film that lasted about an hour. It contained different scenes, photographed at different times. Some of the pictures were surreptitiously taken at the time of the occurrences by Germans who could not resist the temptation to perpetuate the scene; others were taken by the Allied armies, soon after liberation. There was much in this film to give concrete shape to the preceding eight weeks of evidence; people undressing before the open pits, piling up clothes marked with yellow badges, then standing naked at the brink of the pit, their faces showing incredulity and horror. A moment later there was shooting, and they were seen falling into their graves. The camera moved to the shooting squad, immediately behind the victims, and showed the second group of naked figures being pushed forward in their turn. These were the *Einsatzgruppen* murders.

Then came another scene: endless trains rolling on. The scene of loading the cars came, for some reason, afterward. We could see crowds at the railway station, carrying their belongings, being pushed forward and packed inside the cars. A bucket of water was passed inside by an SS man. A minute later the massive doors of the boxcar were locked from the outside. The picture showed the backs of the SS guards and, further, the train starting to roll.

Then the camps were shown, with the electrified barbed-wire fences. Suddenly the camera turned on heaps of naked bodies. It was revolting to see naked human bodies piled up like plucked slaughtered chickens. Among the dead wandered the "Muselmans," morbid dried-out creatures, completely apathetic to their surroundings.

The liberation scenes followed. Germans, who were ordered to carry the decomposed corpses into huge graves, were shown in the performance of the task and, finally, the most sickening sight of all: bulldozers pushing heaps of dead bodies like refuse into a sort of dumping pit. The army was afraid of epidemics; immediate burial was imperative.

I had to give the court short explanations of the scenes as they were shown. Finally the lights were turned on again in the courtroom. The three judges were glued for a moment to their chairs; they looked dazed, and for the first time since the trial had begun, they were seen to have tears in their eyes. They rose abruptly and hurriedly left for their chambers.

We then asked the court to receive in evidence the transcript of the recorded talks between Eichmann and Sassen in Argentina in 1957, which they conducted over a period of five months in order to reduce to writing the essential facts on the "solution" of the Jewish problem, as a preparation for a book on the subject. We had secured sixty-two out of the sixty-seven transcripts of the recorded tapes, as well as additional correction sheets containing, in Eichmann's handwriting, prefatory observations and fifty-two remarks on the text. The typed manuscript contained further hundreds of handwritten corrections and remarks. Eighty-four of these written entries and remarks, spread throughout the manuscript, were definitely identified by a handwriting expert as written by Eichmann; most of the others were also probably his, the expert said, but on these he lacked the scientifically established minimum points of similarity to make a positive identification.

The document was full of Eichmann's characteristic expressions, which he used in his police investigation interviews and in speech. They were what a German observer called a "jargon of violence." But it was not on stylistic similarity that we pinned our claim to the admissibility of the document. The main point was that Eichmann never denied that he had held these talks and that they were recorded on tape at the time and later typed out. He further admitted that Sassen sent him the typewritten pages for correction. But, he claimed, the talks were held in "a saloon atmosphere," since "wine was served from time to time" and he was urged to drink to overcome his reluctance to cough up the details that interested Sassen as a journalist. Dr. Servatius argued that Eichmann had been a "very busy workingman," and did not have time to study every one of these pages seriously; he had consequently given them "only a cursory examination" and made some minor corrections. Occasionally, when he had had more time, he had made more detailed corrections and refutations, counsel said. We were told that the two men had even drawn up a contract providing that the record would not be published till Eichmann had had the opportunity to study it again and to initial each page.

As we were later to learn from Eichmann himself, he never really stopped making the corrections, nor did he ever accuse Sassen of having distorted what he said. He further admitted that he had conducted the talks "in order to establish the truth" and that "what he told Sassen was the truth" though he still claimed that "the truth did not find expression."

Legally, the relevant question was whether Eichmann had actually said the things recorded and transcribed, and not whether, on reconsideration, he would wish to correct or even disclaim them. Since there was no denial that the transcript recorded the talks, I felt it should be admitted as his voluntary statement on the matters with which he was charged. It would then still be open to Eichmann to offer any qualifying explanation he thought fit. So I asked for the inclusion of the document in the court record, without requesting any relaxation of the regular rules of evidence.

To my surprise the application was refused, by a majority decision, mainly on the ground that we had not established a sufficient nexus between Eichmann and the document. "The mere fact that someone puts remarks on a transcript is not unequivocally binding, and does not necessarily mean that he has adopted the statement as coming from him or made by him. . . . If the matter can be argued either way, we prefer, with regard to an instrument offered by the prosecution as a statement by the accused, the more stringent view."

Judge Halevy, in a minority ruling, accepted our argument that, in the circumstances, the origin of the document had been sufficiently proved. The fact that Eichmann had personally corrected statements attributed to him obviously pointed to his acceptance of at least those tape transcriptions on which identifiable handwritten corrections had appeared. "Nobody would insert corrections into statements of talks ascribed to him if the whole thing were a forgery"—which, in any case, Eichmann never claimed. The fact that five tapes and the greater part of the remarks were missing was a circumstance that the court should consider when deciding on the weight of the statement, said the minority ruling, but not when deciding on its admissibility.

By a majority, therefore, the document was excluded, with the exception of the external holographed remarks and the few correction sheets, which, though interesting in themselves, proved useless. The reason I wished to have the document on record was not so much to use it to prove the facts discussed therein. It turned out that in some parts Eichmann had managed to hoodwink even Sassen as could be established by documents, and in any case we had formulated our indictment before we ever got hold of the Sassen document and were confident of our ability to prove our charges without it. What was particularly important was Eichmann's free discussion of his mental attitude toward his job; this emerged from his exchange of words and ideas with Sassen, sometimes in reply to searching questions, sometimes in the course of a heated argument. The unique opportunity "to have a closer look into the inner world of the accused," as Judge Halevy said, was denied the court.

For myself I never entertained any doubt as to either the document's authenticity or its legal admissibility. It is certainly an historic instrument. Now I was able to use only portions of it effectively in cross-examining, since Eichmann, emboldened by the majority's ruling, would usually repeat with the consistency of a gramophone record that the entire statement was a mixture of truth and fiction. He would challenge me to produce the original tapes, and I almost did, as I will describe later.

*

I wanted the last words of the prosecution to be on a different note. It was incumbent upon me to show at least a fraction of what the Jews had been able to do when they had the opportunity to fight the Germans. The trial was recording history, and it would be unpardonable if the superb military effort of the free Jews went unnoticed. The framework of judicial proceedings did not permit any substantial unfolding of the supreme bravery of about a million and a half Jews who fought Hitler on all fronts, under different flags, far exceeding in numbers and military distinction their percentage in the general population.* All these were, under the circumstances, not unnatural feats, since the Jew was fighting his most implacable enemy; but for the sake of the record this story also ought to be mentioned, for it is too often overlooked or glossed over. However, I could properly link with the trial only two aspects of the saga, and even these only on a limited scale. This was better, however, than omitting it altogether.

Some of the heroic feats of the Jewish partisans in the rear of the Germany Army were told by Shalom Cholawski.

It had not been easy to join the fighters, he said. Once the Nazis found out that some Jews had left a ghetto, they often immediately destroyed the entire remaining population. The Soviet partisans, on the other hand, were often distrustful of the Jewish fighters. They would ask, as a proof of loyalty, that each bring firearms with him, preferably taken from a German.

"So we had to form our own units in the woods," Cholawski said. "The first firearms were acquired by ambushing German patrols. Once we had these it was easier to get more. We found in the woods remnants of Jewish villages, people who had escaped and formed family camps, wandering from place to place. We gave them our protection and cared for them. They

* See *Facing the Nazi Enemy* (in Hebrew), telling the story of Jews in the U.S., Polish, Soviet, Palestinian, Czech, Free French, British, Canadian and South African armies and in the fighting resistance movements of Greece, Yugoslavia and Italy.

moved with us and were as mobile as we were, usually moving at night in the dense woods and resting at daytime."

Cholawski described the tactics of the fighting units. "We could rarely enter into an open encounter with large German forces, so we had to rely on guerrilla tactics. We led the Germans into traps and constantly harassed them." Under the circumstances, only a loose coordination existed between the various spontaneously created fighting groups. "We would attempt from time to time to liberate a ghetto and break into a village known to have had a Jewish population. As often as not we found that the Jews had already been destroyed, their houses occupied by others or burnt down, and the synagogues demolished. The Scrolls of the Law were cut up to make parchment for playing cards." Cholawski produced such a card in court.

"From time to time we also had exalting moments of joy, when our actions had a more successful ending," he said.

"How many Jewish fighters would you say there were?" I asked him. "I would say about fifteen thousand fighters, apart from the family camps," was the reply. "We found them everywhere, in the dense forests of Lithuania and of White Russia, among the marshes of Volhynia, in the woods of Polesie, actually all along the front."

The last witness, who also brought to the courtroom a somewhat comforting note, was a Tel Aviv lawyer, Mr. Aharon Hoter-Ishai. He had served with the Jewish Brigade, which fought with the British Army during the war. Fittingly, he was among the first to enter the camps and enclosures where Jews were still lingering. "There were eight million displaced persons and forced laborers in Germany," he said. "They belonged to all European nations. We were searching for the few Jews among them. Our car would enter such a place and inquire about Jews."

Often unforgettable scenes followed.

"In Freimannplatz Kaserne, near Munich, a commotion followed and after a while a group of apparently living people, who were not unlike the dead bodies lying all around, frantically rushed forward and fought with the little strength they had to touch the small Shields of David painted on our cars. Those who could not get close enough kissed the soldiers' boots."

"We found thousands of people already so weak that they could hardly whisper their names. 'Why did you not come before, why only now?' the survivors asked, weeping."

Mr. Hoter-Ishai then described the rehabilitation work undertaken by the Jewish Brigades among the survivors.

With this description of the Shield of David coming to the blood-soaked soil of Europe to rescue the saved remnant of a people, I closed the evidence. This was the last of the 112 witnesses who conveyed the story of our national disaster.

The case for the prosecution lasted fifty-six calendar days, just about the two-month period we had had in mind and informed the court of in advance.

CHAPTER 18

The Case for the Defense

With the case for the prosecution over, the defense was given a week for preparation.

Dr. Servatius said in opening:

"In this case, there are two worlds, the one opposing the other: the world of those who suffer, the victims, and those who are in authority; the victims and the apparatus of the dictator; depths on the one side and, on the other, heights. And the world of the Caesars knows no tears. The machinery of the rulers was described by the prosecution, and the defense will also describe this apparatus.

"The defense will show that the involvement of the accused in the persecution of the Jews was a necessity and a result of the political leadership of his state. For the accused this was a result that could not be avoided.

"It will become clear that the charge that the accused was worse than Hitler was only constructed later. There is no truth in the contention that the accused sabotaged the alleviating orders—this is wrong, as well as the story that Himmler himself feared the accused. . . .

"The proof will be brought into court by hearing the accused himself, and will not be conducted haphazardly, but will follow the documents submitted by the prosecution. The accused himself will testify, and with the aid of these documents will report and account for his position and his activities. He will stand here in evidence, knowing full well that a cross-examination may go very far. He is sure that he will be able to stand his cross-examination. He will describe truthfully all the happenings as he did to the police at the preliminary inquiry. Of his own will and initiative he has stated the important fact: his personal knowledge in regard to the actions of extermination. Documents will prove, once the defense has shown them in their proper light, that responsibility lies on the shoulders of the political leadership of the country. The Ministries created first and foremost a basis for persecution and extermination: the Ministry of the Interior, the Ministry of

Justice, the Ministries of Economy, Finance and other Ministries. These were the institutions that issued the instructions, directions, orders and directives. This was the legal basis and preliminary condition for those persecutions. Without them the accused could not have taken even one step, and he did not even take one step without them. All the government apparatus was a partner, and all had a hand in this terrible harvest. If he is guilty, so much more guilty were those who occupied the high offices, even if they were there as camouflaged resistance agents. . . .

"The defense will prove that the accused is not responsible for the exterminations that took place. It will become clear that he did not give the order and was not the executor. . . .

"It will transpire that as far as he was concerned there was no possibility for him to refuse orders. It will also become clear that the accused attempted, in the only possible way open to him, to stop the persecutions and bring the exterminations to an end by offering, through the usual channels, to enable one million Jews to leave the country."

*

Eichmann stood up, raised his hand and swore by God to tell the truth. He refused to take the oath on the Bible.

One of the observers at the trial said to me during the recess: "It was uncanny to listen to the devil swearing by God."

The opening speech now for the first time clearly demarcated the line of the defense. The facts of the extermination were not disputed, which explained why there had been no cross-examination of the witnesses to the acts. Nor was there any denial of Eichmann's involvement in the operation, but rather an attempt to reduce his role and position to the lowest possible level. Above all, a determined effort was promised to show that all he ever did was done under orders, without the slightest initiative on his part.

Eichmann's position as a mere "transmitter," which he had attempted to bring out during the police interrogation, was now to be further minimized. The "transmitter," it was claimed, had no amplifying power of his own—in fact, no power at all.

This was not an entirely original defense; it had been tried out before in Nuremberg and elsewhere, without spectacular success. But short of a full and truthful admission, it was perhaps the only course he could take in fighting for his life. It would be interesting to see how he would explain away the countless and obvious slips that were visible on every side. Where would he stop in minimizing his own position and authority?

It soon became clear that he would stop at nothing; he would not hesitate to describe himself as a nobody; to believe him, his superiors were endowed with phenomenal capacities, his subordinates were far more active than he was, and the RSHA was so disorganized that it could never have functioned. According to him, everyone in the RSHA dealt with Jewish matters and deportations. All he had to do, as the head of the department in charge of both Jewish affairs and deportations, was "to overcome the difficulties that arose with regard to train timetables" and "to eliminate obstacles by maintaining contact with the directorates of several railway lines." In any case, he never undertook or initiated anything unless specifically told to do so. "I never took any decision by myself, till it became my distinctive feature, about which my subordinates used to complain. . . . I never did anything, great or small, without obtaining in advance express instructions from my superiors." True, many instructions, directives, orders and letters were issued from his office and bore the markings of his department. If these were legally in the nature of confiscatory measures, the "jurists of the department" were responsible for them, he said. Those that were signed by Heydrich, Kaltenbrunner or Mueller emanated from his department only when he was instructed by his superiors to draft them. If hundreds of other documents were signed by him personally, this was always on specific or general instructions.

There was another explanation of how so many binding instructions bore the markings of his department. This was because the records of Jewish affairs were kept there, and the typists would put this archive mark on such documents for filing purposes, he claimed.

He, personally, had never enjoyed any special standing or position, but it was quite different with Rolf Guenther, his deputy. Guenther received "special assignments" from Mueller, the Gestapo Chief, which might explain the department's involvement in several matters with which it should have had nothing to do. That was how they became implicated in the supply of poison gas to the camps, in "this Gerstein business, of which I knew nothing," or the supply of skeletons to Strasbourg, of which he "knew nothing and remembered nothing," but if the matter ever reached his department, "as so many other matters did by mistake," then he must have "referred it to Mueller, the head of the office, as I usually did with such affairs." If his department was later assigned the matter, then Mueller must have asked Guenther to do it.

The same applied to the Lidice children. It was not within his competence, he claimed: "This is one of the orders Guenther received directly." Sterilization measures, too, had nothing to do with him. "It seems that Guenther got this as a confidential, special assignment." Department IV-B-4 had nothing to do with it as such, he claimed. "So why were you present at the sterilization conferences?" asked Dr. Servatius. The reply was: "Because my department had to write down the minutes and have them distributed among participants."

He would from time to time repeat that he had in any case admitted much, and would not have denied "this particular matter" had it been true. Here Eichmann was developing a technique that he had already begun to employ at the pretrial investigation. A partial, usually less damaging, confession was to serve as warranty for the truthfulness of his whole testimony; otherwise, he would ask, with an air of injured innocence at the lengths to which human incredulity could be pushed, why should he have confessed at all?

At one stage, he confessed, he had developed an independent activity. This was in his early Austrian days. He had read Zionist literature, especially *The Jewish State* (though he thought Adolf Boehm the author instead of the founder of Zionism, Theodor Herzl), and said he had been committed "to the policy of giving the Jews firm land under their feet." That was why he promoted emigration from Austria; that was the purpose for which he set up all the institutions there. He was even prepared to assist in getting Herzl's remains transferred from Vienna to Palestine, if Dr. Loewenherz, who desired it, would produce in exchange eight thousand "additional visas for further emigrants."

The entire "efficient, industrious effort" he had created was smashed at one blow, he said. "The *Kristallnacht* shattered all this."

Of course, he had nothing to do with the horrors of that night. Then why did he have to be kept informed of all its events and why did the report of the burning synagogues reach him at 2:20 A.M., as recorded?

"I kept all sorts of files and archives in the outbuildings of the synagogues," said Eichmann with a straight face, "and had to rescue the correspondence, which was absolutely necessary for further emigration work."

He repeatedly stated that the period of his work for Jewish emigration was the happiest in his life. He had been glad to "labor for an ideal," he said. He claimed credit for the lives he had saved by expelling the Jews. In cross-examination he admitted, however, that at the time he was driving Jews out no one had even dreamed of physical annihilation, and that his work was hardly a rescue mission. "But as Jewish leaders were always complaining of hardships this was best for all concerned," he declared. He admitted that there was nothing to be proud of, even in this part of his activity. He also agreed, under questioning, that the horrors of the *Kristallnacht* were quite helpful to him in forcing the Jews to go.

It was a rather unusual examination. At times Dr. Servatius would read parts of one or several documents, make observations on them and then proceed to the next, Eichmann's silence being taken as indicating his assent. Generally, however, Dr. Servatius would ask his client for comments on documents. Eichmann would then embark on a long string of loosely connected phrases, adding numerous explanations and qualifications as he went along. Early in his evidence the court remarked: "His style is his own affair, but if he wants us to understand him he must speak in shorter sentences; otherwise we will not understand at all. The verb in German comes at the end of a sentence, but here it takes too long." Dr. Servatius attempted to curb his client. "Your awkwardly long sentences prevent good translations and hinder understanding," he told him in open court. Sometimes the lawyer would stop his client's tirade and say "Enough." Later the court again complained of "the accused's general lectures." But all these reprimands were useless. It was obvious that Eichmann just could not change his manner of speech.

He would frequently interpolate that what he was saying was "in the documents"—even if it was nothing of the sort.

Before the trial I had listened to several recorded speeches of Hitler, and I was now struck with the curious similarity in voice and style between the two; both used inordinately long sentences and inaccurate expressions that indicated the absence of a systematic education. In spite of his marked effort to impress the judges favorably, Eichmann could not keep away from such typical Nazi expressions as "the Versailles dictate," spoke of the war having been "forced" on Germany, and of "Weizmann's declaration of war on behalf of the Jews."

In dealing with seriously incriminating official German documents, he now went to the length of saying that they were untrue. The attendance list of the fateful conference with Heydrich on September 21, 1939, which contained his name, was incorrect, he said. He was not there. Rademacher's note on Eichmann's order to shoot Jews in Belgrade was not true. "I could not have said it, because this would have seriously overstepped my competence." The Wetzel letter on the use of poison gas was forged, and his name had been inserted by somebody who had just put in "Eichmann" because it was known that he dealt with Jewish affairs. (In cross-examination he said that by putting on both pairs of glasses he found that the name had been wrongly inserted.) The description of him in a document as "Kaltenbrunner's representative on the liquidation of ghettos" showed the draftsman's ignorance of the structure of the police. He had deported Slovenes, that was true. But where a document said that he issued any "instructions" on the matter, this was "no doubt the mistake of the draftsman, who must have been in a hurry." The witnesses who deposed at the Nuremberg Trials on his standing in the hierarchy were lying. The description of him as the plenipotentiary of Himmler and Kaltenbrunner for deportations and all outside contacts on Jewish matters, which was given at Nuremberg by his personal friend, SS Colonel Dr. Rudolf Mildner of the Gestapo, with whom he was later on close terms in Argentina, was, he said, "untrue and impossible under the official allocation of duties at the office."

At this stage, interestingly enough, he did not launch a frontal attack on the heavily incriminating evidence of Rudolf Hoess. All he said on this point was that his visits to the camps had been only for the purpose of "looking, observing and reporting, without comment."

We waited to see how this self-belittlement would be applied to his

Hungarian period. But he clung to it consistently, even in dealing with this last great chapter of his career.

"I had only railway timetables to take care of there, and even this only marginally," he said. "Everything was done by my superiors, Winkelmann and Veesenmayer; I had only to report and to inform my superiors. . . . The Hungarian gendarmery did not need German advisers."

Thus he tried, as it were, to burrow underground and conceal all traces of his activity. In view of the enormous extent of the evidence, however, he felt that some further explanation was called for, so he added: "I know that these things seem incredible. But what can I do? That was the state of affairs."

A discerning observer wrote: "The defense continues. It is patient, plodding, astute. It makes no assault upon the court's emotions. It ignores the derision of public opinion. Its object is to save one man's life. He is a man emotionally parched. Eichmann is frightened."

Throughout Eichmann's evidence the judges kept observing him, the presiding judge with increasingly impatient tolerance, Judge Halevy with infinite patience but with less tolerance, and Judge Raveh with an increasing interest and eager curiosity. For myself, I could not help feeling disgusted with these obvious and systematic lies, accompanied by assurances of veracity. In the old days, Eichmann was well known in Nazi circles for his capacity "to lie in the most convincing manner." Now, in Jerusalem, he was ludicrously unconvincing.

Veesenmayer was wrong, Eichmann said, in attributing to him the attempt to foil the departure of a number of Jews which Hitler had authorized. "I deny the correctness of these things," he said simply, brushing aside an official document. He did not initiate the march from Budapest, nor did he have a hand in its implementation. Of the whole Kistarcsa affair he could "vaguely remember" that a train was once sent back—nothing more. In any case, he had no trucks at his disposal and therefore could not have carried out this or any other deportation. The whole affair was known to him only from literature.

Only once, according to him, did he depart, in Hungary, from this inactivity. This was when Becher spoke of enabling Jews to emigrate. "I was angry . . . that somebody outside the police should deal with emigration matters, on which I was an expert." So he had put out his own feelers, he said, to find out what could be asked of the Jews in return for one or two hundred thousand emigration permits.

"How and when Joel Brand turned up I can't say today, for I don't remember. . . . But I remember I increased the number of emigrants to a million, to be able to put up the scheme to my superiors without being thrown out of the room. . . . Mueller would not listen to a scheme involving, say, ten thousand people, but a million was too much to refuse offhand." And so he put up the notorious deal, which, to his "utter amazement," was approved. "They even approved of the 10 percent condition, which I stipulated"—meaning that 100,000 Jews would be permitted to leave as soon as Brand returned with a favorable reply.

Then, he said, he did all he could to push the whole matter and see it through. He said that he fully understood Brand's rage and grief, adding: "I hope that Joel Brand will also understand my rage and grief, now that he can see, by the documents, that I was not the man responsible for the destruction."

I later learned that Brand almost had a fit when he heard this statement.

Throughout this evidence he implicated many other offices, mainly the Ministry of Interior, "which had to provide the legal basis for the action," and the Foreign Office, whose attitude was "decisive." In the course of the evidence, some of the documents that we had refrained from using were introduced by Dr. Servatius, who had announced that he would fight the charge on the basis of our documentation and "will not seek historic clarifications." It was probably a wise decision. Additional documents, if discovered, would probably add further proof of guilt. As it was, some of the additional instruments that the defense introduced, like the affidavits of Mildner, the Gestapo chief in Upper Silesia and Denmark, Hoffman, of the RSHA, and SS Judge Morgen, or the story of the Dutch lawyer, Mrs. van Taalingen-Dols, though supporting certain aspects of Eichmann's version, ripped it wide open on the main issues. We would have been glad to put in Mildner's and Hoffman's affidavits as part of our case, but these people were, to our knowledge, still alive, and the court would never have accepted their statements without offering the defense the opportunity of cross-examination. This we were not in a position to do, since we knew nothing of their whereabouts. But when Dr. Servatius submitted them as part of his case, we were content and did not object.

Eichmann submitted twenty different charts of the various offices and authorities of the Reich that dealt with Jewish affairs in Germany and the occupied countries. They were heavily marked with lines and arrows, indicating incredibly complicated channels of command. On one of them there even appeared, instead of the usual vertical or horizontal branching-off, a closed circle of command. "This looks like a snake biting its tail," remarked the presiding judge. All this was designed to show that the main arteries of authority did not even pass through Eichmann's department. The all-important Gestapo Section for Jewish Affairs was barely visible on the charts; it was always either on the margin or at the end of the chain. Judging by the charts, it looked as if almost every authority in the Reich had a hand in killing the Jews except the one headed by Eichmann.

The first chart showed Eichmann's career and his various posts. According to this four-page document, which was produced in court, he was posted to Berlin in September, 1939, as soon as the war started.

To conclude his direct examination, Eichmann read a prepared statement, saying that there could be no legal guilt attached to what he had done. The guilt lay only with those who had ordered these acts and who had claimed his obedience. Good leadership was a matter of luck, he said. He had been unlucky. He could not jump over his own shadow or escape. He had to obey. The alternative was suicide.

Like so many other cowardly Nazis on trial, he now actually presented himself as one of the martyrs of the wicked system. It was sickening to listen to.

On the "human" side, however, which had nothing to do with legal paragraphs, "in these high spheres . . . everyone has to judge and sentence himself," he said. "I did so and am still doing it," he concluded. These last phrases were empty talk; I did not believe him. But what he said about the co-responsibility of many others was correct. For it did, in fact, require the mobilization of all the organs of the state to bring about the uprooting and ultimate destruction of the Jews.

He had discussed with Sassen in 1957 a possible trial of the people involved "in the whole complex of matters" of the Final Solution. Had he been in charge of the prosecution, he would accuse, he had then said, the Head of the Security Police, the Chief of the S.S. Economic Office, the Head of the Gestapo, the *Einsatzgruppen* commanders, the Commando of the SS and Police in the General Government, the Head of Office VII and SS General Professor Six (whom, incidentally, he called as a defense witness). Then he named himself as an accused, followed by several other RSHA and SS leaders. The chief figures of the Foreign Ministry came next in line, followed by Hitler's Chancellery, Goebbels' Propaganda Office, the Home Office department chiefs, the Reichstag deputies and all the party leaders. So I had an idea how Eichmann would have done my job had he been in my place.

He actually named all these persons in the course of the investigation and trial, nor did I contradict the wide diffusion of guilt; I merely objected to his own fading away in the process. For he stood among many, but was still outstanding; he had countless assistants, but the job was his. My cross-examination would therefore have to bring him back into the focus of the crowded picture and restore him to his true dimensions, after the reducing measures he had applied in true Alice-in-Wonderland fashion.

*

I began the cross-examination by asking whether he was still ready, as he had said in the pretrial examination, to hang himself in public. He answered that he was. "Do you consider yourself guilty of participation in the murder of millions of Jews?" "Legally not," he replied, "but in the human sense—yes, for I am guilty of having deported them."

I asked him whether this would be a "joyous jumping into the grave" in the knowledge of having dragged millions of Jews with him, as he told his men shortly before his collapse. He said he had never mentioned "Jews" in this context, but had spoken only of "enemies of the Reich," who were then overrunning the country. I showed him his own signed statement at the police interrogation, where he described his "jumping into the grave" speech, and where he added that he had then mentioned "five million Jews whom the war had consumed." Eichmann swallowed hard at this slip. I was later shown a close-up picture of this moment on television. Eichmann's face had a look of utter amazement and, for a moment, of panic. All he managed to say was: "This is an improper interpretation of what I said at the time." Later, in reply to Judge Raveh's questions, he finally admitted it was five million *Jews* he had spoken of at the time.

He had spoken a lot about Germany's struggle, the fight against the Versailles Treaty and so forth.

"But the only front on which you were active all the years from 1937 onward was the fight against the Jews?" I asked.

Eichmann lowered his eyes. "Yes, that is true," he replied.

I knew that he was severely hurt in having to admit that he never served on the battlefield and that all he did was to persecute Jews from behind his writing desk. He continued to maintain that he had taken no initiative. Now he had to drain the medicine of "superior orders" to the last drop; so he claimed that he had never even *suggested* any course of action to his superiors. He would place a problem before them, ask for their instructions and pass these on. It was true that his position and post carried the power of decision and "a certain amount of discretion, but I systematically avoided the use of it." If a document read "Eichmann decided," "this had no special meaning." He made much of the way all his orders, instructions and letters were signed. They all had the words *"Im Auftrage"* ("By Order") or the abbreviation *"I.A."* preceding his signature. This showed, he said, that all he could do was on orders only. There was hardly a single instrument he had signed in any other way.

That much was true, but it meant nothing. For we were able to prove that under the correspondence instructions of the RSHA this was the prescribed formula of signature for all department heads. We showed him this in the internal Gestapo instructions of 1936. "These were later changed," he claimed. This was true again: in 1939, when the RSHA was established, a new set of regulations was issued. But the ruling on signatures remained the same. "So you had to sign all your letters with these prefatory words whether you did consult your superior on the particular matter referred to or not?" was my last question on the subject. "Yes," replied Eichmann.

I distributed my questions on particulars concerning his status all through the cross-examination. This was obviously a preferable technique to a frontal encounter, which he would try to dodge. He agreed with the statement that the "Final Solution" was an enormous venture and that marking, rounding up, concentrating and deporting the Jews was a colossal technical and administrative effort. He further admitted that after the Wannsee Conference all his deportation instructions were part of the "Final Solution," but he still maintained that he had nothing to do with the *Einsatzgruppen* or with affairs in the General Government.

He admitted, however, that he was present at the briefing session of the *Einsatz* leaders, and that he was itching to get an appointment himself. He confessed he had later been in contact with them in the occupied areas by letter and cable, whenever coordination was necessary. This was important to us, as we had proof of only some of the instructions that his department issued to the *Einsatzgruppen.* He admitted, finally, the correspondence with the *Einsatz* commanders in the Riga and Minsk areas, where he sent Jews from the Reich.

He remembered drafting the authorizations to Globocnik about "bringing 250,000 people each time to the Final Solution," and submitting these for Heydrich's signature, and finally taking the signed orders in person to Globocnik. He claimed that these orders had been issued *post factum,* after the Jews were already killed. To my question, "What was the sense, then, of issuing the orders?" he could give no other reason than "Globocnik's macabre burial habits."

He could not explain why the Foreign Office had to consult him prior to the liquidation of the Warsaw ghetto, and why he was described in this correspondence as "the representative of the Head of Police and Security Service." All he could say was: "It was a common mistake at the time." He was unable to tell the court what business he had dealing with death certificates for the Warsaw ghetto, as stated in a document. "I just cannot figure it out," he replied. Nor could he say why he had been requested to countersign instructions concerning this, the biggest ghetto in Europe. But he still maintained that the General Government was none of his affair. If that was so, what business did his department have in sending out instructions not to deport the Jewish employees of the Carpathian Oil Company for the time being, till a replacement could be found for them? "I have no idea," he answered. "I got the order to draft this letter and I drafted it for Mueller's signature." "But was it not decided at Wannsee that problems of Jews throughout Europe, including Poland, were to come under the RSHA?" I pressed him further. Here began one of his long-winded replies, full of "buts" and "thens" and "on the other side," till even the patient presiding judge remarked: "Well, anyway, Poland is in Europe, or is that not clear either?" "Yes, that is clear," was Eichmann's crestfallen reply.

Sometimes it would take half an hour to extract from him a reply confirming a fact that would saddle him with any responsibility, such as the obvious fact that he was the only head of department "for Jewish affairs" in the RSHA, or that his department was centrally responsible for preparing and drafting the Madagascar plan. However, he finally admitted, after prolonged questioning and previous denials, that all Jewish matters—including every individual case of a Jew—had to pass through his department if it pertained to the Gestapo.

Then I proceeded to question him on his position in the Third Reich as reflected in some of the documents. He vehemently claimed that he was just a very ordinary head of department. It did not look like it from the written instruments that I now referred him to, and that he found difficult to explain away.

There was no reason, he said, for the German Foreign Office to apologize to him, as it had done, for acting without his knowledge in a Jewish matter when he was away from Berlin on one occasion. Nor could he account for the Foreign Office addressing "Dear Comrade Eichmann" when it wanted to find out "the wishes of the SS leadership" vis-à-vis the Italian authorities, which were required for a forthcoming meeting between Ribbentrop and Mussolini.

"This was apparently due to negligent drafting and to lack of knowledge," was his reply. Why did the Foreign Office ask him to approach the Wehrmacht on anti-Jewish operations in Denmark? "What has this to do with a transport officer?" "I don't know," was the answer. "It is in the documents, and I cannot say more than I read there." Nor could he explain why his view on Jews in Italian-occupied Greece were submitted to Ribbentrop as "the opinion of the SS leadership."

"How can you deny that the Foreign Office considered and described you in an official document here as the SS leadership on Jewish matters?" I asked. "I don't have to deny it at all," he replied. "I just declare it to be a mistake and not true. Had it been true I would not have lacked the courage to admit it."

Relying on his statement at the pretrial investigation, I asked him whether, in his view, it is the duty of an accused person to give true evidence. He admitted that "according to German usage" the accused had the right to lie, but claimed that he would not avail himself of the privilege.

But he also said he would have to go back on several statements he had made at the police interrogation, for, "having seen the documents, I have had a chance to refresh my memory." When I pressed him to explain why, when questioned by Chief Superintendent Less, he had not rejected the genuineness of a document that he now claimed to be forged, he finally replied: "Why should I have denied things that could perhaps be proved?"

Here was a clue to his general tactics. He took stock of what we had against him and painstakingly provided us with the least offensive picture of himself that, to his mind, could still somehow be compressed into the documentary evidence. The most seriously incriminating documents he would brand as forgeries and so brush them aside. He hoped he would be able to manage somehow with the rest of the material and turn to us the more presentable face of Janus. "As long as the Attorney General sticks to the documents, I am on safe ground," he remarked to one of his guards, as was reported to me.

It was obvious that he had thoroughly studied the documents, but it may be doubted whether he fully realized how damaging cross-examination can be. Perhaps this was due to the extreme difference between our system and the one he was accustomed to. Under the Nazis, questioning by the Gestapo was the most painful part of the process. If anyone had the extraordinary good fortune to emerge alive from this stage and to be placed on trial, the worst was over for him. The trial itself, tough as it might be, was an obvious relief after the tortures in the cellars. Eichmann saw that all Less was asking him to do was to comment on documents.

"I was treated in an extremely fair way by the superintendent who interrogated me," he said in court. What great danger could there be in testifying in court? He did not appreciate that under a democratic system the police must refrain from using even verbal pressure, when the prisoner is more or less at their mercy, while in open court, with everyone watching to ensure fair play, the cross-examiner may wield a double-edged sword.

After the first session of cross-examination, Eichmann claimed that he had had a sleepless night and could not stand the questioning; so the continuation had to be adjourned to the afternoon, to the humorous grumbling of my assistants, who said they had spent many sleepless nights in the course of the trial without asking for adjournments. We were now again having two sessions a day—during the direct examination the court had convened in the mornings only, to allow Dr. Servatius time for briefing sessions with his client.

Though Eichmann now displayed signs of strain, which showed in the haggardness of his face, his more frequent facial twitching and spasmodic movements of his Adam's apple, he lost nothing of his resourcefulness and mental agility. On the spur of the moment he would invent something to patch up a gap. Once, when I let him read aloud a document, he inserted the word "not"—there and then, while reading fluently—changing, of course, the whole tenor of the document. When I questioned him on the addition, he claimed that this was "grammatically necessary." The same thing happened toward the end of the cross-examination, when, while reading aloud a heavily corrected part of the Sassen manuscript, he substituted on the spot the words "Chief of Security Police" for "Reichsfuehrer Himmler" which was in the document. Having followed his reading from my copy, I inquired as to the reason for the substitution. Eichmann now lost his temper and shouted he would not answer any questions on this document, "which was untrue and incorrect." To the presiding judge's quiet statement that the accused would go on answering until released by him, Eichmann protested that this was his wish, adding: "I have the feeling that I am being grilled here until the meat is cooked." Judge Landau looked at his watch and announced a recess. On his way from the courtroom Eichmann had not yet recovered his composure. He said angrily to his guard: "I do not like the Attorney General at all."

It was a portion of the Sassen document that had so upset him. This instrument was obviously playing havoc with his attempt to entrench himself behind the other documents. For from the Sassen talks, on Eichmann's own showing, another face of his was emerging, one he was eager to leave veiled. He could not very well deny everything in the Sassen transcripts, certainly not his evaluations of other persons. One of those referred to Rudolph Hoess. He had told Sassen that Hoess was the "personification of exactness and correctness." "If I said that, it would be the pure truth," he replied to my question. He admitted that they were on good terms and that Hoess had no reason to sling mud at him or to lay the blame for other people's actions at his door. "Why, then, did Hoess write that Mueller gave you a fairly free hand in Jewish matters?" "This is untrue," maintained Eichmann. "Even though Hoess had no reason at all to lie?" I asked. "Though he had no such reason whatsoever" was the answer.

He had maintained contact with Hoess. He admitted that he had visited Auschwitz four or five times, and that Hoess came to see him in Budapest. "What did he talk to you about?" I asked. "It must have also been on these matters," he replied. "Why do you beat about the bush? Say on what matters." "I am not beating about the bush. In Hungary, too, I was a receiver of orders and not a giver of orders. He must have gone first to these who gave the orders."

"Hoess explained that he had no room in Auschwitz to absorb so many Jews from Hungary?" "It is possible, I do not deny it, but . . ." "But he negotiated with you and you wanted to send in more trains, while he didn't want to absorb all of them?"

"I was not the man who demanded more trains. I was not authorized to decide the speed and the tempo of the transports. This was at the discretion of my superiors, as is evident from the documents."

"So why did Hoess contact you in Budapest? Did he come to have a cup of coffee with you?" "No, he was one of the heads and I could give him more details on these matters than my superiors."

So we had got somewhere. Eichmann knew more than his superiors about the big drive of Hungarian Jews to Auschwitz. In the course of this heated exchange of rapidly fired questions I switched to German, since it became exasperating to interrogate Eichmann through an interpreter. On the whole my questioning was in Hebrew, our usual court language, which, during the cross-examination, was filtered through the slow process of consecutive translation.

Eichmann unwittingly provided me with a good opening to examine him on his special standing and powers in the extermination camps. In the pretrial examination, being anxious to display his humane attitude, he had told Superintendent Less that when he had seen in Auschwitz a man called Storfer, whom he knew from Vienna, in a very pitiable condition, he noted in the Auschwitz register that Storfer should be employed in cleaning the gravel paths.

When Eichmann denied in court any authority over the camps, I asked him what authority he had to insert such a note in the Auschwitz books. The reply was that Mueller must have authorized him to do it.

"Didn't you say that the entire RSHA had no authority in Auschwitz?" I asked.

"Mueller must have approached Gluecks" (Head of the Inspectorate for Concentration Camps) was the reply. Eichmann was visibly confused. It was obviously too ridiculous to assume that Eichmann, Mueller and Gluecks would all have to get together to permit a Jew to clean the gravel paths in Auschwitz, where the lives of millions were valueless.

"But how did you know, even before you went there, that Storfer would ask you for permission to clean the gravel paths?" asked Judge Halevy.

Eichmann was at a loss to explain. He mumbled that he must have heard of Storfer's desire to see him, that he had tried to obtain his release, but when this failed he had armed himself in advance with the next best: a permit for light work. This was, of course, a pack of lies, but, as was often the case with Eichmann's evidence, it may have contained a perverted grain of factual substance. Eichmann had, in fact, a certain weakness for Storfer, whom he regarded as cooperative, according to what he told Sassen. It is possible that he wanted to do something for him and, making use of his standing over-all authority, ordered him to be employed in this way. Storfer, having been assigned to a permanent job, ceased to be an ordinary "*Transportjude*." He now had a function, and was not to be killed without special orders. But such special orders were issued by Guenther when Eichmann was in Hungary. "I was angry when I heard of it," said Eichmann.

The questioning on Hoess offered an opportunity to go deeper into Eichmann's attitude toward the whole venture.

A foundation for this had been laid down earlier in the interrogation. One of my first questions to Eichmann was whether, in his view, the judgments passed at Nuremberg on Goering, Frank, Kaltenbrunner and the others were just, and whether they had been rightly condemned and sentenced. This was not an easy question to answer. Had Eichmann doubted the moral validity of the Nuremberg Trials, he would have aligned himself with the proclaimed evildoers. If he justified their condemnation and the penalties meted out to them, as he did, he left himself a very thin thread to hang on to. For in a dictatorship built on the leadership principle everyone below Hitler was a recipient of orders. All officers, in all echelons of authority, received orders from higher up and gave orders to those lower down. Eichmann said that the accused at Nuremberg were rightly sentenced, for they were "order-givers," and it was right to hold them accountable for their deeds. On this assumption I inquired into specific cases.

What about Colonel Rudolf Hoess? He, too, was within Eichmann's interpretation a recipient of orders. In his autobiography Hoess had described himself as "a cog in the wheel of the great extermination machine created by the Third Reich." Would Eichmann now, in Jerusalem, whitewash his friend?

"You saw Hoess at work. Did you think he was a criminal?" I asked.

Eichmann sensed the danger and attempted to parry the blow. "I said I could never have done it," was his reply.

"But this was not my question. Did you, in your heart, consider him to be a murderer?"

"That is a most personal question. What I did not express then I will not disclose now. My inner life I keep in my heart."

"This has nothing to do with your inner life. You saw Hoess killing Jews. What did you think of him?"

"I pitied him and felt sorry for him."

I told Eichmann he would not be able to wriggle out of this dilemma. "So you did not consider Hoess to be a murderer?" I asked.

"I did not say so," he replied.

Obviously he could not say that a self-confessed exterminator of two and a half million people was not a criminal. "When this case is over," he added, "I wish to write a book and there to call the thing by its proper name as a deterrent for this and for future generations." He imagined that he still held one trump: that it would be worthwhile to allow him an opportunity to write that book.

"What you want to write in your book, you will have to say now. It is your duty," said the presiding judge.

"Since you call on me, Mr. President of the Court, I declare that I regard the murder of the Jews as one of the greatest crimes in human history."

This is what he declared at the trial. At the time the acts were committed he could not help himself, he said. "I was in the iron grip of orders," he declared, though even then, so he claimed, he had considered "the whole solution by violence to be a dreadful thing."

He said he gave up National Socialism after the war, but by a slow process, "with many relapses." By 1957, twelve years after Germany's defeat, the "change of mind process" was not yet complete, he confessed. This date was important for us: it was the year of the Sassen talks.

He would still maintain, with a peculiar streak of wishful thinking, that all he had said in court was "supported by documents" and protest that "one of my few virtues was truthfulness."

He was never an anti-Semite, he said. The virulently anti-Semitic expressions contained in a letter I showed him were not his; it had been submitted by another department for his signature. Time and again he would repeat that "rather than incur disbelief or make the impression of shirking responsibility" he would take upon himself the blame for this or that, though he "was not really responsible."

Finally the presiding judge remarked: "You repeat these declarations time after time, and I don't want you to talk here of making an impression. You swore to tell the truth; this and nothing else you should do. . . . You don't have to show any favors to the Attorney General."

This was when I questioned him again on one of "the special assignments," which he ascribed to Guenther. He admitted that there was no intrinsic reason for keeping the supply of poison gas to the camp a secret from him, since he was in any case aware of the process. So why did it have to be a special assignment to his deputy? I asked. "I don't know, I can't understand it or figure it out," was the reply.

He admitted that he had practiced deception on all sides. "It was so ordered," he declared.

"But you carried it out," I said. "Didn't you assure the Slovak authorities that all the stories about the awful fate of the Jews were just horror tales?"

"Yes, there was an order for that."

"And when the Red Cross wanted to inspect a camp you showed them Theresienstadt?"

"Yes."

"And you were telling the Jews that no harm would befall them. In Hungary you promised them they would not be deported if they cooperated."

"Yes, I was so ordered."

He admitted that he sometimes hoodwinked some of the authorities of the Reich itself.

"So the machinery of deception worked in all directions; toward foreign countries, toward some internal bodies and toward the Jews?"

"Yes, that is so with one reservation. The Jews did not always accept what I said. Toward them, I should rather say, toward one of them, I had to be more outspoken."

Eichmann was obviously trying to drag Kastner into the circle of "the initiated."

His true ferocious nature had already pierced through his self-imposed control on a number of occasions. On one such vivid occurrence Joseph Kessel, later of the French Academy, reported in *France-Soir:*

"The submissive Eichmann is growing into a wild beast," he observed, describing Eichmann's reactions to the evidence from abroad.

> He has finally ceased to be a mystery. Most vividly touched by the depositions of his erstwhile accomplices, the former SS colonel forgot to remain an administrative machine, a robot animated solely by the elementary mechanism of cunning and of fear. He spoke with passion and rage. This did not last long, but it sufficed.

Under the livid and hollow mask, under the habitual prudence and pretense, there now appeared the true Eichmann.

I had noticed the same on some other occasions, and knew that the court must have observed them.

*

The cross-examination had now lasted about two weeks. It had achieved, I hoped, the objective of destroying the image of a "victim of orders," who never overstepped his duties. It also showed that Eichmann had lied like a trooper.

From the beginning I told my assistants that this was what I was setting out to achieve by the questioning. It was wiser to "dismantle" him piece by piece than to try to beat him down, though this, too, happened when he claimed that he was being grilled and refused to answer further questions.

I believe that the purpose of cross-examination is to destroy the other side's story, not to bring about his physical breakdown. We all get suspicious whenever "spectacular breakdowns" of the accused occur, as they sometimes do in certain countries. Under our system a witness can occasionally be surprised to the point of collapse when he reaches the extreme limit of self-contradiction. It can rarely occur in the case of an accused who is well informed in advance of what he will have to meet in court and who knows no such limits. This was especially true of Eichmann, who never shrank from denying previous statements or branding official documents as forgeries.

So, to the disappointment of some people who craved to witness Eichmann's collapse under a crushing blow, I aimed only at achieving his complete and utter deflation under constant pressure. This, I felt, had already been accomplished. My feeling was later fully confirmed by the judgment. But as there was still some little wind left in his sails, the original tapes of the Sassen talks would have been useful to bring him to a complete standstill. These I could still put in even at this stage, if I received, while the cross-examination was in progress, not only the transcript, which I had, but the tapes themselves. He could hardly have been able to deny his own voice. There would have been no problem of "insufficient corrections" there.

I asked certain people to try to purchase a set of the tapes abroad from their holders. They demanded twenty thousand dollars for them. It was a great deal of money, but considering their historic importance I approved the expenditure. The prospective purchasers told the holders of the tapes that they wanted to have them played in public. When the deal was about to be closed, I was told that the vendors stipulated that the tapes must not be brought to Israel till the trial was over. I did not wish any part of our evidence to be obtained by false pretenses; so I instructed our people to insist on an unconditional sale. This was on the day when, in reply to a question from the bench, I said that we would finish the cross-examination shortly. The questioning was now touching matters we had covered before, but I kept it going in the hope that the tapes would be flown in at any moment. Time was running out. Late the next day the news arrived that the "exclude Israel" condition was irrevocable, and so the deal was off. The following morning my questioning was concluded.

The re-examination was brief. Dr. Servatius brought out the friendship between Sassen and Eichmann, dating back several years to Otto Skorzeny's visit to Buenos Aires. He then himself read into the record a new portion of the Sassen document (which bore no handwritten corrections), where Eichmann said that he had never held any special power of attorney from Himmler or from the Chief of the Security Police, but that he had always "acted a hundred percent," that he "certainly was not lukewarm in the giving of his orders" and that Mueller had said of him: "Had we had fifty Eichmanns we would have won the war automatically." By this, Eichmann explained to the court, Mueller meant not the capacity to shed the enemy's blood but outstanding ability to get things done and "unconditional loyalty in the execution of orders." Finally, he testified that a criminal investigation had once been launched against him over the alleged disappearance of a bag of diamonds from his office, but he had succeeded in proving that the diamonds had been sent elsewhere before his time. He had insisted on an open apology in front of his men from the judge who had issued the search warrant, which was given.

Questioning from the bench followed to clarify points on which the court required further information. Judge Raveh began by asking Eichmann to cite the Kantian imperative of behavior, which, he had earlier claimed, was his guiding principle in life. He cited the "categorical imperative" more or less correctly: "Let your life be guided by the principle that your will and your actions could become the model for general legislation." He admitted that in expelling Jews he had not conformed to this principle, but he was not free to do as he pleased, since he was not his own master.

The technical functioning of his office and the many things that had to be done there came under closer scrutiny. Judge Raveh wanted to hear how Eichmann's subordinates worked, how drafts of regulations were prepared and how it was possible that Eichmann had never made any suggestions of his own to his superiors. "Did Mueller never ask you what your opinion was on the matter?" "No" was the reply. "If Mueller did not know something, he would in turn go to his superiors for instructions." "It is difficult to swallow what you say," remarked Judge Raveh. "A man of the rank of Oberregierungsrat [Higher Government Counselor] putting up things to his superior and never making a suggestion or being asked for his opinion?" Eichmann stuck to his guns: on the Jewish question all agencies were active and the police had merely to execute the decisions of others; there were no opinions to be expressed.

Judge Raveh compared the working of his department with the procedure of the Foreign Office and traced the German bureaucratic practice by following certain documents we submitted, which proved the decisive importance of the head of department. Eichmann agreed that this was a typical bureaucratic process. But in his department it was different, "for in the Jewish matters there were so many instructions, so many points of contact with central bodies and with the party," that the police had their hands full of work and were never called upon to recommend anything. "Everybody was interfering, requesting and demanding. That is why we had nothing to suggest. . . . This goes for Mueller too."

The Wannsee Conference was then inquired into. Eichmann spoke again of his "Pontius Pilate attitude" and repeated that he had washed his hands of the affair at the time, when he saw his humane methods jettisoned for the Final Solution. "I did what I could by decent methods, but these powers were stronger than I was," he said.

"Mueller said once, so you told us," remarked Judge Raveh smiling, "that a man in the Gestapo called Hartl [hard] should rather be named 'Weichl' [weak]. Did he ever, by any chance, suggest that your own name should rather be 'Weichmann' [weakling]?"

"No, never," replied Eichmann, returning the smile.

Judge Halevy took over. He said that he too, like Judge Raveh, would depart from the accepted customs of the court and would examine Eichmann in German. He reminded Eichmann of his statement that though he was brought to Israel against his will, he was glad to have the opportunity of telling the whole truth. "Yes," said Eichmann. "I want to remove the misinterpretations that have been gathered round my person in the course of fifteen years. I am interested that my family and my sons should know what to answer people whom they meet and who have been influenced by the propaganda against me."

Here, then, we were given another glimpse of Eichmann's motives. What would his children say, what would others say about him? It was a train of thought that has passed through the minds of many accused, including some of the prisoners at Nuremberg. Goering was constantly thinking there what the future schoolbooks would have to say about him. Others were plagued by the thought that their own families and people must abhor them, now that their crimes were fully revealed. Rudolf Hoess wrote in his autobiography:

> My thoughts turn chiefly to my family. Let the public continue to regard me as the bloodthirsty beast, the cruel sadist and the mass murderer; for the masses could never imagine the commander of Auschwitz in any other light. They could never understand that he, too, had a heart and that he was not evil.

So, for the sake of his sons, Eichmann was still suggesting that he had told the truth. Judge Halevy took him up on that: "This about your family and sons tends to complicate matters, because you could certainly wish to appear in the best light to them." Eichmann assured the court that even for this purpose "he would not depart a hair's breadth from veracity."

Judge Halevy now addressed him very quietly and unemotionally: "You have not been questioned with Gestapo methods, and this is not a people's court." Eichmann agreed. The judge reminded him of the few exceptional cases of top Nazis who had had the courage to admit their guilt after the war. Of course it was up to him to speak, but this might be the last chance to prove whether he was a man or wanted simply to wriggle out. The atmosphere in the courtroom was extremely tense. Eichmann was now answering Judge Halevy's specific questions in monosyllables—the first time during the whole trial that he had replied in this way. He admitted he was aware of the Hague rules of warfare. The practical steps in the war against the Jews, he conceded, developed as the operation went on. The Jewish communities were placed under the supervision of the Gestapo. Their leaders were forced to cooperate, first in furthering emigration and later in other matters. The Germans were interested in this, for it saved manpower. The Jewish leadership, he repeated, was deceived and fooled.

Eichmann agreed he had resisted any exceptions for individual cases, since any case, even an unusual one, could turn into a precedent and later into an avalanche.

Then Judge Halevy reminded him of what was said of "civic courage" in Germany. "I lacked it as much as most uniformed people at the time," Eichmann replied.

"Do you have the courage to admit things now and to take responsibility for what you did?" asked the Judge.

"I have already said that I do so from the human point of view. I have my own thoughts and I try myself."

"Do you call this acceptance of responsibility? . . . I mean, for instance, the Sassen talks. You say you were drunk, or that they were forged or improperly transcribed. Were you drunk when you made the corrections?"

"No, I was staying at my ranch at the time, and I put in the corrections there."

"This is what I mean. You mix up two things: the final purpose of the talks and the fact that you did in reality say these things, even if you did not mean them to be final. But you dictated them all the same into the dictaphone."

"I admit that when the evening grew longer and the hour was late I began chattering and thus nationalism broke through my remarks. This was one of the relapses I spoke of."

"But these were actually your words?"

A slight pause followed. Would Eichmann now withdraw his objection to the submission of the Sassen document? We all held our breath.

Eichmann obviously wavered. He jotted down something on a piece of paper for Dr. Servatius. It was clear that he was experiencing one of his rare moments of doubt. But he soon repaired the dent in his armor, and dodged the issue with the usual ruse: "Anyway, I don't want to evade it and to say that I was given alcohol and that I don't know what I said or that my words were forged, because this is not fitting for this place. Though all these objections are true, I declare here, Your Honor, that I would rather take it all upon myself than give the impression that I shirked it."

"This is just empty talk, without any practical conclusion, since after all this talk you do not submit the document," said Judge Halevy, shrugging his shoulders.

Eichmann had resisted the temptation. The Sassen document was not placed on the court's table.

That was on Friday at noon. As we were not sitting on either Saturdays or Sundays, the presiding judge, Justice Landau, started his questioning on Monday morning, speaking in German and himself translating into Hebrew.

Eichmann was now manifestly refreshed; it was obvious that he had resolved not to soften again. From now on his behavior was to be firm and unwavering, though of course it led him into a great many absurdities that could not be concealed.

Now, for instance, he could not remember that it was he who had arrested Dean Grueber. "I always thought before that I did so, on orders, of course, but to my surprise I heard from the Dean that he was arrested by the Gestapo Office in Berlin. Obviously, I am confused on the matter."

His supplementary testimony on the fateful Wannsee Conference was grotesque. "I cannot remember it in detail," he said, "but they spoke there about methods of killing, about liquidation, about extermination. I was busy with my records. I could not prick up my ears and listen to everything that was said. . . . From time to time I heard a word or two."

He was even reduced to disclaiming anti-Semitism as an integral part of National Socialism.

"No," he said, in reply to another question, "one did not have to be an anti-Semite to be an orthodox National Socialist." The virulent anti-Semitic propaganda of the *Voelkischer Beobachter,* which he swallowed every morning, did not affect him. Nor did the Nuremberg Laws alarm him. He thought they would not be fully implemented. "Nothing is ever eaten as hot as it is cooked."

What created a still stranger impression, perhaps, was his contention that one didn't even have to be particularly tough to run the Gestapo. "Mueller was not tough," he said.

Justice Landau found this hard to take. "You mean the head of the Gestapo was not *tough?*"

"Well, not necessarily, though Heydrich, he was."

Eichmann's defense, in short, while perhaps inevitable once he had made up his mind to take a certain line, quickly developed so many implausibilities and blatant impossibilities, both psychological and bureaucratic, that its flimsiness was bound to become apparent. An atmosphere of utter disbelief came to reign throughout the courtroom, and, as we were soon to learn, in the minds of the judges.

CHAPTER

19

The Defense Witnesses

With Eichmann's evidence over, we could turn to his witnesses, whose statements were already coming in. Early in the trial I had made it known that we would be prepared to provide facilities under Israel's arrangements with foreign countries for mutual judicial assistance, should Dr. Servatius desire to call witnesses or to cross-examine persons who had given written evidence on oath in previous trials and whose affidavits we would wish to use. This meant, in practice, that various former Nazis, most of them high-ranking, would appear in court wherever they lived, and have their depositions taken in the presence of representatives of Dr. Servatius and of myself. These statements would be sent back to the prosecution and subsequently become part of the Jerusalem Court's record.

The court accepted this procedure, stating that it would prefer, in principle, to have witnesses appear in person before it, but if a witness did not wish to or could not come, his testimony would be taken abroad.

This course was obviously detrimental to us. It would have been easy for a witness to assist an old comrade like Eichmann by stretching a point or "forgetting" a detail when giving evidence in judge's chambers abroad, with the public and the press excluded. It would have been much more difficult to do so here in Jerusalem, in the full glare of publicity, with everything recorded by television cameras and the statements reported next day in the press all over the world. But this was a chance I had to take. The defense was entitled to call its witnesses and to cross-examine persons who gave statements submitted by us. I could neither force all these people to come here nor could I promise all of them safe-conduct, since they were liable to prosecution under the same law that made Eichmann indictable.

I briefed a German-speaking Israeli lawyer, Mr. Erwin Shimron, to represent me in all the proceedings abroad, and gratefully accepted Dr. Robert Kempner's offer to assist us in handling these witnesses, many of whom he had encountered in Nuremberg as accused years ago when he was

Deputy Chief of Counsel for the U.S. prosecution. Dr. Kempner's help was of great importance, since we had no forensic experience with this kind of person.

We knew that many of them had repeated their protestations of innocence so many times since the end of the war that they now half-believed them. There was reason to assume that some of them were in contact with Nazi groups, which displayed considerable activity on various aspects of the Eichmann trial. If a number of these people had gone out of their way to support Eichmann's story on the microscopic importance of his post and his actions, and these statements had poured into the court's records unchallenged in considerable quantity, it might have presented a problem. The court, not having seen the witnesses, would not be able to judge their credibility by the usual method of watching their demeanor in the box. Doubts might have arisen and, under the usual rule, dubiety works to the benefit of the accused and is resolved in his favor. Eichmann's version, so full of holes as it stood, might thus have received support from a quarter that we were not in a position to counter effectively.

This might have meant no more than increasing the weight of the evidence for the defense against all our documentation and witnesses, against Eichmann's own admissions and hopeless contradictions. Still, we were naturally concerned.

The tribunals abroad were soon ready to hear the various witnesses on the questionnaires prepared by the defense and by us. Mr. Wechtenbruch represented the defense. Altogether sixteen examinations were held abroad. Our court applied in each case, through our Foreign Ministry, to the judicial authority abroad to summon the witness and examine him according to the lists of questions supplied by the parties, and to allow supplementary questioning by the lawyers on both sides. All the foreign authorities approached responded and were most cooperative. Moreover, though some witnesses could not be subpoenaed, they all duly presented themselves to be examined. Some of them, like Professor Franz Six, Hermann Krumey and Richard Baer, appeared with their lawyers, to protect their interests in case they were asked incriminating questions. There were some defense witnesses who could not have come to Jerusalem, even if offered safe-conduct, because they were in prison at the time on criminal charges, mainly war crimes. These were: Franz Slavik and Franz Novak in Austria; Hermann Krumey, Erich von dem Bach-Zelewski and Richard Baer in Germany, and Herbert Kappler in Italy.

After several weeks batches of heavily taped, red-ribboned and sealed statements arrived in Jerusalem in quick succession by diplomatic couriers from sixteen different foreign courts. After we glanced through them we knew we had one worry less on our minds, for none of the witnesses went along all the way with Eichmann's version. To be sure, some of them made a marked attempt to be helpful to him and were obviously inclined to picture his activities in a more favorable light, but even they supported him only up to a point and would not go very far. Others failed him completely.

Almost all these witnesses were concerned with whitewashing their own personalities as far as possible and giving an innocent interpretation of their past activities. Especially those who still had pending procedures to face made an obvious effort at "disentanglement." This would have obviously been even more marked and more prejudicial to their veracity had the whole trial taken place in Germany, as the defense had wished.

In any case, almost all of them left Eichmann alone and unsupported on the one issue that might, legally, have been an arguable ground in mitigation: his claim that he had been a mere will-less tool in the hands of others. On this count he could now rely only on his own unsupported statement.

The evidence from abroad was introduced into the court's records. Most of the statements, though highly interesting, did not attract much attention at the time, for they were only recorded on paper. Important as they were for the court and for historians, they went almost unobserved by the general public, since the living and colorful personalities who made the statements remained hidden behind the walls of sixteen judges' chambers.

❋

Some witnesses made an effort to do something for an ex-comrade. Hermann Krumey, Eichmann's previous close associate, was one of them, but his own pending trial in Frankfurt must have cramped his style.

The only reason why he had written to IV-B-4 on the Lidice children, he claimed, was that these were "transport matters." The fact that the children were delivered to him for "special treatment" did not necessarily mean they were to be killed.

"At that time, we did not, to my mind, construe the word '*Sonderbehandlung*' [special treatment] in the sense of extermination. We meant that these children required some special handling."

"So why did you have to contact Eichmann's department about it at all?" Shimron asked.

"Because they dealt with all our transport matters and the children had to be moved further on. I wanted to know where to."

"But the express instructions in this cable here said that the children were to bring along nothing with them and that they required no extra care. Isn't it obvious what kind of 'special treatment' was in store for them?"

"I cannot remember today having received this cable, and anyway I did look after the children," he replied.

It will be remembered that the greater part of the children perished and were never heard of again.

In Budapest Krumey had been subordinate to Eichmann, though they held the same rank. "I always considered him my superior," he said. Krumey knew that Eichmann had had a hand in the Hungarian deportations, hastening to add: "He did not, on the whole, have much to do in Budapest; he stayed little at the office and led a busy private life."

Krumey remembered having received money from the Jews of Budapest. "Wisliceny was with me at the time," he said. The money was delivered in a leather suitcase. "There must have been some negotiations going on," he added, but he never knew what it was all about. Later, with Hunsche, he received more money, he said.

He never told Joel Brand, as the latter claimed, that apart from Eichmann there were "other decent SS men," like himself. He knew that Becher and Kastner were negotiating abroad; he even escorted them twice into Switzerland. But he did not know what the negotiations were really about. It was some matter of certain trucks. Yes, he confirmed his earlier evidence that he had seen the *Fussmarsch* from Budapest and even spoken to Eichmann about it. "To my remonstrances he replied: 'Forget about it. You did not see anything.' But never did any anti-Semitic remarks fall from Eichmann's lips, nor did he ever maltreat a single Jew."

He admitted having been "sort of Eichmann's deputy in Budapest," but he never dealt with deportations. He certainly did not know what had happened to the deported Jews. He must have heard of it much later, from Kastner. He could not be sure whether the word Auschwitz was mentioned. Anyway, he went to Eichmann to inquire about these revelations, and Eichmann said: "So what!"

"I was later transferred from Hungary, since my friendship for Jews was no longer bearable," Krumey said, managing to keep a straight face. "But it was not Eichmann who had me transferred."

He always had the impression that Eichmann fought shy of responsibility, for when Krumey was still in Litzmannstadt "Eichmann would always demand that requests for trains be put in writing," which Krumey considered "exaggerated."

On this and similar utterances Eichmann later developed a whole theory in his own evidence that it was known "by everybody" and "even held against him" that he never undertook anything of his own initiative.

Krumey said he agreed to testify provided Eichmann was permitted to give evidence for him in his own pending case in Frankfurt. We were approached on this by the West German authorities and made all provisions for a hearing. But Eichmann refused to testify and persisted in his refusal even when directly appealed to by the representative of the Ludwigsburg Center to assist the West German administration of justice.

Apparently Eichmann did not feel obligated to help Krumey; did he expect Krumey, who was more sheltered and less exposed than he was, to take a greater share of the responsibility on himself?

*

There had been two prime witnesses whom Dr. Servatius had been particularly insistent on bringing to Israel in person in order to testify—Walter Huppenkothen and Dr. Wilhelm Hoettl. He claimed that they were vital for the defense, and that if promised safe-conduct they would be willing to come.

They had both been high-ranking Nazis, and allowing them to come and go with impunity involved both legal and political issues. I had wanted to consult the Cabinet, whom I told that for my part I was willing to grant Dr. Servatius' request. No objection was made, so I announced in open court that both Hoettl and Huppenkothen would come to Israel and leave unmolested; they would not be put on trial. "Not even if they incriminate themselves in cross-examination?" Dr. Servatius had inquired. "That is right," I replied. "They will not be charged here for any of their past acts." But though we made elaborate provisions for their safety neither came; they both preferred to testify at home, like all the other defense witnesses.

Wilhelm Hoettl, alias Walter Hagen, lives today at Bad Aussee, Austria, where he is principal of a private high school. During the war he was an SS colonel and a leading officer in the counterespionage services, whose workings he later described in a book entitled *The Secret Front*. His colorful career had its ups and downs and brought him into contact with many important personalities on both sides.

In Rome he observed the disintegration of the Fascist regime and was in close contact with the Vatican. Toward the end of the war he undertook a mysterious mission to Allen Dulles. It is supposed that he disclosed information that saved the lives of Allied soldiers and, in exchange, was promised personal immunity. He was never prosecuted.

Hoettl had been in touch with Eichmann until October, 1941, and two and a half years later in Budapest, where Hoettl was sent in March, 1944, to keep an eye on everything and everybody in Southeast Europe.

He did not know whether Eichmann had ever enjoyed "special powers" outside his department, "but Jewish affairs throughout Germany were certainly his exclusive business." In Hungary Eichmann no doubt enjoyed "a certain special status."

In August, 1944, Eichmann came to see Hoettl in Budapest to learn of the latest developments on the front. He was very nervous and upset, since the Russians had defeated Rumania, where he was going at the time, and were threatening the whole of Southern Europe. Eichmann said that there was no hope for him in the event of a collapse, since he was considered a top war criminal for his share in the destruction of Jews. To Hoettl's question he replied, in confidence, that four million Jews had been liquidated in the camps and two million more by *Einsatzgruppen* shootings. He added that Himmler considered the actual figure to be even higher. Eichmann had been drinking heavily at the time, Hoettl recalled, but he was obviously sober during this conversation. Hoettl went back on his Nuremberg affidavit, in which he swore that Eichmann had admitted having "millions of Jewish lives on his conscience," but still maintained that "the best way to describe Eichmann's job would be to say that he was the great forwarding agent of death."

Hoettl's long evidence is full of historical material, but he too tried to keep away from Eichmann as much as possible.

There is no mystery about Walter Huppenkothen, who is now an official in Cologne and was in his more prosperous days a leading figure at the Gestapo. For over a year he served as Commander of the Security Police in the notorious Lublin District, from which he was transferred to Berlin just when Globocnik was completing his extermination centers there. In the capital, he headed Department IV-E of the RSHA, which dealt with frontier control and espionage. There he rose to be Heinrich Mueller's deputy as Gestapo Chief, with the rank of SS Colonel.

Huppenkothen also tried to do something, though not too much, for a friend in need.

In 1946, in Nuremberg, he had sworn an affidavit that was used in the defense of the Gestapo, which was charged there as an organization. In this statement Huppenkothen had described the functioning of the Gestapo apparatus, deposing, among other things, that Eichmann enjoyed a "special position" (*Sonderstellung*), with the obvious intention of exonerating the organization as a whole from responsibility for Eichmann's deeds. Now he testified that he would rather say that Eichmann enjoyed "a special status"—*besondere Stellung*—("semantic hair-splitting," said our court in its judgment on the distinction) since, in contrast to the other department heads, he was an SD man, whose attachment to the Gestapo was more formal.

"Would you still deny him 'a special position' if you knew that he had direct contacts with Heydrich, Kaltenbrunner and Himmler?" Shimron asked. "Then I would say that he did enjoy an extraordinary status" was the reluctant reply.

Mueller, the head of the office, always kept more important decisions to himself, the witness said; moreover, Mueller too would always ask for instructions from higher quarters on matters outside normal routine. According to Huppenkothen, the dreaded Head of the Gestapo was overcautious—one might say "cowardly." "It is true," said Huppenkothen, "that Mueller sometimes assigned special duties to persons who were not the competent officials for such tasks, and without the knowledge of the directly responsible head of department. This even caused adverse comments in the office. . . . But," he added, "it happened mostly, though not exclusively, in matters pertaining to the fight against Communism, Mueller's special hobby."

"Did it happen to your knowledge in Eichmann's department?"

"I cannot say; I had no close contacts with Eichmann," said Huppenkothen, as anxious as all defense witnesses to place himself at some distance from the accused. "We had no practical common activities. The only close contact I remember was that he took me with him in his car to Prague to attend Heydrich's funeral."

So the defense had some support from this witness for the "special missions" claim.

This argument was played up to the full in his evidence by Eichmann, for whom this sufficed to enable him to speak of Mueller's "notorious habit" of imposing "special tasks" on his favorites. Thus Eichmann now deposited all his most sinister jobs on the doorstep of his deputy Guenther on "the special assignment" theory.

Still, even this evidence was a far cry from what Eichmann really needed.

Another old-time Nazi, Dr. Horst Grell, soft-pedaled some of his earlier statements on Eichmann. He had joined the party in 1929 and the SS in 1933. He was a Foreign Ministry career man, and had climbed the professional ladder until he became a counselor at the embassy in Budapest at a crucial period. He, too, had testified at Nuremberg; now he confirmed that in autumn of 1944 Eichmann had told him in Budapest that he was "Number One" on the Allies' list of war criminals, since he had on his conscience the lives of six million human beings. He did not mention Jews, and Grell had thought at the time, so he now maintained, that this was boasting, on the principle of "the more enemies, the more glory."

On other points Grell was as helpful to the defense as he could be.

"Yes," he replied to a defense question, "it was true that Eichmann was employed exclusively on the technical side of the Jewish transports from Hungary."

"Who was the deciding factor in the carrying out of these deportations?"

"Well, obviously, the Hungarian Government."

"Were they told of the ultimate goal of these deportations?"

"No, and anyway nobody there spoke about deportations. The operations were carried out under the title 'Jewish measures in Hungary.' "

But he did not like Dr. Servatius' referring to him as "the adviser on Jewish affairs" at the embassy in Budapest. "I had nothing to do with Jewish affairs," he said, adding inconsequentially: "My job in Budapest was to separate Jews of neutral and enemy nationalities from local Jews and to keep the Foreign Ministry in Berlin fully informed of all the measures which were taken."

The Kistarcsa operation, he remembered, was all carried out by Eichmann's unit behind the embassy's back and contrary to the agreement between the German and Hungarian authorities; but the statement Grell had given in 1948 for the defense of Veesenmayer, in which he had heavily implicated Eichmann in this affair, was prompted, he now claimed, by "the understandable tendency" to lift the burden from the accused in Nuremberg and blame those who were missing or dead. "It is not, however, an untrue statement," he said; "it is merely incomplete." Now Grell supplemented it by saying that "Eichmann was not and could not be the man of initiative or of decision in his sphere." He was merely implementing orders, though he was "a specially good and ambitious worker who tried to do justice to his duties with all the means at his disposal."

This much "neutralizing" of Eichmann's activity and personality was as far as Grell went in his "understandable tendency" to help him.

But Eichmann was unhappy with this evidence; he had obviously expected Grell to go back on his earlier dangerous assertion about the war criminals list. He gave the lie to Grell. "I could not have said that I had the death of several million people on my head, for I do not even have a single one on my conscience," he remarked bitterly.

*

Among the witnesses who steered a middle course between prosecution and defense was the former Chief of the Jewish Affairs Department at the Foreign Ministry and Eichmann's contact man there, Dr. Eberhard von Thadden.

Before testifying, he wanted to make sure whether giving evidence at the request of a foreign country (Israel) was consistent with his previous position in the German public service. On receiving the examining judge's assurance that this must have been looked into by the competent authorities before he was summoned, this punctilious Nazi admitted that he had been in close touch with Eichmann on various matters, including the deportations.

He could not say, however, whether in any particular matter Eichmann had acted singlehanded or on instructions. In any case, Eichmann had "never overreached his own competence as a department chief."

"Was your office in a position to get him overruled in any specific case?"

"For that the personal intervention of the Foreign Ministry or of the Staatssekretaer [Permanent Under Secretary] was necessary." Even then it was successful only in one case that he could remember. When the Swedes wanted the children of the Bondy family, and Eichmann refused to let them go in spite of the Foreign Office's repeated representations, Eichmann still refused, even in April, 1945, on the very brink of defeat. The Staatssekretaer took it up with Eichmann's superior and the permit was then transmitted from higher up.

"What about the requests for exceptions for Jews in specific cases?"

"Eichmann was most determinedly opposed to any single relaxation, and whenever I pleaded with him for one he would say that I was a weakling," said the witness.

But it was from the Hungarian period that von Thadden had angry recollections. He had been appalled, he said, at Eichmann's scheme for the detention of all the Jews of Budapest, which, for reasons of foreign policy, he had regarded as untenable.

"I personally was furious about that plan," he said. "It originally involved the arrest of all the Jews of Budapest in the course of one night and their internment on an island in the Danube. At the Foreign Ministry we were determined to prevent, or at least delay, it."

"Eichmann's *Sonderkommando* in Hungary was, to my knowledge, independent of Veesenmayer. They acted according to their own firm plans," von Thadden admitted.

Another Foreign Ministry man called by the defense was Dr. Edmund Veesenmayer. He had spent in jail only a fraction of the twenty years' sentence imposed on him in the Ministries Case, but he still had not lived it down. When giving evidence now in Darmstadt he was mainly mindful of his own image. He was "the nonremembering" witness. He could not remember what Eichmann's competence in Hungary had been; he had never been told what Eichmann was sent to Budapest for. He himself had never even received any instructions about his own duties there. They had just put him on a train in Salzburg and told him to proceed to Budapest, where he was an ordinary ambassador, "never a plenipotentiary." He had not even submitted his credentials to Horthy till two weeks after his arrival. He had never taken part in anti-Jewish measures.

Veesenmayer's evidence was simply ludicrous, and I did not ask the court to refer to any part of it. When Dr. Servatius called this defense witness a liar, I did not argue with him.

Kurt Becher's evidence in Bremen did not add much to what he had said years before in Nuremberg. Now a rich businessman, Becher did not like to talk much about his wartime experiences. He claimed to have forgotten many things, but he still "remembered the fight for the Jews in Budapest, and for the survivors of the camps." He openly admitted that he had entered into the negotiations of exchanging Jews for goods on Himmler's express instructions: "Promise them what they want; what we shall keep—we shall see." But then he felt, he said, that Eichmann was sabotaging him for evading even Himmler's orders. So he complained to the Reichsfuehrer and, as a result, Himmler had them both summoned and dramatically made it clear to Eichmann that if he had so far been killing Jews on Himmler's orders he would now have to nurse them, if Himmler so required.

The former chief of military administration of Salonika, Dr. Max Merten, who had been pardoned after receiving a twenty-five-year sentence from a Greek court, was an attorney in Berlin, where he had entered the political arena. A great part of his testimony was taken up with an attempt to reconcile his statements at his own trial with his present evidence. He now claimed that, together with Eichmann, he had saved twenty thousand Jews. This was such an obvious lie that it did not do Eichmann much good, and Dr. Servatius declared that he would not "avail himself" of this evidence at all.

Nor could the defense derive satisfaction from the former commander of the Security Police of Rome, Herbert Kappler, who was serving a sentence of life imprisonment in Italy. He claimed that he was opposed at the time to the arrest and deportation of the Jews of Rome, but Eichmann's man, Theodor Dannecker, had carried out the task all the same. Before 1945 he had never heard of Eichmann, and no orders bearing his name had ever reached him. Kappler admitted that he had received a bribe of fifty kilograms of gold from the Jews of Rome, but he had done so "as a last attempt to avoid the razzia that Dannecker had planned," hoping that Jewish money would avert the disaster.

Franz Novak, in civilian life a printing press expert, had been the transport expert of the Gestapo. It was his task to make sure that the trains allocated to Eichmann in principle were ready to move whenever the office instructed him where the Jews were to be evacuated from and where they had to go. It was he who had drawn up the huge train timetables of the great population movement and maintained contact with the Railroad Directorate.

Germany had had long experience in developing the railroad into a national military machine. "Build no more fortresses, build railroads," was old Moltke's order to the General Staff at the beginning of the century. Novak was assigned to put this strategic master key to good use on the Jewish front, from the beginning of the operations in 1939, and he grew with the job when activities were extended to cover all Europe.

He had stayed with Eichmann all through the war years, though he "usually received orders from Guenther," he said. He could say little about Eichmann's powers and range of duties. As was to be expected, he "had never heard of Kistarcsa and never been to the place." This statement was not surprising for at the time he himself, as well as Krumey and Hunsche, was awaiting trial for complicity in the Kistarcsa affair.

But he did admit having taken part in the decisive railway conference of May, 1944, in Vienna, at which the huge operation of transporting Hungarian Jews to Auschwitz was mapped out. Novak said he never enjoyed any very special status, nor was he called upon to perform extraordinary functions. He had dealt exclusively with transport, he said.

Surely this man's job was the pattern that Eichmann imitated in shaping his own image when he presented himself to the court as a man who could be blamed for no more than supplying information from behind a counter on the departure time of the next train to Auschwitz.

Some of the defense witnesses were, in effect, strongly incriminating.

One such testimony was taken at Nuremberg. General Erich von dem Bach-Zelewski of the Waffen SS, who had managed to steer himself into freedom after numerous quite unorthodox wartime performances, was now under detention there on a charge of having been implicated in the murder of a German civilian before the war. He was the man who boasted of having supplied Hermann Goering with the poison with which he escaped the gallows at the last moment. He got near enough to the Nazi leader to pass over the small vial with a handshake, which was strictly against prison rules. He said he had fooled the guards by practicing for weeks exaggerated salutes and gestures of greeting whenever he passed near Goering in the courthouse detention corridors. Upon being disbelieved he went to the length, some time later, of producing to official investigators a second vial of poison, whose markings were identical with those on glass splinters found in Goering's mouth. So this bragging that he had spared Goering the shame of the gallows seems to have had substance.

Now called as a witness for the defense, Bach-Zelewski claimed that, till the beginning of our case and on the basis of what he had heard in the Nuremberg jail, he "always assumed that Eichmann's name was imaginary." He thought it was a kind of code name for an operation. He had never seen Eichmann in the flesh. He knew that the *Einsatzgruppen* were directed from the RSHA, but could not say whether Eichmann had in any way influenced them.

"I never got the reports of the *Einsatzgruppen*," he said, "though I was in charge of combating partisans and ought to have been informed. If Eichmann was on the distribution list of these reports, it would underline the importance of his office."

"The SS was a knight's order," the general said. "The essential characteristic of a man's position there was the relationship of trust with the superior. Himmler would hand-pick people for jobs from case to case, without any consideration for their ranks. It was the commission which was all-important. A lower rank could not, of course, in the ordinary way issue orders to a higher rank; he would do so on behalf of the superior. In the choice of people for filling important posts, Himmler's confidence, the man's *Weltanschauung* and his personal fitness for the assignment were the qualities that counted."

This explained Eichmann's relatively inconspicuous rank.

The second point in Bach-Zelewski's evidence concerned an SS officer's chance of getting out of a task that he could not stand.

"The possibility of avoiding an assignment by applying for a transfer was open. In a particular case this might involve some disciplinary action, but there was certainly no jeopardy to life."

Eichmann's claim that he could not have got a transfer was thus belied by his own witness.

The former Senior SS and Police Leader in Budapest, General of the Police Otto Winkelmann, was a professional police officer who had served under the Weimar Republic and stayed in office under the Nazis. The choice of a regular police officer as Himmler's personal representative in Budapest was an obvious cover for the "irregular" activities of the SS unit there, mainly Eichmann's. Winkelmann did not deny that he received regular reports of what Eichmann's unit was doing. Nor did he claim that he did anything about it. "I took notice of it and kept my thoughts to myself," he said. Eichmann was attached to him formally, but took orders directly from the RSHA in Berlin. He remembered the dreadful trek on foot from Budapest, to which General Juettner had also drawn his attention. He could not say whether Eichmann's name had been mentioned in this context. (Juettner was examined at the Court of Bad Toelz and testified that Winkelmann had told him at the time that he had nothing to do with the matter, and that Eichmann was the man responsible.) He knew that Himmler gave the order to stop the *Fussmarsch.*

Winkelmann did not like Eichmann. "He had the nature of a subaltern, which means a fellow who uses his power recklessly, without moral restraints. He would certainly overstep his authority if he thought he was acting in the spirit of his commander."

It is interesting that our witness Dean Grueber, testifying in Jerusalem almost at the same time, appraised Eichmann in terms very similar to those used by Winkelmann in Bordersholm. "Eichmann was what we called in German a *Landsknecht,*" said Dean Grueber, "by which we meant a man who, when he puts on his uniform, leaves his conscience and his reason in the wardrobe."

After all these years some witnesses had not forgotten Eichmann's manner of speech in those days. "His jargon was hard," recalled von Thadden. "His dialect was very insolent," said Hoettl. "He was arrogant," said Winkelmann.

Most damaging testimony came from Professor Alfred Six, today an advertising consultant in Kressbronn, and under the Nazis one of the important figures in the SD Head Office, where he attained the rank of brigadier general. A Nazi since 1930, he was professor of law and political science at the universities of Koenigsberg and Berlin, and the commander of *Vorkommando-Moskau* in *Einsatzgruppe* B. At the trial of the *Einsatzgruppen* he was sentenced to twenty years' imprisonment, and escaped conviction on the gravest charge because the court said that "it could not conclude with scientific certitude that Six took an active part in the murder program." Like most of the Nazis convicted at the time, he had served only a small part of the sentence, and had no fear of further prosecutions.

After some time in the *Einsatzgruppen* Six had enough of it, was recalled at his request to Berlin, and ultimately landed in the Foreign Office, where he dealt with intelligence affairs. He had watched Eichmann's career since its beginnings in the SD Head Office in 1937, and later had a good opportunity to observe him in action, on and off, at the RSHA from different vantage points. Nor did Six mince words about him. "Eichmann was an absolute and unconditional believer in National Socialism. His whole outlook was filled with it. It was his world. In case of doubt he would invariably act according to the most extreme interpretation of the party doctrine," he declared.

"It was beyond any doubt," said Six, "that Eichmann had much greater powers than other department chiefs." He had many people working for him, and "the general impression at the RSHA was that he was not really under Mueller's command but was actually quite close to him." It was known, said Six, that Eichmann had direct access to Heydrich and Kaltenbrunner. Since Mueller dealt mainly with internal security and Communists, Eichmann became virtually independent. "When it was found expedient to do something for an individual Jew, I would never go to Eichmann, who was the exponent of the other side." In such a case, Six said, he would approach a chief of the German mission abroad or would go to Schellenberg.

Six also confirmed that it was possible to get a posting from the RSHA and go to the front if one so chose. "I did so myself," he said, "and nothing serious happened to me apart from a personal disagreement with Heydrich. All I suffered was minor discomfort in my career. . . . There were cases of SD leaders who were transferred elsewhere from RSHA at their own request. There was a possibility of getting a transfer to service at the front, or being released for an entirely different assignment."

Six thereby virtually kicked one of Eichmann's main supports from under him.

Other defense witnesses added little new. Richard Baer, the last Commandant of Auschwitz, claimed never to have seen Eichmann. He refused to answer most questions, since these might incriminate him in his own case, which was pending. But he did not live to stand trial; he died in jail before it started.

The evidence abroad was rapidly and efficiently taken. There were fewer mishaps than might have been expected. The judge in Bremen allowed Becher to see the questionnaire in advance, which was unfortunate, for it seriously reduced the value of his evidence. The judge in Bad Aussee, Austria, did not agree to adjourn the hearing of Dr. Hoettl till the parties' representatives could appear before him, but proceeded to take the evidence himself. He not only interrogated the witness on the prepared questions, but plunged deeply into the matter, which resulted in a full three days' hearing and a testimony of historical interest stretching to seventy pages. In conclusion, the judge admonished the witness to remain at the court's disposal till the end of the Jerusalem trial, since the parties might wish to renew the hearing and examine him orally, and declared: "The historic importance of the Eichmann case requires that this court should exhaust all possibilities of helping to find out the truth. . . . It would be most regrettable if anything was neglected in this respect." Both parties found that there was already enough in Hoettl's investigation; we did not need to trouble the Austrian court again.

The evidence for the defense left Eichmann almost where he was before, if not worse off. His disappointment was clearly visible; he obviously felt he had been let down and did not conceal his chagrin. "It is certainly strange if Dr. Six now takes it out on a minor official," he said bitterly. For his former friends and colleagues did not depict him as a minor lackey, as he wanted them to do; nor did any of them take even a part of Eichmann's guilt on himself. Those who were already tried and sentenced, like Six and Veesenmayer, could have done so with relative impunity, but they did not even pass on the blame to the "missing" Guenther, as Eichmann obviously expected them to do. Nobody wanted to stick out his neck for him. As I later learned, his arrogance, hauteur and rough treatment of people had made him so personally unpopular that not a single one of his erstwhile associates and friends wished to come openly to his aid. The very qualities to which he had owed his rise to power now turned against him. When the evidence from abroad was read out in open court, statement after statement, Eichmann was manifestly wrathful and frustrated.

CHAPTER

20

The Summations

The time had come to sum up the case. We were given several days to prepare the final addresses, the hearing of which began on August 8. It was my turn to begin.

I started by reminding the court of the system that in our lifetime has menaced the freedom of man and the life of nations. The shades of Adolf Hitler and his villainous crew, those ghouls whom humanity will always remember as the extreme embodiment of evil, still hovered over the world. Eichmann was like his master, I said: glib-tongued and full of prevarications when it suited him, as a mask for a murderous fury to be unleashed when the time was ripe.

"For two months the survivors of this terrible holocaust have taken their places on the witness stand and given their testimony here; each has told a fraction of that terrible tragedy about which he was asked to testify, until the picture of the great horror emerged. We were shocked to hear of murder, brutality, tortures and atrocities which, had they not been described by living men and women, it would have been impossible to believe were perpetrated by human beings. We have heard of acts of cruelty and lust for evil, degradation, oppression of body and soul, the like of which have never been known in the annals of mankind. We were shaken by Auschwitz, the 'ashen planet' which the Nazis sent into orbit in the skies of Europe, from whose soil Jewish blood welled forth like a fountain. . . .

"I believe that if any man should try to imagine a nightmare, he would not succeed in inventing even one tiny fraction of the appalling tales that have been presented and described here.

"All these things have been heard by the man who sits in the glass dock. It might have been expected that today at least, sixteen years after the heads of the Nazi hydra were severed, he would utter one word of regret and repentance, one syllable of remorse. Instead, he has declared that he does not believe in regret; it would be childish, for the dead cannot be restored to life.

"Later we saw him skulking among the documents, brazenly denying facts that cry out from every piece of evidence, searching for excuses and pretexts, every one of which is designed to conceal and cover up his own liability for the ocean of blood that has been spilled. To achieve this, he has been ready to deny his own statements, to recant his own confessions, to claim that documents have been forged, that witnesses—even his own testimony—are mistaken, that reports are false and that phrases in official papers are incorrect. That is what he has to say in the face of what he himself calls one of the most terrible crimes in the history of humanity. There is no escape from the question that has faced us in this court from the very first day: in what cast were they molded, those whose deeds these were, those who created such realities and who thus defend themselves when the time comes to face justice?"

I reminded the court of the words spoken by the counsel for the defense: "The depth of suffering on the one hand and the heights of power on the other. The world of the Caesars knows no tears," he said.

"True," I replied. "Tears are known only to him who has a human heart within him, who is capable of being moved by the sufferings of his fellow men. He that has a heart of stone is neither moved nor shocked, even when he is brought face to face for over two months with the horror of his hideous actions.

"Indeed, two worlds face each other here. But the world of the dictator is not in the heights of humanity, but in the depths of hatred. It is the world of the victims that has brought to all men on earth the tidings that were proclaimed on Sinai as the supreme command, 'Thou shalt do no murder.'

"Thus Israel has stood from days of yore face to face with men of hatred, vengeance and arrogance. Thus stood the forefathers and thus the children too will stand."

*

The way of the Nazi is a way of no return, I said.

"It is horrifying to realize that whoever set his foot on this path no longer has a way back to human values, for this doctrine destroys his heart and transforms him into a cold block of ice and marble wrapped up in documents, orders, instructions and proclamations. It is with these that the accused and his like try to protect themselves when they find themselves in the hands of the law. Truth and falsehood no longer have any normal meaning for such men. Truth is whatever serves their purpose. Falsehood is whatever hinders them. If there is regret in their hearts, it is because their loathsome work was not completed. If there is sorrow, it is because the means that were chosen were not effective enough to complete this task. After this poison has penetrated into the soul and the subject has broken free from his duty as a human being to weigh moral values and examine his path by the light of conscience, the ground has already been prepared for the phenomenon that was named 'The Final Solution.' There were no more impediments any more, no further brakes on crime. On the contrary, there was justification, enthusiasm and the ardent desire to carry out the evil design loyally to the end. This was the regime that created the 'cyclists,' as Dean Grueber called them, who trampled those beneath them and bowed down to those above them, displaying joyful, heel-clicking, fawning obedience to their superior, whatever his orders might be. This and more: a complete casting off of moral restraints, of what they called 'bourgeois morality,' for the achievement of the supreme goal. For this purpose anything was permissible—falsehood, deceit, slander and murder. In their own eyes and those of their friends they remained decent people and good citizens; not only were they not assailed by pangs of conscience, but they even considered themselves divine figures who could and would carry out the terror to the full."

"This was no mass hypnosis in which men were gripped without possibility of liberation. It was an act of the will, deliberate and conscious. On the part of the gang of criminals who came to power it was also a matter of meticulous and careful calculation. For the wave of evil raised to positions of high authority and tremendous power men who saw in Nazism an opportunity for a career and a share in the administration, a good life for their families and comfortable living conditions for themselves, and who for these ends were prepared to give support to any abominable conspiracy."

Recalling Eichmann's statement, made in Israel, that he should be permitted to hang himself in public as a warning to future generations, I said: "Such ideas did not trouble him when he declared at the end of the war that he would jump laughing into his grave because he had dragged millions of Jews with him. Nor was he later ready to stand trial for his deeds and to face punishment for what he had done; that was why he escaped and went into hiding under an assumed name."

He had "relapsed" from time to the old ways, he said in court, when confronted with the Sassen text. "Relapsed to what?" I asked. Twelve years after the end of the war, when there existed no bond of oath between him and his dead leader, when there was no overhanging fear of orders and punishments, he still adhered to the belief in murder and extermination, expressing to Sassen his profound regret that Jewry had somehow survived, despite all his efforts.

*

Eichmann's deeds now came under review, but from a different angle than in the opening address. It was no longer a sketch of a planned scheme of proof, as it was when I opened the case, but the description of a completed structure. I could now speak of demonstrated facts and proven testimony. The accumulated facts would now fall into their designated places, the documents submitted would be channeled, each to its relevant point, and the answers elicited in cross-examination would assume their indicative meaning. It was the time fully to unveil the construction of the prosecution, painstakingly erected in the course of these months.

This was the summing up. Its purpose was to persuade and convince. It called again for a deliberate effort to argue and to speak without passion. Still, the whole subject was so steeped in drama and tears that I often heard loud sobs behind me from the overcrowded courtroom.

Before reviewing the evidence, I recalled that Eichmann did not deny the holocaust, nor its hideous atrocities. All that was related in court about the ghettos, the tortures, the murders, the malice, the blood lust, the killing of babies, all this he did not question. "That an inferno engulfed Europe—worse than Dante's, for here it was forbidden even to sigh or shed a tear—this he admits too." But he maintains that he was not responsible. Others spilled the blood: Hitler, Himmler, Heydrich, Kaltenbrunner, Mueller, Pohl and Hoess, but not he.

Let us then, I continued, review the facts of the huge conspiracy to exterminate Jewry, which was a multistage process and developed as it went along. First, they threw the Jews out; later they assaulted them, assembled them and deported them; lastly, they destroyed them. "In all these stages Eichmann fulfilled an executive task of first importance."

I began with the already familiar early life of the accused: his days in Vienna, his purge of Jews in Austria. This was the period of his "creative joy." His argument that he had helped the Jews when they were in a tough spot was typical of his cynicism.

"A band of robbers who set fire to a house on all four sides and throw the owners through the window, robbing them in the process, cannot argue that it was better, after all, for the landlord to be thrown out of the window than to be burned alive in the house.

"The conspirators in the early stage of the crime against the Jews, those who dealt with arrests, deportations, setting fire to synagogues, the spoliation of property and forced emigration, were men of the SD and the Gestapo. Each of these scoundrels had a defined task in this conspiracy; all together they created the conditions from which the Jews fled. The whole apparatus of administration and organization to bring about the flight of people from countries where they and their ancestors had lived for centuries was a network of criminal acts."

The accused was already a full-fledged member when the conspiracy passed to its next sinister phases.

On Eichmann's role at these next stages, the statements of leading Nazis were revealing. They all pinpointed him as the driving force of the gigantic enterprise of the Final Solution. It was inconceivable, after all, that everybody should choose him as the one scapegoat in Jewish matters. He was pointed to by people who were incarcerated in different prisons at the time: Wisliceny in Bratislava, Hoess in Cracow, Mildner and Hoffman in Nuremberg, Endre and Baky in Budapest. Could all these have conspired against him? If a scapegoat was being sought, Mueller was a more likely and obvious choice, as it had rightly occurred to Justice Musmanno when he heard some of these statements.

This was confirmed even by evidence submitted by the defense, like the statement of the Dutch lawyer Mrs. van Taalingen-Dols. But the main proof was in the documents.

The Wannsee Conference minutes pointed to him and hundreds of post-Wannsee documents all marked him down as the chief operations officer of the Final Solution. Of course, the chief of operations had legions of people working with and for him. The signal to start the operation came from above, but once it was given, he proceeded relentlessly. "Because of this central position that Eichmann held in the great conspiracy, he bears criminal responsibility for the acts of the robbers, the murderers and the tormentors, who carried out the despicable work in all its manifestations," I said.

"He is responsible, because of his position in the conspiracy, for all that happened to the Jewish people from the shores of the Arctic Ocean to the Aegean Sea, from the Pyrenees to the Urals. His criminal responsibility derives from a legal principle that is very close to the principle of conspiracy, and that is the principle of complicity in crime."

Then I proceeded to analyze the general rules of our law, which follows the accepted common law principle that every person must be presumed to intend the probable consequences of his acts and must be held responsible for them. Each conspirator is, in law, considered an agent for the others. Our Supreme Court has laid down that "once this unholy alliance has been concluded and all the conspirators have agreed among themselves, they become criminal 'Siamese twins,' no longer separable." It is not even necessary that the conspirators act in concert or know each other.

I was well aware that all precedents and examples originating from serious "peacetime causes" sounded hollow and inappropriate in this case, for which there was hardly a precedent. But I had to draw mainly on legal principles established by "ordinary" crimes, with such further illustrations as the postwar trials afforded.

The fact that Eichmann had committed his crimes as a member of the state apparatus was no defense. The International Military Court laid this down with regard to all persons in his position. It said: "They cannot be regarded as innocent because they were used by Hitler if they knew what they were doing. The fact that they were assigned to their task by a dictator does not exonerate them from responsibility for their acts."

The oath of loyalty can be no excuse. I quoted from Justice Musmanno's judgment in the Concentration Camps case:

> Each and every person who took his oath surrendered his personality, gave up his right of individual judgment and self-criticism, threw to the winds his understanding and exposed himself to the winds of moral irresponsibility. This was the poisonous root that brought forth the tree under whose branches the horrible crimes were perpetrated. This oath of loyalty by itself is an act of sacrilege and a base crime and cannot serve either as a justification or an explanation for the crimes which were perpetrated by virtue of this alleged loyalty.

The mere fact that he had kept his post at the Gestapo headquarters during the entire war, as the head of the "Jewish affairs department" for almost six years, without having been transferred or relieved, was in itself proof of his inner attitude to his job. Had he displayed the slightest moral doubts, or given any indication of having grown tired of his post at the nerve center of the Final Solution, his superiors would have replaced him immediately; for it was an enterprise demanding constant effort, calling for callousness, harshness and extraordinary cunning. But he was not replaced; on the contrary, a gigantic death machine was placed at his disposal.

He had admitted in cross-examination having told Sassen: "When I realized that this was necessary, I implemented it with the fanaticism a man would expect of himself as a veteran National Socialist."

*

After expounding the principles of criminal association and complicity, I reviewed the specific evidence that, in addition to his central position in the conspiracy, directly linked Eichmann with the crimes committed on every front of the Final Solution. I showed that he also had a direct hand in all decisive activities, beginning with ghettoization, through the *Einsatzgruppen* killings and the deportations up to the extermination in the concentration camps.

The court inquired, as I knew it would, why we had not submitted more documents connecting Eichmann with the events in Poland. "In Germany this is not surprising—there they did a fairly good job of destroying the documents though a very few local archives were saved. What about local archives in Poland?" asked the presiding judge. "Hans Frank, the Governor General, testified that everything had been destroyed there too; all instruments were burnt, with the exception of his diary, which he carried with him," I replied. Every now and again a few documents were found there. Only in 1960, fifteen years after the war, had the official Polish Committee for the Investigation of Hitlerite Crimes in Poland submitted the documents on the early deportations of 1939-40 and Department IV-D-4 of the Gestapo. The fact had been hitherto unknown.

Then I reviewed Eichmann's over-all authority in the camps, beginning with Theresienstadt and Bergen-Belsen, and passing on to the camps of the Lublin area and to Auschwitz. Everywhere there remained clear imprints either of his authority or of his active participation. "Hoess confirmed that all the '*Transportjuden*'—these were all Jews sent away for no particular 'offense,' all the victims of the Final Solution—were dispatched by Eichmann's office. Their delivery notes invariably bore the markings IV-B-4, RSHA and the remark 'The transport conforms to the standing orders and should be put to *Sonderbehandlung* [special treatment].' *Sonderbehandlung* meant death." Moreover, Hoess had confirmed that Eichmann also had full authority over the fate of those Jews who were temporarily spared for labor.

I surveyed the position in Eastern Europe and in other territories, and summed up: "The campaign to uproot the Jews was carried on in the west and north and south of Europe, and in the capital of each satellite country or occupied territory a representative sat who was formally subordinate to someone else, but who actually received direct instructions from Eichmann. The attack on Jewish centers was carried out in France, Holland, Belgium, Slovakia, Yugoslavia, Bulgaria, Rumania, Norway, Denmark, Greece and Italy. At the very same time actions were continued within the Reich and the Protectorate, and the colossal juggernaut crushed the Jews of Poland and Soviet Russia. The network was spread all over occupied Europe and the Jews were trapped by the millions."

Eichmann laid down the directives as to where the Jews would be deported. When questioned about the aim of these deportations he said: "Whatever the case, I never denied that, to my regret, deported Jews were sent to their deaths. I could never deny this."

"Of course, Eichmann could not deny this," I continued, "because he cannot contradict hundreds of documents, claiming that they were *all* forged, that they were *all* mistakes and that they were *all* attempts to distort facts. We know, and he fully admitted it, that he was the deporting authority to extermination camps.

"The pyramid of documents testifies to the hand that was directing these things, and to the man who held sway over these matters."

Finally, the events in Hungary were reviewed. Eichmann's mission there was to carry out one of the major objectives of the takeover of the country. He himself formulated this as "an accelerated evacuation and deportation of all Jews to Auschwitz, combing Hungary for the purpose from east to west. Speed was of the essence, so that the humiliating experience of the Warsaw ghetto uprising should not recur." I recalled Eichmann's treacherous tactics, his deceptively pleasant talk intermingled with threats. These were the methods of a man immersed in his work up to the neck, and not of one who acted "on instructions only."

Eichmann's rejection of the "directive" issued by Hitler himself, who was prepared to let a few Jews out in exchange for the 300,000 Jews of Budapest, and his resumption of the deportations beyond the scope of his orders and against the will of the Hungarians, were evidence of his stature.

"The Kistarcsa affair throws a true light on the man. His lust to send the last Jews to their death, his inviolable resolution to implement the enterprise, his haughtiness and arrogance in carrying out his designs—this is the true Eichmann. It conforms fully with the picture drawn by those witnesses who had the misfortune to come into contact with him. This, too, is the figure that emerges from the documentation. The man who sits here glassed in, humble and reserved, looking for a rat hole to hide in—that is a sham, a fake Eichmann."

I pointed to the unified system of extermination which, even to the smallest details, was carried out everywhere on the same pattern and through the same stages, for it was all directed from one headquarters: the chief of operations at the Jewish section of the Gestapo.

On his position in the hierarchy of the Reich we had the choice between his version—or whatever remained of it after cross-examination—and the evidence of the sixteen hundred documents and the oral witnesses, including some of his own. I then submitted to the court a written brief which was prepared by Bach and Baror, assisted by some Bureau 06 officers, which linked our documentary exhibits to the charges and showed, generally following the opening statement, which point was supported by each single document.

By this time, after speaking for over two sessions, I hoped that the accused was finally restored to his true proportions, and that the facts had torn to pieces the shrunken caricature of an unobtrusive small official, as he persistently wished to paint himself, on the theory of "the big lie" preached by the Nazis, which taught that any falsehood will find some believers if repeated often enough.

Now was the proper time to tackle the defense of "superior orders." First, I said, to constitute a defense it must be a legal order. For it is a rule of all modern systems of law that a manifestly illegal order offers no shield against an indictment. This had become an accepted principle of behavior for anyone who works within a disciplinary framework. He must not commit obviously illegal acts, even if told to do so by persons of higher rank. The hardships of a soldier confronted with the dilemma of disobeying either the law or his commanding officer had been discussed by such legal minds as Dicey, Stephen, Oppenheimer and hundreds of others. It had been recognized that the principle of blind obedience would ultimately undermine discipline itself. Should a soldier obey his sergeant who orders him to shoot a soldier, or to desert, or traitorously to deliver a post to the enemy? The consensus of legal opinion, at any rate insofar as patent crimes were concerned, was that justice was better served by making the perpetrators fully punishable rather than by allowing them to claim the protection of superior authority.

In our own country we had had a terrible case: a number of Arab villagers, including women and children, had been killed by our frontier police when they unwittingly broke curfew regulations imposed while these villagers were working in the fields. This was on the day the Sinai campaign began in October, 1956, when strict security precautions were being taken all along the borders, and an officer had ordered his men to shoot curfew breakers. Fortunately not all the outposts concerned obeyed the order. "We are not crazy," they claimed later. Those who did obey were brought to justice, and the court, in finding them guilty, said:

> The recognizable sign of a manifestly unlawful order is like a black flag that hovers over it, saying: "Don't." Not a formal, hidden or half-hidden illegality, which only learned jurists can discern, but the obvious, clear and apparent lawlessness of the order, which stabs the eye and revolts the heart, if the eye be not blind and the heart depraved—such lawlessness as renders the order manifestly unlawful.

The defense of "superior orders" had been rejected by all postwar tribunals, beginning with Nuremberg, where the International Military Tribunal said:

> It was also submitted on behalf of most of these defendants that in doing what they did they were acting under the orders of Hitler, and therefore cannot be held responsible for the acts committed by them in carrying out these orders. That a soldier was ordered to kill or torture in violation of the international law of war has never been recognized as a defense to such acts of brutality.

Even in Nazi Germany there were similar provisions. German Military Law laid down in Article 47 that no obedience was due to an order that called for the performance of a crime. This was fully applicable to the SS.

Nor do German courts accept the plea today.

Sometimes the fact of having acted under orders might be urged in mitigation of punishment, but this was only when it could be proved that the accused had done nothing more than was called for by the order, and, moreover, had done all he could to mitigate its evil effects.

But Eichmann had even overstepped his authority; he had acted beyond and above the orders given to him. He had done what he was asked to do to the very last moment and to the bitter end. There was not a single case in which he had allowed a Jew to escape, although there were countless opportunities even within the limits of the Final Solution, had he so wished. All he ever had done was to expedite, enthusiastically and zealously, all measures required within the framework of his orders to the fullest extent, and often beyond their framework.

On the argument that the Jews had declared war on Nazi Germany and that the killing of the Jews was a war measure, I recalled that all Dr. Chaim Weizmann had said was: "The fact is that the Western democracies are also fighting for a minimum living space for Jews; their war is our war, their struggle is our struggle."

I added: "The Nazis did not consider the Jews belligerents. What a pity they did not take the Jews to prisoner-of-war camps. Had they done so, millions of Jews would have been saved. But they did exactly the opposite. They exterminated the Jews, root and branch as the war continued, because it offered them an opportunity to do so, as Eichmann said at the time."

*

I paid a tribute to those Gentiles who helped us. "In the darkness that engulfed Europe there were some shining lights. The Jewish people have a long memory; it will never forget its benefactors as it will not forget its foes." I mentioned the noble help of the whole Danish people; the Belgians and Dutch who risked their lives to hide Jews; the Italians who put a spoke in Mussolini's wheel; the Poles who jeopardized their own safety to save Jews; the Lithuanian women who concealed Jewish children; the Yugoslavs and Hungarians who had helped us; the few humane Germans, like Dean Grueber; the Swedes who received the Danish Jews, and their great son Raoul Wallenberg, who by his own efforts saved thousands in Budapest. These heroes usually came from the rank and file of their nations. Their names would be engraved in our memory forever, as we still bore in thankful memory the name of Cyrus of Persia, who enabled the exiles to return to the promised land.

There were other lights in the darkness, too. The Jewish people, abandoned, beaten, surrounded by walls of hatred, rose to deeds of heroism all over Europe. The revolters, the partisans, the Jewish underground, the escapees, those who went to serve and to liberate—they proclaimed: "Never say this is my last road."

I turned to the particulars of the charge sheet and analyzed the indictment point by point, dwelling on special issues. "Torture is not a lesser crime than murder," I said. "Usually, when a criminal is charged with murder, one does not add the smaller charge of torment. But what this creature did to millions of people by sending them to hideous persecution, to the atrocities of Block 11 at Auschwitz, to the horrors of Treblinka and Sobibór, by humiliating and degrading them, by breaking their souls—this will not be forgiven or passed over. Even those who miraculously survived the martyrdom will never be the same again."

Then I went on to discuss the plunder of Jewish property by all kinds of terrorism, compulsion, theft and treachery. "They even made Jews pay for their deportation to the concentration camps." I spoke of the dreadful sterilization experiments, and the crimes against Poles, Gypsies and the children of Lidice.

Finally, I dealt with Eichmann's membership in criminal organizations, which was the subject of three special counts.

"Thus, Your Honors," I concluded, "we have reviewed the revolution which the Nazis resolved to bring about in Europe and throughout the world, to set back the wheels of process, to wipe off the face of the earth the achievements of civilization, and to establish blind obedience to a dictator as the supreme good. Like Attila the Hun, Hitler was a scourge. . . . Attila bragged that wherever his horses had stood no grass would ever grow. Hitler and his accomplices bragged about their brutality, their cruelty, their capacity to kill human beings without a spark of mercy, to raze cities, exterminate nations and liquidate states. There is a limit to the number of people whom an individual can murder as the result of the bloodthirstiness of his character, but there is no limit to the number of people that can be killed through systematic, calculated decisions based on the categorical imperative.

"The Jewish people, to its great tragedy, was the first victim, although there are many signs that, if the Nazis had been victorious, they would not have been the last. . . .

"Multitudes of the Jewish nation are gone and they cannot be brought back to life. To lament their death and their suffering, and to bewail that part of the nation which has been struck down, a new writer of *Lamentations* must arise. But there must be justice for the crime that was perpetrated. I am proud of the fact that the day has come when a man of Israel can speak the language of justice to a captured evildoer. Here in this state, we do not speak to him with pleading and importunity. There is no need to beg for his mercy, no need to bribe him. We do not flee from him, or have to wander in terror from one country to another. Here law and justice prevail. In this period of the return of the exiles of Judea and Jerusalem, justice is being done here; the trial is taking place here for the blood of the righteous that was spilled, as the Prophet Joel foretold. And again I ask you, Judges of Israel, render a just and truthful verdict."

After a weekend recess, Dr. Servatius, the counsel for the defense, rose to reply. Having submitted a voluminous "closing brief" in writing, he opened by accusing me of having narrowed the issue and pinned the entire guilt of the holocaust on Eichmann. Since I had done nothing of the kind I listened to this with astonishment. He said:

"If the arguments of the Attorney General about the will and the desire of the accused were correct, then this should have provoked satisfaction and joy in many circles. Such a description would have been suitable as a basis for a memorial which Jew-haters all over the world could have erected for the accused. Fortunately, however, this foundation consists only of grains of sand collected from various parts.

"The old followers of Hitler would also have been satisfied. Now we know there was no murder order by the Fuehrer.

"It was not Goering and the great paladins who were the guilty ones. They all pointed to Adolf Eichmann. The 'Jew-helper,' Himmler, need not have committed suicide, and Bormann could now emerge from hiding. Everything is now clear. The great guilty one has been found. This would have been the peculiar result of this case. But this is not the true state of affairs."

Dr. Servatius first dealt with the last points in the indictment, maintaining that our law had erroneously concluded from the Nuremberg judgment that the SS, the SD and the Gestapo were criminal organizations. He continued:

"Therefore the prosecution in this trial must prove that these organizations were criminal and to what extent they were so. This was not done. We dispute the criminal character of these organizations. The political leadership abused these organizations; therefore there is no collective guilt of their members."

Then he added a comparison I found difficult to stomach:

"The persecution of a group of people without proving their guilt but only according to the inclination of the legislator is not admissible; this is precisely what Hitler did to the Jews—he dealt with them without issuing any law, without troubling the jurists; he regarded them as members of a criminal organization. It should not be possible to take up this principle and elevate it to the rank of a law. No group or organization must be persecuted collectively; guilt is personal. This is the exclusive basis of responsibility."

I could not understand how it was possible to put on the same level Hitler's treatment of the Jews as a group and the imputation of guilt for belonging to a group that was found through judicial investigation by an International Tribunal to have been a criminal body.

The accusations concerning Poles, Slovenes, Gypsies and the Lidice children should not be tried in Israel, Dr. Servatius said. In claiming to cover such cases, he argued, our law had wrongly extended the jurisdiction of our courts.

"An expansion of legal jurisdiction is limited by international law, which demands that there should exist at least one link between the punishing state and the alleged offender," Dr. Servatius continued. "Crimes against the State of Israel or its citizens cannot serve as this link here, since at the time of these acts the State of Israel did not yet exist. The circumstance that the man committing the deed had been in the State of Israel might also suffice; but even this link does not exist here. Therefore the acts allegedly committed involving foreigners—counts 9 to 13—must be rejected."

Dr. Servatius was actually repeating his preliminary objection, which had been overruled. The truth of the matter is that any civilized country has both a right and a duty to punish crimes against humanity.

On the merits of the charges, Dr. Servatius maintained that the deportation of Poles was "a mass resettlement connected with the utilization of labor."

"Such a relocation of civilian population," he maintained, "is not explicitly forbidden according to the Hague Convention; it is sometimes required for the regulation of certain relationships, and therefore admissible. Here this resettlement was in the nature of an exchange of populations. The accused was not responsible for either the planning or the execution of this resettlement. . . . The accused was brought into the affair only after catastrophes had occurred as a result of wrong measures adopted due to inexperience. He had to take care of hitches in the transport arrangements, and did so."

The Slovenes were resettled on Hitler's orders, Dr. Servatius said. "Here the accused received orders from Heydrich to perform all the duties in the sphere of transport. The resettlement was carried out in a correct fashion."

The accused denied any share in the killing of the Lidice children, Dr. Servatius said; they had been removed from their village by another department of the RSHA. Krumey, who had received the children in Litzmannstadt, "applied to the accused for advice on further measures concerning the children. He did not receive any reply, and then he approached the competent office Bureau III. . . . He had also applied to Bureau IV-B-4 on the assumption that a special treatment was envisaged for the children."

Counsel added: "The emphasis here must be placed on the point that it was not 'special treatment' but 'a special treatment' that was expected. The man who drew up this letter, witness Krumey, declared that he had in mind a special kind of treatment because the police authorities had no preparations for absorbing these children."

The presiding judge intervened: "Dr. Servatius, I did not understand the distinction you made between the two special treatments. You stressed one word in one expression and then another in the second expression."

Counsel replied: "There does exist a considerable difference from a linguistic point of view. When I speak of 'special treatment,' then I refer to this particular well-known special treatment without any comment. But when the expression is 'a special treatment,' then this implies a choice between several types of special treatment."

What was implied was simple: "special treatment" was the code name for killing Jews "without comments." "A special treatment" as applied to non-Jews might have meant some other way of dealing with them.

On the charge of a war crime, Dr. Servatius claimed that Israel's legislation was an "intervention in the legal sovereignty of the warring states." Since we had not been at war as a state, we had no power to provide by law for the punishment of war crimes, he maintained.

With regard to the plunder of Jewish property, Dr. Servatius said: "It should be noted that in both world wars the plunder of enemy property was a measure adopted by all states. Only with great difficulties did they later on consent to let this property go. It is not charged here against the accused that he himself unduly enriched himself. If indeed robbery did take place, the state committed this plunder. This was done all over the world with regard to enemy property. The accused was not the central person in the seizure of Jewish property. He was engaged side by side with many other central authorities in the execution of legal instructions."

Anyway, it was not a crime against humanity, he claimed, and a Nuremberg precedent to the contrary ought not to be followed.

On the merits of the charge, counsel added that "in Austria the accused had to act in the face of serious opposition from other authorities, in order to ensure that large sums of foreign currency from abroad should be available for emigration."

"Thanks to the endeavors of the accused," he continued, "it was possible for two-thirds of the Jews of Austria to emigrate at that time, and they were in a position to leave the country. True, their condition, previously, was desperate, but this was not the fault of the accused.

"The same applies to the accused's activities in Germany, as well as in Bohemia and Moravia. The accused had no part in the forced contribution of a billion Reichsmarks."

On the extortion of money to feed the Gestapo, known as "donations W account," Dr. Servatius said: "The special character of these contributions was that, in consequence, no more harm befell the Jews. The property from which this contribution was made was blocked, anyway, and the ownership came to an end the moment the owner crossed the border."

Dr. Servatius must have felt how incongruous this sounded, for he added: "These were the strange bureaucratic ways of the Third Reich."

*

Dr. Servatius proceeded to review the charges in the context of what he called "the picture of a sick world," which ought to be examined by philosophers and historians, but could not properly be evaluated "through the loophole of a legal paragraph." The politicians were to blame, not their followers. They always were. This was the difference, in Dr. Servatius' opinion, between the crime of an individual, from which he could abstain at will, and a crime "at the bidding of the collective," which was irresistible. Even Moses the lawgiver, who wrote in the Decalogue "Thou shalt not kill," had to order killings for "political reasons." Genocide had been committed by many peoples: by the settlers in North and South America, by the colonizers of Australia, by the persecutors of the Huguenots in France, and by the Inquisition against the Jews in Spain. Deportations had been by no means uncommon; the French had deported the German population from

Alsace-Lorraine after World War I; the Czechs had expelled them from Czechoslovakia after World War II. Why blame it all on Eichmann?

Every nation plundered "enemy property" in wartime; it was "a favorite measure." Weapons of war had been used indiscriminately on all sides. Who wanted any longer to hear of the destruction of Hiroshima or Dresden? The subject had become a bore. These acts were not judged by their intrinsic "wrongness," but by their ultimate success. "By such means the winner gets a medal; the loser faces the gallows." Heads of state had always resorted to such acts and would do so in the future. Till the establishment of a world government there could be no solution, he said.

Again we were treated to the favorite Nazi defense, which we often hear today. They conveniently forget who had started the war. They gloss over the fact that Hitler was freely elected and enthusiastically served. They claim they could not do anything against him; so in effect they deserve sympathy, for they were his victims as much as the people who were doomed to die at their hands. It was all essentially a matter of inexorable fate and bad luck. It was the Jews' misfortune that they were in Hitler's power—and Eichmann's that he was chosen as his tool.

Turning to the sterilization charge, Dr. Servatius claimed that the documents implicating Eichmann were directed to his deputy. "This is explained by the accused, who believes that this was a special mission assigned to Guenther. In the circumstances, this seems reasonable. In addition, we point to the fact that this same Guenther appears once again in connection with other medical experiments—killing by means of gas and the skeletons affair."

Judge Halevy intervened now: "I assume that you made a mistake when you said that killing by gas was a purely medical matter—this must have been a slip of the tongue."

There was an audible gasp in the packed and shocked courtroom when Dr. Servatius replied: "It was medical inasmuch as it was prepared by medical men. The killing, too, is a medical affair."

On the merits of the charge, he claimed that Eichmann had nothing to do with the matter except "as an observer"; it was dealt with by the Ministry of the Interior.

With regard to deportations, boycott and the enforcement of the yellow badge, the defense maintained: "He was only involved in writing drafts and was engaged simply in the administrative aspects of the problem. Therefore it is absolutely impossible to incriminate the accused here, because all the final decisions were taken by the highest echelon. Even if the RSHA gave orders through the instrumentality of the accused, the accused certainly did not shoulder the main responsibility for these measures.

"People earmarked for deportation were not singled out by the accused; this was determined in accordance with Chapter 5 of the German citizenship law, and the accused had no influence whatsoever on this particular law. So far as the deportations were concerned they were ordered by a higher echelon in accordance with the policy determined by the Reich and adopted in regard to the Jews. This was on the strength of the decision taken at the Wannsee Conference, which flows from a special directive by Goering to Heydrich."

On the labor camps and the horrors of ghettoization:

"All those who dealt with these problems were of higher rank than the defendant. They received the political directives directly from the political authorities. The accused's department would only deal with police measures and would also prepare certain technical matters with regard to the implementation of the purely technical aspect of these orders.

"The accused had no influence whatsoever on these problems. The concentration of ghettos in the East was only the concern of the local authorities where the ghettos were situated. The accused took part in the meeting deciding on the liquidation of the Lódz ghetto, but he was there only as a representative of Himmler. Therefore it is absolutely impossible to draw any conclusion with regard to his personal competence and authority there."

The conditions under which the Jews were transported "to their destination" were "not normal"; that was true. But this was due to the war.

*

Coming now to what he termed the "main count in the indictment"—the charge of the extermination in the death camps—Dr. Servatius said:

"First of all, the distinction must be made here that these camps were not under the jurisdiction of the accused, or under Bureau IV of the RSHA, but, rather, under the jurisdiction of the Head Office for Economy and Administration. Cooperation between these offices was secured by Himmler's personal headquarters.

"The accused stated willingly and of his own initiative during his interrogation that he had repeatedly visited the death camps. Therefore, his statement that he had been sent there by his superiors to report on the nature of the operations must be believed.

"Hoess's charge that the accused passed on to him the order for extermination in the summer of 1941 loses in probative value through the fact that there is no other corroborative evidence. The same applies to the testimony of Gerstein, who was employed by the authorities in obtaining gas. Even if this were correct, if it were correct that Gerstein spoke to Guenther about obtaining gas, this is not certain proof of Eichmann's approval and knowledge. Eichmann visited Auschwitz in order to intervene on behalf of Dr. Storfer, a member of the Vienna Jewish Council, but this does not prove that the camp was under his jurisdiction."

On the Strasbourg skeletons:

"This is a very peculiar procedure, which does not accord with regular bureaucratic procedures. In any case, there is no proof of any kind of order by the accused. In his testimony the accused himself commented on this matter."

Eichmann denied any complicity in the *Einsatzgruppen* shootings. In counsel's opinion Wisliceny's testimony was valueless.

"Wisliceny was sentenced as an accessory to the crime of exterminating Jews. For that reason, his affidavit cannot prove the participation of the accused. . . .

"The presence of the accused, to which he testified himself, during the general briefing session at which the *Einsatzgruppen* commanders were appointed is no proof of the existence of such cooperation. . . .

"Nor is the transmission of the *Einsatzgruppen*'s progress reports any proof of joint action with the *Einsatzgruppen*."

It was admitted that Eichmann was engaged in deportation from various countries named in the indictment, but those responsible for the events in Hungary were Veesenmayer, Winkelmann and Geschke, to whom Eichmann was subordinate, as a professional expert; these leaders approached the Jewish problem "with vigor" and encountered considerable willingness and cooperation on the part of the Hungarians. The accused had to await orders from above—he did not have to influence the Hungarians. The activity of the accused consisted in reporting on the situation. In addition, he had the task of taking over the trains on the German border—these were the trains dispatched by the Hungarians—and of sending these trains on, in accordance with his instructions, to Auschwitz or other destinations.

"Pressure on the Hungarian Government for the resumption of the anti-Jewish measures was brought to bear by Veesenmayer, with the consent of the Foreign Ministry. Winkelmann recalled Eichmann urgently in order to start the deportation of fifty thousand Jews for work in Germany. From this pressure there resulted the notorious march; it was carried out by the Hungarians, and the accused was not in charge of escort personnel. The march was not a secret maneuver executed by the accused, but rather an action agreed upon by the political authorities. The personality of the accused was brought to the fore only after the war by those who were really responsible in order to exonerate themselves.

"These were the facts," Dr. Servatius said hopefully, and he added: "The best evidence in connection with facts is the series of documents presented in court. Without these documents, the accused would have been deprived of any defense. But these documents are only fragments saved from all the material destroyed at the end of the war."

*

On the holocaust witnesses, Dr. Servatius said he had not put any questions to them, for "in general lines there was no room to doubt the description put forward by them. Their suffering was too sacred for me to attack them."

The German witnesses whose affidavits we had used "were dug up in the debris of the Third Reich," Dr. Servatius said. These people were in prison and had other worries than telling the truth, he maintained.

"It was not the truth that was the important thing—this was the slogan. The main object was that they should not be involved.

"We have other testimonies—those of Hoess and Wisliceny. The thing that characterizes Hoess's testimony is that he surrendered. He always uses the style of his accusers and calls his prisoners 'slaves,' something he would not have done before. He does not swim upstream. He is in jail and knows what he has to do. It is still good to shift some of the blame. . . ."

"Now the witness Wisliceny. It is quite evident that he had only one thing in mind, in the multitude of his voluntary statements. He wanted to go free. Repeatedly he offered to help find the accused and his family. He too, came from the Nuremberg jail. In contrast with the usual line of the Nuremberg prisoners, he testified quite differently, and he was promised protection for his relatives from the vengeance of his comrades."

"The archives of the world were not open to the accused," Dr. Servatius said. "Nor was his cause popular," he complained.

"Experts who could have supported him did not want to have any dealings with the defense. The daily fanfares of the press and the trumpets of the periodicals made them shy. They closed their ears."

Dr. Servatius was not overjoyed with his own witnesses either. Those who were promised safe-conduct found that "it would not have been pleasant for them" to appear in Israel and preferred to stay at home. He found fault with the examination of Hoettl, because the examining magistrate went too far. He "writes that he ought to endeavor to help in clarifying the murders. But this was not his task. It was the task of this court. That magistrate had to hear the testimony of the witness and no more."

Then Hoettl was "a fence-sitter." Such people, in Dr. Servatius' opinion, were not to be given credence.

Veesenmayer would not have lied so brazenly, thought Dr. Servatius, had he faced the accused in court. Becher's evidence was unreliable, since the examining judge had shown the witness the questions in advance.

Curiously, counsel offered no explanation of the strongly incriminating evidence of the defense witness Professor Six, or of affidavits of Mildner, Hoffman and Morgen that he himself had submitted, all heavily inculpating Eichmann on some of the main issues.

On the evidence of the accused, Dr. Servatius said: "The prosecution claims that all this testimony is a pack of lies, that he admitted to matters only when documents were shown to him and he was pressed to the wall. I do not think this is quite correct. From the very first day of his police interrogation the accused testified very willingly to every bit of information which was available to him. Who can remember after sixteen years or more every single detail of a proceeding? One needs documents for this.

"It is then contended that the accused did remember many other petty details and that he did not wish to remember matters connected with his official activities. This contention is not justified. All of us remember many trivialities in our past lives, but we do not necessarily remember our official activities."

In fact this was half true, for Eichmann had displayed an extraordinary memory on both; he claimed a black-out just on the most incriminating matters.

It is not clear that the accused shirked answering, Dr. Servatius said. He reported his journeys to the death camps, where he came into contact with the gruesome atrocities. No one could have proved this against him. This sincerity entitles the accused to be given credence in less important matters.

The reasoning behind the argument was that a visit to the camps was no crime and the admission of the trips to Auschwitz was not a confession of guilt. The problem was: for what purpose did he go there—as an innocent observer or as a pacesetter of destruction?

Significantly the version of the allegedly forged official documents was tacitly abandoned. Dr. Servatius did not refer to this any further and did not claim that any part of the written evidence was falsified. Eichmann's "special assignments" theory was only halfheartedly referred to. It was obvious that counsel just could not bring himself to mouth this drivel.

About the Sassen documents, Dr. Servatius said: "True, *a priori,* they seem to be devastating from the point of view of the accused, but their contents do not correspond with reality. There was provocation under alcohol; there was adornment of the truth here and there, to suit the taste of the reader; not truth, but sensation, interesting matters—that was the purpose of the writer. It is surprising that the prosecution did not call Sassen himself as a witness, as the best disproof of the accused's contentions."

I had not called Sassen from Argentina for the obvious reason that I did not want any contact with him. Moreover, since he was under a death sentence passed by a Dutch court, he obviously would not have risked coming to Israel to face a possible application for extradition here.

*

Turning to the legal issues, Dr. Servatius said that Israeli law presupposes "a guilty mind" as a factor in an offense. "It must be proven that the accused knew and approved of the criminal action," he declared.

"The accused was not a partner either at the beginning or at the end of the deed. His actions were confined to the intervening sector. This pertains particularly to the extermination in the death camps. The accused did not order the extermination and did not carry it out. In an individual criminal act it is very difficult to extract one part of the act from the causal train of events; the act of an individual is directed to the whole in which he takes part."

Since Eichmann had been "only a link in the chain," so went the argument, "his actions do not accumulate" to form a complete offense.

I never quite followed this contention. Every single criminal act of Eichmann in the course of the Final Solution was a criminal offense in itself, even if he did not perform the acts of extermination with his own hands.

On the issue of conspiracy Dr. Servatius argued, against the legal authorities, that "there can be no conspiracy between a man and his superior in the execution of orders."

On Eichmann's position, he said: "The accused did not enjoy a position that could have elevated him into the circle of leadership. His executive power was limited. He was independent only in routine work. But here the prosecution tried to elevate the rank of the accused beyond the normal one. The true position is shown only in the plan for the distribution of functions. . . . A chief remains a chief, even when the head of a department endeavors to be his equal.

"The prosecution cannot base itself on documents drafted by the accused. The letterhead showed that in this use of the first person the reference was only to the chief of that office. Through such a collection of circumstantial evidence, the accused cannot be brought into the circle of a conspiracy. Furthermore, the accused did not have the special powers that are alleged. The persons who cooperated most closely with the accused know he had no such special authority. They testified that, quite on the contrary, the accused stuck very closely to the instructions of his superior, Mueller, and always obtained cover from him. But the real position of the accused transpires from the very simple fact that since 1941 he was never promoted. For such allegedly meritorious service not even the decoration which he received was sufficient reward. This is a puzzle . . ."

It was against this background that Dr. Servatius examined Eichmann's activities. Everything he did was inspired by the highest authorities, who enforced his obedience by holding him to his oath. Had Eichmann refused to obey, at great personal cost, others would have carried out the task in any case, and his sacrifice would have been in vain. Had not the machine of destruction pushed on after Heydrich was killed? People saw Eichmann the puppet, but they did not see those behind him pulling the strings, he said. We were reminded again of all the authorities and agencies in Germany that had lent a hand in the venture.

Throughout Dr. Servatius' oral address and the 150-page written summing up, all the familiar names and institutions of the Reich appeared again, like a black forest in which one tree could hardly be distinguished from the other.

"The recipient of orders cannot recognize as criminal acts the deeds of the political leadership, because he is not a member of that leadership. It is the leadership that determines who will be called an enemy and how he will be combated."

It was true, Dr. Servatius conceded, that no war was declared on the Jews, but "there was an intimate contact between the war and the fight against the Jews," he claimed. "In the pre-extermination period Eichmann was well aware of the cool calculations of the politicians of the Western world," and later witnessed the diplomatic chess game following Joel Brand's mission.

(How curious, I thought; did he deport the Jews to death camps because the West did not let them in?)

"He could not have refused to obey, because he was under duress. The action of the state and of its functionaries is not founded, primarily, on the penal code. Voluntary obedience secures the life of a state; that is how the accused acted, willingly and voluntarily on behalf of the state until such time as he learned about the extermination. But after the first steps had been taken, along the way to extermination, there was no way back. The law now imposed obedience."

The presiding judge wanted to know more about this and turned to counsel: "I would like to ask a question: Do we have anything in the testimony of the accused, here in the court, or in his statement to the police, which indicates that he revolted, internally, against the extermination of the Jews?"

The reply was: "As far as I understood the attitude of the accused, in the light of our conversations, he continually repudiated the order, if we consider his internal attitude toward it, but he simply carried it out under duress."

There was no way for a man like Eichmann "to shirk the filthy work," said Dr. Servatius, completely disregarding the voluminous evidence to the contrary. "He could have feigned illness, thereby leaving his comrades to do his job," he said. But there were extremely stern punishments for those who displayed defeatist attitude; even members of the underground did not quit their posts, said Dr. Servatius.

He claimed that since Eichmann had been abducted from Argentina and in that country the period of limitations would have made proceedings impossible, therefore we in Israel should stop the trial.

Finally he appealed for reconciliation. Time must be permitted to heal wounds. There should be an end to eternal collective strife; we should return to self-restraint and humanity. The Jews had formulated the idea of "a holy year" which brought peace and the abandonment of claims. He appealed to the court to render "a Solomonic verdict that will astound the world with the wisdom of the Jewish people."

As usual, it was the victims who were called upon to show forbearance.

With the hearings now closed, after 114 sessions, the three judges retired to their chambers, crammed with documents and records—the history of a nation—to decide on the fate of a man.

Four months later we were back in the courtroom to hear their verdict.

CHAPTER

21

The Judgment

During the fourteen weeks of the trial the judges had mainly listened. Questions occasionally fell from the bench, rulings were given on admissibility of evidence, translations were supervised, but with the course of the trial firmly set, and with the helm strongly in hand, the decks were usually left to the contending parties. The presiding judge watched over the dignity of the trial; he maintained the authority of the bench through the power of his personality and his innate gift of leadership. He made it clear that no audible reactions from the audience would be tolerated. He would severely castigate a laugh or titter at Eichmann's replies, though he was well aware that it was no more than an escape from unbearable tension. With quiet determination, he ordered the removal of the very few members of the public who could not contain their anger and vented on the accused their grief at the loss of their dear ones.

The two other members of the court contributed each his own share to the impressive picture of unflagging judicial decorum that ruled out every consideration but the attainment of scrupulous justice.

A constant concern of the court was to make sure that counsel for the defense got all the necessary facilities and amenities for the performance of his task. The obvious quest of the bench for true impartiality evoked a foreign journalist's remark: "Indeed there are judges in Israel!" This was agreed to by all observers.

The strain on the judges of the need to remain nonpartisan and unbiased in this contest was plainly to be seen. It was a task much more difficult than mine, for I could give some vent to my feelings and those of my people, which was both my right and my duty as the public prosecutor.

At last the time came for the court's final word. It was delivered on December 11, 1961, eight months to the day since the proceedings had opened.

A glance at the overcrowded courtroom revealed many familiar faces of spectators and observers who had been with us from the beginning: the official German delegates, the foreign diplomats, the local and foreign representatives of the press.

Tension soared when Eichmann, flanked by his guards, stepped into his glass cubicle. He was calm, with his familiar expressionless face. Only his nose looked sharper, his eyes narrower. "Now he closely resembles the cartoons of him as a bird of prey," an observer remarked.

Several minutes later the three judges filed in.

"The accused will stand up," ordered the presiding judge, Justice Landau. Eichmann rose to his feet. There was complete stillness. People actually held their breath. "The court finds you guilty of crimes against the Jewish people, of crimes against humanity, of war crimes and of membership in criminal associations. The accused will now sit down." With these few words, the extreme strain of expectation was relieved. Now that the general result was known we could listen more calmly to the historic judgment.

The presiding judge began to read the verdict:

"It is the purpose of every criminal case to clarify whether the charges in the prosecution's indictment against the accused on trial are true and, if the accused is convicted, to mete out due punishment to him. Everything which requires clarification in order that these purposes may be achieved must be determined at the trial, and everything which is foreign to these purposes must be entirely eliminated from the court procedure.

"There was felt a desire—understandable in itself—to give a comprehensive and precise historical description of events which occurred during the catastrophe. There are also those who sought to regard this trial as a platform for the clarification of questions of great import, some of which arose from the catastrophe." Justice Landau listed the array of historical problems that in one way or another were mentioned during the proceedings and continued:

"In this maze of insistent questions, the path of the court was and remains clear. It cannot allow itself to be enticed into provinces which are outside its sphere. The judicial process has ways of its own, laid down by law, which do not change, whatever the subject of the trial may be. Otherwise, the processes of law and of court procedure are bound to be impaired, whereas every effort must be made to adhere to them punctiliously, since they are in themselves of considerable social and educational significance, and the trial otherwise would resemble a rudderless ship tossed about the waves."

Thus the presiding judge explained the course which he and his colleagues had set for the trial. "The path of law," which the judges had narrowed down almost to a knife edge was the characteristic route of the court. Even this trial, to which there was no parallel, was conducted by them like all others.

Before proceeding to the heart of the matter both sides were complimented by the court.

"We desire to express our appreciation to the representatives of both parties, who labored in the presentation of this case. The Attorney General, Mr. Hausner, and his assistants, Dr. Robinson, Mr. Baror, Mr. Bach and Mr. Terlo, who helped him in the conduct of the case, carried an enormous burden on their shoulders and displayed absolute mastery of the huge amount of legal and factual material prepared for them by the police investigators, who toiled before them in a manner which also deserves the utmost praise. The Attorney General himself emerged honorably from the dilemma to which we alluded above, and which he, too, certainly felt in all its full impact. In spite of a slight deviation here and there from the narrow path that the court saw as its duty to set, Mr. Hausner conducted the prosecution in all its stages as a jurist and on a very high professional level.

"In his brilliant opening speech, which was eloquent and broad in perspective, and again in his concluding statement, he gave vent also to the deep feelings which stir the entire nation. Similarly we wish to express our appreciation to the counsel for the defense, Dr. R. Servatius, and his assistant, Mr. Dieter Wechtenbruch. Dr. Servatius, who stood almost alone in his strenuous legal battle, in an unfamiliar environment, always directed himself to the essence of the matter, and refrained from unnecessary controversy over matters which did not seem vital to him for the defense of his client, thereby affording valuable assistance to the court. Thus even some uncalled-for notes in his concluding speech, which jarred on our ears, could not detract from the good and serious impression made by his arguments for the defense as a whole."

The court thus administered a slight rap over the knuckles to Dr. Servatius for his flippancy in treating mass murder as a medical affair.

Now the judgment proceeded to analyze the problems involved. All that had been argued, pleaded, testified and proved returned now once again to the courtroom, but this time in terms of a judgment from an elevated platform and in the shape of final findings.

All contentions and reasonings were now appraised. No argument that did not meet the highest standards of acceptability was approved.

Judge Halevy now took over the reading. Although the judgment was unanimous, each page bearing the signatures of all three judges, we assumed that each of them read out mainly that portion which he had personally elaborated.

Turning first to the legal problems, Judge Halevy said, quoting high authorities, that an *ex post facto* law is often the only way to secure elementary justice, if it puts the stigma of illegality on an act which must be considered as criminal by the notions of the civilized world. No "new prohibitions" were created by these laws; "on the contrary, all the abovementioned crimes constituted crimes under the laws of all civilized nations, including the German people, before and after the Nazi regime, while the 'law' and criminal decrees of Hitler and his regime are no laws and have been set aside with retroactive effect even by the German courts themselves." Of course the perpetrators had guilty knowledge. That was why they went to such lengths to efface the traces of their crimes.

After an analysis of our own and foreign authorities including Roman Law, from the fathers of international law onward, Judge Halevy reached the conclusion that "crimes which afflict the whole of mankind and shock the conscience of nations are grave offenses against the law of nations itself." It followed that, pending the establishment of an international tribunal, "international law is in need of the judicial and legislative authorities of every country to give effect to its penal injunctions and to bring criminals to trial. The authority and jurisdiction to try crimes under international law are universal."

Our Nazi Punishment Law was then compared with the Allied postwar legislation and with the definition of "genocide" in the United Nations declaration, and with the advisory opinion of the International Court of Justice, given at the request of the General Assembly. It was found that our legal definitions and prohibitions tally with the internationally accepted standards. Nor does our law widen the scope of crimes declared to be under universal jurisdiction.

"It is not necessary to recapitulate in Jerusalem," said the court, "fifteen years after Nuremberg, the grounds for the legal rule of the 'crime against humanity,' for these terms are written in blood, in the torrents of the blood of the Jewish people which were shed." Quoting Eugene Aroneanu, the court recalled that "this law was born in the crematoria, and woe to him who will try to stifle it."

The court then turned to other aspects of the problem of jurisdiction, saying:

"We have discussed at length the international character of the crimes in question because this offers the broadest possible, though not the only, basis for Israel's jurisdiction according to the law of nations. No less important from the point of view of international law is the special connection the State of Israel has with such crimes, seeing that the people of Israel [*Am Israel*]—the Jewish people [*Ha'am Ha'yehudi*] (to use the term in the Israeli legislation)—constituted the target and the victim of most of the crimes in question. The State of Israel's 'right to punish' the accused derives, in our view, from two cumulative sources: a universal source (pertaining to the whole of mankind), which vests the right to prosecute and punish crimes of this order in every state within the family of the nations; and a specific or national source, which gives the victim nation the right to try any who assault their existence."

Judge Halevy proceeded to examine this proposition of law in the light of the authorities, which lay down that a "linking point" or "connection" between the act and the prosecutor will confer the right of sitting in judgment. This "linking point" between Israel and the accused "is striking and glaring . . . in the attempt to exterminate the Jewish people. . . . The connection between the State of Israel and the Jewish people needs no explanation," the tribunal proceeded, recalling our Declaration of Independence and the United Nations resolution on the establishment of a Jewish State in Israel.

The judgment continued: "The massacre of millions of Jews by the Nazi criminals which has very nearly led to the extermination of the Jewish people in Europe, was one of the tremendous causes for the establishment of the state of the survivors. The state cannot be cut off from its roots, which lie deep also in the catastrophe of European Jewry."

The Jewish community in Palestine, from which the state grew, was also part of the Jewish people, the court said; the design was to liquidate that community as well. "To argue that there is no connection between the State of Israel and the accused's offenses is like cutting away a tree, root and branch, and saying to its trunk: I have not hurt you."

Thus the State of Israel, through its judiciary, extended a protective wing over the whole of Jewry.

Probing into the kidnaping argument, the court recalled the decisions of the Security Council on the subject (see Appendix I) and laid down:

"It is an established rule of law that a person standing trial for an offense against the laws of the land may not oppose his being tried by reason of the illegality of his arrest or of the means whereby he was brought to the area of jurisdiction of the country. The courts of England, the United States and Israel have ruled continuously that the circumstances of the arrest and the mode of bringing the accused into the area of the state have no relevance to his trial, and they consistently refused in all cases to enter into the examination of these circumstances."

The court reviewed at length numerous local and foreign authorities, all of which support the view that there is no such thing as "territorial immunity"; if an accused has been removed from another jurisdiction by force, it is not his personal right that has been impaired, and he cannot invoke the act in his defense. It is for the injured state alone to pursue or abandon, at will, its right of sovereignty, and the accused is not the foreign state's spokesman for the purpose.

The absolute preponderance of legal opinion was in support of the rule as laid down by the Supreme Court of the United States and the British Court of Appeal.

The court concluded by ruling that according to all these authorities it was duty-bound to try the accused:

"Any plea which assumes that the trial of a fugitive offender or a foreign offender—whether he arrived in the country of his own free will, or was extradited to that country, or was forcibly carried to it—is based on any discretion, is mistaken. The duty of the court to try any accused brought before it for offenses against the laws of the land is based on the rule of law, so that . . . the court must try him in accordance with the charge sheet."

*

Having disposed of the legal problem, the court proceeded to survey the three principal stages of anti-Jewish policy in the Third Reich: from Hitler's rise to power till the outbreak of the war; the period from 1939 to mid-1941; and the last stage, from mid-1941 to the end. Judge Raveh took over the reading. The purpose of the survey was "solely to establish the place of the accused and the degree of his personal responsibility." Judge Raveh chose the chronological method, and began by describing the persecution of the Jews as Hitler's official policy, aimed at depriving them of citizen rights, degrading them, striking fear into their hearts and ousting them from economic and cultural life.

Eichmann's early career was then reviewed till his entry into the SD.

The bench explained in understandable terms the complex structure of the Nazi police and security organs, which had for long puzzled tribunals and writers.

Reverting to Eichmann, Judge Raveh said that his description of "the idyllic fair cooperation in the spirit of mutual understanding" between him and the leaders of the Jewish community was contradicted by the witnesses and the documents. After reviewing the evidence, the court found that "the Jews of Austria lived in an atmosphere of terror ever since the entry of Hitler. . . . Eichmann added threats of his own to increase the pressure . . . for the advancement of his aim to 'purge' Vienna and the whole of Austria of Jews in the shortest possible time."

On the "streamlined financial arrangements" of which Eichmann had boasted in his evidence, the court said:

"The sum total of all these arrangements was that a Jew who was forced to emigrate to another country was allowed to take with him, in addition to his personal effects, only the sum of money which was needed to obtain the entry permit to the country to which he was emigrating [*Vorzeigegeld*]. The rest of his property he had to make over to the German Reich."

On the way Eichmann used Jewish institutions as tools for his schemes, the court said:

"It is true that the accused set the Jewish organizations in Vienna functioning again after they had been closed down by the Gestapo immediately after the annexation of Austria to the Reich. But this was nothing else but the beginning of 'indirect rule,' which the accused developed so cleverly—a system which saved the German ruler manpower and turned the Jewish organizations against their will into an instrument in the hands of the ruler for the realization of his sinister plans."

This is a key fact-finding statement of the court with regard to Jewish so-called "cooperation" with the Germans, and the way in which this cooperation came into being.

"Under this pressure," proceeded the judgment, "Eichmann succeeded in bringing about the emigration of close to 150,000 Jews." He returned to Berlin "crowned with success. . . . It is not surprising, therefore, that from then on central responsibilities were placed on him in regard to the battle against the opponent—Jewry."

After the outbreak of war the second stage began, for "it soon became evident that there was no hope of 'purging' German-ruled territory of the Jews by emigration across the seas, after masses of Jews had been added to them in the Eastern occupied territories. This was a period of mass deportations without a uniform aim, except the desire to get rid of the Jews by all means."

Judge Raveh now reviewed the secret conference held by Heydrich on September 21, 1939, and found as a fact that Eichmann's admission, during the pretrial examination, of his participation in the conference was true and rejected his later attempts to extricate himself with "excuses . . . after he had time to appreciate the serious implications."

With regard to the 1939-40 deportations from the Warthe Province and the means employed, when about a hundred people froze to death in each transport, the court, quoting from Eichmann's directive that "women and children are to be loaded on passenger coaches as far as possible," declared: "This, then, was the measure of the accused's regard for the lives of human beings at the time: men would go on freezing to death; the freezing to death of women and children was to be avoided as far as possible. It should be pointed out here that at a later period even this last spark left the accused, and in all directives he gave there is no longer any mention of any consideration for women and children."

On the Madagascar plan, which Eichmann claimed he worked out with the sole purpose of "putting solid ground under the feet of the Jews and allowing them freedom and statehood," the court said his "version is far from the truth . . . of course, even deportation to Madagascar would have been preferable to the physical extermination that later befell European Jewry. But here again the Madagascar plan must be viewed in terms of the pre-extermination period. It is sufficient to glance through the details of the written plan in order to discover its true significance: the deportation of four million Jews . . . into exile, and their complete isolation from the outer world. . . . This was the RSHA version of the 'Jewish State' plan, the very same plan which the accused dared to mention in one and the same breath with the name of Herzl, from whom, so he says, he drew his inspiration. In fact, there is a direct line leading from the forced emigration organized by the Emigration Centers set up by the accused, via the Nisco plan, to this plan for isolating the Jews in a slave state—a line of increasing severity."

Before the last and decisive stage of the "Final Solution," a reorganization was effected at the RSHA. In March, 1941, several functions were thrown together within the framework of the Gestapo, where they were assigned to department IV-B-4. These were "Jewish affairs," "evacuations," confiscation of property of people hostile to the nation and the state, and "cancellation of German nationality." The head of the department was a man who had already gained much experience in all these matters. It was the accused.

I glanced at Eichmann as his main defenses were now being relentlessly probed and found vulnerable. Though outwardly still calm and collected, the facial contortions he could not control betrayed his mounting nervousness.

From time to time he would seize his pencil and feverishly jot down a few words.

Judge Raveh went on reading in a cool, passionless and matter-of-fact tone.

*

Emigration "ceased to be a practical solution for the removal of masses of Jews," so on July 31, 1941, Goering issued what the court termed "one of the basic documents in the history of the extermination," a directive to Heydrich to take the necessary steps "for the implementation of the Final Solution."

The bench turned to "the central event in the history of the Final Solution"—the Wannsee Conference of the Secretaries of State. After reviewing the proceedings of the Conference, it found that it "carried a more important meaning also for the accused personally, for it was there that his position as the authorized *Referent* of the RSHA in matters connected with the final solution of the Jewish problem was confirmed in the presence of representatives of all the other authorities."

Judge Raveh now proceeded to a brief review of the implementation of the Final Solution, country by country, beginning with Germany. In every case Eichmann's office played a paramount role, either through Eichmann's peremptory instructions or because of the activity of his men on the spot. Full allowance was given to the differing conditions in the various countries, yet Eichmann's pivotal function was illuminated throughout.

Then "the last act in the tragedy of European Jewry under the Hitler regime, the catastrophe which befell Hungarian Jewry," was scrutinized by the Court.

*

At the evening session on the first day of the judgment, the presiding judge, Justice Landau, took over again.

"This chapter," he said, "calls for a special place in the totality of events. This large Jewish community, which until then lived comparatively intact, though an ocean of destruction surrounded it, felt the heavy hand of fate which erased most of its members suddenly from the Book of Life within a few weeks. The Hungarian chapter is different from those which preceded it in other countries also so far as the accused's activities are concerned."

After a survey of the events since the outbreak of war, the court recalled Eichmann's mission to "purge" Hungary of its Jews, and send them all to Auschwitz:

"The accused did his utmost to carry out the order, and if in the end about a third of the Jews of Hungary, and in particular the Jews of Budapest, were saved, it was in spite of his obstinate efforts to complete the operation to the very last Jew."

The judgment proceeded to review the extensive evidence. On the Kistarcsa incident, which reflected Eichmann's initiative and standing, the court ruled:

"The whole incident is very significant as proof of the accused's position in Hungary, and the traits of obstinacy and cunning which characterized his actions."

On the trek of tens of thousands of Hungarian Jews on foot to the Austrian border, the court declared: "Even SS officers who saw the marchers regarded the march as an atrocity."

On the "blood for goods" deal, Justice Landau said:

"We are of the opinion that this whole effort to appear now before this court as the initiator of the above transaction is nothing but a lie. There is no doubt that the order to begin negotiations about the exchange of Jews came from Himmler himself. What caused Himmler to make this proposal, we do not know. Possibly all this was nothing but a maneuver, or he was seeking to prepare an alibi for himself or wanted to show what he could achieve by obtaining essential goods for the Reich. In any case, all these were matters of general high policy, entirely beyond the sphere of activity of the accused, who concentrated all his efforts on the implementation of the Final Solution. On receiving the order to conduct negotiations with the Jews, he carried it out. There is proof that when Brand did not return and the whole matter collapsed, the accused expressed satisfaction. . . . But it is sheer hypocrisy to come now and testify that his reactions to the failure of the negotiations were sorrow, fury and anger, like the feelings of Joel Brand. The entire version was invented by the accused only after he had read Joel Brand's book, from which he thought he could find something to hold on to, in order to show himself in a more favorable light. . . .

"When one compares the accused's evidence in court with what he said in Statement T/37 [the pretrial interrogation] on the same matter, the untruthfulness of his version is glaring. He says there that he received the order to conduct the negotiations directly from Himmler, and that he does not remember who initiated the idea.

"But in his testimony in court," the judgment continued, "everything seems to have become quite clear: he, and he alone, initiated the plan, brought it before Mueller (not directly to Himmler) and received, from and through Mueller, authority to conduct the negotiations.

"We learn from the documents with what kind of plans the accused was concerned after Brand's departure. He was not engaged in preparations for the emigration of 100,000 Jews, as he has had the temerity to allege in his evidence, but in the deportation of all Hungarian Jewry to Auschwitz at an accelerated pace, that is to say, the extermination of those Jews who still remained in German hands and who were to be the subject of barter against goods."

In summing up Eichmann's activities in Budapest, Justice Landau said: "From what has been said, a clear picture emerges. . . . On the German side, which was dominant and made the decisions, the accused was the chief stimulating force in regard to implementing the Final Solution in Hungary. Here, in the actual field of action, he acted with increased energy, initiative and daring, and stubborn determination to complete the work in spite of all the difficulties in his way. It is in this light that the measure of his responsibility for the catastrophe which befell the Jews of Hungary must be evaluated."

*

Next day, at the fourth session of the judgment, Justice Landau referred to the earlier stages of the Final Solution and turned to Eastern Europe—"a valley of death in which millions of Jews were slaughtered by the order of Hitler":

"This is where the Jews, who had been hunted down for this purpose in the other European countries, crammed into trains and brought to the East, were done to death in many different ways. Documents were submitted describing the catastrophe in the East, but the bulk of the evidence consisted of statements by witnesses, brands plucked from the burning, who followed each other in the witness box for days and weeks on end. They spoke simply and the seal of truth was on their words. But there is no doubt that even they themselves could not find the words to describe their suffering in all its depth. . . . And if these be the sufferings of the individual, then the sum total of the suffering of the millions—about a third of the Jewish people, tortured and slaughtered—is certainly beyond human understanding, and who are we to try to give it adequate expression? This is a task for the great authors and poets. Perhaps it is symbolic that even the author who himself went through the hell named Auschwitz could not stand the ordeal in the witness box and collapsed."

The court proceeded to cite excerpts from the "hair-raising" evidence on the *Einsatzgruppen* killings, recalled that the accused had admitted seeing these slaughters, which did not stop him from supplying fifty thousand more Jews to be killed by the Operational Units.

On his contacts with the *Einsatzgruppen,* which Eichmann denied, the court mentioned the evidence of Justice Musmanno, who had it from Schellenberg (since dead) that Eichmann supervised and controlled their activities in regard to the extermination of Jews. While never doubting that Schellenberg had made this statement to the American judge, the court "for reasons of caution refrained from basing a finding of fact upon this version of Schellenberg."

In analyzing further evidence the court pointed out that Eichmann had been singled out as a recipient of the *Einsatzgruppen* reports from June, 1941. This was not to keep him posted but because he needed the information in order to do his job. On his own showing he had to work on these reports and prepare summaries, which he would submit to his superior "for the use of the RSHA command," under whose charge the operational units were.

The court recalled Eichmann's admissions of his contacts with the units, the instructions which his department issued to them. Basing itself on the available evidence, the court found as a fact that "from spring 1942, the accused began to be active in connection with the issuing of operational directives to these units."

The judgment continued:

"Hundreds of thousands, and perhaps a million Jews, were slaughtered by Operational Units by shooting, but this system alone could not have achieved the 'Final Solution,' which meant the extermination of millions, were it not for an additional method, which made possible even more efficient mass killings, and also a 'tidier' way for those who actually dealt in the business of murder. This was the system of mass killing by means of gas."

The evidence of living conditions in the ghettos was reviewed. Judge Halevy took over again and read in a very quiet, barely audible voice. In the chapter on the camps the court let the record speak for itself, adding:

"The extermination of the Jews was connected everywhere with the plunder of their property, down to their clothes and personal belongings which they brought with them on their way to extermination, and including all their other possessions. And, finally, the murderers did not stop short of violating the corpses by removing the gold teeth from the victims' mouths."

After analyzing the political setup in occupied Poland and recalling Eichmann's own version of the matter, the court said:

"The accused alleges that within the General Government, things were run according to special orders from Himmler of which he, the accused, had no knowledge. This is not an easy question, for, on the one hand, many special factors are connected with it, factors which did not exist in other countries, whilst, on the other hand, the evidence brought before us in connection with the General Government area and the measures adopted against the millions of Jews who lived there at the time of the Germans' entry into the area is rather scanty. Among the factors mentioned, the one to be stressed particularly is the very existence of autonomous rule in that area, with a government of its own, headed by Frank. This in itself was an unfailing source of friction between Frank, who jealously guarded his prerogatives as unlimited ruler in the area entrusted to him, and the Reich authorities who strove to centralize power in their own hands."

The court cited several entries from Frank's diary which reflect his struggle with the RSHA, his protests against the direct interference of Himmler and his explanations to his own government that the responsibility for the extermination of the Jews did not lie with the authorities of the General Government, since "the order to exterminate the Jews came from higher authorities."

The court mentioned Eichmann's activity on the various matters on which evidence was found, especially on the Warsaw ghetto, saying:

"Here, therefore, the accused appears as a decision-maker on behalf of the RSHA in matters concerning the Warsaw ghetto, and he certainly had authority to carry out his decisions. This is proof of the fact that he put into practice the authority which was granted to him as a result of the Wannsee Conference."

Judge Halevy minutely reviewed the evidence on the transport of the General Government Jews to the death camps, and summed up:

"To conclude this chapter, we find that the accused and his department were also authorized to deal with matters concerning the Final Solution of the Jewish problem within the area of the General Government, and that according to the evidence, they were also active in fact in this matter from time to time, although it would be true to say that the accused's main activity was not here, but in other places, while in the General Government area there existed also other channels of command, wherein the accused had no part."

On Eichmann's standing in the actual extermination, as distinct from his activities in rounding up and deporting the Jews, the court ruled that this question was actually "of only secondary importance, because the legal and moral responsibility of the man who delivers the victim to his death is, in our opinion, no smaller, and may even be greater, than that of the man who does the victim to death."

With regard to Auschwitz there was more evidence and, having reviewed it, the judgment laid down:

"It follows, therefore, that every trainload of 'Transport Jews' reached the Auschwitz camp with its passengers condemned to death by a general decree given in respect of the transport as a whole by the accused's department. The moment the Jews passed through the camp gates, they came within the power of the camp administration, which had to carry out the death sentence. At the same time, it had authority to postpone the execution of those who were fit for work. . . .

"It has also been proved that it was within the accused's competence to give instructions in advance that a specific transport would not be taken off for immediate extermination, but only after some time had elapsed, as laid down by him."

On the introduction of gas killings as a "cleaner" and more efficient method of killing than mass shooting, the court found that this matter "undoubtedly occupied the attention of the accused as early as the end of the summer and the beginning of the autumn of 1941."

The judgment went on to consider the famous "Wetzel letter," in which Eichmann is mentioned as having given his blessing to the use of gas as an extermination method. As for Eichmann's denial based on the fact that his name appeared only in the final draft of the letter, and not in the handwritten outline that was discovered, the court ruled:

"We do not attribute any value to this denial and so do not accept it. . . . The documents were written in an official office of the German Reich; their formal authenticity is not in doubt. . . . The accused readily admitted the accuracy of their contents, not only spontaneously when the documents were first shown to him, but also a second time on another day, after he had had time to think and volunteered to repeat his confirmation of their accuracy, without having been questioned again on this subject; and again on a third occasion, when shown the same documents he expressed no reservations. This is more than sufficient to convince us. . . . Thus it has been proved that the accused expressed the consent of the RSHA to the use of gas vans in October, 1941, as a substitute for the execution of Jews by shooting. . . . Therefore we find that the accused took part in exchanging the system of execution by shooting for execution by means of gas vans."

The statements of Rudolf Hoess and Dr. Gerstein's documents were then reviewed (see page 403). The court said that it "did not doubt the accuracy of Gerstein's statements" on Guenther's two orders of 'Cyclon B' gas. This corroborated Hoess's account of Eichmann's part in introducing the gas into Auschwitz. Judge Raveh, who read this part of the judgment, said:

"Accordingly, we find that Hoess's deputy began to use Cyclon B in Auschwitz. Hoess informed the accused of this and jointly they decided to introduce this method for the mass killing of Jews in Auschwitz. Guenther—with the knowledge of the accused—made an attempt to introduce this system also in the other extermination camps, and to that end ordered a quantity of Cyclon B from Gerstein in June, 1942.

The judgment proceeded to examine Eichmann's status in the RSHA machinery and the "truly amazing portrait of himself" which he presented. He was a department head, with many subordinates, the court said. Moreover he controlled the advisers on Jewish affairs abroad, "who were themselves persons of considerable status. Yet he asks us to believe that . . . in spite of his being in such a position, he always acted only under explicit instructions received by him in every case. . . . On the other hand, he ascribes to his subordinates no small degree of initiative in their specific fields . . . and as for his deputy Guenther, the accused not only attributes considerable personal initiative to him, but even actions behind the back of the head of his department."

Then the evidence taken abroad was analyzed on this point.

The court summed up, saying:

"All these testimonies and affidavits, even the reserved evidence of Huppenkothen, point to the accused's strong and influential position in the RSHA, and is incompatible with the tendency of the accused to represent himself as having been devoid of any initiative or influence from 1941 onward."

Such corroboration of Eichmann's status the court found in his clash with General Wolff, whom he challenged to a duel (see page 39). This proved that he was "not a minor official without initiative but . . . a man in a position of standing, who knew how to uphold his prestige." Important, too, was Eichmann's reaction to Hitler's directive to allow the emigration of a few thousand Hungarian Jews (see page 142), which shows that he "could not reconcile himself to the order, which was known to him, of the Fuehrer himself, lest some thousands of Jews might escape the general slaughter. Here there is revealed before us not a bureaucratic official, but a man with a will of his own, who feels his own power to the point that even the Fuehrer's order no longer represents an unalterable decision for him."

On the scope of Eichmann's duties, the court made a key finding:

"We reject absolutely the accused's version that he was nothing more than a 'small cog' in the extermination machine. We find that in the RSHA, which was the central authority dealing with the Final Solution of the Jewish question, the accused was at the head of those engaged in carrying out the Final Solution. In fulfilling this task, the accused acted in accordance with general directives from his superiors, but there still remained to him wide powers of discretion which extended also to the planning of operations on his own initiative. He was not a puppet in the hands of others; his place was among those who pulled the strings."

On Eichmann's relatively inconspicuous rank, the court mentioned his own statement that, as a department head, he could not go higher, adding: "It is not rare for a man in an important position—and especially in a position such as that of the accused—to be unwilling to be prominent, or for the ruling powers to wish him not to be prominent."

In the light of these findings, the court, through Justice Landau, applied itself to the examination of the charges and the law under which they were framed. "Crimes against the Jewish people," which were the subject matter of four counts in the indictment, would be committed by a person who killed or grievously harmed Jews, or placed them in conditions calculated to bring about their destruction or devised measures to prevent their birth, *if he did so "with intention to destroy the Jewish people."*

The court now laid down:

"The acts of murder and violence against Jews, committed by the Nazi regime and under its influence from that time onward, were committed without a shadow of doubt with specific intent to destroy the Jewish people as such, and not only Jews as individuals. Hence, also, the ruthlessness shown even toward little children."

The court found that this did not apply to the earlier part of Eichmann's activity in forcing Jewish emigration, since these acts "were not yet accompanied by intent to destroy the Jewish people, but there is no doubt that in the circumstances that have been described these were acts of expulsion of a civilian population which fall within the definition of a 'crime against humanity.'"

A similar finding was made with regard to the "second stage" of the "Final Solution," the early deportations and the expulsions to Nisko.

With regard to the last and decisive stage of the Final Solution, the court preferred my legal conception on criminal complicity in crime to my alternative argument of guilt arising out of the criminal conspiracy as such.

On this point, the court held:

"All the acts perpetrated during the implementation of the Final Solution of the Jewish problem are to be regarded as one single whole, and the accused's criminal responsibility is to be decided upon accordingly. . . .

"Here the basis of the crime lay in Hitler's order to achieve the physical extermination of the Jews. This was not an order to exterminate the Jews of Germany, France, Hungary, Poland, Soviet Russia, each group separately. It was not an order to exterminate first one million Jews and later another million, and so on; but the order was one comprehensive order. . . . The criminal intent was continuous and embraced all activities, until the whole operation had been completed."

Now explicitly endorsing the argument on association in crime, the court based on it Eichmann's criminal responsibility all along the front of the Final Solution:

"The accused was privy to the extermination secret as of June, 1941. As of August, 1941, he began to be active in the furtherance of the extermination campaign, occupying a central place in it. . . .

"Hence, the accused will be convicted of the general crime of the Final Solution in all its forms, as an accomplice to the commitment of a crime, and his conviction will extend to all the many acts forming part of that crime, both the acts in which he took an active part in his own section, as well as the acts committed by his accomplices to the crime in other sections of the same front."

This was, of course, the core of the legal issue on all crimes with the commission of which Eichmann was charged "together with others." The general approach of the prosecution to the problem as reflected in the indictment and in the summing up (see pages 392-393) was vindicated.

The three counts dealing with crimes against humanity were held fully proven.

The court held that the count of plunder was proved for the whole period of Eichmann's activity, from his Viennese beginnings till the end. In all these acts, including the robbery of the deportees' personal belongings in the camps and the desecration of the corpses by the extraction of their teeth, "the accused had a hand, since he was responsible for bringing the victims to the camps where the acts were committed, with the knowledge that these acts would be committed."

The eighth charge—committing a war crime—was proved. So was the count dealing with deportation of Poles. This was not merely "resettlement," as the defense had argued. The plan laid down at Heydrich's conference of November 21, 1939, clearly envisaged a sinister scheme of severely harming the Polish nation.

"Anyone who listened to this speech and plan, and later participated in any form whatsoever in the operation of uprooting the Polish population, will not be allowed to argue that this was an innocent operation of 'resettlement.' This was plain and simple expulsion, accompanied by degradation of the people, and with malicious intent, especially against the educated class."

Even on Eichmann's admission alone, again limited to transportation activity, he could, in the circumstances, be found guilty of the crime as charged.

"But after studying the documents, we have come to the conclusion that his allegation and his evidence in this matter are not in accordance with the truth. It becomes clear that the accused and his department centralized the deportations."

The two waves of deportations, in 1939–40 and in 1942–43, covered about half a million people.

The crimes against humanity of having deported Slovenes and Gypsies were held proved.

The charge of responsibility for the deportation and murder of about one hundred Lidice children had been strongly contested by the defense. We were in no position to prove that these children had actually been murdered or transported to a camp. They had simply disappeared, having been delivered, on the instructions of Eichmann's office, to the Gestapo in Litzmannstadt.

The court held:

"In conclusion, as regards the accused, it has been proved only that he participated in the expulsion of the ninety-three children of Lidice from their homeland, and he thus took part in the commission of a crime against humanity."

Now the last and final question arose. Was there any justification at all which if proved might have excused Eichmann's acts?

Here the court probed into the main defense of obedience to orders. The accused's plea was that "his obedience was based on boundless confidence in the wise judgment of leadership." The court quoted Dr. Servatius' argument that the basic principle of every state is confidence and loyalty, for which the individual becomes accountable in case of failure.

"If by these words," continued Justice Landau, "counsel for the defense intended to describe a totalitarian regime, based on denial of all law, as was Hitler's regime in Germany, then his words are indeed apt. . . . It is also true that under such a regime the criminal, who obeyed a criminal leader, is not punished but, on the contrary, is rewarded, and only when the entire regime collapses will he become amenable to justice."

But a country based on a rule of law will not countenance such arguments.

"The attempt to turn an order for the extermination of millions of innocent people into a political act is of no avail. And do not let counsel for the defense console us with the promise of a world government to come, when such 'Acts of State' will become a thing of the past. We do not have to wait for such a radical change in the relations between nations in order to bring a criminal to judgment, according to his own personal responsibility for his acts, which is the basis of criminal judgment all over the world."

Nor would the argument that "a state of war" existed between Jewry and Germany avail the accused. The court added:

"As the Attorney General said, would that the Jews under the rule of Hitler had been granted the status and privileges of prisoners of war. But this 'war' took the form of deporting helpless people to be slaughtered by citizens of the state in which they lived, without any reason save that of gratuitous hatred and without any aim save that of their extermination."

After a review of the legal authorities on superior orders, the court said:

"Here we shall add that, in civilized countries, the rejection of the defense of 'superior orders' as exempting completely from criminal responsibility has now become general. This was also acknowledged by the General Assembly of the United Nations. . . . Perhaps it is not a vain hope that the more this conviction becomes rooted in the minds of men, the more will they refrain from following criminal leaders, and the rule of law and order in the relations between nations will be strengthened accordingly."

Justice Landau then turned to examine the inner attitude of Eichmann to his work:

"Did these orders disturb his conscience, so that he acted under compulsion from which he saw no escape; or did he act with inner indifference like an obedient automaton; or perhaps he identified himself in his heart with the contents of the order?"

Examining Eichmann's protestations that he had nothing to do with the atrocities, and that he had been ordered to deal with extermination, the court unmasked this argument, saying:

"It means that had he been ordered to throw the gas container among the victims, then his conscience would have waked up, but since it was his duty to hunt down the victims in the countries of Europe and transport them to the gas chambers, his conscience was at peace, and he obeyed orders without hesitation."

It was not even necessary to consider whether he *could have* obtained a posting to another position, had he wished to do so, because "he never thought of giving up his important job behind his desk at RSHA center, a job which he had obtained because of his being an expert on a problem which kept the Third Reich and its heads so busy."

He was merciless in all his deeds. He admitted on cross-examination that he pursued even the "Hungarian deal" for reasons of utility and not as a rescue operation.

"That is to say, it never entered his head that human beings could possibly save their lives in this way. This reveals to us the same block of ice, or block of marble, which Dr. Grueber saw before him when he came to the accused on the humanitarian mission which he had taken upon himself."

"His attempt to argue that he—the expert on Jewish affairs in the Reich Security Head Office—just he himself, was that 'white raven,' the National Socialist who did not hate Jews, cannot hold water."

And the court continued:

"Blind obedience could never have brought him to commit the crime which he committed with such efficiency and devotion as he evinced were it not for his zealous belief that he was thereby fulfilling an important national mission.

"No single case brought to our notice has revealed the accused as showing any sign of human feelings in his dealing in Jewish affairs. . . . In all his activities the accused displayed indefatigable energy, verging on overeagerness, toward advancing the Final Solution, both in his general decisions and in his treatment of individual cases of Jews who wished to escape death. . . .

"Certainly he was not lukewarm in giving his orders nor in his deeds, but energetic, full of initiative and active to the extreme in his efforts to carry out the Final Solution."

On the means he employed, the court added: "When carrying out the final plan, the accused resorted to the psychological warfare tactics of misleading and confusing the enemy."

The judgment illustrated this point with the soothing assurances to Jewish leaders in Hungary that "no harm will befall the Jews and that he wants them to be frank with him as he was with them, while the order for the deportation of Hungarian Jewry to Auschwitz is already in his pocket. Such a measure of viciousness can only be shown by a man who does his criminal job wholeheartedly with all his being."

Relying now on a passage from the Sassen document, which Eichmann had "substantially" admitted on cross-examination, the court said:

"So 'substantially' this attitude of complete identification with his work is correct—his joy in deporting Jews to their deaths. This is not the way a person who did this horrible work with any inner compunction, or even indifference, would have spoken. . . .

"His hatred was cold and calculated, aimed rather against the Jewish people as a whole than against the individual Jews, and just because of this was so poisonous and destructive in all its manifestations. To this task he devoted his alert mind, his great cunning and his organizing skill."

Eichmann had therefore no defense, neither legally nor morally. He had no shield, no justification and no excuse.

On the diffusion of guilt the court held:

"In fact, it is not disputed that in all his activities the accused always acted together with others, and this is how he was charged in the indictment. We shall not see the complete picture if we place the responsibility for the entire extermination campaign only upon the accused. Above him there were the men at the top, beginning with Hitler himself—those who were the initiators of the Final Solution. . . . Many others were active, all of them determined to carry out the Fuehrer's order . . . the Ministries of the Interior and Justice, which laid the main formal groundwork for the persecution of the Jews . . . the Foreign Ministry, which labored unceasingly to spread the poison of anti-Semitism all over the world . . . the Ministry of Finance and the Reichsbank, which took part in plundering the property of the victims; the Fuehrer's Chancellery, which was active in the introduction of the method of killing by gas; and also the German Army Command, which tainted itself by acting in partnership with the SS in the extermination of the Jews in the East, in Greece and in other countries . . . all the authorities of the Reich and of the National Socialist Party, whose sphere of activity touched upon Jewish affairs. . . .

"But all this does not detract from the fact that the accused's department in the RSHA stood at the very center of the Final Solution; and the guilt of the others does not lessen by one iota the personal guilt of the accused."

Turning now to an appreciation of Eichmann's evidence, the bench held:

"His entire testimony was nothing but one consistent effort to deny the truth and to conceal his real share of responsibility, or at least to reduce it to a minimum. His attempt was not unskillful, due to those qualities which he had shown at the time of his actions: an alert mind; the ability to adapt himself to any difficult situation; a cunning and glib tongue. But he did not have the courage to confess to the truth, neither about how things actually happened nor about his inner attitude to the acts he committed. We saw him again and again winding his way under the impact of the cross-examination, retreating from complete to partial denial, and only when left no alternative to admission; but of course always taking refuge in the plea that in all matters great or small he was acting on explicit orders."

All eyes now turned in the direction of the glass dock. Would there be a change in the expression of the man who was now authoritatively branded as a cold-blooded murderer and a brazen liar?

There was nothing to be noticed beyond a somewhat stronger grimace in the region of the mouth.

"Why should you expect the court's condemnation to bother him if the acts he committed did not deprive him of peaceful sleep all these years?" asked one observer.

On Eichmann's partial admission, the court ruled:

"Various theories may be put forward to explain these partial confessions, but this would be futile for the purpose of a legal evaluation of his evidence. Suffice it to say that in our view these confessions did not add credibility to his evidence before us, as regards all those matters in which he was found to be lying."

The court took note of the way we formulated the charge sheet by way of giving illustrative examples. Justice Landau ruled:

"We do not mean to criticize this way of wording the charge sheet. On the contrary, in the nature of things, the description could not be more exhaustive because of the vast dimensions of the activities."

The illustrations in the charge sheet were, of course, not exhaustive, and the court proceeded to say:

"We shall adhere to the general framework of the charge sheet insofar as concerns the description of the statement of offense, and also those parts of the particulars of offense in which appears a general description of the nature of the offense. But as regards all other details we base the conviction of the accused on the detailed description of the facts which we have given in this judgment."

A conviction followed *on all fifteen counts of the indictment*.

*

There remained now the question of sentence.

We were flooded with letters, suggestions and petitions about the punishment to be meted out to Eichmann. Many thought he ought not to be executed. But this, if at all, was a matter to be considered later by the pardoning authority. At this stage I had to perform my duty as public prosecutor and to ask for the penalty imposed by law.

It is a somber, paralyzing responsibility for a man to stand up before his fellow men and ask them for the life of another human being. The first part of my argument was directed to the legal problem: whether the maximum penalty was obligatory. I submitted that it probably was, but even if it were not, it was the only possible penalty in this case, in the light of what had been proved:

"By the enormity of his crime Eichmann has excluded himself from the society of human beings . . . he has shaken off moral restraints, and has given gratification to the basest instincts, against which civilized man has safeguarded himself by a wall of moral bans and injunctions. . . . Even a murderer is still, in spite of the horror of his crime, within the pale of human society. But he who sins against humanity undermines the very existence of society. Such a creature has denied himself the right to walk among human beings, and human society is enjoined to spew him out."

Time had not healed the wounds, I said:

"We are not dealing here with something that is dead and buried; we are not taking scrap metal out of the storehouse of history. Not one of the survivors will ever be the same as he was before; nor will human society again be able to be what it was, before these untouchables came and sent millions to their deaths."

On the resurgence of Nazi theories I said:

"Nazism has not yet vanished from the world. The bearers of the National Socialist message of falsehood are still at large on the earth, and I fear that lately they have regained strength. Among them are not only murderers and criminals, who are perhaps not deterred by the death penalty, but also persons who in cold calculation are out once again to ride the ugly wave of racial hatred. . . .

"Let it be clearly proclaimed: whosoever does the acts of Eichmann will not be cleared of guilt, and will be punished with the utmost severity."

I recalled the sentences passed on Eichmann's subordinates: Wisliceny, Anton Brunner, Seidl and Rahm, his accomplices, Pohl, Hoess and Rauter, his Hungarian partners in crime, Endre and Baky, and the poisoner of world opinion, Julius Streicher, who had all been executed under judgments of various courts.

Turning to Eichmann himself, I continued:

"I pray the court to award the wicked man facing it the penalty that a human and civilized agency is capable of meting out. I know full well that there is no possibility of giving him even a minute fraction of the penalty appropriate to his deeds. Even if he were killed a thousand times, even if he died anew each day, even then there would be no atonement for the suffering he caused to a single child. . . .

"And if it is said now that the execution of a single Nazi criminal, even the Jew-hater Eichmann, will not balance the blood account between the Jewish people and Germany, I would reply that this is certainly true. The account will never be balanced. So long as one Jew is alive in the world, he will carry in his heart the memory of the great catastrophe and the agony inflicted on his people by that bloodstained regime. It will not be wiped out from our hearts and the hearts of our children and our children's children forever. We shall not condone the murders or forgive those whose hands are stained with the blood of our brethren. Too much blood was shed; the wound was too deep. Certainly Eichmann is not the only one who deserves the death sentence. Many of the legions of his assistants have not yet received any appropriate punishment—or any punishment at all. But because we are unable to punish all the wicked as they deserve, should this court refrain from imposing due punishment on the archmurderer who has been captured?"

On the inadequacy of even the maximum penalty, I agreed that there was in practice no greater penalty for the killer of millions than for a killer of one soul. But the court should not reduce the maximum penalty established by law solely because it is impossible to exceed it.

I concluded: "There stands before you a murderer of a people, an enemy of mankind, one who had shed the blood of the innocent. I pray you to judge that this man deserves the capital punishment of death."

In reply Dr. Servatius said:

"It must be borne in mind that the accused did not act according to his own initiative but according to the will of others, who were the leaders of the state. . . .

"In his subordination, the accused did not differ from those around him, and he must be seen within this framework. He was subordinate to the dynamism of this group. His own feelings were driven out, and regimented opinion took their place. Who would not have acted thus? This dreadful experience remains indelibly in his memory, and he has of his own accord referred to it, thus showing what his attitude was. But, after the Wannsee Conference, when he saw what was being done by the rulers, his revolt abated. He capitulated to the influence of mass psychology."

Dr. Servatius referred to "the political hypnosis to which Eichmann had been subjected. "His submission was the result of the constant hammering in of the official image of history, namely, that the political leadership was carrying out an historic act, whereby everybody else had to act in accordance with the orders of the Fuehrer, whose actions were predestined by Providence. 'History is not made with velvet gloves,' they used to proclaim, and: 'Where there is carpentry work, sawdust needs must fall.' The individual was thereby cleared of responsibility, and his will became a meaningless thing. . . .

"The accused cannot serve as a substitute for the guilt of the human organizations, nor for the guilt of the epoch. . . .

"What has happened in the German nation may happen to any nation. The whole civilized world faces this problem. The recognition of this truth should heal, and it ought to teach us to avoid a new catastrophe. . . ."

He sharply criticized the German people and government of the present day for having abandoned Eichmann and for having made him the scapegoat. He added:

"This trial will certainly go down in history. . . . With respect to the accused it does not serve as a deterrent factor, and has no significance. His participation in the acts for which he was convicted was the crime of a government. This government has fallen, and the ideas represented by it have been extinguished in politics. There will be no further ground for an action by the accused in his former position . . . his punishment is not of any significance to the world. . . . The accused himself has changed; this he proved by his life after the war. His inner readjustment will be seen in the book in which he has a special chapter to warn youth. . . . This is the true expiation, the only expiation possible and meaningful. This is also the most effective. . . . It is fitting that the judge who strives for the highest justice should, in his judgment, let mercy predominate."

The accused was now called upon to say his last word. There was a marked change in his tone, and in his attitude toward the court. He was somewhat insolent; there was no longer any need to treat the judges as "superiors."

Eichmann said that his hopes for justice had been disappointed; he could not accept the judgment. And again he declared that he had become involved in misdeeds against his will:

"It was not I who persecuted Jews with avidity and fervor; that was done by the government. The whole persecution could only have been carried out by a government, never by me. . . .

"As I have already stated, it was the ruling circles, to whose ranks I did not belong, who issued the orders." There was nothing for him to confess, he said. Hans Frank had given orders and admitted his guilt. Rudolf Hoess performed mass executions. They had a reason for their confessions, Eichmann had none. "Legally I am innocent," he said.

"The witnesses here have been most untruthful. While the summing up of the testimonies and documents by the court may, at first sight, seem convincing, it is in fact deceptive and misleading. . . . No one came to me and reproached me for my activity in the performance of my duties. . . ."

Then came a calculated sly touch.

"Today, of my own free will," he continued, "I would ask the Jewish people for pardon and would confess that I am bowed down with shame at the thought of the iniquities committed against the Jews and the injustices done to them, but in the light of the grounds given in the judgment this would, in all probability, be construed as hypocrisy.

"I am not the monster I am made out to be. I am the victim of a misconception. . . .

"The reason for this lies in the fact that some of the National Socialists of those days, as well as others, had been spreading untruths about me. They endeavored to rid themselves of responsibility at my expense. . . .

"This lies at the root of the fallacy; this is the cause of my being here."

*

Next day, on December 15, 1961, the courtroom was hushed. Everyone could hear the beating of his own heart and feel the burden of history on his shoulders. The court was to pronounce its sentence.

Eichmann was told to rise. He stood at attention, petrified. His intense emotion was unmistakable.

The court agreed that there was substance in the argument that the death sentence was mandatory, but since the matter was open to some doubt the court preferred to deal with it as though it were discretionary.

"With a deep sense of the responsibility resting upon us, we have considered what is the proper penalty to be meted out to the accused, and have arrived at the conclusion that for the due punishment of the accused, and for the deterrence of others, the maximum penalty laid down by the law has to be imposed in this case. In our judgment we have described the crimes in which the accused participated—crimes of unparalleled enormity in their nature and their extent. The aim of the crimes against the Jewish people of which the accused has been convicted was to blot out an entire people from the face of the earth. . . .

"But at this stage, when the sentence is to be considered, we have to take into account also—and perhaps first and foremost—the injury to the victims as individuals which was involved in these crimes and the untold suffering which they and their families have undergone, and continue to undergo, as the result of these crimes. Indeed, the dispatch by the accused of every train carrying a thousand souls to Auschwitz or to any of the other places of extermination amounted to direct participation by the accused in one thousand acts of premeditated murder, and his legal and moral responsibility for those murders is in no way less than the measure of liability of him who put those persons with his own hands into the gas chambers. . . .

"Even had we found that the accused acted out of blind obedience, as he alleges, yet we would have said that one who had participated in crimes of such dimensions for years on end has to undergo the greatest punishment known to the law, and no order given to him could be a ground even for mitigating his punishment. But in fact we have found that in acting as he did the accused identified himself in his heart with the orders received by him and was actuated by an ardent desire to attain the criminal object. . . .

"This court sentences Adolf Eichmann to death for the crimes against the Jewish people, the crimes against humanity and the war crimes of which he has been found guilty. . . ."

The whole session lasted sixteen minutes.

This was the end of the proceedings, in District Court Case Jerusalem, Number 40/61.

CHAPTER 22

Appeal and Aftermath

After the conclusion of the hearing in the District Court there was a chance to have a second, deeper look into the mail that had poured into my office.

People wrote in various languages, from the four corners of the earth; occasionally even the polyglots of the Ministry's translation department were in difficulties. Many writers, especially from Africa and the Far East, who sounded as if this were the first time they had heard of the Jewish disaster, expressed their intense indignation and dismay. People would give vent to their emotions in different ways, ranging from a few words scribbled on a simple piece of paper in remote Finland to a long cable dispatched from New York. They felt a need and a desire to identify themselves with us and to give some expression to their feelings. We were profoundly touched and grateful.

The greater part of these letters, over five thousand of them, arrived from Israel. It was the overwhelming popular reaction of a nation shocked to the core. Many, probably youngsters, too ashamed to reveal themselves but still wishing to react somehow, expressed their emotions in various ways. Many anonymous letters and postcards of encouragement arrived from different parts of the country, revealing the people's feelings. School classes sent me collective letters, journals and specimens from exhibitions devoted to the subject. Teachers sent selected pupils' compositions and poems, many of them most expressive.

A girl wrote saying she had no uncles and aunts to visit on Saturdays and holidays, like other children, but had never understood before why they were all dead.

"The trial explained to me the behavior of the six million from a human point of view," wrote a youngster of fifteen from Haifa. A girl of seventeen from Ramat Gan went further. "I could not honor all my relatives about whom I heard from my father. I loathed them for letting themselves be slaughtered. Thank you for opening my eyes to what had really happened."

Our youth, who were born or grew up in a free country, could not fully comprehend how deep the national disaster was and how it had come about. Now, when the young Israeli followed the trial, it dawned on him that he was no different from the millions who had perished. They were his own flesh and blood. He was merely fortunate not to have been in Europe himself in Hitler's time; he, too, would have been sent to Auschwitz. Moreover, since it was often a matter of chance who had left Europe in time and who had stayed behind, the Israeli realized that one of those who perished there might have taken his place in Israel. There might have been 600,000 *other* Jews in Israel when we proclaimed the establishment of the Jewish state; then *they* would have fought the War of Independence and secured its survival. Had we, who had the good fortune to be at the time outside the reach of the Nazis, been under their heel, we could not have behaved differently than the Jews of Europe.

There were countless touching expressions of this upsurge of self-identification with the departed part of the nation.

"We were horrified as we listened to the revelations of the trial which brought us face to face with the disaster," wrote children of Kibbutz Bet-Alpha. "I am shattered to the depth of my heart, though I was not there when it had all happened," wrote a girl of fourteen from Tel Aviv. "I follow all the reports of the trial and have a full collection, which I peruse from time to time, though I have to prepare now for my college examinations," wrote another girl. "I hate this kind of letter but cannot refrain from writing to you for I am all shocked," wrote a youngster of Jerusalem. "My boy, Shlomo, shut himself away for hours with the text of your speech. He is devouring everything connected with the trial," wrote a father.

Extensive research undertaken by the Ministry of Education revealed a deep, revolutionary impact of the trial on the minds of the youth of the country.

Adults, too, sent in their expressions of appreciation and good wishes. "I lost my whole family in Europe. They stayed behind when I came to the country as a pioneer. I do not even know where they were buried. Your speech will be their gravestone," wrote a woman from Haifa.

But the most touching and precious letters came to me from the survivors of the catastrophe. Some sent in the yellow badges of ghetto days which they had kept all these years. A man sent me a picture of three little children riding ponies, and wrote: "This is their last picture, from summer 1939. They were all killed in Treblinka, and against the laws of nature I, their father, survived them. I empower you to charge Eichmann also on behalf of these three innocent children."

"I have lived in extreme tension since Eichmann's apprehension," wrote a survivor from Acre. "Perhaps writing to you will reduce my strain."

"When I was discharged from Bergen-Belsen as a girl of fourteen," wrote a woman of Jerusalem, "I always hoped that one day I would be able to avenge the loss of my parents and of my whole family, though I did not know what revenge was. I could do nothing all these years, but now, having listened to the trial, I feel some relief."

There were other letters laden with emotion. "I kept my tears back all these years. I can weep now," wrote a woman saved as a child from the Kovno ghetto. "Our neighbors here will now stop wondering how we managed to survive," wrote a couple in a joint letter.

"I was ten years old when I was liberated," wrote a member of a kibbutz. "Fourteen years of life in this country have corrected much of my distorted childhood, but I had to live and see this trial to relive all the horror, to be able to live it down."

"I relive with you the tragic days," a schoolteacher wrote to me. "I was nine years old that summer in 1942 when my despairing parents, who were about to be deported, delivered me to their Christian neighbors. With their help I survived," wrote a woman who signed with initials only. "I saw and passed through a lot, and later related these things, without ever shedding a tear. It was only when listening to your opening address that the clock was put backward and the tears of the small orphan girl came out now, after nineteen years. Thank you for helping me to cry."

"We feel better now that the story has been told to the world" was a reaction we had from many of the survivors who, through the trial, experienced a kind of emotional catharsis.

By citing a few specimens it is impossible to do justice to all these letters, which my wife collected and devotedly sorted out, and which we both treasure to this day. For each letter revealed the writer's deepest feelings. These messages sustained us both in the difficult, nerve-racking days of strain in court, when the expressions of encouragement and warm appreciation of people from all walks of life were a real comfort and the fullest possible compensation. Now I had the chance also to reply to most of them.

*

There were also, of course, some brickbats and threatening letters. One stenciled letter in German, in the traditional Nazi jargon, was mailed to various persons in Israel, requesting the "subhuman" Jews to stop the trial—or else. . . . Some abusive letters arrived from Germany and other places, all in the *Stuermer* style.

But there were thousands of other messages. Many people were worried that we might not be sufficiently informed of certain facts or acquainted with certain publications. Our library was soon enriched with additional copies of books dealing with the Nazi period and quotations from hundreds of documents. Various approaches to the investigation and interrogation were suggested. We were deeply grateful for these manifestations of interest and goodwill.

Hundreds of letters arrived from Germany; some writers resented the suggestion that the whole German people was involved. "Did you have to bring Eichmann back to life? . . . We were not all Nazis. Now that people are beginning to forget must you remind them again?" wrote a girl of nineteen. But most writers expressed their shock. "I am ashamed of everything I belong to, when I watch the TV these days," wrote a young engineer from Hamburg, "but I am not ashamed of the tears that stream from my eyes as I hear all this."

"Germany is still my country," wrote a twenty-one year-old man. "My friends and I wish to do something to atone for what our elders have done against humanity. If we could only hope to rehabilitate Germany, even partially . . . We wish to work in Israel and offer the best we have. Will you take us?"

Children from Piacenza, Italy, sent me their school journal devoted to the trial, saying they were horrified to hear of the misfortunes that befell the poor Jewish children, and promising to do all they could, when they grew up, to see that nothing of this kind should ever happen again.

There were hundreds of touching manifestations of interest and good wishes. A woman from Germany arranged for flowers to be sent once a month as long as the trial lasted.

Many messages, of different kinds, reached the prison authorities for Eichmann. The Chicago division of the Nazi Party cabled their birthday greetings to Eichmann, assuring him that he "set an example for us to follow." A man from Hamburg wrote that "the spirit of the German nation lives in the Nazi ideas." A man who signed himself Josef Niegast of Salzburg assured Eichmann that "millions of Germans did not consider you a murderer or a knave." The day the trial began a cable in German was received from Gothenburg, Nebraska, U.S.A., saying: "The fight goes on. We belong to you. Perish Judea. Old Comrades."

Some messages were the angry reactions of people who could not contain their feelings on Eichmann's statements in evidence, for example: "How dare you say that the Jews were the enemies of Germany: did your grandfather fight for Germany in 1870–71 and your father in 1914–18? The reward was that you took both my mother and my grandmother away for deportation."

A derisive poem was sent by a lawyer of Wasserburg about the "super-Aryan in the glass cubicle," ending with an expression of regret that "I have to belong to the same nation as he does." There was an angry cable from Winnipeg, Canada: "Drop dead!"

"How can you say you do not regret anything and then be allowed to put down your memoirs in writing?" wrote a lady from Quimperlé, France.

Most of Eichmann's mail was of a religious nature. Many tried to reconcile him to religion by different means. "It will do you good in the loneliness of your cell to communicate with God," wrote a woman from Birmingham,

England, in a Christmas message. "You cannot bring the dead back to life, but I often wonder, if you had the power, would you?" she added.

An English schoolgirl entreated him in warm terms to pray. Twenty children from an orphanage in Worms-Hochheim, told him they were praying for him "on behalf of the Jewish and Gypsy children whom he killed" and who "surely forgave him." What made Gabi, Rita, Hansel, Nora and the other children who signed the letter so sure? Strangely they did not even ask him to repent.

But a German from Aschaffenburg did; and to prove to Eichmann that his correspondent was not a weakling, he appended his picture in uniform, in a German Army camp. "You have to admit you were wrong," he wrote. "This is true courage. Then you will be able to make peace with yourself and with God."

A man from Bordeaux, France, tried to persuade him to admit the justice of the case against him.

A German family, after a visit to the site of Dachau concentration camp, wrote that whatever punishment was meted out to him was not enough.

*

The appeal was now uppermost in Eichmann's mind. Even his last words to the judges before sentence was pronounced were addressed to the Appellate Court. He said that he would challenge the "erroneous conclusions"; it came as no surprise, therefore, that in the fifty-nine-page written appeal, submitted by the counsel for the defense, the judgment of the lower court was attacked all along the line. Every important finding of law and fact was controverted.

The Appellate Tribunal convened on March 22, 1962, with the President of the Supreme Court, Justice Itzhak Olshan, presiding. With him on the bench were the Relieving President, Dr. Simon Agranat, and Justices Dr. Moshe Silberg, Dr. Yoel Sussman and Dr. Alfred Vitkon.

This was the last stage of the great forensic drama; legally it was an important phase since a review of a lower court's decision is a basic part of the judicial process. Otherwise it was anticlimactic since it was in the District Court that the real trial took place, where the witnesses appeared, where the story was told. Any appeal is of necessity limited to a legal review of the lower court's activity from a high altitude. Only the glaring flaws, if any, are noticed and brought out. If no such flaws exist, an appellate tribunal reformulates in authoritative and final terms the main findings of the lower court.

Dr. Servatius' oral address was much shorter than the written plea. He admitted an important point: that the accused had received a fair trial; "The jurists will confirm that it was not a show trial," he said. But, he complained, "there was too much publicity," presenting Eichmann as the central figure in the extermination program, which might have influenced the trial court. "We do not doubt for a moment," he said, "that the judges made efforts to rise above personal feelings which might clash with objective judgment of facts . . . but such efforts are vitiated by psychological considerations."

Then all the legal arguments referred to in the court below were raised again. We were now told, in addition, that Dr. Servatius had requested the West German Government to demand Eichmann's extradition. As this had been refused, he now intended, he said, to petition the Council of Europe to order Germany, as a signatory of the European Convention on Human Rights, to address such a request to Israel. Had Dr. Servatius submitted such a petition, it would certainly have been rejected but might have created a most interesting legal precedent. He never did so, either during the two years preceding the hearing in our Supreme Court or during the ten weeks that passed later, before its judgment was delivered.

Dr. Servatius proceeded to challenge the lower court's findings of fact, including the conclusion, as he put it, that "Eichmann was the gray eminence not blatantly conspicuous" behind the Nazi crimes. Everybody had named Eichmann alone, from the Nuremberg Trials onward, only because they knew he was missing, counsel claimed. That was why they had heaped all their own sins upon him, until he appeared to assume really awesome proportions. It was all in error, he said.

But Dr. Servatius failed to explain how this idea of picking out Eichmann as a scapegoat had occurred simultaneously to so many people, in various places.

Dr. Servatius bitterly contrasted Eichmann's position in the Jerusalem dock with that of Kurt Becher, who, we were told, had become so rich that he paid many millions of German marks in property tax. For this Eichmann lacked the talent, his counsel claimed. Nor did he possess, counsel said, the dexterity of Veesenmayer, who "forgot everything," or the cleverness of Professor Six, who for all his dark deeds in the past had maneuvered himself into a respectable position in the Germany of today.

In this argument Dr. Servatius had my full sympathy. It is indeed appalling how many active participants in the Nazi atrocities have escaped virtually unpunished.

The defense reiterated its position on Eichmann's modest standing, but the court soon put searching questions. If Eichmann was merely "a transport officer," why did he go out of his way to contact the Government of Monaco on some Jewish refugees there, pursuing the matter so insistently that even his own Foreign Office expressed its annoyance and surprise? Why did he issue deportation instructions for Belgium? After a moment's reflection, Dr. Servatius said that he could give no explanation.

On Eichmann's obvious efforts to block all exits for the Hungarian Jews, Dr. Servatius said that there had been differences of opinion on the matter in high quarters, and "when masters are at loggerheads, the servants get dragged into the quarrel."

Dr. Servatius again asked that evidence be heard "to prove that Eichmann's abduction was an action of the State of Israel." He wanted the court to hear evidence of Dr. Hans Globke, as "expert on Nuremberg legislation," to recall Joel Brand on some particulars concerning the "goods for blood" deal, and to call Dr. Seraphim, of the University of Goettingen, as an expert on the problem of whether Eichmann could have obtained a transfer to other duties.

Finally, on the subject of punishment, Dr. Servatius cited Rousseau's view that there is no culprit who cannot be saved from sin. Eichmann was no longer a danger to anyone; on the contrary, if spared he might be an instrument for the "obviation of dangers," he concluded.

*

My reply had again to cover both the written and the oral pleadings. I recalled Eichmann's argument that he had followed the Fuehrer in accordance with his undertaking, in the oath of allegiance, to obey orders and do whatever was necessary for the good of Germany.

But what difference did that make, even if it were true? I asked. His very oath to follow orders wherever they might lead, even to the depths of hell, was among his worst crimes.

Individual responsibility for criminal acts, I claimed, represented justice while the primitive concept of collective irresponsibility was the denial of justice.

Hitler and Himmler could not kill all the Jews by themselves. They had subordinates who served as their eyes, ears and hands. All these were partners in crime.

The main points of law and fact challenged by Dr. Servatius were briefly referred to again.

In reference to the picture of the "peaceful citizen," contrite and repentant, who was no longer a danger to anyone, I recalled Eichmann's confirmation in court of his expression of regret to Sassen, twelve years after the war, that he had not quite finished the total destruction of European Jewry, for "we were implementing a task for our people, our blood and the freedom of nations, in stamping out the most cunning spirit among mankind." These were the regrets of this "peace-loving man," I concluded, saying:

"This wicked man brought down on European Jewry a night of horrors and blood which lasted several years. All through those years this man did nothing else but send people to death after humiliation, torment and torture. For the homes of Israel that were silenced, for a whole diaspora that was destroyed, for a third of a people that was slaughtered, for a million children —the nation's pride and hope—there is no fit punishment. For every child he sent to death he deserved a fourfold death penalty. Let the court sentence him for only one of his deeds, and let history doom him to eternal shame for all the other crimes.

"And let it be proclaimed from Jerusalem, for all to know and hear, that he who chooses Eichmann's path of hatred and murder, he who attains power in the Eichmann way, will be punished by death and end in infamy."

Dr. Servatius replied at length, repeating his earlier arguments. The hearing of the appeal was completed in six sessions. On May 29 the Court of Appeal reconvened to deliver its judgment.

*

Eichmann entered the dock carrying a load of papers. He wore the same dark suit which he had throughout the trial. He bowed to his lawyer, as he usually did, and sat down.

The deputy president delivered the first part of the judgment. Again, the result was clear after the first few sentences.

The manner in which the District Court dealt with the various arguments had been "exhaustive, profound and most convincing," said Justice Agranat on behalf of the five judges of the Supreme Court. He added:

"We should say at once that we fully concur, without hesitation or reserve, in all its conclusions and reasons, because they are fully supported by copious judicial precedents that were cited in the judgment and by the substantial proof culled and abstracted out of the monumental mass of evidence produced to the court. Moreover, we are in duty bound to state that were it not for the grave outcome of the decision of the court constituting the subject of the appeal, we would have seen no need whatever to formulate our opinion separately and in our own language—as we contemplate doing—for the conclusions of the District Court rest on solid foundations."

The legal problems were again reviewed, this time from the angle of an Appellate Court examining from a detached viewpoint the results reached by the court of lower instance. The problem of retroactive legislation was this time dealt with in the following terms:

"As to the *ethical* aspect of the principle, it may be agreed that one's sense of justice . . . recoils from punishing a person for an act committed by him which, at the time of its commission, had not yet been prohibited by law, and in respect of which he could not have known, therefore, that he would become criminally liable. But this cannot extend to the abominable crimes ascribed to the appellant, certainly not if they were committed on the scale and the dimension described in the judgment. In such a case the abovementioned maxim loses its moral value and all moral foundation. One's sense of justice must necessarily recoil even more from the nonpunishment of one who participated in such outrages, for he could not contend—as the appellant could not successfully contend in regard to his share in the execution of the 'Final Solution'—that, at the time of his actions, he was unaware that he was violating deeply rooted universal moral values."

The Supreme Court stated that "the crimes in question must be regarded today as crimes which, even in the past, were banned by the Law of Nations and entailed individual criminal liability."

In support of this proposition the legal authorities and the principles of international law were again reviewed. The Nuremberg principles, the court said, were not merely imposed by the victors; they constituted a development vital for the survival of mankind and the stability of the world order. Crimes against humanity, by their very nature, must necessarily extend beyond the borders of the state to which the perpetrators belong and which tolerated or encouraged their outrages; for such acts can undermine the foundations of the international community as a whole and impair its stability.

Such crimes have always been forbidden by customary international law and for this reason were treated as universal, every country being free to try and punish them. This meant "in essence, that that power is vested in every state regardless of the fact that the offense was committed outside its territory by a person who did not belong to it, provided he is in its custody at the time he is brought to trial."

Justice Agranat surveyed the various legal schools of thought on the subject and concluded that "the state which prosecutes and punishes a person for that offense acts solely as the organ and agent of the international community." After quoting many authorities the Supreme Court added:

"We have also taken into consideration the possible desire of other countries to try the appellant insofar as the crimes included in the indictment were committed in those countries or their evil effects were felt there. . . . It is to be observed that we have not heard of a single protest from any of these countries against conducting the trial in Israel, and it is reasonable to believe that, as Israel has exercised its jurisdiction in this matter, no other state has demanded the right to do so. What is more, it is precisely the fact that the crimes in question and their effects have extended to numerous countries that empties the territorial principle of its content in the present case, and justifies Israel in assuming criminal jurisdiction by virtue of the 'universal' principle. This is so because Israel could not possibly have decided to which particular country the appellant ought to have been extradited without the selection being arbitrary."

The Supreme Court now proceeded to formulate the definition of "*fugitive from justice under the law of nations,*" since the crimes that were attributed to Eichmann were of an international character and had been condemned publicly by the civilized world.

This was a novel and interesting definition, which marks a further step in the development of international law on universal jurisdiction. Such a fugitive—a Cain who has sinned against mankind as a whole—is liable to be tried by any civilized country, which in bringing him to trial enforces international law through its laws and judicial organs. Any court could issue a warrant for his detention and any country could claim the right to try him.

In view of this definition the manner in which such an offender is brought to justice is quite immaterial.

"The moment it is admitted that the State of Israel possesses criminal jurisdiction both according to local law and according to the law of nations it must also be conceded that the court is not bound to investigate the manner and legality of the appellant's detention. This indeed is the conclusion to be drawn from the judgments upon which the District Court has rightly relied."

On the argument of "act of state," the Supreme Court said that even the orthodox "positivists" concede that "lawless laws" which violate basic justice can be no protection.

Nor could Eichmann claim immunity on the ground that he was subject to orders. After a review of the judicial pronouncements on the subject, the Supreme Court held: "The appellant carried out the extermination order . . . with genuine zeal and devotion. Therefore this defense does not apply in any case."

*

Turning to the facts of the case, Justice Silberg spoke for the court:

"The canvas exposed to us in this appeal tells a tale full of blood and tears, the story of the catastrophe that befell European Jewry. No human pen, no human tongue could ever succeed in describing the merest outline of the suffering of the millions who were killed, massacred and burned in the extermination camps and gas chambers through the murderous tools invented and improved by the 'fertile' brains and the perverse imaginations of Nazi scum. Exalted science was harnessed in the service of crime, high education was the nursemaid of brutality and evil—this was the innovation of the school of the Nazi doctrine. Before the rise of Hitler's regime in the thirties of the twentieth century, no one had ever envisaged such a spectacle."

Recalling the Nazi system of administration, built on dictatorship, dominating all arms and spheres of authority, Justice Silberg declared: "They have constructed those arms in the shape of a tapering pyramid, of which the uppermost all-powerful apex was the person of the Fuehrer himself. It follows that the more the pyramid tapered and sharpened, the more numerous were the bottlenecks that were necessarily created, where two or more authorities handled the same job, albeit—very conceivably—from different aspects and approaches, with a good deal of overlapping between them."

But Eichmann's department "had no need of equally ranking partners or associates from outside for his job." Even in relation to his superiors the Supreme Court found, "he held a powerful, virtually independent status." To be sure, he was formally subordinate to Mueller, and Mueller to Heydrich, but in effect and in actual fact these Big Two left to the appellant all affairs regarding Jews.

"His was not at all an inferior status but a high, and indeed exalted, one, and in his capacity he held full sway over all the affairs of the Jews, their lives as well as their property, throughout the sphere of German influence, in Germany itself as well as far beyond its confines. . . . Therefore, he was not vaingloriously bragging when he said to the Commissioner of the International Red Cross that 'in all Jewish affairs he was directly empowered by the SS Reichsfuehrer [Himmler].'"

A few selected facts from the vast mass of evidence were referred to as illustrating Eichmann's zeal and the manner in which he went out of his way to see the Final Solution through. The Supreme Court's conclusion was:

"The facts indicated above also constitute a decisive rebuttal of learned counsel's third contention: namely, that the appellant was acting only on orders from above. . . .

"As a matter of fact, the appellant did not at all receive orders 'from above'; it was he who was the high and mighty one, he who was the commander in all that pertained to Jewish affairs. He ordered and commanded, not only without orders from his superiors in the hierarchy of the service, but also, at times, in absolute conflict with these orders. . . .

"It is clear that the *idea* of the Final Solution was not his own, but the Fuehrer's. Yet that idea might not have assumed so satanic and infernal an expression—in the blood of millions of tortured and martyred Jews—but for the thorough planning, the zeal, the fanatical enthusiasm and the insatiable bloodthirstiness of the appellant and those who did his bidding. We do not here minimize by even one iota the terrible guilt that rests on the heads of many, many others."

And Justice Silberg concluded:

"In deciding to confirm both the judgment and the sentence passed on the appellant we know only too well how utterly inadequate this death sentence is, as compared to the millions of dreadful deaths he inflicted on his victims. Even as there is no word in human speech to designate deeds such as the deeds of the appellant, so there is no punishment in human laws that would fit in its gravity the guilt of the appellant.

"But our knowledge that any treatment meted out to the appellant would be inadequate, that no penalty or retribution inflicted on him would be sufficient, dare not move us to mitigate the punishment. Indeed, there can be so sense in sentencing to death, under the Law of Punishment of Nazis and Nazi Collaborators, he who killed a hundred people, while setting free, or merely keeping under guard and in security, he who killed millions. When, in 1950, the Israeli legislature provided the maximum penalty laid down in the law, it could not have envisaged a criminal greater than Adolf Eichmann; and, if we are not to invalidate the will of the legislature, we must impose on Eichmann the maximum penalty provided in Section 1 of the law, that is: the death penalty.

"The fact that the appellant—by a variety of ruses, escape, hiding, false papers, etc.—succeeded in evading the death sentence that awaited him, along with his comrades, at Nuremberg, cannot afford him relief here, when he at long last stands his trial before an Israel Court of Justice."

The judgment of the Supreme Court took three and a half hours to deliver. It ended the legal proceedings. The mills of justice had done their work. It took them exactly two years.

Dr. Servatius left Israel the next day. He again declared, this time after the final sentence, that "the trial was fair."

*

Eichmann was quick in appealing to the President for mercy.

In his petition Eichmann again reiterated his old plea, on which he pinned his last hopes. "I abhor the atrocities committed on the Jews as the greatest crime, and consider it just that the people responsible should be brought to justice now and in the future," he wrote. "But a line should be drawn between leaders and tools like myself. I was not a responsible leader and therefore do not consider myself guilty. I pray you, Mr. President, to commute the death sentence!"

Thus Adolf Eichmann, for whom the lives of millions had been nothing, was now fighting for his own life to the last by justifying the trials of his leaders and comrades and the death penalties inflicted on them. He even asked for further trials and punishments—but for others, not himself.

The President, the late Itzhak Ben-Zvi, secluded himself with the application and the written opinion of the Minister of Justice, which accompanied it as is the practice with all applications for pardon. There were some university professors, notably the venerable Martin Buber, who maintained that even Eichmann should not cause Israel to put up a gallows, and that it would be "an historic error" to execute him, as this might start a new myth, that of "anti-Christ."

Some people argued that the execution would be an act of revenge. It was an untenable argument. This was not an "eye for an eye" affair. There was no vengeance for the twelve million eyes closed forever. Others argued that his execution would exonerate the German nation as a whole of the crimes. This again did not seem to make sense.

The matter was widely debated in the British press following Professor Norman Bentwich's letter in the *Times* in which he recommended the commutation of the sentence and the deportation of Eichmann to Germany (December 19). *The Economist* felt that what happened to Eichmann was really not important and that it would be unfortunate if his fate were to loom so large as to overshadow the very lesson which the trial attempted to drive home (December 23).

The Israeli press was unanimous in its request that the judgment be carried out.

The organ closest to the government, *Davar,* wrote:

There is no room for clemency or leniency. We say this with the moral force of a people whose legislative assembly has abolished the death penalty, a people which has never, since it became a sovereign nation, carried out an execution. But non-implementation of this verdict will be an affront to justice.

The independent *Ha'aretz* commented:

Even those who generally oppose the death penalty must now admit that in this case it is justified. A man sentenced for such crimes as Eichmann has no right to live.

Labor's *Lamerhav* voiced the same opinion:

Although the implementation of the verdict will not atone for the death of a single innocent victim, we can only express the wish of the entire nation that it be carried out without delay.

The English-language Jerusalem *Post,* while supporting the same view, added:

Israel has applied infinite care to the case of one man of this generation. Germany's own work in this respect is still far from finished and the future safety and security of Europe may depend on its being done with the surgical accuracy and objectivity that have been displayed by the prosecutor and judges here over the past two years.

After hours of solitary deliberation the President decided not to accede to the application.

Now that the judgment had become final it had to be put into effect. There was no reason for delay. Nor was there any sense in putting to the test definite neo-Nazi threats to take hostages for Eichmann. His wife had already seen him between the hearing of the appeal and the sentence. No one else asked to see him, and there were no reasons to put off the execution. The Commissioner for Prisons was immediately informed; he put into operation the arrangements he had made immediately after the dismissal of the appeal. At about 8 P.M. on May 31, 1962, Eichmann was told that his petition had been refused by the President, and that the execution would take place close to midnight. Eichmann asked for a bottle of wine, wrote a few letters to his family, and was ready when Rev. Hull and Mrs. Hull came to see him. He told them he would die in peace because of his belief in Nature as God. All endeavors to reconcile him with religion failed. "The closer Eichmann came to execution, the more defiant he became in rejecting Christianity," declared Rev. Hull.

Even at the last moment he took care of external appearances. He asked for the fetters on his ankles to be loosened as he "could not stand up properly." The government officials prescribed by law, including a doctor as well as four newspapermen, were present. "We shall soon meet," Eichmann said, when he noticed them. He refused the black hood, declared, using the Nazi formula, that he was a *Gottesglaeubiger* (a believer in God), sent his greetings to Germany, Austria and Argentina, "the countries I shall not forget," as well as to his wife and family, and added: "I had to obey the rules of war and my flag." "Obey," "rules," "war" and "flag" were his last words. A moment later the trap door was released and he was dead.

His body was cremated and in the predawn hours of June 1, 1962, his ashes were placed aboard a police boat, which headed out to sea. When it was well beyond the three-mile limit, the pilot cut the boat's engines. The vessel glided for a while over the swell and then Arieh Nir, the Prisons Commissioner, tossed the ashes overboard. The waves of the Mediterranean washed over them just twenty-five years after Eichmann—a rising young SS officer on the first important assignment of a career dedicated to fighting the Jews—had sailed across these same waters en route to Palestine and Egypt on a secret mission.

CHAPTER 23

Reflections—Three Years Later

Three years after the final disposal of the Case of the Attorney General of Israel vs. Eichmann, an attempt can be made to sum up its consequences.

The immediate result of the trial was to compel the world to confront its yesterdays anew. Human nature finds it painful to look unflinchingly at the horrors of the past; it is very quick to forget them. It is astonishing how men tend to gloss over the most obvious lessons of their lives, condemning themselves to repeat their own mistakes.

This is what had happened with the appalling chapter of Hitlerism, "What good will it do to remember?" many people said. They found it convenient to label Nazism an atavistic outburst from some hidden stratum of bestiality; they cherished the belief that the menace had been successfully subdued, and the lid firmly clamped down over the weak spots to prevent further eruptions. Thus the dead past was left to bury its dead, and the world left happily free to enjoy the present.

The Jerusalem trial and its revelations shattered this complacency. Its drama commanded attention; the disclosures as they unfolded pricked many bubbles. There were noticeable repercussions in Germany and the world at large; there was a sharp impact on the Jewish scene.

The inspection at close range of the techniques employed in the systematic extermination of a nation shocked the world. It was the human details that made the events real, for the mere statistical facts were well known. The revelation of the technical feasibility of the cold-blooded, calculated annihilation of a whole nation including the deliberate murder of its children, the details of how it was done, the realization that the criminals were able to do their work unhindered, were horrifying.

It so happened that the trial began at the time when Gagarin, the Russian cosmonaut, made his first flight into space, and the hearings were concluded when Carpenter of America had just performed a similar feat. Were we, then, heading for the stars, or were we standing on the brink of an abyss of self-destruction? Were these shattering events the last convulsions of a horrible past or the forerunners of an even more disastrous future?

No one, as yet, can answer these questions. But the principle of personal responsibility, proclaimed afresh from Jerusalem, may prove a factor of great, perhaps decisive, importance. At the Eichmann trial the rule was publicly pronounced by an authoritative and universally accepted tribunal that the perpetrator of mass murder will not find shelter in the orders of his superiors, but will be held personally accountable for his deeds.

That was why, basically, the verdict was generally acclaimed and accepted by public opinion. The doctrine that a criminal order is no excuse can no longer be seriously challenged, certainly not at the bar of a court. It has become a principle, well illustrated and, it is to be hoped, deeply implanted in the minds of men.

It may well take some time before a criminal is brought to justice. In Eichmann's case it took fifteen years, since he had gone into hiding, but he was ultimately found, exposed to the obloquy of mankind and executed. Neither the passage of time nor the distance of asylum saved him. These facts are worth bearing in mind.

Moreover, it was salutary that it was the operational executive of the Final Solution who was brought to trial. The executors, the men responsible for the perpetration of dreadful deeds are not less—indeed, often more—dangerous than the men who evolve ideas, who make the plans and give the orders. It is for the men in the field, in the first place, that a striking and deterrent example was established by this trial.

Moreover, it was proved that the criminal's confidence in ultimate victory may well be groundless. When Eichmann first embarked on his career, he was undoubtedly sure of German victory.

In this confused century this was an important lesson. Fittingly, I think, it came from Jerusalem. If kept fresh in the minds of men, it may have a sobering effect one day when another adventurer, confident of victory, orders his followers to unleash destruction on the nations.

In the general and legal literature, Eichmann is already becoming more than a name. He is developing into a concept signifying the type of evildoer who joyfully follows a leader and carries out his orders with redoubled zeal.

The Jerusalem trial thus brought out clearly once again the basic notions of right and wrong and drove them home with exemplary force, in the hope that if a man finds himself in the future entrusted with a task similar to Eichmann's he will stop in his tracks to reflect whether he may not share Eichmann's fate. In this alone the trial has performed a service to humanity.

*

There have also been other, indirect repercussions on the international scene.

A grave moral indictment was registered at the Jerusalem proceedings against the free world: that it stood by inactive before the war when a nation was tortured and did not offer refuge or react when a nation was later led to the slaughter. I avoided playing up this aspect of the case; the court was trying the murderer, not those who looked on while his crimes were being committed. It would have done my case little good to join hands expressly with Eichmann in blaming other nations for his acts. But I placed the material on record and it heavily incriminated the free world.

There was no immediate direct reply to the charge, but it produced a widespread admission of moral guilt, which may have been partly responsible for strengthening the prevailing resolution not to allow the Arabs to complete what Hitler started by attacking Israel, the country of the remnant which was delivered from his clutches. The democracies cannot, without losing the last vestige of decency and honor, repeat the callousness they so recently showed.

Prejudice, however, lives long and dies slowly. Anti-Semitism is still a powerful and dangerous evil, though not so widely in vogue in intellectual quarters today. Some violent anti-Jewish outbursts followed Eichmann's execution in various parts of the world, mainly in Argentina; a Jewish girl even paid with her life. The Jew-haters reacted like a snake whose lair has been exposed. On the whole, however, the exposure to strong light had a disastrous effect on them; they cannot stand the light for long.

In some quarters, especially in the Catholic Church, voices have been raised to demand the rectification of the millennial wrong toward the Jews, which has been responsible for the spilling of an ocean of innocent blood throughout the ages. It has long been realized that the absurd doctrine of deicide has been responsible for implanting bottomless hatred against the Jew. In a way, it even made the Final Solution more easily acceptable, for if a Jew *is* an agent of Satan, why shrink from the last conclusion—even though it is forbidden by the Church—that he must be destroyed? It was thus possible for the Jew-baiter, by twisting Christian doctrine, to exploit its terrible latent potentialities.

The fact that the Supreme Pontiff and the overwhelming majority of the clergy held their peace while the crimes were being committed disturbed many consciences. Moreover, it was proved that a strong and courageous stand on the part of the Church against another Nazi crime, the destruction of the insane, did stop the murders. This will be recorded to the credit of Bishop (later Cardinal) von Galen. We can only speculate heartbreakingly how many Jewish lives could have been saved by a similar stand on the part of Rome through an encyclical expressly forbidding Catholics to murder the innocent Jews.

The problem of the Church's moral responsibility for its silence has been widely debated. Hochhuth's successful play, *The Deputy,* which directly accuses Rome, has provoked angry retorts.

The Church acts very slowly, through its century-old channels, but there is positive evidence that the revelations of the Jerusalem trial have had a deep impact on its liberal elements, which are resolved to withdraw the ancient, terrible and false accusation of deicide against Jewry. At the Ecumenical Council held in the Vatican in 1964-65, some steps were taken in this direction under the leadership of Augustus Cardinal von Bea of Germany, who made a valiant attempt to bring Roman Catholic thought into harmony with our own era by formally exculpating Jewry of any guilt for the death of Jesus. Unfortunately, the Princes of the Church went only half way in their historical "resolution." Only the future can tell whether these steps will ever be carried to their logical conclusion. It is an historic test for the Church itself. Actually, it is Christianity which needs exoneration.

"Was all this possible only in Germany?" is a recurrent question.

The Germans prefer to believe that almost anyone, everywhere, if adequately conditioned by the propaganda of a dictatorship, could become a concentration-camp murderer, but they fail to add that this conditioning took place and was possible in Germany after over a century of indoctrination by the glorification of war and racial hatred. It was this nation that freely gave the largest number of votes to a ruler who had openly proclaimed that he would unflinchingly plunge the country into war, who announced in advance that he would suffer no democratic nonsense but would govern by the *Fuehrerprinzip.* One resolve the future Fuehrer made crystal-clear: that he would fight Jewry to the end.

This man could have gained the free support of over thirteen million electors only because the nation had beforehand been thoroughly corrupted by so many nationalist thinkers, and this was clearly illuminated in the course of the Jerusalem trial.

Whether the same thing could have happened in another country, after similar preparation, is debatable. Perhaps it could. But it *did* happen to Germany, which committed the unprecedented act of genocide, and which started two aggressive world wars in one generation.

It is naïve to assume that a pathological condition which developed so long and corroded the national soul so deeply could be cured in twenty years, even had Germany worked on the moral readjustment and rehabilitation of her people with a greater tenacity of purpose than she has in fact done. The assumption that present-day Germany is an entirely new nation, immune to the perils of the past, is therefore as dangerous as it is false. Of course there are no concentration camps and no Fuehrer. Of course there are free elections. There has even been a marked decline in the membership of neo-Nazi organizations and a corresponding drop in the number of anti-

Semitic outbursts since the peak they reached in 1959. But these are not the points at issue; under the Kaiser and the Weimar Republic also things looked promising on the surface, and still the latent tendencies were there all the time. The problem is whether the national spirit of Germany has radically and irrevocably changed. Of this I am more than doubtful. Such changes in national traits do occur in peoples, as every student of social history knows. But it is a gradual, long-drawn-out process.

In summer 1964, I publicly expressed the view that Germany's moral rehabilitation is incomplete, and that if a Fuehrer appeared now the nation would be ready to march behind him. A popular newspaper, *Abendpost*, took up the issue with some leading German personalities. Many said that I was "understandably" wrong; others categorically rejected my analysis; but numerous democratic leaders and clergymen of all denominations supported my view.

There are unfortunately forces at work to counteract Germany's moral recovery. Among them is the power politics of the West, which is responsible for remilitarizing Germany and injecting her organism once again with the germs to which she is constitutionally susceptible.

The recent widespread desire of many Germans to put an end to the further investigation of war crimes was an alarming omen. Another bad sign is the fact that some of the perpetrators, especially those who belonged to the Wehrmacht, are again being spared exposure. The folly of the attempt to "save the army's honor," which was committed after World War I, is being repeated.

It was only under the strongest pressure from public opinion, both domestic and international, that the German authorities compromised on a brief postponement of the deadline for the statute of limitations, a statute that in effect meant an amnesty for all war crimes after a certain date. By failing to abolish the deadline altogether the German authorities missed the opportunity of proclaiming the Nazi crimes so abominable that the ordinary rules of human forgiveness could not apply to them. Moreover, the more recent war crimes trials, many of them stimulated by the Eichmann trial, often fail to live up to their educational possibilities. Public opinion might easily be focused repeatedly on each of these trials as a renewed demonstration of an evil to be faced, denounced and abhorred. Instead, the proceedings are too often a matter of mere lip service. Occasionally this results in astonishing acquittals or ridiculously inadequate sentences.

There are true democratic elements in Germany, who strive sincerely for the rebirth of their country. I maintain contact with some of them; some come to Israel from time to time, seeking their rehabilitation among the people their country so grievously wronged, and they surely deserve every encouragement.

The Jerusalem trial had a marked effect on many of these people, especially of the younger generation; many have written that this was a turning point for them. The trial also had a marked effect in leading to the renewal of abandoned investigations in Germany and the opening of many new proceedings. "An avalanche of prosecutions will now have to follow," said a senior official of the German machinery of justice, when the revelations from Jerusalem burst on the world. Official German publications acknowledge that the trial awakened public interest in the fate of the criminals so far untouched.

The Nazi doctrine, what it represented and stood for, was a powerful and corrosive poison. In most cases it destroyed the character beyond all possibility of rehabilitation. Experience proves that there are few genuine cases of ex-Nazis. There are, however, large numbers of free Nazis who ought to be apprehended, tried and punished.

On the whole, Germany still stands in need of self-purification as a duty to herself and for the peace of the world. It will be very dangerous for her to forget it.

*

On the Jewish scene the response to the trial was, of course, more immediate than elsewhere.

Delving into the terrible past facilitated a more correct appreciation of the present and, strange as it may seem, a more confident approach to the future. A better and more intimate knowledge of the facts leads to the inescapable conclusion that the usual moral yardsticks for the acts and reactions of the victims are totally fallacious. No one can possibly know what he would have done in similar situations. Can anyone say how he would behave in an earthquake, with a stream of lava pouring over his house? Would he first alarm his neighbors, or try to protect the house, or just flee for his life? Which course is the right one?

Moral standards and imperatives, the call for proper foresight and true appreciation of the situation, which are normally expected of public figures, have little application in the face of such a calamity. The very few extreme collaborators were traitors and must be pilloried. All others were unfortunate victims.

The Jewish tragedy is so profound that it has no parallel, though it was not the first time that Jews had served as the experimental laboratory of history, starting with the dawn of national existence, through the spiritual struggle in search of monotheism and social justice, all the way down to recent events. The nation suffered grievously for its perpetual and consistent nonconformism. But it was rewarded with a unique prize: uninterrupted survival from early antiquity.

The recent loss of blood was almost fatal. When the extent of the tragedy became fully known, surviving Jewry fell into dark despair. But for the establishment of a new center of national inspiration in Israel, Hitler's war aim, the annihilation of Jewry, might well have succeeded. The sections physically surviving after the holocaust, including even the impressive American Jewry, were not yet strong or cohesive enough to replace the destroyed communities and thus to maintain the continuity of Jewish existence. Israel created a new focal point of struggle and interest, thus preserving Jewishness both for its own inhabitants and for those who live outside its boundaries. All this was dramatically demonstrated by the trial.

It came as a discovery to many that we are actually a nation of survivors. The editor of a leading newspaper told me, after listening to the shattering evidence of a woman witness in court: "For years I have been living next to this woman, without so much as an inkling of who she was." It now transpired that almost everyone in Israel had such a neighbor.

The reaction of the youth, who followed the trial with great interest, was summed up in a phrase that recurred in many letters and school essays: "Our eyes have been opened." The trial thus proved to be a strong educational factor in strengthening Jewish consciousness. The interest of the younger people in the events of the Nazi holocaust continues unabated. Israel's education authorities are trying out various means of maintaining this upsurge of identification with the nation's past. Schools are "adopting" communities that have perished and, by studying their history and outstanding personalities, carrying out the honorable duty of preserving their memory. Youngsters visit the survivors and collect evidence about the communities they have "adopted." A number of memorial books have already been written by schoolchildren on the basis of material accumulated in this way.

Important also was the realization that the only reason it was possible to hold the trial at all was that there is now a Jewish state on the map. Fifteen years earlier Dr. Chaim Weizmann had pleaded with the American Chief Counsel at Nuremberg, Robert Jackson, to be allowed to appear as a Jewish witness to unfold the great tragedy at the trial of the war criminals. Jackson politely refused, saying that his office had already assembled a great collection of material on the persecution of the Jews. "I am convinced," he wrote Dr. Weizmann, "that for the future position of the Jews in Europe, it has been better to prove our case in this manner than to have proved it by testimony."

Now it was the Jews themselves who could decide what was best for their position. They could do so because they had their own machinery of justice, their own prosecutors and their own policemen. The trial was thus, in itself, an overwhelming manifestation of the revolution in the position of the Jewish people that has taken place in this generation.

Some of the witnesses at the trial were symbolic of this transformation. Rivka Yoselewska, the woman miraculously saved from the dead, had lost everything in the mass grave at Zagorodskie, yet she survived, remarried, and, in spite of a heart condition, gave birth to two other children (see pages 73–74).

Here was a Jewish rebirth reflected in the destiny of an individual. The nation, cut off from the land of the living, seemed doomed. Yet somehow it raised itself from the sepulcher and survived. Today it continues an honorable existence in its own country. It is still deeply wounded; it is the only nation in the world that has not yet made up its terrible wartime losses. All others have benefited from the "population explosion" of the fifties and have long since surpassed their prewar figures; the Jews, who entered the war with seventeen million, still do not number more than thirteen million all over the world. But we exist and create; we are producing a new, healthy generation.

Some time ago I went as a delegate to Warsaw for the commemoration of the twentieth anniversary of the ghetto revolt. Jews came from all over the world. On Saturday we met in the only synagogue left, and after the service we sang the songs of the ghettos and of the uprising; we concluded with "*Am Yisrael Hai*" ("The People of Israel Live"). The Nazi design has been thwarted.

The trial thus brought home to everyone in Israel the basic facts and lessons of our time. But even more significant was the feeling of self-assurance and confidence that swept the nation. If Hitler, for all his fiendish powers, enormous resources and unrelenting efforts, did not succeed in wiping out Jewry when he had it at his mercy, then the age-old belief in the eternity of Israel was reaffirmed before our very eyes. The Jews had survived their mightiest enemy. The prophetic assurance bequeathed by Isaiah to the Jewish people—"No weapon that is formed against thee shall prosper"—was once again proved true. In comparison with Hitler's might the present-day anti-Semites and foes of Jewry and of Israel, formidable as they may be, still look less menacing. There can be no complacency in facing them, but there is a valid and reasonable hope of overcoming them.

Thus the great national disaster has also been a fountain of new strength, and it holds out new hope for a better future.

APPENDIX I:

Reactions to the Trial

The problems presented by the capture and trial of Adolf Eichmann evoked widespread interest. Many writers supported our position from the outset. Some observers, critical at first, gradually adopted a more understanding approach in the course of the trial; most ended with almost unreserved approval.

From more than one point of view, the process was of interest. Following are a few excerpts.

Reactions to the Principle of the Trial

Some of the most virulent attacks were launched against us by two or three leading American papers. Prejudging the basic issues in the name of fair trial, the Washington *Post* announced that "anything connected with the indictment of Eichmann is tainted with lawlessness," and that Israel was "doing a grave disservice to Jews of other nationalities" by holding the trial. (May 27, 1960)

Others, continuing along the lines of conventional arguments in the face of an unprecedented situation, chastised us for Eichmann's abduction. "No immoral or illegal act justifies another," they reminded us. "The rule of law must protect the most depraved criminals," said the *New York Times*. (June 18, 1960)

There were also, to be sure, many different voices in America and elsewhere. Many people realized that in "the choice between rules of legality and the demands of justice" it was more just to stretch an arm across the ocean to apprehend Eichmann than to let him remain free. (New York *Herald Tribune*, June 11, 1960)

"Had there been no Israeli state, Eichmann would still be at large, haunted and hunted but still mocking the process of justice." (New York *Journal-American*, June 2, 1960)

A plea for an international court was raised, even by a distinguished Jewish leader, Dr. Nahum Goldmann, President of the World Zionist Organization and the World Jewish Congress. Without doubting for a moment the legal competence of the Israeli courts, he thought the Jews could render a unique service to the principle of international cooperation by placing Eichmann at the bar of an international tribunal. He forgot, however, that no such tribunal was in existence or could have been effectively set up while the West-East breach continued. We were soon presented with an eloquent demonstration of what such a tribunal would have degenerated into, when the United Nations Security Council dealt with the problem.

Other Jewish personalities came out in defense of an Israeli court, saying that "only if Eichmann is tried in Israel will this great moral lesson of retributive justice be impressed upon the minds of the world" (Dr. Joachim Prinz, President of the American Jewish Congress, New York *Herald Tribune*, June 24, 1960), and that "there was no doubt it would be an impartial trial" (Sir Barnett Janner, President of the Board of Deputies of British Jewry, the *Jewish Chronicle*, June 24, 1960).

Some French jurists insisted that only Germany was competent to try Eichmann, implying that the nation which spawned him should bear the shame of dealing with him. Others claimed that he ought to be returned to Argentina (*Le Figaro*, June 16, 1960). One of the ablest experts on international law, Eugene Aroneanu, replied that he was "astonished to see law solemnly invoked not on the side of justice but in favor of crime." He added:

> In the state of International affairs as given, with crime prevailing rather than law, with a United Nations organization incapable of making a united stand, in short, in a world dominated by anarchy, scrupulous respect for procedure is of little value or significance. If we seek to establish the rule of law we must first find the path to righteousness. (*Le Monde*, June 11, 1960)

Israel was solidly behind the government. The Israeli press from right to left was united in its conviction that Eichmann must be tried in Israel. Public opinion was typified by an outstanding cartoonist who pictured little Israel holding a writhing serpent by the throat, while the ghosts of six million dead stand behind, putting their hands on the boy's shoulders and saying: "Keep hold of the snake!" (*Ma'ariv*, June 10, 1960)

Some typical comments were:

> The "Final Solution" was not carried out against Russians, Poles or Czechs, but only against Jews. We, the Jewish people in our own land, therefore have the right to try Eichmann, with our judges and according to our law—not forgetting that no other state made a supreme effort to apprehend him and bring him to justice. (*Ha'aretz*, June 3, 1960)

> It is only natural that the relatives of the victims should see to it that justice be done if the criminals are not turned over to the people against which their crimes were committed. The murderer of the Jewish people must be tried by Jewish judges in the Jewish State. (*Hatzofe*, June 5, 1960)

A popular evening paper addressed itself "To our Argentine friends":

> Please forgive us, dear friends, but are you really sure, quite sure, that you would have arrested Eichmann at the request of the Israel Government? If you had received such a request, would you have acted immediately upon it? Would you not have wanted, before issuing the warrant of arrest, to make certain that the facts were true? And would you not have stuck to all the formalities? And would you not have given this heinous criminal at least ten opportunities to escape, change his identity and vanish?
>
> We wanted to be sure, and that is the reason we violated the law, and now we want to be sure that the criminal will not escape from the hands of justice.
>
> And that is the reason we will not give him back. (*Ma'ariv*, June 10, 1960)

There were, of course, other countries that could have claimed the right to try Eichmann. In fact, eighteen European countries, where Eichmann's dragnets had been spread to catch Jews, might have done so.

The formerly occupied states were in favor of Israel's jurisdiction.

> All the world is grateful for the opportunity afforded to humanity to mete out justice to this monster. The court will be composed not only of citizens of the young state of Israel but also of millions slaughtered at Auschwitz, Theresienstadt, Warsaw and all the ghettos of Europe

wrote a leading Dutch newspaper (*Arnhems Dagblad,* May 25, 1960).

Similar voices were heard on all sides; it was soon obvious that there would be no request for extradition from these countries. This still left two possible claimants for Eichmann's person, who might have embarrassed us by a formal demand: Germany and Argentina.

There were, indeed, some German voices asking for Eichmann. Among them was *Der Stern,* two of whose representatives arrived in Israel soon after Eichmann and failed in the attempt to get a scoop by interviewing him, though they came with a letter from his son. (The letter contained a phrase that had all the appearance of a secret message. It spoke of "a deep fertilizing" applied to the birch tree in the garden at home. "There is no such tree there," I was told by the man who had kept this garden under observation for many days.) *Der Stern* claimed that the verdict on Eichmann should be rendered by "an indubitably independent court." (June 25, 1960)

But the majority of commentators in both parts of Germany were in our favor. The East German *Bauern Echo* said: "Israel is among the countries most competent to try Eichmann" (June 1), and the *Frankfurter Allgemeine Zeitung* wrote: "We failed to bring Eichmann to trial before our courts; we must now trust the Israeli judiciary" (June 9, 1960).

Finally, Schaeffer, the West German Minister of Justice, announced that there would be no request for extradition (*Neu-Ruhr Zeitung,* June 10, 1960).

Some of Israel's best and staunchest non-Jewish supporters voiced their skepticism. Guy Mollet, the former Prime Minister of France, who had proved his friendship in a hundred ways and stood by us in an hour of direct need, wrote:

> Many outstanding jurists declare that Israel had the right to apprehend Eichmann. Their arguments seem well founded and still they evoke resentment. . . . I wish, because I am a friend of Israel, that its Government would accept and suggest of itself an international control of the Eichmann case. (*Koelnische Rundschau,* September 10, 1960)

Richard Crossman, M.P., the well-known intellectual and Labour Party leader, a friend of old standing, expressed his doubts. He wrote:

> As the Eichmann trial approaches, I feel more and more uneasy. . . . The first gleeful announcement of the abduction came as a shock, but it was nothing compared with the press conference which the Israeli Prime Minister gave a few days ago. . . .
>
> Of course the Israeli Prime Minister can find excellent legal precedents for putting a man on trial who has been abducted and for charging him with the crimes committed in another country. . . . But the political framework within which Ben-Gurion has decided to set the trial is such a perturbing combination of Old Testament ethics and modern sensationalism that, though what is done will no doubt be justice, what is *seen* to be done may well look more like an act of tribal vengeance. . . .
>
> In the Christian world, where anti-Semitism is endemic, this danger (of

brutalizing people's instincts instead of rousing their moral indignation) is increased if the victims are Jews. I know of no evidence to suggest that anti-Semitism is quenched by retailing the horrors of the pogrom. I know of a good deal of evidence that it thrives on them. But the danger is increased when it is Jews who are conducting the propaganda. (*New Statesman and Nation*, March 31, 1961)

Two of the ex-prosecuting attorneys at Nuremberg crossed swords. Mr. Alfred Coste-Floret, the French prosecutor, held that Israel was undoubtedly authorized to try Eichmann since Jewish Palestine had been recognized internationally for years and the "extermination of the Jews was a real threat also to the State of Israel, which would have ceased to exist had this genocide met with full success" (*Bulletin Juif d'Information*, June 10, 1960).

The former American Chief Counsel at Nuremberg, Brigadier General Telford Taylor, took the opposite view. The Nuremberg Trials, he said, were a necessity, since there was no other way to handle the problem of "what to do" with the surviving Nazi leaders. "But this was not the case with Eichmann," he argued, who, in his opinion, ought to be tried in Germany, "to enlighten the public and especially the post-war generation, in a way and to a degree that perhaps no other means would afford."

According to Mr. Taylor, "the principles of Nuremberg were strongly criticized because of the fact that they were held under the auspices of the victorious powers. . . . But future international tribunals should surely be more broadly constituted." He was certain that "Eichmann's trial in Israel will be even more susceptible than Nuremberg to this attack." This prejudgment of the issue was followed by a shocking comparison:

> The victims of the Nazi "final solution of the Jewish problem" in which Eichmann is implicated, were in the power of the Third Reich then, just as Eichmann is now in the power of Israel. If Israel as a sovereign nation is not "answerable to any external authority" for its handling of Eichmann, neither was the Third Reich (or Eichmann) for its handling of the Jews. ("Large Questions in the Eichmann Case," the *New York Times Magazine*, January 22, 1961)

Jurists of international standing fell out. Professor Milton Katz of Harvard Law School defended our position all along the line against a vehement attack by Professor Herbert Wechsler of Columbia Law School. Professor L. C. Green of University College, London, supported our legal point of view on the cardinal issues. The *American Journal of International Law* published an extensive and analytical article by Professor Helen Silving, of the University of Puerto Rico, under the title: "In re Eichmann: Dilemma of Law and Morality." When I later read this learned and richly documented essay, reviewing German, Argentinean, English and American authorities, supporting our arguments to the hilt, I was sorry it had appeared too late to be used in my arguments. Our courts were later to pay Professor Silving a rare tribute. Both District and Appellate Courts mentioned her article in their judgments, though it is not usual for a tribunal to refer to works written directly on an issue involved in a pending trial.

The two-installment, richly illustrated abbreviation of the Sassen document carried by *Life* was prefaced with an editorial saying:

> The sickening confession of Adolf Eichmann on these pages is a major historical document, but why read it? Some people can't bear to be reminded that these crimes happened in our own era, or to face the puzzle of the hideous personality that perpetrated them. Others recoil from his arrogant self-justification, his "I regret nothing," his "little cog in the machinery" plea. But we believe it is healthier to look this monster in the face and hear him out, for the lesson he personifies applies to every man and time. (January 9, 1961)

Soon interest reached new heights. The charge sheet was given wide publicity in the world press. The information services of Poland, Bulgaria, Yugoslavia and Hungary published, both at home and through their embassies abroad, extensive bulletins and pamphlets on the crimes Eichmann had committed on their territories.

While some papers reminded their readers of the Nazi horrors and of Eichmann's biography, others deplored "the opening of old wounds." "Justice for the Monster," read headlines in the British press. "A Trial of Everybody's Responsibility," the Italian papers wrote. In Germany and Austria the headlines were: "We Tensely Await the Beginning," "Will an Atom Bomb of Hatred of Germany Explode?," "A Search of Conscience Is About to Start," "The Trial of the Century," "Eichmann and Us," "Racial Hatred on Trial."

Victor Gollancz, the British Jewish publisher and author, published an extraordinary pamphlet, in which he deplored the whole idea of hunting Eichmann down over a period of over fifteen years, because he thought it was wrong to dwell on the sins of the past. He went so far as calling the Nuremberg precedent "an evil example," adding that he was "unaware that it had ever been regarded, by legal opinion or the common feeling of mankind, as establishing a principle thereafter valid for international law."

Mr. Gollancz was sure the trial would stir up hatreds that were better forgotten, and that Eichmann could not have a fair trial in Israel.

The *Jewish Chronicle,* the organ of British Jewry, promptly replied that Gollancz did not represent the views of Anglo-Jewry.

This sort of give-and-take went on in a number of places.

Even in South America, responsible voices, though siding with Argentina in its claim of an injury to its sovereignty by Eichmann's abduction, felt the moral dilemma involved. "Which weighs more: six million victims or a legal paragraph?" asked *El Espectador* of Colombia (June 10). "How can Israel be requested to return a man who was never in Argentina legally and was never knowingly granted asylum there?" soberly inquired *Jornal do Brasil* (June 10, 1960). "The only country really interested in trying Eichmann is Israel, representing the millions of Jews sacrified to Hitler's mania. For the Israelis, respect for the rules of etiquette cannot secure satisfaction if it involved impunity for genocide" (the Guatemalan *Prensa Libre,* June 13, 1960).

There were similar voices even in Argentina itself. "How can we not admire a group of brave men who have, during the years, endangered their lives in searching throughout the world for this criminal and who yet had the honesty to deliver him up for trial by a judicial tribunal instead of being impelled by an impulse of revenge to finish him off on the spot?" wrote the influential *El Mundo* (June 17, 1960).

Nevertheless a diplomatic altercation between Argentina and Israel was soon in full swing, as shown below.

The International Framework

The capture of Eichmann had instantly created a diplomatic and political problem with Argentina, where Eichmann had been seized.

There were internal developments in Argentina that drove its government to adopt a stiff attitude. Israel's Prime Minister, David Ben-Gurion, wrote to Argentine President Arturo Frondizi:

> I do not underestimate the seriousness of the formal violation of Argentine law committed by those who at last ended their long search with the capture of Eichmann; but I am confident that there can be very few people in the world who have failed to understand the profound motives and the supreme moral justification for this act.

In conclusion, the Prime Minister pleaded for understanding, saying:

> I am convinced, Mr. President, that you will understand the supreme moral force of these aspects of the problem. You yourself fought dictatorship untiringly and have constantly displayed your profound respect for human values. I am sure that no one will understand better than yourself our true feelings; that you will accept the expression of our most sincere regret for any violation of the laws of the Argentine Republic which may have been committed at the bidding of an irresistible inner force.

But Argentina's Foreign Minister, Diogenes Taboada, took a strong stand. He declared that, though his country "has a most emphatic condemnation of the mass crimes committed by the agents of Hitlerism," it protested against the violation of its territorial sovereignty through the act of the people who captured Eichmann, and for whose action "the State of Israel bears the responsibility arising from its express approval of those individuals' action." He asked that Israel should show respect for the sovereignty of a friendly state, presented his "most explicit protest," and asked for the return of Eichmann and for the punishment of the persons responsible for the violation of Argentine law. Consequently on June 15, 1960, Argentina presented a complaint to the Security Council of the United Nations, requesting "an urgent meeting to consider the violation of its sovereign rights creating an atmosphere of insecurity and mistrust incompatible with the preservation of international peace" (*Security Council Official Records, 15th Year,* Supplement for April, May and June, 1960, p. 27).

It was the first time the United Nations had been faced with such a problem. The Council was convened a week later and Mario Amadeo, the Permanent Representative of Argentina to the U.N., presented his case. He recalled the friendly and cordial relations that had so far existed between the two countries, but described Israel's act as an "inexplicable affront." He called on Israel to punish the perpetrators and "make reparations for violations of territorial sovereignty committed by its nationals abroad," for which the Israel Government, by condoning their actions, was responsible. Eichmann's illegal sojourn in Argentina had nothing to do with the question, he said. Nor was he defending the crimes of which "the protagonist in this case" was accused. What he could not accept, he said, was "that Eichmann should be brought to justice as the direct result of the violation of law."

Yet, significantly, there was no more talk of returning Eichmann. In the draft resolution that Mr. Amadeo submitted to the Council, Israel was requested to make "appropriate reparations" (*Security Council Official Records,* 865th meeting, June 22, 1960). What this meant was never spelled out. By clever diplomacy Argentina adopted a formula that could be utilized either for further pressure or for an honorable retreat, as circumstances dictated.

In a tense atmosphere, charged with deep emotion, the Foreign Minister of Israel, Mrs. Golda Meir, rose to reply. She, too, regretted that the matter had had to be brought before the Council, repeated Israel's apology for a breach of Argentine laws by the persons who captured Eichmann, and proceeded to introduce "the protagonist" to the sentinels of world peace. She recalled what the International Military Tribunal had said about Eichmann and briefly reviewed the evidence adduced against him at Nuremberg.

"What wonder," she continued, "that many Jews could find no rest until they ascertained whether he was alive and tracked him down? Are these the 'armed bands' referred to in the statement of the representative of Argentina this morning?"

Then she proceeded to deal with the argument that Israel's act might constitute a dangerous precedent. "But modern history knows of no such monster as Adolf Eichmann. The representative of Argentina has sought to contrast the norms of ordinary legal procedure on the one hand with resort to lynching and mob violence on the other. Insofar as he sought, in the latter connection, to draw an analogy with the apprehension of Eichmann there is no analogy."

This was the core of the reply. If there was no precedent for what Israel had done, there was no precedent for Eichmann's guilt.

Mrs. Meir went on: "Far from lynching Eichmann or hanging him on the nearest tree, those who pursued him over fifteen years and finally seized him have handed him over to the process and judgment of the courts of law. The reference to mob passions and lawless justice in this context is unwarranted and provocative." (*Security Council Official Records,* 866th meeting, June 22, 1960)

Mr. Arkady A. Sobolev then spoke for the Soviet Union; he had little to say on the issue:

"The Soviet Union stands for the strict observance of the universally recognized principle of sovereignty in relations between states and shares the Argentine position that violation was inadmissible under any circumstances and can in no way be justified."

The representative of the United States, Mr. Henry Cabot Lodge, then took the floor. "Clearly," he said, "the way in which Eichmann was apprehended has been the cause of a strain in relation between two friendly countries," and the United States was anxious to see a fair settlement. But the matter could not be considered apart from the monstrous acts with which Eichmann was charged. He recalled that for years Eichmann had been on the lists of war criminals compiled by the United Nations Commission. Still, he said, Argentina's complaint was legitimate. He intended, therefore, to vote for her resolution, but suggested an important improvement by adding that the Security Council was "mindful . . .

of the concern of people in all countries *that Eichmann should be brought to appropriate justice* for the crimes of which he is accused." (My italics.)

The representative of Great Britain was even more conciliatory. "It would be wrong for the Council," he said, "to underestimate the strength of the feeling on this matter among Jewish people everywhere." He pointed out that there was basic agreement between all concerned on the principles involved; the difficulty lay only in applying to the issue on hand.

In the course of the evening recess the diplomatic machinery went to work. It was obvious that there was unanimous support for the formal claim that Argentina's sovereign rights had been violated, but everybody thought it might have been wiser not to pursue the claim to the limit. The problem was how to make amends to Argentina for the injury to her pride and still to ensure that Eichmann would be tried.

Next day Mr. Lodge came up with the solution. The debate in the Security Council, coupled with Israel's apology, would in themselves constitute the "appropriate reparation" that was called for.

This was the turning point. France came out in support of the American solution, Mr. Armand Bérard recalling the recent fifteenth anniversary of the United Nations Charter, which expressed the determination to save mankind in the future from the untold sufferings of the past. Eichmann's activities must be rapidly and fully judged in all fairness, he said. Mr. Correa, of Ecuador, was of the same opinion. It was impossible, he said, to let Eichmann escape the consequences. (*Ibid.*, 867th meeting, June 23, 1960)

Mr. Sobolev wanted to know whether Argentina still requested the return of Eichmann, as part of her "reparations." Mr. Amadeo replied that "neither Argentina nor any other member of the Council has a special obligation to supply an interpretation of the resolutions." But both France and Great Britain declared that they would vote for the resolution as amended on the understanding that it meant just what Mr. Lodge had explained. Eichmann ought not to be returned.

And so the resolution was carried unanimously, with Russia and Poland abstaining. Mr. Lewandowski, for Poland, said that he had abstained for fear that the ambiguity of the phrasing might give rise to an interpretation that could be used in favor of Eichmann or other war criminals. Echoing this view, Mr. Sobolev charged NATO states with allowing ex-Nazi generals to occupy leading positions, and West Germany with appointing to ministerial posts the same individuals who under the Nazis carried out the policy of extermination; he mentioned by name Dr. Oberlaender, Dr. Schroeder and General Speidel. Mr. Lodge replied that West Germany was bringing ex-Nazis to trial, while East Germany did nothing of the kind. He charged that the President of the East German Supreme Court, Dr. Schumann, and the chairman of the Law Committee of the People's Chamber, Siegfried Dallmann, were both ex-Nazis, and cited a pamphlet disclosing that there were two hundred ex-Nazis holding posts under the Communist regime in East Germany. To this Mr. Sobolev rejoined that there were 1,146 ex-Nazi judges and prosecutors in service in West Germany, according to a bulletin from which he read. Mr. Lodge retorted that Speidel had turned against Hitler, while an East German general, Arno von Lenski, had been photographed in Nazi uniform.

The President remarked that the debate had gone off at a tangent, and the session was soon closed (*Security Council Official Records,* 868th meeting, June 23, 1960). The last exchange, however, furnished a striking illustration of what would have occurred in the International Tribunal had we yielded to the temptation to request the United Nations to set up such a court for the trial of Eichmann. It might have provided another platform for mutual recriminations between West and East, but it would hardly have been a fitting forum for the trial, with dignity and under judicial standards, of a crime that cost us one-third of our people.

The matter was now left to Israel and Argentina to settle between them, and notes were again exchanged. The authorities in Buenos Aires did not accept the expression of Israel's regrets as sufficient amends, and they declared our Ambassador, Arieh Levavi, *persona non grata,* without, however, breaking off diplomatic relations. This, apparently, provided a sufficient vent for hurt feelings and the atmosphere was cleared for the resumption of normal international ties.

A visit to Buenos Aires by the legal adviser to our Foreign Ministry, Ambassador Shabtai Rosenne, was the occasion for the final clearing of the air. He saw President Frondizi and ultimately, on August 5, 1960, a joint communiqué was issued saying that both governments, "imbued with the wish to give effect to the resolution of the Security Council," which expressed the hope for the advancement of the "traditionally friendly relations between them," had decided to regard as closed the incident that had arisen out of the action taken by Israel nationals "which infringed fundamental rights of the State of Argentina." (T/4)

The diplomatic battle was thus over, and the international tension it had created was eased. But for the real impact on the world we had to wait for the unfolding of the trial itself.

Public Reactions During the Trial

An observer reported:

> In Jerusalem I sought out two famous journalists who had been critical of the Eichmann arrest and trial and found they had changed their minds after the first week of testimony. The dignity of the trial communicated its purpose at once. By the first of June there were few journalists and lawyers in the Western World who were not satisfied that this story not only had to be recorded for history, but that it was being told at the right time and in the right place and under the correct conditions. (Harry Golden, *The Carolina Israelite,* May-June, 1961)

My opening statement was favorably received. A correspondent wrote:

> Instantly Hausner rose to his feet, black and predatory, with a pride so harnessed but so patent with burning Jewishness so hunted but so hunting, that for a few seconds we seemed posed on some plane outside time or space, where the voices of all the Jews of all the centuries could speak at once and in unison.
>
> For me it was as though a shutter had been opened, if only temporarily, through which we Gentiles could peer into the heart of Jewry and out of which the Jews could speak with dignity. This was the meaning of the trial and is, perhaps, the meaning of Israel. (*The Guardian,* Manchester, April 19, 1961)

Eichmann's personality appeared in a new light. Professor Trevor-Roper wrote:

> There emerged a picture of Eichmann which contrasts dramatically with the spectacle of the grey lifeless robot behind the glass. We see Eichmann—if we

can abstract our minds from the grim field of his activity—as an administrator of genius. For it needed something like genius for a mere S.S. Lieutenant-Colonel to organize, in the middle of the war, and through human instruments, against the conscience of the world, and in fierce competition for the essential resources, the transport, concentration and murder of millions of people. (*Sunday Times*, April 23, 1961)

The same thought was voiced by other foreign observers. Patrick O'Donovan reported:

There were many who thought that Adolf Eichmann was not suited to the role given him by the Jews. He was too small, too insignificant a man. It does not do to punish minor civil servants for the crimes of a whole regime.

But any suspicion of inadequacy on the part of Eichmann has been put at rest this week. He will do. He was big enough and did enough evil.

This week the facts of his career have begun to emerge. (*The Observer*, April 23, 1961)

Still, world public opinion kept watching us closely. In May, when the trial was well on its way, Gallup Polls were held to test the reactions of the public in America, Britain and Switzerland. The gist of the results was published in the New York *Herald Tribune* (May 19, 21, 27, 1961):

The American public believes that the Israeli Government is doing the right thing in trying Adolf Eichmann before a court in that nation. Such a course is preferred to possible alternatives which the Israelis might have taken after their agents captured the former Nazi officer. . . .

This is one of the major findings in studies in the United States by the American Gallup Poll—supported by the separate studies in British Gallup Poll —to measure the reaction to the Eichmann trial. . . .

A heavy majority—62 per cent—of the American public believes Adolf Eichmann is getting a fair hearing.

An even greater majority of the British public—70 per cent—approves of the way Eichmann's trial is being handled. Only 5 per cent disagree while 25 per cent had no opinion.

In the special two-nation study Gallup Poll reporters throughout the United States and Great Britain were assigned to ask this question of a cross-section of the public in each nation.

Focusing world attention on the past horrors of the Nazi era—as the Adolf Eichmann trial has done—is regarded as a good thing by the American public. Americans' views on the merits of letting the world hear again the gruesome details of the World War II concentration camps are shared by the people of Britain and Switzerland.

Previous critics changed their views. The Washington *Post* now said, "Hausner has painstakingly laid a legal groundwork for this nation's case" (April 19, 1961) and later admitted, "In balance the trial is right" (April 24, 1961). Telford Taylor too gave expression to his gradually altering attitude. "That these proceedings have so colorless an inception is a great tribute to the sense and integrity of the Israel authorities," he commented on the legal arguments phase. Later he took a further step: "No visitor can fail to be impressed by the dignity of the proceedings." And finally, though still holding some features of the trial "controversial," he said that "it is an important increment to international law" (*The Spectator,* April 21, May 28, 1961, January 5, 1962). The charge he had leveled a year earlier that the trial was irreconcilable with the very idea of international law was thus tacitly withdrawn.

Mr. Guy Mollet also expressed a changed view. He now praised Israel for "turning the proceedings into a trial of the system," adding: "The younger generation must now learn, since the system was not yet done with. That is why the trial is a necessity" (*Démocratie,* April 20, 1961).

Another writer, with his usual courage and candor, publicly confessed that he had been wrong in his predictions and criticisms. This was Richard Crossman, who wrote in a devastating article on the Arendt book,* which was strongly critical of the trial:

> But what are we to make of Miss Arendt's sensational conclusions? Before the trial, my own attitude was not unlike hers.
>
> I still think our fears were reasonable enough at the time. But none of them was substantiated by the trial itself. Yet whereas the rest of us were frank enough to admit we were wrong in our predictions Miss Arendt has preferred to retreat to a new position. She now criticises those responsible for the trial. . . .
>
> By the end of the trial, indeed, it was clear that Eichmann was a far stronger and more malignant character than many of us had supposed. Miss Arendt, however, could not abandon her theory about his banality because it was essential to her main theme. (*The Observer,* October 13, 1963)

The reports of the trial itself continued to be published and assessed in many places all over the world. We received clippings from sixty-three countries.

Almost all European countries followed the progress of the trial throughout, with France, Italy and Holland displaying special and continuous interest.

French papers and statesmen repeatedly declared that the trial was of vital importance. "This is the trial of a system . . . and mankind can be proud that a state was found that undertook to expose it and to prove that morals and law are basic values of mankind," announced Jacques Soustelle.

The Spanish press was at first skeptical of the reports that Spain's ex-ally, Nazi Germany, had operated gas chambers. "I am sure that these were used only for testing gas masks" wrote Rodrigo Royo, editor of *Arriba.* "The Jews had invented a certain Eichmann in Argentina, had chased him all around the place and dressed him up now as a clown for a Sunday show."

Later on, however, the Spanish press grudgingly approved Israel's efforts to maintain justice.

The Latin-American papers accompanied the trial with extensive coverage and genuinely thoughtful articles.

A Japanese conclusion was: "Coexistence between races is imperative. This is true for the 850 million 'whites' and 1,900 million 'colored' for the future existence of the world" (the *Mainichi Daily News,* May 27, 1961). The *Times of Vietnam Magazine* called the trial "the biggest murder trial of the century."

Of the Communist countries, Yugoslavia displayed great interest and followed

* Hannah Arendt's *Eichmann in Jerusalem* has been refuted by many reviewers, most recently in a comprehensive point-by-point rebuttal in Dr. Jacob Robinson's *And the Crooked Shall Be Made Straight* (The Macmillan Company, New York, 1965).

Consequently I refrain from dealing with her book at all in these pages.

the trial consistently. The Polish papers were, naturally, most interested, as the murders had been committed on Polish soil. Their coverage was continuous and generally approving, and their correspondents showed full understanding of the way we were handling the trial, including the initial legal battle. Like other journalists from the Eastern bloc, however, they followed the Communist line on Dr. Hans Globke, who was, at the time, Chancellor Adenauer's right-hand man.

(Since we had included all relevant documents, including those incriminating people living in Germany today, many scandals ensued. Two documents we had submitted heavily incriminated Globke in the devising of measures for robbing Jews of their property, and the Bonn authorities immediately issued a statement attempting to exculpate him. Chancellor Adenauer kept him in office in spite of a storm of protest, not only from the Eastern bloc countries. Globke's Nazi past was incontestable, and though various explanations were offered for his career under Hitler I must say I found none of them convincing. The Communist world of course wanted to use the Eichmann trial as a platform from which Globke could be denounced; a lawyer from East Berlin, Dr. Friedrich Kaul, even arrived in Jerusalem demanding to be admitted as a civil claimant, though Israeli law provides that in offenses punishable by death civil claimants must seek their remedy through separate proceedings. Even after producing the documents incriminating Globke we were accused by Communists of working in "collusion" with Bonn to shield Globke and suppress evidence on other influential Nazis.)

The reaction in Germany itself was, perhaps, the most interesting. There was widespread soul-searching; it was certainly more intense than it would have been had the trial been conducted in Germany. The proceedings were widely shown on German television and given prominence in the press. Children were reported to be asking their parents and teachers embarrassing questions as to what they had been doing under the Nazis. The usual leitmotif of the reply was: "We did not know," but a debate was unleashed on the extent to which "knowledge" of Nazi crimes had been current in Germany. Many said that it did not really matter: everyone who had voted for Hitler was guilty.

One paper wrote: "The problem is whether we feel secure from our past only because we have become used in the last fifteen years to be considered as solid, solvent and urgently needed partners of the free world" (*Stuttgarter Zeitung*, June 12, 1961).

Germans looked into the mirror of the trial to find out whether the figure reflected still wore the Nazi uniform. The replies varied; it would be impossible to reduce them to a common denominator.

There were different reactions, too, in readers' letters. Some wrote: "We have heard enough of it," or "We can't be ashamed of ourselves for the rest of our lives." But to judge by the published selections, most people wrote in the vein of: "Thank heaven the trial is in Israel and not in Bonn, so that we can hear what really happened," or "There are still too many Eichmanns among us," and—a recurring reaction: "We are ashamed."

The German people were now being told the truth, which differed sharply from the thousands of articles, essays and research studies emanating from institutes, research groups and semiofficial agencies, which had been devoting their efforts for years to the task of whitewashing the devil by a slow and systematic process of concealment and distortion. With every new work of "research," the circle of the wrongdoers had been narrowed, many state agencies becoming less sinful and the Germans as a whole somewhat less guilty. The trial, which brought the true facts to life, came as a shock just when the "research" institutes had half-succeeded in clipping the devil's nails, cropping his horns and camouflaging his tail. So it was from Jerusalem that the Germans were reminded that all branches of their authorities, including the army, had played an active part in the crimes. The German press noted, with surprise, the need for "some necessary corrections of history."

"In Nuremberg the accused denied everything," the papers said.

> Nobody knew. In Jerusalem this is gone like straw in the wind. No one can quibble about it now. All the officialdom of the Ministries knew. . . . A second officialdom of the Ministries knew. . . . A second officially doled-out thesis is that the army was not implicated. Now it is proved that it set the pace of the extermination. . . . Another official version on which we are fed was that only a few hand-picked SS men did the job. It is now clearly established that every single link in the long chain of administration not only knew but had its assigned share in the criminal acts. . . . Methodically the Jerusalem trial examines the events of the last thirty years. . . . The emerging facts are not confined to a new assessment of the past, but strongly penetrate into our present. (*Deutsche Woche*, Munich, May 31, 1961)

An interesting two-way process of observation developed during the trial While foreign correspondents in Germany reported German reactions, the German press was keeping a watchful eye on the way the trial affected the free world and Germany's standing there. In the middle of June the *Stuttgarter Zeitung* rounded up reactions from its correspondents in New York, London, Paris, Rome, The Hague and Copenhagen. Almost all the reports start stereotypically: "The interest in the trial is unabated," but while it was reported that in America the basic assessment of present-day Germany remained unchanged, the correspondents were not so sure about other centers. "We should not be surprised if we get fewer tourists from Holland this year," wrote a practical-minded reporter. "Our standing is undermined here and something must be done about it," wrote the correspondent from Denmark.

Toward the end of the trial a leading daily summed it up in an article: "Our Burden and Our Task."

> It will be impossible to say that German public opinion has not been told now, by press, radio and television, what our younger generation has to know. . . . The effects of the trial will be something only future generations will be able to tell. More important than the generation that still belonged to the Hitler youth groups is the problem of the youth who were born when the war started. It is all-important to instruct them. They must know what it was. They must learn why it could have happened. . . . They need clarity and determination to find confidence in the knowledge of the misfortune and their fathers' burden of sin, to bear it for a better future. (*Frankfurter Allgemeine Zeitung*, August 4, 1961)

One cannot help asking oneself, when reading this obviously sincere statement, what the Germans were doing to instruct their youth in the true facts before we caught up with Eichmann and put him on trial, and what they have been doing since the trial. Will the process of exonerating the Nazis by small, subtle, systematic inroads on truth continue, or will there be a true catharsis?

Reactions to the Judgment

The judgment produced a spate of press comment and correspondence in many countries. Most writers expressed wholehearted approval, though the death penalty remained a matter of controversy. An official statement by the German Press Bureau stated: "There is not a person in Germany who considers the judgment unjust" (*Official Bulletin of Press and Information*, December 20, 1961).

The New York *Herald Tribune* wrote under the heading: *Justice Is Done in Jerusalem:*

> It is not with a sense of vengeance accomplished but of justice done that one received the news from the modern state of Israel. Vengeance is the Lord's—justice is man's—at least in so far as he, in the deepest honesty of his mind and soul, can mete it out. . . . There can be no doubt that justice has been accomplished in Jerusalem. . . .
>
> And so the great trial, conducted with scrupulous fairness, held admirably in restraint, has come to an end. . . . That this would all end in a courtroom in Jerusalem before a tribunal of the people he had so cruelly and irreparably wronged could never have crossed his mind in his days of glory and might. And yet it has come to pass just so, and this may be the ultimate justice of all. (December 13, 1961)

The *New York Times* carried three pages of excerpts from the judgment and the sentence in full.

Under the title "Judges in Israel" the London *Times* wrote: "The dignity and discipline of the Court's proceedings and of the Israelis' reaction to them have won respect" (December 16, 1961).

Rev. James Parkes, who has devoted his life to the study of relations between the Jews and other peoples, examined in the light of the judgment the lesson humanity must derive from the trial, of a man "in whose person the universal elements of evil are focused."

The story is "part and parcel of Jewish life," Rev. Parkes wrote. "Jews can forget anti-Semitism only when Christians and humanists remember it" (*The Observer*, December 19, 1961).

Edward Crankshaw, a historian of the Nazi movement and institutions, wrote: "The judges tore his defence to pieces. . . . Long and painstaking judgement showed [Eichmann] was a human dynamo stretching himself to the limit (*The Observer*, December 17, 1961).

In the professional literature the conduct of the trial and the provisions of our law were more carefully analyzed from various angles. Some of the commentators had dealt with the problems involved even before the judgment was given, and several of these deserve a brief mention. Professor L. C. Green, then still of University College, London, wrote in October, 1960, supporting our legal point of view on the two cardinal issues: abduction and jurisdiction (*Modern Law Review*, 1960, Vol. 23, p. 507).

Most legal reviews that have come to my notice upheld our legal approach either entirely or on the main issues: Professor Milton Katz in *Harvard Law Review* (Vol. 32, February, 1961, p. 9); Professor Hans W. Baade in *Duke Law*

Journal, 1961, No. 3, p. 400; Judge Michael A. Musmanno in *Temple Law Quarterly* (Fall, 1961); George R. Parson, in *Cornell Law Quarterly* (Vol. 46, No. 2, pp. 326–336); Nicholas N. Kittrie in *The Journal of Criminal Law, Criminology and Police Science* (March, 1961); Zad Leavy, in *Los Angeles Bar Bulletin* (February, 1961, p. 113). So did J. A. Cesar Salgada, Attorney of Justice of the State of São Paulo, Brazil, in his booklet: *O Caso Eichmann a luz da Moral a do direito* (*The Eichmann Case in the Light of Morality and Justice,* São Paulo, 1961).

Different views were taken by Professor Herbert Wechsler in *N. Y. County L. B. Bulletin* 101 (1962) and by Yosal Rogat in *The Eichmann Trial and the Rule of Law* (1961).

Julius Stone, Professor of International Law at the University of Sydney and author of important works in the subject, summed up his impressions for the Australian section of the International Commission of Jurists, on whose behalf he had attended the trial:

> While in a fuller account I would embrace two or three minor criticisms of the organization and procedure of the trial, my general conclusion obviously was that the trial has been a fair one based on lawful jurisdiction. And because I myself entertained criticism before I attended the Court, which I now think groundless, I have wondered since my return from Jerusalem why all of us, Jew or Gentile, have tended at moments to be rather carping in a technical way about the whole business. My analysis of myself, which I put forward tentatively as a rational if somewhat Freudian explanation of a phenomenon not easily explicable in other ways, is that we all knew of the nature of the horrors which the evidence would thrust before our eyes for weeks and months in the press, on the radio and on television, and that subconsciously we resisted.
>
> The Eichmann trial may have registered a number of important advances both in the theory and practice of the enforcement of human rights. . . .
>
> The trial has shown, moreover, in the observer's opinion, that if certain conditions are observed, particularly those of a truly public hearing, before independent judges, a fair trial can be had even in the State to which the victims naturally look for protection, for instance, the State of which they are nationals. And it deserves to be said with great emphasis that a State whose nationals have been victims of mass murder is far more likely to make the law effective by enforcement than the State of the territory where the alleged crimes were committed. (International Commission of Jurists, Sidney, 1961)

After the judgment was delivered the matter was again taken up in the professional literature.

Professor Georg Schwarzenberger, of the University of London, found that, on the level of international law, our law was not in conflict with accepted rules. "It is possible to acclaim the three substantive provisions of Israel's Nazi Punishment law as much as its jurisdictional section . . . as a revindication of the standard of civilisation against a totalitarian relapse into barbarism of diabolical dimensions," he wrote. "Thus both the Eichmann trial and the judgement pass the tests of international law and the standard of civilization with flying colours" (*Current Law Problems,* 1962). Professor Jean Graven, of the Law Faculty of Geneva University, a world-famous authority on the subject, author of books on international criminal law and chairman of the International Association of Penal

Law, wrote a long article on "How to Judge the Eichmann Judgment." He called it "a veritable monument," and said that it "carefully dealt with and answered every argument" (*Revue internationale de Criminologie et de Police Technique*, Geneva, Vol. 16, p. 19).

In a second article on the trial, Professor L. G. Green, then Vice-Dean of the Faculty of Law at the University of Singapore, analyzed the main principles of the judgment against a wide background of legislation and judicial pronouncements on war criminals, and accepted them *in toto* (*Tulane Law Review*, June, 1963, p. 641).

The only authoritative minority view which came to my notice was expressed by Professor Robert K. Woetzel, of New York University, author of books on the Nuremberg Trials. He maintained that

> there is no overwhelming consensus of opinion among lawyers in favor of the basis claimed for the trial. . . . It must be concluded that the court in the Eichmann case was not justified in claiming a basis in customary international law for the extension of the universal principle of jurisdiction to crimes against humanity involving genocide. (*The Criminal Law Review*, October, 1962, p. 671)

However, the official observer at the trial for the International Commission of Jurists, Professor Peter Papadatos, of the Law Faculty at the University of Athens, commented:

> Let me point out that the controversy about the right of Israel to punish Eichmann ended in a categorical and well-founded declaration by the District Court in its judgement, to the effect that genocide, by its very nature as well as by its gravity, is a crime subject to universal jurisdiction. This declaration, which has served to strengthen the view already prevailing among authoritative writers, is of very special importance. . . . The Eichmann trial will undoubtedly occupy a leading place amongst the great trials of our century concerned with international penal law. (*Bulletin of the International Commission of Jurists*, October, 1962, p. 3)

Professor Norman Bentwich, erstwhile Attorney General of Palestine, wrote in *The Solicitor Quarterly* that "the trial was a unique historical demonstration. It could be claimed with reason that this was a unique case, and must be tried as unique. . . . The judgement added to the thorough analysis of international criminal law, particularly in relation to jurisdiction." Professor Bentwich saw the significance of the trial in the moral issues, and the lesson he derived was the need for an International Criminal Court for the establishment of which "Israel has taken a lead" (October, 1962).

A noted author on military law, G. I. A. D. Draper, lecturer on international and constitutional law and the editor of the *Official Manual of the Law of War*, wrote:

> The indictment against Eichmann and the ensuing judgement are based upon a complicated mosaic of legal rules. . . . The legal craftsmanship reflected in the judgements of both tribunals is impressive. . . .
>
> The legal reasoning upon which the decision of the two Courts (the District Court and the Court of Appeal) rests presents a coherent and convincing whole.

Attempts to destroy this framework of legal reasoning will undoubtedly be made, but it is open to considerable doubt whether such attempts will command much weight with jurists of repute. . . . Out of the great catastrophe in the history of the Jewish race a judicial precedent has been forged that can stand without fear as a lasting tribute to Jewish justice and as an event of which the State of Israel may justifiably be proud. (*International Affairs,* 1962, p. 485)

Reactions to the Appeal and Its Rejection

Israel itself reacted to the conclusion of the whole drama with a feeling of great relief; the trial had been a continuous trauma.

The reactions all over the world were generally in support of Israel. "A sombre necessity," said the BBC commentator. "A general relief," said Radio Hague. "Justice was done," said Radio Moscow.

The press reactions were also generally favorable.

Public opinion realized that mercy to Eichmann would have been interpreted as a forgiveness of the crimes.

The New York *Herald Tribune* said:

> The execution of Adolf Eichmann, if any execution can be, is an act of justice and of remembrance. . . .
>
> We on earth administer man's justice, not God's, and by man's justice it is eminently fitting that Eichmann, after a fair, complete, and scrupulous hearing, should be hanged like a common criminal among a people whose kin he so ruthlessly persecuted and murdered. (June 1, 1962)

The Philadelphia *Inquirer* wrote:

> Clemency for this defiant, unrepentant, less-than-human homicide, was clearly out of place. He pleaded for it, of course, and it is strictly in character for one who had never shown mercy to a single one of his victims to ask, in the shadow of the gallows, that his own mean life be spared. . . .
>
> No man can remain unsickened by Adolf Eichmann's bloodied hands. The world would have been better if he had never lived in it. It is a cleaner place today now that his ashes have been scattered on the sea. (June 2, 1962)

In London, the *Times* commented:

> The world must hope that the calculations of the Israel authorities will prove correct that the long, grim process of Eichmann's arrest, trial and execution will have given Israelis a sense of atonement which they need, and that the course of history will never again require a symbol of anti-Semitism to appear differently. (June 2, 1962)

The *Daily Herald* of London wrote:

> By killing Eichmann Israel earned no shame or guilt. It committed an act of understandable political necessity. . . . If Eichmann's life had been spared it would have been the greatest act of clemency in the history of the world. No State would have shown such clemency and only because we still think of Jews as a Chosen People of unique moral purpose, we dared to hope they would act differently. (June 2, 1962)

The Canberra *Times* sized it up: "Eichmann's vileness left mankind no choice" (June 2, 1962), and Professor Julius Stone said of the verdict:

The speed with which Adolf Eichmann was executed after his conviction surprised me at first. But more delays would have but prolonged the agony.

I realized that it was a bit foolish to expect the Israel authorities to allow further long delays after an investigation and trial that have already spread over more than two years. (The Sydney *Morning Herald*, June 4, 1962)

The only official dissenting voice was an Argentinian communiqué, expressing abhorrence of the crimes but maintaining that Israel should have taken into account the fact that under the law of Argentina Eichmann was not liable to the death penalty. The Falangista press in Spain reverted to its previous attitude saying that the hanging was a crime. The Arab press hailed Eichmann as a martyr.

Voices were heard from all over the world. "Justice has been done," wrote the *Herald* of Addis Ababa after the execution (June 2, 1962). "Justice was delayed but was done at last," wrote *El Imparcial* of Guatemala City (June 1), *Trybuna Ludu* of Warsaw (June 3), the *Chronicle* of Manila (June 3) and *Corriere della Sera* of Milan (June 3). "We asked for clemency," wrote the *Jornal do Brasil* (June 4), "but we admit that it was not a human but a superhuman request." The press of all Eastern bloc countries published the news with comments expressing full approval.

The German press also approved. The *Koelnische Rundschau* wrote, "This will not expiate the crimes" (June 3). "Guilt was established beyond any doubt," said the *Frankfurter Allgemeine Zeitung*. "We must be grateful that the judges from Jerusalem avoided any undertone of hatred against the German people and of revenge against Eichmann," wrote the *Koelner Stadt-Anzeiger*.

I thought one of the finest and most moving summings up was that of Martha Gellhorn, a well-known American writer and humanist:

> The trial was essential, to every human being now alive, and to all who follow us; and, despite its length, its carefulness, the trial furnishes only a partial record—for the scene of the crime was a whole continent, the victims were a whole nation, the methodical savages who committed the crimes were as clever as they were evil, ingenious, brilliant organizers, addicts to paperwork. This is the best record we and our descendants will ever have; and we owe the state of Israel an immeasurable debt for proving it. No one who tries to understand our times, now or in the future, can overlook this documentation of a way of life and death which will stain our century forever. No one will see the complete dimensions of twentieth-century men—and that includes all of us, I insist—without studying the Eichmann trial. (*The Atlantic,* February, 1962)

APPENDIX II:

Notes

The proceedings in the Eichmann trial were recorded verbatim in Hebrew. The simultaneous translations in English, French and German, as well as an abridged version in Yiddish, were also recorded. All this material was made available to the institutes and documentation centers which deal with the events of the Second World War. The official record is now in preparation. The available record is, naturally, the most accurate, and references are therefore made here to the Hebrew minutes by session and page numbers.

References to the court exhibits are by their official designation, bearing the letters T/ (for prosecution exhibits) or N/ (for defense exhibits), followed by the number given to them by the court. The markings given to some of these exhibits in the Nuremberg proceedings are added. These are identified by the initials ND (for Nuremberg Documents) together with their accepted international markings (PS or NG or NO or L or EC, etc., preceded or followed by a number).

The statements of witnesses who gave evidence abroad are marked by the Roman numerals given to each statement by the court. Whenever parts of such statements were read in court, the relevant session and page numbers are added.

The tape-recorded Eichmann-Sassen talks held in Argentina during five months in 1957 have not yet been published. The quoted passages are referred to by tape and page number of the available transcript.

The pretrial interrogation of Eichmann was made a court exhibit. It is marked T/37.

The following abbreviations are used: IMT for the official publication of the proceedings before the International Military Tribunal; TWC for the Trials of War Criminals (the *Green Series*).

CHAPTER 1. *The Mask*

PAGE

8 I am not interested in Jewish stories: William Hull, *The Struggle for a Soul,* New York, Doubleday, 1963, p. 140.

9 To obey is the highest command: T/44 ("My Memoirs," written by Eichmann in prison), p. 7. See also T/37, p. 360.

9 A hoax about alleged genocide: Guido Heimann, "Die Luege von den sechs Millionen," *Der Weg,* 1954, p. 479.

9 The Jews were kept in camps: Wolfram Sievers, "Die Endloesung der Judenfrage," *Der Weg,* 1957, p. 235.

10 Either the German people will live: Sassen, tape 39, p. 2.

10 Diabolically clever Jewish scheme: Sassen, tape 39, p. 7; tape 36, p. 3.

10 Kastner's "statement": Sassen, tape 38, p. 6.

10 The battlefields of this war: Sassen, tape 36, p. 2.

11 It gave me uncommon joy: Sassen, tape 1, p. 2.

PAGE
11 I lived in this stuff: Sassen, tape 1, p. 11.
11 I thought it over: Sassen, tape 3, p. 3.
11 But the Jews were actually right: Sassen, tape 5, p. 4.
11 Personally I never had any bad experience: Sassen, tape 17, p. 7.
11 I worked 100 percent: Sassen, tape 11, p. 9.
11 To be frank with you: Sassen, tape 67, p. 9.
12 But these things had better be omitted: Sassen, tape 67, p. 10.
12 I had many detailed discussions: Rudolf Hoess, *Commandant of Auschwitz,* New York, Popular Library, p. 145.
12 He showed himself: *ibid.*, p. 205.
12 Eichmann on Hoess: Sassen, tape 17, pp. 5–6; confirmed by Eichmann in cross-examination: "If I described Hoess to Sassen as the incarnation of truth and punctuality, then I was right." (Session 95, p. 27.)
13 A coward at heart: T/84, p. 14.
13 His character and personality: T/57, p. 5.
13 Dean Grueber's evidence: Session 41, p. 31.
13 Loesener on Eichmann: *Vierteljahrshefte fuer Zeitgeschichte*, July, 1961, p. 265.

CHAPTER 2. *The Pathology of Hatred and Its Organization*

15 Luther's statement: Martin Luther, *Von Juden und ihren Luegen,* Wittemberg, 1543.
15 Kaiser Wilhelm to H. S. Chamberlain: Shirer, *Rise and Fall of the Third Reich,* New York, Crest Books, 1962, p. 157.
16 Statement of von Caprivi: *Judenfeindschaft,* Fischer, 1963, p. 234.
16 The odor of these people: *Mein Kampf* (translated by John Murphy), London, Hurst and Blackett, 1939, p. 60.
16 Then his mind, never quite normal: Bullock; *Hitler, a Study in Tyranny,* New York, 1962, Bantam Books, pp. 342 ff.
17 Responsibility of Jews for white-slave traffic: *Mein Kampf, op. cit.*, p. 61.
17 Influence of Lenz von Liebensfeld: See Wilfried Daim, *Der Mann der Hitler die Ideen gab,* Munich, Isar Verlag, 1958.
17 From being a softhearted cosmopolitan: *Mein Kampf, op. cit.*, p. 65.
17 It is true we are barbarians: Rauschning, *Hitler Speaks,* London, T. Butterworth, 1940, p. 87.
17 Jews had no intention to build a state: *Mein Kampf, op. cit.*, p. 253.
17 Hitler declared war on Jews: *Mein Kampf, op. cit.*, p. 65.
17 Hitler's testament: ND 3569-PS.
18 Importance of terror: *Mein Kampf, op. cit.*, p. 49.
18 No race in scientific sense: Rauschning, *op. cit.*, p. 229.
20 Perfumed National Socialism: Wilhelm Roepke, *Die Deutsche Frage,* Erlenbach-Zurich, E. Rentsch, 1948. (Translated into English under the title *The German Question,* London, G. Allen, 1946, and also as *The Solution of the German Problem,* New York, G. P. Putnam, 1947.)
20 The Professor was always subserviently helpful: *ibid.*, p. 82.
20 German physics: Max Weinrich, *Hitler's Professors,* New York, Institute for Jewish Research, 1946, pp. 11–14.
20 It was a scene of prostitution: Roepke, *op. cit.*, p. 90.
20 Various reasons and many excuses: Karl Jaspers, *The Question of German Guilt,* New York, Dial Press, 1948, p. 70.

PAGE
21 Blindness to the misfortunes of others: *ibid.*, p. 70.
21 Regimental education officer: Bullock, *op. cit.*, p. 39.
22 One of those terrifying human beings: Edward Crankshaw, *Gestapo,* London, Putnam, 1956, p. 21.
22 How can you find any pleasure in shooting?: Felix Kersten, *Memoirs,* London, Hutchinson & Co., pp. 115–116. (Translated from the German, *Totenkopf und Treue,* Hamburg, Robert Moelisch, 1952.)
22 I still respect and admire him: Sassen, tape 2, p. 6.
22 History may prove that he was the most demonic: Charles Wighton, *Heydrich,* Odham ed., London, Odham, 1962, p. 90.
22 I never knew a cooler dog: Sassen, tape 46, p. 10.
22 Such people could still be used: Kersten, *op. cit.*, p. 97.
22 Eichmann told Sassen: Sassen, tape 4, p. 4, and tape 64, p. 3.
22 He was the hidden pivot: Walter Schellenberg, *Memoirs,* London, André Deutsch, 1956, p. 31.
23 Himmler asked the former naval officer: Wighton, *op. cit.*, p. 37.
24 The organization of the police under the Nazis: Crankshaw, *op. cit.*, Chapter 6, "Confusion as an Art."
24 Behind the apparently iron front of Teutonic organization: *ibid.*, p. 63.
24 It was so usual for the members of the Gestapo: Gisevius, *To the Bitter End,* London, Jonathan Cape, 1948, p. 61.

Chapter 3. *The Beginnings of a Man and Bureaucrat*

27 The same history teacher: T/84, p. 2.
27 He was decisive for my whole later life: *Mein Kampf, op. cit.*, p. 26.
28 The years of my youth were quite sunny: Sassen, tape 29, p. 2.
28 The Nazi Party in Linz: Sassen, tape 30, pp. 2–3.
28 To break off his engagement: Sassen, tape 30, p. 4.
29 Imagine: one day he came to see me: Sassen, tape 67, p. 2.
29 During the interrogation and trial: T/37, pp. 114 ff.; Session 105, pp. 15–16.
29 In 1945, I heard that Fritz saw my children: Sassen, tape 67, p. 3.
29 Naturally, they showed me the door: Sassen, tape 29, p. 6.
30 I still remember how glad and proud I was: Sassen, tape 30, p. 3.
31 This impressed me favorably: Sassen, tape 30, p. 4.
32 Don't they trust me enough?: Session 75, p. 91.
32 An economic chaos: T/124.

Chapter 4. *Overture to Destruction: Eichmann Wins His Spurs*

34 At the entrance to many towns signboards appeared: Shirer, *op. cit.*, p. 320.
35 I did not recognize the man: Session 17, pp. 52–55.
35 He had shouted obscenities at Dr. Stahl: Session 15, p. 27.
35 Fleischmann on Chief Rabbi Taglicht: Session 17, pp. 17–20.
36 Any resistance would be brutally crushed: Session 16, pp. 91–95.
37 We exchanged astonished looks: Session 16, pp. 91–95.
37 They believed it about my birthplace: T/84, p. 5.
38 Tomorrow I shall again inspect the offices: T/130.
39 Recognized specialist: T/55; Promotion to Obersturmbannfuehrer on January 30, 1939.

PAGE
39 Visits of high officials: T/37, p. 110.
40 It was terrible, terrible: Session 17, pp. 56–57.
40 I had to be everywhere: Sassen, tape 2, p. 4.
40 Sent Jewish leaders abroad: T/149.
40 Got almost ten million dollars: T/185, p. 5.
40 Migration turned into good business: Session 90, p. 12.
40 Heydrich's congratulation: Sassen, tape 42, p. 7.
40 I suggested these words: Sassen, tape 26, p. 8.
40 I used it in my travels: Sassen, tape 26, p. 7.
41 Ransom was openly required: Frederic Morton, *Rothschilds,* London, Secker and Warburg, 1962, p. 259.
41 Grynszpan's evidence in court: Session 14, p. 46.
42 The President of the People's Court wrote: Lucien Steinberg, "Documents allemands sur l'Affaire Grynszpan," *Le Monde Juif*, April–June, 1964.
42 Eichmann interrogated Grynszpan: T/37, pp. 2464 ff.
42 Heydrich teletyped instructions: ND 3051-PS.
42 Eichmann was immediately alerted in Vienna: Session 90, p. 14.
42 I could not believe my eyes: Session 15, p. 17–20.
43 The events of the *Kristallnacht* described in T/137; T/140; N/34.
43 Heydrich's report: T/113 (ND 3058-PS).
43 Buch's report: Shirer, *op. cit.*, 582.
43 Minutes of meeting: T/114 (ND 1816-PS).
43–44 Goering's, Goebbels' and Heydrich's statements: *ibid.*
44 *Kristallnacht* in Vienna: Session 17, pp. 31–35.
45 Report, prepared in 1945: T/154, p. 9 (ND 3934-PS).
45 Mueller director of Central Emigration Office: T/116.
45 Eichmann summoned the leaders: Session 15, p. 27.
46 By tomorrow morning: *ibid.*
46 At the next meeting: T/142.
46 Hitler's and Ribbentrop's talks with Chvalkovski: Eugene V. Erdely, *Germany's First European Protectorate,* London, Robert Hale, 1943, p. 141.
46 Description of Emigration Office in Prague: Session 19, p. 13.
47 When we knew he was about to come: Session 19, p. 21.
47 Eichmann compares Vienna, Prague and Berlin offices: Sassen, tape 60, p. 2.
47 He stopped all releases from Buchenwald: T/154, p. 8 (ND 3934-PS).
47 Order by telephone: T/797.
47 Guenther is still alive: Sassen, tape 40, p. 11.
48 Jews will be Germany's best protection: Rauschning, *op. cit.*, p. 94.
48 War means annihilation of Jewish race in Europe: T/117 (ND 2663-PS).
49 Conference of May 23, 1939: ND L-79.
49 Naujocks testified at Nuremberg: IMT, Vol. 31, p. 90.

CHAPTER 5. *Deportation into Ghettos*

54 Ada Lichtman's story: Session 20, pp. 71 ff.
55 In Sanok the first thing the Germans did: Session 21, p. 27.
55 Heydrich originally opposed to ghettoization: T/114, p. 24 (ND 1816-PS).
55 Lieutenant Colonel Lahousen's report: T/358 (ND 3047-PS).
55 Heydrich called a halt to the shootings: T/164, p. 5.
55 This originated with me: Sassen, tape 23, pp. 6–7.
55 Wisliceny on Eichmann and ghettoization: T/85

PAGE
55 Heydrich originally opposed to ghettoization: T/114, p. 24 (ND 1816-PS).
55 Heydrich announced there and then: T/164, p. 4
55 All this was in its main outlines: Franz Halder, *Kriegstagebuch*, Stuttgart, Kohlhammerverlag, 1962, Vol. I, pp. 79, 81.
55 Heydrich issued urgent detailed instructions: T/165 (ND 3363-PS, EC 307-1).
56 Eichmann's remarks on Heydrich's instruction: T/37, pp. 3142–3149.
56 It obviously can no longer be doubted: T/37, p. 3151.
57 Eichmann and Stahlecker visit Nisko: Sassen, tape 43, p. 1.
57 Eichmann addressed the arrivals: Session 19, p. 31.
58 All those who were considered "unfit": Session 19, p. 31.
58 Those who stayed behind: Session 19, p. 36.
58 Occupied Poland was especially recommended: T/164, p. 3.
58 Himmler ruled that all Jews: T/169.
58 Creation of IV-D-4: T/170.
58 Globocnik's biography: Eugen Kogon, *Der SS-Staat,* Frankfurt 2.M., Europaeische Verlagsanstalt, 1947, p. 222.
59 He was told in very vague terms: T/253 (ND 2233-PS).
59 Fully laden with people: T/253 (ND 2233-PS).
59 Meeting of January 30, 1940: T/166 (ND NO-5322).
60 Ley's announcement in Lódz: Ludwik Landau, *Kronika lat wojny i okupacji,* Warsaw, Państwowe Wydawnictwo Naukowe, 1962, Vol. 1, p. 143 (Polish).
60 Report of Polish-Jewish Aid Society: T/210 (ND NG-2490).
60 *Politiken* story: T/666.
60 Deportees allowed one hundred zloty: T/171.
60-61 The General Government authorities later requested: T/211.
61 Stop of deportations: T/383.
61 To cover up the failure: T/801.
61 Eichmann even continued his deportations: T/384; T/808; T/809; T/810.
62 Eichmann's grudge against Frank: Sassen, tape 43, p. 2.
62 It was meant as a possible temporary solution: T/37, p. 124.
62 Professor Peter Heinz Seraphim: *Bevoelkerungs und Wirtschaftspolitische Probleme einer Europaeischen Gestamtloesung der Judenfrage,* Munich, Hoheneichenverlag, 1941, pp. 25–26.
62 Hitler awaited news of England's capitulation: *Documents on German Foreign Policy, 1918–1945,* Washington, D.C., Government Printing Office, 1957, Series D, Vol. 10, p. 82.
63 Emigration would not do: T/173.
63 Eichmann interested in Madagascar scheme: T/111.
63 Frank announced in 1940: T/253, p. 15 (ND 2233-PS).
63 Eichmann's detailed scheme (but without most appendices) in T/174 (ND NG-2586, NG-5764).
63 Got the idea from Herzl and Boehm: Session 91, p. 22.
64 Frank averts serious new influx of deportees: Raul Hilberg, *The Destruction of the European Jews,* Chicago, Quadrangle Books, 1961, p. 141.
64 Kidnapings for labor: Session 25, p. 7.
64 The Polish mob was encouraged to plunder: Emanuel Ringelblum, *Diaries of the Warsaw Ghetto,* Warsaw, Jewish Historical Institute, 1961, Vol. 1, p. 105 (Yiddish). A partial translation into English was published under the title *Notes from the Warsaw Ghetto,* New York, McGraw-Hill Book Co., 1958.
65 Their purpose is clear: Landau, *op. cit.,* p. 370.

PAGE

65 At first we had to face laws: Session 25, p. 6.

66 Boast of General Government authorities: T/253 (Selections from the *Diaries of Hans Frank*, Warsaw, Wydawnictwo Prawnicze, 1957).

66 Uebelhoer's orders: *Dokumenty i Materjaly*, Vol. III, p. 31.

66 The evidence of Henryk Ross: Session 23, p. 91.

66 Hoeppner's warning of July 16, 1941: T/219.

66 Memorandum of German Mayor: T/221.

67 Uebelhoer's profits: T/219, p. 3.

67 He sent a long telegram: T/220.

67 Uebelhoer told me: T/222.

67 The whole population is on the move: Landau, *op. cit.*, entry of August 8, 1940, Vol. I, p. 652.

67 Zivia Lubetkin Zukerman recalled: Session 25, p. 11.

68 It was behind the Vistula: Session 26, p. 27.

CHAPTER 6. *Slaughterhouse on Wheels: The "Einsatzgruppen"*

69 Minutes of conference in Prague on October 10, 1941: T/294.

69 In cross-examination I asked him: Session 98, p. 30.

70 This will be a war of annihilation: Halder, *op. cit.*, Vol. 2, p. 227.

70 Commissars' Order: ND NOKW-484.

70 Keitel's directive: ND 886-PS.

70 Brauchitsch's directive: T/175 (ND NOKW-2080).

70 Then *Einsatzgruppen* commanders were briefed: T/37, pp. 249, 2119–2121; Session 102, pp. 10–11.

70 Ohlendorf's evidence in Nuremberg: T/312 (ND 2620-PS).

70 Blume's statement: T/306 (ND NO-4145).

70 "Kill all Jews": ND NO-3414; TWC, Vol. 4, p. 130; and T/312, *op cit.*

70 Hitler on inferior races: Rauschning, *op. cit.*, p. 140.

71 When Barbarossa commences: ND 872-PS.

71 The evidence of Avraham Aviel: Session 29, pp. 36 ff.

73 The evidence of Rivka Yoselewska: Session 30, pp. 26 ff.

74 Graebe's affidavit: T/334 (ND 2992-PS).

75 Gustav, aim well!: Ulm trial, Stuttgart, I.S. 1/56, *Anklageschrift*, p. 92.

75 We have only two days for Sluck: T/340 (ND 1104-PS).

75 It is one minute after twelve: Max Kaufmann, *Churbn Lettland: Die Vernichtung der Judend Lettlands*, Munich, Selbstverlag, 1947, p. 116.

75 Eichmann inspects *Einsatzgruppen:* Sassen, tape 5, p. 7.

75 The army cooperated fully: T/330 (ND NO-3157).

75 Report from Tarnopol: ND NO-2940.

75 Dr. Stahlecker's report: T/304 (ND L-180).

75 Dr. Ohlendorf's report: ND NOKW-3234.

75 Soldiers should not gaze curiously: ND NOKW-2523.

76 Photographs smuggled out: Hilberg, *op. cit.*, p. 255.

76 Nor did the local population present difficulties: T/332 (ND NO-2832).

76 Gave their approval to the measure: T/327 (ND NO-3140).

76 We are deluged with denunciations: T/332 (ND NO-2832).

76 The population is hostile to the Jews: T/335 (ND NO-2828).

76 On the whole they were most reliable: T/304 (ND L-180).

76 Beating people to death with clubs: ND NO-3149 and NO-2943.

76 Their salaries were often paid: T/322 (ND NO-3154).

76 Some ethnic Germans: ND NO-4997.

PAGE
76 Accepted with thanks the solution: T/323 (ND NO-3153).
76–77 Stahlecker's report on Lithuania, Esthonia and Latvia: T/304 (ND L-180).
77 Senitsa Werszowsky, the Mayor of Kremenchug: ND NO-3405.
77 The complete elimination of Jews: T/304 (ND L-180).
77 If we shoot the Jews: T/339 (ND 3257-PS).
77 A Jewish committee was told: T/304 (ND L-180).
77 *Einsatzgruppe* C had to exclude for the time being: T/326 (ND NO-3146).
77 Map marked with coffins: ND 2273-PS.
77 Expert laborers must be spared: T/340 (ND 1104-PS).
78 In a private letter to Lohse: Weinreich, *op. cit.*, p. 153.
78 Lohse inquired in Berlin: ND 3663-PS; Weinreich, *op. cit.*, p. 149.
78 The Ministry for Eastern Territories replied: ND 3663-PS; Weinreich, *op. cit.*, p. 155.
78 Heydrich on redrafting the Brown Portfolio: T/297 (ND NO-4882).
78 Eichmann's amended version: T/298.
79 The Duesseldorf police file: T/1395-1398.
79 It begins with an order: T/302.
79 The captain in charge of the transported submitted a nine-page report: T/303.
79 Evidence of Leona Neumann: Session 30, pp. 2 ff.
79 The *Einsatzgruppe* to Eichmann: T/305 (ND NO-3257).
80 The trucks were camouflaged: T/309 (ND 501-PS).
80 Janów ghetto: Hilberg, *op. cit.*, p. 250.
80 An SS man would sink his fist: ND NO-5558.
80 Kube was subdued: T/342 (ND 3428-PS).
80 Kube and Italian officials: T/341.
80 Kube's altercation with Strauch: ND NO-4317.
80 Himmler on Kube's death: See *Aufbau*, New York, September 6, 1946.
80 Eichmann's department's instructions on foreign Jews: T/310 (ND NG-2652-A).
80 The department later ruled: T/784 (ND 3319-PS, NG 2652-H).
81 Conference on *Mischlinge*: T/299 (ND NG-5035).
81 Heydrich on doubtful cases: T/301.
81 Himmler on silly definitions: ND NO-626.
81 Affair of Jenni Cozzi: T/348-T/354.
82 Judgment of Nuremberg Military Tribunal: Case IX, TWC, Vol. 4, pp. 416 ff.
82 Nosske's evidence: T/307.
82 Jews of Kamenets Podolsk executed: T/322 (ND NO-3154).
82 Jews of Kiev massacred: T/326 (ND NO-3146).
82 Report of Group A, October 15, 1941: T/304 (ND L-180).
82 Report of Group D, December 12, 1941: T/335 (ND NO-2828).
82 Report of Group B., November 3, 1941: T/330 (ND NO-3157).
82 Judgment on cash register: Case IX, TWC, Vol. 4, p. 439.
83 Total number of *Einsatzgruppen* victims: Hilberg, *op. cit.*, p. 256.

CHAPTER 7. *The Final Solution*

84 For months Eichmann kept informing: T/732; T/733; T/683; T/395.
84 Change of title of department: T/99 (ND L-185).
85 Goering's directive to Heydrich: T/179 (ND 710-PS, NG-2586-E).

PAGE

85 Heydrich appointed Eichmann competent authority: T/186.

85 Goering's self-hypnotic instructions: Werner Bross, *Gespraeche mit Hermann Goering waehrend der Nuernberger Prozesses,* Flensburg and Hamburg, Verlagshaus Christian Wolff, 1950, p. 143.

86 Cross-examination by Justice Jackson: IMT, Vol. 9, pp. 518–520.

86 Jackson wanted to resign: Francis Biddle, *In Brief Authority,* New York, Doubleday, 1962 p. 410.

86 Goering's boast he had outmaneuvered Jackson: Bross, *op. cit.,* p. 236.

86 Goering kept repeating: Gustave M. Gilbert, *Nuremberg Diary,* New York, New American Library, 1947, p. 193; T/1168.

86 Kaltenbrunner denied giving orders: *ibid.,* p. 234; T/1168.

87 Eichmann drafted Goering's historic directive: Sassen, tape 50, p. 6.

87 Apparently he also kept another order: T/58, p. 6.

87 Globocnik wanted order in writing: Sassen, tape 35, p. 1; Session 96, p. 25.

87 Eichmann himself complained that these people: Sassen, tape 3, p. 7; T/37 p. 214.

87–88 Himmler observed execution at Minsk: Hilberg, *op. cit.* pp. 218–219.

88 But only three years earlier: Sassen, tape 40, p. 40.

88 The Fuehrer was right: Sassen, tape 47, p. 4.

89 Killing of Jews outside the norm of authority: Sassen, tape 46, p. 12.

89 What was good for Germany: Sassen, tape 47, p. 5.

89 More Jews returned after each shooting: T/330, p. 4 (ND NO-3157).

89 Eichmann's visit to Chelmno: T/37, p. 176; Sassen, tape 3, p. 6.

90 Hitler authorized mercy killing: ND 630-PS.

90 Wirth employed in euthanasia program: N/95 (ND SS-67).

90 Dr. Wetzel reported on October 25, 1941: T/308 (ND NO-365, NO-996, NO-997).

90 This being the exclusive duty of the Security Police: T/1414 (ND NO-2673).

90 Hoess was engaged in experiments: T/90; T/45, p. 173.

91 Wirth regarded Hoess as his "untalented pupil": N/95 (ND 55-67).

91 Hoess pointed to greater speed of his method: T/45, p. 187.

91 Von Otter transmitted Gerstein's story to Sweden: T/1312.

92 Goebbels obtained the Fuehrer's consent: Hilberg, *op. cit.,* p. 120.

92 Heydrich's order on yellow badge: T/635.

92 Two Secret Police regulations: T/209.

92 It became Eichmann's responsibility: Session 97, p. 17.

92 Interministerial conference of January 1, 1941: T/676 (ND NG-300).

92 Regulation 11: T/637.

93 Goebbels' article of November 16, 1941: Robert M. W. Kempner, *Eichmann und Komplizen,* Zurich, Stuttgart, Vienna, Europa Verlag, 1961, p. 115.

93 Himmler ordered the stopping of all emigration: T/394; T/395.

94 Heydrich instructed Eichmann to invite each dignitary: T/182 and Sassen, tape 50, pp. 7, 12.

94 Luther's brief: T/183 (ND NG-2586-F).

94 Wannsee Conference minutes: T/185 (ND NG-2586-G).

94 Rolf Guenther was there as Eichmann's aide: T/44, p. 114.

94 Heydrich's draft prepared by Eichmann: T/37, pp. 408 ff.; Sassen, tape 50, pp. 11 ff.

95 Kastein's *Geschichte der Juden:* T/82. The quotation was from p. 16 of the book.

PAGE

95 They evolved complicated tables: T/185, p. 12 (ND NG-2586-G).
95 A *Mischling* possessed leadership qualities: T/1381 (ND NG-2586-1).
95 On Eichmann's and Reischauer's views: T/526; Loesener's memoirs, *Vierteljarshefte fuer Zeitgeschichte,* Stuttgart, July, 1961, p. 298; T/693 (ND NG-1944-A).
95 Finally both matters were deferred: T/185.
96 Debate on different killing methods: Session 106, p. 11.
96 Department head specified by name: T/186.
96 Wannsee meeting called "Enabling Conference": T/44.
96 Kempner's interrogation of participants: Kempner, *op. cit.,* pp. 151–159.

CHAPTER 8. *The Great Deporter I: Germany and Occupied Europe*

99 Advisers on Jewish affairs subjected directly to Eichmann: Session 96, p. 15.
99 He was brutal to his subordinates: T/84, p. 15.
100 Our job was to detain: Sassen, tape 27, pp. 6–7.
100 The territorial principle: T/193; T/194 (ND NG-424); T/195 (ND NG-4892).
100 Payment for transport of Jews: T/404 (ND RF-1216); T/1074.
100 At first they would throw us their Jews: Sassen, tape 2, p. 6.
101 The German Foreign Office insisted that nationals: T/762; T/103 (ND NG-2652-D); T/781.
101 Eichmann admitted cheating: Session 104, p. 23.
101 It also kept him informed of anti-Jewish atrocities: T/1285.
101 Eichmann on Prince Eugene of Sweden: T/601.
101 Minutes of second and third Final Solution conferences: T/100 (ND NG-2586-H); T/190 (ND NG-2586-M).
101 We must meet the other side halfway: Loesener, *op. cit.,* pp. 298 ff.
102 Himmler's interest in sterilization experiments: T/816 (ND NO-440).
102 Eichmann's office to keep in close touch: T/1379 (ND NO-050).
102 Recommendations of second Final Solution conference: T/100 (ND NG-2586-H).
102 Proposal to sterilize all *Mischlinge:* T/190 (ND NG-2586-M).
103 Hitler decided to defer measures against *Mischlinge:* T/526.
103 Department IV-B-4 was most heavily involved: T/37, p. 2872.
103 Eichmann on Brack's request: Session 98, p. 35.
103 The great forwarding agent of death: Hoettl's evidence in Austria, p. 64, Statement No. I, Session 85, pp. 13 ff.
103 Notification to police offices: T/730.
103 Directives for seizure of property: T/729.
104 Ansbacher's evidence: Session 38, p. 8.
104 There was usually no way to escape: Session 37, p. 31.
105 People arrested at work: Session 37, p. 46.
105 Eichmann planned deportations from Vienna: T/810; T/811.
105 Evidence of Ernst Recht: Session 44, p. 46.
105 Special care was given to objects of art: T/712.
105 Takeover of Jewish public property: T/665.
106 Interchange of letters between Eichmann and Foreign Office: T/402 (ND NG-024, NG-4954).
106 Eichmann's instructions for deportations from France: T/407.
106 Query on Yugoslav citizens: T/409.

PAGE
106 Eichmann ordered introduction of yellow badge in France: T/405.
106 Imposition of yellow badge: T/413.
106 Eichmann ruled on deportation of 100,000 Jews: T/419 (ND RF-1217).
106 Meeting of Eichmann and Dannecker in Paris: T/428 (ND RF-1223).
106 Timetable for deportations: T/429 (ND RF-1222).
106 Minutes of telephone conversation between Eichmann and Roethke: T/436 (ND RF-1226).
107 Roethke placated Eichmann with large-scale arrests: T/441.
107 Laval encouraged the Germans: T/433.
107 Meeting of Pastor Boegner with Laval: Alexander Werth, *France 1940–1955,* London, Robert Hale, 1956, p. 62.
107 Evidence of Professor Wellers: Session 32, p. 36.
107 Eichmann has decided: T/439 (ND RF-1233).
107 Children sent to Auschwitz: T/443; T/444.
108 Eichmann on fate of transports to Chelm: Session 93, p. 33.
108 Eichmann's ruling of August 28, 1942: T/451 (ND NG-1965).
108 French to hand over naturalized Jews: T/453.
108 Roundup of all badge-bearers: T/454.
108 Knochen urged discretion: T/471 (ND NG-4956).
108 Roethke applied to Wehrmacht: T/472.
108 Promised denaturalization: T/485.
108 Roethke's report on Laval meeting: T/487.
108 Over fifty thousand Jews deported: T/488.
109 Wellers on Alois Brunner: Session 32, p. 51.
109 Order of April 14, 1944: T/506 (ND NO-1411).
109 Roethke reported 75 deportation trains: Gerald Reitlinger, *The Final Solution,* London, Valentine, Mitchell, 1953, p. 328. (German translation: *Die Endloesung,* Berlin, Colloquium Verlag, 1960.)
109 Report on René Blum's deportation: T/455.
109 Order for arrest of Max Gollub: T/496.
109 Refusal to let Rosenthal stay: T/491.
109–110 Eichmann's ruling on Abraham Weiss: T/499.
110 Eichmann and SS General Reeder: T/511.
110 Eichmann's ruling on Belgium's quota: T/419 (ND RF-1217).
110 There is too little understanding of Jewish matters here: T/512 (ND NG-5209).
110 Belgian report on arrival of train in Malines: T/520, p. 29.
111 We shall never forget Breendonck: T/520, p. 22.
111 Raid of September 3, 1943: T/519; T/520, p. 6.
111 Breach of promise to Queen Elisabeth: T/520, p. 6.
111 It was a very meager affair in Belgium: Sassen, tape 58, p. 5.
111 Seyss-Inquart's inauguration address: Werner Warmbrunn, *The Dutch under the German Occupation,* Stanford, University Press, p. 27.
111 Rauter's announcement: Reitlinger, *op. cit.,* p. 336.
112 The NSB raid on the Jewish quarters: Warmbrunn, *op. cit.,* p. 107.
112 Melkman on Edelstein: Session 34, p. 18.
112 Melkman on Center for Jewish Emigration: Session 34, p. 18.
112 The initial deportation quota: T/422 (ND NG-183).
112 Weekly trains for Auschwitz: T/572 (ND 1726-PS).
112 The Tuesday selections: Session 34, p. 28.
113 Pressure to increase prizes for informers: T/563.
113 The story of the Van Dam boy: Session 34, p. 31.

PAGE
113 Mail lost through enemy action: T/559; T/611.
113 Passports sent for rescue of Jews were fake: T/550.
113 Eichmann delegated SS Captain Moes: T/559.
113 Eichmann and NSB Jews: T/528.
113 Converted Jews to be the last deported: T/558.
113 Rauter's report on Jews in Vught camp: T/531.
114 A similar request to spare the Vught camp: T/554, p. 6.
114 Eichmann's office rejected request: T/554, p. 6.
114 The Vught camp Jews could work: T/557.
114 It is preposterous: T/562.
114 Request of the Arms and Ammunitions Office: T/565.
114 Eichmann's office said no: T/566.
114 Rajakowitsch and expropriation of Jewish property: T/525 (ND NID-13414); T/37, p. 2359.
114 Statistics of looted Jewish property in occupied West: T/508 (ND L-188).
114 The affair of the Jewish hospital at Apeldoorn: T/538; Session 34, p. 32.
114 The German Foreign Office intervened for Andreas Michaelis: T/548.
114 Eichmann said he would not do it: T/549.
114–115 Eichmann's refusal to reprieve Caroline Simmons: T/552.
115 Emigration for ransom: T/1138 (ND NO-2408); T/535.
115 Refusal to let Professor E. H. Meyers leave: T/534; T/535.
115 Final report from Holland: T/577.
115 Eichmann on deportations from Holland: Sassen, tape 34, pp. 4–5.
116 Wisliceny on his first duty in Slovakia: T/56, interrogation of November 14, 1945, p. 10.
116 Wisliceny toured Jewish labor camp: T/1075; T/57.
116 He showed them how the machinery worked: T/56, interrogation of November 15, 1945, p. 6.
116 Introduction of a Jewish Code: ND NG-4409.
116 Wisliceny submitted detailed plan: T/1077.
116 Slovaks suggested sending families of deportees: T/1074, p. 2.
116 By June about 52,000 Slovak Jews deported: T/1101. See T/58 for destination of deportations.
116 Eichmann went off to Bratislava: T/1090.
116 Eichmann summed up his Bratislava visit: Sassen, tape 22, p. 17.
117 Eichmann told of attempt on Heydrich's life: T/1074, p. 7.
117 Fialla dispatched to Auschwitz: T/1118.
117 Mail suddenly arrived too: Session 49, p. 36.
117 Evidence of Hoess at the Cracow trial: T/1356, p. 52.
117 Wisliceny's negotiations on a "Europa plan": Session 49, p. 47.
117 Reaction of Slovak Jews: Session 49, p. 47.
117 Support of camp deportees by working groups: Session 49, p. 31.
118 The end of Gizi Fleischmann: Session 49, p. 42.
118 Wisliceny called for by Ludin: T/1122.
118 The Germans got ten thousand additional Jews: T/1130.
118 Total number of deported Slovak Jews: Session 50, p. 41.
118 For me the political horizon was the important thing: Sassen, tape 25, p. 1.
118 King Victor Emmanuel expressed his pity for the Jews: Galeazzo Ciano, *Hidden Diary, 1937–1938*, New York, E. P. Dutton, 1953, p. 199.
118 Evidence of Dr. Hulda Campigniano: Session 36, pp. 62 ff.

PAGE
119 Italian Fourth Army liberated arrested Jews: T/474 (ND RF-1230).
119 Alarm from Zagreb: T/904 (ND NG-2345).
119 Italians assisting good-looking Jewish girls: T/906.
119 Wisliceny had troubles: T/985; T/986.
119 Italian attitude as an excuse for their own slowdown: T/611 (ND NG-4956).
119 Ribbentrop requested the SS Command: T/610 (ND NG-4956).
119 Von Hahn asking for concretization of SS wishes: T/612.
119 Eichmann's reply to von Hahn: T/613.
119 Outrage was expressed: T/611 (ND NG-4956).
119 Italy asked to join in the total European measures: T/613.
119 The Duce said his generals had a different mentality: ND D-734.
119 Eichmann invited Lo Spinoso: T/482.
119 Lo Spinoso declined: T/483.
119 His detention is of extreme importance: T/497.
120 Italians proposed internment of Jews on an island: T/990 (ND NG-5051).
120 Eichmann insisted on transfer to the East: T/991 (ND NG-5051).
120 Eichmann dispatched Dannecker: Examination of Kappler in Italy, Statement No. XV, p. 2.; Session 108, pp. 17 ff; T/615.
120 Arrest of Jews from the front line northward: T/617.
120 Ion Antonescu praised by Hitler: Reitlinger, *op. cit.*, p. 84.
121 Eichmann threatened police measure: T/1013 (ND NG-4817).
121 Eichmann admitted 28,000 Jews were killed: T/37, p. 3074. For number, see T/1014 (ND NG-4817).
121 Killinger's outburst: T/1029 (ND NG-2195).
121 Eichmann was amused: Sassen, tape 33, p. 4.
122 Allocation of trains to Bełżec camp: T/1284.
122 Richter published articles against "Jew slaves": T/1035; Session 48, p. 56.
122 Chief Rabbi Dr. Shafran called on Queen Mother and others: T/1072.
122 Richter on Mihail Antonescu's embarrassment: T/1039.
122 The Rumanians were wavering: T/1041 (ND NG-2200).
122 Killinger suggested Eichmann come to Bucharest: T/1030; T/1042; T/1043.
122 Eichmann declined: T/1044.
122–123 Eichmann frustrated emigration of five thousand Jewish children: T/1055.
123 The German Government would not lend its support: T/1256.
123 Eichmann's somber warning: T/1055.
123 Mihail Antonescu prepared imaginary minutes: ND NG-2704; Hilberg, *op. cit.*, p. 508.
123 Dannecker sent to Sofia: T/929; T/930.
124 Bulgaria signed a written contract: T/938.
124 In lambskin camps: Reitlinger, *op. cit.*, p. 381.
124 Dannecker on his talk with Eichmann: T/939.
124 Pesheff's petition: T/937.
124 Deportations from Bulgaria proper stopped: T/941.
124 This was just the first required step: T/942.
124–125 Eichmann's campaign against Jewish emigration: T/928.
125 Every piece of information about an intended refugee ship: T/946; T/952.
125 Benzler inquired what to do with them: T/870 (ND NG-2723, NG-3354).

PAGE
125 Foreign Office replied Jews should be put into camps: T/872 (ND NG-3354).
125 Benzler cabled back: T/874 (ND NG-3354).
125 Benzler wanted a quick and draconic solution: T/873 (ND NG-3354).
125 Benzler inquired on possibility of transport to East: T/874 (ND NG-3354).
125 Eichmann proposes shooting: T/874 (ND NG-3354).
125 Rademacher questioned in Nuremberg: T/875.
125 Suhr and Stuschka went with Rademacher: T/882.
125 Rademacher's detailed report: T/883 (ND NG-3354).
125 Turner's letter to a friend: ND NO-5810; Hilberg, *op. cit.*, p. 440.
126 The directives came from Eichmann: T/894.
126 Gas vans used exclusively for Jews: T/896.
126 Eichmann sent Abromeit to Zagreb: T/37, p. 1442.
126 Croatia would pay thirty marks per Jew: T/903 (ND NG-2367).
126 By and large the Jewish problem in Croatia: T/921 (ND NG-2349).
127 The evidence of Itzhak Nehama: Session 47, p. 42.
127 Eichmann delegated Guenther to Salonika: T/958.
127 Guenther replaced by Wisliceny: T/959.
127 He will need six to eight weeks: T/959.
127 Within a month Wisliceny had them in a ghetto: T/970.
127–128 Life in the Salonika ghetto: Session 47, p. 47.
128 Jews fooled by German temptations: Michael Molho, *In Memoriam*, Salonika, N. Nicolaides, 1948, p. 81.
128 Wisliceny reported the deportations: T/994.
128 The German report from Athens: T/996.
128 Jews on Dodecanese islands put on old barges: T/999 (ND NOKW-1715).
128 Uprooting of Slovenes: T/898 (ND NG-4897); T/899.
128 Deportation of Slovenes to Poland: T/370.
128 Poles are to be allowed to die naturally: T/382.
128 Priests should normally be sent to a concentration camp: T/378.
128 Polish children were trained for "germanization": T/375.
128 Other Poles transferred for work in Germany: T/374.
128 Polish children died en route: T/381.
128–129 Operation planned for 140,000 people: T/371.
129 Its scope was later reduced: T/376.
129 Five thousand Gypsies pushed into Litzmannstadt: T/221; T/222.
129 Eichmann had them transported to Auschwitz: T/37, p. 1163; Novak's evidence in Austria, Statement No. XII, Session 108, pp. 3 ff.
129 Removal of Lidice children for "germanization": Evidence of Maria Hanfova: TWC, Vol. 4, p. 1033.
129 Krumey informed IV-B-4: T/1094.
129 Infants of under two years: T/1091.
129 Children arrived without luggage: T/1093.
129 No need to take special care: Krumey's evidence, Statement No. IX, Session 107, pp. 125 ff.
129 Eichmann had a telephone talk with Krumey: T/1093.
130 Brack detailed some of his men: T/1375 (ND NO-205).
130 Strain on railway administration: T/251 (ND NO-2207).
130 5,000 men of the chosen people: T/252 (ND NO-2207).
130 At a high-level conference: T/1284.

PAGE

130 It was decided to reduce Bialystok ghetto: T/292 (ND 1472-PS).
130 Guenther got his ten thousand Jews: T/293, p. 21.
131 Eichmann was delegated to represent Kaltenbrunner: T/247 (ND NO-519).
131 He had Dr. Max Horn on his side: T/248 (ND NO-519).
131 Differences of reasoning between Horn and Eichmann: T/248 (ND NO-519), *supra*.
131 Greiser requested compensation: ND NO-519 (memorandum of Volk).
131 The ghetto would be gradually reduced: T/249 (ND NO-519).

CHAPTER 9. *The Great Deporter II: Hungary*

132 Jeckeln undertook to complete the liquidation: ND 197-PS.
133 Guenther's complaint of the Jewish laborers: T/1140.
133 A Jew had accosted a German police sergeant: ND NG-3522.
133 Tungsram declined to accept further German orders: Hilberg, *op. cit.*, p. 515.
133 In a reply dated September 25, 1942: T/1136.
133 Kállay opposed imprisonment of Jews: T/1139.
134 Luther to Sztojay: ND NG-1798.
134 Hungarians hesitated to deliver the Jews: ND NG-628.
134 Kállay instructed Sztojay to placate the Germans: Jenö Levai, *Eichmann in Hungary*, Budapest, Pannonia Press, 1961, p. 48.
135 Veesenmayer advocated strong measures: T/1144 (ND NG–5560), p. 28.
135 RSHA was ordered to draw up a list: ND D-679.
135 Send the Master in person: Session 103, p. 3.
135 Hungarian gendarmery wanted to clear Budapest first: T/37, pp. 272–274.
135 Veesenmayer arrived as Plenipotentiary of the Reich: T/1145 (ND NG-5524).
136 We asked the Hungarian authorities: Session 51, p. 46.
136 Krumey said: T/1155.
136 Written instructions were issued: Levai, *op. cit.*, p. 68.
136 Wisliceny was the main speaker: Session 52, p. 2.
136 Do as the Germans ask: T/1113, p. 19. (This is the document known as the Kastner Report, published under the title *Der Kastner-Bericht*, Munich, Kindler Verlag, 1961.)
137 Baky ordered to put gendarmery at Eichmann's disposal: T/1113, p. 18.
137 Report of meeting of March 31, 1944: T/1156.
138 Otto Komoly had sounded Jewish war veterans on resistance: T/1113, p. 22.
138 Unusual speed under local conditions: Hilberg, *op. cit.*, p. 531.
138 Personal contact and influence of Eichmann's unit: T/1184 (ND NG-5725).
138 The *Sondereinsatzkommando* was showering it: Session 52, p. 11.
138 Meeting of April 4, 1944: Levai, *op. cit.*, p. 71.
139 They would meet the fate of rumormongers: *ibid.*, p. 88.
139 I have ordered ghettoization: Session 52, p. 21.
139 Sanitation conditions in Užhorod ghetto: Session 53, p. 36.
139 Eichmann visited the larger ghettos: Session 53, p. 52.
139 Endre said that the Jews: Levai, *op. cit.*, p. 79.
139–140 To find out whether the camp was in a condition "to stomach" the Jews: T/37, p. 1321.

PAGE
140 He accompanied the first transport: T/1356, p. 168.
148 Torturing of deportees: Levai, *op. cit.*, p. 106.
148 Pack them in like herrings: T/1162.
148 It was a voyage of horrors: Session 53, p. 42.
148 Children did not need much air: Session 58, p. 17.
148 Stop bothering me with horror stories: T/1113, p. 47.
140 A campaign of deception continued: Session 53, p. 43.
141 The Waldsee postcard: Freudiger's evidence, Session 52, p. 32.
141 They finally agreed on a schedule: T/1356, p. 168.
141 Veesenmayer summed up the final total figures: T/1213.
141 Ferenczy's report: T/1166.
141 The pamphlet addressed to the Hungarian people: Levai, *op. cit.*, p. 114.
141 Petitions to the government and the Regent: Levai, *op. cit.*, p. 115.
141 Plans for a great final knock-out: T/1195 (ND NG-2190).
142 The German Foreign Office had its apprehension: T/1199 (ND NG-2424).
142 Veesenmayer's reply to the Foreign Office: T/1200 (ND NG-2260).
142 Horthy suddenly got cold feet: T/1212 (ND NG-5523).
143 Veesenmayer's report of July 25, 1944: T/1215 (ND NG-1806).
143 This can't be tolerated: Levai, *op. cit.*, p. 126.
144 Dr. Brody's evidence on Kistarcsa camp: Session 52, p. 101.
144 The Jewish Council was ordered to appear: Session 52, p. 46.
144 But at Kistarcsa something else was happening: Session 52, p. 106; Session 53, p. 1.
145 He saw Freudiger next day: Session 52, p. 47.
145 Eichmann got his train out by a trick: T/691 (ND Veesenmayer-216), p. 8.
145 We have protested most sharply: Levai, *op. cit.*, p. 129.
145 He wrote to his deputy, Guenther: T/1216.
145 He appealed to Himmler on conceded exceptions: T/1217.
146 Now I have to go to Minister Jaros: T/1113, p. 41.
146 He decided that the Jews would supply it: T/1116, p. 6.
146 Wisliceny delivered message from Rabbi Weissmandel: Session 52, p. 6.
146 A virtual contest between Germans and Hungarians: Session 56, p. 16.
147 The loser in this game is also called a traitor: T/1113, p. 43.
147 You may promise the Jews what they want: T/689; Becher's interrogation of March 2, 1948, p. 2.
148 A million Jews for ten thousand trucks: Session 56, p. 32.
148 Today I start deporting: Session 56, p. 41.
148 My hands are now free: Session 58, p. 36.
148 I knew Eichmann's mind: T/1116, p. 5.
149 I'll set the mills of Auschwitz in full operation: T/1113, p. 47.
149 I would not even have thought of it: Sassen, tape 12, p. 9.
149 Eichmann admitted general correctness of the passage: Session 103, p. 18.
149 Sharett's report: T/1176.
149 During the police investigation he said he could not remember: T/37, pp. 294, 295.
149 It was prompted by material considerations: Session 103, p. 19.
149–150 Veesenmayer's reply to Ribbentrop: T/1191 (ND NG-2994).
150 In any case, the Hungarians must have had little doubt: Levai, *op. cit.*, p. 135.
150 The Germans replied that they would be glad: Levai, *op. cit.*, p. 138.

PAGE
151 Eichmann expected Jewish armed resistance: T/1217.
151 SS parade in Budapest: Levai, *op. cit.*, p. 139.
151 Horthy gave consent to limited deportation from Budapest: T/1218.
151 Eichmann was mad with rage: Levai, *op. cit.*, p. 140.
151 Eichmann suggested he might be recalled from Budapest: T/1219.
151 Becher reminded Himmler of "goods for blood" negotiations: T/1220.
151 Becher was instructed to go ahead: T/1221.
151 Wisliceny called in Kastner: T/1113, p. 92.
151 Deportations would begin on September, 2: T/1223.
151 His Commando was finally dissolved: T/1225 (ND NG-4985).
151 Himmler awarded him an Iron Cross; Levai, *op. cit.*, p. 143.
152 I am back, you see: T/1113, p. 109.
152 Eichmann would take urgent steps for immediate ghettoization: T/1234.
152 Eichmann intends to send fifty thousand more: T/1235.
152 Ribbentrop wrote back that the new setup: ND NG-4986.
152 October 20 collection of the labor force: Session 58, p. 41.
152 The premises of the Jewish Council: Levai, *op. cit.*, p. 153.
153 The foot march: Evidence of Aviva Fleischmann, Session 61, p. 72.
153 International Red Cross report: Levai, *op. cit.*, p. 165.
153 Juettner saw the march: T/692 (ND NG-5216).
153 Becher said the march was "clear murder": T/689; interrogation on July 10, 1947, p. 5.
153 Veesenmayer on the number of marchers: T/1247.
154 Szálasi ruled that Hungarian Jews: Levai, *op. cit.*, p. 157.
154 The "vehicle ruling" worried the Germans: T/1242 (ND NG-4987).
154 Vajna Gabor on his meetings with Eichmann: T/1245 (ND NO-1874).
154 Himmler summoned Eichmann to Berlin: T/689; interrogation of Becher on July 10, 1947, p. 10.
154 Kaltenbrunner had gone to Hitler: T/1248.
154 Eichmann awarded Cross of War Merits: T/55.
154 This mollified him a great deal: T/689, interrogation of Becher on July 10, 1947, p. 10; Becher's evidence, Statement No. VI, p. 27.
154 Armed resistance by the Jews: T/1113, p. 108; Levai, *op. cit.*, p. 175.
154 The suffering of the Budapest Jews: Levai, *op. cit.*, p. 178.
155 Eichmann to Sassen on the foot march: Sassen, tape 15, p. 2.

CHAPTER 10. *The Death Camps*

156 The camps became an essential part of the "SS State": Eugen Kojon, *op. cit.*
157 As early as October 10, 1941: T/37, p. 117.
157 Minutes of conference of October 10, 1941: T/294.
158 Hitler claimed the swine got their distinctions: Reitlinger, *op. cit.*, p. 165.
158 On January 19, 1942, Eichmann inspected Theresienstadt: T/846.
158 At a conference with police chiefs: T/734.
158 The propaganda camp: T/537.
158 Eichmann called it a signboard: T/37, p. 254.
158 Whenever these visitors arrived: Session 38, p. 47.
158 Two days after our arrival: Session 38, p. 12.
159 Theresienstadt was an assembly deportation camp: Interrogation of Seidl, T/842.

PAGE

159 Figures on fate of inmates: H. G. Adler, *Theresienstadt 1941–1945,* Tuebingen, 1955, J. C. B. Mohr (Paul Siebeck), 1955, 2nd ed., p. 59.

159 Sixteen Jews were hanged: Interrogation of Seidl, T/842.

159 But I wrote only to my grandmother: Adler, *op. cit.*, p. 87.

159 Himmler on Theresienstadt: Reitlinger, *op. cit.*, p. 167.

159 Bearing children in Theresienstadt: T/863

159 Gas chambers in Theresienstadt: Session 45, p. 34.

160 Foreign office asked Eichmann to set aside thirty thousand Jews: T/762.

160 A reminder followed: T/775 (ND NG-2652-D).

160 Von Thadden on intentions of the Gestapo in Bergen-Belsen: T/789.

160 Foreign Office's message to Eichmann: T/790.

160 "Sojourn camp": T/557.

160 Dr. Melkman on conditions in Bergen-Belsen: Session 34, p. 36.

160 International Red Cross asked for permission to visit Bergen-Belsen: T/79.

160 Eichmann finally refused: T/865, p. 3.

161 Evidence of Dr. Mordechai Chen: Session 71, pp. 56 ff. The Bergen-Belsen photographs: T/1347-T/1355.

161 Dr. Hadassa Bimko Rosensaft's description: Raymond Phillips., ed., *The Belsen Trial,* London, William Hodge, 1949, p. 69.

161 Asocial elements will be removed: T/197 (ND 654-PS).

162 Finally even a law was promulgated. T/643.

162 The code words "special treatment of Jews": T/201.

162 Dr. Leon Wells's evidence on Janowska camp: Session 22, pp. 12 ff.

162–163 Dr. Moshe Beisky's evidence on Plaszów camp: Session 21, pp. 76 ff.

163 Yitzhak Zuckerman on Kampinos camp: Session 25, p. 5.

163 Noah Zabludowicz's evidence: Session 24, p. 47.

163–164 Dr. Bużminsky's evidence: Session 24, p. 32.

166 A smiling SS man demanded deep inhalation: T/1309, p. 6 (ND 1553-PS).

166–167 Dr. Kurt Gerstein's evidence: T/1309, p. 7 (ND 1553-PS).

167 "Entrance to the Jewish State": Session 66, p. 41.

167 "This is the gate of the Lord": Session 66, p. 96.

167 The procedure in the Chelmno camp: Evidence of Michael Podchlevnik and Mordechai Zurawski, Session 65.

167 Treatment of a rebellious transport: Session 64, p. 57.

168 Kalman Teigman on a train from Grodno: Session 66, p. 63.

168 Abraham Lindwasser on his attempted suicide: Session 66, p. 96.

168 SS "sport": Session 64, p. 52.

168 They kept dogs specially trained: Session 64, p. 42.

169 I was a dentist in Treblinka: Session 66, p. 93.

169 Michael Podchlevnik's evidence: Session 65, p. 33.

169 The victims used to help and encourage each other: Session 64, p. 51.

169–170 Description of Auschwitz-Birkenau: T/1358 (Jan Sehn, *Concentration Camp Oświecim-Brzezinka,* Warsaw, Wydawnictwo Prawnicze, 1960, is the official report of the Polish Commission on Investigation of Hitlerite Crimes in Poland).

170 Statistics on crematoria: Ota Kraus and Erich Kulka, *The Mills of Death–Auschwitz,* Jerusalem, Yad Vashem, 1960, p. 125 (Hebrew).

170 According to the register no one in the camp: Session 70, p. 11.

170 One day a letter came from the Oldenburg bureau: Raya Kagan, *Hell's Office Women,* Merchaviah, Kibbutz Avtai Shomer Tzaiv, 1947 (Hebrew), p. 158.

PAGE

171 The evidence of K. Zetnik: Session 68, p. 1.

171 "Transport Jews" and "detained prisoners": T/470; T/1280 (ND NO-1553); Session 70, p. 12.

172 The selections were the weekly terror: Session 70, p. 51.

172 Joseph Kleinman's evidence: Session 68, p. 12.

172 Mengele wanted to show us: Session 68, p. 16.

173 The evidence of Dr. Aharon Beilin: Session 69, p. 16.

173 A well-known psychiatrist, himself a prisoner, wrote: Viktor Emil Frankl, *From Death-Camp to Existentialism*, Boston, Beacon Press, 1959, pp. 20–21.

173–174 Nahum Hoch's evidence: Session 71, p. 21.

174 Number of prisoners on January 17, 1945: Kraus and Kulka, *op. cit.*, p. 247.

174–175 The trek from Auschwitz: Session 69, p. 36.

175 At the rate of twenty carloads per week: Session 71, p. 41.

Chapter 11. *Under the Heel*

176–177 Evidence of Dr. Moshe Beisky: Session 21, pp. 61 ff.

178 Hans Frank told a gleeful audience: *Diaries of Hans Frank*, Warsaw, 1957, p. 320 (German and Polish).

178 Night and Fog decree: ND 389-PS; ND 1733-PS.

178 This land will forever be an annex: Hans Frank, *op. cit.*, p. 272.

178–179 The blood-red deeds of terror do not stop: Landau, *op. cit.*, Vol. 3, p. 325 (Polish).

179 He who had no part: Andrzej Ropelewski, *Memoirs of the Home Army*, Warsaw, 1957, p. 110 (Polish).

179 I looked on: Marek Sadzewicz, *Oflag*, Warsaw, Spodzielnia Wydawnicza Wiedza, 1948, p. 68 (Polish).

179 Frank informed his government December 14, 1943: Landau, *op. cit.*, Vol. 3, p. 481 (photostat of Frank's diary).

179–180 Landau records mass shootings: *ibid.*, p. 584.

180 The doomed people had to dig a long ditch: Simon Datner, *The Crimes of the Wehrmacht on Prisoners of War*, Warsaw, Zachodnia Agencja Prasowa, 1964, p. 80 (Polish).

180 This is now the end, I thought: Tadeusz Klimaszewski, *Verbrennungskommando Warschau*, Warsaw, Czytelnik, 1959, p. 17 (Polish).

180 General Boehme ordered his units in Servia: Hostage Case, TWC, Vol. XI, p. 1265.

180–181 The taking of civilian hostages: *ibid.*, p. 825.

181 Under the Commissars' Decree: IMT, Vol. IV, p. 353.

181 Treatment of Russian prisoners of war: Alexander Dallin, *German Rule in Russia, 1941–1945*, London, Macmillan, 1957, p. 425.

181 All 20,000 prisoners are doomed to die: ND NOKW-3140.

181 Death rate in Pskov camp: TWC, Vol. X, p. 32.

181 The Bolshevik soldier has lost all claim: ND 1519-PS.

181 Liquidation of three-quarters of the inmates of certain camps: Gerald Reitlinger, *House Built on Sand*, London, Weidenfeld and Nicolson, 1960, p. 122.

181 Admission of Wilhelm Schubert: Heinrich Teoplitz, *S. S. in Einsatz*, Berlin, Kongres-Verlag, 1957, p. 18 (German).

181 About 150 people crept into every ditch: Datner, *op. cit.*, p. 142 (Polish).

PAGE

182 Figures on fate of Russian prisoners of war: Dallin, *op. cit.,* p. 427. On strength of Vlasov's army, see *ibid.,* pp. 583–584 and ND 172-L.

182 Resistance of wounded Russian prisoners of war near Zhitomir: ND USSR-311.

182 Evidence of Dr. Eugene Kivelisha: IMT, Vol. 8, p. 270.

183 Dr. Kivelisha's description of treatment inside the camp: *ibid.,* p. 275.

183 Commando Decree: ND 498-PS.

183 There was no possibility of escorting them: ND 757-PS.

183 There were notorious massacres: Lord Russell of Liverpool, *The Scourge of the Swastika,* London, Cassel, 1954, p. 35.

183 German prisoners had only one request: Moshe Kahanovich, *The Fighting of the Jewish Partisans in Eastern Europe,* Tel-Aviv, Ayanot, 1954, p. 303 (Hebrew).

184 They often claimed to be of Jewish ancestry: *ibid.,* p. 304.

184 The Jews here are remarkably ill-informed: Hilberg, *op. cit.,* p. 207.

184 Resistance in Kaunas: T/304 (ND L-180), p. 5.

184 At the execution of all Zagare Jews: T/337 (ND NO-3279), p. 7.

184 On Zadok Slapoberskis and Abraham Weintraub: Ephroim Oshry, *The Destruction of Lithuania,* New York–Montreal, Rabbi E. Oshry Committee, 1951, p. 391 (Yiddish); *The Fights of the Ghettos Book,* p. 494 (Hebrew).

184 In other cases Jews would at least spit: Betty Ajzenstain, *The Underground Movement in Ghettos and Camps,* pp. 50 ff. (Polish).

184 What heroes will you be: *ibid.,* p. 47.

184 Your end is near: *The Fights of the Ghettos Book,* p. 457.

185 The behavior of the Jews in Dombrowa: Ajzenstain, *op. cit.,* p. 44.

185 The last speeches of Rabbi Nachum and Joseph Avrech: *Book of Kowel,* p. 417 (Hebrew).

185 The behavior of Rabbi Daniel Mowsowic: Bar-On and Dov Levin, *The Story of an Underground,* Jerusalem, Yad Vashem, 1962, p. 52 (Hebrew).

185 Blobel found a psychological explanation: TWC, Vol. 4, p. 497.

185 They were often tracked down: ND NOKW-95.

185 Jews were escaping deeper into Russia: T/322 (ND NO-2832, p. 23).

185 Warned by the excesses: T/323 (ND NO-3153, p. 13).

185 The Jews of Nieświez resist: Ajzenstain, *op. cit.,* pp. 103–107.

186 Resistance in Lachwa: *The First to Revolt—The Book of Lachwa, Encyclopedia of the Jewish Diaspora,* Jerusalem–Tel-Aviv, 1957, pp. 34 ff. (Hebrew); Ajzenstain, *op. cit.,* p. 94.

186 Resistance in Tuczyń: Ajzenstain, *op. cit.,* p. 100.

186 Resistance in Minsk-Mazowiecki: *The Fights of the Ghettos Book,* p. 491.

186 Resistance in other places: *ibid.,* pp. 474 ff.

187 The revolt in Treblinka: Session 66, pp. 66 ff.; *The Fights of the Ghettos Book,* pp. 533 ff.

187–188 The revolt in Sobibór: Session 64, pp. 36 ff.; Session 65, pp. 1–29.

188 Globocnik had all surviving Jews shot at Majdanek: Session 67, p. 56.

189 In this hell of Auschwitz: Evidence of Raya Kagan, Session 70, p. 41.

189 We smuggled into the camp: Evidence of Gedalya Ben-Zvi, Session 71, p. 42.

189 Vera Alexander's evidence: Session 71, p. 11.

189 Sometimes lives were risked for other purposes: Evidence of Joseph Zalman Kleinman, Session 68, p. 7.

PAGE

190 Sabbath candles in Auschwitz: Evidence of Rivka Kuper, Session 26, p. 31.

190 *Matzot* baking in the labor camp: Evidence of Professor Wdowinski, Session 67, p. 61.

190 The rebellious train from Bendzin-Sosnowiec: Session 71, p. 46.

191 The story of Mala Zimetbaum: Evidence of Raya Kagan: Session 70, pp. 21–23. See also Raya Kagan, *op. cit.*, pp. 208–210 (Hebrew).

191 The underground in Auschwitz and the revolt of October 6, 1944: Evidence of Israel Gutman, Session 63, p. 116.

192 The crematorium on fire: Evidence of Yehuda Bakon: Session 68, p. 36.

192 Ninety-six death certificates certifying "Shot in attempt to escape": Session 70, p. 27.

192 Rosa Robota tortured: Raya Kagan, *op. cit.*, p. 228.

192 The hanging of Rosa Robota: Evidence of Israel Gutman: Session 63, p. 117.

194 Only a few Jews availed themselves of this opportunity: Dr. Lenski, *Life of the Jews in the Warsaw Ghetto,* Jerusalem, Sifriat Shoah, 1961 (?), p. 45 (Hebrew).

194 Fear of expulsion by the Germans: Ringelblum, *op. cit.*, Vol. 1, p. 48 (Yiddish).

194 Establishment of public kitchens: YISA Report, *Pages of History,* 1948, p. 3 (Yiddish).

194 There was not a single instance: Yaacov Maltiel, *There Was No Vengeance,* Tel-Aviv, Am Oved, 1947, p. 75 (Hebrew).

195 We just could not imagine: Evidence of Zivia Lubetkin Zuckerman, Session 25, p. 31.

195 Evidence of Dr. Dvorjetski: Session 27, p. 31.

196 He [the General] announced that the Lithuanians: Leib Garfunkel, *The Destruction of Kovno's Jewry,* Jerusalem, Yad Vashem, 1959, p. 43 (Hebrew).

196–197 Dr. Elhanan Elkes persuaded to head the Kaunas Council: *ibid.*, p. 48.

197 The murder of the head and members of Jewish Councils in Galicia: Joseph Kermish, article in *Book of Galicia,* p. 447 (Hebrew); Philip Friedman, *Yad Vashem Studies,* Jerusalem, Vol. 2, 1960, p. 85 (Hebrew).

197 The execution of the Council chairman in Stanislawów, *The Book of Stanislawów,* p. 400 (Hebrew).

197–198 The end of the Jewish councils in Bereza Kartuska and Mlawa: *A Chronicle of Destroyed Communities: Pružana, Bereza, Mlawa,* p. 407 (Yiddish).

198 Dr. Jacob Lemberg shot: Gruenbaum: *Face of the Age,* Jerusalem, Zionist Library, 1957–61, p. 392 (Hebrew).

198 The members of the Jewish Council in Pružana murdered and deported: *Pružana Yiskor Book,* p. 23 (Hebrew).

198 Resolute stand in Shavli: Eliezer Yerushalmi, *Pinkas Shavli,* Jerusalem, Mosad Bialik, 1958, p. 107 (Hebrew).

199 The desire to survive: Philip Friedman, *Martyrs and Fighters,* New York, Frederick A. Praeger, 1954, p. 99.

199 Goering rules in favor of Jewish labor formations: Hilberg, *op. cit.*, p. 236.

PAGE

200 Eichmann a determined opponent of selecting Jews fit for work: Hoess, *op. cit.*, p. 205.

200 We know we are doomed: Garfunkel, *op. cit.*, p. 261.

200 We have only one purpose: Nachman Blumenthal, *Conduct and Actions of a Judenrat, Documents from the Bialystok Ghetto,* Yad Vashem, Jerusalem, 1962, p. 748.

200 We are about to produce boots: *ibid.*, p. 108.

200 Barasz defends his policy: *ibid.*, p. 148.

200 Proclamation issued in the ghetto of Wilno: Dr. Marc Dvorjetski: *Wilno in Defiance and Disaster,* Tel-Aviv, Mapai, 1951, p. 114 (Hebrew), (T/275).

200 We work as on half-holidays: Kermish, *op. cit.*, p. 446.

200 The password P. P.: Jacob Poznański, *Memoirs of the Ghetto Lódz,* Lódz, Wydawnictwo Lódzkie, 1960, p. 152 (Polish).

200–201 Uniforms reminiscent of the Gestapo: Reizl (Ruzka) Korchak, *Flames in the Ash,* Machavia Sifriat Poalim, 1965, 3rd ed., p. 121.

201 It was a difficult and tortuous way: Jan Mabolt, "The Ordnungsdienst in the Warsaw Ghetto," *Yediot Beit Lohamey Hagetaot,* April, 1960, p. 35 (Hebrew).

201 The hanging of Jewish policemen in Stanislawów: *Book of Stanislawów,* p. 400.

201 Criminal record a recommendation for police employment: *Book of Brody,* p. 402 (Hebrew).

202 Jacob Gens defends employing Jewish police to round up Jews: R. Korchak, *op. cit.*, p. 125.

202 We did not know yet whether to curse him or bless him: *ibid.*, p. 124.

202 Gens answered them: Dvorjetski, *op. cit.*, p. 400 (T/275).

202 I have saved the young: *ibid.*, p. 401 (T/275).

202 The surrender of Izik Wittenberg: Evidence of Abba Kovner, Session 27, p. 91.

202 Reports that Gens supported the partisans: Dvorjetski, *op. cit.*, p. 404 (T/275).

203 If I, the head of the ghetto, escape: *ibid.*

203 Jewish police in Shavli ordered to round up children: Yerushalmi, *op. cit.*, p. 305.

203 "He is our greatest disaster": Shlomo Frank, *Diary of the Lódz Ghetto,* Buenos Aires, Tzentral Farband fuer Polische Yidden in Argentine, 1958, pp. 34–35 (Yiddish).

204 Opinions of ghetto inmates on Rumkowski: *ibid.*, pp. 354 ff.

204 Even Rumkowski's severest critics: Isaiah Trunk, *The Ghetto of Lódz,* p. 373 (Yiddish).

204 Rumkowski voluntarily boarded the train: Sol Bloom, "Dictator of Lódz Ghetto," *Commentary,* February, 1947, pp. 110–122; Trunk, *op. cit.*, p. 374.

204 Czestochowa Jews disregarded Dr. Eck's warning: Nathan Eck, *Wandering on the Roads of Death.* Jerusalem. Yad Vashem, 1960, p. 180 (Hebrew).

205 One dies only once: Friedman, *op. cit.*, p. 68.

205 Czerniakow's suicide and farewell letter: *ibid.*, pp. 148–149.

205 Social activities in the Warsaw ghetto: Session 26, p. 3.

205 Lwów Gestapo forbade use of abbreviation JSS: Michal Weichert, "Jewish Mutual Assistance, 1941–1945," *Memoirs-War,* Vol. 3, Tel-Aviv, Ha-Menorah, 1963, p. 50 (Yiddish).

206 The Jews will have either to die out: *ibid.*, p. 238.

PAGE

206 They required every family that cooked a meal: Evidence of Rachel Auerbach, Session 26, p. 3.

206 Dissolution of all Jewish self-aid groups: Weichert, *op. cit.*, p. 376.

206 Reports on vocational training: Unpublished documents of Jewish Historical Institute, Warsaw.

206 The vocational training system in Slovakia: Oskar Neumann, *In the Shadow of Death,* Tel-Aviv, A. S. Stein, 1958, p. 105 (Hebrew).

206 We organized lectures: Evidence of Rachel Auerbach, Session 26, p. 6.

206–207 Cultural activities in Theresienstadt: Evidence of Mordechai Ansbacher, Session 38, p. 17.

207 "Ghetto Encyclopedia": Zvi Schner: *History of Cultural Life in Ghetto Lódz, 1940–41, Pages for the Study of Catastrophe and Revolt,* 1951, p. 89 (Hebrew); Trunk, *op. cit.*, pp. 396 ff.

207 Cultural activities at Janowska camp: Kermisz, in *Book of Galicia,* p. 444 v.

208 The sermons of Rabbi Kalman Shapira: T/258.

208 Sabbath evening service in Lódz: Judah Loeb Girst, *From the Depths,* Jerusalem, Spero Foundation, 1949, p. 124 (Hebrew).

209 They declined the offer: K. Shabbetai, *As Sheep to the Slaughter,* Bet Dagan: Keshev Press, 1962, pp. 59 ff.

209 The end of Rabbi Zvi Yecheskiel Michelson: Rachel Auerbach, *In the Streets of Warsaw 1939–1943,* Tel-Aviv, Am Oved, 1954, p. 145 (T/257).

209 Good news discussed: Hillel Seidman, *Diary of the Warsaw Ghetto,* Tel-Aviv, Umah Umoledeth, 1946, pp. 73, 228 ff. (Hebrew).

210 The world will ask: Ringelblum, *op. cit.*, p. 380.

210 I plunged with fervor and joy: Friedman, *op. cit.*, p. 134.

211 At least our descriptions will be left over: *ibid.*, p. 136.

211 The concealed bunkers: Evidence of Dr. Dvorjetski, Session 27, p. 32.

211 Katzmann on bunkers: T/215 (ND L-18), p. 2.

211 The Fuehrer needs all the remaining Jews: Evidence of Jacob Gurfein, Session 21, pp. 28 ff.

212 We assumed that the enemy: Eck, *op. cit.*, p. 89.

213 Mother, what shall I do?: Evidence of Dr. Dvorjetski, Session 27, p. 36.

213 In fateful hours the Jewish women: Aharon Peretz: *No Crying in the Camps,* Tel-Aviv, Masadah, 1960, pp. 35–36 (Hebrew).

213 We were astonished that three- or four-year-old children: Evidence of Dr. Peretz, Session 28, p. 31.

213 They were the little breadwinners: Friedman, *op. cit.*, pp 52–57.

214 At least 75 percent of the children: Session 26, p. 13.

214 Conspiratorial network of schools established: Eck, *op. cit.*, p. 37.

214 Children's theaters in Wilno ghetto: Dr. Dvorjetski, *op. cit.*, p. 219 (T/275).

214 Teachers disguised as "labor inspectors": Girst, *op. cit.*, p. 113.

214 I remember the famous educator: Evidence of Dr. Adolf Berman, Session 26, p. 17.

215 Few suicides among Polish Jews: Seidman, *op. cit.*, p. 134.

215 Nothing can force a Jew to lay hands on himself: Friedman, *op. cit.*, p. 98.

215 The youth movements became centers of an underground conspiracy: Session 27, p. 21.

215 We wanted to live: Gusta Dawidson-Drenger, *Diary of Justina,* trans. from the Polish by Moses Singer, Tel-Aviv, Kibbutz HaMeuchad, 1953, p. 25; T/259 (Hebrew).

PAGE
215 We wanted to preserve a human and Jewish image: Evidence of Zivia Lubetkin Zuckerman, Session 25, p. 22.
215 Whether we were wiser or more courageous: Session 25, p. 32.
216 He that has left the ghetto gates: T/289.
216 Evidence of Abba Kovner: Session 27.
216 This spark will kindle the smoldering fire: Dawidson-Drenger, *op. cit.*, pp. 36–37.
216 Defense plan for Kaunas ghetto: Bar-On and Dov Levin, *op. cit.*, pp. 118 ff.
217 The heroism of Lisa Magun: Korchak, *op. cit.*, p. 64.
217 Hela Rufeisen's evidence: Session 26, p. 37.
217 Anyone who saw Hela on the train: Dawidson-Drenger, *op. cit.*, p. 48.
218 They accept the most difficult missions: Ringelblum, *op. cit.*, p. 221.
218 We, the young and strong, could not leave the ghetto: Evidence of Yitzhak Zuckerman, Session 25, p. 87.
218 I explained to him: Evidence of Abba Kovner, Session 27, p. 67.
218 They had to decide when the fighting should start: Yitzhak Zuckerman, *The Fights of the Ghettos Book*, p. 113 (Hebrew).
218 Let us die honorably: Dawidson-Drenger, *op. cit.*, p. 110.
218–219 The attack on the Germans in Cracow: Aryeh Bauminger, *The Book of Cracow,* Jerusalem, Mosad Harav Kook, 1959, p. 423 (Hebrew).
219 Heinrich Mueller reported that the Jewish terrorists: T/254.
219 The fate of Gusta and Shimon Drenger: Bauminger, *op. cit.*, p. 428.
219 I now go to the big conference: Mordechai Tenenbaum-Tamaroff, *Pages from the Blaze,* Tel-Aviv, Kibbutz Meuchad, 1948, pp. 61 ff. (Hebrew).
220 Nonsensical optimistic news: *ibid.*, p. 82.
220 On August 15, 1943: Haike Grossman, *The Men of the Underground People,* Merhaviah, Sifriyat Poalim, 1950, p. 308 (Hebrew), T/293.
220 The first homemade hand grenades in Czestochowa: L. Brener, *Resistance and Death in the Ghetto of Czestochowa,* Warsaw, Jewish Historical Institute, 1951, p. 121 (Yiddish).
220 The fighting in Czestochowa: Ajzenstain, *op. cit.*, p. 66.
221 In Wilno they sabotaged railroads: Evidence of Abba Kovner, Session 27, p. 86.
221 Jewish resistance in Kaunas: Bar-On and Levin, *op. cit.*
221 Jewish resistance in Riga: Evidence of Eliezer Kerstadt, Session 29, p. 26.
221 In many other places: Kermish, *op. cit.*, p. 450.
221 Katzmann reported finding: T/215 (ND L-18), pp. 23–24.
221–222 "We were ashamed": Evidence of Yitzhak Zuckerman, Session 25, p. 76.
222 The fighting of January 18, 1943: Session 25, p. 72; Tuvia Borzykowski: *Between Falling Walls,* Warsaw, HeChalutz in Poland, 1949, p. 22 (Hebrew, translated from Yiddish).
222 Himmler's order: T/274 (ND NO-2514).
222 The Gestapo sent their contact men: Evidence of Yitzhak Zuckerman, Session 25, p. 37.
222 The manifesto of the underground: Israel Gutman, *The Revolt of the Besieged,* Merchavia, Sifriat Poalim, 1963, p. 287 (Hebrew).
223 Our most daring expectations were surpassed: T/255.
223 We were happy and laughing: Evidence of Zivia Lubetkin Zuckerman, Session 25, p. 41.
224 General Stroop on stubbornness of the Jewish bandits: T/274 (ND 1061-PS).

PAGE

224 On May 1, Goebbels recorded in his diary: Joseph Goebbels, *The Goebbels Diaries,* London, Hamish Hamilton, 1948, p. 273.

224 Let us kill ourselves: Gutman, *op. cit.,* p. 396.

224 Stroop reports: T/274 (ND 1061-PS).

224 The battle of the Warsaw ghetto continues: Goebbels, *op. cit.,* p. 307.

225 Eichmann was sent out to the spot: Sassen, tape 23, p 5.

225 Our losses were several thousand: Sassen, tape 23, p. 3.

CHAPTER 12. *The Great Powers and the Little Man*

227 In his letter of resignation, December 27, 1935: James G. McDonald, letter of resignation, London, 1936.

228 Myron C. Taylor's plea: *Documents on American Foreign Relations, 1938,* Boston, World Peace Foundation, Vol. 1, p. 438.

228 Setting up of Intergovernmental Committee on Refugees: Arieh Tartakower and Kurt R. Grossmann, *The Jewish Refugee,* New York, Institute of Jewish Affairs, World Jewish Congress, 1944, p. 415.

228 Rublee reports failure: *Documents on American Foreign Relations, 1938,* Vol. 1, p. 796.

228 Ribbentrop-Bonnet talk: *Documents on German Foreign Policy, 1918–1945,* Washington, D.C., Government Printing Office, 1957, Series D, Vol. 4, p. 481.

228 Switzerland complained: *Documents on German Foreign Policy, 1918–1945,* Series D, Vol. 5, pp. 895–896.

228 Hitler derided the democratic world: Norman H. Baynes, ed., *Speeches of Adolf Hitler,* London, Oxford University Press, 1943, Vol. 1, p. 736.

229 One of the chief difficulties: *Documents on British Foreign Policy,* Third Series, Vol. III, p. 295.

229 We are going to step up our anti-Semitic propaganda: Joseph Goebbels, *Tagebuecher aus den Jahren 1942–43,* Zurich, Atlantis Verlag, 1948, p. 302 (German).

229 President Roosevelt recalled the U.S. Ambassador: *Documents on American Foreign Relations, 1938,* Vol. 1, p. 450.

229 Rublee's tentative plan rejected: Artur Eisenbach, *Hitler's Policy of Extermination of Jews,* Warsaw, 1961, pp. 85–86 (Polish).

229 Roosevelt's cable to Myron Taylor: *Documents on American Foreign Relations, 1939,* Boston, World Peace Foundation, Vol. 2, p. 66.

229 Mussolini's refusal to let Jews settle in Ethiopia: *The Ciano Diaries, 1939–1943,* New York, Garden City Publishing Co., 1947, p. 5; *Documents on German Foreign Policy, 1918–1945,* Series D, Vol. 4, p. 548.

230 Refusal of British Government to approach Portugal: *Documents on American Foreign Relations, 1939,* Vol. 2, p. 88.

230 Germany exports anti-Semitism: *Documents on German Foreign Policy, 1918–1945,* Series D, Vol. 4, p. 340.

230 Barter for human misery: *Documents on American Foreign Relations, 1938,* Vol. 1, p. 876.

230 The fate of the *St. Louis's* passengers: *American Jewish Year Book 1939–1940,* New York, American Jewish Committee, Vol. 41, p. 356.

231 The news of the first massacres reached America: *American Jewish Year Book 1940–1941,* New York, American Jewish Committee, Vol. 42, p. 371.

231 The Dominican Republic project: *ibid.,* pp. 445, 446.

PAGE

231 Nor did America's policy change when it was reported: *ibid.*, p. 450.

231 Our interest continues to be in a great Jewish emigration: T/645.

231 Evacuation scheme of children to America abandoned: Winston Churchill, *The Second World War,* Vol. 2, *Their Finest Hour,* Boston, Houghton Mifflin Company, 1949, p. 646.

231 A most gratifying response: *Pets Magazine,* Chicago, 1940. Confirmed to author by ex-editor, Mr. Bernard Davis of New York, now of Davis Publications Ltd.

232 U.S. Government agreed to assist in transporting Polish children: *Documents on American Foreign Relations, 1942,* Vol. 3, p. 152.

232 Cordell Hull informs Eden about transportation to Mexico of Polish refugees: *Documents on American Foreign Relations, 1943,* Vol. 3, p. 29.

232 Eden told Roosevelt: *ibid.*, p. 38.

232 Eden pleaded with the Americans: *ibid.*, p. 39.

232 The British were, therefore, not at all certain: *Parliamentary Debates, House of Lords,* March 23, 1943, Vol. 126, No. 41, pp. 854–855.

232 There will be repercussions in America: ND NG-4406.

232 The American Government lodged a protest: *Documents on American Foreign Relations, 1940,* Vol. 2, pp. 568–570.

233 Churchill on *Einsatzgruppen* murders: *Documents on American Foreign Relations, 1942–1943,* Vol. 5, pp. 662–663; *War Speeches of Winston Churchill,* London, Cassell & Co., 1952, Vol. 2, pp. 59–66.

233 Inter-Allied Conference, January 13, 1942: *Punishment for War Crimes, the Inter-Allied Declaration,* London, H.M. Stationery Office, 1942, p. 11 (including minutes of conference).

233 Roosevelt castigated Hitlerism: *Documents on American Foreign Policy,* Vol. 4, pp. 664 ff.

233 The British press carried partial reports: A. Sharf, *The British Press and the Holocaust, Yad Vashem Studies,* Jerusalem, Vol. 5, p. 135 (Hebrew).

233 Report on early deportations from Berlin: *Die Zeit,* October 14, 1941; T/1419.

232 Churchill's *Jewish Chronicle* centenary message: *Jewish Chronicle,* London, November 14, 1941.

233 Churchill's Balfour Declaration Day message to be treated as private: Cable to Chaim Weizmann, November 2, 1942 (by courtesy of the Weizmann Archives, Rehovoth).

234 The fate of the *Struma:* Leib Kuperstein, *The Fall of Struma,* Tel-Aviv, Am Oved, 1944 (Hebrew).

235 Lord Cranborne's reply: *Parliamentary Debates, House of Lords,* March 10, 1942, Vol. 122, No. 33.

235 American Under Secretary of State uses "planted spies" excuse: Sumner Welles to Eleanor Roosevelt, March 14, 1941 (by courtesy of the Weizmann Archives).

235 State Department's rejection of Turkish plan: Memorandum of the Division of European Affairs, November 12, 1941: *Documents on American Foreign Relations, 1941,* Vol. 2, p. 875.

235 Roosevelt's message to Madison Square Garden demonstration; Churchill's confirmation of mass butchery story: *Jewish Chronicle,* July 24, 1942.

236 Dr. Wise quoted White House sources: Keesing's *Contemporary Archives,* London, Vol. 4, 1940–1943, p. 5506.

236 Jan Karski tells of the massacres: Jan Karski, *Story of a Secret State,* Boston, Houghton Mifflin, 1944, pp. 383–387.

PAGE

236 Churchill's message to the Royal Albert Hall meeting: *Jewish Chronicle,* November 6, 1942.

236 The letter of Archbishop of Canterbury: The *Times,* December 5, 1942.

237 Major General Neill's letter: The *Times,* December 22, 1942.

237 Fundamentally, however, I believe: Goebbels, *op. cit.* (German, p. 222; English, p. 181).

237 Lord Cranborne read joint Anglo-American statement: *Parliamentary Debates, House of Lords,* Vol. 126, No. 41, March 23, 1943.

238 Official figures "deceptive": *American Jewish Year Book, 1943–1944,* Vol. 45, p. 357.

238 The choice of place of the conference: *ibid.,* p. 358.

238 The opinion of conference participants: *ibid.,* p. 359.

238 Emanuel Celler's statements: Emanuel Celler, *You Never Leave Brooklyn,* New York, John Day Co., 1953, p. 88.

238 A monument of moral callousness: *Unity in Dispersion,* New York, World Jewish Congress, p. 165.

238 Eleanor R. Rathborn again took the lead: Eleanor R. Rathborn, *Rescue the Perishing,* London, 1943.

238–239 The inactivity of other countries, and other quotations: *Parliamentary Debates, House of Commons,* May 19, 1943, Vol. 389, No. 67 (debate, pp. 1117–1196; Eden's reply, pp. 1196 ff.).

239 Save a million Jews?: Joel Brand, *Advocate for the Dead, the Story of Alex Weisberg,* London, A. Deutsch, 1958, p. 167. (Translated from the German, *Die Geschichte von Joel Brand.*)

239 Shmuel Zygelbojm's farewell letter: *Jewish Chronicle,* May 21, 1943.

239 A partial rescue effort failed: T/1055 (ND NG-1794, NG-4747).

239 Senator William Langer in the Senate: *Congressional Record,* Vol. 89, Part 6, p. 8125.

239 Representative Sommers in the House: *ibid.,* Part 8, p. 10783.

239 Senator Gillette's resolution: *ibid.,* Part 7, p. 9305.

239 Representatives Baldwin, Rogers and Celler: *ibid.,* Part 9, p. A 907.

240 She proved that America: Mercedes M. Randall, *The Voice of Thy Brother's Blood,* Washington, D.C., Women's International League for Peace and Freedom, 1944.

240 Representative Hamilton Fish: *Congressional Record,* Vol. 88, Part 7, p. 9537.

240 Roosevelt announced coming of one thousand refugees: Message to Congress, June 12, 1944.

240 Exchange of letters between Attorney General Francis Biddle and Senator Robert E. Reynolds, June 14 to June 23, 1944 (by courtesy of Jewish Agency Archives).

240 State Department attempted to suppress further news: Stephen Wise, *Challenging Years,* New York, Putnam, 1949, pp. 276–277; "The Morgenthau Diaries, Part VI," *Collier's,* November, 1947.

241 Officials dodged their grim responsibilities: *ibid.*

241 Nothing was done owing to shocking delay: Wise, *op. cit.,* pp. 278–279.

242 London simply did not know what was happening: Ringelblum, *op. cit.,* p. 377 (Yiddish) (pp. 295–297 of the English version, *Notes from the Warsaw Ghetto, op. cit.*).

242 In October, 1942, two Jewish representatives: Karski, *op. cit.,* pp. 320 ff.

243 People are gradually beginning to lose courage: Goebbels, *op. cit.,* p. 311.

PAGE

243 Dr. Weizmann's demand to bomb Auschwitz and the British reply: T/1177.

243 Bewilderment of M.P.'s and the promise of the Prime Minister to disclose the available documents: *Parliamentary Debates, House of Commons,* Vol. 642, pp. 202–203. See also the *Guardian,* June 5, 1961.

243 The statement of Sir Arthur Harris: *Jewish Chronicle,* November 16, 1962; January 11, 1963, p. 7.

243 Statement of Group Captain Leonard Cheshire, V.C.: *Sunday Telegraph,* June 4, 1961.

243–244 Letter of John J. McCloy to Dr. Kubowitski (now Dr. Kubovi, chairman of YKAD Vashem): *Unity in Dispersion, op. cit.,* p. 167.

244 The bombing of industrial installations around Auschwitz: *Jewish Chronicle,* February 1, 1963.

244 Foreign and colonial offices interfered: T/1117.

245 Dr. Nahum Goldmann admitted as much in public: *In the Dispersion,* World Zionist Organization, 1963, No. 2, pp. 9–10 (Hebrew).

245 A message for their brothers: Karski, *op. cit.,* p. 336.

246 We preferred to risk a way of escape: Menahem Bader, *Sad Missions,* Merchavia, Sifriat Poalim, 1954, p. 95 (Hebrew). For further material on rescue, see Eliahu Dobkin, *Migration and Rescue in the Years of the Holocaust,* Jerusalem, Rubin Maas, 1946 (Hebrew); Chaim Barlasz, *Report on Rescue;* the Jewish Agency for Palestine, *Emissaries to the Diaspora* (Hebrew).

248 W. O'Dwyer's report: *Final Summary Report to Executive Director, War Refugee Board,* Washington, D.C., September 15, 1945.

248 Pressure on Rumania to break up camp in Transnistria: Ira A. Hirschmann, *Life Line to a Promised Land,* New York, Vanguard Press, 1946, pp. 51 ff.

248 The War Refugee Board prompted Roosevelt: *Final Summary Report, op. cit.,* p. 49.

249 "The offer comes from high up": Minutes of conference, June 7, 1944 (by the courtesy of the Jewish Agency Archives).

249 Churchill himself ruled: Winston S. Churchill, *The Second World War,* Vol. 6, *Triumph and Tragedy,* Boston, Houghton Mifflin, 1953, p. 693.

249 Weizmann's pressing request rejected: T/1177.

249 Eichmann recalled it all: Sassen, tape 44, p. 5.

249 Landsbischof Wurm fearlessly told the Nazis: *Der Lautlose Aufstand,* p. 46.

250 Metropolitan Szeptycki condemned compatriots: Philip Friedman, *Their Brothers' Keepers,* New York, Crown Publishers, 1957, p. 135; Itzhak Levin, *I Arrived from Specia,* trans. from the Polish by Dov Stock Tel-Aviv, Am Oved, 1947 (Hebrew).

250 Pius XII's encyclical *Summi Pontificatus: New York Times,* October 28, 1939.

250 All the Holy See would say in reply: *U.S. Diplomatic Papers, 1942,* Vol. III, pp. 772–777; Guenter Lewy, *The Catholic Church and Nazi Germany,* McGraw-Hill Book Company, 1964, pp. 298–299.

250 Pius XII to Berlin correspondent of *Osservatore Romano:* Guenther Levy, *op. cit.,* pp. 303–304.

250 Even Cardinal Faulhaber of Munich: Filip Friedman, *Das Andere Deutschland: Die Kirchen,* Berlin, Arani, 1960, p. 13 (German); Guenther Levy, "Pius XII, the Jews and the German Catholic Church," *Commentary,* February,

PAGE

1964, p. 24; and also Guenther Levy, *The Catholic Church and Nazi Germany,* p. 276.

250–251 Catholics did not come out in defense of the Jews: *Der Lautlose Aufstand, op. cit.,* pp. 47 ff.

251 Papal Nuncio "groped around" to the subject: Hilberg, *op. cit.,* p. 440.

251 Intervention of Nuncio in Rumania: Theodor Lavi, *Rumanian Jewry in World War II,* Jerusalem, Yad Vashem and Union of Rumanian Jews, 1965, pp. 85 and 111 (Hebrew).

251 Archbishop de Jonge of Utrecht: Warmbrunn, *op. cit.,* p. 161.

251 Monsignor Chattel wore the yellow badge: *Wiener Library Bulletin,* Vol. 8 (1954), No. 5–6, pp. 40–42.

251 Underground fighters in convent near Wilno: Korchak, *op. cit.,* p. 64.

251 Father Chaillet arrested: ND NG-5127.

251 To Marshal Pétain's inquiry: Léon Poliakov, "The Vatican and the Jewish Question," *Commentary,* November, 1950, p. 445; Levy, *The Catholic Church and Nazi Germany,* p. 297.

251–252 Laval had no patience with his own priests: Hilberg, *op. cit.,* p. 409.

252 Pius XII welcomed Father Tiso as a "dear son": Livia Rotkirchen, *Destruction of the Slovak Jews,* Jerusalem, Yad Vashem, 1961, p. 28 (Hebrew); Karol Sidor, *Sest rokov pri Vatikane,* Scranton, Pa., Obrana Press, 1947, p. 64 (Slovakian).

252 The Pope blessed Sidor in his own language: Sidor, *op. cit.,* p. 38.

252 Holy See told the Bratislava authorities of annihilation of Jews: *ibid.,* pp. 141 ff.; Hilberg, *op. cit.,* pp. 469–470.

252 Jews were being mobilized for labor: Rotkirchen, *op. cit.,* p. 29.

252 Intervention of Monsignor Roncalli: Chaim Barlas, "John XXIII and His Attitude to the Jews," *Davar* (Hebrew daily), November 4, 1959.

252 This time the deportations were stopped: Rotkirchen, *op. cit.,* p. 33.

252 Monsignor Roncalli intervenes against mopping-up operations: *ibid.,* p. 29.

252 Lukewarm *note verbale* of Vatican: Sidor, *op. cit.,* p. 148.

252 Goebbels bared his teeth: Goebbels, *op. cit.,* p. 118.

252 Pope not so opposed to National Socialism: *Goebbels Tagebuecher, op. cit.,* p. 246 (German ed.); omitted from English edition.

252 The Pope is possibly closer to us: *ibid.,* p. 233 (English ed.).

252 A further test for the Vatican: ND NG-5027; Hilberg, *op. cit.,* p. 429. See also Saul Friedlander, *Pie XII and le III[e] Reich,* Paris, Editions du Seuil, 1964.

253 Intervention of Bishop Hudal: T/620 (ND NG-5207); Guenther Levy, *op. cit.,* p. 301.

253 Pope not drawn into demonstrative censure: ND NG-5027; Levy, *op. cit.,* p. 302.

253 Asylum given a few dozen refugees in Vatican: Poliakov, *Commentary, op. cit.,* p. 441.

253 Eichmann on reaction of the Catholic Church: Sassen, tape 25, p. 5.

253 Reason for the Vatican's silence: *Summa Iniuria or Should the Pope Have Kept Silent?,* Rowohlt Taschenbuch Verlag (German).

253 The world keeps silent: W. Bartoszewski, *Conspiratory Polish Publications on Jewish Matters, 1939–44,* Warsaw, Twórczość, 1962, No. 9.

254 Refusal of Finnish Foreign Minister to give up Jews: Kersten, *op. cit.* (German ed.), p. 180 (English ed., p. 145).

254 Himmler furious: *ibid.,* pp. 172 ff. (German ed.), (English ed., p. 141).

PAGE

254 Result of Danish elections, March, 1943: *Hitler's Europe,* Survey of International Affairs, 1939–1946, Toronto, Oxford University Press, p. 527.

255 Warning of King Christian X: T/581.

255 The reaction of a Copenhagen cab driver: Kurt R. Grossmann, *Die Unbesungenen Helden,* Berlin, Arani Verlag, 1957, p. 374.

255 Danish police helped evacuation of Jews: Evidence of David Melchior, Session 35, p. 37.

256 I will ask for the heads of the saboteurs: T/584 (ND Steengracht-35).

256 Reich's plenipotentiary blamed the Army: T/586 (ND NG-3920).

258 The case of Sergeant Anton Schmidt: Session 27, pp. 81 ff.

258 SS Lieutenant Schwarz of Sobibór: Session 64, p. 61.

259–260 Assistance to people in hiding in Holland: By the courtesy of Yad Vashem archives. See also Grossmann, *op. cit.,* and Friedman, *Their Brothers' Keepers.*

260–261 Eichmann and Wallenberg: T/1234; T/1244.

CHAPTER 13. *Escape and Capture*

266 Himmler promised estate in Bohemia: T/84, p. 16.

266 Eichmann saw no sense: T/86, p. 3.

266 If, in the course of the evacuation: T/1113, p. 149

266 Some of the commanders were idiotic enough: Quoted by Kastner in T/1113, p. 149; confirmed by Wisliceny to be a true "word for word repetition" of his conversation with Eichmann: T/1116, p. 17.

266 To remain the man behind the scenes: T/84, p. 14.

266 He was hurt at their never inviting him: T/37, p. 306.

266 Hitler vacillated between hope and despair: IMT, Vol. 16, p. 498.

267 Eichmann reflected those moods: T/84, p. 17.

267 I will jump with joy into my grave: T/57, para 10; T/58, p. 22.

267 So he dramatically pointed to his gun: Sassen, tape 3, pp. 1–2.

267 He provided his wife with poison: Sassen, tape 13, p. 7.

268 You can't surrender: Sassen, tape 48, p. 2.

268 I later found out: Sassen, tape 65, p. 12.

268 They looked after the money more carefully: Sassen, tape 48, p. 8.

268 Eichmann was relieved when Kaltenbrunner: Sassen, tape 48, p. 7.

268 We have discussed the matter: Sassen, tape 48, p. 10; Session 88, p. 26.

269 He wore the uniform of an airman: *Der Stern,* June 25, 1960.

269 I was just a shade cleverer: Sassen, tape 4, p. 3.

270 That Wisliceny is just a little swine: T/1168; G. M. Gilbert, *op. cit.,* p. 102.

270 He was granted approval: Sassen, tape 11, p. 1.

270 Eichmann worked his way up: *Der Stern,* June 25, 1960.

270 The International Nuremberg Tribunal branded him: IMT, Vol. 22, p. 496.

270 The sinister figure: IMT, Vol. 19, p. 405.

271 A month later he landed in Buenos Aires: *Der Stern,* June 25, 1960.

271 The National-Socialist belief in God: *Der Stern,* July 9, 1960.

271 Reaction to the *Stern* articles (T/46): T/37, pp. 2682–2683.

271 His marginal notes were his own affair: *ibid.*

272 We analyzed everything minutely: T/37, p. 397.

272 I am no longer being pursued: Sassen, tape 3, p. 3.

PAGE

272 Telford Taylor's statement (Nuremberg and Jerusalem), Jerusalem *Post,* April 19, 1961, p. 4.

275 Eichmann's statement in Buenos Aires: T/3; Gideon Hausner, *6,000,000 Accusers,* Jerusalem, Jerusalem *Post,* 1961, p. 184.

CHAPTER 14. *The Preparation of a Case*

278 A roll was given there extra: T/44.
278 I am prepared, unreservedly: T/37, p. 360.
279 This knowledge alone: T/37, p. 360–361.
279 I did nothing wrong: Hull, *op. cit.,* pp. 83 and 116.
280 Repentance is a matter for small children: Session 96, p. 7.
280–281 Eichmann's interrogation by Less: T/37, pp. 368–371.
282 No, no, Mr. Chief Inspector: T/37, p. 410.
282 I never took part in deportations: T/37, p. 941.
282 Because of the stupidity of those fellows: Sassen, tape 37, p. 9.
282 This IV-D-4 here: T/37, p. 1646.
283 I am slowly getting befogged: T/37, pp. 1646–1648.
283 The minutes of a meeting of January 4, 1940: T/166 (ND NO-5322).
283 It is entirely strange to me: T/37, p. 1658.
283 I see by my own name: T/37, pp. 1659–1662.
283 Finally, he had to admit: T/37, p. 1676.
284 Léon Poliakov, *Harvest of Hate,* Syracuse, Syracuse University Press, 1954.
284 Gerald Reitlinger, *op. cit.,* p. 27.
284 Joseph Tenenbaum, *Race and Reich,* New York: Twayne Publishers, 1956, p. 242

CHAPTER 15. *Some Prosecution Problems*

296 Evidence of Jacob Friedmann: Session 64, p. 26.
302 I assume he has experience in these matters: T/37, p. 1273.

CHAPTER 16. *The Opening Battle*

307 Televising the trial: For America, especially in New York, see *American Jewish Year Book,* 1962, pp. 95–97. See also *The Eichmann Case in the American Press,* American Jewish Committee, Institute of Human Relations Press, 1962.

310 The preliminary objections of the defense: Session 1, pp. 26 ff.; also Hausner, *op. cit.,* pp. 179 ff.

312 In reply to the arguments of the defense: Session 1, pp. 46 ff.; Hausner, *op. cit.,* pp. 186 ff.

312 The reparations agreement: *United Nations Treaty Series,* Vol. 162, p. 165.

313 The mere fact, if true: *U.S.* v. *Insull,* 8. Fed. Sup., 310.

313 This court has never departed: *Frisbie* v. *Collins,* 1952, 96 L. ed., p. 541.

313 If a person is arrested abroad: *R.* v. *Officer Commanding Depot Battalion, R.A.S.C., Colchester, ex parte Elliot* (1949), 1 *All England Law Reports,* p. 373.

PAGE

313 Dr. Robinson's appearances before U.N.: U.N. Document A/2136; U.N. Document A/2645.

314 *The "Lotus" Case,* Publications of the Permanent Court of International Justice, Series A, No. 10.

314 An enemy of mankind at large: Blackstone, *Commentaries on the Laws of England,* 12th ed., Book IV, p. 71; Grotius, *De jure belli ac pacis,* Book Two, Chapter 20, para 40 (Translated by L. R. Loomis, New York, 1949).

314 The perpetrator of a crime against humanity: Morris Greenspan, *The Modern Law of Land Warfare,* University of California Press, 1959, p. 503; *Re Piracy Jure Gentium* (1934) Appeal Cases, p. 586; *British Year Book of International Law,* Vol. 28 (1951), p. 392.

315 Israel recognized as a cobelligerent: T/51.

315 The case of a Japanese warrant officer: *Law Reports of Trials of War Criminals,* Vol. 1, p.106.

316 On trials in various zones of occupation and in West Germany: See Reinhard Henkys, *Die Nationalsozialistichen Gewaltverbrechen,* Stuttgart-Berlin, Kreuz-Verlag, 1964, p. 189.

316 Not only defiance of well-established principles: Judgment, IMT, Vol. I, p. 227.

317 Humanity is the sovereignty: Judgment in *U.S.* v. *Ohlendorf and others* (Case 9), TWC, Vol. 4, p. 459.

317 But the jurisdiction of the Tribunal: *ibid.,* p. 497.

318 International Law Commission: U.N. Document A/1306, *Yearbook of the International Law Commission, 1950,* Vol. 2, p. 364.

318 The Germans have become so accustomed: Judgment in *U.S.* v. *Pohl and others* (Case 4), TWC, Vol. 5, p. 968.

318 Dr. Servatius replied briefly: Session 5, pp. 16 ff.

319 The present trial is concerned: Session 6, p. 1.

320 Hausner's arguments could, according to experts: *Yedioth Aharonoth,* April 16, 1961.

321 Professor Trevor-Roper remarked: *Sunday Times,* April 16, 1961.

321 S. L. A. Marshall wrote: New York *Herald Tribune,* April 15, 1961.

321 Patrick O'Donovan showed a deep insight: *The Observer,* April 13, 1961.

321 The Earl of Birkenhead summed up: the *Daily Telegraph,* April 19, 1961.

CHAPTER 17. *The Case for the Prosecution*

323 The opening address is reported verbatim in Hausner, *6,000,000 Accusers;* Sessions 6–8.

325–326 Evidence of Chief Inspector Less: Session 9, pp. 41 ff.

326 Professor Salo Baron's evidence: Session 12, pp. 31 ff.

326 Evidence of Zindel Shmuel Grynszpan: Session 14, pp. 41 ff.

326 Evidence of Dr. Benno Cohen: Session 14, pp. 56 ff.

326 Bear with pride the yellow star: T/60.

326–327 Evidence of Moritz Fleischmann: Session 16, pp. 81 ff.

327 Evidence of Dr. David Meretz: Session 19, pp. 6 ff.

327 Evidence of Zvi Pechter: Session 21, pp. 1 ff.

328 Evidence of Dr. Leon Wells: Session 22, p. 12.

328 Eichmann had directed Blobel's activities: Statement of Hoess, T/90, p. 6; T/217 (ND NO-4498-B); statement of Wisliceny: T/84, p. 17; T/85, p. 9.

PAGE
328 Evidence of Zivia Lubetkin Zuckerman: Session 25, pp. 6 ff.
329 Evidence of Judge Beisky: Session 21, pp. 61 ff.
330 Evidence of Leona Neumann: Session 30, pp. 2 ff.
330 Evidence of Dr. Aharon Peretz: Session 28, pp. 22 ff.
331 I have no objection whatsoever: Session 37, p. 21.
334–335 Evidence of Dean Grueber: Session 41, p. 22 ff.
335 Evidence of Judge Michael A. Musmanno: Session 39, p. 31.
336 Affidavits submitted in the *Einsatzgruppen* case: T/687; T/688.
337 Himmler's speech in Posen: ND 1919-PS. Excerpts from it submitted by the prosecution and marked T/1288.
337 Eichmann said: "No, never": Sassen, tape 47, p. 11.
337 Eichmann's guiding idea on staff policy: T/84, p. 9.
337 We can only cleanse our stables: Sassen, tape 1, pp. 7–8.
337 When I examined Eichmann: Session 95, pp. 29–30.
337 Eichmann on his rank: R/37, p. 250; Sassen, tape 62, p. 5.
338 The job was rotten: Sassen, tape 62, p. 5.
338 Eichmann had full authority over Jews: Hoess evidence in Nuremberg, T/1357 (IMT, Vol. 11, p. 438 ff); Hoess evidence in Cracow, T/1356.
338 Eichmann's program will continue: T/90.
338 Eichmann arrived with a further order: *ibid.*
338 I hear for the first time: Sassen, T/38, p. 2.
338 In the pretrial interrogation: T/37, p. 176.
338 Pohl and his subordinates cleared: Judgment in *U.S.* v. *Pohl and others* (Case 4), TWC, Vol. 5, p. 981.
338 Evidence of Professor Gustave M. Gilbert: Session 55, pp. 1 ff.
339 Goering wants to know: T/1170.
339 Supply of skeletons and skulls to Strasbourg University: T/1362-T/1371 (ND NO-085–089, NO-538, NO-303, NO-807).
340 Twenty-one macabre photographs: T/1372.
342 Evidence of Freudiger: Session 51, pp. 32 ff.
342 Evidence of Dr. Alexander Brody: Session 52, pp. 90 ff.
342 Evidence of Margot Reich: Session 53, pp. 26 ff.
342 Reich's letters and postcard: T/1148-T/1150.
343 Evidence of Abraham Gordon: Session 54, p. 1.
343 I have to clear the provinces: T/1113, p. 43.
344 Evidence of Slavik in Vienna: Statement No. XVI.
344 Evidence of Joel Brand: Session 56, pp. 2 ff. Session 57, p. 11 ff.
345 The catastrophe is right on them: Weizmann to Eden, interview, July 6, 1944, T/1177.
345 We are consulting with Russia and America: Foreign Office to Moshe Sharett (Shertok), interview of July 12, 1944, T/1177.
345 Bomb the camps: *Aide-mémoire* of July 6, 1944, T/1177.
345 Foreign Office reply, July 15, 1944: T/1177.
345 We can assure you that both His Majesty's Government: T/1177.
345 Haj Amin al Husseini to Ribbentrop: T/1261.
345 The Arab nation will appreciate: T/1263.
345 The ex-Mufti's request for a personal adviser: T/89.
345 The biggest friend of the Arabs: T/1267, T/1268; and see evidence of Chief Inspector Haggag, Session 74, pp. 6–7.
345 The personal ties continued: T/37, pp. 568–569.
346 The evidence of Mrs. Gerstein: T/1311.
346–347 The evidence of the priest Hecklinger: T/1315.
347 The statement of the Swedish Foreign Office: T/1312.

PAGE
347 The French death certificate: T/1306.
349 Court's ruling on the Sassen document: Session 74, p. 1, and Session 88, pp. 15–16.
350 Evidence of Shalom Cholawski: Session 73, pp. 51 ff.
351 Evidence of Aharon Hoter-Ishai: Session 73, pp. 58 ff.

CHAPTER 18. *The Case for the Defense*

352 Opening speech of Dr. Servatius: Session 75, pp. 61 ff.
353 Everyone in the RSHA dealt with Jewish matters: Session 76, pp. 1–20.
354 I never took any decision: Session 79, p. 3.
354 The jurists of the department were responsible: Session 77, pp. 56, 68.
354 He was instructed by his superiors to draft them: Session 79, p. 4.
354 The typist would put this archive mark: Session 79, p. 4.
354 Guenther's special assignments: Session 79, pp. 13, 24.
354 This Gerstein business: Session 87, p. 24.
355 The horrors of the *Kristallnacht* were quite helpful: Session 90, p. 14.
355 Eichmann's silence taken as indicating assent: Session 76, p. 36.
355 His style is his own affair: Session 76, p. 16.
356 Your awkwardly long sentences: Session 76, p. 21.
356 The accused general lectures: Session 82, p. 1.
356 The attendance list of the fateful conference: Session 76, p. 81.
356 I could not have said it: Session 83, p. 17.
356 The Wetzel letter was forged: Session 78, p. 17.
356 Putting on both pairs of glasses: Session 98, p. 37.
356 No doubt the mistake of the draftsman: Session 81, p. 3.
356 Draftsman's hurry: Session 87, pp. 4–5.
359 Himmler's and Kaltenbrunner's plenipotentiary: N/97 (ND 2376-PS).
356 Untrue and impossible under the official allocation: Session 87, p. 12.
356 Looking, observing and reporting: Session 87, p. 22.
357 I know that these things seem incredible: Session 86, p. 18.
357 The defense continues: Jerusalem *Post,* June 30, 1961.
357 In the old days, Eichmann: See Becher's interrogation on July 7, 1947, T/689, p. 17.
357 I deny the correctness of these things: Session 86, p. 18.
357 He could vaguely remember: Session 87, p. 1.
357 I was angry: Session 86, p. 12.
357 How and when Joel Brand turned up: Session 86, p. 13.
358 I hope that Joel Brand: Session 86, p. 15.
358 On the Ministry of the Interior: Session 78, p. 11.
358 On the Foreign Office: Session 82, p. 7.
358 Will not seek historic clarifications: Session 75, p. 66.
358 A chart with a closed circle of command: N/20.
358 The first chart showed Eichmann's career: N/2.
358–359 To conclude his direct examination: Session 88.
359 He had discussed with Sassen in 1957: Tape 42, pp. 1–2.
360 This is an improper interpretation: Session 88, p. 23.
360 Later, in reply to Judge Raveh: Session 105, p. 21.
360 But the only front on which you were active: Session 90, pp. 1–2.
360 Now he had to drain the medicine: Session 97, pp. 7–8.
360 A certain amount of discretion: Session 97, p. 7.
360 If a document read: Session 94, p. 23.

PAGE
360 Internal Gestapo instructions: T/94.
360 The ruling on signatures remained the same: T/97 (ND L-361).
360 So you had to sign all your letters: Session 92, p. 1.
360 The Final Solution was an enormous venture: Session 94, p. 2.
361 He admitted that he was present: Session 102, p. 10.
361 He confessed he had later been in contact: Session 98, p. 30.
361 The department's instructions to the *Einsatzgruppen:* T/310 (ND NG-2652-A).
361 He admitted, finally, the correspondence: Session 98, p. 30.
361 Drafting the authorizations to Globocnik: Session 99, p. 5.
361 Warsaw ghetto liquidation: G/268.
361 It was a common mistake: Session 99, p. 13.
361 I just cannot figure it out: Session 99, p. 15.
361 Instructions to the Carpathian Oil Company: T/266.
361 I have no idea: Session 99, p. 21.
361 Poland is in Europe: Session 99, p. 23.
361 The only head of department for Jewish affairs: Session 92, pp. 15 ff.
361 Drafting the Madagascar plan: Session 91, pp. 21 ff.
362 Including every individual case of a Jew: Session 98, p. 29.
362 The Foreign Office apologized: T/469.
362 Dear Comrade Eichmann: T/612.
362 Due to negligent drafting: Session 93, p. 5.
362 It is in the documents: Session 97, p. 16.
362 As the opinion of the SS leadership: T/991 (ND NG-5051).
362 I just declare it to be a mistake: Session 93, p. 5.
362 The accused had the right to lie: Session 91, p. 21.
362 He would have to go back on several statements: Session 91, p. 9.
362 Why should I have denied things: Session 98, p. 39.
363 I was treated in an extremely fair way: Session 79, p. 8.
363 This was grammatically necessary: Session 93, p. 24.
363 I am being grilled: Session 102, p. 15.
364 It would be the pure truth: Session 95, p. 27.
364 Why, then, did Hoess write: Hoess, *op. cit.*, p. 207.
364 This is untrue: Session 95, p. 25.
364 Admitted visits to Auschwitz: Session 93, p. 25.
364 Hoess came to see him in Budapest: *ibid.*
364–365 Eichmann on Storfer in the pretrial examination: T/37, p. 224.
365 Eichmann was at a loss to explain: Session 99, p. 9.
365 I was angry when I heard of it: *ibid.*
365 The accused at Nuremberg were rightly sentenced: Session 88, p. 26.
366 Did you think he was a criminal?: Session 95, p. 33.
366 One of the greatest crimes in human history: Session 95, p. 35.
366 The whole solution by violence a dreadful thing: Session 95, p. 35.
366 He gave up National Socialism with many relapses: Session 95, p. 29.
366 By 1957 the change of mind process was not yet complete: Session 96, p. 7.
366 One of my few virtues: Session 91, p. 20.
366 Submitted by another department for his signature: Session 88, p. 28.
367 You don't have to show any favors: Session 98, p. 39.
367 I can't figure it out: Session 95, p. 17.
367 He admitted he had practiced deception: Session 104, p. 24.
367 He has finally ceased to be a mystery: *France-Soir,* July 7, 1961.
369 He certainly was not lukewarm in the giving of orders: Session 105, p. 6.

PAGE
369 He had insisted on an open apology: Session 105, p. 12.
369 He was not his own master: Session 105, p. 17.
369 Judge Raveh's questioning: Session 106.
370 Everybody was interfering: Session 106, p. 11.
370 My thoughts turn chiefly to my family: Hoess, *op. cit.*, pp. 170–171.
370–371 Judge Halevy's questioning: Session 106.
372 Judge Landau's questioning Monday morning: Session 107.

CHAPTER 19. *The Defense Witnesses*

374 The court accepted this procedure: Session 20, pp. 2–3.
376 The evidence of Hermann Krumey: Statement No. IX, Session 107, pp. 125 ff.
378 They will not be charged here: Session 30, p. 1.
378–379 The evidence of Hoettl: Statement No. I, Session 85, pp. 13 ff.
379 The evidence of Huppenkothen: Statement No. II, Session 85, pp. 12 ff.
379 Huppenkothen's Nuremberg affidavit: T/159 (ND Gestapo-39[A].
380–381 The evidence of Dr. Horst Grell: Statement No. V, Session 85, p. 20 ff.
381 He gave the lie to Grell: Session 88, p. 8.
381–382 The evidence of Dr. Eberhard von Thadden: Statement No. III, Session 85, p. 14.
382 The evidence of Dr. Edmund Veesenmayer: Statement No. XIII, Session 108, pp. 3 ff.
382 Dr. Servatius called this defense witness a liar: Session 108, p. 13.
382 The evidence of Kurt Becher: Statement No. VI, Session 85, p. 21.
382 The evidence of Dr. Max Merten: Statement No. VIII, Session 107, p. 25.
382 Dr. Servatius declared that he would not avail himself: Session 114, p. 31.
383 The evidence of Herbert Kappler: Statement No. XV, Session 108, pp. 17 ff.
383 Evidence of Franz Novak: Statement No. XII, Session 108, pp. 3 ff.
383–384 Evidence of Eric von dem Bach-Zelewski: Statement No. XIV, Session 108, pp. 13 ff.
383–384 Von dem Bach-Zelewski and Goering's suicide: Joe J. Haydecker and Johannes Leeb, *Der Nürnberger Prozess; Bilanz der 1000 Jahre,* Kiepenheuer und Witsch, 1960, p. 520 (German).
384–385 The evidence of Otto Winkelmann: Statement No. XI, Session 108, p. 1.
385 The evidence of Juettner: Statement No. IV, Session 85, p. 19.
385 Dean Grueber on the *Landsknecht:* Session 41, p. 76.
385–386 Evidence of Alfred Six: Statement No. VII, Session 107, pp. 21 ff.
386 Evidence of Richard Baer: Statement No. X, Session 107, pp. 33 ff.
386 It is certainly strange if Dr. Six: Session 101, p. 15.

CHAPTER 20. *The Summations*

388–398 Summation of the Attorney General: Sessions 110–113.
398–408 Summation of Dr. Servatius: Session 114. See also Verteidigung, *Adolf Eichmann, Plädoyer von Dr. Robert Servatius,* Verlag Ferdinand Harrach, 1961.

CHAPTER 21. *The Judgment*

All references (with five exceptions) in this chapter are to the judgment delivered by the Jerusalem District Court, identified by the paragraph number of the official Hebrew text.

PAGE

410 There was felt a desire: para 1.
410 The path of the court: para 2.
411 Compliments to prosecution and defense: para 3.
411 *Ex post facto* law is often the only way: para 7.
412 Of course the perpetrators had guilty knowledge: para 7.
412 Crimes which afflict the whole of mankind: para 12.
412 The authority and jurisdiction to try crimes under international law: para 2.
412 It is not necessary to recapitulate in Jerusalem: para 26.
412 This law was born in the crematoria: Eugene Aroneanu, *Le Crime contre l'Humanité,* Paris, Librairie Daloz, 1961.
412 We have discussed at length: para 30.
412 This linking point: para 33.
412 The connection between the State of Israel and the Jewish people: para 34.
412 The massacre of millions of Jews: para 34.
412 To argue that there is no connection: para 35.
413 It is an established rule of law: para 41.
413 Any plea which assumes: para 53.
414 The bench explained in understandable terms: para 60.
414 The idyllic fair cooperation: para 63.
414 The Jews of Austria lived in an atmosphere: para 64.
414 The sum total of all these arrangements: para 64.
414 It is true that the accused set: para 65.
414 Under this pressure: para 65.
414 He returned to Berlin crowned with success: para 67.
415 It soon became evident that there was no hope: para 68.
415 This, then, was the measure: para 73.
415 His version is far from the truth: para 76.
415 This was the RSHA version: para 76.
416 One of the basic documents: para 81.
416 The central event in the history of the Final Solution: para 86.
416 Carried a more important meaning: para 88.
416 The last act in the tragedy: para 111.
416 This chapter calls for a special place: para 111.
417 The accused did his utmost: para 111.
417 The whole incident is very significant: para 113.
417 Even SS officers who saw the marchers: para 115.
417 We are of the opinion: para 116.
418 We learn from the documents: para 116.
418 From what has been said: para 117.
418 This is where the Jews: para 119.
419 The court for reasons of caution refrained: para 139.
419 Preparation of summaries for the use of the RSHA: para 139.
419 From spring 1942, the accused began to be active: para 139.
419 Hundreds of thousands, and perhaps a million Jews: para 122.

PAGE
419 The extermination of the Jews was connected: para 131.
419 The accused alleges that within the General Government: para 135.
420 The order to exterminate the Jews came from higher authorities: para 135.
420 Here, therefore, the accused appears: para 136.
420 To conclude this chapter: para 137.
420 This question was actually of only secondary importance: para 141.
420 It follows therefore that every trainload: para 145.
421 This matter undoubtedly occupied the attention: para 166.
421 We do not attribute any value to this denial: para 167.
421 Did not doubt the accuracy of Gerstein's statements: para 169.
421 Accordingly, we find that Hoess's deputy: para 169.
421 Who were themselves persons of considerable status: para 170.
422 All these testimonies and affidavits: para 176.
422 Not a minor official without initiative: para 176.
422 Could not reconcile himself to the order: para 176.
422 We reject absolutely the accused's version: para 180.
422 It is not rare for a man in an important position: para 180.
423 With intention to destroy the Jewish people: para 182.
423 The acts of murder and violence against Jews: para 182.
423 Were not yet accompanied by intent to destroy: para 185.
423 The early deportations and expulsions to Nisko: para 186.
423 All the acts perpetrated during the implementation: para 190.
423 Here the basis of the crime lay in Hitler's order: para 192.
423 The accused was privy to the extermination secret: para 195.
423 Hence, the accused will be convicted: para 195.
424 The accused had a hand: para 205.
424 Anyone who listened to this speech: para 208.
424 But after studying the documents: para 208.
424 The crimes against humanity of having deported: para 210 and para 211.
424 In conclusion, as regards the accused: para 213.
425 If by these words: para 216.
425 The attempt to turn an order for the extermination: para 216.
425 As the Attorney General said: para 217.
425 Here we shall add: para 220.
425 Did these orders disturb his conscience: para 222.
426 It means that had he been ordered to throw: para 225.
426 He never thought of giving up: para 226.
426 That is to say, it never entered his head: para 227.
426 His attempt to argue: para 229.
426 Blind obedience could never have brought him: para 231.
426 No single case brought to our notice: para 233.
426 Certainly he was not lukewarm: para 235.
426 When carrying out the final plan: para 237.
427 So substantially this attitude of complete identification: para 238.
427 His hatred was cold and calculated: para 241.
427 In fact, it is not disputed: para 242.
427 His entire testimony was nothing but one consistent effort: para 243.
428 Various theories may be put forward: para 243.
428 We do not mean to criticize: para 244.
428 We shall adhere to the general framework: para 244.

PAGE
429–430 Address of the Attorney General on sentence: Session 120, pp. 1 ff.
430–431 Address of Counsel for Defense on mitigation of sentence: Session 120, pp. 31 ff.
431 Eichmann's last word: Session 120, pp. 54 ff.
432 The sentence of the court: Session 121.

CHAPTER 22. *Appeal and Aftermath*

437 The jurists will confirm that it was not a show trial: Dr. Servatius, Court of Appeal, Session 1.
438 Eichmann's contacts with Monaco: T/492–495 (ND NG-4978).
438 Eichmann's instructions for Belgium: T/513.
438 Dr. Servatius said he could give no explanation: Court of Appeal, Session 1, p. 21.
439 When masters are at loggerheads: Court of Appeal, Session 2, p. 12.
439 We were implementing a task for our people: Sassen, tape 67, p. 9; referred to in cross-examination, Session 104, pp. 26–27.
439 This wicked man brought down: Court of Appeal, Session 5.

The following quotations from the judgment of the Appeal Court are according to the authorized English translation:

440 We should say at once that we fully concur: Part I, para 5.
440 As to the ethical aspects of the principle: Part I, para 8.
441 The crimes in question must be regarded today: Part I, para 11.
441 This meant in essence, that the power is vested: Part I, para 12(a).
441 The state which prosecutes and punishes: Part I, para 12(b).
441 We have also taken into consideration: Part I, para 12(d).
441 Fugitive from justice under the law of nations: Part I, para 13(8)(a).
442 The moment it is admitted: *ibid.*
442 On the argument of "act of state": Part I, para 14.
442 The appellant carried out the extermination order: Part I, para 15(d), p. 35.
442 The canvas exposed to us in this appeal: Part III, para 1.
442 They have constructed those arms: Part III, para 7.
442 But Eichmann's department had no need: Part III, para 8.
443 He held a powerful, virtually independent status: Part III, para 13.
443 He was formally subordinate: *ibid.*
443 His was not at all an inferior status: Part III, para 15.
443 Therefore, he was not vaingloriously bragging: *ibid.*
443 The facts indicated above: Part III, para 17.
443 In deciding to confirm both the judgment: Part III, para 18.
444 The trial was fair: Jerusalem *Post*, May 31, 1962.

CHAPTER 23. *Reflections—Three Years Later*

451 A popular newspaper took up the issue: *Abendpost*, June 23, 24, 1964.
453 Fifteen years earlier Dr. Chaim Weizmann: Letter of Jackson to Weizmann of January 7, 1946 (by the courtesy of the Weizmann Archives).

APPENDIX III:

Bibliography

The judgments of both courts, the opening speech, the closing address and the evidence of the witnesses were all published verbatim in Hebrew. The opening speech was also published in Yiddish, English, German, French, Russian, Italian and Spanish.

Below are a number of works dealing with the trial at some length.

Arendt, Hannah, *Eichmann in Jerusalem,* New York, The Viking Press, 1963 — English

Barlasz, Blumenthal, and Kermish, *The Holocaust and the Trial* (3 vol.) — Hebrew

Dezzö, Shön, *A Jeruzalemi Per,* Jerusalem, Ujkelet-Kiadás, 1962 — Hungarian

Gouri, Haim, *La cage de verre,* Paris, A. Michel, 1964 — French

Grun, Herbert, *Proces Jeruzalemu,* Ljubljana, Mladiska Knjiga, 1961 — Slovenian

Hamrin, Agne, *Bokslut i Jerusalem,* Stockholm, Bonniers, 1961 — Swedish

Herzberg, Abel J., *Eichmann in Jerusalem,* The Hague, B. Bakker, 1962 — Dutch

Kakol, Kazimierz, *Adolfa Eichmanna droga do Bejt Haam,* Warsaw, Iskry, 1962 — Polish

Kaul, Friedrich S., "Der Fall Eichmann," *Das neue Berlin,* 1963 — German

Kempner, Robert M. W., *Eichmann und Komplizen,* Zurich, Europa Verlag, 1961 — German

Mňačko, Ladislav, *Ja, Adolf Eichmann,* Bratislava, 1962 — Czech

Mulisch, Harry, *De zaak 40/61. Een reportage,* Amsterdam, Uitgeverij de Bezige Bij, 1963 — Dutch

Nellessen, Bernd, *Der Prozess von Jerusalem,* Duesseldorf, Econ Verlag, 1964 — German

Papadatos, Peter, *The Eichmann Trial,* London, Stevens, 1964 — English

Pardo, Paul, *Processo al tertio Reich, Il processo Eichmann giorno per giorno,* Rome, Editori Riuniti, 1962 — Italian

Pearlman, Maurice, *The Capture and Trial of Adolf Eichmann,* New York, Simon and Schuster, 1963 — English

Poliakov, Léon, *Le procès de Jérusalem,* Paris, Calmann-Lévy, 1963 — French

Robinson, Jacob, *And the Crooked Shall Be Made Straight,* New York, Macmillan, 1965 — English

Russell, Lord Edward Frederick Langley, *The Trial of Adolf Eichmann,* London, W. Heinemann, 1962 — English

Santander, Silvano, *El Gran Proceso,* Buenos Aires, Ediciones Silva, 1961 — Spanish

Schmorak, Dr. Dov B., *Sieben sagen aus,* Berlin-Grunewald, Arani, 1962 — German

On the trial in the world press:

The Eichmann Case in the American Press, The American Jewish Committee, Institute of Human Relations Press, 1962 — English

"The Eichmann Case—Reactions in West Germany," *Midstream,* 1961 (reprint) — English

Der Eichmann Process in der deutschen oeffentlichen Meinung, Frankfurt a.M., Ner-Tamid, 1961 — German

INDEX

Abduction (*See* Kidnaping)
Abeles, Dr. Ernst, quoted, 116–117
Abendpost, 451
Abortion, 213
Abromeit, SS Captain Franz, 126, 135
"Action Reinhard," 129–130, 188
Adenauer, Chancellor, 319, 466
Agranat, Simon, 437
  quoted, 440–441
Alexander, Renate, 60
Alexander, Vera, quoted, 189
Allied Documentation Center, 285
Allied nationals, exchange of, 160
Allied service men, 378
  massacre of, 183, 355
Allies, the, 109, 149, 188, 232, 242–243, 268–269, 272–273, 288, 315–316, 337, 347
Alsace-Lorraine, 226
Altman, Tosia, 218
Amadeo, Mario, quoted, 460–462
American Broadcasting Corporation, 307
American Jewish Committee, 238
American Joint Distribution Committee, 117
Amin al Husseini, 345
Amsterdam, 112, 114
Angola, 229–230
Anilewicz, Mordechai, 222–227
  quoted, 223
Ansbacher, Mordechai, quoted, 104, 158, 206–207
Anschluss, the, 34
Anti-Semitism, 14–15, 17–19, 62, 100, 118, 227, 229–230, 234, 239, 259, 279–280, 324, 326, 366, 372, 449–451
Antonescu, Ion, 120
Antonescu, Mihail, 122–123
Antwerp, 111
Apeldoorn, Holland, 114
Arabs, 231, 235, 345–346, 396
Arendt, Hannah, 465
Argentina, 4, 30, 289, 348, 449, 459–463
  Eichmann's escape to, 271
Argentina (*Continued*)
  Eichmann's life in, 271–274
  Hitler Youth in, 9
  Nazis in, 9
Aroneanu, Eugene, 412
Arrow Cross Party (Hungary), 133, 152–154
Atom, The, Kahn, 271
Atrocities, 54–55, 64–65, 71–80, 87–90, 102, 107, 109, 112–113, 127–129, 134, 140, 144–145, 152–157, 161–175, 177, 179, 182–191, 195, 214, 233, 327, 329–331, 339–340, 343–344, 347–348, 391, 397, 415, 417, 438
Auerbach, Rachel, 293
  quoted, 205, 210–211
Aus dem Fuenten, 112
Auschwitz camp, 12, 90–91, 106–109, 112–118, 128–130, 135, 138–142, 145, 148–150, 161, 169–175, 189–192, 258, 280–281, 296, 338, 340, 342, 345–347, 364–365, 377, 383, 394, 397, 403, 417–418, 420–421, 432
  bombing of, 243–244
Australia, 229
Austria, 27, 30, 37, 58–59, 98, 105, 226, 401
  Eichmann in, 34–42, 44–45, 391, 414–415
  (*See also* Vienna)
Avenue of the Righteous Gentiles, Jerusalem, 261
Aviel, Avraham, 331
  quoted, 71–73
Avrech, Joseph, quoted, 185

Baade, Hans W., 468
Babi Yar, 76
Bach, Gabriel, 286, 302–304, 334, 341, 395, 411
Bach-Zelewski, SS General Erich von dem, 152, 375, 383
  quoted, 88, 384

Bader, Menahem, 249
quoted, 246
Badoglio, Marshal Pietro, 120
Baeck, Fanny, 29
Baer, Richard, 375, 386
Bakon, Yehuda, quoted, 192
Baky, Lászlo, 137–139, 142
Balaban, Meyer, quoted, 209
Baldwin, Representative, 239
Balfour Declarations, 193, 233, 315
Baltic States, 58, 76
Barasz, Ephraim, 220
quoted, 200, 220
Barlas, Chaim, 246
Barmann, Jean, 114
Baron, Salo, 193, 326
Baron Hirsch camp, 127
Baror, Jacob, 286, 301, 303–304, 327, 395, 411
Barth, Adolf Karl (*see* Eichmann, aliases of)
Bartoszewski, Wladyslaw, 259
Bauer, Bruno, 15
Bavaria, 21, 24–25, 59
BBC, 235, 249
Bea, Augustus Cardinal von, 450
Beaune la Rolande camp, 106
Bech, Joseph, 233
Becher, Kurt, 147, 149, 151–154, 248, 341, 357, 377, 382, 386, 438
Beilin, Aharon, quoted, 173–175
Beisky, Moshe, 176
quoted, 162–163, 177, 329–330
Bekasmagyer, Hungary, 150
Belczycka, Mrs. Stefania, 214
Beleff, Alexander, 124
Belgium, 99, 438
Jews in, 110–111, 257
Belsen, 157
(*See also* Bergen-Belsen camp)
Bełżec camp, 91, 122, 130, 165, 236, 346–347
Bendzin, Poland, 212
Ben-Gurion, David, 277, 289
quoted, 460
Bentwich, Norman, 444
quoted, 470
Benzler, Felix, 125
Ben-Zvi, Gedalya, quoted, 173, 189–191
Ben-Zvi, Itzhak, 444
Bérard, Armand, 462
Bérard, Léon, quoted, 251
Bereza Kartuska, Poland, 197
Bergen-Belsen camp, 109, 159–162, 394
Bergson, Henri, quoted, 194
Berlin, 105, 258, 283, 358
suicide in, 104
Berlin, Rabbi Meir, 245
Berlin Document Center Archives, 284
Berman, Adolf, quoted, 214
Bermuda Conference, 238
Bernadotte, Count, 248
Best, Werner, 255
Bialystok, Poland, 130, 219–220
Biddle, Francis, quoted, 240
Biebow, Hans, 131, 198
Bigart, Homer, 308
Bird, Robert S., 308
Birkenau camp, 150,169, 191
Birkenhead, Earl of, 308
quoted, 321
Blackmail, 150–151
Blobel, SS Colonel Paul, 328
quoted, 185
Bloch, Captain Zelo, 187
Blood, purity of, 16–17, 33
"Blood for goods" deal, 344, 357–358, 417, 426
Blum, René, 107, 109
Blume, Walter, quoted, 70
Boda, Ernö, 137
Boegner, Pastor Marc, 107
Boehm, Adolf, 37, 63, 355
Boehme, General Franz, 180
Boetticher, Paul, quoted, 15
Bogaard, Johannes, 261
Bohemia, 30, 46 ,157, 401
Boldt, Gerhard, 271
Bolek, 30–31
Bonnet, Georges, 228
Book burning, 21
Bordeaux, 107
Boris, King, 123–124
Bormann, Martin, 306
Bosnia, 128
Boy Scouts, Danish, 255
Boycott Day, 226
Brack, Colonel Victor, 90, 130
quoted, 103
Brand, Joel, 149, 239, 248, 344–345, 357–358, 377, 408, 417–418, 439
quoted, 146–148
Brand, Mrs. Joel, quoted, 148
Brandt, Karl, 90, 302
Brant (teacher), 27
Bratislava, 116–118, 252
Brauchitsch, Field Marshal Walter von, 70
Braun, Eva, 147
Brawer, Dr. David, 197
Breendonck camp, 110–111
Brody, Alexander, 144–145, 342
quoted, 144–145
"Brown Portfolio," 78
Bru, Laredo, 230
Brunner, Alois, 108–109, 117
Buber, Martin, quoted, 444
Buch, Walter, quoted, 43
Bucharest, 151

Buchenwald camp, 34, 47, 81
Budapest, 136, 141–143, 146–147, 150–155, 248, 260, 265, 340, 342, 344, 364, 376–378, 380–382, 394, 417–418
Buehler, Dr. Joseph, 90, 94–95
 quoted, 95–96
Buenos Aires, 273–275
Bulgaria, 125–126, 246
 Jews in, 123–125
Bunkers, 211, 223–224
Burger, Anton, 46, 135, 272
 quoted, 268
Burger, Catharina, 256
Burger, Max, 57
Bużminsky, Jacob, 163–164

Camouflage, 187
Campert, Jan, quoted, 254
Campigniano, Hulda, 334
 quoted, 118–120
Canada, 231
Cannibalism, 160
Canterbury, Archbishop of, quoted, 236–237
Capital Cities Broadcasting Corporation, 307
Caprivi, Chancellor von, quoted, 16
Carbon monoxide, 90–91
Carpathian Oil Company, 361
Cassulo, Andreía, 122, 251
Catholic Church, 449
 German, 250–253
 Polish, 258–259
Cazalet, Colonel, 239
Celler, Emanuel, 239
 quoted, 238, 240
Central Bureau for Jewish Emigration, 5, 36, 40, 44–45, 48
Chacza, Edward, 257
Chaillet, Father, 251
Chamberlain, Houston Stewart, 15–16
Chamberlain, Neville, 41
 quoted, 229
Chattel, Monsignor, 251
Chelmno (Kulm) camp, 89, 167, 169, 296, 322
Chen, Mordechai, quoted, 161
Cheshire, Group Captain Leonard, quoted, 243
Childbirth, 153, 159, 211, 300
Children, 38, 55, 60, 71, 75, 113, 123, 140, 147, 153–155, 158, 166, 172, 182, 189, 330, 415
 British, 231
 Czech, 301
 ghetto, 66, 213–214, 324
 Jewish refugee, 239, 247–248, 251, 260, 345
Children (*Continued*)
 Lidice, 129, 301, 354, 376, 397, 400, 424
 Polish, 232, 259, 330, 347
Cholawski, Shalom, quoted, 350–351
Choms, Wladyslawa, 259
Choronżycki, Dr. Julian, 187
Christian X, King, quoted, 255
Churchill, Winston, 231, 235, 242–243, 245
 quoted, 41, 233, 236, 249
Chvalkovski, Dr. Frantisek, 46
Ciano, Count Galeazzo, 24
Cluj, Hungary, 147
Cohen, Benno, quoted, 33, 42–43, 46
Cohen, Erich, 159
Cold War, 271
"Commando Decree," 183
Commandos, 76, 82, 88, 135, 151, 183, 221
"Commissars' Order," 70, 181
Communists, 70, 75, 82
Compiègne Armistice, 62–63
Compiègne camp, 106
Concentration camps, 80, 92, 102, 131, 156, 300, 393–395, 397
 French, 106
 (*See also* names of camps, as Buchenwald)
Consette, Alphonse and Emilie, quoted, 257
Convention of Refugees, 1951, 317
Copenhagen, 255–256
Correo, Representative, 462
Coste-Floret, Alfred, quoted, 458
Council of Assistance, 259
Council of Europe, 438
Councils of Elders, 55–56
Coward, Charles, 260
Cozzi, Jenni, 81–82
Cracow, Poland, 61, 68, 218–219
Cranborne, Lord, quoted, 235, 237
Crankshaw, Edward, quoted, 24, 468
Crematoria (*see* Gas chambers)
Crestianu, Ambassador, 248
Crimea, the, 76
Croatia, 119, 125–126
Crossman, Richard, quoted, 457–458, 465
Cuba, 230
"Cyclon B" gas, 91, 421
Czajkowski, Bronislawa, 256–257
Czechoslovakia, 41, 46, 49, 57–58, 129, 230, 265, 286, 327
Czerniakow, Adam, quoted, 205
Czestochowa, Poland, 204, 211, 220

Dachau camp, 25, 31, 34–36, 47, 249
Dahlerus, Birger, 57
Daladier, Éduard, 41, 229
Daluege, Kurt, 25
Dannecker, SS Captain Theodor, 32, 59, 105–106, 120, 123–124, 135, 383
 quoted, 107

Danzig, 49
Davar, 445
Davis, Lord, quoted, 234–235
Dawidowicz, quoted, 207
Davidson-Drenger, Gusta, 218, 219
quoted, 215, 217
Dayan, Chief Inspector Pinchas, 286
Death camps, 53, 103, 108, 156–175, 188, 243–244, 295, 328–329, 346–347, 403–404, 420
(*See also* Gas chambers; names of camps)
Death vans, 80
Delitzsch, Friedrich, 15
Democracy, 18
Denmark, 115, 254–256, 362
Deportation, 26, 35–36, 40–42, 45–48, 57, 79, 401–403, 415, 424
from Germany and Occupied Europe, 98–131
from ghettos, 48–68
from Hungary, 132–155
Deputy, The, Hochhuth, 450
Detained prisoners, 171–172
Dicey, Albert, 395
Dictatorship, 19
Dinur, Yehiel, quoted, 171, 347
Divorce, compulsory, 102
Documents, incriminating, 210–211, 284–285, 356, 358, 393, 404–406, 418
safety guaranteed by, 212
Dodds, Harold, quoted, 238
Dogs, 169, 173, 177
refugee British, 231
Dombrowa, Poland, 185
Dominican Republic, 231
Donati, Angelo (banker), 119
"Donations W account," 401
Drancy camp, 106–108, 110
Draper, G. I. A. D., quoted, 470–471
Dreksler, Maria (SS woman), 191
Drenger, Shimon, 219
quoted, 216
Dubinska, Poland, 54
Dubnow, Simon, quoted, 210
Duehring, Eugen, 15
Duesseldorf, 79
Dulles, Allen, 378
Dutch Fascist Party (NSB), 112–113
Dutch underground, 259
Dvorjetski, Dr. Marc, quoted, 195
Dysentery, 153

Eck, Nathan, 211
quoted, 204, 212
Eckmann, Otto (*see* Eichmann, aliases of)
Economist, The, 444
Edelstein, Jacob, 112
Eden, Anthony, 236–237, 249, 345
quoted, 232, 236, 269
Education in ghettos, 214
Eichmann, Adolf, 4, 24, 26, 62
aliases of, 269–271
in Argentina, 271–275
in Austria, 34–41, 44–45, 47–48
character of, 4–6, 8, 13, 27
confession of, 275, 280
and death camps, 158
defense counsel for, 301–303, 310–311
descriptions of, 8, 309–310, 320, 332, 363, 367–368, 410, 416, 428, 446
and *Einsatzgruppen*, 75, 78, 80–81
escape and capture of, 265–276
execution of, 446
and Final Solution (*see* "Final Solution")
and ghettoization, 64, 68
and Hungarian Jews, 132–155
and Jews, 11–13, 28, 35, 45–49, 53, 69, 79–81, 233
life of, 27–32
and Madagascar scheme, 63
and *Mischlinge*, 102
and Nazi Party, 9, 11, 28, 30, 39
and Poland, 55–58, 61, 66–67
in Prague, 46–47
prosecutors of, 303–304
psychiatric examination of, 6–7
quoted, 11–12, 22, 28–31, 37–41, 45–46, 55–57, 62, 69, 75, 78, 81–82, 87–89, 100, 103–104, 108–111, 114–116, 120–122, 125, 133, 137, 139–140, 143, 145–146, 148–149, 152, 155, 158, 160, 225, 249, 253, 256, 260–261, 266–269, 271–272, 275, 277–281, 338, 343
(*See also* Eichmann trial, Eichmann's testimony at)
and religion, 8–9, 14–15, 28
role of, in deportations, 98–155
and RSHA, 58–59, 78, 87
tracking of, 272–275
and Trusteeship Office–East, 60
Eichmann, Adolf Karl and Marie, 27–28
Eichmann, Dieter, 267, 271
Eichmann, Horst, 271
Eichmann, Klaus, 271
Eichmann, Ricardo Francisco, 272
Eichmann, Mrs. Vera, 30, 267, 271, 273, 445
Eichmann in Jerusalem, Arendt, 465*n*.
Eichmann trial, 243–244
appeal from judgment at, 437–444
bibliography on, 473
case for defense in, 352–373
case for prosecution in, 322–351
cross-examination in, 359–373
defense witnesses in, 374–387
Eichmann's testimony at, 337, 353–359, 431
fairness, of, 310–315

Eichmann trial (*Continued*)
judges at, 305, 318–320, 325, 333, 348–349, 357, 366–367, 386, 408–432, 437
judgment passed in, 409–432
letters about, 433–437
non-Jewish witnesses in, 297–298, 397
observers at, 307–308, 321
opening battle in, 305–321
preparing case for, 277–287
press and, 444–445, 455–459, 463–472
prosecution's problems at, 288–304
reactions to, 455–472
reflections on, 447–454
sentence pronounced at, 428–432
summations at, 388–408
Eicke, Theodor, 31
Einsatzgruppen, the, 69–83, 87–89, 94, 118, 121, 126, 180–181, 185–186, 199, 233, 299, 331, 333–334, 336–337, 347, 361, 378, 384–385, 404, 418–419
Eisenhower, General Dwight D., 248
Elisabeth of Belgium, Queen, 111
Elkes, Elhanan, 196–197
Endre, Lászlo, 137–139, 142, 152, 155
Engelstein, Adolf, quoted, 159
England (*see* Great Britain)
Epidemics, 68, 139, 207
Esthonia, 77
Ethiopia, 229
Eugene of Sweden, Prince, 101
"Europa plan," 117
European Convention on Human Rights, 317, 438
Euthanasia, 90, 130, 250
Evian, Switzerland, 227
Extermination centers (*see* Death camps)
Extortion, 117, 146, 149

Facing the Nazi Enemy, 350*n*.
Falkenhausen, General Alexander von, 111
Fascists, 100, 118–120
Dutch, 112
Faulhaber, Michael Cardinal, 250
Faust, Goethe, 20
Fegelein, SS General Hermann, 147
Feldhaendler, Leon, 188
Ferenczy, Lieutenant Colonel Lászlo, 137–138, 151
Feuchtensleben, Ernst von, 144
Fialla, Fritz, quoted, 117
Fichte, Johann Gottlieb, 19
Fighting Pioneer, 219
Filderman, Dr. Wilhelm, 122
"Final Solution," 8–12, 24, 40–41, 53, 56, 84–99, 101, 125, 131, 156, 227, 234, 270, 277, 282, 284, 299, 324–325, 333, 339, 345, 359–361, 370, 390–
"Final Solution" (*Continued*)
394, 407, 416–419, 422–423, 426–427, 445, 448–449
Finland, 254
Fish, Hamilton, quoted, 240
Fisz, Moses, 186
Fleischmann, Aviva, quoted, 153
Fleischmann, Gizi, 117, 146
quoted, 118
Fleischmann, Moritz, 45, 326
quoted, 35, 37–38, 44, 327
Fleissig, Mrs. Sandor, 145
Florant, Léon, 258
Földi, Martin, quoted, 139–140
Forster, SS Major, 203
Foundations of the Nineteenth Century, Chamberlain, 16, 19
France, 19, 56–57, 63, 228–229, 314
fall of, 62
Jews in, 105–110, 119
Frank, Anne, 113, 211
Frank, Hans, 59, 61–64, 87, 93–94, 96, 179, 269, 365, 393, 420, 431
quoted, 59, 178–179, 199
Franz, SS Lieutenant Kurt, 187
Free World, 238
Freisler, Dr. Roland, 94
French underground, 257
Freudiger, Pinchas, 137, 341
quoted, 136, 140–141, 144, 146, 342
Freund, quoted, 204
Friediger, Dr. Maks, 255
Friedmann, Jacob, 296
Friedmann, Tuvia, 273, 284
Fries, Jacob, 15
Fritzsche, Eberhard, 9
Fritz, Uncle (Eichmann's), 28–29
Fuchs, Colonel Dr. Wilhelm, 126

Gabor, Janos, 137, 143
Gabor, Vajna, 152, 154–155
Gailani, Rashid Ali, 345
Galen, Cardinal von, 449
Galewski, 187
Galicia, 211–212
Gallup Polls, 289, 464
Garfunkel, Leib, quoted, 196, 200
Gas chambers, 37, 86, 157, 159, 166–168, 172–174, 187, 190–192, 345–347, 421, 426
(*See also* Death camps)
Gauleiters, 39, 58, 93, 96
Gebauer, SS Lieutenant Colonel Fritz G., 162
Gellhorn, Martha, quoted, 472
Genoa, 271–272
Genocide, 401, 412
Genocide Convention, 317
Gens, Jacob, quoted, 201–203

Gentiles, 178, 195, 397
German Army, 21, 25, 55, 69, 75, 89, 99, 102–103, 212, 258, 302, 336, 362
German Foreign Office, 63, 81–82, 93, 96, 101, 114, 119, 123, 133, 142, 159–160, 284–285, 361–362, 370
German War Documentation Project, 284
Germany, 31, 312, 318, 401
  anti-Semitism in, 14–15, 17–19, 229–230, 450–452
  bombing of, 242–243
  Bureaus of Vital Statistics in, 170
  Catholic Church in, 250–253, 450
  collapse of, 265–267
  and deportation of Jews (*see* Deportation)
  and Jewish problem, 10, 425
  pre-Nazi, 24
  Protestant Church in, 249–250
  universities in, 19–20
  and world domination, 18–19
  and world opinion, 226–261
  (*See also* Third Reich; West Germany)
Gerstein, Kurt, 91–92, 166–167, 243, 251, 346, 354, 403, 421
Geschke, Dr. Hans Ulrich, 146, 404
Gestapo, 24–26, 34–36, 46, 49, 61, 71, 79, 84, 92, 98, 103–104, 111, 129, 136, 156–157, 160, 190–191, 197–198, 203, 216–217, 219, 222, 255–258, 260, 267, 299, 301, 324, 337, 358, 363, 371–372, 379, 383, 391, 395, 399, 401
"Ghetto Encyclopedia," 207
"Ghetto passports," 212
Ghettos, 44, 71–72, 77, 79–81, 127, 129–131, 134, 138–139, 147, 154–155, 184–185, 196–197, 241–244, 403, 419–420
  cultural activities in, 207–208
  deportation to, 53–68
  education in, 214
  Jewish Councils in, 196–200
  and Jewish police, 200–204
  life in, 210–213
Gilbert, Gustave M., 86
  quoted, 338–339
Gillette, Senator, 239
Gimenfeld, Mayer, quoted, 186
Giorgetti, Ezio, 257
Gisevius, Dr. Hans B. (Gestapo member), quoted, 24–25
Globke, Hans, 92, 439, 466
Globocnik, Odilo, 58–59, 87, 89–90, 129, 164, 188, 299, 361
Gluecks, Inspector Richard, 87, 339, 365
Gobineau, Arthur, 16
Goddard, Lord Chief Justice, quoted, 313
Goebbels, Joseph, 19, 21, 39, 43–44, 92, 227, 239
  quoted, 93, 224, 237, 243, 252
Goering, Hermann, 21, 24–25, 39–40, 43–44, 60–61, 63, 85, 87, 92, 199, 227, 269, 335, 338–339, 365, 370, 383–384, 403, 416
  quoted, 43–44, 86, 270
Goethe, 20
Gold teeth, 165, 167, 169, 419, 424
Golden, Harry, quoted, 463
Goldmann, Michael, 164, 286, 293
Goldmann, Nahum, 249, 455
  quoted, 245
Goldstein, Esther, quoted, 172
Goldstein, Mordechai, 197
Gollancz, Victor, quoted, 459
Gollub, Max, 109
Gordon, Abraham, quoted, 343–344
Gortenkranc, Henoch, 186
Graebe, Hermann Friedrich, quoted, 74–75
Graf, SS Master Sergeant Mathias, 336
Graven, Jean, 469
  quoted, 470
Graves, reopening of, 328
Great Britain, 19, 57, 62, 193, 228–239, 241–244, 313, 315, 345, 413, 444
Greece, 99, 119–120, 362
  Jews in, 126–128
Green, L. C., 458, 466, 470
Greiser, Governor Arthur, 131
Grell, Horst, 380
  quoted, 150, 380–381
Grese, Irma, 189
Grinberg, Menashe, 177, 183, 186
Grodno, Poland, 197
Grossman, Haike, 218
Grosz, Bandi, 148
Grude, Liese, quoted, 310
Grueber, Heinrich Karl, 249, 297, 372, 426
  quoted, 13, 334–335, 385, 390
Grueber, Margarette, 249
Grynszpan, Herszel, 42, 326
Grynszpan, Zindel Shmuel, 41–42, 326
  quoted, 41
Guarnieri, Professor, 114
Guenther, Hans, 46–47
Guenther, Rolf, 47, 59, 81, 91, 94, 104, 115, 127, 130, 133, 135, 280, 354, 365, 367, 402–403, 421–422
Gurfein, Jacob, quoted, 55
Gutman, Israel, quoted, 191–192
Gypsies, 59, 66, 129, 301, 397, 424

Ha'aretz, 445
Hácha, President Emil, 46
Hagana, the, 244
Hagen, Herbert, 32

Hague, The, 114–115, 313–314
Hague Conventions, 400
Hahn, Counselor von, 119
Halevy, Benjamin, 305, 357, 370, 411
  quoted, 318, 349–350, 365, 370–372, 402, 412–413, 419–421
"Half-breeds," 95, 101–103
Hamilton, Bermuda, 238
Hamilton, Duke of, 227
Handtke, Untersturmfuehrer, 329
Hanging, 162, 168–169, 178, 191–192, 197–198, 201, 279–280
Harris, Sir Arthur, quoted, 243
Harrison, Leland, 240
Harster, SS Major General Wilhelm, 111–112
Hassid, Gideon, 308
Hausner, Gideon, 320, 323–351, 411, 463–464
  quoted, 323–325, 339, 351, 428–430, 439–440
Hecklinger (a priest), 346
Hegel, Friedrich, 15, 19
Helsinki, 254
Henschel, Mrs. Hildegard, 334
  quoted, 104–105
Herzl, Theodor, 63, 355, 415
Hess, Rudolf, 227
Heydrich, Reinhard, 21–25, 34, 36, 39–43, 45–46, 55–59, 61–64, 67, 71, 81, 85–88, 93, 97, 117, 129, 158, 227, 281, 354, 356, 361, 372, 380, 386, 400, 403, 407, 416, 443
  quoted, 44, 67, 78, 94–96
Hill, A. V., quoted, 239
Himmler, Heinrich, 21–23, 25, 39, 58–59, 61, 67, 80, 85–88, 90, 93, 99, 101–102, 113, 131, 134, 143, 145, 147–149, 151, 153–154, 156, 160–161, 222, 248, 266–267, 337–339, 352, 356, 382, 384–385, 403, 417, 419–420, 439, 443
  quoted, 22, 81, 90, 135, 159, 254, 338
Hirsch, Fredi, 206
Hirschmann, Ira A., 248
Hirth, Professor, 339–340
Hitler, Adolf, 16–18, 20–21, 25, 27, 33, 39, 41, 43, 46, 48, 58, 61–64, 96, 99, 102–103, 124, 135, 142–143, 145, 154, 184, 219, 316, 318, 356–357, 398–400, 402, 439
  fall of, 265–267
  and Jews, 48, 64, 84, 86–88, 90, 92, 176–225, 228, 230, 232, 414–416, 422–423, 425–427
  men surrounding, 21–22
  and peace, 226
  quoted, 16–18, 22, 27, 48–49, 70–71, 134, 154, 158, 181, 228, 230, 266
Hitlerism, 447
  international reaction to, 226, 233
Hoch, Nahum, quoted, 173–174
Hoeppner, SS Major Rolf Heinz, quoted, 66
Hoess, Rudolf, 12, 90, 135, 141, 281, 338–339, 357, 364–366, 394, 403, 405, 421, 431
  quoted, 90–91, 117, 200, 370
Hoettl, Wilhelm, 378, 386, 405
  quoted, 378–379, 385
Hoffman, Otto, 358, 405
Hofstaedter, Ephraim, 285
  quoted, 277
Holland, 99, 146, 250, 259–260
  Jews in, 111–115
  (*See also* entries under Dutch)
Holy See, the, 250, 252
  (*See also* Vatican)
Horn, Max, 131
Horowitz, Markus, 197
Horthy, Regent Miklós, 134–136, 142–145, 151–152
Hostages, 179–181
Hoter-Ishai, Aharon, quoted, 351
Hudal, Bishop Luigi, quoted, 253
Hull, Cordell, 232, 238
Hull, the Rev. and Mrs. William, 8, 279, 445–446
Hungary, 30, 125, 244, 246, 295, 357, 365, 378, 394–395, 404
  Committee for Assistance and Rescue, 146
  deportation from, 132–155
  Jewish Councils in, 136–139, 144–145, 147, 150–152
  Jews in, 249, 325, 340–345, 364, 367, 380–383, 416–418, 422, 426
Hunger, 64, 66, 127, 153, 155, 158, 160–161, 173, 256, 329
Hunsche, Otto, 103, 135–136, 138, 144–145, 377, 383
  quoted, 140, 145
Huppenkothen, Walter, 378, 422
  quoted, 379–380

Ihne, Ingrid von, 30
Insane, killing of, 103
Insurance companies, 43
Intellectuals, German, 19–21
  Jewish, 193–194
Inter-Allied Conference of 1942, 233
Intergovernmental Committee on Refugees, 228, 231
International Commission of Jurists, 307
International Military Tribunal, 286, 298, 301–302, 316, 392, 396
  (*See also* Nuremberg trials)
Interpol, 227

Israel, 250, 259–260, 276, 312, 314–315, 319–320, 325, 331, 340, 406, 412–413
and Eichmann trial, 275, 288–289, 399–408, 413
Government Press Office, 309
Knesset, 273, 277, 302
(*See also* Jerusalem)
Israeli Secret Service, 273
Italy, 81–82, 118–120, 126, 128, 240, 250, 257, 383

Jackson, Justice Robert H., 85, 303
quoted, 86, 453
Jaenisch, Adjutant Rudolf, 269–270
Jaffe, Leib, quoted, 245
Janów, Poland, 80
Janowska camp, 162, 207
Jaros, Andor, 137, 146, 151
Jasenovac camp, 126
Jaspers, Karl, 20
Jeckeln, Friedrich, 132
Jerusalem, 3–4, 13, 261
Appellate Court, 437, 440
District Court, 6, 301, 306–307, 440
ex-Mufti of, 345
Supreme Court, 437, 440–442
Jerusalem *Post*, 445
Jewish Agency, 234, 244, 246
Jewish Brigade, 351
Jewish Chronicle, 233
Jewish Councils, 196–200, 216, 221–222, 295, 330, 403
Hungarian, 136–139, 144–145, 147, 150–152, 341–342
Jewish holidays, 172, 208
Jewish Martyrs' and Heroes' Memorial Authority, 261
Jewish nationals, 80–81, 101, 209
Jewish partisans, 350–351
Jewish Rescue Committee, 117
Jewish resistance, 184–188, 190–192, 215–225, 243, 333
Jewish State, The, Herzl, 355
Jewish underground, 191, 216–225, 258
(*See also* Jewish resistance)
Jewish women, 65, 73–74, 81–82, 329, 415
courage of, 213
(*See also* entries under Women)
Jewry, Dutch, 325
before the Nazis, 193–194
and oppression, 177
Palestinian, 245
Rumanian, 234
and the SS, 176–225
world, 10, 48
(*See also* Jews)
Jews, Austrian (*see* Austria)
Communist, 70, 75, 82
Jews, Austrian (*Continued*)
Czechoslovakian, 46–47
Danish, 254–256
and death camps, 156–175
deception of, 36–38, 47, 57, 112, 165, 195, 329, 367, 427
deportation of (*see* Deportation)
Finnish, 254
French, 105–110
denaturalization of, 108
Germany and, 10–11, 14–15, 17–19, 42–49, 226–261
ghettoization of, 53–68, 138–139, 152, 154
hiding of, 256–261
Hitler and, 16–18, 33–34, 226–261
Hungarian (*see* Hungary)
as intellectuals, 193–194
isolation of, 209–210
kidnaping of, 35, 64
in labor force, 95, 102, 104, 116, 129, 131, 133–134, 137, 150, 154, 161–162, 199–200, 211, 221, 343, 400
liquidation of, 4–5, 7–9, 11–12, 17, 40, 69–97
Palestinian, 244, 246
Polish (*see* Poland)
pro-Communist, 184
stateless, 106–107
sterilization of, 95, 101–102, 300, 346, 354, 397, 402
Joachimowicz, A., quoted, 204
Joel, 3, 398
John XXIII, Pope, 251
Jonge, Archbishop de, 251
Juedische Rundschau, Die, 326
Juettner, SS General Hans, 385
quoted, 153
Julags (*see* Labor camps)

Kafka, Emil, 327
Kagan, Raya, quoted, 189, 191–192
Kahn, Fritz, 271
Kállay, Prime Minister Miklós, 132–136
quoted, 133–134
Kallmeyer, Dr. Walter, 90
Kaltenbrunner, Ernst, 12, 30–31, 131, 154, 266–267, 269, 335, 356, 365, 386
quoted, 86, 267
Kamenets Podolsk, Poland, 82
Kameradenwerk, 9
Kampinos camp, 163
Kann, Marja, quoted, 259
Kapos, 160, 169–170, 174, 189
Kappler, Herbert, 375, 383
Karski, Jan, 236
quoted, 242, 245
Kassa, Hungary, 140
Kastein, 95

Kastner, Israel (Rezsö), 142, 146–152, 284, 340–341, 343, 367, 377
Katz, Aharon, 198
Katz, Milton, 458, 466
Katzmann, SS Major General Fritz, 221
quoted, 211–212
Katznelson, Yitzhak, quoted, 207–222
Kaul, Friedrich, 466
Kaunas, Lithuania, 77, 184, 195, 203, 216, 221, 330
Keitel, Field Marshal Wilhelm, 269
quoted, 70
Kempner, Robert M. W., 96–97, 287, 374–375
Kempner, Witka, 218
Kerstadt, Eliezer, quoted, 221
Kersten, Felix, 22
Kessel, Joseph, 308
quoted, 367–368
Kibbutz Lohamei Hageta'ot, 286, 294
Kidnaping, 35, 64, 119, 178–179, 288, 311–312, 319, 321, 413
Kiev, 82
Killbach, SS Captain, 182
Killinger, Ambassador Manfred von, 121–122
Kistarcsa camp, 143–144, 295, 340, 357, 380, 383, 395, 417
Kittrie, Nicholas N., 469
Kivelisha, Eugene Alexandrovich, quoted, 182–183
Kleck, Poland, 186
Kleinman, Joseph Zalman, quoted, 172
Klement, Ricardo (*see* Eichmann, aliases of)
Klopfer, Colonel Gerhard, 94, 96
Knochen, SS Colonel Helmut, 106, 108–109
Knopf, SS Staff Sergeant Fritz, 182
Koch, Erich, 64
Koller, General Karl, 335
Kolomyja, Poland, 197
Komoly, Otto, 138, 146
Korchak, Ruzka, quoted, 202
Korczak, Janusz, 214
Koretz, Dr. Zvi, 128
Kosów, Ukrainia, 257
Kovner, Abba, 217, 333
quoted, 202, 216, 218
Kramer, Joseph, 340
quoted, 160
Kristallnacht (*see* "Night of Broken Glass")
Kritzinger, Friedrich Wilhelm, 94, 97
Krueger, Friedrich Wilhelm, 61
Krumey, SS Lieutenant Colonel Hermann, 129, 135, 138, 146, 375, 383, 400
quoted, 136, 141, 376–377
Kube, Wilhelm, quoted, 77–78, 80
Kubowitzki (Kubovi), Dr. Leon, 243
Kuechler, General Georg von, 181
Kuper, Rivka, quoted, 68, 190, 217
Kutschera, Margit, 30

Labor camps, 133, 154, 157, 162–163, 188, 195, 197, 200, 329–330, 403
Labor cards, 212, 328–329
Lachwa, Poland, 186
Lahousen, Lieutenant Colonel Erwin, 55
Lakatos, General Geza, 151
Lamerhav, 445
Landau, Ludwik, quoted, 65, 67, 178–180
Landau, Moshe, 305, 323, 363, 372
quoted, 410, 416–418, 422–423, 425, 428
Landor, David, 308
Landsberg, Dr. Henryk, 197
Langner, William, quoted, 239
Last Days of the Reichkanzlei, The, Boldt, 271
Latin America, 247
Latvia, 77, 81
Laval, Pierre, 105, 107–108, 251
quoted, 107
Law of Nations, 441
League of Nations, 226
Leavy, Zad, 469
Lebensraum, 18, 94
Lechatov, Poland, 197
Lechfeld, Germany, 31
Liebbrandt, Dr. Georg, 94, 97
Leibovič, Mendel, 198
Leitman, Salomon, 188
Leitner, Dr., 187
Lemberg, Jacob, quoted, 198
Lenard, Philipp, 20
Lenski, M., quoted, 194
Leopold III, King, 110
Less, Chief Inspector Abner, 56, 277–278, 326, 362–363, 365
quoted, 280–283
Lewandowski, Representative, 462
Ley, Dr. Robert, quoted, 60
Lichtenberg, Bernard, 251
Lichtenstein, Israel, quoted, 210
Lichtman, Ada, 54
quoted, 54–55
Lidice, 129, 301, 354, 376, 397, 400, 424
Liebensfeld, Lenz von, 17
Liebeskind, Dolek, 217, 218, 219
quoted, 218
Liebeskind, Mina, 218
Liebl, Vera (*see* Eichmann, Mrs. Vera)
"Life cards," 212
Life magazine, 10, 302, 458
Lindwasser, Abraham, quoted, 168
Linz, Austria, 27–29, 31
Lithuania, 76, 221, 330, 351

Litzmannstadt, Poland, 129–130, 167, 203, 377, 400, 424
Livai, Jeno, 295
LO (underground), 259
Lodge, Henry Cabot, quoted, 461–462
Lódz, Poland, 65, 200, 207, 220, 403
Lodzyk, Marie, 257
Loesener, Bernhard, 101
quoted, 13
Loewenherz, Joseph, 37–38, 45–46, 355
quoted, 45
Lohse, Hinrich, 77–78
London, 233, 236, 242–243
London *Daily Telegraph*, 235
London *Times*, 249, 444
Lopatynski, Wasyl, quoted, 257
Lo Spinoso, 119
Lotus (French ship), 314
Lublin, Poland, 58–60, 62, 89–90, 108, 164–165, 188, 326, 379
Ludin, Ambassador Hans, 116, 118
Luther, Martin, 15
Luther, Undersecretary, 94
quoted, 134
Lutz, Carl, 260
Lwów, Poland, 197, 200, 207, 211, 250, 347

Maas, Pastor Hermann, 249
Mabolt, Jan, quoted, 201
McClelland, Roswell D., 248
McCloy, John J., quoted, 243–244
McDonald, James G., quoted, 227
Mach, Sano, 116–117
Madagascar scheme, 63, 84, 361, 415
Madison Square Garden, New York, 235, 245
Magun, Lisa, quoted, 217
Majdanek camp, 164, 188, 296
Malinas (shelters), 211
Malines camp, 110
Mandel, Maria, 191
Mannerheim, Marshal, 254
Manthei (police commander), 185
Marr, Wilhelm, 15
Marshall, S. L. A., quoted, 321
Martin, John, quoted, 345
Masaryk, Rudolf, 187
Masaryk, Tomáš G., 187
Mass executions, 180–183, 198, 231, 242, 300, 421
Masur, Norbert, 159, 248
Mauthausen camp, 34, 36, 112, 135, 152
Mein Kampf, Hitler, 17, 21
Meir, Mrs. Golda, quoted, 461
Meisner, SS General August, quoted, 126
Melchior, David, 255, 334
Melkman, Josef, 334
quoted, 112–113, 160
Memel, Lithuania, 49
Mengele, Dr. Josef, 172, 347
Mercy bullets, 173
Mercy killing (*see* Euthanasia)
Meretz, David, 327
Merin, Moshe, quoted, 203
Merten, Max, 382
Mexico, 232
Meyer, Alfred, 94
Meyer, Franz Eliezer, quoted, 35
Meyers, E. H., 115
Meyzel, Rabbi, quoted, 223
Mice, 168
Michael, King, of Rumania, 151
Michaelis, Andreas, 114
Michelson, Rabbi Zvi Yečheskiel, 209
Mielec, Poland, 54
Miete, August, quoted, 167–168
Mila 18, 223–224
Mildner, SS Colonel Rudolf, 272, 356, 358, 405
Minorities, rights of, 193
Minsk, 78–80, 186
Mirer, Gola, 218
Mischlinge, 95, 101–103, 250, 256
Mixed marriages, 95, 102–103
Mlawa, Poland, 198
Moes, SS Captain Ernst, 113
Moldavia, 151
Mollet, Guy, quoted, 457, 465
Monaco, 438
Moravia, 46, 157, 401
Moreali, Giuseppe, 257
Morgen, SS Judge Konrad, 358, 405
Morgenthau, Henry, Jr., quoted, 241
Mount of Memory, Jerusalem, 261
Mowsowic, Rabbi Daniel, quoted, 185
Moyne, Lord, 248
quoted, 239
Mueller, Bishop Ludwig, 249
Mueller, Heinrich, 5, 25–26, 39, 45–46, 71, 94, 96, 108, 219, 225, 337, 354, 357, 361, 365, 372, 379, 386, 392, 407, 418, 443
quoted, 369–370
Mueller, Wilhelm, 20
Munich, 41, 46, 48
Munich *Putsch,* 21
Munkács, Hungary, 139–141
Murmelstein, Benjamin, 204
"Muselmans," 172–173, 348
Musmanno, Judge Michael Angelo, 297–298, 334, 336, 392, 419, 469
quoted, 317, 335, 393
Mussolini, Benito, 118, 120, 128, 152, 252, 362
quoted, 229
Myth of the Twentieth Century, Rosenberg, 19

Nachum, Rabbi, quoted, 185
National Socialism, 20, 70, 156, 252, 267, 271, 335, 366, 372, 385, 427, 429, 431
Nationalism, German, 28, 30
Naujocks, Alfred Helmut, 49
Naumann, SS Brigadier Erich, 112
Nazi and Nazi Collaborators (Punishment) Law, 301, 311, 320, 412, 445
Nazi Party, 9, 11, 28, 30–31, 42, 302
Nazis, 3–4, 8–9, 39, 80, 87, 90, 120, 133, 187, 216
in Argentina, 9
destruction caused by, 193–225
and police, 24–25
and power, 19, 31
propaganda of, 19–20, 49
world reaction to, 226–261
and World War II, 53
Nebe, Arthur, 26, 69, 87–88
Nehama, Itzhak, quoted, 127
Neill, Major General, 236
quoted, 237
Neumann, Leona, 79
quoted, 330
Neumann, Secretary of State Erich, 94, 97
Neurath, Constantin von, 85
New York City, 235–236, 307
Nieśwież, Poland, 185
Nietzsche, Friedrich, 19
quoted, 15
"Night of Broken Glass" (*Kristallnacht*), 42, 44, 226, 229, 326–327, 355
Night and Fog decree, 178
Nisko, Poland, 57–58, 61–62, 423
Nisko plan, 58–62, 415
Nobel Prize winners, Jewish, 193
North Africa, 247
Norway, 115
Norwegian underground, 256
Nosske, SS Lieutenant Colonel Gustav, 82, 337
Novak, Franz, 135, 138, 144, 280, 375
quoted, 383
Nuremberg, 12, 32–33
Nuremberg Laws, 43, 81, 116, 315–318
Nuremberg trials, 13, 45, 49, 56, 59, 74, 82, 85–86, 96, 125, 180, 244, 269–270, 272–273, 288, 290–291, 303, 311, 335, 338–339, 346, 353, 356, 365, 379–380, 383, 396, 399, 453, 458
Nyiregyháza, Hungary, 139

Obedience to superiors, 395–396, 425–427, 439
Occupied Europe, deportation of Jews from, 98–131
Gentiles, in, 178
Jews in ghettos of, 241–244, 394
ODESSA, the, 270
O'Donovan, Patrick, 308
quoted, 321, 464
O'Dwyer, William, 248
Ohlendorf, Otto, 26, 181
quoted, 70, 75
Olshan, Itzhak, 437
Olympic Games of 1936, 34, 227
"Operation Barbarossa," 70
Oppenback, Lieutenant Colonel, quoted, 270
Oppenheim, Baron von, 146–147
Oppenheimer, Lassa, 395
Ordnungspolizie (Orpo), 25
Ostara, 17
OSTI, 131
Ostjanowski, Ignacy, quoted, 259
Ostland, 77–78
Ostrovski-Cohen, Mrs. Victoria, 293
Otter, Baron von, 91, 243, 347

Palestine, 32, 37, 118, 122–123, 193, 206, 228, 230, 234–235, 241, 244–246, 315, 345
Papadatos, Peter, 307
quoted, 470
Parachutists, Palestinian Jew, 244, 246
Paris, 107–109, 257
Parker, the Rev. James, quoted, 468
Parnas, Joseph, quoted, 197
Parson, George R., 469
Passports, foreign, 113
"ghetto," 212
Paul VI, Pope, 253
Paulus, Friedrich von, 134
Pavelic, Ante, 126
Pawlowska, Kleopatra, quoted, 257
Pechorsky, Alexander (Sasha), 188
Pechter, Zvi, quoted, 327
Peretz, Aharon, quoted, 330–331
Permanent Court of International Justice, 313–314
Pesheff, Dimiter, quoted, 124
Pétain, Marshal Henri, 105, 108, 251
Petö, Ernö, 137
Pets Magazine, 231
Pfannenstiel, Dr., quoted, 167
Pier (Ben-Nathan), Arthur, 273
Pirow, Defense Minister Oswald, 230
Pithiviers camp, 106
Pius XI, Pope, quoted, 250
Pius XII, Pope, 252–253, 449
quoted, 250, 252
Plaszów camp, 162, 176, 183, 258, 330
Pleiger, Paul, 302
Podchlevnik, Michael, quoted, 169
Poets, ghetto, 207
Poetsch, Leopold, 27
Pogroms, 42, 44–45, 229
Pohl, SS Lieutenant General Oswald, 338

Poison gas, 90–91, 347, 402–403, 421, 426–427
Poland, 19, 41, 49, 56–65, 76, 103, 121, 128, 134, 137, 160, 164, 286, 299, 393
anti-Jewish propaganda in, 258
deportation from, 301, 424
ghetto police in, 201–204
Jewish Councils in, 196–200, 295
Jews in, 41, 54–56, 58, 64–68, 71–75, 117, 178–180, 184–188, 231, 236, 239–240, 242, 258–259, 293, 327–331, 333, 361, 394, 397, 400
in World War II, 54, 93, 206, 265
(*See also entries beginning* "Polish . . .")
Poliakov, Léon, quoted, 284
Police, 24–25, 99, 162
Danish, 255
French, 108–109
Hungarian, 138
Israeli, 277, 293, 346
Jewish, 200–204, 216, 223–224
(*See also* Security police)
Polish Committee for the Investigation of Hitlerite Crimes, 393
Polish-Jewish Aid Society, 60
Polish underground, 180, 190, 216–225, 236, 242, 253
Ponar camp, 195
Portugal, 229–230
Posen, 337
Poznański, Jacob, quoted, 200
Prague, 30, 46, 62, 105
Prayer, 189–190
Prinz, Joachim, quoted, 455
Prisoners of war, 183
German, 183–184
Polish, 179
Soviet, 181–183, 188
Propaganda, anti-Jewish, 258
Nazi, 19–20, 49
Property, confiscation of, 64, 92, 99–100, 103, 105, 110–111, 114, 116, 129, 138, 175, 300, 397, 400–402, 419, 424
Protectorate, the, 104
Protestant Church, German, 249, 334
Prussia, 24–25
Prużana, Poland, 198
Pskov camp, 181

Quislings, 59

Rabbis, 208–209
Race, concept of, 16–18, 60, 324
Racial laws, 226
Rademacher, Franz, 356
quoted, 125
Radom, Poland, 57, 62
RAF, 242
Rajakowitsch, Dr. Erich, 59, 92, 103, 114
Randall, Mrs. Mercedes M., quoted, 240
Ransom, 115, 145–147, 154, 246
Rasch, SS Brigadier Otto, 69
Rath, Ernst vom, 42
Rathborn, Eleanor R., 238
Raucke (SS man), 330–331
Rauter, Hanns Albin, 112
quoted, 111, 113
Raveh, Yitzhak, 305, 357, 360
quoted, 369, 414–416, 421
Ravenbrueck camp, 81, 129
Razzias, 251–252, 383
Recht, Ernst, quoted, 105
Records (*see* Documents)
Red Army, 152, 155
Red Cross, 150, 153, 158, 160, 248, 367
Reeder, SS General Eggert Hans, quoted, 110
Refugees, 227–261
Reich, Jacob, quoted, 342
Reich, Margot, 342
Reich Security Head Office (RSHA), 12, 25, 58, 70–71, 77–78, 82, 87, 103, 130–131, 135, 160, 231, 299, 338, 353, 359–361, 379, 384–386, 400, 402–403, 415–416, 420–422, 426–427
Reichsbank, 39–40, 165
Reinecke, Lieutenant General Hermann, quoted, 181
Reischauer, 95
Reitlinger, Gerald, quoted, 284
Religion, 8–9, 14–15, 28
Religious institutions, reactivation of, 208
Reprisals, 125, 197–198, 243
Rescue the Perishing, Rathborn, 238
Reshef, Chief Inspector Yehuda, 285–286
Reynolds, Robert, 240
Ribbentrop, Joachim von, 24, 46, 61, 63, 119, 134, 149, 152, 227, 269, 362
quoted, 228
Ribbentrop-Molotov Pact, 49
Richter, Emma, 258
Richter, Gustav, 121–122
Ridley, quoted, 238
Riegner, Gerhard, 240
Riga, Latvia, 75, 79, 81, 90, 221, 330
Ringelblum, Emanuel, 64, 205
quoted, 194, 210, 215, 218, 242
Robinson, Jacob, 303–304, 313, 333, 411, 465*n*.
Robota, Rosa, 192
Rochczyn, Yitzhak, quoted, 186
Roehm, Ernst, 21, 25
Roepke, Wilhelm, quoted, 20
Roethke, Heinz, 106–110
quoted, 108, 119

Rogat, Yosal, 469
Rogers, Representative, 239
Rome, 120, 252, 378, 383
Roncalli, Cardinal (later Pope John XXIII), 251
Roosevelt, Eleanor, 235
Roosevelt, Franklin D., 228–229, 236, 241, 247–248
quoted, 229, 231, 233, 235, 240
Rosen, Pinchas, 290, 301
Rosenberg, Adolf, quoted, 118
Rosenberg, Alfred, 19, 21, 63, 87
Rosenne, Shabtai, 463
Rosensaft, Hadassa Bimko, quoted, 161, 175
Rosensaft, Josef, quoted, 190
Rosenstein, quoted, 204
Rosenthal, 109
Ross, Henryk, quoted, 66
Rothschild, Baron Louis von, 34
Rottweil, Germany, 91, 346
Royo, Rodrigo, quoted, 465
Rublee, George, 228–230
Rufeisen, Hela, quoted, 217
Rufer (Raphael), Gideon, 273
Rumania, 125, 151, 246, 248, 378
Jews in, 120–123
Rumkowski, Mordechai Chaim, 203–204
Russell, Lord, 308
Russia (*see* Soviet Russia; White Russia)
RZ (*Reichszentrale*), 283

SA (*Sturmabteilung*), 21, 23, 25, 28
Sabotage, 200, 203, 221, 254
Sachsenhausen camp, 13, 42
St. John, Robert, 308
St. Louis (boat), 230
St. Nicolai, Austria, 29
Salgado, J. A. Cesar, 469
Saliège, Archbishop, 251
"Salon Kitty," 24
Salonika, 126–127
Sanok, Poland, 55
Sapir, Zeev, quoted, 140
Sassen, Willem Antonius Maria, 9–11, 22, 28–30, 40, 47, 55, 62, 87–88, 111, 115, 121, 149, 225, 253, 272, 296, 337–338, 359, 368–369, 393, 406, 439
Sassen document, 12, 302, 348–350, 363–364, 369, 371–372, 390, 406, 427, 458
Satellite countries, 98–99, 101, 115
Sauckel, Fritz, 302
quoted, 178
Schacht, Dr. Hjalmar, 39
Schellenberg, SS General Walter, 147, 386, 419
quoted, 22, 336
Schillinger, 190
Schindler, Oscar, 258
Schirach, Baldur von, 64
Schmidt, Sergeant Anton, 258
Schmukler, Rabbi Jacob Moshe, quoted, 196–197
Schneidermuehl, Poland, 60
Schubert, Wilhelm, 181
Schulz, Erwin, 336
Schuschnigg, Dr. Kurt V., 34
Schwartz, Heinrich, 116
Schwarz, SS Lieutenant, quoted, 258
Schwarze Korps, Das, 227
Schwarzenberger, Georg, quoted, 469
Schwenk, Superintendent, 286
Scroll of Lamentations, 326
SD (*Sicherheitsdienst*), 11, 22–26, 31–32, 34–35, 42–43, 46, 49, 94, 96, 178, 221, 284, 301, 336, 385, 391, 399
Sebestyan, Arpad, 116
Secret Front, The, Hoettl, 378
Security Police (Sipo), 25, 81, 90, 95–96, 99, 111, 138, 146, 324, 379
Seidl, Siegfried, 135
quoted, 159
Selbar, Harry, 28
Self-preservation, 174
Selinger, Commander Abraham, 277, 286–287, 346
Seraphim, Hans Guenther, 337, 439
Seraphim, Peter Heinz, 62
Serbia, 99, 126, 180
Sered camp, 118
Servatius, Robert, 7, 301–303, 307, 315, 317, 332, 334, 344, 363, 369, 374, 378, 382, 411, 424, 444
quoted, 310–311, 318–319, 331, 335, 348, 352–354, 356, 358, 378, 380, 398–408, 430–431, 437–439
Seyss-Inquart, Arthur, 59, 111, 114
Shafran, Chief Rabbi Alexander, 122
Shapira, Rabbi Kalman, quoted, 208
Sharett, Moshe, 148
Shaw, Irwin, 308
Shield of David, 33, 351
Shimron, Erwin, 374
quoted, 376, 379
Shipper, Yitzhak, 209
Shtetls, 325
Siauliai (Shavli), Poland, 198, 203
Sidor, Ambassador, 252
Sievers, Wolfram, 339
Silber, Rosa, 218
Silber, Sara, 218
Silberg, Moshe, 437
quoted, 442–444
Silesia, 169
Silverman, Sidney, 236
Silving, Helen, 458

Sima, Horia, 268–269
Simmons, Caroline, 114–115
Singapore, 315
Singer, Katia, 189
Siplet, Fernand, 257
Six, Alfred, 26, 386–387, 405, 438
Six, Major Franz, 32, 337, 375
Skeletons, 339–340, 354, 403
Skorzeny, SS Lieutenant Colonel Otto, 120, 152, 369
Skorzeny's desperadoes, 265
Skrzepicki and Feifel, quoted, 204
Slang, ghetto, 210
Slapoberskis, Zadok, 184
Slave labor, 133, 178
(*See also* Labor camps)
Slavik, Franz, 343, 375
quoted, 344
Slovakia, 115–116, 126, 146, 206, 252, 336
Slovenes, 128, 300, 400, 424
Sluck, Poland, 75
"Sluice, the," 104
Sobibór camp, 112, 165, 187–188, 258, 397
Sobolev, Arkady A., quoted, 461–462
Social aid societies, 205–206
Socony Vacuum Company, 28–29, 31
Solingen, Germany, 27
Solomon (Hungarian boy), 343–344
Sommers, Representative, quoted, 239
Soustelle, Jacques, quoted, 465
South Africa, 232
Soviet Russia, 19, 48–49, 57–58, 69–70, 93, 194, 232, 254, 286, 299, 331, 345, 394
and SS, 181–186
Spaak, Suzette, quoted, 257
Spain, 231, 247, 252
"Special Operation Group Eichmann," 135
Speer, Albert, 87
Spies, 192, 235
Spinne, Die, 270
Springman, Samuel, 146
SS (*Schutzstaffel*), 9, 22–23, 25, 31–32, 34–35, 39, 41, 46, 54, 58–61, 65, 73–75, 78, 80, 85, 90, 94, 104–105, 109, 119, 121, 127–128, 136, 144–147, 156–157, 161–170, 173–174, 258, 284, 295, 301, 324, 329–331, 337, 347, 362, 377–379, 384, 399, 417
Economic Office, 131, 338
Jewry under heels of, 176–225
Stahell, General, 253
Stahl, Dr. Heinrich, 35, 45–46
Stahlecker, Dr. Walter, 30, 35, 46, 57, 184, 195
quoted, 75–77
Stanislawów, Poland, 197, 201
Stark, Johannes, 20
State, the, 19
Stawki camp, 221
Stein, Dr., 209
Stephen, Sir James, 395
Sterilization, 95, 101–102, 300, 346, 354, 397, 402
Stern, Jacques, 107
Stern, Samuel, 137
Stettin, Poland, 60
Stettinius, Edward, quoted, 248–249
Stone, Julius, 307, 471
quoted, 469, 472
Storey, Colonel, 285
Storfer, Bertold, 365, 403
Strasbourg University "Institute of Ancestral Heredity," 339–340, 354, 403
Strauch, SS Lieutenant Colonel Eduard, 80
Strechenbach, Bruno, 61
Streicher, Julius, 19, 21, 32, 39, 87, 429
Strikes, 112
Stroop, General Juergen, 128, 223
quoted, 224
Stuckart, Wilhelm, 39, 94, 96, 101–102
Students, Danish, 255
Stuermer, Der, 32
Sturma (ship), 234–235, 246
Stuschka, SS Lieutenant Franz, 125
Sudetenland, 46, 258
Suhr, SS Major, 81, 103, 125
Suicide, 35, 104, 168–169, 177, 187, 189, 197, 205, 215, 224, 239, 306, 359
Sussman, Yoel, 437
Sweden, 91, 248, 255–256, 261, 347
Switzerland, 109, 113–114, 227–228, 241, 247–248, 256
Sylten, Pastor Werner, 249
Synagogues, burning of, 42–43, 47, 55
Szálasi, Prime Minister Ferenc, 152–154
Szapiro, Rabbi David, 208
Szenes, Mrs. Elisheva, quoted, 144
Szeptycki, Andrzej, quoted, 250
Szondi, Lipot, 6–7
Sztojay, Ambassador, 134, 137
quoted, 142
Sztokhauer, Rabbi Shimshon, 208

Taboada, Diogenes, quoted, 460
Taglicht, Chief Rabbi Josef, 35
Tanganyika, 229
Tattoos, 170, 191
Taylor, Myron C., 229
quoted, 228
Taylor, Telford, 308
quoted, 272, 458
Teigman, Kalman, quoted, 168
Teitel (Eichmann's driver), 343–344
Tenenbaum, Joseph, quoted, 284
Tenenbaum, Yehuda, 219

Tenenbaum-Tamaroff, Mordechai, quoted, 219–220
Terlo, Zvi, 304, 411
Tevavi, Arieh, 463
Thadden, Eberhard von, quoted, 160, 381–382, 385
Theresienstadt camp, 103, 115, 157–159, 206, 255–256, 258, 267, 330, 367, 394
Thierack, Otto von, quoted, 161
Third Reich, 4, 48, 227
  anti-Jewish policy of, 414–416
  Main Security Office, 5, 11
  (*See also* German)
Tiso, Father Josef, 116, 252
Tito, 126, 152
Toebbens, Walter, 222
"Top, the," 109
Torture, 109, 154, 161, 187, 191, 215, 397
  (*See also* Atrocities)
Totenkopfverbaende, 25
Transnistrian camps, 248
Transport Jews, 171, 394, 420
Trawniki camp, 188
Treblinka camp, 130, 165, 169, 187–188, 218, 328, 397
Treitschke, Heinrich von, 15, 19
Trevor-Roper, Hugh, 307
  quoted, 320, 463–464
Trusteeship Office–East (*Treubandstelle-Ost*), 60
Tuczyń, Poland, 186
Turkey, 148, 150, 234–235, 246, 248, 314
Turner, Harald, quoted, 125
Typhoid fever, 153, 160, 162, 173, 189

Uebelhoer, Friedrich, 67
  quoted, 66
Ukraine, the, 48, 76–77, 218
Underground, Dutch, 259
  French, 257
  Jewish, 191, 216–225, 258
  Norwegian, 256
  Polish, 180, 190, 216–225, 236, 242, 253
Union of Front Fighters, 28
United Nations, 246, 412–413
  Committee on International Criminal Jurisdiction, 313
  General Assembly, 313
  International Law Commissoin, 318
  Security Council, 289, 316, 413, 455, 460, 463
  War Crimes Commission, 272
United States, 93–94, 345
  and Jewish refugees, 228–243, 247
United States Court of Appeals, 312–313
United States National Archives, 184
United States State Department, 235, 240–241
United States Supreme Court, 313, 413
Universal Declaration on Human Rights, 317
Universities, German, 19–20
Upper Silesia, 116

Valley of Decision, 3–4
Van Dam (child), 113
Van Roey, Cardinal, 111, 251
Van Taalingen-Dols, Mrs. L. M. I. L., 358, 392
  quoted, 115
Vasdenyei, Istvan, 144–145
Vatican, the, 252–253, 378, 450
  (*See also* Holy See)
Veesenmayer, Edmund, 134–135, 138, 141–142, 149–153, 155, 357, 380, 382, 387, 404–405, 438
  quoted, 143, 152–154
Ventzki, Werner, 66–67
Vichy, France, 105
Victor Emmanuel, King, 118
Vienna, 16–17, 34–40, 42, 44–47, 55, 59, 105, 326–327, 383, 391, 414
Vitkon, Alfred, 437
Vlasov, General Andrei, 182
Voelkischer Beobachter, 372
Voice of Thy Brother's Blood, The, Randall, 240
Volhynia, Poland, 58, 186, 351
Vught camp 113–114

Wagner, Richard, 16, 20
Walbaum, Dr., quoted, 206
Waldsee, Austria, 140–141
Wallenberg, Raoul, 397
  quoted, 260
Wannsee Conference, 94–98, 101–102, 105 131, 234, 281, 284, 361, 370, 372, 392, 403, 416, 420
War criminals, 268–269, 272
  prosecution of, 315–321
  (*See also* Nuremberg trials)
War Refugee Board, 247–248
Warsaw, 65, 67, 163, 178–180, 194, 205–209, 213, 243, 253, 328–329, 420
  ghetto revolt in, 128, 134, 163, 187, 195, 217, 221–225, 236, 258, 293–294, 394, 454
Wechsler, Herbert, 458, 469
Wechtenbruch, Dieter, 303, 375, 411
Wedgwood, Lord, 234–235
Weg, Der, 9
Wehrmacht (*see* German Army)
Weintraub, Abraham, 184
Weiss, Abraham, 109–110
Weiss, Baron, 146–147
Weissmandel, Rabbi Michael Dov, 117, 146

Weizmann, Chaim, 194, 233, 244, 344, 453
quoted, 235, 243, 245–246, 345, 397
Weizsaecker, Ambassador Ernst von, 253
quoted, 252–253
Welczek, Count Johannes von, 42
Wellers, Professor George, 334
quoted, 107–109
Wells, Leon, quoted, 162, 328
Wells, Sumner, 240
Werszowsky, Senitsa, 77
West Germany, 286, 307, 438
Westerbork camp, 112–113
Westerweel, Joop, 259
quoted, 260
Wetzel, Erhard, 90, 356
"Wetzel letter," 421
White Russia, 77, 184, 218, 351
Wieliczka, Poland, 54
Wiesenthal, Shimon, 273
Wighton, Charles, quoted, 22
Wilhelm, Kaiser, 18
quoted, 15
Wilhelm, Karl, 137
Willhaus, SS Second Lieutenant Gustav, 162
Wilner, Arieh, quoted, 224
Wilno, Poland, 200, 201–202, 207, 211, 214, 216, 218, 221, 324, 333
Winkelmann, Police Chief Otto, 151, 153, 155, 357, 384, 404
quoted, 385
Winterton, Lord, 228
Wirth, Kriminalkomissar Christian, 90–91
Wise, Rabbi Stephen, 236, 240–241
Wisliceny, Dieter, 12, 32, 37, 55, 117–119, 123, 127–128, 135–136, 138, 144, 146, 151, 270, 284, 377, 404–405
quoted, 13, 87, 99, 116, 136, 145–147, 151, 337
Wittenberg, Izik, 202
Witting, Foreign Minister Rolf, quoted, 254
Woerl, Ludwig, 258
Woetzel, Robert K., quoted, 470
Wohltat, Helmut, 40
Wolff, General Karl, 39, 422
Women prisoners, 163
Women's hair, 165–166, 168
World Jewish Congress, 235, 240
World Jewry, 10, 48
World War I ,19, 27–28, 60, 158, 195
World War II, 4, 49, 130, 402
World Zionist Organization, 194
Wurm, Landsbischof, 249
WVHA, 131

Yad Vashem, 261, 284–286, 293, 296
Yellow badges, 53, 64, 92, 106, 110, 127, 137, 141, 152, 232, 251, 326, 402
Yerushalmi, Eliezer, quoted, 203
York, Archbishop of, quoted, 237
Yoselewska, Rivka, 331, 453
quoted, 73–74
Yost, Heinz, 26
Youth movements, 215–218, 246
Yugoslavia, 119, 128, 286
Jews in, 125–126

Zabludowicz, Noah, quoted, 163, 192
Zagare, Lithuania, 184
Zbonszyn, Poland, 41
Zdunska Wola, Poland, 198
Zeit, Die, London, 233
Zelikowicz, Josef, quoted, 204
Zemba, Rabbi Menachem, 208–209
Zentralstelle (Vienna), 38–40
Zetnik, K. (Yehiel Dinur), quoted, 171, 347
Zimet, Walli, quoted, 46
Zimetbaum, Mala, 191
Zionism, 10, 37–39, 193–194, 355
Zloczów, Poland, 197
Zucker, Fritzi, 207
Zuckerman, Yitzhak, 217, 218, 223, 294
quoted, 163, 218, 221–222, 294
Zuckerman, Zivia Lubetkin, 294
quoted, 67–68, 195, 215, 223, 295, 328
Zygelbojm, Shmuel, 235
quoted, 239, 245

ABOUT THE AUTHOR

Gideon Hausner, Chief Prosecutor at the trial of Adolf Eichmann, came to Israel from his native Poland in 1927.

During Israel's war of liberation (1947–48), he was first military prosecutor and later president of the military court. From 1960 to 1963 he was Attorney General of Israel.

At present he is in private law practice in Jerusalem. He also is Advocate and Lecturer of Commercial Law at Hebrew University and serves as legal consultant and adviser to national institutions and legal firms. In the fall of 1965 he was elected a member of the Knesset on the ticket of the Independent Liberal Party.